Case Law in the Making

The Techniques and Methods of Judicial Records and Law Reports

Volume 1: Essays

Comparative Studies
in Continental and Anglo-American Legal History
Vergleichende Untersuchungen zur kontinentaleuropäischen
und anglo-amerikanischen Rechtsgeschichte

Herausgegeben von

Prof. Dr. Dr. h. c. mult. Helmut Coing

und

Prof. Dr. Dr. h. c. Knut Wolfgang Nörr

Band 17/I

Case Law in the Making

The Techniques and Methods of Judicial Records and Law Reports

Volume 1: Essays

Edited by

Prof. Dr. Dr. Alain Wijffels

Duncker & Humblot · Berlin

Gedruckt mit Unterstützung der Gerda Henkel Stiftung, Düsseldorf

Die Deutsche Bibliothek – CIP-Einheitsaufnahme

Case law in the making : the techniques and methods of judicial records and law reports / ed. by Alain Wijffels. – Berlin : Duncker und Humblot
Vol. 1. Essays. – 1997
(Comparative studies in continental and Anglo-American legal history ; Bd. 17,1)
ISBN 3-428-09075-6

Fremddatenübernahme: Klaus-Dieter Voigt, Berlin
Druck: Druckerei Gerike GmbH, Berlin
Printed in Germany

ISSN 0935-1167
ISBN 3-428-09075-6

Gedruckt auf alterungsbeständigem (säurefreiem) Papier
entsprechend ISO 9706 ♾

Preface

The present volumes (Part 1: Essays; Part 2: Documents) are the sequel to the volume *Judicial Records, Law Reports, and the Growth of Case Law* (J. H. Baker ed.), published as Vol. 5 of the *Comparative Studies in Continental and Anglo-American Legal History* in 1989. While that volume was still at the press, there was a consensus among the contributors that the project ought to be continued. For a while, Prof. J. Hilaire, then Director of the Centre d'Etude d'Histoire Juridique in Paris (C.N.R.S.), kept the flame alive, but eventually, practical considerations led me to act as the general coordinator of the project. From the table of contents and the list of contributors in these new volumes, it will be clear that there is a strong continuity between the present publication and its 1989 predecessor. Most of the contributors to the earlier project agreed to participate in the new project. Except for the municipal *Schöffensprüche* in northern Germany (Prof. F. Ebel's contribution to the previous volume) and for the judicial system in Russia (Prof. W. E. Butler's essay in the same volume), the jurisdictions dealt with in 1989 appear again in the present contributions. Prof. R. Jacob first considered contributing to the present project with a study of local courts in the French territories governed by customary law *(pays de coutumes);* other commitments prevented him from carrying out this plan, but the collaboration nevertheless proved profitable: in September 1993, he organised a successful international conference in Paris on the theme: 'Le juge et le jugement', where several members of the present project also presented papers, and the proceedings of that conference will probably appear shortly before the present publication. Prof. J. Hilaire and Dr. C. Bloch were no longer in a position to contribute to the new project, but the participation of the Centre d'Etude d'Histoire Juridique and of the Centre National de la Recherche Scientifique was ensured by Dr. B. Auzary-Schmaltz and Dr. S. Dauchy, who wrote the essays on the *Parlement* of Paris. For the papers on the Low Countries, young scholars were found ready to support the 'old guard' (Drs. C. Verhas for the Dutch Supreme Court, and Mr. C. H. van Rhee for the Great Council of Malines).

It will also be obvious that our venture was considerably strengthened by the participation of other new members to the project. In the previous volume, Prof. J. H. Baker had not only carried the burden of coordinating the project and editing the volume, but he had also had the task of representing the English legal tradition on his own. As the general aim and the title of the series in which this work appears suggest, the English system deserves to be approached in more than one contribution. The most striking innovation of this sequel is no doubt that the main historical traditions of the English legal system are now dealt with by different scholars. For the Common Law, Prof. Baker himself focuses specifically on the Year Books, while Dr. D. J. Ibbetson deals with the early-modern reports. For Equity Law, Prof. W. H. Bryson (whose new contribution on Virginia law reports also ensures that the American leg of the project remains represented) kindly accepted to provide an essay, drawing on his expertise and more recent research in Chancery and other Equity records. Finally, the English civil lawyers' practice in the ecclesiastical courts is studied by Prof. R. H. Helmholz. For France, I was keen to include a separate study on at least one 'provincial' *Parlement;* Prof. J. Bart and Dr. M. Petitjean provide us now with new insights in the records and reports related to the *Parlement* of Dijon. Clearly, other territories and legal systems might also have been included in the present collection; I personally miss very much contributions on the courts in some of the major territories within the *Reich,* and at least one contribution on the practice in Spain; Scotland, too, would certainly have deserved a separate paper in a legal-historical comparative perspective, and a similar point could no doubt be argued for early-modern developments in Scandinavian and in Eastern European countries.

At first sight, the approach followed in the different essays may seem very different from one legal system to another. Here again, however, the present essays need to be envisaged with respect to those published in 1989. In some cases, the authors had already provided in their first paper a general survey of the records and of the reports, which made it possible to consider more in detail particular aspects of the specific theme of the new project; whereas in other cases, such a general survey and outline of the court was still needed. For courts which originated or developed only towards the end of the middle ages or later (e. g. the *Reichskammergericht,* the Great Council of Malines, the Dutch *Hoge Raad*), it may have been expedient for the authors to direct their attention to a particular feature of, say, the drafting of a judgment (cf. the Great Council of Malines) or of the *relatio* (cf. the very stimulating and innovative essay on the Imperial Chamber of Justice, in which Prof. F. Ranieri also emphasises the importance of the technique in present-day German legal education). For some of the 'great European courts' which had already acquired a respectable status before the early-modern period (the Roman Rota, the Royal High Court of Sicily, the *Parlement* of Paris), the emphasis is different; for those jurisdictions, the reader will be reminded of relevant institutional developments; in the case of the Roman Rota, Prof. Dolezalek effectively succeeded in presenting an extremely clear and original synthesis of early-modern developments, which will no doubt serve in the future as a work of reference for many students and scholars, and which provides a valuable complement to his essay in the previous volume. For Southern Italy, Prof. G. Vallone somewhat shifted his interest *ratione temporis et loci* from his earlier essay on Matteo d'Afflitto and the court in Naples; while Prof. A. Romano's substantial contribution on the Royal Court in Sicily forcefully helps to equilibrate a collection which, in general, is still tainted by a Northern European bias. Prof. M. Ascheri's recent reprint of *Tribunali, giuristi e istituzioni dal medioevo all'età moderna* already addresses some of the central themes of the present volumes, and has the advantage of providing comparative perspectives for the Northern territories of the Italian peninsula; however, even in his present essay, which is more specifically focused on Siena and Tuscany, the author pursues his wider comparative regional approach with some general considerations regarding the practice in Northern Italian 'Rotæ'.

In spite of these differences in emphasis, a unity of approach was preserved thanks to the active cooperation of all the members of the project. A meeting was held at Leiden on 5 - 6 July, 1993,[1] and it provided an adequate opportunity to discuss both the essential options of the new project and the more practical concept of the two volumes to be produced.

In a comparative collection as the present one, a separate volume containing almost exclusively sample documents is not a luxury. Since the emphasis of the new project was to be on the technical aspects of day-to-day drafting of judicial records and law reports (or their continental counterparts: collections of 'decisiones' etc.), which are inevitably solidly embedded in particular 'styles' and institution-bound practices, the risks of misunderstandings or plainly unintelligible methods are not small. The risk of confusion is even greater when the authors, each well-acquainted with the court system they present, are writing in their own language, for some terms of art they use – possibly even for referring to very ordinary and

[1] The meeting was attended by B. Auzary, J. H. Baker, W. H. Bryson, J. Th. de Smidt, G. Dolezalek, R. H. Helmholz, D. Ibbetson, R. Jacob, K. W. Nörr, F. Ranieri, C. H. van Rhee, C. Verhas and A. Wijffels. The organization was greatly facilitated by the support of Dr. F. Egmond. The meeting immediately preceded the 11th British Legal History Conference, held in Exeter, where papers were presented by several contributors to the present volumes. The theme of the conference was closely related to that of our project and Leiden meeting: cf. the proceedings published under the title: Law Reporting in England (*Ch. Stebbings,* ed.) (London/Rio Grande 1995). These proceedings include inter alia a contribution on the High Court of Admiralty in London, which originally had been intended for the present project; thanks to Prof. Helmholz's study, an additional essay on an English civil lawyers' preserve in the present collection became redundant.

trivial practices – are so intimately related to the clerical habits of the court in question that the very language used becomes idiosyncratic; needless to say, no translation (barring a system of comprehensive and cumbersome paraphrases) could prevent this pitfall, well familiar to any comparative lawyer or legal historian. Once again, the old scholastic saw that 'nothing reaches the mind, unless it has gone through the senses' pointed the way to a practical solution: specific sample documents would illustrate and exemplify the general (and inevitably, to some degree abstract) features and principles developed and presented in the essays. Unquestionably, a printed version of a transcript from an extract of a judicial record is a very pale and inadequate reflection of the real thing! It may be impossible to grasp the materiality of a 'roll' in an English judicial record until one has actually seen such a document being unrolled and consulted on a long side-table at the Public Records Office in London; or that of continental 'registers' recording the various stages and aspects of the written proceedings inherited from the Roman-canonical procedure, unless one has been granted access to the depots where, literally, hundreds or even thousands of metres of archives from a single court, amassed over several centuries, can be visualised. One of the contributors to the project suggested that a collection of photographs might be more appropriate;[2] indeed, new publishing techniques which make it possible to gain a computer-steered 'animated' access to the most complex source-material make it possible to envisage even more sophisticated data-bases opening up serial judicial archives. In comparison, the present volumes remain very modest and highly conventional. Nevertheless, it is hoped that by providing for each court-system examples of both records and reports, precisely the technical aspects of these documents may be better understood. English Year Books and early reports, even when modern editions are available, are still scarce in continental European libraries, while even popular *ius commune* collections of *Decisiones* are not always readily accessible in specialised academic institutions; when records have been published by a modern author, the aim of the publication has seldom been to highlight the formal aspects of the drafting-technique. In this context, the second volume now published may offer a rudimentary, yet indispensable instrument for understanding the inner working of foreign judicial recording methods. During the discussions, pertinent objections were raised as regards the possibility

---

[2] Some photographs of records and reports are reproduced in the lavishly illustrated volume: Frieden durch Recht. Das Reichskammergericht von 1495 bis 1806. (*I. Scheurmann* ed.) (Mainz 1994), including contributions on German courts, the English central Royal courts, the *Parlement* of Paris, the Great Council of Malines, early-modern Italian supreme courts, Swedish royal courts, and Polish jurisdictions. Again, one will note that among the authors, the present contributors are strongly represented.

of selecting 'typical' or 'representative' samples from the records or reports. Moreover, the problem was acerbated when I suggested that each contributor might attempt to produce a collation of records and reports relating to the same case. Considering the nature of the source-material or its accessibility in some of the jurisdictions under review, the practical difficulties of such a scheme were deemed to be insuperable. Yet, the discussion itself, which is echoed in several passages throughout the different contributions, where the authors explain why such a collation would have been impractical or vain, or what restrictions they had to take into account, may serve the comparative purpose of the present collection of essays. Also, a general introduction aims to highlight and compare some of the features discussed in the various essays.[3]

These two volumes appear at a time when the interest of (legal) historians for judicial records, at least in continental Europe, is perhaps much greater than ever before. In England (and Common Law countries in general), the importance of the judiciary in the law-making process means that legal historians have always privileged such sources; and historians have traditionally also regarded legal sources as primary material for their investigations. By contrast, on the European continent, comparable sources have long been neglected and are, even today, only to a limited extent readily available or accessible; the systematic use of forensic records and materials by legal historians is a comparatively recent, and on the whole still marginal phenomenon; for historians at large, the perceived 'threshold' to gain access to legal material is apparently often still too high.[4] Meanwhile, continental-European initiatives in the area of 'judicial history' have thrived, and one may wonder whether the development of a *histoire de la justice (histoire judiciaire), Rechtsprechungsgeschichte, rechtspraakgeschiedenis* etc. (to mention only a few of the commonly used designations) as a specialised and institutionalised discipline, with its distinct journals, chairs, societies, conferences, and all other attributes of an established academic subject, is fully warranted. Admittedly, the study of judicial historical sources in continental Europe still needs special attention in order to catch up with other, better investigated fields of historical research. However, one should always bear in mind that, in the end, judicial history should not serve an independent purpose, but only makes sense when it is ultimately regarded as a *science auxiliaire* for both histo-

---

[3] I am very grateful to David Ibbetson for accepting to co-write that introduction according to a set plan.

[4] One of the members of the present project has initiated practical steps to reverse this mentality: cf. *S. Dauchy* (ed.), Ter overwinning van een historische drempelvrees. De historicus en juridische bronnen. L'historien face aux sources juridiques. [Iuris Scripta Historica VII] (Brussels 1994).

rians and legal historians in general. The most lasting value of the present contributions may well be that their authors have been keenly aware of that ancillary role of their study.[5]

Easter 1996. *Alain Wijffels*

[5] It is a pleasure to acknowledge the financial support of the Gerda Henkel Foundation (Düsseldorf) and of the Nederlandse Organisatie voor Wetenschappelijk Onderzoek (N.W.O., The Hague), which subsidised the Leiden meeting on 5 - 6 July 1994; the former's support also made possible the present publication. We are much indebted to Prof. K. W. Nörr, whose interest for the project allowed us to consider the two volumes in their present format. Dr. D. Waibel should be thanked for acting as an efficient advisor and intermediary between the editor and the publisher.

Contents

DAVID IBBETSON AND ALAIN WIJFFELS*

Case Law in the Making: The Techniques and Methods of Judicial Records and Law Reports

Any assessment of case law as a source of law, i.e. an authority which contributes to create new law, whether by interpreting existing rules or by formulating a principle which had hitherto not been expressed, depends on the more or less systematically elaborated theory of legal authorities which prevails at any given time in a particular legal system. Every complex legal system is marked by a plurality of different types of authorities and sources. Conflicts of laws not only occur when different systems are involved, but they are also an essential feature of any internal legal system. Indeed, 'external legal history' is to a large extent the history of the emergence and decline of the different sources of law, and of the ever-changing relationship between these sources. 'Internal legal history' (or *Dogmengeschichte*) can only ignore the shifts between legal sources at its peril. Thus, standard text-books on continental legal history are still often widely based on statute law and doctrine, and, when possible and appropriate, on customary law. Comparatively few works attach commensurate attention to judicial decisions.

Admittedly, a theory of legal sources is an elusive concept. It may even be argued that, jurisprudential attempts notwithstanding, accurate systematic elaborations of such theories are more often wanting, and that, both for ancient and modern law, the literature available does not necessarily reflect the prevailing ideas or practice of its time. Even nowadays, both academic jurists and practitioners would usually find it difficult to express such a theory in any detail, assuming that a conscious consensus might be found among the legal profession of a particular legal system. Moreover, the hierarchy of legal authorities, which such theories imply, may differ, depending on the vantage point; one thing is to consider which authority overrules another, another to decide which authorities are required to be referred to

* The introduction and the section on continental European traditions were written by A. Wijffels, the section on the English and American traditions and the conclusion by D. Ibbetson.

in court, or of which authorities judicial notice should be assumed, and for which proof is required, and, if so, how such a burden of proof can be met with. Such practical considerations may fundamentally affect the contribution of any legal source to the development of the law at different times in history.

There may also be a discrepancy between more or less generally acknowledged principles regarding the authority of different sources and the practice both *in scholis* and *in curiis*. Although the continental European cliché is still that the English Common Law developed as a judge-made law, this would hardly have been the view proposed by the medieval and early-modern judges who may have deemed more political to present the role of the judiciary as that of a 'repository' of the Common Law. The 19th-century Exegetic School (in France and Belgium) may have on the whole proclaimed, through the mouthpieces of both doctrine and the judiciary, that the only authoritative source of law was *'la loi'*, but, at the same time, it produced massive multi-volume commentaries of the codes and, for the first time, systematic and periodical publications of the courts' judgments.

A recurrent doubt in respect with the authority of precedents is that, for the medieval and early modern periods, the evidence generally ignores or repudiates a firm doctrine of 'stare decisis'; precedents, it is alleged, were not *binding* precedents. Perhaps that view betrays some paradox, for the same stringent test does not always seem to be applied to other sources of law. Yet, it is known that for the proof of controversial rules of customary law, judicial precedents could be required, which could suggest that, per se, the binding authority of such rules was questionable. Even for statute law, the evidence is that, in practice, even when the legislator's political power (whether a municipal authority, a modern state's monarch, or the acts of a representative body) was well established, the implementation of its statutes could be imperfect. One does not necessarily need to agree with the commonly held view that frequent repetitions of the same or similar statutory provisions, in particular in continental European systems, reflect the legislative power's frustrations with the application of these provisions, for the reiteration of previously enacted rules was often part and parcel of the legislative technique. Nevertheless, the approach to statute law in practice often shows how, at various times in history, its binding character was by no means absolute, but depended on the relative authority attributed to the different other sources of the legal system. Moreover, the paradox of case law is that, although the extent of its authority is often questioned, in any political system which tends to abide by the rule of law, the binding character of *any* rule of law largely depends on its enforcement through judicial decisions. Also, the development of a legal system is not the sum total of formulations of positive rules, but rather the result of incrementally extending sets of rules through various forms of practice, stemming from both official and non-official groups within society.

The following essays reflect the ambiguities and the uneasiness as regards the place of case law in the development of law. In order to facilitate a comparative basis to assess the possible role of case law in various systems, a more pedestrian approach than the jurisprudential question as to the theoretical authority of judicial precedents was opted for. Therefore, the essays focus on the material aspects of how case law (whether normative or not) developed, *viz.* on the prerequisites for the affirmation of legal principles via judicial, or at least litigation-related decisions. They deal exclusively with superior, often supreme courts (in the sense of *cours souveraines,* whose decisions could not be challenged through 'ordinary' remedies) during the later middle ages and the early-modern period.

All these courts developed, sometimes at an early, sometimes at a later stage, some system of records. The essays attempt to set out the recording techniques, insofar as these may shed some light on the purposes of the courts' records. The courts' decisions, generally in the form of a judgment, are of obvious interest for case law, but all other records dealing with the legal aspects of a case, alleging or establishing (whether as part of a creative process or not) legal principles, are also relevant. The crucial question is whether these records can in a way be related to the emergence of case law, i.e. whether they can provide a material reference which may be later adduced as evidence or authority sui generis of a legal rule.

In the various legal systems and traditions under consideration, the generic term 'reports' is used for a variety of sources which are not entirely homogeneous. The term refers here both to reports in the strict and traditional sense, as it has long been well established in the Common Law system, but also as a convenient shorthand for what is usually referred to (in continental Europe) as *recueils de jurisprudence* (or, in the languages used in the various legal systems referred to in the following essays, *raccolte di giurisprudenza, Rechtsprechungssammlungen, rechtspraakverzamelingen*), in early modern literature generally published under titles as *Decisiones..., Arrêts...,* or more original titles during the later centuries of the Ancien Régime, but forming, on the whole, a fairly established and more or less well-defined category for the purpose of legal-historical research. As the essays and the documents here published emphasize, the object of such publications may nevertheless vary considerably, even within the same tradition. The vexed question regarding this literature pertains to its degree of 'proximity' to the opinions held by the judges of the cases involved, or at least by the intellectual authors of the decisions. When they cling to the cases, old reports may still seem, to a modern lawyer, to tell more about 'how' a case was decided, relating the facts and the proceedings, than 'why' they were decided as reported. As regards reports, the crux for the legal historian is to determine whether they provide any grounds beyond the assessment of facts, *viz.* whether they enable the historian to determine the legal grounds of the decision. The notion that judicial decisions are at least implicitly based on a legal reasoning, and on the application of a legal rule, is not self-evident, and may well be challenged. The adjudication of a case, it may be argued, can be based on a variety of considerations, which do not necessarily include the application of legal rules. Even when judges are trained, professional lawyers, and in particular when the decision is – formally or informally – a collegiate conclusion, the decision in any particular case of some complexity can often be reached at through different, sometimes even mutually inconsistent, legal reasonings.

There seems to be little doubt that, for all practical purposes, the 'reports' (in the widest sense, as above) have been instrumental in the development of case law as one of the sources which directly or indirectly contribute to the formulation, and possibly the elaboration, of the law. Whereas few questions have been raised regarding the historical reliability of court records, the 'authenticity' of the reports, particularly as to the legal principles it purports to establish, has been much debated. Inevitably, the value and intrinsic qualities of reports can only be assessed on a case to case basis. One aspect of this assessment, which has been attempted in several of the following contributions, consists in comparing the presentation of a particular case in a report with the corresponding records. Thus some insight may be gained into the various elements which were deemed worth relating, both by the clerical administration of the court and in the mind of the reporter. The comparison highlights, in various ways, how the techniques of recording and reporting a case may greatly differ, and how that difference can be largely explained by the contrasting purposes of the respective authors.

I. Continental European Traditions

1. Legal authorities and judicial precedents

The position of case law among the sources of law is not easy to determine. Partly, this may be due to the emphasis traditionally reserved to some of the other sources. To some historians, the main development has been a gradual shift of balance between customary law (in the earlier middle ages, by far the predominant form of law) and statute law (the prevailing source in modern bureaucratic states). Case law, in such a perspective, can only be given (as in the case of doctrine) an ancillary role, although for the sake of symmetry, some may be tempted to situate conveniently between the medieval 'ère de la coutume' and the 19th-century 'ère de la loi' an 'ère des arrêtistes' – a formula which may have the advantage of maintaining some equivocation as regards the respective importance of case law proper and practice-related doctrine. Obviously, such over-simplified characterisations may express some basic insights in the changing balance between the various sources, but it may be equally evident that the importance of the works by 'arrêtistes' during the early modern period did never match that of customary law during the middle ages or the primacy of legislation and codes last century, at least in some 'paradigmatic' legal systems such as France. Neither does such a presentation satisfy the needs to confer an adequate role to *ius commune* – a complex entity in itself, since it encompasses not only the fundamental authorities of the texts in the *corpora iuris,* but also a large part of medieval and early-modern doctrine, and, through various forms of 'receptions', it impressed its mark on customs, statutes, and judicial decisions. However, whichever model prevails, judicial decisions are not perceived, for any period, to have been a major formal source of law commanding the orientations or the expression of the legal system. With respect to the other main sources – customary law, statute law, doctrine, *ius commune* –, its role is usually characterised as a confirmatory one. This also means that perhaps to a greater extent than any of these other sources, its own characteristics are more closely linked to the particular way each of these sources is developing at any given time.

These considerations may to some degree explain the ambivalence expressed in most of the continental European essays in the present volume. Considering either the theoretical positions or the practice of the courts, the authors who deal with medieval developments in Italy and France tend to confirm that, as a matter of principle, judicial precedents enjoyed only a limited authority, and that the contemporary view was hostile to the concept of 'binding' precedents. Institutional developments of the judiciary could influence the progress and the specific character of a court's ability or willingness to contribute actively and consciously to the law-making process. *G. Vallone* calls our attention to territories of southern Italy, such as the principality of Tarento, where the development of superior tribunals and appellate jurisdictions could be a very gradual process, closely linked to the local and regional power structures; the emergence of a superior court exercising effective control over lower tribunals, which were often steeped in traditional institutions or associated with established offices, could be impeded in various ways, and an original feature in the southern Italian development seems to have been the creation of several successive remedies which were all but in name early forms of appeals within what remained considered to be technically the same instance. At such stage of the institutional development, it may be gathered, the superior court's main concern may have been to acquire a grip over the various proceedings, rather than to impose its authority on points of substantive law. However, as *B. Auzary-Schmaltz* points out for the medieval Parlement in Paris, the reluctance to develop a set of 'binding' precedents on questions of substantive law did not prevent that court, at the same time, developing a more marked form of case law on points of adjective law, *viz.* both jurisdictional and procedural questions. In medieval Sicily, no binding force could be attributed to a judicial decision at the level of the royal court, unless such a decision had been reached after the intervention of the sovereign; apparently entirely in conformity with the prevailing doctrine, the authority of the decision was that of the sovereign's ruling, while the court could not in its own right presume to create law through its precedents *(A. Romano).*

Traditionally, the superior courts have been credited with a more decisive influence in the various legal systems from the later middle ages onwards, and particularly during the early-modern period, when, at different stages (depending on the political situation in each country), those courts' fortunes can more closely be linked with the development of the 'modern state'. However, constitutional developments can only partly explain the manifest rise of case law. Other developments, such as the fundamental changes in the methods of the learned law, would necessarily have affected the standing of decisions by a territory's superior courts and supreme tribunal. Here again, the connections between case law and *ius commune* doctrines will require much further research before one may venture any confident assessment. Some of the essays nevertheless strongly suggest the importance of *ius commune* doctrines for the authority of judicial precedents. The medieval learned law's restrictive views on the authority of judicial decisions have been the subject-matter of well-known studies and need not be further discussed here. Much less attention has been given to the effects of the early-modern developments of *ius commune* on the role of judicial decisions in the various legal systems, probably because under the regime of *usus modernus,* a combination of substantive rules of both *ius commune* and *iura propria* became a characteristic feature of legal reasoning. The articulation of that new approach was largely realised through doctrine, in particular the practice-oriented legal literature. Precisely because it became necessary to express the balanced blend of *ius commune* and particular law with regard to the latter's own institutional context, the decisions of a territory's supreme court often provided the most adequate reference which enabled it to include both political authority (because of the link between the court and the territory's sovereign) and scholarly creativity. Moreover, this practice-related literature could be sufficiently flexible to take into account the various (mostly, territorial) levels of *usus modernus* variations on *ius commune.* At the same time, the adaptation of the *decisiones*-literature to the *usus modernus* standards meant that the appeal of these works became increasingly confined to their own territorial legal systems. There is some paradox in considering that late-medieval or sixteenth-century collections of *decisiones* related as they were to comparatively peripheral courts (as, for example, the Parlements of Grenoble and Bordeaux), still attained a European-wide audience and were quoted in civil law courts throughout the continent (and England), but that some *recueils d'arrêts* from the end of the Ancien Régime which purported to express the case law of the entire French realm could only aspire to enjoy a similar authority mainly within those political borders, and that the authority of collections related to regional Parlements was henceforth on the whole limited to the territory of their jurisdiction, except for comparative purposes, again mainly limited to the realm. *M. Ascheri*'s essay on the Sienese Rota shows that during the sixteenth century, *ius commune* doctrinal authorities were predominant, whereas the court's own precedents were not quoted as authorities; in the Sienese system, this may to some extent be explained by the short period of tenure enjoyed by the Rota judges (*viz.* a three-years' term). By the eighteenth century, however, a 'Tuscan' case law seems well-established and referred to in Sienese legal practice. *Ascheri* expresses the view that the rise of a (territorial) case law coincided with the decline and crisis of *ius commune,* but that may express too strict a concept of *ius commune,* and underrate the contribution of *usus modernus* to the common European legal culture; at any rate, *Ascheri*'s observation for Siena is not inconsistent with the general tendency of a marked role of the *decisiones*-literature and increasingly frequent references to precedents within their territorial, i.e. regional or national, legal systems.

Some authors (and prominently, in the present volume, *A. Romano* and *M. Petitjean,* for, respectively, Sicily's Royal Court and the Parlement of Dijon) make a strong case for the effects of a court's (or its judges') 'prestige' on the authority of its decisions. The prestige referred to presumably includes both social and political status and a recognised prominence among the legal profession. At the same time, one may strongly suspect from the source-material attesting that status that it was concocted and maintained within a social and professional group which largely shared the same interests. The alleged prestige was, in other words, to a large extent the result of self-advertising, and would therefore rather express the self-consciousness of the judiciary and the legal professions involved in quoting and using their own precedents. Even so, such self-assurance (and the conditions it implied) will no doubt have been a non-negligible prerequisite for the development of case law in legal practice.

By the last centuries of the Ancien Régime, even when the binding authority of precedents was in theory still questionable, the practice of referring to them was wide-spread in many jurisdictions. In some courts, such as the Paris Parlement, the practice may already have been established at a much earlier time. At the *Reichskammergericht, F. Ranieri* found that individual judges, the rejection of a doctrine acknowledging some binding *consuetudo iudicandi* notwithstanding, could be tempted to confer in their vota a more stringent authority to precedents, though this practice apparently did not impose itself in general. The Roman Rota's practice, which for the continental tradition of case-reporting had been paradigmatic, is particularly revealing as it illustrates both the importance of precedents and the judges' discretion in acknowledging their authority. *G. Dolezalek*'s essay, which, for the early-modern period, offers an indispensable addition to his contribution on the medieval Rota (published in the previous volume), recalls the particular character of the Rota as a collegiate court and of the procedural role of the 'decisiones'. Although the decisions were issued by an individual auditor, an elaborate system of concertation ensured that opinions remained in tune with as large a consensus as possible among the members of the court. The constitution 'In throno justitiae' (1561) provided that the Rota's judges would only depart from printed precedents under restrictively defined circumstances, the procedure for which strived to ensure, once again, concertation and a relative consensus among the members of the court. The very illustrative sample case edited by *Dolezalek* (a litigation opposing the bishops of Chiemsee and Salzburg, 1701 - 1705, *coram Scotto*) shows in any event that, in the exchanges between counsel, both published and unpublished cases were adduced in impressively great quantities – in excess, it would seem, of the numbers which the court might have been willing to consider.

2. Technical prerequisites for the development of case law

In very general terms, the modern concept of case law implies a material and an intellectual element. The material condition is the availability of the decisions for future reference. The intellectual prerequisite is the expression of a ratio decidendi in the form, at the very least, of the specific legal principles on which the decision is based. For the modern lawyer, it has become evident that both aspects of the information are at his disposal, all the more so since the extensive study of case law are now part and parcel of the legal curriculum. For medieval and early-modern lawyers, the same information was mostly unavailable.

The actual texts of the decisions (here in the sense of: judgments) enjoyed on the whole only exceptionally, and mostly to a very limited extent, circulation among the legal profession. Until the end of the Ancien Régime, periodical publications reproducing judgments were not a regular feature of legal literature. Collections reproducing judgments as such were scarce. In some legal systems, judicial opinions which cannot, as a rule, be assimilated to judgments, were, on the other hand, wide-spread and successful; the Rota's *Decisiones* are possibly the most important example of such publications.

Neither did the practice of recording judgments, a common (though not universal) practice among superior courts by the end of the middle ages, necessarily facilitate its availability to practitioners at large. For several courts, it is established that access to these records was restricted, and their consultation by the judges themselves would also appear to have been limited. Copies of the judgments delivered to the parties did not generate systematic references to these decisions as judicial precedents (except, as we shall see, when their authority as *res judicatae* could be invoked).

An obvious reason for this disaffection would have been that these decisions lacked the second prerequisite for any case law, *viz.* the intellectual element, or legal reasoning on which the decisions were based. If, on the whole, the continental tradition was hostile to motivation of judgments, provisions were made, either by *ius commune* doctrine or in some particular legal systems, to ensure that, under certain circumstances, a ratio decidendi would be expressed and, possibly, recorded. *M. Ascheri,* whose previous research on late-medieval and early-modern Central and Northern Italian practice had already established the effect of such provisions, recalls here how, at Siena, a dissenting opinion by a collegiate judge was to be put into writing and had to be motivated.

Most superior continental courts abided by the principle, first developed in roman-canonical procedure, that every stage of the proceedings had to be recorded – *quod non est in actis, non est in mundo.* For the legal historian, it is extremely frustrating that, in many cases, the *relatio* and its discussion are not, or very unsatisfactorily, recorded. It may be argued that, for our understanding of the types of legal reasoning that led to collegiate decisions in collegiate courts, the deliberation following the account of the *juge-rapporteur* may well have been the crucial stage of the proceedings. The report *(relatio)* provides a model of reasoning and argumentation which could be (and no doubt frequently was) followed by a majority of the court. It may still be an oblique source to the (legal) grounds of the decision, but it is much more closely linked to the actual decision than other sources which are sometimes referred to as possible patterns of motivation (such as, e. g., learned legal opinions, advocates' *plaidoyers,* or other documents presented by the litigants). In most secular courts under consideration in this volume, the *relatio* remained unrecorded, and records of the discussions of the court *in camera* provide little insight in the actual reasonings (see, for example, the transcripts by *C. Verhas* of recorded discussions from the *Resoluties* at the Dutch *Hoge Raad*).

F. Ranieri's contribution on the *relatio* at the Reichskammergericht opens new perspectives, though the *Kameralpraxis* developed at Speyer and Wetzlar should certainly not be projected as a general style practised in foreign courts. Even so, the general pattern of the *relatio* at the Empire's court, and its more formal method of elaboration (illustrated, in *Ranieri*'s selection of source material, by the extracts from Rosencorb's manual), probably offer the most accurate insight in the formal and legal aspects of judicial decision-making process during the early-modern period.

Finally, it must be reiterated that the very concept of a legal reasoning supporting judicial decisions is largely speculative, as other (*viz.* non-legal) considerations could carry the decision. Moreover, even in cases where controversial legal questions were raised, in the absence of a general duty to express the legal grounds of a judgment, the decisions of collegiate tribunals could more conveniently be reached through possibly contrasting reasonings, as these were not expressed. Sovereign courts could also, as *S. Dauchy* reminds us for the Paris Parlement, lay aside strictly legal considerations in favour of an 'equitable' judicial settlement of the litigation.

3. Recording the practice and decisions of superior courts

By the end of the middle ages, the various stages of the superior courts' practice were generally being recorded according to established rules. Mostly, the court had its own official records, which were accessible to senior members of the court only, or under their supervision. Even at the Roman Rota, where the keeping of records was more closely linked to the staff of individual judges, later early-modern developments (analysed by *G. Dolezalek*) tended to confirm earlier practices while ensuring that the clerical personnel and their recordings came henceforth more strictly under the control of the institution. However, even when, at the Roman Rota, the organisation of records was different from that at other courts, all these records appear to show much in common as regards their nature and finality.

Of all the courts discussed in the present volume, the Regia Gran Corte of Sicily provides us here with the most complete view of the various stages of the records' emergence and development. *A. Romano*'s essay surveys the development from the era of oral proceedings until, by the end of the middle ages, elaborate serial records were produced which form, at the present-day, a massive, if still largely inadequately accessible, documentation of the court's workings throughout the early-modern times. *Romano*'s evocation of the court's records at the Palermo Archives will no doubt sound suggestive to many a historian who has had the experience of visualising the archivistic holdings of ancient courts. Anyone who has been admitted to the large hall at the Archives Nationales in Paris where the bulk of the remaining records of the Parlement are preserved, realises that the thousands of *registres* filling the shelves reflect a myriad of facets of Ancien Régime society. Does it, however, also reflect legal developments?

In Sicily, throughout the changes from the twelfth century onwards, it would seem that the foremost purpose of drafting instruments was to convey proof of the process of law to which the litigation has been subjected, and, when a formal decision had been reached, to safeguard the *res iudicata* in its various aspects. At the beginning, when oral proceedings prevailed, decisions may not have been recorded, yet written instruments were delivered to the parties so that their rights, as settled by the court, might be authenticated 'ad perpetuam memoriam'. Later, as witnessed in Frederic II's legislation, it became a matter of principle that judgments should be proferred in written form, and, in conformity with the general development in roman-canonical procedure, other stages of the proceedings were being recorded. By the 14th century, the court kept records of all or most stages of the proceedings. The judgments themselves, as they were recorded or 'registered', remained brief and did not mention any grounds. From his study of the source-material, *A. Romano* concludes that the most likely purposes of these records were to secure the audit of fees due, and the control of the regularity of the proceedings; apart from this procedural safeguard, the records do not appear to have fulfilled any legal purposes, or to have provided a repository for judicial precedents.

Similar patterns and considerations appear in the other continental European courts, but, inevitably, with important variations, in particular during later periods. The sixteenth-century Italian 'mos rotalis' referred to by *M. Ascheri* may highlight how the records of proceedings expressed the *Verhandlungsmaxime* as the fundamental tenet of *ius commune* inspired procedure of superior courts, but the way this principle was applied at Siena to the recording of legal reasonings advanced by counsel during their arguments would not seem to have had its equivalent in Northern Europe. The recording techniques applied at Siena would suggest that these records were meant to be retrievable for future reference, but the early practice of the court does not indicate that much notice was taken from its own archives. *M. Ascheri*'s findings are that *ius commune* sources, and printed legal sources in general, played a far greater role than Sienese case law, even for questions where Sienese *ius proprium* was at stake. Possibly, as the author surmises, this disregard of Sienese particular statute and case law may be explained (as already mentioned) by the Rota judges' limited tenure of three years, which favoured reliance on *ius commune*. In France and in the Low Countries, where customary law was strongly rooted and had strengthened its capacity to resist *ius commune* influences after the homologation of customs and the subsequent rise of scholarship in connection with customary law, and where appointments in the superior courts were not subjected to restrictions of tenure, the development of case law in relation to *iura propria* was much more pronounced. Eventually, even at Siena, we learn, the appearance of legal imprints dealing with local or regional law fostered its recognition in the Rota's practice.

Several authors believe that the records' use was largely confined to the court's internal administration. For the medieval Paris Parlement, *B. Auzary-Schmaltz* notes that, as access to the records was strictly limited to qualified members of the courts, counsel for the litigants had to rely on their own means to find out and prove precedents which they wished to refer to in their arguments. Not surprisingly, the scope of these alleged precedents was limited; more often, a previous decision was not called upon to establish that the court had acknowledged or applied an abstract rule of law, but to argue that their client could claim that the case was *res iudicata* – not, however, in the sense of estoppel by record. Particularly where institutional (or quasi-institutional) parties disputed over long-term, recurrent grievances, which, perhaps under slightly different circumstances, were repeatedly submitted to the court, *res iudicata* was a convenient argument. Moreover, it could be combined with the conventional lines on possession, one of the most versatile and common legal concepts in forensic *ius commune* arguments under *mos italicus* influence. The practice of the Great Council of Malines – which, certainly at its beginnings, was modelled on the Paris Parlement – reflects the same findings *(A. Wijffels).* At another regional court influenced by the Paris standard, the Parlement of Dijon, the domestic finality of the records is also illustrated by the variety of its series, which reflect the internal organization of the court and its peculiarities, rather than any 'Cartesian' distinction regarding jurisdiction and procedures; in spite of these restrictions, decisions at the Burgundian Parlement were not only kept as drafts *(minutes),* but also in more formal, 'solemn' registers *(J. Bart).*

G. Dolezalek's remarks on the practice of the Roman Rota around 1700 perhaps reinforces a contrario the importance attached to the records of the proceedings and judgments for establishing the exact effect of *res iudicata.* Here, too, the methods of recording the various stages of the proceedings (which seem to apply the *Verhandlungsmaxime* with a vengeance), culminating in the *registrum,* appear to serve the purpose of overseeing the proceedings. At the stage of the decision, however, there is a double paradox. First, the judgments did not include any legal grounds, apparently for the same, mainly procedural, reasons generally given in support of the omission. At the same time, the Rotal *decisio* in its technical sense, an elaborate opinion drafted by the judge in charge and based on the collegiate deliberations on the case, was communicated to the parties, partly in order to encourage an amicable solution, partly to ensure a full adversarial approach to all aspects of the case, including the treatment of specific legal questions. The second paradox is that precisely these *decisiones* which encompassed the answers to the legal *dubia* were not technically included in the records, and did not affect the *res iudicata*. Yet they were collected and, in printed or unpublished form, they represent one of the most accomplished examples of case law in the Ancien Régime civil law tradition.

4. Reporting the practice and decisions of superior courts

The continental 'reports' are, in spite of some (very few) late-medieval and (more abundant) sixteenth-century examples, an early-modern phenomenon. In several legal systems considered in the present volume, printed reports came late, although the court and the court's practice they referred to had been well-established for a long time. This seems particularly true in Sicily *(A. Romano)* and in the Low Countries *(A. Wijffels, J. Th. de Smidt);* the late start of printed reports at Siena was largely due to the particular political context in Tuscany *(M. Ascheri)*. However, the most striking feature is the magnitude of the development during the last centuries of the Ancien Régime in most legal systems. *G. Dolezalek*'s long list for the Roman Rota seems to testify to a virtually systematic attempt to make *decisiones* available in print. In France, the numbers and weight of publications related to the practice of the Paris Parlement reflect the court's importance beyond its own jurisdiction for the whole realm *(S. Dauchy)*, but at the same time, provincial courts (such as the Dijon Parlement) took their cue from their illustrious model in the capital and developed a similar literature at regional levels *(M. Petitjean)*. These 'reports', moreover, are but one aspect of an even much greater body of early-modern legal literature, which, in various guises, is characterised by its reliance on legal practice, especially with respect to the superior courts' proceedings and decisions. In addition, many doctrinal works tended to include an increasing amount of references to that practice-related literature. In Holland, a primer for law practitioners as the *Inleidinge* was often bound with blank pages between Grotius's text so that it could be complemented with material gathered during the court's hearings *(J. Th. de Smidt)*.

Most of the contributions focus their attention on printed collections, but it is clear that in many of the jurisdictions under survey, one has to take into account a 'dark number' of unpublished collections, some of which, on the strength of the numbers of manuscript copies preserved, enjoyed nevertheless a considerable success. In fact, in some of the legal systems where the first imprints of reports were late to appear, the evidence is that manuscript collections had been circulating for a few generations. Nor did the publication of a collection in a particular jurisdictional area stop practitioners from starting their own, unpublished collection.

In general, the technique of continental collections owed much to the prevailing methods of legal scholarship at the time. As a result, their approach follows by and large the major changes which affected the mainstream legal literature of the civil law tradition. Scarce as they may be, the medieval examples show that they adopted existing moulds. Inevitably, this was the case when a collection of cases was incorporated in a commentary on procedural or customary law, but also when the author attempted greater originality and was breaking new ground. This was the case with the Parisian advocate Jean le Cocq, whose *Quæstiones* were clearly conceived and inspired by a traditional academic model *(B. Auzary-Schmaltz).* Sixteenth-century (and still many early seventeenth-century) collections of *Decisiones* were mostly entirely in the *mos italicus* tradition, while later collections embody the fundamental changes brought about by the *usus modernus.* These changes are not only reflected in the methods and scholarship which appear in the treatment of the individual *decisiones* or the legal issues to which they gave rise, but sometimes also in the general arrangement of the *decisiones,* though few collections ever followed a general order *ratione materiæ.* Perhaps the most striking development regarding later collections is their ability to combine *ius commune* and *ius proprium,* and their contribution to the formulation of the latter. The role of the Parlement of Paris in elaborating and establishing a *droit coutumier commun* in (the customary law regions of) France, thereby strongly buttressing a project set out by sixteenth-century jurists in their doctrinal works, is one of the best-known examples of such an influence. In the Low Countries, both minor collections (e.g. that by De Grysperre) and major collections (for Holland, cf. *J. Th. de Smidt*) often reveal a proclivity to concentrate on *ius proprium* rules; for the superior courts sitting in The Hague (Court of Holland and *Hoge Raad*) *De Smidt*'s emphasis on the strong links between reports or other practice-related works and the development of Roman-Dutch law (which should be understood as a Dutch variation on *usus modernus*) reminds us that a comparable function can be attributed in very different political systems, where the rapport between *ius proprium* and *ius commune* could be decisively closer than in the French *pays de coutumes.*

Much research still needs to be done regarding the materials which were used by the authors of *Decisiones*-collections. To some degree, the authorship offers a clue as to the sources pressed into service. The vast majority of authors were clearly steeped in day-to-day practice, either as advocates or as judges. Local traditions may have played a part, which may perhaps explain why in Burgundy, most *recueils* seem to have stemmed from the Bar, and only few from the Bench *(M. Petitjean)*. The authorship does not necessarily guarantee a distinct form of treatment. At the Great Council of Malines, the cases reported by De Grysperre provide at best only very general insight in the reasoning and discussions which led to the judgment, even when the author had been sitting as a judge or had presented the *relatio;* on the other hand, the most important *Decisiones*-collection published in connection with the Great Council was written by P. Christinaeus, an advocate, and a contemporary of De Grysperre, and its reputation and success was due to the breadth of legal scholarship displayed in a practical format and perspective, although Christinaeus generally did not presume to present any 'authentic' *rationes decidendi (C. H. van Rhee)*. Both judges and advocates not only referred to printed, widely available legal literature, but also to the opinions of the judges in the case referred to. In most of the legal systems here considered, neither the judges nor the advocates could warrant the authenticity of their information regarding what had happened *in camera (S. Dauchy)*, though information by a judge will perforce often appear to be *prima facie* more reliable. Whatever the position of the authors, they frequently used (and reprocessed) argumentative documents which had been produced during the proceedings. At the Roman Rota, the *Decisio* proferred relied heavily on the advocates' *informationes* (in particular the arguments proposed by the advocate of the party whom the court was inclined to favour). At the Royal Great Court of Sicily, *A. Romano* suggests that some authors of *Decisiones*-collections may have relied on the *vota*. In Paris, *S. Dauchy* mentions the advocates' opinions *(plaidoiries)*, which were recorded; the (elusive) reports by the *rapporteurs;* and also the court's records, though, as a matter of caution, these were not reproduced literally. In Paris and elswehere, the authenticity of *rationes decidendi* proposed by the authors of private collections remained doubtful – whatever the claims expressed on title-pages and in prefaces –, and sometimes, as in Burgundy, the lack of authenticity was a pretext to criticise the publication (though *M. Petitjean*'s essay seems to imply that at Dijon, fellow-lawyers showed a more general propensity to make scathing comments on the works by their Burgundian colleagues).

If, overwhelmingly, collections of case law were written by members of the legal profession, it would also seem that the finality of these collections can be characterised in general terms as written for members of the legal profession – these were works by practitioners, for practitioners. The phrase 'ad utilitatem advocatorum, ad usum studendi et commodum practicorum et curialium', quoted by *A. Romano* from Sicilian collections, sums up the essential purposes expressed by authors, editors and publishers of collections throughout Europe. Of course, such aims were shared with other practice-related literature. Therefore, the most striking feature of this literature is perhaps that its orientation to legal practice implied that it did not purport to contribute (as other contemporary genres of legal literature) to academic legal scholarship. Yet, at the same time, it meant to fulfil a definite educational function on behalf of practitioners *(S. Dauchy)* and its approach was usually closer to the prevailing modes of academic scholarship than to the basic manuals of a more clerical type. Thus a form of legal scholarship *sui generis* developed, the main purpose of which was not, however, to provide more or less 'binding' precedents for future cases *(G. Dolezalek).*

The development of these doctrinal collections of case law in most continental legal systems gave rise to a massive bulk of literature, which was bound to influence the assessment of judicial decisions in the law-creating process. While statute law, under the systematising influences of both *usus modernus* and *Vernunftrecht* in general tended towards a greater degree of abstraction, the *recueils de jurisprudence* often tended to assert more strongly their case-based origins. At the Roman Rota, *G. Dolezalek* observes that, whereas at an earlier stage, the drafting of *decisiones* focused on abstract legal issues, it gradually included more information about the specific aspects of the cases. *M. Petitjean* relates that an author like J. Melenet, practising and writing during the seventeenth century, still held the traditional view that collections reporting on decisions in individual cases were not helpful in understanding the law. By the early nineteenth century, however, the time was ripe for a concept and presentation of case law publications based on a full (and often literal) account of the factual and procedural circumstances, as witnessed by the quote from the preface to J. van der Linden's collection published in 1803 *(J. Th. de Smidt).*

II. The English and American Traditions

1. Legal authorities and judicial precedents

Anglo-American law does not reveal the same ambivalence towards the position of case law among the other sources of law as is found in continental European systems. This does not mean, though, that case reports have always had a uniform weight among the sources of law, or that a form of a doctrine of more or less binding precedent existed back into the early roots of the English legal system. *J. H. Baker* shows that reference to previous decisions is found in legal arguments in the early fourteenth century, though at this stage the citation is to case law remembered by the judge and counsel rather than to case law found in any written report. By the sixteenth and seventeenth century citations to previous cases are frequent *(D. J. Ibbetson, W. H. Bryson).* Normally these are to cases found in printed texts – the Year

Books or the later 'nominate' reports – though reference to cases remembered by counsel or found in manuscript collections is by no means uncommon. Moreover, by this time, cases are increasingly seen as 'precedents' which serve in some way to define what the law is. While it is not until the eighteenth century (at the earliest) that any doctrine of the binding force of such precedents is articulated, by the end of the sixteenth century there is a clear shift in the direction of treating reported cases as 'authority'; the weight of case law is coming to displace 'reason' as the most forceful form of legal argument. In part there is only a difference of degree between the citation of cases in the early fourteenth century and in the early seventeenth century: the far wider availability of the printed text compared to the manuscript, the uniformity of production permitting uniformity of citation, the growth of the legal profession reducing the extent to which reliance could be placed on generally accepted 'common learning', all strengthened the reliance on previous case law on the surface of legal argumentation. In part, though, it is a difference in substance: lawyers are increasingly treating previous cases as the starting point of legal argument, not simply as points on which an argument by analogy can be anchored.

The parallel studies of *Ibbetson* and *Bryson* show this development occurring in both the Common law courts and the Court of Chancery. By contrast, there is no such reliance on previous case law in the English ecclesiastical courts. *R. H. Helmholz* shows that the practice of reporting decisions began here far later than in comparable secular courts, and that forensic arguments are typically bolstered by reference to commentators on the learned laws rather than to any case law generated by the court, though as elsewhere in Europe the jurisprudence of the Rota did have some part to play in the courts' decision-making processes. Doctrine and *ius commune* play a significant part here; they are almost entirely absent from the English secular courts.

Anglo-American reporting is very heavily biased towards the courts at the top of the legal hierarchy. In Virginia, for example, *Bryson* notes that almost no reports survive from the county courts, though several sets survive from appellate courts. Exactly the same is true of England: the number of reports emanating from anywhere other than sittings of the King's courts in Westminster Hall is tiny. These central courts were undoubtedly more significant than the mass of local courts throughout England, and the law articulated in them was commensurately more influential. It is noteworthy that perhaps the most widely circulating set of manuscript reports in the late sixteenth century was the so-called Cases in Camera Scaccarii, containing reports of cases decided in the Court of Exchequer Chamber which had been created by statute in 1585 as essentially the highest appellate court in England. In addition, as is shown by *Baker* in the previous volume and *Ibbetson* in the present one, reporting had some educational function, and the lawyers who were being educated were predominantly those who aspired to practise in the superior courts.

Within the superior courts, it is worth noting that there is a very strong bias towards the reporting of cases in the Common law courts of Common Pleas and King's Bench rather than in the Chancery: very few reports from the latter court survive from the period before 1600, and even after that date the number of Chancery reports is consistently dwarfed by the number of Common law reports. There is little comparable bias in favour of reports taken by prominent judges or lawyers. The medieval Year Books circulated anonymously, and it is only recently that legal historians have begun to identify some of their authors. Similarly, many of the surviving compilations of reports from the Common law courts of the sixteenth and seventeenth centuries have no names attached to them; while there is some reason to believe that their authorship was known to contemporaries, the absence of any explicit attribution in most of the surviving manuscripts suggests that at this time the value of the report was not dependent on the prestige of the reporter. There may have been some shift in this regard in the seventeenth century, particularly when many volumes of reports came to be printed. Sir Edward Coke's Reports, published from 1600, enjoyed a significant measure of authority related to Coke's own authority as a lawyer; and the reports coming into print in the second half of the century are commonly attributed (not always accurately or even plausibly) to judges and advocates of the previous generations. In the same way, *Bryson* observes that it is not until the end of the seventeenth century that reports associated with strong Chancery judges are found, and *Helmholz* notes that there are no reports linked to well-known ecclesiastical lawyers.

2. Recording the practice and decisions of the superior courts

As in continental Europe, within the Anglo-American tradition the records of cases were hardly adequate to permit the development of any sophisticated concept of case law. Their function was not to provide material for future legal argument but to record the stages of process of a dispute (in the English Court of Common Pleas, for example), or at least those stages of process which had involved appearance before judges or legal officials (as in the Court of Chancery). Indeed, the final outcome of the dispute seems to have been of less concern to the recording clerks than were its interlocutory stages; in the Common law courts, where the formal stages of process would have occurred at Westminster but the actual trial of the issue – typically by jury – would have taken place in the region where the action had arisen, the initiative for causing the decision in the case to be recorded lay with the victorious party, and it was perhaps only if he needed to enforce the judgment or wished to establish *res iudicata* that he would go to the trouble and expense of procuring the enrolment of the decision. Thus, in the case transcribed by *Ibbetson,* it is only from the reports and not from the record that we are able to learn what the judgment of the court was. Similarly in the English ecclesiastical courts *Helmholz* notes that the sentence of the court would not necessarily be recorded, though the process in the Court of Chancery described by *Bryson* was perhaps more regular in this respect.

Though the principal function of the courts' records was to maintain and lubricate the courts' own internal administrative procedures, access to them seems not to have been limited to the judges and officials of the courts. *Ibbetson,* for example, observes that at the end of the sixteenth century the reference to the court's record of a case might frequently be included in a report of the arguments in the case, that a reporter might note that he had himself verified the record of the case, and that arguments in subsequent cases might occasionally be based on earlier decisions cited by counsel apparently from the records of the court. None the less, although the access to the courts' records may not have been restricted their utility can hardly have been great. As has been seen, all too frequently they do not record what the judgment of the court was, and when the judgment of the court is recorded the reasons which lay behind it never appear. If the continental tradition was hostile to the motivation of judgments, the Common law tradition was no less so. In practice, therefore, it was only where the parties had themselves formulated their dispute with extreme precision, where there was no need for the determination of any extraneous material facts, and where the judgment of the court had actually been recorded, that the court's record could ever have been used as a formal precedent; such cases are exceedingly rare.

3. Reporting the practice and decisions of superior courts

Case reports occupy a more central position in the Anglo-American tradition than in continental Europe. Though an abstract doctrinal literature did exist by the late medieval period (principally in the form of readings – lecturae – on statutes) this was relatively insignificant, and there is nothing at all to parallel the collections of consilia found elsewhere in Europe.

The Year Books, described by *Baker* in the previous volume, exist from the second half of the thirteenth century, and by the middle of the fourteenth century there is some reason to think that their production was the result of more than the chance initiative of individual lawyers. For whatever reason, the arrival of printing in the late fifteenth century coincided with the end of the regular production of Year Books, though they continued to be printed and reprinted into the seventeenth century. They had, and were perceived to have, an educational function; at times this may have been explicitly pedagogical, but in any event they were the principal vehicle for the transmission of legal knowledge and legal ideas from generation to generation. In purely functional terms, they are the equivalent of the doctrinal literature of continental Europe.

The decline of the production of Year Books did not reflect any decline in the practice of reporting: through the sixteenth century – and beyond – lawyers made their own manuscript collections of reports, and there is abundant evidence that many of these collections circulated within the legal community in London *(Ibbetson, Bryson)*. Two of these collections were printed in the sixteenth century – those of Plowden and Dyer – and many more came into print in the seventeenth and eighteenth centuries. From a purely English perspective the law reports of the sixteenth to eighteenth centuries can be seen to represent the continuation of the practice of reporting of the thirteenth to fifteenth centuries, but from a wider European point of view they can be seen as part of the main stream of *decisiones*-literature found throughout the continent at this time.

It is, however, as well not to over-emphasise the similarity between English and continental European materials. The medieval Year Books contain remarkably little that can with justice be described as decisiones: their focus is firmly on the arguments of advocates and the extempore responses to those arguments by the judges. This was inevitable given the nature of medieval English legal process, for the concern of the court was firmly centred on the way on which a legal question was to be put to thc jury, not on the way in which it was to be answered. Judges were hardly deciding cases in any way which would be recognisable to a modern lawyer, or to a medieval lawyer in continental Europe. Where there was no decisio, we seek in vain for any ratio decidendi. This is not to say that there was no scope for case law in medieval England, for just as lawyers were primarily concerned with what manoeuvres were permissible in the game of legal chess (an analogy which was explicitly drawn: *Baker*) so the Year Books gave guidance on precisely this matter. Changes in legal process around the beginning of the sixteenth century meant that judges increasingly came to decide cases, not simply to supervise the putting of questions to the jury; none the less, in most of the surviving corpus of reports the emphasis continues to be placed on the arguments in the case rather than on the reasons for the judgment of the court. There may be no more than an insignificant difference of style between the English and continental collections of reports: the English reporter faced the same problem as did his continental counterpart, that he would normally have no means of knowing the precise basis on which a judgment had been reached (though, as elsewhere, a report made by a judge in the case might claim to be prima facie more reliable in this respect than one made by an advocate or a person not directly involved in it). Some reporters – English or continental – might have constructed their own reasons for the court's decision. Others, more honestly, might have attempted to reconstruct them from the arguments presented; the continental reporter, perhaps with access to a written summary of arguments in the dossier of the case, would be best able to reconstruct those reasons ex post facto, whereas in England, where all argument continued to be oral, the reporter might most easily record the arguments as they were made and append the judgment of the court at the end of his report, leaving the fundamental problem of identifying the ratio decidendi of the case to the reader.

Some Comparative Conclusions

The similarities between the Anglo-American experience and that of continental European courts is marked. To begin with, while in general superior courts came to keep records of their business at some point in the medieval or early-modern periods, these records were primarily designed to satisfy the demands of the internal administrative procedures of the courts. The decision of the court would normally be recorded (though it should be noted that this was not inevitable), but if precise reasons for the decision existed they would invariably be omitted from the record of the case. However useful it would have been to lawyers to have known the basis on which a case had been decided, such information was of little relevance in the context of the courts' administration. In continental Europe this phenomenon might have been justified by reference to the *ius commune* rule that explicit reasons for a decision ought not to be given since they might provide a ground to appeal against a judgment if it could be argued that they were legally inadequate; in England it might have been explained by the fact that the way in which the legal process operated before the sixteenth century served to minimise judicial involvement in the making of judgments; whatever the reason, from the standpoint of the courts' records judgments throughout Europe were apparently unmotivated.

The response to this inadequacy on the part of the records of the superior courts was again pan-European. Those concerned to ensure that legal norms be applied consistently, be they advocates or judges, began to take their own notes, notes which might have circulated among interested lawyers. Such manuscripts are found very early in England, and only slightly later from the Paris Parlement and the Roman Rota. In the early-modern period, more slowly in some states than in others, collections of these notes were printed and hence achieved a far wider audience than would ever have been possible when dissemination was exclusively in the form of manuscripts. While decisions known solely from manuscript collections might have been citable in some courts, in general (and unsurprisingly) the printed texts were afforded a privileged status, so much so that printed reports of cases decided in other jurisdictions might sometimes have been referred to in court in preference to local decisions which had not circulated in printed form. We see this, for example, with citations of the French Jean le Coq and Guy Pape in De Grysperre's reports from Malines, of the French Jehan Papon in Neostadius' notes from the Dutch *Hoge Raad,* of Guy Pape in Meichsner's *Decisiones* from the German *Reichskammergericht,* or of the Neapolitan Matteo d'Afflitto in Siena; a fortiori it was the case with the decisions of the Roman Rota, for these had pretensions to general applicability found in the decisions of no other court.

These reports were unofficial: they were made by interested lawyers for their own use and for the use of other lawyers. Even where the compiler was a judge his reports were still essentially private collections which enjoyed no more de jure authority than the collections of any other lawyers. As private collections, their style varied considerably. This was not predominantly a variation between regions or states; it was a variation between individuals. Thus, where different reports of the same case are found the stylistic differences between them may be no less marked than those existing between reports of cases from different states or from the same state in different periods. Stylistic factors might have affected the degree of influence exerted by any particular volume of reports. The closer they moved towards the clear formulation of a ratio decidendi for a case, whether or not this represented the actual basis on which the case had been decided, the more likely it was that they would be cited as evidence of legal rules – though other factors, such as the extent to which a particular volume was regarded as reliable (which may have been a completely different thing from the extent to which that volume was in fact accurate), came into play too.

These similarities in the material form of records and reports of the decisions of superior courts of the different European states did not entail that case law functioned in the same way as a source of law in the different jurisdictions. Central to the variation between them was the role played by doctrine, and in particular the doctrine of the learned laws and the *ius commune.* Most obviously, where the learned laws were recognised as a formal source of law there was comparatively less scope for arguments derived from the practice of the courts than where there was no such acceptance of the validity of the learned laws. In an extreme form, case law might have been admitted as a source of law only where other sources (the learned laws, local statutory laws, custom) were silent or inconclusive; less extremely, case law was still only one source among many, and the relatively small volume of available case reports meant that it would normally be overshadowed by arguments derived from the learned laws.

More tentatively, we might suspect that where legal argument was primarily based on received doctrine arguments based on case law would function in very much the same way. It was of central importance therefore to identify what was being decided by the court and the reasons which lay behind it – the ratio decidendi of the case – for it was only this that could have the status of a rule, albeit a rule without formally binding authority. Thus it is that the *Decisiones* of Paulus Christinaeus or the cases reported by Cornelius Neostadius, for example, bear a close resemblance to the style of civilian consilia, and those emanating from the Roman Rota or the Paris collection of Jean le Coq, for example, specify at their head the precise legal question in dispute. By contrast, in England, where received doctrine is not recognisable as a formal source of law outside the ecclesiastical courts, the reporters are more concerned to extract elements from the oral arguments produced to the court and little attempt is ever made to formulate the ratio decidendi of a case. Equally, where cases are cited by De Grysperre, Christinaeus, or Neostadius they are not formally distinguished from citations from the learned laws or from the printed commentaries on customary law; whereas in late-sixteenth century England the citation of previous cases was more concerned with the establishment of analogy than authority, and analogy could be drawn with any part of an argument, not simply from the ratio decidendi of a case.

We are left, therefore, with a paradox. In the continental tradition, especially when dominated by the *mos italicus,* case law was simply one source among many, and arguments from case law would most commonly be subsidiary to arguments from other sources. This contrasts with the Common law tradition within which case law was already the primary source before the early-modern period. On the other hand, continental lawyers were more concerned than their counterparts in the Common law with the derivation of formal legal rules from cases and with the application of these rules alongside other sources of law. For the Common lawyer the absence of any determinate ratio decidendi meant that case law was, and remains today, an inherently dynamic source of law. By the last two centuries of the Ancien Régime we may recognise throughout Europe (and, at the end of this period, America) the operation of a system of case law; while the details of this varied from jurisdiction to jurisdiction, nowhere was the goal of achieving formal consistency between like cases allowed to stand in the way of a degree of flexibility in argument which permitted the law to change over time.

Part One

English and American Traditions

J. H. BAKER

The Common-Law Courts of Medieval England: Year Books and Plea Rolls

Introduction

Given the many thousands of cases reported in the year books, and the hundreds of miles of parchment rolls filled with the records of the superior courts in England during the year-book period (*c.* 1270 - 1535),[1] it is impracticable to think in terms of a 'typical' case and difficult even to identify typical categories of case. Part of the problem, as our examples will demonstrate, is that the relationship between the report and record is not constant. As a general rule, the record is a formal minute of all the stages in a suit which the parties chose to have recorded. Most entries on the rolls stop short of a judgment, presumably as a result of a private settlement, the abandonment of hope, or the exhaustion of finance. In those cases where a judgment is entered, the record stands as incontrovertible evidence of what the successful party has won, and for this purpose the previous pleadings are important as establishing exactly what property, wrong, contract, or whatever, was in dispute. It may incidentally serve as a precedent for other litigants in the future by indicating judicial recognition of a particular action, or of the forms whereby a certain result can be achieved, or of a particular mode of pleading. But it was not part of the raison d'être of the record to explain the result, by setting out the legal arguments made by the parties or the authorities on which they relied. The vast majority of records are in fact quite useless as precedents, because the entries were made in common form and vary from each other only in particulars of people, places, things, and dates, matters which – however historically interesting they may be – are of no legal consequence.

A common form of entry on the plea roll in an action of trespass,[2] for instance, will begin by stating that the defendant was attached to answer

[1] The plea rolls of the two central courts of common law – the King's Bench and Common Pleas – are in the Public Record Office (classes KB 27 and CP 40 respectively). For their format, see 5 CSC 15 - 17.

[2] The action of trespass (L. *transgressio*) was used for the recovery of monetary damages for a wrong done. The example given here is of the species called 'assault

the plaintiff in a plea that he, on such a day, and in such a place, with force and arms, namely with swords and staves (or staves and knives), assaulted, beat and wounded the plaintiff so that his life was despaired of, and inflicted other outrages upon him, against the peace of the lord king, to the plaintiff's damage. This opening pleading by the plaintiff was called the 'declaration' or 'count' *(narratio),* and its object was to add narrative detail to the bare assertion in the writ *(breve),* the Chancery document which authorised the suit to commence.[3] The declaration had to follow the writ exactly, or the latter might be quashed. But here we may pause to remark that the allegations of fact made in the declaration are not all to be taken literally. The swords, staves and knives are invariably fictional: the particulars of 'force and arms' were always given in the same way, listing dangerous weapons, without regard to the actual force used, and even where the trespass involved nothing more violent than the munching of grass by placid cows. Similarly, the 'life despaired of' and 'other outrages' *(alia enormia)* were common-form phrases put into every declaration for battery. The same formula served not only for a vicious armed attack but also for a road accident or the abduction by a paramour of a willingly adulterous wife. What the plaintiff had to allege formally in his declaration was not the same as what he had to prove by evidence at the trial. The legal fiction is more frequently encountered in trespass than in other actions, but in various forms it is encountered in many other areas of the common law.[4]

The record will continue after the declaration with the defendant's appearance and plea *(placitum).* Although this was the defendant's opportunity to tell his side of the story, in the vast majority of trespass cases he was supposed to take 'the general issue': that is, 'he denies the force and wrong etc. and whatever is against the peace of the lord king, and says that he is no way guilty of the alleged trespass'. By these words – the plea of Not guilty – the whole of the plaintiff's case was denied. And that brought the pleadings to a close, because there was now a dispute for trial: what common lawyers call an issue *(exitus).* The next stage was therefore to order the sheriff (by writ of *venire facias juratores*) to summon a jury to try the issue and say whether the defendant was guilty or not. This might take a good deal of parchment and wax, especially if there was laxity or a suspicion of bias on the part of the sheriff or his officers, and the steps

---

and battery'. Text 4 shows the form of the Latin entry in a trespass action for beating a servant.

[3] The writ itself was put on file, but was not copied verbatim onto the roll. There is a summary of the writ immediately before the declaration.

[4] This is a problem which bedevils, in particular, the history of negligence in tort: see, e.g., *J. H. Baker,* Introduction to English Legal History (3rd ed., 1990), 456 - 463. For some examples of fictions, see ibid., 230 - 232, 650. See also: The Use of Assumpsit for Restitutionary Money Claims (1995) 15 CSC 31 - 57.

taken to produce 'twelve good men and true' in court at the assizes might actually take up more space in the record than the pleadings. If and when the jury finally comes, its verdict will be recorded in the simplest terms: 'the jurors, having been sworn to say the truth concerning the foregoing matters, say upon their oath that the defendant is guilty [*or* not guilty, *as the case may be*] of the trespass' and assess the damages and costs to be awarded as so many pounds, shillings and pence. The judgment follows, with similar brevity: 'Therefore it is considered that the plaintiff do recover against the defendant his damages and costs as assessed by the jury in manner aforesaid'. Such is the most straightforward kind of entry; and such clerical straightforwardness is extremely common even as late as the sixteenth century. Neither the plaintiff nor the defendant, nor the jury, has placed on record any specific facts which might raise interesting legal questions. All we learn as a matter of principle from such an entry is that a plaintiff may recover damages for a serious attack with armed force. We may read ten thousand such entries and learn no more law than that. Nor shall we ever know the true range of facts underlying the recorded cases except in the case of a 'special plea', whereby a defendant set out some of the facts of the particular case.[5] Special pleading was most common in the case of real property, and often raised intricate questions of title to land. In other branches of the law, it was much less common.[6] A special plea would normally require a response: a replication from the plaintiff, a rejoinder from the defendant, and so on until issue was reached.

The record served the turn of the parties perfectly well in its undeveloped form. But it would be of value to posterity for the purposes of precedent only when it diverged in some way from the simplest common forms. For example, the plaintiff brings some new kind of action, or alleges facts which have not been considered before, or perhaps omits something which has always been alleged before (such as the 'force and arms' in trespass); or the defendant tries to plead a new kind of defence; or the jury finds the

---

[5] For some year-book examples of special pleas in trespass, see *J. H. Baker and S. F. C. Milsom,* Sources of English Legal History: private law to 1750 (1986), pp. 310 (abduction of a divorced wife), 311 (treatment given to man having a fit), 312 (distrained horse strangling itself), 314 (custom to turn plough on neighbouring headland), 316 (tithe corn put in barn by neighbour to save it from cattle).

[6] For some commentary on pleading and its relationship to the factual and legal issues in dispute, see *S. F. C. Milsom,* Law and Fact in Legal Development (1967) 17 Univ. Toronto Law Journ. 1 - 19 (reprinted in: Studies in the History of the Common Law (1985), pp. 171 - 189); *J. H. Baker,* Joinder of Issue: the mechanics of pleading, in: 94 Selden Soc. *92 - 103;* Pleading and Litigation as Sources of Law, ibid. *142 - 163;* Introduction to English Legal History (3rd ed.), pp. 84 - 110; *M. S. Arnold,* Law and Fact in the Medieval Jury Trial: out of sight, out of mind (1974) 18 Amer. Journ. Legal Hist. 267 - 280; The Medieval Rules of Pleading (1985), in: 100 Selden Soc. x - xx.

facts in detail. Such variations produce legal questions on the face of the record, and – if judgment follows – the record furnishes an authoritative answer to a specific question.

Sometimes the legal question was raised explicitly by a 'demurrer' *(moratio in lege),* whereby a party admitted all the facts alleged by his opponent but chose to rest his case on the legal proposition that the facts did not entitle the opponent to succeed. Such a proceeding was obviously risky, and until the sixteenth century it was relatively rare. Moreover, the judges were unwilling to give judgment upon demurrer unless they could achieve near unanimity, and so the formal demurrer as often as not reinforced a doubt without resolving it. In the absence of a demurrer, on the other hand, one can never be sure from the record alone whether the legal question which occurs to our minds was explicitly raised at all. It may have been overlooked, or the parties may have agreed not to take it. Only a current of similar examples will carry much force. The precedential value of the record in the year-book period is therefore limited. Many miles of parchment may yield only a few inches of law.

Reports are usually quite different.[7] The year books are important as providing a more direct insight into what happened in court, how cases were argued, and on what grounds they were decided. Only a tiny proportion of cases reached the pages of a law report, but the intellectual value of a report is generally greater than that of the record. Not that year-book reports are without defects of their own. The manuscripts are often corrupt. They omit factual details which would be historically interesting, and indeed often mutilate the facts as formally pleaded and recorded. They are often taken up with minutiae of procedure, or with practical moves in pleading, rather than with general principles of law. But the last observation might equally be made of many modern law reports. At no stage in history is the reporter, any more than the clerk who kept the record, working to facilitate legal history; and the counsel whose arguments he reports are practical men who know when procedural dexterity or technicality will serve a client better than fine jurisprudence.

To a considerable extent, legal historians use reports and records separately, for the practical reason that it is a highly laborious and sometimes fruitless exercise to try to match them up. Nevertheless, it has long been recognised that it is extremely helpful to locate the record of a reported case in order to obtain as complete a picture as possible of a particular piece of litigation. In our first illustrative case, *Corbet* v. *Scurye*

[7] For the origins and earlier history of law reporting in England, see *Baker,* Records, Reports and the Origins of Case-law in England, in: Judicial Records, Law Reports, and the Growth of Case Law (1989) 5 CSC 15 - 46.

(1292),[8] it was necessary to combine the information in two different reports with the record before the case could be understood. In other instances there may be a number of distinct but related cases which need to be put together from the rolls for greater enlightenment. From the fifteenth century onwards, there is the added possibility of finding parallel cases in the Chancery, Star Chamber or Court of Requests. Because of the more liberal use in those courts of detailed factual allegations, augmented by written depositions and interrogatories, such parallel material may throw considerable light on cases recorded more enigmatically in the common-law plea rolls. These other courts are, however, beyond the scope of the present essay.

The four cases chosen to accompany this volume, together with the specimen report and record from the 1292 eyre of Shropshire, printed in our previous volume, represent different degrees of sophistication as well as different relationships between report and record. They are not placed in chronological order, because it is not the intention to imply that the differences represent changes which can be dated. Cases of the simplest kind may still be found in the sixteenth century, while cases of considerable sophistication – especially in the sphere of property law – may be found in the thirteenth and fourteenth centuries. The cases have been chosen to illustrate some of the different functions of the reports and records in simple cases of contract, tort and criminal law. This means, almost by definition, that they are untypical, since the majority of reported cases concerned land law; but English land law is hardly the best context for comparative work of the present kind, and it has been thought safest to exclude it from consideration completely. It is hoped that the legal questions raised by the selected cases will, with the aid of the following commentaries, be comprehended without too much difficulty by readers who have no previous acquaintance with the common law.

I. Chaloner v. Moresle (1329)

The first case is of elemental simplicity. It is an action of trespass taken from a report of the proceedings at one of the last eyres ever commissoned in England.[9] A simplified form of procedure was available before justices in eyre for local complainants of trespass, who were given access to the

[8] *Baker,* Records, Reports and the Origins of Case-law in England, at pp. 42 - 44 (with commentary at pp. 34 - 36).

[9] An eyre (*iter* in Latin) was a peripatetic royal court acting under a commission which empowered the justices to exercise a wide jurisdiction. In the 12th century the eyres had been perceived as the regular royal courts, but with the rise of the two benches they had declined towards extinction.

justices sitting in their own county without the need for an original writ from the Chancery (which was de rigueur in the Common Pleas).[10] The informal complaint was made in a 'bill', a written petition which was supposed to follow the same general form as a writ of trespass but was not enrolled on the record and not preserved. Neither were the pleadings enrolled. The entry on the eyre roll is therefore considerably shorter than the entry of a similar case would be in the King's Bench or Common Pleas. It is, in effect, no more than a memorandum of the verdict, enrolled in the words presumably contained in the bill of complaint, and the judgment. From the verdict in our selected case we can deduce that the plaintiff, Walter le Chaloner, had complained by bill of an assault and battery in the suburbs of Northampton on 8 September 1329,[11] when the defendant struck him two blows across the two middle fingers of his left hand and another blow across his nose. The bill was laid before the justices in eyre when they sat at Northampton later in 1329; and the defendant pleaded Not guilty. The jury found the defendant guilty, damages were assessed by the discretion of the justices at ten marks (£6. 13s. 4d.), and judgment was given for the plaintiff to recover that sum, enforceable by writ of *capias ad satisfaciendum.* Despite the terminology of 'conviction' of a wrong against the king's peace, this was what we should call a civil action for damages. The particular story told, in contrast with the imaginary swords and staves of the standard declaration as used at Westminster, is intended as the truth; and the jury finds it to be true, or at least substantially so.

The report in this case is shorter than the record, and it may be typified as a note of what happened in court, for future reference as a guide to procedure. No argument is mentioned on either side. No specific words are attributed to anyone. Yet the report does add something significant which the bare record conceals beneath the words *per discretionem justiciariorum.* The reporter tells us that the jury had been minded to award two and a half marks (£1. 13s. 4d.), and that this award was increased by £5 because the court could see from its own inspection of the plaintiff that he had been seriously injured. We may guess that his nose was permanently scarred and his hand maimed. Elsewhere in the reports of the same eyre we find damages of £5 increased to £6. 13s. 4d. for putting out an eye, so this latter sum (ten marks) may have been the going rate for a serious wound.[12] Now, it was axiomatic under the common-law system that any question of fact was for the jury, not the court, to decide; and the quantum of damages

---

10 Some litigation in eyre was by writ, and the proceedings could be just as formal as those in the benches at Westminster.

11 The feast of the Nativity of the Blessed Mary, 3 Edw. III. Dates in common-law records were usually expressed by reference to feast-days and regnal years.

12 *Carter* v. *Knoston,* 97 Selden Soc. 159.

depended on fact. The case is thus an early precedent of what became a well-established exception to the general rule, confined in practice to cases of serious personal injury, which permitted the court to increase damages on the basis of its own inspection of the injured party.[13]

II. R. v. Bury (1321)

Our second case is a more elaborate example of the same kind of report, taken from the Crown side of the eyre of London in 1321. Criminal cases are not prominent in the later year books, but they are quite plentiful in the fourteenth century and often provide a lively impression of interchanges at trials.[14] Since most Common Pleas cases – and therefore the vast majority of year-book cases – are reported at the pre-trial stage, these criminal cases have a special value in providing insights into the way judges handled cases at trial. The case of Isabel Bury raised three separate questions of law. Her indictment, as summarised in the eyre roll, shows that she was charged with felonious homicide in killing a clergyman who had tried to throw her out of All Hallows' church, Broad Street, London, for making a noise. An indictment was a formal accusation of a criminal offence, on behalf of the Crown, made either by a 'grand jury' sworn to present all offences known to them or by a coroner's inquest *super visum corporis,* investigating a sudden death. The present case arose from a coroner's inquest.

The first point raised by Isabel was that she had been forcibly removed from the church in breach of the privilege of sanctuary.[15] Normally such a claim, if proved, would entitle the prisoner to be returned to the sanctuary without trial; but in this case the ordinary, having been asked by the judges, produces the decretal[16] which establishes that the privilege does not avail those who commit homicide or mayhem in churches. The report sets out the decretal, in Latin, whereas the record merely states that she was expelled from the church by the churchwardens *pro delicto suo* and taken to Newgate prison. The record was not here designed to serve as a prece-

[13] Later authorities in the vulgate year books are *Anon.* (1348) Mich. 22 Edw. III, fo. 11, pl. 10; *Anon.* (1365) Mich. 39 Edw. III, fo. 20; Mich. 39 Edw. III, fo. 26; *Anon.* (1401) Mich. 3 Hen. IV, fo. 4, pl. 16; *Anon.* (1408) Pas. 9 Hen. IV, fo. 23, pl. 9.

[14] See *J. H. Baker,* Some Early Newgate Reports (1313 - 28), in: *C. Stebbings* ed., Law Reporting in England (1995) 35 - 53.

[15] The report refers to this, rather oddly, as *privilegium clericale.* For the general legal context, see *J. H. Baker,* The English Law of Sanctuary (1990) 2 Eccles. Law Journal 8 - 13.

[16] X. 3.49.10.

dent for the application of the decretal in England. The report, on the other hand, served as the leading case on the subject until the abolition of sanctuary.[17] Her preliminary objection having failed, Isabel Bury was arraigned for felony and refused to plead. Apparently her previous objection had not been made in person, because the justices were unsure whether she was dumb for natural causes or was (in our later terminology) 'standing mute of malice'. If a prisoner obstinately stood mute on arraignment for felony he was liable to the awful *peine forte et dure,* which involved pressing to death without trial. Since the explanation for a defendant's dumbness was a question of fact, it was necessary to swear in a jury to establish whether or not the prisoner was able to speak. The court in the present case was reminded of the procedure by the clerk of the court, and a jury was duly sworn in; but the judge attempted in the mean time to persuade her to speak, pointing out that if the jury found that she could speak she would have waived the opportunity of a trial. At this point she called for mercy, making further enquiry unnecessary. The court did not, however, sentence her to the *peine forte et dure* but allowed her to plead to the felony. The reporter thought the court had been generous on account of her sex, and that a man would not have been given the same indulgence. The record, we may note, says nothing of this exchange.

Isabel's third move was to assert that she had killed the cleric in self-defence. No doubt he had laid hands on her first, but that would not in itself be a reason for killing him; she would have to show that the force used to defend herself was appropriate to the circumstances. This was a question of fact for a jury, but it could not be pleaded specially in a criminal case; in other words, it was a matter to be given in evidence, not entered on the record. The court therefore pressed her to plead Not guilty in general terms, so that she could put her case to the jury. So she did; but the report and the record both show that she did not convince them, and that she was sentenced to death. On conviction of felony, a felon's property was forfeit to the Crown. The record of Bury's case mentions goods worth £6. 15s. 6d., for which the sheriff was to answer. Further on in the principal manuscript which reports the case there is an epilogue, arising from a claim to some of these goods. Isabel's maid-servant, Joan, established that some of them were her own, and she had them returned; a more substantial claim is made by one Richard le Blaket, who says that he had left some of his things in Joan's custody. The reporter here is interested not in the fate of the individuals or their property but in the procedure for establishing property in such a claim against the Crown.[18]

[17] Because of its inclusion in Sir Anthony Fitzherbert's Graunde Abridgement (*c.* 1514), tit. *Corone,* pl. 420.

[18] 85 Selden Soc. 83 (from Brit. Lib. MS. Harley 453, fo. 33v).

III. Randolf v. Abbot of Hailes (1311)

Our next case is an action of debt.[19] Debt was one of the commonest forms of action, and by the end of the year-book period was by far the most common. However, the vast majority of debt cases did not involve disputes of law or even of fact. They were simply a matter of debt-collection. The great volume of debt cases did not therefore generate a particularly sophisticated law of contract. Most of the reported cases raised questions of procedure and evidence rather than substantive law in the modern sense.

The case of *Corbet* v. *Scurye* (1292), already discussed in our previous volume,[20] illustrates very well the practice of 'tentative pleading'. Pleadings were not originally written documents settled in advance of an oral hearing, as they were by the early modern period, but were made orally at the bar of the court and were open to challenge and discussion. The defendant's pleader comes to court armed not with a single draft plea, but with a series of fall-back positions worked out in advance. At any point he could stick with a particular plea, and have it formally entered; but if there was any likelihood of successful challenge – by means of a demurrer – he would have been well advised to pay heed to the prevailing opinion expressed in discussion and move on to his next position. Corbet had sued Scurye in the Shropshire eyre, without writ, upon an agreement to borrow a horse for jousting, and to return the horse in good condition or £20. This was no ordinary horse-dealing; a £20 horse was a highly prized charger, suitable for a display of prowess by a gentleman of substance such as Scurye, who was to become a member of Parliament three years later. Serjeant Louther, appearing for Scurye, comes prepared with four successive lines of attack. He argues that an action for more than £2 requires a writ rather than a mere bill; that the plaintiff should produce written evidence of the contract; and that the matter belongs to the jurisdiction of the earl marshal, since it touches a feat of arms. All three submissions having failed to persuade the court, he pleads that the horse was returned in good condition, and thereupon issue is joined. The report omits to inform us that the issue was never tried because the parties settled, on the terms that Scurye would pay £13. 6s. 8d. The interest of the case to legal historians is in showing that the rule requiring written evidence was not yet universal. The eyre reporter was more interested in Louther's defence strategy. But the bare record, without the additional details supplied by the reports, is of interest only in the history of jousting.

---

[19] Debt was an action to recover a sum of money, or a fixed quantity of fungibles, owed to the plaintiff.

[20] Records, Reports and the Origins of Case-law in England, in: 5 CSC 15 - 46 at pp. 34 - 36.

The case of the abbot of Hailes likewise illustrates how a number of legally interesting moves might be made in court without being noticed in the record. The record here is almost wholly lacking in legal interest, since it ends with an adjournment before any plea is entered. John Randolf has brought a writ of debt against the abbot for the price of wool sold to Brother John the Blond, one of his monks, the wool having been sold to the use of the abbot *(ad opus abbatis)* and having come into his hands for the benefit of the house. It was common enough for monks to make contracts in this way as agents for religious houses. A monk cannot be sued himself, since upon profession he is dead to the world *(civiliter mortuus)*; but an abbot, though under the same personal disability, as a professed religious, may sue and be sued as representative of his house, which has corporate status.

The report shows that the abbot is represented in the Common Pleas by no less than four serjeants at law (John Stonor, Robert Malberthorpe, Walter Friskney and Gilbert Toudeby), three of whom later became judges. The first objection, taken by Serjeant Stonor, is that the original writ of debt was sent to the sheriff of Gloucestershire (the county where Hailes Abbey is situated) whereas the plaintiff has counted on a contract made in another county, Wiltshire. Staunton J. says that once upon a time that would have been a good objection, but nowadays writs are no longer quashed on this ground. No explanation is forthcoming, but Stonor acquiesces and Malberthorpe takes the second point. The plaintiff has declared upon a sale, and the abbot wishes to plead that he was never party to any sale. The plaintiff responds by producing a written document which records (in the presence of numerous witnesses) that the monk made the contract to the use of the abbey. Malberthorpe objects that the monk could only bind the abbey if he had written authority to do so, and no such authority has been produced. To this the plaintiff answers that the monk had an office – the record calls him the abbot's caretaker *(procurator abbatis)* – which entitled him to make contracts without specific authority on each occasion. The chief justice intervenes to point out that there is nothing special about religious houses in this regard; if Malberthorpe were to send his own servant to buy goods at a market or fair, he would be responsible for settling the bill. Malberthorpe, by now running out of arguments, raises once more the geographical problem; the monk was an official of an abbey in Gloucestershire, and so his authority could not extend to making a contract in Wiltshire. He is nevertheless pressed to say whether the wool came to the use of the house,[21] Staunton J. referring to an earlier case of a similar kind concerning the abbot of Selby. The cited case may be identified in the year books for 1307, when the defendant abbot tried to plead that the

[21] It seems that the transaction with the monk was taken as proved by the writing.

monk who made the written contract had since defected from his religious habit – *evasit a religio suo* – but was forced to join issue on whether the money in question had come to the use of the house.[22] Malberthorpe does not think it wise to join issue in this way, and offers to 'imparl': that is, to have the case adjourned for further consultation. The report then shows Serjeant Friskney, possibly on a later occasion, offering to wage law. A defendant in debt for the price of goods sold was normally allowed to wage his law, that is, to take an oath that he did not owe the money or any penny thereof; if he produced eleven compurgators to support his oath, he was discharged. But the plaintiff in the present case sought to resist this procedure on the grounds that the issue was not whether a contract had been made but whether the goods had come to the use of the abbey. Although Bereford C.J. seems in the report to be in favour of wager of law, another report of the case suggests that the abbot was not allowed to do it, and that Serjeant Toudeby persuaded his client to settle rather than have the case put to a jury. In this case, by way of contrast with Corbet's, the settlement is mentioned in the report but not in the record.[23] The lack of any firm decision would, to modern English thinking, deny the case any precedential value. In the year-book period, however, the presence or absence of a judgment was largely immaterial. The case of the abbot of Hailes stood in the books as authority for the proposition that a religious house could be sued on a contract made on its behalf by one of its monks, if the goods came to the use of the house. It was evidently not the first case in point.[24] Nor did it prevent the point from being discussed again by the next generation.[25] But as a well known decision[26] it contributed somewhat to the establishment of the law of agency and perhaps (less directly) of restitution. Until the dissolution of the monasteries in the 1530s, it remained the common and necessary form of pleading in an action against a religious house on a contract made by a monk, or by a predecessor of the present head, to assert that the goods came to the use of the house.[27]

[22] *Brayton* v. *Abbot of Selby* (1307) Y. B. Trin. 35 Edw. I (Rolls Series), pp. 567 - 569; CP 40/164, m. 197. This case was identified from the plea rolls by Dr Paul Brand, to whom we are most grateful for a note from the record. In the 1311 report, there is a suggestion that 'Sir Henry' [Scrope] was a party, but his involvement does not appear from the record or the year book of 1307.

[23] Most records end without any final decision being entered, and one may guess that many of them were settled; but this is rarely stated in the later rolls.

[24] See *Brayton* v. *Abbot of Selby* (1307), noted above.

[25] There were similar debates in *Anon.* (1348) Y. B. Trin. 22 Edw. III, fo. 8, pl. 16 (also a monk holding an office); *Anon.* (1352) Pas. 26 Edw. III, fo. 1, pl. 1.

[26] The case was printed in A. Fitzherbert, Graunde Abridgement, tit. *Dette,* pl. 168.

[27] A late example is *Thornton* v. *Master of Sutton College* (1535) CP 40/1087, m. 330d (issue joined as to whether the goods came to the use of the house).

IV. Fyloll v. Ashley (1520)

Our final case comes from the end of the year-book period and provides a striking contrast with the tentative pleading of two centuries earlier. It is an action of trespass, which is still recorded with archaic formalism, including the obligatory (but imaginary) staves and knives. There has evidently been some kind of quarrel among the hunting classes of Dorset. Sir William Fyloll (d. 1527), knight, one of the justices of the peace for that county, and a member of the Middle Temple, complains that Henry Ashley (d. 1549), esquire,[28] assaulted and beat his servant so severely that he was unable to work for three months, and took the plaintiff's bloodhound. Of these two allegations, the assault on the servant might seem the more serious, but the facts were disputed and in the event the plaintiff waived that part of his claim. The action was therefore essentially a claim for damages for taking a bloodhound. This suggested to the legal mind of 1520 an arguable point of law. Can a mere dog be the subject of an action for damages? The defendant's counsel decided to stake everything on this question by entering a formal demurrer to the declaration.

The demurrer, as entered in common form, does not reveal the nature of the objection in law, but asserts that (with respect to the bloodhound) *breve et narratio minus sufficientes in lege existunt* and that he has no need to answer. The effect of demurring is that the defendant gives up any opportunity to have the facts tried by jury. It now has to be assumed, for the purpose of this suit, that the defendant did indeed take the dog as alleged. The question is purely one of law, and it will be argued in the Common Pleas.

The report is from a series covering the years 1520 - 1523[29] in which virtually all the cases arise from questions of law being formally raised upon the record. There is no tentative pleading here. The pleadings as entered on the record in effect pose a question for the court, and the court's answer (in the form of a judgment) sets a precedent. This is the way all typical suits will look in the future, but our anonymous reporter of 1520 is unusual in having decided already that only such cases are worthy of attention. As in the earlier cases, we see more than one serjeant (in this instance two) speaking on each side. Whether they have all received instructions

---

[28] Seated at Wimborne St Giles. His son Henry was a member of Parliament and twice sheriff of Dorset: *S. T. Bindoff* ed., The House of Commons 1509 - 1558 (1982), vol. I, p. 342.

[29] I.e. the year books 12 - 14 Hen. VIII, which exist only in the printed editions first published in the late 1520s. Most of the records corresponding to the cases in these years have been located and transcribed by the present writer, with a view to printing a modern edition.

and fees, or whether it is the custom for everyone present to join in debate, remains unclear. What we do see clearly is a set-piece debate following an orderly pattern. The defendant begins, since he has to assign reasons in support of the demurrer. His objections are first to the form of pleading, and then to the substantive question of law *(le mater)*. The plaintiff responds in the same order. The defendant's second serjeant replies. Then the judges speak, in reverse order of seniority, ending with the chief justice. The judges likewise address themselves first to the form and then the substance. There is reason to believe that this is the way students were taught to argue at moots in the inns of court, though the earlier year books do not show the same formality – perhaps because it was appropriate only when arguing a formal demurrer.

The formal pleading point arose from a statute of 1389 which was passed to prevent the lower orders from self-indulgence in hunting. Because, said the statute, working people and servants had been hunting on Sundays – *quant bones Cristiens sont as esglises oiantz divine service* – and had sometimes even used hunting as a pretext for unlawful political assemblies, it was ordered (amongst other things) that no layman worth less than 40s. a year in land should keep any greyhound, lurcher, or other hunting dog *(leverer ne lerce n'autre chien pur chacer)*, on pain of imprisonment.[30] Of course, this measure was not directed at the likes of Sir William Fyloll, and it must have been a potential irritation to him – if not a calculated insult – that the point was argued at all. But the point was that Fyloll had not stated in his declaration that he was worth 40s. a year in land. The judges could not presume that he was, even though he was a knight, and (because of the demurrer) the case was never going to reach a jury, who alone could try facts. Was the declaration therefore bad, in not showing that the plaintiff was legally entitled to have a bloodhound in the first place? This was not a very strong argument, since the statute only created a criminal offence and was not material to the cause of action, and in any case it could be argued that any objection should come from the defendant's side:[31] it had similarly been accepted in the monastic contract cases that the plaintiff need not necessarily allege that the goods came to the use of the house, since the defendant could plead as a defence that they did not.[32] Only one of the judges saw any merit in the submission, which was rejected by the majority.

30 13 Ric. II, stat. 1, c. 13.

31 I.e. the defendant would have to plead that the plaintiff was not qualified according to the statute. But this would mean staking his case on that point, since he was only allowed one plea.

32 Y. B. Trin. 35 Edw. I (Rolls Ser.), 566 (point questioned); *Anon.* (1444) Y. B. Trin. 22 Hen. VI, fo. 56, pl. 2.

The point of substance is whether an action of trespass may be brought for a dog, which is said to be of no legal value. There is no previous reported case on this point. We know that in fact such actions had been brought for dogs in the past,[33] but the old precedents are probably not known in 1520 and they are not cited. Counsel for the defendant points out that a man may not be hanged for stealing a dog,[34] and by the same argument he should not be liable in trespass. The law draws a distinction, it is argued, between things of value and things of pleasure; no notice should be taken of the latter. If an action could be brought for a hunting dog, it might equally be brought for a lady's lap-dog or a parrot.

The debate touches overtly on questions of policy. What is meant by 'value' in the eyes of the law? The law of theft is rejected as an analogy, because there are many things which cannot be stolen but which may nevertheless be the subject of trespass actions: for instance, trees and wild game. But are there cases where one can cause harm without being liable to an action for damages? If one suffers loss in respect of one's sport or recreation, is that *damnum absque injuria,* an irremediable wrong? Or should recreation be regarded as truly valuable, since it enhances bodily health which is worth more than all other riches? The arguments range far and wide. There are even reflections on the origins of property in animals. Cases are cited, and Biblical allusions made, albeit without references. It was still the practice to cite cases by name, as in 1311, or by year, but the reporter does not always remember them or regard them as important, and scripture was presumably treated as common knowledge.

The conclusion, again by three judges to one, is that the action will lie; and judgment is given accordingly. Yet neither the report nor the record answer the question which necessarily presents itself to the curious historian: why should two wealthy landowners employ four of the best lawyers of the day to argue about a dog? That is not a legal question, though it is the kind of question which detailed record research may sometimes answer. Here the plea rolls do provide several clues. It is only the record of the present case in the rolls which identifies the defendant as Henry Ashley, his name having been edited out of the printed year book. Reading through other rolls reveals that four years later the tables were turned when Ashley sued Fyloll for taking two bloodhounds; Fyloll claimed they were taken as

---

33 E.g. two 14th-century cases (1357 and 1397) in *M. S. Arnold* ed., Select Cases of Trespass from the King's Courts 1307 - 1399, vol. I (100 Selden Soc., 1985), p. lxiii n. 457 and n. 460; vol. II (103 Selden Soc., 1988), p. 266. An action of trespass against a forest official for taking greyhounds is mentioned in a Chancery suit in the 1480s: *Tame* v. *Swetman,* C1/109/69. A battery was justified in defence of a dog in 1500: KB 27/956, m. 35.

34 See *Baker,* The Reports of Sir John Spelman, vol. II (94 Selden Soc., 1978), Introduction, pp. *317 - 318.*

strays, and there was another demurrer, though no judgment.[35] Then, in 1525, Fyloll sued Ashley again, this time for killing and taking hunting dogs and greyhounds. This third action finally gives the game away: the underlying feud concerned hunting rights.[36] Hunting rights, though in a sense purely recreational, were quite valuable enough in the real world to justify expensive litigation and to explain the ingenious attempts to trip up the plaintiff on an unusual point of law. But that is beside our present point. The rolls have always been of historical value, provided allowance is made for the opaqueness of the legal forms and the pleaders' economy with the facts. We now see them, in the early sixteenth century, becoming slightly more valuable as sources of law.

Since the 1520 judgment was given upon demurrer, and entered on the roll, the record stands as explicit authority for a legal proposition, in a way that our previous records do not. The writ and declaration have been given the stamp of judicial approval by the Court of Common Pleas, after a formal challenge and an adjournment for careful consideration. The record is therefore of some legal value as confirming what the year book states. But it would be impossible to know, without the report, what had actually been argued and whether the decision was unanimous, unambiguous and unqualified; we would not even know whether the case was decided on the 'matter' – the point of substance – or on the point of form. The record of the 1520 decision does not prevent the same question being raised again. As far as we know it was always followed[37] and is still law today, though the decision left open the possibility of a distinction between hunting dogs, which performed useful work,[38] and pet dogs which were kept purely for company.[39]

---

[35] *Assheley* v. *Fyloll* (1524) CP 40/1044, m. 537.

[36] *Fyloll* v. *Assheley and others* (1525) CP 40/1045, m. 720. Ashley pleaded a royal grant of a 'chase', and a jury was summoned, but no verdict is recorded.

[37] The matter was raised again on demurrer, but with the same result, in *Cary* v. *Braye* (1527) CP 40/1055, m. 430d (trespass for taking two greyhounds; demurrer to the declaration; judgment for the plaintiff). James Hales, in his Gray's Inn reading of 1537 (Brit. Lib. MS. Hargrave 92, fo. 33r), said detinue would also lie for things of pleasure: 'Si home done a moy un grehownd, jeo avera action de detynu pur luy. Mesme ley sil done a moy un tame popinjay, saffer, ruby ou turkas'.

[38] Cf. *Boyden* v. *Alspath* (1308/09) 2 Edw. II, pl. 29, in 17 Selden Soc. 87; CP 40/173, m. 233: replevin for a ferret and three nets used in catching rabbits.

[39] See *Bollez* v. *Risseley* (1544), reported in the Gell MS. in the Library of Congress, Washington, sub dat. Trin. 36 Hen. VIII, fo. 44, where this very distinction was made in opposing an action of replevin for a 'greybiche'; but the report ends with counsel apparently wondering whether to risk a demurrer. The judges there recalled a case of 2 Edw. II where replevin was brought for three greyhounds. Cf. *Goldwyn* v. *Wulberde* (*c.* 1536) C1/803/29, where detinue was brought in the city of London courts for a 'whistling linnet ... of great pleasure', said to be worth twenty marks.

And it does not add anything of juristic importance to the very full report, a report written in the new style which will eventually prevail over that of the classical year books.

D. J. IBBETSON

Report and Record in Early-Modern Common Law

I. Introduction

The formal sources of English legal history may neatly be divided into the official records of cases and the unofficial reports of forensic arguments. Professor Baker has provided a full survey of this material,[1] which it would serve little point to repeat. The present paper, therefore, aims rather to show the use that legal historians can make of these sources, and their limitations, and to illustrate this by reference to a sample case of 1595.

II. The Record

The formal records of litigation in common law courts, from the end of the twelfth century to the present day, survive almost completely in the Public Record Office in London. It is possible to discover the details of nearly every law-suit in the early modern period enrolled on the plea rolls of the appropriate court – King's Bench, Common Pleas, or Exchequer – although in practice the tedium of wading through the many miles of badly-indexed vellum membranes frequently deters the researcher from doing so. On the face of it, they should constitute a superlatively useful resource for the legal historian.

The reality is, inevitably, rather different. They are invariably highly formalistic in their language, rarely reflecting in anything other than the most superficial sense the legal (or factual) issues underlying the claim. The same standard phrases occur in case after case, for century after century. Their structure is highly stereotyped: the plaintiff's claim is formulated in the declaration; the defendant's plea – most commonly a simple denial of liability in standard form (the general issue), less frequently a denial of the legal sufficiency of the claim (a demurrer) or a special plea – follows; in the relatively few cases where the defendant does something other than

---

[1] *J. H. Baker,* Records, Reports and the Origins of Case-Law in England, in: Judicial Records, Law Reports, and the Growth of Case Law, 15.

demur or plead the general issue, the pleadings continue until some triable issue is joined between the parties and the sheriff of the county where the case arose is instructed to summon a jury.[2] Frequently the record will end at this point: the plaintiff may have discontinued the case; the parties may have settled the dispute informally; or the victorious party might not have taken the trouble to pay the appropriate fee to have the verdict of the jury entered on the plea roll, for it was only if legal process to enforce the judgment was instituted that it was necessary to cause it to be enrolled. In many cases, therefore, we know nothing other than the names of the parties and the bare outline of the dispute between them, and even in those cases where the judgment is entered on the roll the only thing it adds is the identity of the victorious party and the amount of damages awarded.

It follows from this that the plea roll, the record of the case, is of very little utility to the historian of the law, for only in the rarest of cases will the nature of any legal argument that has taken place be discoverable from it. The only real exception to this in the early modern period occurred where the defendant demurred, for in this situation he was required by a statute of 1585[3] to specify the grounds on which the plaintiff's declaration was said to be insufficient.[4] Yet, as the transcribed case shows, even this did not demand any elaboration of the reasons for its alleged insufficiency,[5] and the record will never reveal to the historian which of several reasons alleged may have been thought relevant by the court.

III. The Reports

The reports of cases, by contrast with the records, do provide a very valuable resource for the legal historian. They exist in bewildering profusion in the early modern period,[6] and most of those dating from before the second half of the seventeenth century remain in manuscript. Superficially they bear a strong resemblance to the mediaeval Year Books.[7] They are invariably written in French, although unlike the language of the earlier

---

[2] Other forms of trial were possible, but trial by jury was by far the most common by the early modern period. See *J. H. Baker,* Introduction to English Legal History, 84 - 90.

[3] Stat. 27 Eliz cap. 5.

[4] Similarly where there was a writ of error from an inferior court the plaintiff in error had to specify the grounds of the alleged error: *J. H. Baker,* Spelman's Reports, ii (Selden Society, vol. 94), *119 - 123.*

[5] See the record of the case, defendant's response.

[6] *D. J. Ibbetson,* Law Reporting in the 1590s, in: *C. Stebbings* ed., Law Reporting in England (1995), 73.

[7] See *Baker*'s essay in the present volume.

Year Books, it is a highly degenerate version of the language with little recognisable syntax, and which pays scant respect to gender, number, tense or mood. It is not clear why French should have been used for the reports, for by this time the language used in the courts was English. It is hard to give credence to Edward Coke's explanation that the technical terms of the mediaeval law could not be translated unambiguously into English,[8] and it may be more convincing to see it as a form of private language which served to unite and define the lawyers as a professional group.[9]

It is not simply in their language that there is an apparent similarity between the early modern reports and the mediaeval Year Books, for both consist largely of reports of the oral interchanges between counsel and judges. This does, however, mask a very significant difference between them. The interchanges contained in the Year Books are rarely conclusive, and often reflect the tentative moves of lawyers each trying to manoeuvre the pleadings in order to ensure that the case is put to the jury in the way that best furthers their own client's interest. By the sixteenth century the pleadings were invariably settled in writing by the parties' lawyers and the judges only became involved at a later stage of the proceedings, either after the jury had delivered its verdict or after the defendant had demurred to the plaintiff's declaration. The arguments were consequently more like modern forensic debates: well-structured presentations by counsel for each side, sometimes with interjections from the judges or other lawyers, followed by the judges' own opinions and either an adjournment for further argument or the giving of judgment in the case. The reports of the sixteenth century and after inevitably reflect this change in the nature of legal argument.

While in its ideal form an early modern report will follow the structure of the forensic debate – statement of facts, counsels' argument, judges' opinions, decision – in practice many reports depart from this. Some merely give the facts and judgment;[10] some omit counsels' arguments[11] or the judges' opinions;[12] and some add a more or less lengthy commentary on the question in issue, not always distinguishing between what was said in court and what was thought by the reporter.[13] The historian must be sensi-

---

[8] Coke on Littleton (1823 edition), Preface, xxxix - xl.

[9] Cf. *E. Eisenstein,* The Printing Press as an Agent of Change, 362. Yet lawyers might keep not only professional literature but also their private diaries in law French: see for example *W. Prest* ed., The Diary of Sir Richard Hutton (Selden Society Supplementary Series, vol. 9), and Sir Thomas Walmsley's commonplace book (Lancashire County Record Office, DD/Pt/46/1).

[10] E.g. the transcribed case, Texts D and J.

[11] E.g. the transcribed case, Texts A, C, H and K.

[12] E.g. the transcribed case, Text G.

[13] Sir Edward Coke, in particular, was criticised for this: The Lord Chancellor Egertons Observacions upon Ye Lord Cookes Reportes, in: *L. A. Knafla,* Law and

tive to these differences, but by juxtaposing a range of reports of a single case it is possible to have some confidence that the composite so produced is a fairly reliable reflection of what actually went on in court.

In order to understand the function of the reports and their limitations, it is important to recognise that until 1865 there was no such thing as an 'official' report of a case,[14] although an unsuccessful attempt was made to initiate such a system in the second decade of the seventeenth century.[15] All of the reports of the early modern period are therefore unofficial, taken by men who happened to be in court when the case was discussed. Such people might have a range of different reasons for taking reports, not to mention a range of different competences to understand what was occurring. 'Reporters' would operate under different physical conditions. At the one extreme were the judges who sat at a long table, and who could therefore take contemporaneous notes with ease. At the other extreme were the student observers who were crushed into galleries from which they might hardly be able to hear; they had no possibility of taking notes, but had to write up their reports from memory afterwards.[16]

The appended texts give a good indication of the different types of reports and their different styles. We may distinguish five distinct forms:

1. Reports prepared with a view to publication;
2. Reports made on a regular basis throughout a lawyer's career;
3. Practitioners' notebooks;
4. Reports made by junior lawyers in preparation for practice at the bar;
5. Students' notebooks.[17]

1. Reports prepared with a view to publication

Text A, Edward Coke's report, is a very good example of this genre. By the time that this report was made Coke was Attorney-General, and probably the most respected (and feared) lawyer in practice. He had been taking

Politics in Jacobean England, 297; *J. H. Baker,* Coke's Notebooks and the Sources of His Reports [1972] CLJ 59, 70 n. 64.

[14] It was in this year that the Incorporated Council of Law Reporting was set up.

[15] *G. J. Turner,* Year Books 4 Edward II (Selden Society vol. 26), xi - xii; *E. M. Wells,* Common Law Reporting in England (University of Oxford D. Phil. thesis, 1995). The only set of reports identified as the product of this system of official reporting is Suffolk Record Office HA 93/8/116.

[16] *Ibbetson,* Law Reporting in the 1590s, in: *C. Stebbings* ed., Law Reporting in England, 73.

[17] We might add a sixth, lengthy transcriptions of individual arguments circulated (in manuscript form) apparently by their authors; but these are relatively uncommon, and they represent a wholly different genre of legal literature.

notes of cases throughout his career, and by the 1590s had probably already determined to put them into print.[18] He regarded his printed Reports as essentially pedagogic and sometimes added substantial comments of his own to the arguments that were put forward in court, without always taking the trouble to distinguish between his views and those of counsel or judges.[19] The present case is an uncomplicated example of his style. As well as being brief, it confines itself to the central issues of the case, and contains no extraneous matter of Coke's own fancy. Comparison with the autograph manuscript, text A1, reveals that it was substantially edited (by Coke himself) for publication: there are numerous verbal changes; and the discussion of the second point is reduced to a single bland sentence, further sharpening the focus on the principal issue.

2. Reports made on a regular basis throughout a lawyer's career

Texts B and C are examples of the work of practitioners who took reports throughout their careers, both of whom were well established by the time of the present case. B is the work of George Croke, who was by this time aged 35, and who had been called to the bar in 1584. His reports begin in about 1580, and continue until 1641;[20] they were published posthumously.[21] The author of C is almost certainly Sir Nicholas Overbury,[22] a practitioner of a similar degree of seniority to Croke: he was a member of the Middle Temple, called to the bar in 1582. His reports begin in 1583 (possibly 1579), and continue until 1622.[23] There are stylistic similarities between the two reports: both focus reasonably sharply on the two main issues discussed in the case, and neither is too concerned to go through the arguments of judges or counsel in any great detail. They are essentially workmanlike, practical tools which enabled their authors to keep them-

---

[18] *Baker,* Coke's Notebooks and the Sources of His Reports [1972] CLJ 59, 65; cf. *Crispe* v. *Frier,* CUL MS Gg 6.29 f. 125: "Coke Attorney-General prist un note de ceo case in ses tables, disant, hoc facit pro nobis".

[19] Supra, n. 13.

[20] His notebooks survive in the Hertfordshire Record Office, MSS Verulam XII. A. 6a - 6e and XII. A. 14. The first volume is largely a compilation of materials drawn from other sources, and it is likely that the second volume, beginning in 1583, marks the start of Croke's personal reporting of cases.

[21] For a full description and discussion of Croke's work see *Wells,* Common Law Reporting in England.

[22] The author speaks of himself as counsel in *Bowle* v. *Winston* (BL MS Add 35952 f. 100v). Overbury is referred to by name as counsel in the parallel report of the case in BL MS Lansd 1075 f. 275v; other counsel did appear in the case, but for various reasons none of them is a candidate for the authorship of these reports.

[23] BL MSS Add 35949 - 35952.

selves up to date with legal developments, as well as providing themselves with ammunition for use in legal argument.[24]

3. Practitioners' notebooks

Text D is the work of John Harris,[25] who had been called to the bar in 1590; like George Croke, the author of text B, he was a member of the Inner Temple, though some years Croke's junior. We might characterise him, like Croke, as a lawyer who took reports throughout his career; but his reports are stylistically so different from Croke's that we should suspect that they had a different function, as little more than an aide-mémoire. Their severe style reflects an unremittingly practical nature. Most of them, the present case included, are very brief and confine themselves to a concise statement of the facts and the points of law involved, and there is rarely any attempt to re-create the arguments, even when the author was himself counsel.

4. Reports made by junior lawyers in preparation for practice at the bar

Texts E, F, G, H, and I are representatives of a type of reports that became very common in the late sixteenth and early seventeenth century, which are of enormous value to our understanding of the law of the period. All are the work of lawyers at the beginning of their careers, whose reports cover the period just before and just after their call to the bar.[26] It seems that 'reporting' in the King's Bench – attending the court and taking notes of cases heard there – was a normal preliminary to practice. In part, attending court allowed these young lawyers to learn the conventions of legal argumentation; but probably more importantly it enabled them to gain a good grounding in the law that was actually being applied in the courts.[27]

---

24 For examples of Croke citing from MS reports see below, n. 53.

25 There are a number of examples of the author of the manuscript noting that he was counsel in a case, including *Agard* v. *King* (f. 175v). In a parallel report of the case (B. L. MS Add 35951 f. 126) counsel is referred to not simply as Harris (there were several lawyers of this name), but more specifically as John Harris. In addition, at f. 1 of the MS there is the epigram "Volenti nichil difficile/quod [?] Jo: Harryes". In the light of the internal evidence of the manuscript, we may see this as an authorial signature.

26 By this time call to the bar was the essential prerequisite for practice in the Court of King's Bench; *J. H. Baker,* Solicitors and the Law of Maintenance 1590 to 1640 [1973] CLJ 56.

27 Formal legal education, through readings and moots in the Inns of Court, was at this time not at all practical; there was as yet no regular system of apprentice-

Taking notes of cases was one way of committing them to memory; the same would have been true of copying other lawyers' notes, and in this case the act of transcription might have gone hand in hand with the process of comprehension. As well as this, however, they would inevitably have acted as a source of future reference.[28] Despite their frequent lack of such basic bibliographical tools as indexes or internal cross-references between different stages of argument of a single case – and where these do appear they are commonly in a much later hand than the original text – it is likely that they were prepared at least in part with a view to their utility. Sometimes an author or copyist omits a case or argument, noting that it is better reported elsewhere;[29] reporters might go to some lengths to check cited references[30] or make a note to verify what had been said in a case;[31] or they might include their own comments on the arguments in a case[32] or references to analogous cases.[33]

It is not at all easy to identify the authors of these texts, and all of the following are in some measure hypothetical:

Text E: Humphrey Were, admitted to the Inner Temple in 1588, called to the bar in 1597.

Text F: 'W. C. and H. G.', identifiable as: Henry Goldsmith, admitted to Gray's Inn in 1589, called to the bar in 1595;[34] and (probably) William Cobbe, admitted to Gray's Inn in 1587 and called to the bar in 1594 or 1595.[35] Text F1 is almost certainly a precis of text F, although the points are re-ordered.

---

ship; and the available legal literature was wholly inadequate to give any useful base for legal practice. See *Ibbetson,* Law Reporting in the 1590s, in: *C. Stebbings* ed., Law Reporting in England, 73.

28 They were not infrequently cited in court: below, Part IV.

29 Cf. BL MS Lansd 1060 f. 79 (marginal instruction, presumably to a copyist, to omit the report of a case because it was well reported by Coke).

30 E.g. *Anon.* (BL MS Lansd 1106 f. 54); see too the interpolated note of the reporter in text F (note 13) of the transcribed case.

31 E.g. *Anon.* (BL MS Lansd 1061 f. 15) (note to check with counsel in the case).

32 E.g. *Andros* v. *Eden* (BL MS Lansd. 1101 f. 57v); BL MS Lansd. 1061 f. 14 (commenting on accuracy of a cited Year Book case); *Waule's Case* (BL MS Lansd. 1061 f. 44) (noting that this was "un mult dangerous case").

33 *Ibbetson,* Coventry's Reports (1995) 16 JLH 281, 285, 290.

34 For the identification of Goldsmith, compare the reports of *Buskin* v. *Edmunds* in B. L. MS Harl 6745 f. 156v and C. U. L. MS Ii 5.24 f. 185v.

35 There were members of Inns of Court with the initials WC, but Cobbe is the most likely of them to have been responsible for the reports. None of the others is known to have practised as a lawyer.

Text G: James Kirton, admitted to the Middle Temple in 1585, called to the bar in 1596.[36]

Text H: Unidentified, but perhaps a member of the Inner Temple, called to the bar in 1595.[37]

Text I: Unidentified.

More or less common to all of these reports is that their authors were less in control of their material than were the authors of texts A - D. This is hardly surprising given their relative inexperience, but paradoxically it is this that gives these texts their greatest value to the historian. Each contains material not in any of the others, material which is from a purely practical point of view not strictly relevant and which would have looked rather out of place in the more polished reports of Croke and the like. The arguments, of both counsel and judges, are detailed, but frequently not easy to follow as they stand. Sometimes the language of the text appears garbled; but this is perhaps no more than should be expected when a bastard language without any identifiable syntax is written by an inexpert writer, copied by an inexpert copyist, and read by an inexpert reader. Arguments may be transposed or misattributed. Yet all of these difficulties can be overcome by the comparison of different reports, and the composite text so created provides a wealth of detail about both the law of the period and the canons of legal argument.

5. Students' notebooks

Texts J and K appear to be examples of the final type of report found in the early modern period, the student's notebook. Neither author has been identified. From early in his legal training, a prospective lawyer might transcribe or abstract notes from other printed or manuscript books and jot down near-random pieces of legal information. Equally he might take down crude notes of cases he had heard about or witnessed in court, although they are often so brief that we cannot normally distinguish between first-hand and second-hand reports unless the author of the manuscript takes the trouble to tell us. These notes are rarely of significant value to the historian, unless they happen to contain references to good texts which have otherwise disappeared.

---

36 For the identification of Kirton, see *Wells,* Common Law Reporting in England.

37 There is a list of Inner Templars called to the bar in Easter term that year at f. 71, but no comparable list for any other year or any other Inn.

IV. Report and Record in Legal Argument

The relatively large number of volumes of reports that have survived from the later years of the sixteenth century, mostly notes of cases taken down by eye-witnesses to them, enables us to gain a good idea of the nature of legal argument. From these we may gain some idea of the way in which reports (both printed and manuscript) and records were used by lawyers in the course of forensic debate.

It is clear by the end of the sixteenth century that the existence of an earlier decision of a court might carry considerable weight. In a case in 1592, for example, Fenner J is reported as wanting to consult his 'books' before giving an opinion.[38] In 1588 in the Common Pleas we find Serjeant Puckering as counsel citing a precedent decided in the King's Bench two years previously: "and they relied on the report of this precedent brought by Puckering in giving judgment".[39] In 1595 Fenner J, not believing a case cited to him, demanded to see if the record supported counsel's citation.[40] In another case the record of a cited case was brought into court for the perusal of the judges; after examining it they thought it was a strong case to prove counsel's argument.[41] In *Atkinson* v. *Atkinson* in 1595, Doughty of Gray's Inn relied on the case of *Chamberlain* v. *Nicholls* which had been decided only the previous day in the court of Exchequer Chamber, arguing that the present case should be governed by this precedent; discussion was adjourned to check precisely what had been decided.[42] In a revealing report of 1596, counsel cited an earlier case:

> "but the court replied that no opinion had been given in the said case, and so it cannot be a 'directory' to this case, but this case rests as a new case without authority".[43]

While it would be wrong to elevate this into any strict doctrine of precedent such as is found in the later Common Law, it is clear that authority is displacing reason as the fundamental source of legal argument.

In the light of this we can make some observations of the use that is made of reports and records in legal argument. Reconstructing the details of arguments as well as we are able from the surviving reports of Michael-

---

[38] B. L. MS Harl 1697 f. 9.

[39] *Anon.* (BL MS Lansd. 1076 f. 129).

[40] *Vicary* v. *Farthing* (BL MS Harl. 4998 f. 124 (Were's report)). Similarly in *Bowyer* v. *Jenkins* (BL MS Harl. 4552 f. 32 (Escourt's report)) the court stayed judgment in order to look at a case which had been cited to them.

[41] *Pembroke* v. *Barclay* (BL MS Harl. 1697 f. 78v; BL MS Harl. 1624 f. 253 at f. 254v, f. 256v).

[42] BL MS Harl. 6745 f. 166 at f. 166v (WC & HG's report).

[43] BL MS Harl. 1697 f. 96v.

mas term 1595, it is possible to gain a reasonably good impression of the relative importance of the different sources.[44] The majority of citations (approximately 350) were from the printed Year Books, which covered cases argued between the reigns of Edward III (1327 - 1377) and Henry VIII (1509 - 1547):

Year Book	*Citations*	*Citations per 100 folios*[45]
Edw III[46]	109	6.5
Hen IV / Hen V[47]	24	6.1
Hen VI[48]	69	6.5
Edw IV[49]	64	9.3
Edw V / Ric III / Hen VII[50]	60	13.1
Hen VIII[51]	17	16.9

The variations in the absolute numbers of citations is put into perspective by the figures in the last column: if anything there is a gentle increase in the rate of citation of relatively recent cases, though it is better to explain this by the fact that the more recent Year Books contained more obviously relevant material rather than by reference to any preference for citing new cases ahead of old. The increasing relevance of more recent material is brought out by the citations from the two volumes of reports printed in the second half of the sixteenth century – Plowden and Dyer – together with

44 Whilst it would be dangerous to draw any conclusions about the absolute number of citations – we cannot assume that all cases were reported, nor that reporters noted all authorities cited – the sample size is sufficiently large that we may have a fair degree of confidence in the relative frequencies.

45 The Year Books were printed in a uniform series in 1678 - 1679, so there is no need to correct these figures to take account of any variations in type size or page length.

46 1327 - 1377.

47 1399 - 1422; n.b. that there was no printed text of the Year Books of the reign of Richard II (1377 - 1399), though manuscripts existed. Some reports from this reign are found in Fitzherbert's Graunde Abridgment, and there are occasional citations from this source.

48 1422 - 1461 and 1470 - 1471.

49 1461 - 1473.

50 1483 - 1509.

51 1509 - 1547 (but the printed Year Book covered only the years 1520 - 1523, 1527, and 1534 - 1535).

more recent cases culled from Brooke's Abridgement. These three works produce a total of some 120 citations.[52]

By the side of these citations from printed sources, the reports reveal a range of citations apparently from unprinted sources. At the very least this reveals that there was no sense in which the printed reports constituted an exclusive canon of source-material. Some of these cases are apparently being cited from memory – as where counsel or a judge refers to a recently decided case without giving any further reference for it[53] – and they should consequently be left out of calculation if we are attempting to assess the role of reports and records. Even taking a maximal view of what might be a citation from memory, we are still left with some 80 references which appear to have come from manuscripts. Of these, perhaps ten are from the reports of William Bendlowes,[54] which by this time were clearly circulating widely;[55] this is the only set of manuscript reports to be regularly cited by name. For the rest, individual lawyers were clearly happy to cite from manuscript reports which they had either taken themselves or had copied from the collections of other lawyers. Such citations are clearly less widespread than citations from the printed canon of Year Books and the reports of Dyer, Plowden, and Brooke, and we should not underestimate the difficulties and hazards associated with them: they were not especially easy to use, usually lacking any index; they were of unreliable quality, so that a judge or opposing counsel might simply deny the accuracy of the cited case[56] and they were invariably a good deal less easy to read than was the printed text.

It is more difficult to assess the function of the official record in legal argumentation. It is clear that the record had some value to lawyers. Reports of cases commonly cross-refer to their reference in the plea rolls,

---

52 The lack of any uniform editions of these works makes it impossible to produce meaningful figures for the frequency of citation comparable to those derived from the Year Books.

53 To take examples from Escourt's reports (BL MS Harl. 4552): *Harbin* v. *Barton* (f. 25v) (citations by Croke); *Downall* v. *Catesby* (f. 26v) (citations by Tanfield and Atkinson); *Edmunds* v. *Buskin* (f. 29) (citation by Popham C. J.); *Richardson* v. *Yardley* (f. 31) (citations by Heron and Croke); *Bragg* v. *Bannings* (f. 35) (citation by Foster); *Hillyard* v. *Constable* (f. 38) (citation by Popham C. J.); *Woodliff* v. *Drewery* (f. 38) (citations by Coke and Popham C. J.); *Johnson* v. *Pees* (?) (f. 39) (citation by Fenner J.).

54 *L. W. Abbott,* Law Reporting in England 1485 - 1585, 62 - 103.

55 The earliest explicit citation to Bendlowes reports that I have noticed is in 1582: Bodl MS Eng Hist c 486 f. 69v. It may therefore already have been circulating in the legal profession a decade or more before the period on which we are focusing.

56 For examples of the problems that might arise see *Ibbetson,* Law Reporting in the 1590s, in *C. Stebbings* ed., Law Reporting in England, 73.

and the better series of printed reports (Plowden, Coke) commonly included a transcript of the record as well as the reports of forensic arguments. More explicit evidence pointing to the same conclusion is the relatively common practice of the judges having recourse to the record of a cited case in order to verify some point made by counsel, or the frequency of reporters' notes that they themselves had examined the records of such cases. In a sprinkling of examples, though, counsel is reported as citing a case by reference to the plea roll, and it would not be unreasonable to deduce from this that the primary referent here was indeed the record rather than a report of the case. We should be hesitant before reaching any such conclusion. To begin with, the plea rolls themselves were so unwieldy, and their indexes so useless, that it is a priori wildly unlikely that a busy lawyer seeking persuasive authority in his client's cause would undertake a trawl through the plea rolls in the hope of coming across something useful. Secondly, as we have seen, the plea roll would often not contain the desired information. Thirdly, we should note that this type of citation is found only in arguments attributed to a very small number of barristers – within our sample, to Lawrence Tanfield (five examples), George Croke, John Walter, Randle Crewe,[57] and Robert Atkinson (one example each) – and it is possible that these references indicate an unusual quirk rather than a normal practice. The case cited by Croke, in fact, is reported in his own notebook (together with the reference to the plea roll), and it is far more likely that he was using in his own notes rather than the record as his source.[58] While the record was the ultimate authority, it seems more likely that its function was essentially no more than verificatory.

V. An Illustrative Case

The case taken to illustrate the different types and functions of record and reports, *Samon* v. *Pitt,* has been selected as a very straightforward example of a case from the last decade of the sixteenth century. There are no factual disputes or ambiguities, and the principal legal issues are clear. The case was heard in the court of King's Bench in Michaelmas term 1595. It was argued and resolved at a single sitting, unlike many cases which could be debated time and time again, so we may be sure that all the reporters are dealing with the same set of arguments.

The facts of the case appear in full at the start of the record and in a more or less brief form in all of the reports, except in text F1 where they

---

57 In the sample case, text E.

58 The case cited, *Grace* v. *Lorcrosse* P33 El rot 211, is in Hertfordshire Record Office Verulam MS XII. A. 6b at the beginning of Michaelmas term 1592.

are left to be deduced from the legal arguments. In brief, the plaintiff and defendant had submitted certain disputes to arbitration, and the defendant had promised to pay £200 should he fail to perform the award to be made by the arbitrators. The arbitrators awarded that the defendant should enter into a bond that the plaintiff and his wife should have the land (except seventeen acres) during the life of the wife, and that subsequently the plaintiff should have it for the rest of his life if he happened to survive the wife, without any disturbance from the defendant or his son. The plaintiff now alleged that the defendant had failed to carry out the award, nor paid the £200 that he had promised to pay in the event of non-performance of the award. To this the defendant demurred, admitting all the facts as alleged but denying that they gave the plaintiff any claim in law.

Two principal reasons for the insufficiency of the plaintiff's claim were put forward and debated.[59]

First was the argument that the award was void for uncertainty. Most significantly, the arbitrators had awarded simply that the defendant should enter into a bond to pay a penalty without specifying the amount of the penalty. It followed from this that, given that the award was void, the defendant's promise to perform it was ineffective. This argument is found in most reports, put by the defendant's counsel Randle Crewe,[60] together with the counter-arguments of the plaintiff's counsel Lawrence Tanfield.[61] The judges' apparent acceptance of the argument is reported in all of the texts, and it is sometimes stated as the principal reason for which judgment was given for the defendant.[62] It should be noted in passing that the record itself has no note of the judgment; we are wholly dependent on the reports for this.

Although this is the only uncertainty referred to explicitly in the record, the reports show that two related points were canvassed in argument:

(1) the lands in dispute were not delineated specifically enough; this argument did not meet with judicial favour;[63]

(2) the arbitrators had not specified which seventeen acres were excepted from the award in the plaintiff's favour;[64]

The second principal point, explicitly articulated in the record, was that the award was also void in that it purported to extend to individuals who were

59 They are stated in the record, defendant's response.

60 Texts E, F, G (not attributed), I.

61 Texts B, E, F (but attributed only in F1), G (not attributed).

62 Texts B, E, F.

63 Texts C, F, H, K.

64 Texts H, I.

not parties to the submission to arbitration. Most obviously, the arbitrators had awarded that the plaintiff and his wife should enjoy the lands, notwithstanding that the wife was not party to the submission. Argument,[65] counter-argument,[66] and judicial opinion[67] are found in most reports; on this occasion the judges seem to have favoured the plaintiff. Related to this was a second aspect, that it had been awarded that the plaintiff should have the land unhindered by the defendant or his son, notwithstanding that the son was not a party to the submission. Although this argument is attributed to the defendant's counsel in several texts[68] there is no reference either to counter-argument or judicial opinion: we are left to deduce for ourselves that it was not favoured.

Finally, from some reports we learn that a third argument was made, although it was not one of the causes for the demurrer articulated in the record and was hence probably technically improper. The submission to arbitration was said to have concerned the 'title and possession' of certain lands, whereas the award had dealt only with the possession and was therefore not a final determination of the matters submitted to the arbitrators. The point is only referred to in a minority of reports, and it clearly met with judicial disfavour.[69] It was perhaps treated as a variant of the first argument, that the award was void for uncertainty, but it does seem to be logically distinct and to have been argued independently.

[65] Texts B, E, F, G.

[66] Texts B, E, F, G.

[67] Texts A, B, C, E, F, G, H, J.

[68] Texts D, F, G, J.

[69] Texts C, F.

W. H. BRYSON

Equity Reports and Records in Early-Modern England

I. The Court of Chancery

The municipal law of England is divided into common law and equity. This is so because in the middle ages, the judges of the courts of common law (the Court of Common Pleas and the Court of King's Bench) believed that they could not expand the existing law in order to solve new problems. They thought that they were bound by the established law as found in their own earlier judicial opinions. Furthermore, they felt that it was the function of Parliament to change the law; therefore, it would be an unconstitutional usurpation of the legislative power for the courts to expand the law. Since Parliament in the middle ages was not an efficient instrument for law reform, the common law began to stagnate.

The impasse was broken by the rise of an equity jurisdiction in the Court of Chancery. The Court of Chancery avoided the problems of the common law courts by ordering the parties to litigation to act in a just manner, even though the common law may have allowed them to act in an unjust manner in a particular situation. The Court of Chancery required the parties to act according to good conscience, and thus the court has been called a 'court of conscience.' But the reference to conscience, although it may originally have had some religious connotations, soon became institutionalized and objective. Lord Nottingham, the celebrated Chancellor of the seventeenth century, explained that the reference to conscience was not to the personal conscience of the parties, the Chancellor, or the King, but to the civic conscience of the legal system of England.[1]

Thus the Court of Chancery did not declare common law rights or change the common law where it was deficient; it only required the parties to act according to justice and good conscience. Equity was said to act on the person, not on the property in dispute. *(Aequitas agit in personam non*

---

[1] *Cook* v. *Fountain,* 3 Swanston 585 at 600, 36 English Reports 984 at 990 (Ch. 1676). Today, it can be said that "Equity is a complex system of established law and is not merely a reflection of the chancellor's sense of what is just or appropriate". *Tiller* v. *Owen,* 243 Va. 176, 179, 413 S.E.2d 51, 53 (1992).

in rem.) For example, if a certain person in justice and fairness ought to own a certain piece of land, the courts of common law would declare that person to be the owner, but the equity courts would order the person with common law title to make a common law conveyance of the property to that person who ought to own it. Thus the common law ownership was transferred not by the equity court but by the party who had it wrongfully. Thus, there was no conflict with the power of Parliament to legislate and to change the law, nor was there any conflict with the common law courts to declare who had what common law rights.

The Court of Chancery could be resorted to only where there was no complete and adequate remedy for the plaintiff in the courts of common law. The inadequacy of a common law remedy could be one of substantive or procedural law. If the defendant could show that the plaintiff had an adequate remedy in the common law courts, the equity court would dismiss the case on the grounds of lack of jurisdiction. Thus equitable remedies are said to be 'extraordinary' remedies, not in the sense of unusual but in the sense of not the first resort because the ordinary remedies to be looked to first were the remedies available in the courts of common law. In practice, the extraordinary remedies of the courts of equity were frequently resorted to because of the lack of adequate remedies at common law for a wide variety of problems.

Thus, there was no genuine conflict with the older courts of Common Pleas and King's Bench as to the administration of the common law of England.[2] Equity supplements and completes the common law of the older courts.

II. The Court of Exchequer

In the middle of the sixteenth century, the Court of Exchequer began to give equitable remedies, as well as common law remedies. The Exchequer was a part of the royal treasury department dating back to the middle ages. The medieval Exchequer had a court of law to hear disputes over revenue payments. Also in the middle ages, the Exchequer had a court to hear common law disputes where a debtor of the king was attempting to collect money from another private person so that he could pay his own debts to the king. These two jurisdictions were known as the revenue side and the common law side of the Court of Exchequer. In the sixteenth century, the

---

[2] For the Court of Chancery in the early modern period, see *J. A. Guy,* The Public Career of Sir Thomas More (1980); *W. J. Jones,* The Elizabethan Court of Chancery (1967); *L. A. Knafla,* Law and Politics in Jacobean England (1977); *D. E. C. Yale,* Lord Nottingham's 'Manual of Chancery Practice' (1965).

Court of Exchequer developed its equity side in order to further the collection of the royal revenues by giving to the debtors and accountants to the crown equitable remedies against their own debtors.

The equitable procedures and remedies of the Court of Exchequer were the same as those of the Court of Chancery. This essay will consider equally the equity records and reports of the Court of Chancery and the Court of Exchequer.[3]

III. The Minor Courts of Equity

There were several other courts of equity in the sixteenth and seventeenth centuries, but most of them were of limited jurisdiction.

The Court of Requests was a court of equity that was set up to hear the disputes of poor people involving small sums of money. Even though it later came to hear cases where large sums were disputed, it was not a high court and its decrees were not well respected by the other royal courts. It fell into disuse in the 1640s.[4]

Two regional courts were set up in the time of Henry VIII to provide justice conveniently to the inhabitants of the northern and western parts of England and Wales. These were the Council of the North, which sat at York, and the Council of the Marches of Wales, which sat at Ludlow. Both of these courts administered equitable remedies. They fell into disuse when their criminal jurisdictions were abolished by statute in 1641.[5]

Moreover, for disputes involving land lying in Durham, Lancashire, and Cheshire, equitable remedies were available in the Chancery Court of the County Palatine of Durham,[6] the Court of the County Palatine of Lancashire, the Court of Duchy Chamber of Lancaster,[7] and the Court of Exchequer of the County Palatine of Chester. These courts were abolished in modern times.

---

[3] For the Court of Exchequer in early modern times, see *W. H. Bryson,* The Equity Side of the Exchequer (1975).

[4] *I. S. Leadam* ed., Select Cases in the Court of Requests [Selden Society, vol. 12 (1898)], pp. l, li.

[5] Stat. 16 Car. I, c. 10, ss. 2, 7, Statutes of the Realm, vol. 5, pp. 110, 111; *R. R. Reid,* The King's Council in the North (1921), pp. 445 - 449; *C. A. J. Skeel,* The Council in the Marches of Wales (1904), pp. 158 - 165; note also *P. Williams,* The Council in the Marches of Wales under Elizabeth I (1958).

[6] See: The Practice of the Court of Chancery of the County Palatine of Durham (1807).

[7] *R. Somerville,* The Palatinate Courts in Lancashire, in: *A. Harding,* Law-making and Law-makers (1980), pp. 54 - 63.

In addition, there were several revenue courts that administered common law rights by means of equitable remedies. These were the short-lived Court of Augmentation[8] and the Court of First Fruits and Tenths and the important Court of Wards and Liveries.[9] The first two were merged into the Court of Exchequer in 1554, and the latter disappeared in the middle of the seventeenth century when military tenure of land was abolished.

Finally, there was the Court of Star Chamber. This was a court of criminal common law that operated by equity procedure. The result of this unique combination of common law and equity was that criminal defendants were denied the traditional right of trial by jury. By the sixteenth century, trial by jury was a procedure whose flaws in practice were obvious, and many branches of equity jurisdiction were created in order to avoid the vagaries of juries. However, on the criminal side of the common law courts, trial by jury was considered to be a safeguard against overzealous prosecutions and royal tyranny.

The Court of Star Chamber was composed of the members of the Privy Council, who were always the political supporters of the King, and there was no jury. During the reign of Charles I, the Court of Star Chamber became a conspicuous instrument of political and religious oppression, and, when Parliament got the upper hand over the King in 1641, this court was abolished.[10]

It is to be noted that the Court of Chancery and the Court of Exchequer never had any criminal jurisdiction, and they had always been careful not to move in that direction. These equity courts would not even enforce civil penalties or civil forfeitures.

IV. The Records of the Courts of Equity

The records of the courts of Chancery and Exchequer have been well preserved since the middle ages. They are now to be found in the Public Record Office in London. The basic records of a suit in equity were written in the vernacular language, which was English from the end of the middle ages onwards. These records are as follows.

The first class of records was the pleadings, which were drafted by the lawyers on behalf of their clients, the parties to the lawsuit. The plaintiff began by filing in court a written 'bill of complaint', in which he set forth

---

[8] See generally, *W. C. Richardson,* History of the Court of Augmentations 1536 - 1554 (1961).

[9] See generally, *H. E. Bell,* History and Records of the Court of Wards and Liveries (1953).

[10] Stat. 16 Car. I, c. 10, s. 1, Statutes of the Realm, vol. 5, pp. 110, 111.

his claim against the defendant. The defendant then filed either a 'demurrer' or an 'answer'. A demurrer was the type of pleading used to deny the plaintiff's theory of legal right; an answer was the type of pleading used to deny the truth of the plaintiff's statement of facts. There could be further written pleadings if the parties thought it necessary and the rules of pleading permitted it. The general purpose of the pleadings was to state and to define the dispute between the parties. They are similar in function to the 'positiones' and 'responsiones' of the Romano-canonical practice. The pleadings in the courts of equity are long and full of conflicting allegations of facts. While they may shed light on the dispute between the parties, they do not help much to understand the legal reasons that underlie the final decision of the court. Therefore, no transcriptions of any of them will be published in this work.

The next major set of records in a suit in equity is the evidence. In the equity courts, as opposite to the common law courts, the evidence was presented to the court entirely in a written form. (In the courts of common law, the evidence of the witnesses was presented orally to the jury, and thus the evidence has not been preserved not having been officially written down.) In the courts of equity, the method of collecting the evidence was as follows. The court appointed a commissioner or several commissioners, who were laymen and not formally connected with the court but who lived near the witnesses. The parties to the lawsuit then gave lists of written questions, 'interrogatories', to the commissioners. The commissioners thereupon summoned the witnesses, read the questions to them, took down their answers in writing, the 'depositions', and then sent the interrogatories and the depositions back to the court in Westminster.

When the parties were ready to present their cases to the judges for a decision, the pleadings and the evidence were read aloud in open court and the lawyers presented their arguments. The judges in most cases gave an oral decision then and there, but sometimes they adjourned the matter for private debate among themselves and perhaps to do some legal research. Even an adjourned case resulted in an oral decree in the seventeenth century except in the most rare situation.

After the judge had rendered his judgment, the clerk in court who was representing the prevailing party drafted a written decree for the judge's signature. Since the decree was drawn up by a clerk and not the judge, the reasons for it were not often given. The decrees were then copied into the official decree book of the court. Several sample decrees have been transcribed. The decrees and orders are the only records that were generated by the judges, and they thus correspond to the reports of them that were made by the lawyers in court. Numerous of these equity orders and decrees have been published in *Cecil Monro,* Acta Cancellariae (1847), which covers the period 1545 to 1625, and in *John Ritchie,* Reports of Cases Decided by Francis Bacon (1932), which covers the period 1617 to 1621.

While much factual information may be found in the written pleadings and in the written evidence, this is all partisan and must be sifted carefully to discover the truth of the case. This, of course, was the job of the judge, but it is equally the burden of the modern legal historian. Because these records are very long and not very useful as compared even to the orders and decrees, no sample pleadings and depositions have been transcribed or published here.

V. Reports of Equity Cases

Even though the official records of the courts of equity only infrequently give the judges' ratio decidendi, the judges usually gave their reasons in court orally. The frequency in the seventeenth century of these pronouncements or comments from the bench cannot be known precisely. However, the lawyers and law students present in court sometimes made notes of them. These notes would then be written out later in the form of reports of cases. In the sixteenth and seventeenth centuries, these reports might be very brief notes of legal points or they might be extensive transcripts of the argument of counsel and the speeches of the judges. Some of these reports found their way into print. Of those manuscripts that were not printed, many must have been lost, but some have survived.

The following list of reports gives all of the reports that were limited to equity cases, that have been printed, and that cover the period before 1714. This list gives the names of the reporters or reports, the dates of first publication, and the dates of the equity cases reported.

Sir George Cary (Carew) (1650) 1557 - 1604
Choyce Cases in Chancery (1652) 1557 - 1606
John Dickens (1803) 1559 - 1798
Reports in Chancery (1693 - 1716) 1625 - 1710
William Nelson (1717) 1625 - 1693
Hutton Wood (1798 - 1799) 1650 - 1797
Cases in Chancery (1735) 1660 - 1698
Richard Freeman (1742) 1660 - 1706
Equity Cases Abridged (1792) 1667 - 1744
Reports tempore Finch (1725) 1673 - 1680
D. E. C. Yale, Lord Nottingham's Chancery Cases (1957, 1961) 1673 - 1682
Thomas Vernon (1726 - 1728) 1680 - 1719
Precedents in Chancery (1733) 1689 - 1722
William Peere Williams (1740) 1695 - 1735
Sir Jeffrey Gilbert (1734) 1705 - 1727

Compared to the printed reports of common law cases, this list is short indeed. However, many of the common law reports include a selection of important equity cases. The most notable of the reports that do are those of Sir Edward Coke, Sir Francis Moore, Sir Thomas Hardres, and John Rayner.

The following cases (reports and records) were chosen for publication in the companion volume to this work.

1.

Attorney General v. Bond (Ex. 1587)

The case of *Attorney General v. Bond* (Ex. 1587) was selected for several reasons. It is one of the earliest reports of an equity case in the Court of Exchequer. There are three reports of the case, only one of which has been previously printed. It is to be noted that these reports are rather short, as indeed are the orders of the court. Note also that the orders of the court contain no preamble giving summaries of the facts and no reasons for the orders.

It is interesting to note that the Lord Treasurer was sitting with the barons of the Exchequer as a judge. Although the Lord Treasurer and the Chancellor of the Exchequer could sit on the Exchequer bench as judges when the court was hearing equity cases, they only infrequently did so, as a matter of practice. Note also that the unsuccessful defendant refused to obey two orders of the court, and the court had to appoint several people to carry out its order.

In this case, James Bond, who had leased a part of the manor of Thorpe from the Queen, had built a dove house there in order to have a plentiful supply of game to hunt. John Wooley (or Wolley) and other inhabitants of the manor complained to the Queen because Bond's birds were eating up their grain, which they considered to be a nuisance. The Attorney General acting on behalf of the Queen sued in the Court of Exchequer for an injunction ordering Bond to abate the nuisance by removing the dove house or stopping up the louvers so that the birds could not get inside to roost safely. The court ruled in favor of the plaintiff, the Attorney General.

The Court of Exchequer had jurisdiction over the case because it involved a royal manor and thus, though indirectly, the rents and revenues of the crown. This was an appropriate case for the equity jurisdiction of the court in that it was a continuing and ongoing nuisance, a tort, and money damages at common law to compensate for past harm would be an inadequate remedy to prevent the future harm of the tenants' crops being eaten by the defendant's birds. Thus an injunction, an equitable remedy, was needed to do complete justice to the Queen and the inhabitants of her manor lands. As a matter of substantive law, only the lord of a manor (here the Queen) or the parson of the parish church could maintain a dove house within a manor, and James Bond was neither being only a lessee of the lord of the manor.

He was ordered to abate the nuisance by blocking up the building. He refused (or neglected to act) and was found in contempt of court, and the agents of the equity court were ordered to act for him. By this last order, the equity court appears to be acting *in rem,* a questionable practice.

2.

The remainder of the cases were chosen to illustrate some of the steps along the way of the development of the rules of res judicata. This was a very serious issue in the first years of the seventeenth century, and it resulted in a clash of personalities and of courts in England at that time.

The original purpose of the courts of equity was to provide a just remedy where the courts of common law failed to give one. Thus where different remedies were available or different results would obtain, the remedy of the courts of equity would, and will, prevail. Thus, for example, if a person is induced through fraud to enter into a contract and that person is then sued in a court of common law in such a procedural manner that the defence of fraud cannot be asserted there, that person can then resort to a court of equity for relief. The court of equity will forbid by means of an injunction the prosecution of the lawsuit in the common law court but allow it in the equity court where the defence of fraud can be asserted and proved. Thus, the suit was removed from the common law court to the equity court at the beginning of the legal proceedings.

However, in the late sixteenth and early seventeenth centuries, defendants were remaining in the common law court and taking their chances with a jury verdict, and then if the jury ruled for the plaintiff, the defendant would get an injunction and remove the case to a court of equity and have a new trial. Not only was this inefficient and wasteful of time and money, but it appeared to give to the courts of equity an appellate review of the common law court's actions. Such an appeal was not a part of the traditional organization of the court system of England. This matter led to a bitter public dispute between Sir Edward Coke, the Chief Justice of the Court of King's Bench, and Thomas Egerton, Lord Ellesmere, the Chancellor of the Court of Chancery. The dispute was temporarily settled in 1616 by King James I himself, who was being advised by Sir Francis Bacon.

Bacon was a great rival of Coke, and he soon succeeded Ellesmere as Chancellor.[11]

Even though there was an end to the public dispute in 1616, it took perhaps a century for the issue to be worked out properly. The cases published here show that the law was still not settled in 1655.

The issue is not a question of an appeal but is one of res judicata. When the dispute between the parties has proceeded to a final judgment, it should not be relitigated, neither in a different court nor in the same court, unless an appellate court reverses that lower court judgment. Thus if a defendant in a common law court elects to proceed to a final judgment in that court, he should not be allowed to relitigate it anywhere. Thus in modern practice, an injunction after a final judgment will be refused at common law or in equity on the grounds of res judicata.

Unfortunately, life is not so simple. In the famous case of Richard Glanville in 1616,[12] the original defendant, who had been the victim of fraud, had neither the opportunity to present a defence nor the chance to remove the case to an equity court before final judgment because he had been defrauded into releasing those rights. This presents the distinction between intrinsic and extrinsic fraud. This is a distinction that is understood today but was not in the seventeenth century. Intrinsic fraud, as where a person enters into a contract through deceit, is covered by the doctrine of res judicata and cannot be considered in later litigation. On the other hand, extrinsic fraud, as where a defendant is prevented by deceit from going into court to make any defence, is separate from the contract in dispute and is not covered by res judicata. Other examples of extrinsic fraud would be deceit as to the period of the statute of limitations, a judge who had been bribed, and a lawyer who deliberately betrayed his client. Other grounds for an injunction after a final judgment are accident, surprise, and breach of trust, which are well established grounds for equity jurisdiction.

The following is a good explanation of the proper balance between finality of judgments and relief from final judgments in cases of injustice. "Where a party has had a day [in a court of common law] in which he could make his defence in the proper form before a verdict and judgment against him, equity will not entertain him and grant relief after such verdict

---

[11] *J. H. Baker,* The Common Lawyers and the Chancery: 1616, in: The Legal Profession and the Common Law (1986), pp. 205 - 229; *C. M. Gray,* The Boundaries of the Equitable Function, American Journal of Legal History, vol. 20 (1976), pp. 192 - 226; *J. P. Dawson,* Coke and Ellesmere Disinterred: The Attack on the Chancery in 1616, Illinois Law Review, vol. 36 (1941), pp. 127 - 152.

[12] 1 Rolle's Reports 111, 219, 81 English Reports 365, 444; Croke (Jac.) 343, 79 English Reports 294; 2 Bulstrode 301, 80 English Reports 1139; Moore (K. B.) 838, 72 English Reports 939; Hobart 115, 80 English Reports 264.

and judgment, unless in case of fraud, accident, or surprise, or some adventitious circumstance unmixed with negligence on his part which shall sufficiently account for the omission to seek its intervention before the judgment."[13]

These cases were chosen to demonstrate some of these points.[14] It is also hoped that these reports and decrees will show the development of the English common law through reports of lawsuits.

Ayliffe v. Duke (Ch. 1655)

The Chancery case of *Ayliffe v. Duke* (Ch. 1655) was chosen for inclusion because it is an example of a court of equity granting relief following a final judgment at common law for the same matter. The two reports of the case are very similar and can perhaps be considered different versions of the same report. In this case, the official record of the case gives many more facts and details than the private reports of the case.

In this case, a series of bonds had been given in favor of various members of two families as part of a marriage contract. Later, due to economic hardships that followed the English Civil War, some of these bonds became unenforceable leaving George and Elizabeth Duke destitute. Mrs. Ayliffe agreed to make a large gift to them, Elizabeth Duke being of her kin. Then George Duke's father forced him to give a bond to his brother, John, so that Mrs. Ayliffe's gift would eventually end up in the hands of John rather than those of the intended donees. When Mrs. Ayliffe heard of this attempted fraud, she refused to go through with the gift. George, thereupon, gave the bond to her, and she cancelled it by tearing it up. Then she gave the money to George and Elizabeth.

Four years later after the money had been paid, John Duke sued Mrs. Ayliffe in a court of common law for destroying the bond in which he was the payee. The jury gave a verdict for John, and final judgment was entered by the court. Mrs. Ayliffe then sued in the Court of Chancery for equitable relief against the common law judgment, and the Court of Chancery granted it in order to prevent a double payment and fraud.

Since Mrs. Ayliffe was aware of the fraud before the common law action was begun, she should have removed the common law case into the court of equity by means of a routine common injunction before the verdict. Then she could have asserted her equitable defences against John Duke.

---

13 *Haseltine & Walton* v. *Brickey,* 16 Grattan 116, 120 (Va. 1860).

14 Note also *Pickett* v. *Morris* (Va. 1796), which is printed in the companion to this volume, and the discussion below in 'Virginia Law Reports and Records, 1776 - 1800'.

Perhaps, she could have shown the fraud in evidence at common law. Having failed to do this, the rules of res judicata, as understood today, would have prevented her from suing in equity after the common law judgment but this would have allowed a great hardship and fraud to be committed against her.

Morehead v. Douglas (Ex. 1655)

In the Exchequer case of *Morehead v. Douglas* (Ex. 1655), the defendant had secretly obtained a default judgment at common law, and the plaintiff in the present case had not known about the common law case until it was too late to make his defences there. The plaintiff in equity then sued to have relief against the common law judgment on the grounds of fraud.

The defendant thereupon pleaded by means of demurrer that the judgment at common law was final and res judicata and the court of equity could not relieve against it. The defendant in equity alleged that there were several acts of Parliament to this effect, but this author could not find any such act.[15]

The plaintiff in equity said that there were many precedents of injunctions in equity granting relief against common law judgments. When the Court of Exchequer asked for precedents to be shown, the plaintiff could only show precedents from the Court of Chancery but none from the Exchequer, the barons of the Exchequer said that they were not bound by Chancery cases and dismissed the case.

It is the opinion of this author that, though Chancery cases may not have been binding on the Court of Exchequer, they should have been persuasive, and because of the fraud committed (assuming it could have been proved) upon the plaintiff, he should have been relieved. This assumes that there was no such act of Parliament prohibiting it.

Curtis v. Smallridge (Ch. 1664)

In the case of *Curtis v. Smallridge* (Ch. 1664), Mrs. Smallridge had pawned Mr. Smallridge's property to Curtis. Mr. Smallridge then sued Curtis at common law for the wrongful taking of his property because Mrs. Smallridge, his wife, had no authority to give it to Curtis, as a pledge or otherwise. The common law court held for Mr. Smallridge and awarded damages for the value of the property received by Curtis.

---

[15] The Act of 21 August 1654, chapters 27 to 30, is not on point, but it may have been the statute referred to.

After this, Curtis discovered that Mrs. Smallridge did have her husband's authority to enter into the transaction and that she gave the money to him. The common law action was thus a fraud upon Curtis. Moreover, Mr. Smallridge ended up with the money loaned and the common law damages for the property that had been pledged as security for the loan.

Curtis thereupon sued in equity. However, the Court of Chancery refused him relief because he could have pleaded Mr. Smallridge's fraud as a bar to the action at common law. The Court of Chancery said that Curtis was not prevented by any accident from having his witnesses present at the common law trial. The other issue was that of after-discovered evidence, but the court ruled against the plaintiff because the evidence was available before the common law trial and it was not discovered or not used through the negligence of the plaintiff.

Robinson v. Bell (Ch. 1690)

In the case of *Robinson v. Bell* (Ch. 1690), Robinson was sued in a court of common law for money received as the executor of a decedent's estate. He instructed his attorney in the common law court, a court official, to enter a special defence, but a general defence was entered through the mistake of the attorney. In addition, Robinson wrote a letter to Bell, the claimant of the estate and plaintiff at common law, saying that he had received money due to the decedent when in fact he had not nor ever would receive the money. Because of these two mistakes, the court of common law ruled for Bell and ordered Robinson to pay her the money. Robinson then sued in a court of equity, and there he was relieved from payment of the common law judgment for the reasons of the two mistakes.

It is the opinion of this writer that the first mistake, that of the attorney, was a true surprise or accident over which Robinson had no control and was a sufficient ground for equitable relief against the final judgment at common law. He would not have been liable for the second mistake and would not have been ordered to pay money that he had not received from the decedent's estate had he pleaded a special defence. However, admitting receiving money which he had not received appears to have been his own negligence, against which a court of equity would not relieve.

This case was included because it was cited in *Pickett v. Morris* (Va. 1796), which is printed in the companion to this volume in 'Virginia Law Reports and Records, 1776 - 1800'. Note also that Sir George Hutchins, one of the Commissioners to hold the Great Seal until a chancellor could be chosen and appointed, cited two earlier Chancery cases. Neither of them was in print; he may have had personal knowledge of the case of *Cryer v. Goodhand* (Ch. 1673 x 1682).

Crane v. Hill (Ex. 1695)

In the case of *Crane v. Hill* (Ex. 1695), Crane was a creditor of Hill and of Hill's insolvent father. When Hill's father died, Crane and Hill came to an agreement as to the debts owed to Crane. As a part of this agreement, Hill conveyed to Crane the rectory of the parish church of Hales, which included the right to receive tithes, the rent of the glebe lands, and various other income. Afterwards, Hill acquired a precedent and superior right to the rectory, and he sued Crane in an action at common law and recovered the property.

Crane then sued Hill in the equity side of the Court of Exchequer to be relieved against the common law judgment. The equity court granted Crane's petition and required Hill to give up his title and possession. The reason of the equity court was that it was unfair and wrong for Hill to have a double recovery by setting up his new right against his own conveyance of that same right. Hill's common law judgment operated as a fraud upon Crane because of Hill's earlier conveyance to Crane; Crane could not plead this in the common law action of ejectment against him; therefore, relief in equity was granted to him.

This case was chosen for inclusion because the report was compiled by one of the judges who decided the case. Edward Ward began making reports of cases when he was a law student. He continued this practice throughout the rest of his life, as a barrister, Attorney General, and Chief Baron of the Court of Exchequer.

Kent v. Bridgman (Ch. 1704)

In the case of *Kent v. Bridgman* (Ch. 1704), Kent, the sheriff's bailiff or deputy, had levied on property owned by Bridgman's father pursuant to a court order. Bridgman then sued Kent in a common law court alleging falsely that the property taken by Kent was his property and not that of his father. At the trial at common law, Kent proved that the property that he had officially seized was in fact owned by Bridgman's father, the judgment debtor. However, Kent failed to have with him a copy of the court order to prove that the taking was lawful, and for the failure to prove that technical fact, which was never in dispute, the common law judgment was for Bridgman. Kent thereupon resorted to the court of equity, and he was relieved against the final judgment at common law.

The reasoning of the Court of Chancery is not set out in the reports of the case. (Perhaps this report is no more than a later extract from the official decree.) However, one can surmise that the ground for forbidding the enforcement of the common law judgment was that Kent was surprised at having to prove the technical fact that he was acting under court order by producing an official copy of that order. He, no doubt, assumed that that fact could be proved by oral evidence or that it need not be proved at all, and it was an accident and not negligence that he had no witness present in court to prove it.

It is not a very good report. This case was chosen for inclusion because it was cited in *Pickett v. Morris* (Va. 1796), which is printed in the companion to this volume.

In editing these records and reports, modern spelling and punctuation have been used. This is consistent with the rule of idem sonans, which is that a word is the spoken word, not the written word.

R. H. HELMHOLZ

Records and Reports: The English Ecclesiastical Courts

Introduction

A description of the records and reports of the English ecclesiastical courts must begin with a word about the Church's jurisdiction. Without it, the scope and utility of either the records or the reports cannot be fully comprehensible.[1] The English Church exercised jurisdiction over significant areas of human life during the Middle Ages and into the sixteenth and seventeenth centuries. Indeed a considerable part of this jurisdiction was retained until the nineteenth century, when statute removed all but a few vestiges of its earlier jurisdiction from the ecclesiastical system. The jurisdiction was, from first to last, organized by legal subject matter. The records of the courts themselves show this in their regular division of the cases heard before them into separate subject-matter categories, much as the English common law organized itself into separate 'forms of action'. Thus, a case in any of the court records might be listed as a 'causa testamentaria', a 'causa matrimonii', or any of the other areas of law that came within the courts' subject-matter competence. With few minor exceptions, the English Church did not attempt to exercise jurisdiction *ratione personae,* as did the ecclesiastical tribunals in many places on the Continent. Still less did it seek to exercise the jurisdiction *ratione peccati* that one finds as the source of expansive claims and sharp conflict with temporal authorities in the historical record of the Western Church.

Besides dictating the nature of the records, this restriction to jurisdiction *ratione materiae* meant that the English courts could not exercise the full scope of the canon law found in the texts of the Corpus iuris canonici. This may have been counted as unfortunate by the medieval English ecclesiastical lawyers themselves. However, it helps to explain the comparative peacefulness of relations between the courts of Church and State in medieval England, and it also offers a plausible explanation for the retention of most

[1] See the pertinent remarks by *Charles Donahue* Jr., in: The Records of the Medieval Ecclesiastical Courts, Part I: the Continent (Berlin 1989) 24 - 26.

areas of jurisdiction by the English Church during the sixteenth century Reformation. There were conflicts between *regnum* and *sacerdotium* all along, but there was never an upheaval, and there was always a certain level of agreement among common lawyers and the civilians. The comparative completeness and continuity that characterize the early modern records of the period provide documentary and eloquent testimony to that relative concord.

Ecclesiastical jurisdiction in England was customarily split between an *ex officio* side and an instance side, and again the court records reflect this division. The two sides were often kept in separate act books, at least where the volume of litigation warranted it. The former included actions brought at least formally in the name of the court itself to enforce the disciplinary side of ecclesiastical jurisdiction. It included, but was not limited to, the public offenses of the clerical order. Thus adultery and fornication, blasphemy, false swearing, heresy and contempt of the clergy, sacrilege, usury and witchcraft fell within the *ex officio* side. Both clergy and laity were subject to it. The instance side embraced actions brought by individual parties, normally to vindicate their own interests. Marriage and divorce, testaments and succession (generally limited however to personal property), defamation, tithes and oblations, and parochial law generally constituted the major heads of litigation on this side of the English Church's jurisdiction.

The English Church was divided into only two provinces, the large southern province of Canterbury and the much smaller northern province of York. The former contained eighteen dioceses during the Middle Ages (four more after 1540); the latter only three (two more after 1540). Each diocese within these two provinces possessed a consistory court, with staffs of lawyers and regular places of sitting, and most also had courts belonging to archdeacons and rural deans. Appeals lay to the provincial courts in York and in London (and thence to Rome before the 1530s, afterwards to the Court of Delegates in London). London became a particular center for English ecclesiastical lawyers because of the organization there of a college of advocates, normally called Doctors' Commons, around the start of the sixteenth century.[2] Some of the reports to be discussed below emanated from that center of the profession, and we would certainly have many more had the Library and records of Doctors' Commons been preserved. However, in most aspects the diocesan structure of the Church's tribunal has determined the way in which the records and reports have been kept. Most are now kept in local diocesan archives, or in the county record offices located within the appropriate diocese of the Church. There has been no centraliza-

---

2 The standard work on the subject is *G. D. Squibb,* Doctors' Commons (Oxford 1977).

tion or general consolidation of these records or reports over the years, though there has been a general movement in the last fifty years to put them into the hands of competent archivists.

The Records

Under this archival class fall the official acts of the ecclesiastical courts. The earliest examples extant come from around the year 1200.[3] These early records are very incomplete, however, and it is questionable whether one can actually speak of 'official' *acta* from this period before the consistory courts had been organized as regularly sitting courts of law. That step was not taken until the second half of the thirteenth century, or at least very shortly before.

Considerable numbers of records survive from the end of the fourteenth century, and by the fifteenth century they exist in some quantities.[4] From the last quarter of the sixteenth century forwards, they survive in regular and mostly unbroken sequence, with the unfortunate exception of almost all of the London tribunals save the Commissary court. The prevailing opinion holds that the other records were destroyed in the Great Fire of 1666. All the surviving records can, without too much distortion of the facts, be divided into one of three classes: act books, cause papers, and miscellaneous documents. The first two are much the more frequent survivals, and also the most important.

Act books

Act books are the most regular class of records from the ecclesiastical courts to have come down to us, particularly for the medieval period. The canon law required that the courts employ a scribe to record all the formal acts of the court, this being to preclude later questioning of the validity of the action taken by the courts. The Fourth Lateran Council (1215), which enacted this rule, laid down no set form for recording the *acta,* and the act books we have do differ in form, both over the course of time and between dioceses. Their compilation was undertaken by a court official called the court Registrar, or by his deputy. The Registrar, usually also a Notary

[3] See: Select Cases from the Ecclesiastical Courts of the Province of Canterbury c. 1200 - 1301, eds. *Norma Adams* and *Charles Donahue,* Jr. (Selden Society, Vol. 95, 1978 - 79) 1 - 48.

[4] A list, although an incomplete one, is included in *R. H. Helmholz,* Marriage Litigation in Medieval England (Cambridge 1975) 233 - 35. A much fuller listing appears in: The Records of the Medieval Ecclesiastical Courts, Part II: England, ed. *Charles Donahue,* Jr. (Berlin 1994).

Public, kept the act book for future reference as required by the Lateran Council's decree. Indeed, it seems to have been one of the Registrar's most important functions to preserve the records of his consistory court.

Some generalizations about the nature of these act books can be put forward. Virtually all of them can be described as the day-to-day records of the procedure in all the cases heard by a particular court. Often, but not always, the nature of the cause and some of the evidence introduced was also recorded in these books. However, they excluded any record of the substantive or procedural law. No arguments of the advocates were included and no legal authorities were cited in the act books, although they did sometimes record that a term for such arguments was set. It is therefore hard to draw firm conclusions about the law being applied. Sentences in the canonical tradition contained none of the legal reasons that moved the judges to reach the result they did. Thus, it is only by indirection and surmise that the modern historian can make use of these records to describe the law enforced in the spiritual tribunals.

The English act books were compiled in codex form, and divided internally into sessions, usually called consistories. Under the heading for each session was recorded the title for each case heard on that day and the action taken in it. For a particular case, for example, the first recorded entry may note the constitution of proctors and the giving of the libel by the plaintiff. Under the second, the defendant's answer to the libel may be recorded; under the third, the plaintiff's introduction of articles and his production of several witnesses. And so on through to the final sentence and taxation of costs. Thus, tracing the full hearing of a specific action often requires a search through many folios of an act book. It is virtually impossible to use the records if one is required to use a microfilm reader rather than being allowed to consult the original. One simply must leaf backwards and forwards in the book or books that contain the case to follow its course. Unfortunately some record offices are now imposing that requirement.

The headings of each court session and title of each case in an act book were normally written in advance of each sitting by the scribe. The action taken was recorded either at the time of hearing or shortly thereafter, and placed under the appropriate case title. The use of this method is obvious because in most instances the individual cases were laid out regularly on each folio of the act book. Every case was, in other words, given a set amount of space in advance. Entries of the actual steps of the procedure taken appear sometimes in a different ink from that used for the heading, and often not enough was done to fill the space which had been left under the heading. For this reason, blank areas appear on many folios. Occasionally, too much was done in a session to be fitted into the space available.

The entry for one case then spilled over onto a following folio, inserted by the scribe in the blank space left from a less active case. The continuation were usually marked by a cross, or some other convenient symbol, to lead the reader to the appropriate place. This system thus provides one more incidental indication that the act books were meant to be used in the future. Otherwise there would have been no need for the symbols.

It is true that not all act books were compiled in precisely like fashion. In the diocese of Hereford, for instance, the headings for each case were not set down in advance of the court session. Instead, they were either recorded at the same time as the matter was heard or put together later from the scribe's notes. At York, each case was identified by a notation in the left-hand margin above the normal entry giving the names of the parties, and no explicit record was made of the case's subject. At Canterbury, on the other hand, each case was identified by the parish of the parties, and the subject was almost invariably stated expressly. These seem trivial differences, no doubt, but they show that there was room for continuing and differing traditions of record keeping within the dioceses.[5] They also warn that the most one can hope to do is to offer generalizations that generally hold true for the act books, without confidence that they will be complete or everywhere applicable.

Although most of the earliest act books were kept chronologically, a few were not. It may be that they were preserved as formularies more than simply records. The remaining book from Bath and Wells, for example, from which an example is included in the Appendix (No. 2), does not have its entries arranged on a strictly day-by-day basis. The cases recorded in it also cover a long period of time, from 1458 - 1498, so that it may have been put together at the latter date from existing materials. There was also notable variation in contents. Some act books combined instance litigation, that is actions begun on the initiative of private parties, with *ex officio* business.[6] This tended to be true when the level of business was light. A few books contain the depositions of witnesses. Most do not. There are, as just stated, no absolutely firm rules about the content and manner of composition of the English act books. But, in general, it is fair to think of them as systematic records of all the cases which came before a particular court, normally arranged chronologically and separately for each case.

The history of the standards and completeness in recording within the instance act books is one of apparent decline. It is a virtual rule that the earlier the act book, the more useful information is to be found in it. The

---

[5] *Dorothy M. Owen,* The Records of the Established Church in England excluding parochial records (London 1970) 9.

[6] E. g., The Courts of the Archdeaconry of Buckingham 1483 - 1523, *E. M. Elvey* ed. (Buckinghamshire Record Society 19, 1975).

middle of the fifteenth century marks a turning point of sorts. In the act books from before that time, the scribe usually recorded each case fairly thoroughly. He gave the opening steps and followed the suit through to its final disposition, whether the sentence, dismissal or flight by one party. A good deal about the cases can usually be recovered from the early records. After the middle of the century, however, cases were often left incompletely recorded.

The gradual decline in completeness is probably best explained as an incidental effort of progress. It occurred because of a growing legal sophistication of record keeping procedures in the courts. Act books came to be rigorously separated from the Cause papers described below and the Cause papers more regularly preserved. When this happened, the Cause papers could be relied upon for information about the nature of the case. The act books did not need to contain information that was easily to be found in the other kind of formal record.

This means that in the fourteenth-century books, which survive from Canterbury, Ely, and York, the substance of the claim was almost invariably recorded. For example, one can learn that a plaintiff sought a decree of nullity because he had been coerced into marriage, or claimed that someone had slandered him with words that were recorded verbatim in English. Often, some of the evidence was recorded in the act book. Likewise, the substance of the court's sentence was usually recorded in the book itself, and sometimes it was given in full. Early fifteenth-century instance act books continued to give fairly full details of the actions heard, though with somewhat greater abbreviation. After the 1450s however, only the barest of procedural steps were normally recorded. For the sixteenth century and later, the routine and substantively uninformative character of these books became all but invariable.

In concrete terms, this means that instead of knowing what the exact claim was in cases involving marriage or testaments, one learns simply that some sort of marriage or testamentary litigation had begun between two parties. One can only guess at what was actually at issue. There are inevitably some exceptions to this rule. An occasional case was more fully recorded, and some act books are more informative than others. The *ex officio* act books in particular continued to provide a good deal of information about the crimes with which defendants were charged and often the individual's response to that charge. In general, however, the concrete information about the facts behind each case recorded in the act books came to be quite small.

The standard of handwriting of the act books deteriorated markedly over the course of the fifteenth century, though there was some improvement in the last quarter of the sixteenth. In the 1480s or the 1520s, for example, the records of the Church courts look very messy indeed, and a prominent historian once described them as 'among the more repulsive of all the relics of the past'.[7] It is difficult to disagree with his assessment, although it is not fair to say that the act books from after the middle years of the fifteenth century are without value. They can normally be deciphered. They almost always give the names of the parties, the general type of case, the parishes of the parties, and the procedural steps taken by the court. They provide much incidental information that can be valuable for understanding the nature of the jurisdiction exercised by these courts. About the facts and exact points of law at issue in each case, however, they are most uninformative. For more information one must turn, where possible, to the Cause papers described below.

The rate of survival of act books is virtually complete in England from the last quarter of the sixteenth century. The consistory court of the diocese of Ely, near Cambridge, provides a fairly typical example, and it has the advantage of possessing an excellent guide to its records.[8] Although it possesses one of the earliest Act books (1374 - 81), the next surviving instance book comes only from the sixteenth century (1580 - 81). In between, a few court records still exist, but they are not act books properly speaking, and they are very uneven as to date. There is nothing at all, for example, from the fifteenth century that could be put into this class. From the end of the sixteenth and particularly from first decade of the seventeenth century, however, the number of surviving act books picks up dramatically, and it continues thereafter. A few gaps exist, but not many. And from the 1620s forwards the series is virtually complete. This same pattern is found in most of the English dioceses.[9]

The *ex officio* act books at Ely follow roughly the same pattern in survival as the instance records. There is one, not terribly regular, document left from the fifteenth century, a total of three from the last quarter of the sixteenth, and a regular series beginning in the first decade of the next century. At Ely, these *ex officio* books contained both the presentments made at visitations and those heard in the ordinary course of business as a result of private 'informations' or by 'promotion' of the judge's office. In some dioceses, however, the two were kept separate in the records. There also

---

[7] *G. R. Elton,* England 1200 - 1640 (Ithaca, N. Y. 1969) 105.

[8] *Dorothy M. Owen,* A Catalogue of the Records of the Bishop and Archdeacon of Ely (Cambridge 1971) 21 - 27. See also *Isabel M. Kirby,* Diocese of Gloucester: A Catalogue of the Records of the Bishop and Archdeacons (Gloucester 1968) and *Francis W. Steer,* Diocese of Chichester: A Catalogue of the Records of the Bishop, Archdeacons and Former Exempt Jurisdictions (Chichester 1966).

[9] See, e. g., *Ralph Houlbrooke,* Church Courts and the People during the English Reformation 1520 - 1570 (Oxford 1979) 283 - 84 and *Martin Ingram,* Church Courts, Sex and Marriage in England, 1570 - 1640 (Cambridge 1987) 377 - 78.

seems to be no separate probate act books for Ely, unlike the situation in many dioceses where these records were recorded separately from the act books used in instance and *ex officio* cases. In any event, by the early years of the seventeenth century, the pattern of record keeping and preservation had reached a stable situation. It is only in the later eighteenth century that things changed dramatically, and this seems to have occurred because of the diminution of business in the spiritual courts. No one has yet investigated these later records with any care, although the subject would be well worth undertaking.

Cause papers

Cause papers were the documents used in the course of litigation, and they are the source of most of our detailed knowledge of the litigation heard by the English spiritual courts, at least after the middle of the fifteenth century, when they begin to survive in quantity, and before the late sixteenth century, when the ecclesiastical reports came into existence. Most of the cause papers were produced by the parties themselves, rather than the court scribes. One copy was to be given to the court, one to the other party, and one retained. They were written on separate pieces of paper or parchment, and were sometimes stitched together at the top corner, presumably at the conclusion of litigation, by the court officials. Except for deposition books noted below, the Cause papers were nowhere compiled in codex form, as were the act books. The *codices* compiled for purposes of appeal, which did include these documents and which are found in many Continental archives, begin to be used in English practice only towards the end of the sixteenth century. Thus, when there was an English appeal in earlier centuries, either a long roll or a separate file containing all the documents stitched together was customarily used to transmit the process.

For the medieval period and into the first half of the sixteenth century, the only sizable collections of Cause papers surviving come from the metropolitan sees, Canterbury and York.[10] For the period after the 1580s, however, the collections are geographically much fuller. Not only do Canterbury and York have copious survivals, smaller dioceses are also well represented. Coventry and Lichfield is fairly typical.[11] A very small quantity of material has survived from the period before 1589. However, from

[10] For York, see *D. M. Smith,* Ecclesiastical Cause Papers at York: the Court of York 1301 - 1399 (Borthwick Texts and Calendars 14, 1988). For Canterbury, see Select Canterbury Cases (above note 3).

[11] What follows is based on the author's experience in the Record Office, on the help of the wonderful staff there, and on a guide: Staffordshire Record Office, Cumulative Hand List Part I: Lichfield Jt. Record Office, Diocesan Probate and Church Commissioners' Records (1970) 15.

1590 forwards the volume picks up markedly. We do not yet know whether it is in any sense complete. There are clearly cases in the act books for which no cause papers survive. Nor can we be sure whether what remains is representative. No one has yet worked through these papers and the contemporary act books carefully enough to have formed a good judgment.

At the present time, the Cause papers at Lichfield are arranged by year, and this appears to have been the original system of filing. There is an annual bundle, which must have been put together by a registrar or his assistant towards the end of each year, containing all the Cause papers for that year. This too represents a challenge for the historian, as it does for the archivist. The system can be difficult (though by no means impossible) to use, since there is no internal means of reference to a case found in an act book other than looking through all papers for any of the years covered by the book's entries. However, today it is equally difficult to be sure how to improve the system in the interest of accessibility. Particularly since one would often be disturbing an arrangement of very long-standing if one were to 'rationalize' the organization of these files, one might easily find he had only made things worse. Some experiments in that direction – such as arranging them by parish or rural deanery – have done exactly that.

The different types of cause papers surviving mirror the steps of Romano-canonical procedure. Many of the forms found in the early *ordines iudiciarii,* some of which were printed at the start of this century by Ludwig Wahrmund,[12] appear in the English archives, although the fit is not exact in every situation. For example, a document frequently found at the front of cause files is the constitution of proctors,[13] and most of these follow in form and substance what appears in contemporary procedural literature of the *ius commune.* On the other hand, the formal citations of parties, from both instance and *ex officio* matters, seem mostly to have disappeared over the course of centuries. It is not clear why, because citations were a fundamental part of the *ordo iuris.* The English courts did not ignore this requirement, since many mandates from the courts to rural deans and curates directing them to cite named parties to appear before the court are mentioned in the records and a few of them have survived in documents.

The principal types of Cause papers now surviving include the following: libels, positions, articles, *responsa personalia,* interrogatories, exceptions, depositions, and definitive sentences. For the most part, these follow the forms found in the *ordines* or in the *Speculum iudiciale* of William Dur-

---

[12] Quellen zur Geschichte des römisch-kanonischen Prozeßes im Mittelalter (5 vols., 1914, repr. 1962).

[13] Die Summa aurea des Wilhelmus de Drokeda, in id., II, 103.

antis and require no particular comment here. Most of them, as stated above, were prepared by the parties themselves, and all of them were eventually paid for by the parties. At some point during the Middle Ages this became the practice even as to the definitive sentences. Both parties introduced draft sentences, and one of them was 'porrected' by the judge to embody his decision. Indeed, some of the surviving documents were physically altered in the course of the end of litigation – as by adding or changing words and amounts – almost certainly to bring the document into line with the judge's substantive determination.

As time went on in English practice, there was a tendency to combine the first three of the documents just named, the libel, positions and articles. Although in theory each served a distinct function in litigation, these functions were close enough that in practice often it would have been quite otiose to differentiate and duplicate the three. It would have served merely to waste time and money. The issue of this development was what was later called the 'articulated libel', in which the complainant's claim was divided into its component parts. This document was used to fill all the functions of the three separate documents, and thus for initiation of the case, for the *responsa personalia* of the defendant, and for examination of the witnesses. By the late sixteenth century, these 'articulated libels' were ubiquitous in the English records. An example is found in the Appendix volume (No. 6).

Of the Cause papers the *responsa personalia* of the parties and the depositions of witnesses, or attestations as they were often called, were the only documents customarily prepared by the court officials themselves. This was necessary because examination of the parties and the witnesses was conducted privately by a court official, and the results then published by reading them aloud and providing the parties with a copy. Customarily, the answers to the interrogatories were combined on the same document with the attestations of witnesses, the former coming second. In several places the results were collected together into books and preserved as part of the court records. Otherwise, they appear on separate sheets of parchment or paper and were kept with the other Cause papers.

Definitive sentences contain elaborate recitations of the procedural steps followed in litigation, coupled with a finding in favor of one party or the other. They were formal documents, and unlike modern judicial opinions, they never articulated the legal reasoning used by the judge to reach his decision. This would have been contrary to the traditions of the *ius commune,* the habitual guide for the English spiritual courts. As noted above, a draft of the sentence was normally prepared by each party and submitted to the court for approval and promulgation. Taxation of the expenses of litigation, assessed against the losing party, occurred at the end of most instance cases, and many files of cause papers also contain this document. However, few written appeals in the archives survive; perhaps because appeals could be made orally *apud acta.*

Miscellaneous records

Over the course of centuries, the numbers and types of court records used and preserved multiplied. Particularly from the 1580s and afterwards, the variety of miscellaneous documents connected to litigation in the consistory courts to be found in the ecclesiastical archives is very great. Not all of these records would have been found there a hundred years previously. Examples of new classes of documents are: schedules of penance, *cautiones* or caveats used to prevent administrative action, citation books, excommunication books, appointments of apparitors, churchwardens' presentments and returns from visitations, fee books, sequestration orders, license and faculty books, and bonds of various sorts. Examples of continuing records are registers of wills, inventories of the assets of the estates of decedents, and precedent books or formularies. For these, the only multiplication that occurred was in their numbers. Even for the others, mostly it was the creation of a separate class of records that was new. Few resulted from actual changes in the procedure used in the consistory courts; they resulted rather from more thorough and complete habits of record keeping. The argument has been advanced that the English ecclesiastical courts were at their height in the seventeenth century. The argument is debatable. By then, the courts had lost a significant part of their medieval jurisdiction. From the point of view of the preservation and quality of the records of the consistory courts, however, the statement is definitely true.

The Reports

There is less to be said about the tradition of law reporting in the courts of the English Church than there is about the court records. This is true for several reasons. The first is quantitative. There are many, many fewer reports extant than there are surviving records. The ratio must be several hundreds to one in favor of records. There is no doubt that some early reports have been lost, particularly those kept at Doctors' Commons in London. We can be certain that losses have occurred, since there are occasional references within those that remain to other, presumably similar, books which cannot now be traced.[14]

---

[14] E. g., Cathedral Library, Canterbury, MS. Z. 5.4, f. 12, containing a marginal reference to "M. Parker's Book intitulate Tomus secundus fol. 1844". No trace of such a book is apparent today in the Cathedral archives.

Second, the reports extend over a much shorter period of time than the surviving records. The first reports (at least so far discovered) come from the last quarter of the sixteenth century. None exists from the medieval period, whereas the survival rate of medieval ecclesiastical records is considerable. And, at least from what has been learned to date, it appears that the total number from the period between 1580 and the 1640s, when the courts were temporarily closed by the outbreak of the Civil War and the ensuing Interregnum period, probably does not exceed twenty in all.[15]

The sixteenth century reports seem to have been innovations in English ecclesiastical court practice. There is nothing like the Yearbook tradition of the common law for the spiritual tribunals. Although English ecclesiastical lawyers during the Middle Ages produced memoranda of law relating to litigation being heard in their courts, so far as is presently known, none of these was ever collected into a report. There are no medieval English collections of *decisiones.* Nor do we have English *consilia* connected to actual cases and collected together. The legal memoranda that survive from before the sixteenth century were kept as isolated documents, then either recorded in a formulary,[16] or kept among the Cause papers of a particular case.[17]

The second reason for the brevity of the second part of this contribution grows out of the nature of these reports, once they do begin in the sixteenth century. It would not be unfair to describe most of them as closer to the reports of the English common law courts than they are to the famous Continental *decisiones* or *consilia.* The Continental literature was certainly known in England. The *decisiones* of the Roman Rota and the important collection from the see of Toulouse circulated widely within the English Church.[18] However, the Continental products were not imitated, or at least not imitated very exactly. The English reports are less elaborate and systematic in presentation. They were compiled by men who knew, but were not following, the style of most of the Continental *decisiones.*

---

[15] A preliminary list is found in *R. H. Helmholz,* Roman Canon Law in Reformation England (Cambridge 1990) 198 - 99. Since the date of that book some new case reports have been found in Cambridge University Library, Add. MS. 8866, fols. 1 - 50, and in Wiltshire Record Office, Trowbridge, MS. D 5/24/1, fols. 17 - 38v. Doubtless there is more to be discovered.

[16] E.g., John Lydford's Book, *Dorothy M. Owen* ed. (London 1974) No. 305; Hemingby's Register, *Helena M. Chew* ed. (Wiltshire Archaeological and Natural History Society 18, 1962) no. 229.

[17] E.g., Select Canterbury Cases, above note 3, No. D.19.3.

[18] E.g., *Cragges c. Glover,* in Colmore's Book, Durham Diocesan Records, DDR XVIII/3, fols. 235v - 36, reference to the *decisiones* of the Capella Tolosana in a marriage cause.

In seeking to characterize the surviving reports, one might define the majority as recollections by the reporter of important or interesting points raised by a particular case, sometimes coupling these points with the citation of learned authorities from the *ius commune.* The reports were probably not based upon the official records. At least they do not refer to records either directly or by indirection in their account of cases. It also appears virtually certain that the ecclesiastical reporters were not acting officially in any sense. They were not recording cases as the official of any court, as was the case with the act books and cause papers.

Authorship of the surviving reports is uncertain. They are anonymous for the most part, although internal clues from the manuscript often gives clues allowing us to identify the reporter. In one instance, it is possible to identify the reporter as the judge of an ecclesiastical court from which the cases were drawn.[19] More often it appears that someone other than a judge did the collecting. Several of the prominent English civilians who were also judges wrote treatises, many of which were stimulated by the contemporary conflicts with the English common lawyers. However in no case can one identify these great names (e.g., Swinburne, Ridley, Cosin) with a surviving collection of reports. Thus, while we associate the English common law reports with the great judges who wrote them (e.g., Coke, Dyer, Croke), the same association is lacking for the ecclesiastical reports.

Despite the lack of connection with the judges of the ecclesiastical courts, the frequent inclusion of learned authorities from the *ius commune* suggests that advocates rather than proctors were more frequently the reporters of the surviving works, though this statement is not without exception. That is, they came from the same class that would produce the judges. The precedent book or formulary, compiling the various forms used in litigation, was the document of choice for the future use of proctors. These have not been counted as reports, even though most of the forms found within them came from identifiable cases.

It is difficult to generalize about the contents of the remaining ecclesiastical reports, though it is surely worth stating that the *ius commune* remained the touchstone of the law found in them. Procedural questions, which were particularly frequently raised and discussed at length in the surviving reports, were uniformly treated according to law found in the Continental treatises. And the same is true for most of the substantive areas of law. Citations to the English common law were very rare, at least before 1640, although not entirely absent. It is evident that the English civilians

---

[19] Clement Colmore, chancellor of the diocese of Durham, 1582 - 1619, was responsible for collecting the material in University of Durham, Dept. of Palaeography and Diplomatic, DDR XVIII/3.

were fully in contact with the latest developments within the *ius commune*. Even the effects of the *Usus modernus pandectarum* are apparent in some of the reports.

The reports very often included the salient facts of the cases upon which they commented. However, this was not an invariable rule. More so even than the Common law reporters, the English ecclesiastical reporters descended into simply collecting miscellaneous points of law. Sometimes these comments were interspersed with actual cases, sometimes they were collected without the cases. Although the comments and the legal rules may have been raised within the context of court practice, many seem not to have been connected specifically to an actual case by the reporter. One can appreciate their utility for an English advocate or proctor, who would need to know and remember the applicable law. But perhaps it would not be accurate to describe some of the comments found in the manuscripts as actual reports. The Appendix provides one example (No. 8).

The fullest surviving report so far discovered – one that is firmly tied to actual cases – is found in the Bodleian Library, Oxford.[20] This is a manuscript of more than 200 folios, and the cases in it extend from 1597 to 1604. The best reports of the individual cases in it give the names of the parties, a brief statement of the facts, the point of law at issue, the arguments made by the advocates in it, the learned authorities cited, and (usually) the definitive sentence. Yet, for all its interest, this manuscript nonetheless lacks the regularity and the professionalism of a Continental collection of *decisiones*. Its compiler did not follow any firm pattern in the presentation of material. Sometimes material was inserted seemingly almost as an *aide memoire* for him, without any attempt to make it accessible to other lawyers. And certainly that is true of most of the lesser examples of reports to be found today in the English archives. Some of them – for instance an elementary collection of cases, relatively brief and almost entirely without citation of authorities that is now found in the Suffolk Record Office at Bury St. Edmunds[21] – were surely never meant for print. It does seem likely, nonetheless, that such reports as these were designed to be used in the future practice of the anonymous ecclesiastical lawyer who compiled them.

At least in the present state of knowledge, it is impossible to speak with assurance about the circulation of these reports. We know that there was movement of forms and personnel between dioceses. Forms inserted into precedent books, elementary works of procedure designed for use by proctors, and manuscript copies of Francis Clerke's *Praxis in curiis ecclesiasticis*

---

[20] Tanner MS. 427; noticed briefly in *J. H. Baker,* English Legal Manuscripts, Vol. II (Zug 1978) 150.

[21] MS. E 14/11/7, 36 fols. (1623 - 40).

clearly did circulate widely within the English Church. There was also some circulation of the reports. A manuscript now found in the Library of Congress, in Washington D.C., for example, contains material identical to that found in an early report from the diocese of Ely now kept in the Borthwick Institute in York.[22] This is not the only example. However there was not enough copying and duplication for one to speak of circulation anywhere approaching the scale of the reports of the English common law. On virtually all fronts, therefore, the ecclesiastical reports cut a poor figure compared with either their Common law counterparts or Continental *decisiones.*

The limitations in the sources being admitted, it is nevertheless true that the reports that have survived are extremely valuable, and that they deserve to be taken into account in assessing the wider history of English law. The show the vitality of the civilians, and the learning possible among them, during the post-Reformation period. The first printed reports from the ecclesiastical courts come only from the eighteenth century[23] but this gives a misleading impression of a collapse of learning among the civilians of an earlier period. Evidently, however, the appearance is to some extent an accident of what happened to be printed, rather than a judgment that the ecclesiastical courts produced nothing worthy of report prior to that date.

Moreover, it seems virtually certain that there is more to be discovered about the English ecclesiastical law from these reports. Few scholars have mined the manuscript tradition of this part of the Church's jurisdiction, and there are also several known examples of reports from the period after the courts were restored in the 1660s that no one has looked at with any care. Probably what is known so far is the tip of a smallish iceberg. For example, several reports beginning with cases from before the Civil War and continuing, without any pause, with cases from after 1660 exists, now in the Cambridge University Library.[24] No survey of these later manuscript reports has yet been conducted, but it is clear already that there is a great deal of useful information to be uncovered in them and that their number is not inconsequential. Reports from the spiritual courts exist, for example, as far away from their original place of production as the Spencer Research Library at the University of Kansas, Lawrence,[25] and the Free Library in Philadelphia.[26] The Codrington Library at All Souls' College, Oxford, and

---

22 Library of Congress, Law MS. 27, pages 215 et seq. and Borthwick Institute, York, MS. Prec. Bk. 11.

23 The first printed reports were the decisions of Sir George Lee (1752 - 58) (*Joseph Phillimore* ed., 2 vols.) reprinted in Vol. 161 of the English Reports.

24 CUL, Add. MS. 8866. The first fifty pages come from the earlier period; the later period takes up the rest of the volume.

25 MS. E 181 (18th century cases).

26 MS. LC. 14/54.

the University Library in Cambridge both contain several valuable manuscript reports from the post-Reformation period.[27] No doubt more exist in other likely repositories. They remain to be discovered, or at least adequately catalogued and described, for use by historians of the law.

[27] All Souls' MS. 230, entitled 'Jus regis ecclesiasticum'.

W. H. BRYSON

Virginia Law Reports and Records, 1776 - 1800

In 1607 Virginia was settled by a London-based corporation, and the English settlers brought with them the municipal law and legal institutions of England.[1] It was specifically required by the instructions to the Virginia Company that litigation was to be settled "as near to the common laws of England and the equity thereof as may be".[2] In 1632 when commissioners were appointed to hold the monthly courts (later renamed the county courts), their commissions required them to execute the office of justice of the peace and to act "as near as may be after the laws of the realm of England and the statutes thereof made".[3] When the statutes of Virginia were recodified in 1662, the common law of England was acknowledged to be in force.[4] When independence from Great Britain was declared in 1776, a statute was enacted which stated that the general common law of England remained in force,[5] and this provision has been continued in substance by every Virginia code since.[6] Thus, one should not be surprised to see the lawyers and judges in *Downman v. Downman* (1791) and *Pickett v. Morris* (1796) relying upon English cases as precedents.

In eighteenth century Virginia before independence in 1776, the basic court structure was a county court for each county and a central court in Williamsburg called the General Court. The General Court had appellate jurisdiction over the county courts and original jurisdiction as well. Appeals lay from the General Court to the Privy Council in London. Although some of the justices of the peace in the county courts may have had legal train-

---

[1] See generally, *W. H. Bryson,* English Common Law in Virginia, Journal of Legal History, vol. 6 (1985), pp. 249 - 256; *W. H. Bryson,* Law Reporting and Legal Records in Virginia, 1607 - 1800, in: *J. H. Baker,* Judicial Records, Law Reports, and the Growth of Case Law (1989), pp. 319 - 335.

[2] 'Articles, Instructions and Orders' (20 November 1606), *W. W. Hening,* Statutes at Large of Virginia, vol. 1, p. 68 [hereinafter cited as: Hening's Statutes].

[3] Act of February 1631/32, chap. 33, Hening's Statutes, vol. 1, p. 169.

[4] Act of March 1662, preamble, Hening's Statutes, vol. 2, p. 43.

[5] Act of May 1776, chap. 5, § 6, Hening's Statutes, vol. 9, p. 127.

[6] Virginia Revised Code, vol. 1, p. 135, chap. 38 (1819); Virginia Code, p. 98, chap. 16, § 1 (1849); Virginia Code § 2 (1887); Virginia Code § 2 (1919); Virginia Code Annotated § 1 - 10 (Repl. Vol. 1992).

ing, the large majority were laymen similarly to the English Quarter Sessions, upon which the Virginia county courts were modelled. Also most of the judges of the General Court were not professionally trained. The General Court was composed of twelve gentlemen appointed for life and presided over by the royal governor. This same group also sat in legislative and executive sessions.

After 1776, the place of the Privy Council was given to a new court, the Court of Appeals of Virginia (since renamed the Supreme Court of Virginia). Then in 1777 the equity jurisdiction of the General Court was transferred to a new parallel High Court of Chancery. In 1788 the members of the General Court were required to ride circuit and hold sessions throughout the state in the new appellate district courts. After 1776 all of the judges above the county court level were required to be members of the bar and thus to be professionally qualified.[7] It is to be noted that the county courts and the Court of Appeals were fused courts having jurisdiction over cases at common law and in equity similarly to the English Court of Exchequer.

It should, therefore, come as no surprise to find that the operation of the Virginia courts at the clerical level was quite similar to that of the English courts. Every court at every level of jurisdiction had a clerk, who was trained as such as an apprentice to an older experienced clerk. The best training available in colonial Virginia was in the office of the Secretary of State in Williamsburg, the Secretary being the official clerk of the General Court.[8] In the eighteenth century before Independence, the clerks of the county courts were appointed by the Secretary and served in the capacity of his deputies.[9] After 1776, the clerks were appointed by the judges in whose court they acted. It is an indication of the importance of these officials that, once appointed, they held office during good behavior and not at the will of the judges.[10]

The clerks had the general responsibility for managing the office and the records of the courts. The clerk of the county court was a very significant official in that he heard routine procedural motions at rule days[11] and generally guided the lay justices of the peace through the court procedures.

---

[7] *M. V. Nelson,* A Study of Judicial Review in Virginia, 1789 - 1928 (1947), pp. 13 - 29.

[8] The Secretary delegated this duty to a deputy, who was assisted by under clerks. *O. P. Chitwood,* Justice in Colonial Virginia (1905), pp. 114 - 115; *L. R. Heaton,* 'This Excellent Man' Littleton Waller Tazewell's Sketch of Benjamin Waller, Virginia Magazine of History and Biography, vol. 89 (1981), pp. 143 - 152.

[9] *A. G. Roeber,* Faithful Magistrates and Republican Lawyers (1981), pp. 47, 69; *P. A. Bruce,* Institutional History of Virginia in the Seventeenth Century (1910), vol. 1, pp. 588 - 591, vol. 2, pp. 397 - 399.

[10] Virginia Constitution of 1776, chap. 2, § 15, Hening's Statutes, vol. 9, p. 117.

[11] Hening's Statutes, vol. 6, p. 335, vol. 12, p. 33.

The court records kept by the clerks of all of the courts, trial courts and appellate courts, that are relevant to this essay are the order books. In these books, the clerk of the court entered copies of all of the orders made by the court. The orders at this period, 1776 to 1800, were drafted by the clerk or his deputy rather than by a judge or the lawyer representing a party. The orders were entered into the order books chronologically similarly to the order books of the English courts of Chancery and Exchequer and the acta books of the English ecclesiastical courts. Thus the order of the court will normally be a formal note of the action of the court devoid of any reason therefor. Moreover, there are usually few or no facts of the case given.

Thus the modern researcher must rely on the reports of the decisions of the judges. During this period in Virginia, the county court judges rarely gave any opinions for their rulings, or if they did, none were written down. (The only exception to this rule is the small handful of cases reported by David Watson.) This is not surprising because these courts were composed of lay magistrates, and they were composed of several of them who acted upon a majority.

On the other hand, we do have reports of cases from the appellate courts. The judicial routine in these courts at this time was for the court to hear the arguments of the lawyers and then to adjourn to consider their judgment. The court was later reconvened, and the judges each gave their individual opinions orally *seriatim.* These opinions were then noted down by anyone in the courtroom who cared to do so. Sometimes the judges had written notes from which to deliver their opinions; sometimes not. When the judges wrote out their opinions, they might gave them to the reporter of decisions after they had been read in court. Indeed, Edmund Pendleton made his notes available to Bushrod Washington.[12] It was not until 1820, however, that the Court of Appeals of Virginia was provided with an official salaried reporter of decisions.

Thus the reports of Virginia cases before 1800 were taken down in open court. At the end of the day, the notes taken in court would be expanded to include a statement of the facts, the arguments of the lawyers, and the reasons for the opinions of the judges. Therefore, it is not surprising that there are errors in proper names, in numerals, and in citations, matters which cannot be corrected by any grammatical context.

Since the reports at this time were created by private persons unofficially, there is not much uniformity to them. Some cases are reported in much greater length than others. If the reporter was representing one of the parties or if he was particularly interested in the case for whatever reason,

[12] 1 Washington [v] (1798). Note also 4 Call [iv] (1833).

there might be a very thorough report of it. Otherwise, it might be very cursory. Moreover, it was in the reporter's sole discretion or whim as to which cases to report and which not. The clerk of court was, of course, required to enter an official record of every case decided by the court.

From the materials copied in the companion volume, we see that the lawyers and the judges relied upon earlier reports, both Virginian and English, but there was no mention of the official records of any case. The records were never printed and were thus unavailable, as a practical matter. They were not printed and published because they normally did not shed any light on the legal reasons given by the judges to support their judgments.

For the period 1776 to 1800, the following reports have survived.[13]

1. Bushrod Washington published two volumes of reports of cases in the Court of Appeals dating from 1790 to 1796. They were first printed in 1798 and 1799.

2. Daniel Call's *Reports* also cover the Court of Appeals. Volumes one and two systematically cover the years 1797 to 1800 and later; these two volumes were published in 1801 and 1802. Volumes three, four, and six contain a miscellaneous selection of cases dating from 1779 to 1800 and later; they were printed in 1805 and 1833.

3. John Brown, the clerk of the Court of Appeals, made reports of cases in that court covering the period 1791 to 1799. These were published in 1977 primarily for the benefit of historians.

4. George Wythe, the Chancellor of the High Court of Chancery, published reports of cases in his court dating from 1788 to 1799. The first edition was published in 1795 by Chancellor Wythe; the second edition was printed in 1852.

5. William Brockenbrough and Hugh Holmes reported cases in the General Court during the period 1789 to 1800 and later. These reports appeared in 1815.

6. Charles Lee's reports include cases from many different Virginia courts but not many cases from any single one. They date from 1784 to 1794 or 1795. They were printed along with Brown's reports in 1977.

7. James Hughes reported twenty-two cases from the Virginia Supreme Court for the District of Kentucky from 1785 to 1792. They were first published in 1803.

---

[13] See generally, *W. H. Bryson,* The Virginia Law Reporters Before 1880 (1977), and *W. H. Bryson,* Miscellaneous Virginia Law Reports (1992).

8. David Watson's reports include a few cases from the Louisa County Court and the Fluvanna County Court from 1799 and 1800 and five cases from the year 1800 in the District Court at Charlottesville. These were first edited and printed in 1992.
9. St. George Tucker compiled a series of reports of cases from the Court of Appeals and the General Court from the year 1786 to 1800 and later. They remain in manuscript form at the College of William and Mary in Williamsburg.

In addition, the following county court records have been transcribed and published.

10. *Boyd Crumrine* ed., Virginia Court Records in Southwestern Pennsylvania: Records of the District of West Augusta and Ohio and Yohogania Counties, Virginia, 1775 - 1780 (1981).
11. *Marshall Wingfield* ed., An Old Virginia Court: Being a Transcript of the Records of the First Court of Franklin County, Virginia, 1786 - 1789 (1948).

The following records and reports are copied in the companion volume to this work. For this edition, modern spelling and punctuation have been used.

Downman v. Downman (1791)

In the case of *Downman v. Downman* (1791), the defendant owed a debt to the plaintiffs; the defendant offered to pay the debt with paper money; the plaintiffs refused to accept the paper money because it was not legal money; the plaintiffs then sued in the Northumberland District Court for the debt; the defendant failed to respond within the time allowed by law; default judgment was entered against him; and the defendant then requested the court to set aside the default judgment and allow him to respond that he had offered to pay the debt. Then the plaintiffs argued that the default judgment in their favor should stand and this was for two reasons: (1) the defendant cannot respond with a plea of tender after an office (i.e. default) judgment and (2) when the paper money was tendered (i.e. offered), it was not legal money and they had no obligation to receive it in discharge of the debt. The Northumberland District Court refused to allow the defendant to respond late and ordered the debt to be paid. The defendant appealed to the Court of Appeals of Virginia, and this appellate court affirmed the decision of the lower court because the paper money tendered was not legal currency.[14]

[14] Later proceedings in this case on another issue are reported in St. George Tucker's manuscript reports, vol. 1, p. 242 (1794), and at 2 Washington 189 (1796).

The record of this case is unusual in that the District Court Order of 3 April 1790 gives many, but not all, of the facts of the case. This was done only because the procedural posture of the case required that the proposed defense be copied into the record. Normally, the statement of facts taken from the proposed defense would not appear in any order of the court. It is also unusual in that the District Court put its reasons for its order into the order.

The other unusual thing about this case is that the Court of Appeals put its reason in its order. This was done after prodding from the lawyers and a tart reply from the presiding judge, as John Brown notes in his report of this case. But this little exchange makes it clear that the official orders in the order books did not normally include any reason which might have been given orally in open court.

The other motivation for transcribing this case is that it is one of only a very few which were reported by more than one reporter.

Turner v. Wright (1794)

In the case of *Turner v. Wright* (1794), the Halseys conveyed land to Stip, and Stip leased it to Wright. However, Turner was in possession of the land, and so Wright, asserting the rights of Stip, sued Turner in the Berkeley County Court to get possession of the land. Turner's defense was that Stip did not own the land because the deed of conveyance of the land from the Halseys to him was invalid because it was not properly recorded in the county clerk's office. The County Court agreed with Turner and refused to allow Wright to have a trial to prove his right to possession. Wright thereupon appealed to the Winchester District Court on the ground that, while the improperly recorded deed may have been invalid as against creditors and subsequent purchasers, it was valid against the Halseys, the sellers, and against Turner, a trespasser not claiming under the Halseys. The District Court agreed with Wright, the lessee, and reversed the County Court. Turner then appealed to the Court of Appeals of Virginia. The Court of Appeals affirmed the District Court, and the case was remanded so that Wright could have a trial to prove his case.

This case was chosen for publication because it was reported by more than one reporter. It is interesting to note that the lawyers for both parties on the second appeal and the clerk of the Court of Appeals were the three reporters of this case. Bushrod Washington, being the lawyer for the appellee, gave a particularly full report of the arguments of the attorneys.

Pickett v. Morris (1796)

In the case of *Pickett v. Morris* (1796), Pickett sued Morris in the Henrico County Court at common law for a debt. Morris offered to prove that he had a discount against the amount due to Pickett, but the County Court refused to allow him to prove it, and the jury gave its verdict for Pickett. Morris then sued in the High Court of Chancery in equity for an injunction to stay execution on the common law verdict and judgment because he was not allowed to prove his discount to the jury and for other procedural errors. The equity court ruled for Morris. Thereupon, Pickett appealed from the High Court of Chancery to the Court of Appeals because the discount should not have been allowed by the High Court of Chancery and because that court did not have jurisdiction to grant relief after the final judgment at common law.

After the Court of Appeals had heard the arguments of the lawyers on both sides, they adjourned to consider their judgment. They were troubled by the erroneous judgment of the common law court in denying the right of discount in Morris and by the procedural errors of the County Court and of the lawyers there, and they requested the appellate lawyers to reargue the point of the jurisdiction of the equity court. They did so having dredged up what English authority they could find, and the Court of Appeals thereupon affirmed the chancellor's interference in the matter because of the errors of law and procedure in the common law court. Thus do 'hard cases make bad law'.

Although it is the opinion of this author that this case was wrongly decided because the court of equity did not have sufficient grounds for jurisdiction, this case was chosen for inclusion because it discusses the boundaries of common law and equity jurisdiction. It is included also because it demonstrates the reliance of the Virginia lawyers and judges in the eighteenth century on English cases as precedents. Moreover, it is a thoroughly typical lengthy unofficial report with a very short and uninformative official court order.

As to the liberality of allowing the equity court to grant a remedy after the final judgment at common law, there are several points to be made. Even though the common law court was in error, the error should have been corrected upon appeal, and the common law judgment should have been res judicata until reversed on appeal. The Court of Appeals strains here the concepts of surprise and accident as a matter of the facts in this case in order to affirm the equity court's jurisdiction. The refusal of the common law court to correctly instruct the jury, grant a new trial, or sign the bill of exceptions was not, in this author's opinion, sufficient to justify the equity court's actions.

However, at that time in Virginia, the county courts and the Court of Appeals had both common law and equity jurisdiction, and thus there were no personal judicial rivalries in this regard. Nor had there ever been in Virginia; Coke and Ellesmere had died a long time ago a long way away.[15] Moreover, the Virginia legal profession did not fear equity courts. The county courts were composed of lay justices, who were not highly regarded for their legal acumen by the professional bar and the appellate courts. In this case, they had given a clearly erroneous judgment. In this case, justice ultimately triumphed over the strict interpretation of the law of res judicata and the limits on equitable jurisdiction.

In fact, there was recent Virginia precedent for this. In the case of *Smith and Moreton v. Wallace* (1794),[16] the Court of Appeals held as follows.

> "The court are of opinion that the bail piece was sufficient and must have been so considered if it had been objected to, at the time it was offered. The clerk therefore mistook the law when he rejected it and entered a plea for the sheriff. That court might, and most certainly would, have corrected this mistake at any time if it had been moved to do so. But the party was ill advised when instead of doing this, he applied for a supersedeas to the judgment, since the record furnished a superior court with no ground for an interference.
>
> However, we are fully satisfied upon the equity of this case. A more complete surprise can hardly be conceived. It would be strange if an accident so mischievous as this in its effects were beyond the reach of that court whose peculiar province it is to grant relief in such cases. The negligence with which the appellee is charged is fully excused by the agreement of the counsel and the mistake which followed and, therefore, cannot be urged as a ground for denying the relief which has been extended to him".

In the case of *Norton v. Rose* (1796),[17] the Court of Appeals held that an equitable right could be asserted against a debt that had been assigned. Here, the debtor had had a common law judgment go against him before suing in equity to assert his equitable rights. The debtor should have removed the case to the equity side of the court by means of a common injunction before the final judgment. However, this issue of equity jurisdiction was mentioned by neither the lawyers nor the judges.

In the case of *Ambler v. Wyld* (1794),[18] there was a suit in equity after a final judgment at common law. The plaintiff in equity was asserting that certain papers should not have been considered by the common law jury.

---

[15] See 'Equity Reports and Records in Early Modern England' and the authority cited there, which is printed above.

[16] 1 Washington 254; this case is also reported by John Brown at Miscellaneous Virginia Law Reports, p. 50.

[17] 2 Washington 233 (1796).

[18] Wythe's Reports 235, 2 Washington 36.

The equity judge, George Wythe, ruled that this was not a sufficient ground for equity jurisdiction, but since all parties had consented, he would and did hear the case.

In the case of *Cochran v. Street* (1791, 1792), after a verdict and final judgment at common law, four members of the jury said that they did not agree with the verdict but believed that they were bound by the vote of the majority and were unaware that the verdict must have been unanimous. The defendant at common law thereupon sued in equity in the same county court to have the common law execution stayed. An injunction was granted on the grounds that the false verdict was a surprise on the defendant that was not discovered until after the entry of the final judgment. (Surprise is a good ground for equitable jurisdiction.) This decree in equity was appealed to the High Court of Chancery, and Chancellor Wythe reversed the County Court and dismissed the bill in equity because the 'surprise' in this case was not sufficient.[19] Upon a further appeal to the Court of Appeals, the High Court of Chancery was reversed, and the suit in equity was reinstated.[20] Edmund Pendleton, President of the Court of Appeals, held that "as to the unfairness of the trial on the score of surprise, there is no doubt, but that if it were proved, it would afford good ground for granting a new trial...".

In more recent times, the boundaries between common law and equity in reference to injunctions after final judgment at common law have been well defined. "The elements of this [suit for an injunction] in equity are (1) a [common law] judgment which ought not, in equity and good conscience, to be enforced; (2) a good defense to the alleged cause of action on which the judgment is founded; (3) fraud, accident or mistake which prevented the defendant in the judgment from obtaining the benefit of his defense; (4) the absence of fault or negligence on the part of the defendant; and (5) the absence of any adequate remedy at law".[21]

The reference to fraud, however, is to extrinsic fraud only. Extrinsic fraud is fraud that is collateral to the issues before the court. Whether perjury and matters that go to the veracity of the evidence is extrinsic fraud on the court or whether this is intrinsic fraud to be decided by the trier of fact while weighing the evidence is a dispute that has been settled in favor of the latter definition. Otherwise, few judgments would be final because most litigants contest the truth of their opponents' evidence.[22]

---

19 Wythe's Reports 133.

20 1 Washington 79.

21 *Charles v. Precision Tune, Inc.*, 243 Va. 313, 317 - 318, 414 S.E.2d 831 (1992).

22 *Rowe v. Big Sandy Coal Corp.*, 197 Va. 136, 143, 87 S.E.2d 763 (1955); *McClung v. Folks*, 126 Va. 259, 268 - 272, 101 S.E. 345 (1919).

An example of extrinsic fraud is the case of *O'Neill v. Cole.* In this case, a teenage infant was deceived by her father as to the contents of her uncle's will so that she did not defend her interests in the suit to settle the estate, in which she was a defendant. This was "extrinsic and collateral fraud which precluded her from presenting her true case and rights to the court for adjudication".[23]

Fraud which produces false evidence is intrinsic fraud, but fraud which prevents the consideration of evidence is extrinsic fraud. An example of this distinction is where a condemnor withheld from the court and from the condemnee information showing that the proposed condemnation was for a private purpose so that the condemnee-defendant could not argue against the false allegations of the condemnor.[24]

"[A] court of equity ... relieves against judgments at [common] law, not because they were wrong but because of some new matter, which the court of law did not, or could not, pronounce a judgment on, or which, for some just cause, the party could not bring to the consideration of the court of law".[25]

---

[23] *O'Neill v. Cole,* 194 Va. 50, 57, 72 S.E.2d 382, 385 (1952). See also *Lee v. Baird,* 14 Va. (4 Hening & Munford) 453 (1809), where the defendant at common law was deceived into not making a defence.

[24] *Justice v. Georgia Industrial Realty Co.,* 109 Va. 366, 63 S.E. 1084 (1909).

[25] *Garland v. Rives,* 25 Va. (4 Randolph) 282, 316 (1826). Other examples of original bills after final judgment at common law are noted in *C. Robinson,* Practice in the Courts of Law and Equity in Virginia, vol. 2 (1835), pp. 212 - 222, and in *R. T. Barton,* Pleading and Practice in the Courts of Chancery, vol. 1 (1926), pp. 604 - 611.

Part Two

Continental European Traditions

ANDREA ROMANO

La Regia Gran Corte del Regno di Sicilia

> «... Magna Curia dicitur aliarum curiarum caput et velut exemplar, ... id quod servat M. C. totum Regnum servare debet, unde dicitur etiam curia veritatis in cognoscendo rei originem et originalem iustitiam prout quod quid est, et sic secundum veritatem et non secundum rigorem...»
>
> *Petri de Gregorio,* De iuditiis causarum feudalium tractatus

Una delle più antiche e autorevoli magistrature del Regno di Sicilia può senza dubbio considerarsi il tribunale della Regia Gran Corte. Istituito in epoca normanna, esso affondava le sue più remote radici nella *Curia Regis* normanna, risultando dalla 'specializzazione' di quel supremo collegio che col tempo era venuto acquisendo esclusive competenze giurisdizionali[1].

Evolutasi nel tempo, attraverso l'apporto di più dinastie di sovrani, la Regia Gran Corte veniva ad assumere un ruolo di primo piano nel quadro del sistema giurisdizionale siciliano riuscendo a mantenere intatto tutto il suo prestigio, derivante anche dalla presenza di giudici dottori di diritto, fino all'entrata in vigore nell'isola della grande riforma borbonica del 1819.

Se riveste interesse ricostruire le fila delle vicende dell'alto tribunale, dei suoi giudici, delle sue procedure e della normativa che ne regolava il funzionamento, appare altrettanto utile potere soffermare l'attenzione sulla produzione di quella corte, in particolare sulle sentenze, e sul rilievo e l'autorità cui quella produzione assurgeva in un sistema normativo su base codicistica, espressione di un ordinamento politicamente accentrato, come quello rappresentato dal Regno di Sicilia.

Appare peraltro utile, anche in una prospettiva comparata tesa a ricostruire i lineamenti e la portata di un diritto giurisprudenziale comune 'europeo', risultante proprio dal diffondersi delle *decisiones* dei tribunali

---

[1] Sul processo di transizione dalla *Curia Regis* alla *Magna Regia Curia,* con interessanti elementi di comparazione fra le coeve realtà dei regni di Sicilia e d'Inghilterra, cfr. *Mario Caravale,* Ordinamenti giuridici dell'Europa medievale (Bologna 1994) 333 - 4, 341 - 5, 357 - 8, e *Errico Cuozzo,* La 'Magna Curia' al tempo di Federico II di Svevia, in: «1989» Rivista di Diritto Pubblico e Scienze Politiche, V. 1 (1995), 23 - 31. Per la problematica storica generale e bibliografia cfr. *Donald Matthew,* The Norman Kingdom of Sicily (Cambridge 1992) 178 s. e *passim.*

maggiori e dal ruolo assunto dalla giurisprudenza delle corti supreme, un'analisi 'dinamica' della produzione della Regia Gran Corte siciliana, del suo ruolo all'interno del sistema normativo-giurisdizionale siciliano e delle fonti attraverso le quali quella trovava diffusione, diventando conoscibile sia in Sicilia che al di fuori dell'isola.

I. *Curia Regis* e *magistri iusticiarii*: la genesi del supremo tribunale del *Regnum Siciliae*

Annota Romualdo Salernitano, nei suoi *Annales,* che «Rogerius in regno suo perfectae pacis tranquillitate potitus, pro conservanda pace Camerarios et Justiciarios per totam terram instituit, leges a se noviter conditas promulgavit, malas consuetudines de medio abstulit»[2]. L'attento cronista, ponendo l'accento sul desiderio del re di Sicilia di conservare la pace *(pro conservanda pace)* finalmente raggiunta *(perfecte pacis tranquillitate),* dà notizia di un deciso intervento regio secondo una triplice direttiva: l'istituzione diffusa di funzionari fiscali e giudiziari; la promulgazione di proprie nuove leggi; la revisione della normativa consuetudinaria.

Sappiamo che la promulgazione del *corpus* normativo del sovrano normanno (il codice delle Assise) avveniva nel parlamento tenutosi ad Ariano nel 1140[3], quando Ruggero, in seguito al rientro in Germania dell'imperatore Lotario III ed alla pacificazione con il pontefice Innocenzo II, si poneva l'obiettivo di dare una salda struttura al proprio regno attraverso l'imposizione della propria legge e della propria giurisdizione, disegnando a tal fine un sistema che andava decisamente oltre i confini del vecchio assetto comitale per concretizzare una nuova visione monarchico-imperializzante. Chiara affermazione della propria *voluntas,* quindi, attraverso l'imposizione di nuove norme (pur nel rispetto di *mores, consuetudines et leges* vigenti, purché non fossero in evidente contrasto con le leggi regie)[4], la

---

2 *Romualdo Salernitano,* Annales, a cura di *W. Arndt,* in: Monumenta Germaniae Historica. Scriptores, 19 (Hannover 1866) 423 e, con varianti, *Id.,* Chronicon, in: *Giuseppe Del Re,* Cronisti e scrittori sincroni napoletani editi e inediti, 2 v., Storia della monarchia ... Normanni, I (Napoli 1845) 13.

3 In generale sulla legislazione delle assise, cfr. *Francesco Brandileone,* Il diritto romano nelle leggi normanne e sveve del regno di Sicilia (Torino 1884) 94 - 138 e, di recente, *Andrea Romano,* Diritto romano e diritto longobardo nella legislazione delle Assise dei re normanni, in: Le Assise di Ariano 1140 - 1990, a cura di *O. Zecchino* (Roma 1994) 179 - 202, e in *Id.,* Diritto e Società in Sicilia, Materiali per una storia delle istituzioni giuridiche e politiche medievali moderne e contemporanee, Studi 4 (Soveria Mannelli 1994) 1 - 19.

4 Ass. De legum interpretatione, in: *Brandileone,* Il diritto romano, 95 - 6. Una più recente edizione delle assise, con traduzione italiana a fronte, si legge in: *Ortensio Zecchino,* Le assise di Ruggero II. I testi (Napoli 1984) 24 - 133.

revisione dei privilegi già concessi in precedenza[5], la delineazione di un sistema giudiziario espressione dell'esclusiva *iurisdictio* sovrana[6]. Un principio, quest'ultimo, che si affermava anche col riconoscimento normativo di un particolare *status* ai funzionari regi, che si volevano inviolabili in quanto voce del sovrano ed espressione della sua *potestas*, e con la regolamentazione di un sistema ordinario di appelli contro le sentenze ritenute 'ingiuste'[7]

Ugo Falcando narra che avendo il regio cancelliere Stefano de Perche convocato la Regia Gran Corte per giudicare il conte Riccardo di Mandra, questi contestava la sentenza pronunciata in nome del re dal conte Boemondo di Monopoli protestando che «iniuste se gravari; odium equitati manifeste preferri; paratum se probare quod iniquam falsamque protulisset sententiam». Si trattava di una contestazione della 'giustizia' della sentenza resa dalla corte regia condotta secondo l'antico costume della *blasfematio iudicii*, che Boemondo immediatamente troncava proibendo ai giudici della corte di rispondere in quanto «iniuriam hanc non in eos qui iudicaverant, sed in caput regium principaliter redundare». Un'osservazione assai grave, fondata sulla lettera dell'assisa regia, che veniva ad avere tristi conseguenze per il conte di Mandra che «non solum de terra sua, verum etiam de membris et corpore regis misericordie subiacere, eo quod iudicium curie falsum dicere presumpsisset». Riccardo di Mandra era condannato alla perdita dei beni e della vita non per effetto della prima sentenza, che pur lo riconosceva colpevole, ma per avere osato accusare di 'falso giudizio' un tribunale regio. Siamo intorno al 1167: della corte facevano parte Boemondo conte di Monopoli, Roberto del Lauro conte di Caserta, Ruggero del Lauro conte di Tricarico, Ruggero conte di Avellino, Simone conte di Sangro, Ruggero conte di Gerace, il mastro connestabile Ruggero di Tirone ed ancora il giudice Tarentino e Addenago figlio di Annibale «qui magistri erant iusticiarii»[8]. Il racconto del Falcando risulta di notevole interesse per

---

[5] Cfr., in particolare, i diplomi del 1144 di Ruggero editi in: *Carlo Alberto Garufi*, I documenti inediti dell'epoca normanna in Sicilia, in: Documenti per Servire alla Storia di Sicilia. Fonti, XVIII (Palermo 1899) 45 - 49. Sul punto *Paul Scheffer-Boichorst*, Das Gesetz Kaisers Friedrich's II. «De resignandis privilegiis», in: Sitzungsberichte der Königlichen preußischen Akademie der Wissenschaft zu Berlin, I (Berlin 1900) 132, e *Mario Caravale*, Il Regno normanno di Sicilia (Milano 1966) 189.

[6] Sul rapporto *consuetudo - lex*, con riferimento anche agli elementi di novità prospettati dalla *iurisdictio regia* nel regno di Sicilia, cfr. *Paolo Grossi*, L'ordine giuridico medievale (Bari 1995) 94 - 6, 130 - 5.

[7] Cfr. *Andrea Romano*, Tribunali, Giudici e Sentenze nel 'Regnum Siciliae' (1130 - 1516), in: Judicial Records, Law Reports, and the Growth of Case Law, ed. by *J. H. Baker* (Berlin 1989) 222.

[8] *Ugone Falcando*, La Historia o Liber de regno Siciliae, a cura di *G. B. Siragusa*, in: Fonti per la Storia d'Italia, 22 (Roma 1897) 141.

più ordini di motivi. Innanzi tutto ci dà notizia di una *Regia Curia* funzionante come corte giudicante, formata da funzionari dell'amministrazione, giudici e vassalli forse facenti parte del *consilium regis* ma, comunque, non delegati della feudalità[9]. Una corte dalla composizione non predeterminata e non stabile, chiamata a pronunciarsi sui giudizi più rilevanti o con funzioni di appello. Di poi ci conferma la presenza in quell'alta corte dei *magistri iusticiarii,* funzionari che, istituiti con compiti di accertamento dei privilegi e dei diritti controversi, progressivamente andavano assorbendo anche le competenze in materia giurisdizionale esercitate dalla *Curia Regis*[10]. Infine attesta l'assenza di una corte dei pari, formata da soli feudatari, con competenza sulle cause feudali e l'affermarsi, ai livelli supremi, di una giurisdizione unica esercitata da tribunali formati da 'funzionari' o *fideles* regi.

Appare documentato, comunque, che intorno alla fine degli anni '60 del secolo XII i giustizieri facevano stabilmente e regolarmente parte della *Curia Regis,* riunita con funzioni giudicanti, con competenza estesa alle controversie di qualsiasi natura[11], organo al quale intervenivano anche in precedenza, come documenta la presenza del *judex Tarentinus* nel 1156 e di Rinaldo da Tusa *magister iusticiarius Regiae Magnae Curiae* nel 1159[12]. Dopo tale data, peraltro, troviamo, con una certa regolarità, espresso riferi-

---

[9] In questo senso *Caravale,* Il Regno, 91 - 6; cfr. altresì *Cuozzo,* La 'Magna Curia', 26 ss.

[10] La presenza dei giustizieri nella *Curia Regis* appare documentata a partire dal 1144. Dal 1145 le fonti attestano con una certa regolarità l'ufficio dei giustizieri di corte ai quali erano assegnate, almeno alle origini, prevalentemente funzioni di accertamento *in loco* delle specifiche situazioni di diritto. Si trattava, quindi, di funzionari regi ai quali erano affidate delle *inquisitiones* al fine dell'accertamento di diritti contestati e dell'eventuale soluzione di controversie. Cfr. *Caravale,* Il Regno, 160 - 163. Sulle strutture del governo normanno cfr. la recente sintesi di *Hiroshi Takayama,* The Administration of the Norman Kindom of Sicily (Leiden-New York-Köln 1993).

[11] Secondo *Ferdinand Chalandon,* Histoire de la domination normande en Italie et Sicilie, II (Paris 1909) 632, i gran giustizieri divengono membri stabili delle curie giudiziarie del regno a datare dal 1172. *Cuozzo,* La 'Magna Curia', 29 ss., precisa come questa magistratura si riuniva in sedute plenarie, sotto la presidenza del sovrano o di un suo delegato, rappresentando in tale composizione il supremo organo giudiziario del regno, e in sedute ordinarie, sotto la presidenza di un maestro giustiziere, per giudicare delle questioni civili e penali insorte fra i sudditi o che vedevano coinvolto un funzionario regio.

[12] *Garufi,* I documenti inediti, 82. L'attività di questo giustiziere regio, nel medesimo torno d'anni, è documentata anche in *Charles Homar Haskins,* England and Sicily in the twelfth century, in: The English Historical Review, 26 (1911), 642. Sul giudice *Tarentinus* cfr. *Evelyn Jamison,* Judex Tarentinus. The career of Judex Tarentinus 'magne curie justiciarius' and the emergence of the Sicilian 'regalis magna curia' under William I and the regency of Margaret of Navarre, 1156 - 1172, in: Proceedings of the British Academy, I.3 (London 1968) 289 - 344.

mento alla *Regia 'Magna Curia'*. Così, ad esempio, nel 1172 viene sottoposta a tre *supreme curie magni iudices* la soluzione di una controversia fra il vescovo di Messina e Leo Chelones[13], nel 1176 sappiamo di un «Persicus regie magne curie magister iusticiarius»[14], nel 1183 abbiamo notizia di un «Guillelmus de Malconvenant regie magne curie magister iustitiarius»[15]. Certamente, dopo il 1140, viene posto l'impianto di un vasto progetto di riforme politico-amministrative e giudiziarie mirante, fra l'altro, alla definizione di un *regius ordo iudiciarius* valido per tutto il regno e teso a limitare le giurisdizioni cittadine e baronali.

Elementi portanti di questa nuova articolata struttura sono a livello cittadino i baiuli, giudici locali con competenze erariali ed amministrative oltre che di giurisdizione penale minore e talvolta anche civile, che operano con l'assistenza di giudici-assessori[16].

A livello provinciale espletano, invece, la loro giurisdizione i giustizieri ed i camerari, magistrati, secondo la testimonianza di Romualdo Salernitano, istituiti da re Ruggero perseguendo i suoi disegni di ordine e pacificazione («pro conservanda pace camerarios et iusticiarios per totam terram instituit»)[17]. I secondi (giustizieri)[18], assistiti da una propria curia, con competenza di primo grado nelle materie penali più rilevanti e nelle liti relative ai feudi non quaternati (ovvero non registrati nei *quaterni* della *Dohana baronum*[19]) e talora d'appello avverso alle sentenze pronunciate

---

[13] Cfr. *Raffaele Starrabba,* I diplomi della cattedrale di Messina, in: Documenti per Servire alla Storia di Sicilia. Fonti, I (Palermo 1876) 399 - 405, cit. in *Romano,* Tribunali, 227.

[14] *Carlo Alberto Garufi,* Catalogo illustrato del Tabulario di S. Maria Nuova in Monreale, in: Documenti per Servire alla Storia di Sicilia. Fonti, XIX (Palermo 1902) 165.

[15] *Garufi,* I documenti inediti, 191.

[16] Cfr. *Luigi Genuardi,* L'ordinamento giudiziario in Sicilia sotto la monarchia Normanna e Sveva, in: Il Circolo Giuridico «L. Sampolo» di Palermo (= Circ. Giur.), 36 (1905) 268 - 71; *Caravale,* Il Regno, 341 - 55; *Romano,* Tribunali, 223 - 4.

[17] Si tratta di magistrature entrambe probabilmente istituite intorno al 1140, anche se compiutamente definite nella loro struttura solo in età successiva. In generale, diffusamente, su tale problematica cfr. *Caravale,* Il Regno, *ad ind.* È opportuno notare, per evitare errori dovuti ad indebite generalizzazioni, che sia le competenze che il funzionamento delle varie magistrature non sono né uniformi né coeve in tutte le province del Regno e, in particolare, che possono rilevarsi significative difformità con riferimento alla Sicilia.

[18] Cfr. *Genuardi,* L'ordinamento, 262 - 5; *Caravale,* Il Regno, 221 - 234, 248 - 250, 260 - 7; *Romano,* Tribunali, 224 - 5.

[19] «Feuda quaternata dicebantur magna feuda quae in quaternionibus seu codicibus Regni tabularii erant inscripta» (giusto quanto previsto in cost. I.40.2 e 44, cfr. Constitutiones Regum Regni Siciliae Libri III (Neapoli 1786) 39, 45 = rist. an. a cura e con Introduzione di *A. Romano,* in: Monumenta Iuridica Siciliensia, I (Messina 1992) *ib.*).

dai magistrati cittadini[20]. I primi (camerari)[21] con giurisdizione in materia civile e finanziaria e competenze di natura amministrativa. Di particolare rilievo per definire le competenze delle varie magistrature risulta l'ass. 36 di Ruggero, nella quale si dispone: «Sancimus ut latrocinia, fracture domorum, insultus viarum, vis mulieribus illata, duella, homicidia, leges parabiles, calumpnie criminum, incendia, forisfacte omnes de quibus quilibet de corpore et rebus suis mercedi curie debeat subiacere a iusticiariis iudicentur, clamoribus supradictorum baiulis depositis, cetera vero a baiulis poterunt detineri»[22]. La norma sembra, infatti, identificare chiaramente una giurisdizione civile da una penale, distinguedo quest'ultima in alta e bassa e affidando la prima ai giustizieri provinciali e la seconda ai baiuli[23]. La giurisdizione dei giustizieri veniva così a concorrere con quella feudale, che il sovrano non voleva senza limiti, riservando in ogni caso ai suoi giudici sia il giudizio sugli abitanti delle città demaniali e delle terre non infeudate, sia il giudizio su reati indicati come *reservata maiestatis,* anche se commessi da soggetti sottoposti alla giurisdizione signorile. È così, ad esempio, che nella concessione del mero e misto imperio sugli abitanti *in terra Turchii* fatta nel 1177 all'archimandrita del S. Salvatore di Messina, Onofrio, il sovrano escludeva espressamente ogni giurisdizione in «illis iurisfacturis et iudiciis que specialiter ad cohercionem magne regie curie pertinerent que in manibus et potestate dicte sue curie idem rex reservavit»[24].

Tutte queste magistrature sembrano trovare riscontro gerarchico, almeno a partire dagli ultimi anni del regno di Ruggero II, nella presenza di funzionari che partecipavano al 'governo del re'. Al vertice dei giustizieri provinciali (magistrati introdotti in Sicilia probabilmente verso gli inizi del regno di Guglielmo I)[25], ad esempio, si trovavano tre (o quattro) maestri giusti-

---

20 Cfr. *Evelyn Jamison,* The Norman administration of Apulia and Capua more especially under Roger II and William I, in: Papers of the British School at Rome, 6 (1913) 322.

21 Cfr. *Genuardi,* L'ordinamento, 264 - 5; *Caravale,* Il Regno, 235 - 43, 250 - 54, 275 - 83; *Romano,* Tribunali, 225.

22 Cfr. Ass. 36 (testo cassinese), Que sit potestas iustitiarii, in: *Brandileone,* Il diritto, 136.

23 Utili riferimenti al sistema giudiziario normanno in Inghilterra in *Caravale,* Ordinamenti, 336 - 45.

24 Cfr. *Garufi,* I documenti inediti, 168.

25 I giustizieri provinciali non si trovano, significativamente, menzionati in un privilegio del 1145 concesso da Ruggero II al monastero di S. Filippo Maggiore: «Propter hoc praecipimus nostris strategotis, foresteriis, capitaneis et vicecomitibus, procuratoribus et omnibus degentibus sub nostra potestate» (in: *Rocco Pirro,* Sicilia sacra disquisitionibus et notitiis illustrata (Panormi 1733) II, 1030) ed ancora in un ordine del medesimo anno riguardante la custodia dei privilegi di S. Maria di Mandanici indirizzato dal sovrano ai «forestariis, comitibus, baronibus, capitaneis, procuratoribus et omnibus existentibus sub nostra potestate» (*Pirro,* Sicilia sacra, II,

zieri (o giustizieri centrali) che sovrintendevano, probabilmente con funzioni di coordinamento e controllo e con assetto itinerante, ai giustizierati (valli) in cui era divisa amministrativamente la Sicilia e quindi, forse, un gran giustiziere, con presenza stabile a corte, che presiedeva per delega regia la Gran Corte[26]. Le funzioni giurisdizionali dei maestri giustizieri, come quelle dei giustizieri, peraltro, si vanno completamente definendo solo nell'ultimo trentennio del secolo XII e, se in un primo tempo appaiono attestati quali incaricati regi di *inquisitiones* sull'esistenza di specifici diritti o per l'accertamento di situazioni di fatto contestate, successivamente acquistano una ben precisa specializzazione andando a ricoprire le funzioni giurisdizionali proprie della *Curia Regis,* organo cui sembrano legarsi sempre più anche nel titolo che ne accompagna il nome specificandone la funzione: *Regiae Magnae Curiae magister iusticiarius*[27].

È, comunque, opportuno distinguere i giustizieri periferici dai giustizieri centrali formanti la Gran Corte Regia dato che, fino a quando la magistratura non avrà una propria fisionomia, risulta possibile il sovrapporsi delle diverse competenze[28].

Probabilmente, è Guglielmo II che, intorno al 1170, rende stabile, all'interno della *Curia Regis,* la *Magna Regia Curia,* precisandone le funzioni giurisdizionali e strutturandola come un tribunale presieduto, in Sicilia, dal vice gran giustiziere e formato da giudici di nomina regia (anche se certamente non tecnici del diritto) con competenza a giudicare in materia di feudi quaternati e, in grado d'appello, sulle sentenze feudali, civili e penali

---

1046 - 7), mentre in un diploma del 1154 si legge «venimus nos Avenellus et Bartholomeus Favariu iusticiarii terre Castrijanni nobiscum venit Rogerius Maletta iusticiarius Demennae» (*Starrabba,* I diplomi della cattedrale, 384). Sul punto cfr. *Caravale,* Il Regno, 226 - 7, 244.

[26] In tal senso *Garufi,* I documenti inediti, 152 - 4 e *Chalandon,* Histoire, II, 682; giustificate riserve sono espresse in *Caravale,* Il Regno, 274.

[27] Così, ad esempio, appare qualificato, in un diploma del 1159 Rinaldo di Tusa (*Garufi,* I documenti inediti, 81 - 2) ed in un altro, del 1176, *Persicus* (*Garufi,* Catalogo illustrato, 165). *Cuozzo,* La 'Magna Curia', 27, sottolinea come la *Curia Regis* (ad-diwan al-ma'mur), riformata intorno al 1145, comprendeva tre *magistri iustitiarii* che costituivano la *Magna Curia Regis.*

[28] Sulle possibilità di confusione fra le due magistrature e i possibili effetti che ne possono derivare, cfr. *Julius Ficker,* Forschungen zur Reichs- und Rechtsgeschichte Italiens, II (Innsbruck 1868) 351 - 4, e *Caravale,* Il Regno, 226, 234. In tale errore, con riferimento alla Sicilia, sembrerebbero caduti sia *Ernst Mayer,* Italienische Verfassungsgeschichte von der Gothenzeit bis zur Zunftherrschaft (Leipzig 1909) 404, che lo *Haskins,* England and Sicily, 644, come anche *Chalandon,* Histoire, II, 678, sostenendo l'esistenza in Sicilia di giustizieri provinciali già negli anni di Ruggero II. La costituzione della curia regia quale «organo del governo centrale gerarchicamente organizzato», quantunque «non ancora istituzionalizzato e fisso nella sua composizione» è convincentemente riportato all'età di Guglielmo I da *Cuozzo,* La 'Magna Curia', 26.

pronunciate dai giustizieri periferici. La data dell'apparizione in Sicilia di una magistratura suprema composta da soli giudici 'specializzati' è, peraltro, controversa e se C. H. Haskins è incline a collocarla nel 1168[29], anticipandola di qualche anno rispetto a F. Chalandon, che la porrebbe nel 1172[30], è certo che anche dopo quegli anni – ad esempio, ancora nel 1183 – troviamo corti regie giudicanti alle quali partecipano, oltre ad un giustiziere, dei *fideles et familiares regii*[31].

A conclusione di un processo evolutivo abbastanza complesso, negli anni '70 del secolo dodicesimo, l'organo primitivo della *Curia Regis* conosceva una differenziazione fra funzioni di natura amministrativa e funzioni giurisdizionali, acquistando una sua specializzazione 'tecnica', che si manifestava nella composizione limitata ai soli giustizieri quando come *magna curia* assumeva le funzioni di massimo organo giurisdizionale. I giustizieri regi, del pari, assumevano il ruolo di *magni iudices* ai quali il sovrano non esitava ad affidare, quando la natura dei fatti lo richiedeva, anche compiti di fiducia in occasione di eventi criminosi particolarmente gravi, incarichi in qualche misura riportabili alle antiche *inquisitiones* tendenti all'accertamento della natura giuridica di privilegi vantati da città, feudatari, enti ecclesiastici[32]. Una 'suprema curia', quindi, formata da *magni iudices* – come attestano le fonti – che nasceva e si evolveva mantenendo una struttura collegiale che, opportunamente, M. Caravale ha individuato come unica nell'organizzazione degli uffici centrali normanni ed originale[33].

Tribunale senza sede fissa, poteva riunirsi nella 'residenza del re' e quindi sia nel palazzo regio, nella capitale[34] o in altra sede[35], sia ove occasional-

---

29 *Haskins,* England and Sicily, 642 - 3.

30 *Chalandon,* Histoire, II, 632.

31 Così risulta, ad esempio, la curia innanzi alla quale compaiono i coniugi Ruggero e Maria di Tarsia, cfr. *Garufi,* I documenti, 191.

32 Così, ad esempio, il giustiziere Burgundione, nel 1168 in occasione della congiura del vescovo di Agrigento contro il cancelliere Stefano de Perche, è inviato dal re Guglielmo II e dalla regina «cum licteris regiis Agrigentum ... precipientes Agrigentinis ut episcopum tanquam proditorem sub eiusdem Burgundii custodia Panormum transmicterent» (*Falcando,* La Historia o Liber de regno Sicilie, 146) e nel 1188 il giustiziere Goffredo di Martorana viene inviato «ex mandato domini nostri serenissimi Regis ... ad investigandas divisas generales Viccari et ad specificandas distincte divisas ecclesiarum, baronum et militum» (*Carlo Alberto Garufi,* Monete e conii nella storia del diritto siculo dagli Arabi ai Martini, Parte I, in: Archivio Storico Siciliano (= A. S. S.), n. s., 23 (1898), 150 - 1). Sul punto cfr. *Caravale,* Il Regno, 163 - 5.

33 *Caravale,* Il Regno, 166, ed anche *Cuozzo,* La 'Magna Curia', 29 - 31.

34 Così, ad esempio, da una *charta* del 1156 sappiamo che la corte regia pronuncia la sua sentenza «in palatio nostro huius urbis Panormi» (cfr. *Carl Andreas Kehr,* Die Urkunden der normannisch-sicilischen Könige (Innsbruck 1902) 433).

mente si trovava il sovrano[36] o, su mandato regio, ovunque fosse chiamato dalla necessità[37], potendo, probabilmente, giudicare sia sulle vertenze espressamente demandategli dal sovrano o, per le materie rientranti nella propria competenza, sulle controversie direttamente propostegli, anche in appello avverso sentenze dei giudici cittadini o provinciali.[38]

Le procedure adottate dalla Regia Gran Corte normanna nelle sue sessioni ordinarie, di fatto limitate alla sola Sicilia[39], non sembra seguissero formalità uniformi e puntualmente predefinite e trovano sommaria documentazione negli atti predisposti dal notaio-cancelliere della corte, al quale era affidato il compito di redigere per iscritto le *cartae iudicati* o *scripta memoriae*[40] che le parti potevano richiedere come prova del loro buon diritto («factum est presens ad perpetuam memoriam instrumentum»[41]) o che la corte riteneva opportuno rilasciare «ne de his terminis *aliqua in posterum suboriatur dubitacio*»[42]. I procedimenti civili innanzi al sommo tribu-

---

35 Da una *charta* del 1172 apprendiamo di un procedimento discusso «in magna urbe Messanae ... in magna curia» (cfr. *Starrabba,* I diplomi, 399).

36 In una *charta iudicati* del 1142, ad esempio, leggiamo «cum ego comes Symon et Georgius amiras coeterique proceres essemus cum patruo meo et domino rege Rogerio in Monte Linariorum, animi causa venit una Gipertus Pirollius et accusationem contra episcopum Robertum proposuit» (cfr. *Starrabba,* I diplomi, 365).

37 Sappiamo, ad esempio, che nel 1172 il mastro giustiziere della Val di Noto, Goffredo de Mohac, «regio precepto» deve recarsi «a Syracusia usque ad terminos terre Notae ... pro dirimenda et finienda quadam controversia et contencione que diu fuerat inter homines Notae et canonicos Cephaludi» (cfr. *Garufi,* I documenti, 152). Sulla prassi di discutere e risolvere le liti «sul luogo istesso della contesa», cfr. *Rosario Gregorio,* Considerazioni sopra la storia di Sicilia dai tempi dei normanni sino ai presenti, in *Id.,* Opere rare ed inedite riguardanti la Sicilia (Palermo 1873, rist. anast. Sala Bolognese 1977) 101. Le Considerazioni del Gregorio si possono leggere anche con Introduzione di *A. Saitta* (Palermo 1972).

38 Cfr. *Gregorio,* Considerazioni, 154 - 5; *Vito La Mantia,* Storia della legislazione civile e criminale di Sicilia, I (Palermo 1866) 195 - 6; *Genuardi,* L'ordinamento, 262 - 5.

39 Così *Cuozzo,* La 'Magna Curia' 31.

40 Si noti che le carte di giudicato, di norma, non si limitavano a riportare il dispositivo della sentenza ma, come si è osservato, riportavano una sintesi di tutte le fasi della lite, compresa la sentenza, assumendo una forma di atti notarili, come attestano le caratteristiche diplomatiche che li caratterizzano. Cfr. *Pietro Burgarella,* Nozioni di diplomatica siciliana (Palermo 1978) 189 - 92.

41 Così, ad esempio, si legge nella sentenza pronunciata dalla Regia Gran Corte a Messina nel 1172 nella lite fra Leo Chelones ed il vescovo di Messina. Cfr. *Romano,* Tribunali, 288.

42 Così si legge nel citato *scriptum memoriae* fatto redigere, nel 1172, dal mastro giustiziere Goffredo de Moach («hanc memoriam scribi feci»). Non dissimilmente, nel 1159, il gran giustiziere Raimondo di Tusa ordinava la stesura di una sentenza, sotto forma di carta bipartita, motivando: «ad perpetuam autem concordiam utriusque ecclesiae praesens scriptum utique dedimus ecclesiae mediantibus quibus-

nale si iniziavano con la presentazione al sovrano, o ad un suo *familiaris,* di *quaerimonie,* mentre quelli penali erano attivati dall'*accusatio* proposta dalla parte lesa o dalla *curia.* Una procedura istruttoria avviava il dibattimento con la costituzione della corte giudicante, cui era affidata la *solutio* della questione con sentenza valida solo nei confronti delle parti e pronunciata in nome del re. Le sentenze, comunque, concludendo un procedimento totalmente orale, non erano obbligatoriamente redatte in forma scritta, né trovavano registrazione in appositi *volumina* custoditi dal notaio agli atti del tribunale, anche se dobbiamo ritenere che l'esigenza della scrittura cominciasse ad evidenziarsi proprio negli anni del regno di Guglielmo II, contemporaneamente all'altra esigenza, della quale si è detto, di creare un organo giudiziario stabile da inserire al vertice dell'*ordo iudiciarius* del *Regnum.*

II. Strutture ed evoluzione del tribunale della Regia Gran Corte

È Federico II di Svevia, in conformità con il disegno efficacemente delineato nella *const. Pacis cultum,* in forza della quale «nullus auctoritate propria de iniuriis et excessibus dudum factis vel faciendis, in posterum se debeat vindicare, nec presalias seu represalias facere, vel guerram in Regno movere, sed coram magistro iustitiario et iustitiariis regionum vel locorum camerariis vel baiulis et dominis, prout ad unumquemque eorum causae cognitio pertinet, causam suam ordine iudiciario prosequatur»[43], a provvedere alla strutturazione di un *ordo iudiciarius* organico ed uniforme, funzionale ad un progetto politico che, traendo spunto dall'impianto normanno, ne rafforza la portata.

L'opera di riforma dell'apparato giudiziario del *Regnum,* contrariamente a quanto si è affermato da chi ha sostenuto una sorta d'intervento di tipo 'codicistico', veniva portato a compimento dallo svevo nell'arco di oltre vent'anni, concretamente dalle *assisae* di Capua del 1220 fino alle *novellae* del 1240[44]. Apparentemente il sovrano svevo, nel suo *Liber Constitutionum* promulgato nel 1231, non sembra volere creare nuove magistrature, ma semplicemente ridare vigore a quelle già istituite dai suoi antenati, affer-

dam apicibus qui partiti fuerunt ut si quando de predictis divisis oriretur discordia per munimentum huius scripti sopiretur» (cfr. *Garufi,* I documenti, 83).

[43] Cfr. C. I. 8 (Constitutiones, 10).

[44] Con specifico riferimento alla *'Magna Curia',* il lungo *iter* riformatore fridericiano è assai bene documentato da *Cuozzo,* La 'Magna Curia', 31 - 72, che con puntualità evidenzia alcuni errori nella traduzione del testo normativo delle costituzioni fridericiane che possono assumersi all'origine di imprecise ricostruzioni storiografiche.

mando a chiare lettere la suprema *iurisdictio regia.* Venivano così espressamente abrogate tutte le precedenti norme non comprese nel nuovo codice, si poneva fine alla prassi della personalità del diritto, era perseguita qualsiasi giurisdizione o fonte normativa concorrente a quella regia, fatte salve quelle espressamente ammesse per privilegio.

In questa prospettiva, precisando l'ambito della giurisdizione feudale[45], venivano chiaramente distinte una giurisdizione civile ed una penale, così come erano ben definite le competenze dei vari giudici, la durata del loro ufficio, che non si voleva più perpetuo, nonché il loro salario, corrisposto *de camera regia,* il loro numero e la loro distribuzione sul territorio[46].

Tutti i giudici erano sottoposti a 'sindacato' nei cinquanta giorni successivi alla scadenza del loro mandato, normalmente di durata annuale. Eleggere un giudice, come farsi giustizia privata, era reato gravissimo contro la *maiestas* e l'*auctoritas* del sovrano e pertanto punito in maniera esemplare, come esemplarmente dovevano essere puniti quanti avessero offeso un magistrato, nella persona o nelle decisioni, configurando un reato considerato «par sacrilegio»[47].

Il vero connettivo del sistema giudiziario siciliano, nell'età sveva, era di fatto costituito dai tribunali dei mastri giustizieri (provinciali), due per l'intera Sicilia, aventi competenza uno per la parte *citra flumen Salsum* e l'altro per la parte *ultra Salsum,* probabilmente istituiti verso la fine del secolo XIII[48]. Queste corti, formate da un giudice ed un notaio agli atti che assistevano il giustiziere[49], oltre ad avere giurisdizione d'appello avverso le sentenze dei giudici cittadini e provinciali (baiuli, strategoti, giustizieri provinciali, giustizieri locali), conoscevano in primo grado delle liti civili non esaminate da quei magistrati o proposte «in defectu etiam camerariorum et baiulorum». Oltre a giudicare in prima istanza delle materie dell'alta giurisdizione penale, espressamente previste nella *const. Iusti-*

---

[45] Particolarmente alle giurisdizioni feudali sono dedicate le prescrizioni di cui alle C. I. 8, Pacis cultum; C. I. 44, Iustitiarii nomen; C. II. 18, Dilationes e C. III. 42, Varietates (Constitutiones, 10, 44, 130, 195).

[46] Per una rapida sintesi sull'organizzazione giudiziaria sveva, ed ulteriore bibliografia, cfr. *Romano,* Tribunali, 231 - 6.

[47] Significativamente la C. I. 4, Disputare, prescriveva che: «Disputare de Regis iudicio, consiliis et institutionibus factis non oportet. Est enim pars sacrilegii disputare de eius iudiciis factis et constitutionibus atque consiliis, et an dignus sit quem Rex elegit et decrevit» (Constitutiones, 6 - 7).

[48] Sul punto si vedano, principalmente, le puntualizzazioni di *Paolo Colliva,* Ricerche sul principio di legalità nell'amministrazione del Regno di Sicilia al tempo di Federico II. I. Gli organi centrali e regionali (Milano 1964) 141, e *Cuozzo,* La 'Magna Curia', 70.

[49] Prevede la C. I. 95, Occupatis nobis: «iustitiarius quilibet iudicem unum continuum et notarium unum actorum habebit» (Constitutiones, 99).

tiarii nomen («latrocinia scilicet, magna furta, fracturae domorum, insultus excogitati, incendia, incisiones arborum fructiferarum et vitium, vis mulieribus illata, duella, crimina maiestatis, arma molita, defensae impositae [...] et generaliter omnia de quibus convicti poenam sui corporis vel mutilationem membrorum sustinere deberent»), essi potevano inoltre avocare a sé i processi in corso presso le corti inferiori e non definiti entro sessanta giorni ed erano competenti a giudicare delle controversie fra vassalli e baroni, oltre che ad istruire le cause relative ai feudi minori, ovvero non quaternati, («De feudis etiam et rebus feudalibus ipsi cognoscant, praeter quaestiones de castris et baroniis et magnis feudis quae in quaternionibus dohanae nostrae scripta sunt; quae omnia singulariter cognitioni nostrae curiae reservamus»)[50].

Al vertice degli uffici giudiziari dell'isola, ma con compiti anche politici e di alta amministrazione, almeno dopo le riforme del 1239 - 40 (se non già dal 1235)[51], era posto il *magister iustitiarius magnae regiae curiae,* o gran giustiziere, che Federico II non esitava a definire *iustitiae speculum,* sottolineandone il rilievo[52]. Dapprima solo componente dell'antica *Curia Regis,* egli era venuto assumendo, attraverso un processo di concentrazione-semplificazione, le competenze dei tre maestri giustizieri normanni, dando vita, di fatto, ad un ufficio sostanzialmente nuovo[53]. A questo magistrato, del quale si occupavano principalmente le *const. Magnae Curiae* e *Magister iustitiarius*[54], era affidato il compito di sovrintendere al buon andamento

[50] C. I. 44 (Constitutiones, 45). Sulle competenze di questi magistrati vanno tenute presenti anche le costituzioni I. 46, Inter cetera; I. 51, Iustitiarii per provincias; I. 52, Iustitiarii non per calendas; I. 53.1, Inquisitiones; I. 53.3, Item dira; I. 53.4, Praesenti; I. 54, Apud iustitiarios; I. 55, Iustitiarios regionum; I. 63, Quaestiones; I. 95, Occupatis nobis (Constitutiones, 46, 50 - 53, 56 - 58, 66, 98). Per notizie più dettagliate e ulteriore bibliografia, cfr. *Colliva,* Ricerche, 63 - 152; *Romano,* Tribunali, 234 - 5; *Cuozzo,* La 'Magna Curia', 31 ss.

[51] La più tarda datazione è proposta da *Cuozzo,* La 'Magna Curia', 69.

[52] Sottolineando differenze esistenti fra la parte continentale del *Regnum* e l'isola, va detto che il giustiziere della Sicilia è indicato, anche nei documenti più antichi, comunemente come *magister iustitiarius,* appellativo, questo, riservato all'alto magistrato siciliano o, forse, attribuito ai giustizieri provinciali (l'identificazione fra *magistri iustitiarii* e giustizieri provinciali è in *Cuozzo,* La 'Magna Curia', 47).

[53] A questa conclusione giunge, dopo una convincente puntuale analisi dei testi delle costituzioni regie, *Cuozzo,* La 'Magna Curia', 44 ss. Ma su quest'ultimo si vedano anche le note di *R. Neumann,* Parteibildungen im Königreich Sizilien während der Unmündigkeit Friedrichs II. (1198 - 1208) (Frankfurt-Bern-New York 1986) 176 ss., e *Theo Kölze,* 'Magna Imperialis Curia'. Die Zentralverwaltung im Königreich Sizilien unter Friedrich II., in: Historisches Jahrbuch, 114 (1995).

[54] C. I. 40.2 e I. 42. Ma si vedano anche le 'constitutiones' *Nihil veterum,* I. 38.1; *Statuimus,* I. 38.2; *Praecipimus,* I. 39.2; *Causas,* I. 42.2; *Capitaneorum,* I. 43; *Iustitiarii nomen,* I. 44 (Constitutiones, 34 - 7, 38, 41 - 5), nonché le norme evidenziate in *Cuozzo,* La 'Magna Curia', 31 ss.

della giustizia nel regno. Annualmente egli era tenuto a 'visitare' tutte le *universitates* demaniali per raccogliere eventuali lagnanze e concludere le cause non definite dai vari tribunali locali entro i termini previsti. Lo stesso sovraintendeva anche all'opera dei secreti e dei castellani, nelle materie di loro competenza. Gli era consentito rettificare le sentenze dei giudici locali, che in caso di mancanze gravi poteva anche destituire dall'ufficio. L'alto magistrato, alla cui presenza qualsiasi altro «silere debebit utpute minori lumine per luminare maius superveniens obscurato»[55], aveva altresì piena giurisdizione su qualsiasi reato commesso nei luoghi ove era presente, com'era anche competente a decidere delle impugnative propostegli contro le sentenze dei giudici periferici. Era altresì competente a procedere, secondo quanto previsto dalla *const. Magnae Curiae,* anche per via d'inquisizione, nelle cause feudali comprese quelle «de comitatibus videlicet baroniis, civitatibus, castris et magnis feudis quae in quaternionibus dohanae nostrae baronum inveniuntur inscriptis»[56].

Nelle sue funzioni il mastro giustiziere del re, tenuto a stare a contatto con la *Curia Regis,* era assistito da quattro giudici formanti la Regia Gran Corte, che, almeno a partire dal 1239, veniva a proporsi come organo collegiale e come massimo tribunale stabile del regno con competenza a giudicare di ogni causa, civile, penale o feudale che fosse, oltre che delle cause appositamente ad esso delegate dal sovrano. Alla Regia Gran Corte erano affidati anche compiti di giustizia amministrativa. L'organico del tribunale prevedeva, altresì, un mastro notaio con funzioni di cancelliere ed un archivista. Si tratta – come efficacemente delineato da E. Cuozzo – di una magistratura che risulta frutto di un perfezionamento fridericiano del sistema giudiziario del *Regnum.* È da ritenere, infatti, che fino a dopo la promulgazione delle costituzioni melfitane sopravvivesse la *'Magna Curia' Regis* d'impianto normanno, della quale era membro il *magister iustitiarius* di corte[57], assistito da quattro o cinque giudici *a latere* scelti fra i principali giuristi del Regno[58].

---

[55] Così prescriveva la *const. Honorem,* C. I. 41 (Constitutiones, 40).

[56] C. I. 40.2 (Constitutiones, 39).

[57] La sopravvivenza della *'Magna Curia' Regis,* con compiti giurisdizionali, è attestata nelle *assisae* sveve di Capua (1220), mentre – almeno a parere di Cuozzo – i riferimenti ai maestri giustizieri contenuti nelle costituzioni melfitane sono dovuti in parte ad errori di traduzione, trattandosi realmente di riferimenti ai giustizieri provinciali, indicati anche come *magistri iustitiarii,* cfr. *Cuozzo,* La 'Magna Curia', 44 ss. Dopo il '20, comunque, quel tribunale conosce una progressiva ristrutturazione che, probabilmente, si conclude con le costituzioni di Foggia del '40, quando diviene un tribunale stabile presso la corte del sovrano. Così *Julius Ficker,* Forschungen zur Reichs- und Rechtsgeschichte Italiens (Innsbruck 1868 - 74, rist. anastatica Graz 1961) I, 349 ss.; III, 175 ss., ma anche *Wilhelm Heupel,* Der sizilische Grosshof unter Kaiser Friedrich II. Eine verwaltungsgeschichtliche Studie (Stuttgart 1940) 83 ss., e *Cuozzo,* La 'Magna Curia', 65 ss.

Le competenze e la giurisdizione della Regia Gran Corte venivano indicate principalmente dalla *novella const. Statuimus*[59], ove si prescrive: «Magnae curiae nostrae magister iustitiarius nobiscum in curia commoretur, cui quatuor iudices volumus assidere et ut magister iustitiarius curiae nostrae supradictus de crimine laesae maiestatis nostrae et de feudis quaternatis et de quota parte ipsorum feudorum, et de appellationibus ordinariorum seu delegatorum nostrorum ad nostram curiam interiectis et de quaestionibus nostrorum curialium qui immediate nobis assistunt, de speciali conscientia nostra in curia commorantium, qui de curia nostra sine speciali mandato nostro non possunt recedere, nec non et miserabilium personarum, quarum est privilegium forum eligere corporali praestito sacramento quod adversariorum suorum forte potentiam perhorrescunt, causas audiat et iustitia mediante decidat. Consultationes inferiorum iudicum pro sua iurisdictione recipiat, de iure consulentibus responsurus. In aliis autem nulli liceat adversarium suum in nostra curia evocare sed apud civiles et criminales iudices, prout eorum quilibet de causa cognoscere ex officio suo potest adversarios suos citandi licentia concedatur. Hoc addito, quod de crimine laesae maietatis nostrae apud iustitiarios regionum, si hoc accusator elegerit, causas audiri volumus et decidi». Ancora le *novellae const. Nihil veterum, Litteras* e *Hac lege*[60] definivano, intorno al 1240, ruolo e competenza del gran giustiziere di corte e della sua *'Magna Curia'.*

Contemporaneamente alla proposizione di un *regius ordo iudiciarius,* sostanzialmente di nuovo impianto, il sovrano svevo, cosciente dell'importanza della forma, ne regolava minuziosamente le procedure ponendo dei capisaldi di notevole portata.

Tutte le fasi del processo, dalla citazione alla contumacia, dalla costituzione alla *litis contestatio,* dall'acquisizione delle prove all'escussione dei testi, dalla proponibilità di eccezioni ad eventuali pronunzie interlocutorie, venivano meticolosamente regolate prevedendo, al termine di processi che si volevano definiti in un breve arco di tempo, sentenze motivate redatte, a pena di nullità, in forma scritta: «Ab omnibus Regni nostri fidelibus quemcunque dignitatis gradum aut iurisdictionis obtineant, observare praecipimus

---

[58] Di questi giudici conosciamo, ad esempio, Leone Mancino da Bari, Roffredo da Benevento, Enrico di Tocco, Pietro delle Vigne, Taddeo da Sessa, Benedetto d'Isernia, Andrea da Capua, Durando da Brindisi, Roberto da Palermo. Giuristi noti, alcuni dei quali maestri dello studio napoletano sin dalla fondazione fridericiana (1224); cfr., per tutti, *Eduard Maurits Meijers,* Iuris interpretes saec. XIII, curantibus scholaribus Leidensibus septingentesimo anno Studii Neapolitani (Napoli 1925) e, anche per ulteriore bibliografia, *Andrea Romano,* Federico II e lo 'Studium generale' di Napoli, in: Federico II e l'Italia (Roma 1995) 149-55.

[59] C. I. 38.2 (Constitutiones, 35 - 36).

[60] C. I. 38.1; I. 39.1; I. 40.1 (Constitutiones, 34, 37 - 39).

quod omnes sententias definitivas in scriptis proferant»[61]. Incerta è l'efficacia delle sentenze pronunciate da questo tribunale, anche se è presumibile che si limitasse alle parti. Diverso poteva essere il peso delle sentenze pubblicate *de voluntate imperatoris* su problemi di diritto. Per le sentenze di maggiore rilievo politico, infatti, o comportanti soluzioni incerte *de iure,* era previsto il ricorso al sovrano, cui venivano trasmessi gli atti per richiederne l'intervento chiarificatore e per sollecitarne quell'*interpretatio necessaria* che poteva risolvere i problemi originati da lacune dell'ordinamento o da difformità di opinioni in dottrina[62].

Si trattava di un 'sistema giudiziario', sostanzialmente di natura accusatoria, largamente informato ai principi del processo romano-canonico[63], che riusciva a mantenere la sua armonica compattezza solo in presenza di un apparato statale funzionante, ma pronto ad entrare in crisi con il venir meno della saldezza di quell'apparato. Cosa che in Sicilia, probabilmente, avveniva già negli ultimi anni del regno di Federico II e che, certamente, fu acuita dalle successive vicende politiche che attraverso vari accadimenti portarono al passaggio della Sicilia, dapprima regione di un più vasto *Regnum,* sotto la dinastia angioina e quindi, dopo la ribellione dei Vespri del 1282, costituendo essa da sola un regno sovrano, sotto la dinastia aragonese con il re Pietro.

La dinastia aragonese, peraltro impegnata in una grave guerra con gli angioini di Napoli, non riusciva a garantire né uno stabile sistema di potere politico né un apparato giudiziario funzionante, restando costretta a venire a patti e con la feudalità e con le *universitates* demaniali maggiori, che non esiteranno ad erodere la debole giurisdizione regia che solo con Federico III (asceso al trono nel 1296) e Martino I (asceso al trono nel 1402) potrà essere riaffermata.

Una delle magistrature che per prima entra in crisi, cadendo anche in tentazioni autocratiche, è quella dei maestri giustizieri che, specie se collegati a gruppi parentali potenti, tendono a rendere perpetuo il loro ufficio e illimitati i loro poteri, non esitando dal compromettersi in frequenti episodi di prevaricazioni, violenze e corruzioni, come si può ricavare da alcuni provvedimenti dei primi sovrani della dinastia aragonese (Giacomo, Federico)

---

61 Così disponeva la *const. Ab omnibus,* C. I. 77 (Constitutiones, 80) che, in caso di inosservanza, imponeva al giudice di risarcire «de suo damnum quodlibet et expensas litigantibus».

62 Cfr. *Heupel,* Der sizilische Grosshof, 83 - 109, part. d. 29. La trasmissione degli atti al re non era invece richiesta nelle sentenze che non presentavano problemi interpretativi, come parrebbe ritenere *Cuozzo,* La 'Magna Curia', 69.

63 Per una rapida informazione cfr. *Adriana Campitelli,* Processo (diritto intermedio), in: Enciclopedia del Diritto, 36 (Milano 1987) 93 - 100.

databili al decennio 1285 - 1296 ed ancor prima di Carlo d'Angiò[64]. Si capisce così l'iniziativa di Federico III che, elevando a quattro il numero dei mastri giustizieri provinciali, tende a restringere la loro giurisdizione limitandola a quella penale maggiore e togliendo loro ogni competenza sugli appelli avverso le sentenze dei giustizieri locali e dei baiuli, che sarà invece attribuita al tribunale della Regia Gran Corte[65]. La stessa Gran Corte, nel criminale, funzionerà come giudice d'appello contro le sentenze dei giustizieri o dei capitani feudali.

Il disegno concepito da Martino il Giovane, a fine Trecento, di ripristinare la *iurisdictio regia* non poteva non interessare anche la Gran Corte, probabilmente assai compressa nelle sue funzioni. E, significativamente, nel 1394 il sovrano, rinnovando i giudici di quel tribunale, notava che «propter ribellionem et guerram imminentiam nostra magna curia quasi vacat ad presens»[66]. Difficile dire se Martino lamentasse una contingenza assolutamente momentanea o una situazione che era venuta protraendosi nel tempo; le vicende politiche dell'isola porterebbero tuttavia a credere come maggiormente verosimile la seconda ipotesi.

Precisando i poteri ispettivi del regio mastro giustiziere, Martino I disponeva che il tribunale della Regia Gran Corte venisse presieduto stabilmente da un luogotenente del regio mastro giustiziere, coll'appellativo di mastro giustiziere della Regia Gran Corte.

Al sommo tribunale veniva confermata la competenza esclusiva sulle cause feudali e criminali più gravi nonché la giuridizione d'appello per tutte le liti decise dai tribunali inferiori e per quelle profferite, anche in seconda istanza, dai *Comites, Barones et Feudatariis* provvisti di *merum et*

---

[64] Si possono vedere, in particolare, i capitoli 48, di re Giacomo del 1286, e 7 e 8, di re Federico del 1296 (cfr. Capitula Regni Siciliae quae ad hodiernum diem lata sunt, I (Panormi 1741) 29 e 51 - 2).

[65] Cfr. cap. 7 Friderici II (Capitula, I, 51): «Edicto perpetuo valituro censemus, ut in tota Sicilia, prout alias fieri assolet, exceptis civitatibus Panhormi et Messanae, quatuor iustitiarii, nobiles et regnicolae pollentes divitiis debeant anno quolibet ordinari». I mastri giustizieri provinciali spariranno intorno alla metà del secolo XIV e neanche un tentativo operato da Martino I nel 1403 riuscirà a ripristinare la magistratura.

[66] Cfr. Palermo, Archivio di Stato, Real Cancelleria, 1393 - 5, 23, 60r, cit. in *Romano,* Tribunali, 242. Si tenga conto, peraltro, che l'alto tribunale subiva non poche limitazioni dai privilegi delle città politicamente più importanti e, segnatamente, di Palermo e Messina, come si può agevolmente riscontrare dalle collezioni di *privilegia* editi in *Michael De Vio,* Felicis et fidelissimae urbis Panormitanae selecta aliquot privilegia (Panormi 1706, rist. an. con Premesa di *R. Giuffrida,* Palermo 1990) *passim,* e *Camillo Giardina,* Capitoli e privilegi di Messina (Palermo 1937) *passim.* In forza di tali privilegi il tribunale non ha, sostanzialmente, una sede fissa fino al secolo XVII, così come la Corte.

mistum imperium[67]. Si disponeva inoltre che i giudici della Regia Gran Corte, a partire dal 1433 previsti stabilmente nel numero di quattro[68], dovessero riferire settimanalmente al sovrano, o ad un suo vicario, sulle cause di maggiore rilievo[69]. L'alto rango della magistratura veniva confermato dal fatto che uno dei suoi giudici era chiamato a fare parte del Consiglio Regio. Il rilievo 'politico' del tribunale era confermato dalla circostanza che dalle città più influenti era costantemente rivendicata una presenza paritaria in esso, per cui un giudice doveva essere palermitano, un secondo messinese, un terzo catanese ed il quarto *de Regno*[70].

Risultava così che la Regia Gran Corte veniva ad essere, ad un tempo, tribunale di primo grado e tribunale d'appello, seppure per materie diverse. Il problema dell'appellabilità delle sentenze della Regia Gran Corte veniva organicamente affrontato da Alfonso V il Magnanimo, che nel 1446, nel suo *Ritus Magnae Curiae,* disponendo che le sentenze interlocutorie potessero essere appellate innanzi al viceré che poteva o valutarle personalmente, sentito il Sacro Regio Consiglio, o affidarne l'esame ad un giudice appositamente delegato, gradito ad entrambe le parti[71]. Avverso questa sentenza definitiva si poteva proporre appello al tribunale originariamente monocratico della Sacra Regia Coscienza, che Alfonso il Magnanimo inte-

---

67 Cfr. cap. 47 Martini e 457 Alphonsi (Capitula, I, 159, 384).

68 «Statuimus igitur nostrae Magnae Curiae quatuor iudices tantum praeesse», cfr. cap. 1 Alphonsi; disposizione ribadita nel cap. 76 del medesimo sovrano, ove si legge: «statuimo et ordinamo, che in la dicta Gran Curti siano solum quattro iudici et non plui, et si per inadvertentia, oi importunitati inde creasimo alcuno altro, volimo et ordinamo che tali creationi de altri iudici ultra lu dictu numeru sia ipso iure nulla» (Capitula, I, 206, 232).

69 «Item li iudici de la Gran Curti faczano ogni venerdì collationi de arduis, cum quilli di lu Consigliu et si necessario sarrà lu casu, con la dicta regina, maxime in iudicio de morti, et causi de terri, et de castelli». Cfr. cap. 67 Martini I (Capitula, I, 186).

70 Così, ad esempio, si ribadiva nel cap. 366 di Alfonso del 1456 (Capitula, I, 340). Ma a seconda del variare degli equilibri poteva capitare che una delle città maggiori avesse due giudici nella Gran Corte (così, ad esempio, Palermo a fine '300: cfr. *Andrea Romano,* Guglielmo Perno da Siracusa cittadino palermitano, in: Studi in memoria di M. Condorelli, v. III (Milano 1988) 287) o che quelli fossero suddivisi fra le città maggiori, fino ad essere, complessivamente, tre palermitani, due messinesi ed un catanese, con alternanza numerica fra queste due ultime città. Sul punto, per una realtà che si protrae fino agli inizi del sec. XIX, cfr. *Francesco Candini,* Codex iuris publici siculi, II.1 (Panormi 1804) 6.

71 Il celebre quanto importante *Ritus* alfonsino, approntato dal protonotaro del Regno Leonardo di Bartolomeo, si legge in Capitula, I, 240 ss. Quella normativa diveniva subito oggetto di una travagliata esegesi da parte della locale dottrina e, comunque, dei principali giuristi interessati ai problemi della pratica forense. Per indicazioni su quella letteratura, cfr. *Andrea Romano,* 'Legum doctores' e cultura giuridica nella Sicilia aragonese. Tendenze, opere, ruoli (Milano 1984) 249 - 50 e *infra* nt. 117.

grerà con due giuristi graditi alle parti tratti dal Regio Consiglio[72]. Non consentivano appello le sentenze della Regia Gran Corte pronunciate a conclusione di procedimenti sommari *per viam confessionis, ingiuntionis* o *ex scripturarum visione* ed *ex abrupto.* Alcune sentenze non appellabili potevano però essere ammesse a gravame innanzi al sovrano.

Al viceré ed alla Regia Gran Corte era affidato il compito di vigilare sul funzionamento dell'apparato giudiziario[73], mentre il controllo sulla corretta amministrazione della giustizia nel suo complesso da parte dei singoli magistrati era normalmente affidato ad un 'sindacatore'[74], che, nonostante le richieste che volevano fosse un siciliano («quod officiales Regni non possint syndacari per exteros»), dall'età di Carlo V sarà stabilmente uno straniero, per confidare di più sulla sua imparzialità[75].

Proprio in tarda età aragonese, intorno al 1447, la Regia Gran Corte, che normalmente aveva trovato sede a Palermo o, con alternanza semestrale, a Messina, tornava ad avere sede, come nell'età dei Martini (seppure ancora per un periodo relativamente breve), a Catania, la città fedelissima dei catalani e della corona, ove doveva stabilirsi per tutto l'anno, fatti salvi i periodi in cui era impegnata dell'annuale visita a tutte le *universitates* del regno prevista dai capitoli[76].

Il definitivo assetto del tribunale della Regia Gran Corte, regolarmente presieduto da un luogotenente del mastro regio giustiziere di nomina regia, si ebbe con la grande riforma dell'apparato giudiziario voluta da Filippo II[77].

---

[72] Sulla composizione del tribunale della Sacra Regia Coscienza cfr. i cap. 18, 367, 422 Alphonsi (Capitula, I, 212, 341, 365).

[73] Cfr. cap. 363 Alphonsi (Capitula, I, 338).

[74] Il sindacato dei magistrati attirava l'attenzione della dottrina e su quella pratica ci restano delle utili trattazioni; in particolare si possono vedere *Girolamo Giorlando,* Practica sindicatus ... valde perutilis cum nonnullis questionibus (Messanae 1553), e *Giuseppe Cumia,* Practica sindicatus cum theorica summariis atque numeris unicuique capiti apte distinctis (Catinae 1568).

[75] Cfr. cap. 22 e 363 Alphonsi (Capitula, I, 214, 338) e cap. 169 e 209 Caroli V (Capitula, II Panormi 1743, 126, 169). Sull'ufficio dei sindacatori cfr. i cap. 22, 106 Ferdinandi II nonché i cap. 63, 119, 169, 209 Caroli V (Capitula, I, 527, 584 e II, 49, 89). Utili note in *Camillo Giardina,* L'istituto del viceré di Sicilia, (1415 - 1798), in: A.S.S., n.s., 51 (1931), 277 - 80, e *Pietro Burgarella – Grazia Fallico,* L'archivio dei visitatori generali di Sicilia (Roma 1977) 21 - 6.

[76] Cfr. cap. 362 Alphonsi (relativo alle visite annuali) e 10 Ioannis (Capitula, I, 338, 436 - 7).

[77] Sulle strutture giudiziarie siciliane cfr. *Garsia Mastrillo,* De magistratibus eorum imperio et iurisdictione tractatus in duas partes distinctus (Panormi 1616), e *Giuseppe Riccio,* De publicis iudiciis in genere (Panormi 1656); *Id.,* De publicis iudiciis in specie (Panormi 1664), ed anche *Francesco Candini,* Codex iuris publici siculi (Panormi 1804). In generale sulle riforme dell'ordinamento giudiziario siciliano, cfr. *Gigliola Parrino Piccione,* I 'Capitula Regni Siciliae' in tema di riforme dell'ordinamento giudiziario, in: A.S.S., ser. III, 19 (1969), 33 - 115; in particolare

Dei problemi della giustizia e del funzionamento dei tribunali si erano occupati, particolarmente, i parlamenti del 1534 - 35 e del 1562, ma la riforma sarà promulgata dal sovrano con suo atto normativo nel 1569 costituendo la prammatica *De reformatione tribunalium*[78], che di fatto veniva a costituire il momento conclusivo di una vasta serie d'interventi, ora proposti dai sovrani ora richiesti dai parlamenti (ma non sempre andati a buon fine) a partire dagli inizi del secolo XV.

Innanzi tutto veniva stabilmente confermata l'articolazione della Regia Gran Corte in due sezioni, una civile ed una penale, così come stabilito da Carlo V. Sia la sezione civile che quella penale erano costituite da un presidente assistito da tre giudici[79]. Entrambe le sezioni prevedevano la presenza di un avvocato fiscale, di nomina regia, *rei publicae tuendae causa.* Peraltro, essendo richiesta la presenza di quattro giudici per la trattazione delle liti di carattere feudale, in tali procedimenti la corte civile era integrata da un quarto giudice (il più anziano) tratto dall'altra sezione[80]. Le sentenze della Regia Gran Corte, in sede civile, potevano essere appellate innanzi al tribunale del Concistoro della Sacra Regia Coscienza e delle Cause Delegate, formato da tre giudici e da un presidente[81]. Quelle in sede penale potevano, invece, essere rinviate dal viceré, ma per grazia, al riesame del Sacro Regio Consiglio.

---

sulla riforma di Filippo II, cfr. *Helmut G. Koenigsberger,* The governement of Sicily under Philip II of Spain (London 1951); *Id.,* The Practice of Empire (Ithaca-New York 1969); *Vittorio Sciuti Russi,* Il governo della Sicilia in due relazioni del primo Seicento (Napoli 1984) 17 - 25; *Id.,* Astrea in Sicilia. Il ministero togato nella società siciliana dei secoli XVI e XVII (Napoli 1983), particolarmente 79, 216 ss.

78 Il testo della prammatica si legge in: Regni Siciliae pragmaticarum sanctionum ... tomus secundus, a cura di *R. Ramundetta* (Panhormi 1576) 1 - 4; Pragmaticarum Regni Siciliae novissima collectio tomus secundus, a cura di *P. Amico, C. Fimia* e *R. Potenzano* (Panormi 1637) 1 - 7, e in: Pragmaticae Sanctiones Regni Siciliae, a cura di *F. P. Di Blasi,* II (Panormi 1793). Sul parlamento del 1534 - 35, utili note in *Sciuti Russi,* Astrea in Sicilia, 22 - 8.

79 Cfr. cap. 168, 213, 231 Caroli V (Capitula, II, 125, 175, 195). La riforma carolina del 1535 accoglieva una reiterata richiesta del braccio demaniale del parlamento motivata dall'eccessiva lentezza dei giudizi derivante dall'alto carico di lavoro. Lo stesso Carlo V respingeva, invece, la richiesta sorretta dalle medesime motivazioni (contenuta nel cap. 231) di elevare ad otto il numero dei giudici. In generale cfr. *Candini,* Codex, II.1, 3 ss.

80 Per tutti, cfr. *Candini,* Codex, II.1, 34 s., ove si dà notizia anche delle norme specifiche.

81 Questo tribunale traeva origine dall'antico *iudex Sacrae Regiae Conscientiae,* la cui attività appare documentata a datare dal secolo XIV, assumeva anche la funzione di giudice d'appello nelle sentenze pronunziate dal Tribunale del Real Patrimonio, purché non vi fossero interessi del regio fisco, o dal giudice della Regia Monarchia di Sicilia. In quest'ultimo caso ai tre giudici propri si aggiungeva un quarto giudice ecclesiastico. Lo stesso fungeva altresì da tribunale speciale per le cause delegate.

L'intero sistema degli appelli, comunque, risultava alquanto complesso e, ai massimi livelli, di fatto coinvolgeva tutte le supreme magistrature, anche per la circostanza che (conformemente a quanto previsto da C.7. 10. 1) erano necessari tre giudizi per ottenere il passaggio in giudicato di una sentenza. Era così che le sentenze della Regia Gran Corte potevano essere impugnate innanzi al Concistoro della Sacra Coscienza; quelle del Concistoro della Sacra Coscienza potevano essere appellate innanzi alla sezione criminale della Regia Gran Corte; le sentenze di questa potevano essere impugnate innanzi alla Regia Gran Corte, nella composizione di tribunale per le cause delegate; le sentenze di quest'ultima potevano essere appellate innanzi al Concistoro della Sacra Coscienza, nella composizione di tribunale per le cause delegate[82].

L'insieme di tutti i giudici del tribunale della Regia Gran Corte, del tribunale del Concistoro della Sacra Coscienza e del tribunale del Real Patrimonio (massima magistratura con competenza contabile e fiscale che con la riforma di Filippo II veniva a sostituire l'antica *'Magna Curia' Rationum* o Gran Corte dei Razionali)[83] costituiva il Sacro Regio Consiglio, organo di considerevole rilievo politico, anche se con prevalenti funzioni consultive, presieduto dal viceré e del quale era segretario il protonotaro del Regno[84].

Un assetto, questo, rimasto sostanzialmente senza significative variazioni (nonostante le non poche critiche), fino all'abolizione del sistema delle 'autorità giudiziarie ... oltre il Faro', avutasi con l'approvazione prima della legge 22 dicembre 1818 e quindi con l'entrata in vigore in Sicilia della *Legge organica dell'ordine giudiziario* promulgata da Ferdinando di Borbone nel 1819[85].

---

82 Per una sintesi del sistema giudiziario siciliano, con specifico riferimento alla materia delle impugnazioni, cfr. *La Mantia,* Storia, I, 193ss.

83 Cfr. *Adelaide Baviera Albanese,* L'istituzione dell'ufficio di conservatore del Real Patrimonio e gli organi finanziari del Regno di Sicilia nel sec. XV. Contributo alla storia delle magistrature siciliane, in: Circ. Giur., n. s., 29 (1958), 332 - 63.

84 Per le vaste competenze del Sacro Regio Consiglio cfr., principalmente, *Giardina,* L'istituto del viceré, 272 - 5; *Adelaide Baviera Albanese,* L'ufficio del Consultore del Viceré nel quadro delle riforme della organizzazione giudiziaria del secolo XVI in Sicilia, in: Rassegna degli Archivi di Stato, XX. 2 (1960), 181 ss., ora in *Id.,* Scritti minori (Soveria Mannelli 1992) 111 - 52; *Id.,* Diritto pubblico e istituzioni amministrative in Sicilia, Le fonti (Roma 1981) 99 - 100.

85 Cfr. Collezione delle leggi e de' decreti reali del Regno delle Due Sicilie, anno 1819, n. 1612.

III. I giudici

Sotto il profilo della composizione soggettiva il tribunale della Regia Gran Corte conobbe una lenta ma decisa evoluzione, risentendo inizialmente della sua origine di *Curia Regis*.

È certo, infatti, che anche quando la *Magna Regia Curia* assume la fisionomia di magistratura stabile con competenze essenzialmente giurisdizionali (anche se in senso lato) i suoi componenti non sono definiti né nel numero né nella qualifica.

Se, infatti, almeno a datare dagli inizi degli anni '70 del secolo XII, troviamo normalmente presenti fra i componenti quella Corte i maestri giustizieri (ma non esclusivamente quelli, come vorrebbe lo Chalandon), è anche vero che accanto ad essi rinveniamo ancora a lungo altri funzionari e *fideles regii,* e comunque non dei professionisti esperti di diritto o giudici specializzati, come sembrerebbe sostenere l'Haskins.

Una composizione stabile di questa magistratura, come si è detto, si ebbe solo con Federico II, contemporaneamente alla definizione della *magna curia.* Presieduta dal *magister iustitiarius,* o da un suo vicario, la Gran Corte risultava formata da quattro giudici di nomina regia, assistiti da un notaio *ad acta* con funzione di cancelliere. Si trattava di giudici professionisti – regi per nomina – dei quali, però, si prescriveva la rotazione annuale a garanzia di un sistema d'imparzialità strutturato anche per impedire la formazione di 'gruppi di potere' all'interno dell'apparato regio. La stessa costituzione fridericiana che imponeva l'annualità degli uffici giudiziari prescriveva anche dei requisiti tecnici per i giudici: «Iudices ubique locorum, remotis perpetuis hactenus ordinatis ut est dictum, annui viri industres et fideles et iurisperiti, si unquam in regno reperiantur idonei decernantur»[86]. Requisiti comuni a tutti i magistrati risultavano l'essere «industres et fideles et iurisperiti» per costituire così un corpo 'mobile' di funzionari tecnicamente preparati e fedeli alla corona, indipendentemente dal ceto di appartenenza. I giudici fridericiani, anche quelli del supremo tribunale, erano dei *fideles* ma non apparivano più tratti esclusivamente dal rango dei *milites,* come avveniva in precedenza. Si aprivano, nel contempo, grandi possibilità per gli esperti di diritto, soprattutto per gli *iuris doctores* che potevano nutrire fondate prospettive di occupare le più alte magistrature[87].

La revisione alfonsina della composizione della Regia Gran Corte portava alla durata biennale dell'ufficio, con obbligo di almeno una *vacatio*

---

[86] *Const. Iudices,* C. I. 95.3 (Constitutiones, 100).

[87] Su questa problematica cfr. *Romano,* 'Legum doctores', 47 ss. e *passim.*

biennalis[88], mentre i quattro giudici dovevano essere scelti fra i maggiori dottori di diritto dell'isola e provenire uno da Palermo, uno da Messina, uno da Catania ed il quarto *de Regno,* tratto cioè dai dottori residenti nelle altre città demaniali[89]. Prescrizione quest'ultima non sempre puntualmente osservata, o meglio elusa attraverso un sistema di irregolari mutamenti di cittadinanza[90]. Certamente ormai i giudici dell'alto tribunale regio (dal 1569 presieduto stabilmente dal luogotenente del maestro giustiziere che assumeva il titolo di presidente della Regia Gran Corte: «Preses ipsius tribunalis dicatur»[91]) erano dei tecnici, dei dottori di diritto, come veniva più volte ribadito in diversi provvedimenti normativi e a più riprese richiesto al sovrano dalle stesse città che, ad esempio, ancora nel 1457 sollecitavano Alfonso a stabilire che i giudici della Gran Corte fossero «docturi idonei, pratichi, virtuusi et suficienti a lu officio»[92]. Peraltro, già nel 1451, con formula più generale estesa a tutti i giudici del regno, era stato richiesto che in «tucti cittati et terri de lo dicto Regno in li quali sonno docturi in numero sufficiente non poczano esseri iudici oi assessuri notarii ne iurisperiti ma li docturi»[93]. Per i giudici della Gran Corte che non potevano farsi sostituire nel loro ufficio da delegati[94] non si richiedeva soltanto lo specifico titolo dottorale ma, altresì, che fossero virtuosi e dotati di esperienza.

L'antica norma fridericiana in forza della quale i giudici dovevano essere retribuiti *de camera*[95], ovvero dallo stato nel cui interesse esercitavano il loro ufficio, era dapprima confermata da Alfonso il Magnanimo nel 1433,

---

88 Il sovrano nel 1446 respingeva una richiesta di *vacatio triennalis,* cfr. cap. 366 Alphonsi (Capitula, I, 340). Ferdinando II, nel 1514, accettava invece la *vacatio quatriennalis,* ovvero l'esclusione del medesimo dottore per due mandati dall'ufficio, cfr. cap. 111 Ferdinandi (Capitula, I, 588), prescrizione infine emendata da Filippo II nella prammatica *De reformatione tribunalium,* con la riammissione della *vacatio biennalis.*

89 Cfr. cap. 366, 501 Alphonsi, 14 Ioannis (Capitula, I, 340, 406, 439).

90 Un sintomo evidente di tali elusioni (talvolta anche facilitate da interventi regi: «in fraudem dicti capituli aliqui fuerint iudices facti ex privilegio indulto per Regiam Maiestatem et aliqui qui nullam habuerant habitationem in dicta civitate») risulta, ad esempio, dal cap. 43 Ioannis (Capitula, I, 454), ove, fra l'altro, si stabiliva che i dottori per essere considerati cittadini di un'*universitas* dovessero essere «cives originarii dictarum civitatum vel per ductionem uxoris et ibi habitantes».

91 Cfr. *De reformatione tribunalium pragmatica unica,* §. 2 (Regni Siciliae pragmaticarum sanctionum, II, 2), ove si fissa un salario di «scuti mille anno quolibet».

92 Cfr. cap. 501 Alphonsi (Capitula, I, 406).

93 Cfr. cap. 412 Alphonsi (Capitula, I, 362).

94 Cfr., ad esempio, cap. 502 Alphonsi (Capitula, I, 407), ove si legge «Item, perché in lo officio de lo locutenenti et iudici de la Gran Curti videtur esse electa industria et iudicium personarum che sua Maiestà si digni providiri, che de caetero li dicti officii de locutenenti et iudici non se digiano ne poczano exerciri per substituto».

95 Cfr. *const. Cum iuxta,* C. I. 74 (Constitutiones, 76). La *ratio* della norma si fondava sulla necessità di «viam praecidere cupiditatibus cupientes».

quando, accogliendo una richiesta del parlamento, confermava l'alto salario annuo di ottanta onze, disponendo che «non poczano haviri altri emolumenti pro causa delo dicto officio dali litiganti directe vel indirecte aut quovis quaesito colore ... et che non poczano haviri provisioni ne officio de qual si voglia persuna altra, si non dela nostra maiestati»[96], ma subiva una parziale modifica nel 1446 ad opera dello stesso Alfonso, che recepiva il sistema previsto dalle *ordinationes* viceregie sui diritti di curia del 1420[97]. Questi, infatti, abolito il sistema degli stipendi, prescriveva che andassero ai giudici i 'diritti' dovuti dai contendenti, per cui quelli venivano compensati con le provvigioni e le propine versate dalle parti[98]. Lentamente s'innescava un meccanismo senza apparente soluzione che sarebbe sfociato, più tardi, nella prassi della 'venalità' delle magistrature vendute 'a vita' a soggetti che se le aggiudicavano per trarre profitto proprio da quelle 'propine', che non di rado erano anche arbitrariamente estorte[99]. Certamente un sintomo di cattivo funzionamento della magistratura sembra trasparire da un capitolo richiesto a Carlo V nel quale, al fine di 'moralizzare' il comportamento dei giudici, si richiedeva di reintrodurre il sistema dello stipendio regio, da elevare a ben trecento onze annue, togliendo però loro ogni emolumento, attribuito secondo un sistema che si riteneva fosse servito a prolungare all'infinito la durata dei processi[100]. Cambiamento del sistema delle retribuzioni ed aumento del numero dei giudici divengono i motivi ricorrenti di una polemica che lamentava il divenire delle liti «immortali et infinite», come si legge nel cap. 134 dell'imperatore Carlo V *Quod iudices Magnae Regiae Curie non possint percipere iura provisionum nisi tantum eorum salarium.*

Non sappiamo se in conseguenza del nuovo sistema di retribuzione o se, piuttosto, della rilevante mole di lavoro che si andava accumulando, certo è comunque che le cause discusse innanzi all'alto tribunale si protraevano ben oltre i termini previsti dalla normativa, fino a diventare «infinite ed immortali», come lamentato con sempre maggiore frequenza ed espressamente denunciato nel parlamento del 1534[101].

---

96 Cfr. cap. 2, 17, 77, 90 Alphonsi (Capitula, I, 207, 212, 233, 237), sostanzialmente ribadito dal cap. 234 Caroli V (Capitula, II, 101). L'entità della retribuzione spettante ai giudici della Gran Corte risulta, anche, dal confronto con il salario attribuito al mastro notaio dello stesso tribunale, ammontante a 15 onze, e all'archivista, di 6 onze, per i quali cfr. i cap. 15 e 88 Alphonsi (Capitula, I, 211, 236).

97 Cfr. *Ordinationes factae per magnificos et potentes dominos vicereges regnante serenissimo rege Alphonso ... super iuribus solvendis curialibus regiis,* cap. 205 ss. Alphonsi (Capitula, I, 273 ss.).

98 Cfr. cap. 366 Alphonsi (Capitula, I, 340).

99 In generale, sul problema, cfr. *Sciuti Russi,* Astrea in Sicilia, 11 e *passim.*

100 Cfr. cap. 134 Caroli V (Capitula, II, 101).

Problemi nascevano anche dalla prevista biennalità dell'ufficio, dato che di fatto si veniva a creare una sorta di rotazione fra pochi dottori di diritto con la possibilità, non infrequente (tenendo conto che parecchie liti – al di là di qualsiasi previsione normativa – si protraevano per anni: in genere oltre due per grado), che il medesimo soggetto potesse essere agli inizi patrocinatore in una lite, quindi avvocato fiscale nel medesimo processo e, in fine, potesse essere chiamato a decidere, quale giudice, della controversia che lo aveva visto avvocato di parte, nonostante i non pochi divieti in proposito[102].

Come rimedio per accelerare lo smaltimento dei numerosi processi giacenti innanzi alla corte regia si chiedeva, con forza, l'aumento del numero dei giudici, che nel 1535 da Carlo V venivano portati a sei, tre per il penale e tre per il civile, con previsione (successivamente abbandonata) dell'avvicendamento annuo fra gli incaricati degli uffici civili e criminali[103]. Nelle cause feudali (che prevedevano una corte giudicante di quattro componenti) i tre giudici della sezione civile venivano integrati da un quarto tratto dall'altra sezione.

La prammatica *De reformatione tribunalium* di Filippo II confermava tre giudici per la sezione civile e tre per la sezione criminale, oltre un avvocato fiscale, disponendo la durata biennale dell'ufficio (quindi, annuale nel 1599), senza così raccogliere le osservazioni contro la *vacatio* provenienti dal foro siciliano, di cui si era reso autorevole portavoce il Cutelli, convinto sostenitore dell'opportunità tecnica e politica di rendere stabili nel loro ufficio almeno i giudici dei tribunali supremi[104]. Va osservato,

---

[101] Lamentele in tal senso emergono, ad esempio, nei cap. 33 Ferdinandi (Capitula, I, 535) e 134 Caroli V (Capitula, II, 101). In generale, *Gregorio,* Considerazioni, 476 - 9.

[102] Cfr., ad esempio, cap. 136 Caroli V (Capitula, II, 103). Sul problema cfr. anche *Sciuti Russi,* Astrea in Sicilia, 220 - 3.

[103] Le richieste di aumento del numero dei giudici del massimo tribunale siciliano, alle quali non erano probabilmente estranei i numerosi *iuris doctores,* continueranno anche successivamente all'ampliamento carolino, cfr. cap. 168, 213, 231 Caroli V (Capitula, II, 125, 175, 195). La spinta, proveniente dal braccio demaniale del Parlamento, verso l'incremento dei giudici della Gran Corte veniva motivata in forza dell'eccessiva mole di lavoro giacente innanzi a quel tribunale, ed infatti «in la Regia Gran Corte di questo Regno sono tanto cresciuti li negotii et cause, così civili, come criminali, che li negotii, parte per la moltitudine delle facende occurrenti in detta Regia Gran Corte, alle quali non bastano li quattro giudici di quella supplire, parte ancora per essere mista et confusa la negociatione civile con la criminale». Pertanto «le cause si protraheno in longo in grave danno, pregiudicio et interesse delli regnicoli li quali alle volte, benché ottenghino le sententie delle cause che agitano in favore loro, consumano tanto tempo et danari in seguir dette cause che li saria meglio di non haverle fatto»; cfr. cap. 213 Caroli V (Capitula, II, 175).

[104] *Mario Cutelli,* Codicis legum sicularum libri quattuor (Messanae 1636) 254 - 9. Sul tema cfr. *Sciuti Russi,* Astrea in Sicilia, 216 - 222.

comunque, che la riforma degli uffici giudiziari promossa da Filippo II di fatto tendeva anche alla creazione di una solida rete di 'funzionari statali' di buona professionalità e più legati agli interessi della monarchia che a quelli della feudalità. Tuttavia, anche per l'ambiguità di alcune delle soluzioni adottate, la riforma del 1569 doveva rivelarsi poco efficace, quando non addirittura peggiorativa della situazione preesistente. Le linee d'intervento risultavano, infatti, concretamente informate ad un rigorismo più apparente che reale, determinando in breve una vera e propria corsa al conseguimento del titolo dottorale e una sorta di 'inflazione' di *doctores iuris,* spesso forniti di un titolo non adeguatamente supportato da idonei contenuti culturali e professionali[105].

Il sistema giudiziario siciliano sembra avere maturato sempre più nel tempo una reale 'specializzazione', reggendosi in effetti su tecnici del diritto. L'amministrazione della giustizia – almeno ai livelli più alti – era costantemente gestita, sempre in nome del re, ad opera di *legum doctores* ed il parere *(votum)* di un dottore di diritto confortava persino le sentenze più gravi dei 'commissari' o giudici delegati a procedere «ex abrupto, nullo iuris ordine servato»[106]. Una realtà che contribuiva decisamente ad un'approfondita elaborazione giurisprudenziale, potremmo dire di livello europeo, del diritto siciliano, ma che nel contempo rendeva politicamente assai influente il 'ceto' dei giuristi, che in Sicilia veniva non di rado a sostenere rigide posizioni di conservazione a fronte di ogni mutamento politico-istituzionale che potesse in qualche misura intaccare le prerogative non solo proprie ma anche del 'ceto' nobiliare, cui esso era assai spesso strutturalmente legato per provenienza e comunanza d'interessi.

---

[105] Sul punto, diffusamente, *Sciuti Russi,* Astrea in Sicilia, 112 - 7, anche con particolare riferimento alla «decadenza dell'Università di Catania», e *Daniela Novarese,* Studi giuridici, apparati amministrativi e dinamiche dei ceti. La realtà della Sicilia nell'età moderna, relazione al Seminario internazionale «Contesti e dinamiche della mobilità sociale in età medievale e moderna: figure professionali, strategie familiari, onorificenze, retribuzioni» (Venezia – Fondazione Cini – 22 - 24 maggio 1995).

[106] La richiesta di parere allo *iuris doctor* in ordine alla comminazione di una sentenza capitale pronunciata *ex abrupto* (inappellabile ed immediatamente eseguibile) fungeva da garanzia per il corretto funzionamento della giustizia e sollevava il giudice 'speciale', delegato regio o viceregio, da qualsiasi responsabilità in ordine alla sentenza stessa. Sul procedimento penale *ex abrupto,* in particolare, cfr. *Mauro Burgio,* Methodi criminalis de modo procedendi ex abrupto (Panormi 1611; Panormi 1646).

IV. Le procedure

Se nell'età normanna le procedure seguite nei giudizi innanzi alla Regia Gran Corte probabilmente non erano rigide ed uniformi, almeno nei tempi più antichi, purtuttavia le superstiti carte di giudicato ci attestano l'esistenza di un processo di carattere accusatorio che si svolgeva oralmente ovunque fosse convocata la Corte: nell'aula regia, in una chiesa, sui luoghi delle contese.

Le parti potevano farsi assistere da un 'causidico' nelle vesti di procuratore, la citazione era affidata all'istante che si costituiva in giudizio ed il libello esposto oralmente e senza precise formalità dinanzi alla corte. Da una carta processuale del 1133, riguardante una lite fra gli abitanti di Patti ed il vescovo di Lipari discussa nel palazzo reale di Messina, apprendiamo, ad esempio, che il vescovo era assistito da causidici appositamente convocati in giudizio («congregata itaque sicut diximus idoneorum virorum nostrorum curia et praenominato episcopo ipsiusque causidicis convocatis»[107]). Da una diversa carta del 1142, relativa ad una vertenza fra Gilberto Perollo ed il vescovo di Messina Roberto, risulta che Gilberto compariva innanzi al re Ruggero, riunito con la sua Corte formata dal «comes Symeon et Georgius amiras coeteresque proceres», e «accusationem contra episcopum Robertum proposuit itaque dixit» ed immediatamente «respondit episcopus», dopo di che il conte Simone, sentiti i testimoni, pronunziava la sentenza[108]. Costituitesi le parti, dopo la proposizione delle azioni e delle eccezioni, l'escussione dei testimoni e l'acquisizione delle prove, il giudice pronunciava alla presenza dei contendenti o dei loro procuratori la 'sentenza regia' che «ad perpetuam memoriam», o anche «ne de his terminis aliqua in perpetuum suboriatur dubitacio», poteva venire fissata per iscritto su una pergamena ad opera del notaio della curia[109].

Significative innovazioni si hanno con Federico II che, regolando minutamente tutte le fasi del procedimento, pone – a pena di nullità e con responsabilità del giudice – l'obbligo della forma scritta per le sentenze («omnes sententias definitivas in scriptis proferant»: *const. Ab omnibus regni*[110]) che dovevano comunque pronunziarsi nel termine di due mesi se civili e di tre se criminali[111]. Secondo il dettato fridericiano, tutte le fasi del procedimento sottostavano, peraltro, all'obbligo della scrittura mentre era compito

---

[107] La carta si legge pubblicata in *Gregorio,* Considerazioni, 116.

[108] Per il testo cfr. *Starrabba,* I diplomi, 365.

[109] In generale sulle procedure seguite, cfr. *Genuardi,* L'ordinamento, 261 - 78; *Id.,* La procedura civile in Sicilia dall'epoca normanna al 1446 (Palermo 1906), ed anche, per linee generali, *André Guillou,* Lo svolgimento della giustizia nell'Italia meridionale, 67 - 78.

[110] C. I. 77 (Constitutiones, 80).

di un *regius notarius ad acta* assicurare la tenuta dei registri del tribunale, con l'incarico di redigere i verbali di tutte le fasi del processo e di raccogliere gli allegati. E puntualmente in una carta del 1276 riguardante una sentenza del giustiziere *citra flumen Salsum* Roberto de Sancto Yano riscontriamo l'esplicita annotazione: «condemnamus sententialiter et in scriptis»[112], mentre la pergamena costituiva una documentazione data alle parti «ad futuram memoriam», dovendosi chiaramente distinguere la sentenza registrata, *ad substantiam,* nei *libri curiae* dallo *scriptum memoriae,* pur esso redatto in forma ufficiale dal *notarius actorum curiae de mandato iudicum* e sottoscritto da giudici e testimoni, rilasciato alle parti affinché potessero servirsene per i loro fini.

È certo, comunque, come attesta una documentazione concorde, che in età aragonese le parti venivano regolarmente assistite da procuratori e avvocati che erano convocati anche per la lettura delle sentenze, ormai stabilmente redatte per iscritto e formalmente lette dal giudice nel tribunale. Federico III, nel 1296, abolendo la procedura inquisitoria nei processi criminali, prescriveva che, fatti salvi i crimini maggiori, si potesse agire solo ad istanza dell'offeso[113]. Da una pergamena del 1340[114], ad esempio, apprendiamo che il tribunale della Regia Gran Corte continuava a rilasciare carte di giudicato a documentazione dei diritti dei contendenti e, contemporaneamente al maturare di una diffusa esigenza di registrazione degli atti 'giuridici' ed 'amministrativi' di maggiore interesse che portava alla costituzione dei primi archivi organici dei principali uffici, restano tracce di una prassi di regolare registrazione degli atti giudiziari della Gran Corte attestata dall'esistenza di appositi *registra*[115]. Sappiamo ancora, ad esempio, che nel 1326 il notaio Rinaldo Picigna ed il giudice Nicolò Palazzo da Castrogiovanni (Enna) transuntavano una cedola della Regia Gran Corte da un «quodam quaterno, cedularius appellato, in quo huiusmodi cedule registrantur»[116].

Sostanzialmente è con Alfonso il Magnanimo che, nel 1446, si ha un'organica riforma della procedura giudiziaria del regno, con la stabile determinazione di un *ritus* che, rivisto e completato dalla riforma elaborata dal viceré Pignatelli nel 1530, costituirà un vero e proprio 'testo unico' di

---

111 Per ulteriori notizie, cfr. *Gregorio,* Considerazioni, 240 - 3; *La Mantia,* Storia, I, 211 ss.; *Genuardi,* La procedura, 64 - 5.

112 La sentenza si legge edita in *Romano,* Tribunali, 289.

113 Cfr. cap. 10 Friderici (Capitula, I, 52).

114 Palermo, Archivio di Stato, Tabulario S. Maria di Malfinò, perg. 238.

115 Sui procedimenti di registrazione, cfr. *Burgarella,* Diplomatica, 196. Numerosi sono gli esempi documentati di *quaterni sententiarum* tenuti anche dai tribunali locali, dai quali vengono estratte, all'occorrenza, copie. Cfr. *Romano,* Tribunali, 244 - 5.

116 Palermo, Archivio di Sato, Tabulario di Polizzi, perg. 29.

diritto processuale siciliano, essenzialmente vigente fino all'entrata in vigore del codice borbonico nel 1819[117].

Quel supremo tribunale aveva competenza in materia civile, penale e feudale, sia in prima che in seconda istanza[118]. In prima istanza, in sede civile, conosceva, infatti, le cause concernenti le controversie per valori eccedenti le ottanta onze; in sede penale decideva le cause relative a crimini che potevano comportare la pena di morte, la mutilazione o la deportazione[119]; mentre, fatte salve alcune eccezioni, esercitava l'esclusiva giurisdizione nelle materie feudali[120]. In tal caso le sentenze della Gran Corte, ove non si

---

117 Sul *Ritus Magnae Curiae et totius Regni Siciliae Curiarum* elaborato dallo *iuris doctor* Leonardo di Bartolomeo, cfr. *Vito La Mantia,* Storia della legislazione civile e criminale di Sicilia, II (Palermo 1874) 202 - 26, e *Romano,* Tribunali, 252 - 6, ove sono citati anche gli scritti della più importante dottrina dei secoli XVI e XVII. Dopo la promulgazione del *ritus* alfonsino si ha il fiorire di una vasta letteratura (sono indicati come 'ritualisti' i giuristi che dedicano particolare attenzione ai temi processualistici) che porterà all'approfondimento dello studio delle procedure e dell'ordinamento giudiziario in genere. Solo nel XVII secolo, però, con l'accentuarsi del formalismo e con il definitivo stabilizzarsi – e deciso complicarsi – delle procedure anche per il sovrapporsi di continui provvedimenti normativi, si assiste alla pubblicazione di un consistente numero di trattati, anche di complessa struttura, che troveranno larghissima diffusione. Fra i più noti trattati sul *modus procedendi* si possono utilmente ricordare, anche ai fini di eventuali riscontri: *Carlo Caruso,* Praxis circa modum procedendi in civilibus super ritu Regni Siciliae non minus utilis quam necessaria (Panormi 1655; anche: Panormi 1662; Panormi 1663); *Id.,* Praxis circa modum procedendi in criminalibus super ritu Regni Siciliae, non minus utilis quam necessaria (Panormi 1655; anche: Panormi 1662; Panormi 1663); *Leonardo Cimino,* Sol ritus Regni Siciliae eiusque commentarii ad Cumiam (Panormi 1617); *Id.,* Theoripraxis de contrario imperio ad ritum Regni Siciliae ex iure communi digesta a nemine alio hucusque tractata (Panormi 1618); *Id.,* Praxis quinquaginta septem §§., in quibus conditae sunt ordinationes et declarationes illustrissimi et excellentissimi domini d. Francisci de Castro, olim in hoc Siciliae Regno proregis vigilantissimi (Panormi 1630); *Ottavio Corsetto,* Quaestiones forenses in ritu Magnae Regiae Curiae Regni Siciliae (Panormi 1615; anche: Panormi 1621); *Mariano Maringo,* Practica super ritu Magnae Regiae Curiae ac caeterarum totius Regni Siciliae curiarum (Panormi 1597; anche: Panormi 1598; Panormi 1619). Sul *Ritus* cfr. anche *supra* nt. 71.

118 I vari problemi inerenti alle competenze della Gran Corte sono trattati, in particolare, da *Corsetto,* Quaestiones forenses super ritu. Ancora nel 1804, peraltro, a quest'importante magistratura sono dedicati numerosi fondamentali capitoli del secondo volume dell'opera di *Candini,* Codex juris publici siculi academicus et forensis.

119 In generale sulla formazione e sulle competenze della Regia Gran Corte, cfr. *Candini,* Codex, II.1, 3 - 76.

120 Cfr. cap. 169 Alphonsi (Capitula, I, 256 - 7). Sull'argomento, in particolare, si soffermano *Pietro De Gregorio,* De iuditiis causarum feudalium tractatus cum additionibus d. Garsiae Mastrilli, in *Id.,* Tractatus de vita et militia... (Panormi 1596) 149 - 283, e *Benedetto Barbagallo,* Practica novissima ac theorica super ritu Magnae Regiae Curiae Regni Siciliae in sex partes divisa (Panormi 1667; e Panormi

trattasse di procedure con rito sommario, erano appellabili innanzi al tribunale del Concistorio della Sacra Regia Coscienza[121]. In seconda istanza, definiva gli appelli avverso le sentenze (ove appellabili) dei tribunali inferiori e, forse, anche dei consoli esteri[122]. Estendeva, altresì, per antico privilegio la propria giurisdizione alle controversie che interessavano vedove e pupilli, nonché *pauperes* e curiali[123].

Tutte le fasi del procedimento erano previste in lingua latina e andavano registrate a cura del mastro notaio del tribunale e custodite da un archivista. Le sentenze dovevano essere lette personalmente dal giudice, in piedi, con gli occhi rivolti al cielo e tenendo innanzi i santi Evangeli, alla presenza delle parti appositamente convocate. Lo stesso giudice doveva rammentare che la decisione era «lata in scriptis»[124]. A cura del mastro notaio doveva essere tenuto un registro dei processi 'iscritti a ruolo' *(liber processuum)*[125];

1785, da cui si cita) 209 - 34. È il Barbagallo (p. 218) ad osservare: «Per constitutiones Regni erant – sc. *competentes in causa feudali* – magister iustitiarius et quatuor iudices M.R.C. sed per pragmaticam Regni 13. tit. 2, de Officio iudicum M.R.C., tom. I, edita anno 1548, fuit provisum quod causae feudales expediantur per tres iudices civiles et unum criminalem seniorem, et si suspectus partibus fuerit, sit alter habita semper ratione ad aetatis praerogativam, sed ex privilegio iudices huius felicis urbis Panormi et similiter iudices nobilis urbis Maessanae cognoscunt de causis feudalibus in prima instantia tantum ut per cap. Regni Regis Philippi 2, cap. 4, concessum anno 1559 [...] et si dubitaretur si causa sit feudalis cognitio est ipsius M.R.C.».

[121] Cfr. cap. 18 Alphonsi (Capitula, I, 212). Sulle modalità dell'appello e sui procedimenti di revisione, cfr. *Barbagallo,* Practica novissima, 179 - 89.

[122] Cfr. *De Gregorio,* De iuditiis, 151. Il De Gregorio osserva che in virtù dei capitoli di Alfonso d'Aragona la Magna Regia Corte era competente «etiam de sententiis consulum nationum Regni ex commissione Viceregis, ut in capitu. Ritus de sententiis consulum». Non sappiamo se l'autorevole giurista facesse riferimento ad una prassi andatasi consolidando, dobbiamo però osservare che il capitolo ricordato (187, De sententiis consulum) non fa cenno ad un possibile affidamento degli appelli contro le sentenze dei consoli stranieri alla Gran Corte, bensì «licet secundum formam eorum privilegiorum a sententiis consulum non appelletur neque supplicetur, nihilominus causa eadem per vicereges in Regno solet committi mercatoribus non suspectis per ipsos decidenda, facta prius relatione in consilio de evidenti iniquitate» (Capitula, I, 268).

[123] Cfr. *De Gregorio,* De iuditiis, 150; *Candini,* Codex, II.1, 185 - 6.

[124] Le formule delle sentenze sono analizzate, sotto l'aspetto paleografico, in *Burgarella,* Diplomatica, 189 - 92. Per le formule ricorrenti si può consultare *Giovan Battista Rocchetti,* Ordine dei giudizi civili nel Regno di Sicilia colla esposizione delle leggi civili, canoniche e sicule che v'hanno relazione e ridotte agli usi del foro, II.4 (Palermo 1805) 296, nonché *Maringo,* Practica super ritu Magnae Regiae Curiae, ad v. 'Utile', anche per un'esatta comprensione della terminologia, risulta l'opera di *Onofrio Buscemi,* Practica ritualis seu explanatio terminorum et vocabulorum ritus forensis (Panormi 1779; e Panormi 1785).

[125] Cfr. la prag. *De officio magistri notarii Magnae Regiae Curiae,* §. 4 (in Regni Siciliae Pragmaticarum Sanctionum, 75).

del pari forse esistevano anche dei *registra sententiarum*, nei quali venivano annotate le sentenze, anche se l'esemplare di *liber sententiarum* allo stato noto si presenta più che altro come una 'giuliana' in cui appaiono sinteticamente riportate le notizie dei vari processi discussi con l'annotazione dell'esito[126]. L'esistenza di un 'archivio' contenente le sentenze risulta, comunque, seppure indirettamente, provata dal cap. 244 del re Alfonso nel quale si fissano le competenze da pagare per ottenere la copia ordinaria di una sentenza (grani 10) o «pro redigendo sententiam in formam publicam» (3 tarì, per cause di valore inferiore alle 50 onze; 6 tarì per le altre)[127].

Il consolidamento della forma scritta in tutte le varie fasi del procedimento aveva come conseguenza la produzione, per ogni lite, di una notevole documentazione che, in distinti fascicoli, era conservata agli atti del tribunale formando imponenti archivi. Necessità di scrittura ed uso della lingua latina, introdotti in un sistema processuale di tipo accusatorio, imponevano altresì l'indispensabile assistenza di avvocati esperti di diritto che, nel caso dei procedimenti innanzi alla Gran Corte, e almeno a partire dalla fine del Trecento, erano degli *iuris doctores*. L'esasperato formalismo, peraltro, contribuiva certamente a dilatare i tempi necessari per arrivare alla definizione di una lite, che nemmeno nei procedimenti *summarie ad litis ingressum* si riusciva a chiudere nei due mesi previsti dal cap. 137 di Alfonso[128], mentre appariva una mera speranza la disposizione per la quale «visti che siano li processi per li iudici se digiano spachiare e dare sententia ad altius infra termino de iorni deci»[129].

La presenza di dottori di diritto in tutte le fasi del procedimento della Regia Corte, ora come patrocinatori ora come giudici, e la particolare competenza della medesima corte, riservata alle materie di maggiore rilievo sia sotto il profilo sostanziale che giuridico-formale, avevano come conseguenza che le decisioni della Gran Corte, anche per il prestigio dei giudici, fossero rivestite di notevole autorità, sicché la loro conservazione veniva a rilevare al di là della pura documentazione dell'ufficio. In maniera particolarmente eloquente il *feudista magnus* e *consiliarius benemeritus* di Ferdinando e Carlo V, Pietro De Gregorio, riecheggiando Andrea d'Isernia, non esitava ad affermare: «'Magna Curia' dicitur aliarum curiarum caput et

---

[126] Un «Liber sentenciarum anni prime indicionis 1497» si conserva a Palermo, Archivio di Stato, Tribunale del real Patrimonio, Sentenze, b. 1/d (cfr. Romano, Tribunali, 256, 297 - 300) e, probabilmente, si tratta di un registro tenuto per scopi fiscali dal real Patrimonio.

[127] Cfr., ad esempio, cap. 244 Alphonsi (Capitula, I, 281).

[128] Cap. 137 Alphonsi (Capitula, I, 253).

[129] Cfr. cap. 3, 4, 78, 79 Alphonsi (Capitula, I, 207, 208, 233). In particolare il cap. 3 prescriveva «quod iudices cum omni diligentia et sollicitudine partes expediant et postquam processus missus est ad aliquem iudicem, iudex ad altius debeat vidisse et curiae restituisse infra tempus dierum duodecim».

velut exemplar, ut dicitur in prohemio Ritus, et ex hoc dicit idem Andreas in Constitutione Si quis in posterum, in 4. coll. in tit. De feud. impos., lib. I, quod id quod servat M. C. totum Regnum servare debet, unde dicitur etiam curia veritatis in cognoscendo rei originem et originalem iustitiam prout quod quid est et sic secundum veritatem et non secundum rigorem, ut voluit glosa in Auth. de instr. cauth. et fid., coll. 6»[130], mentre il non meno autorevole Niccolò Intrigliolo definisce quel tribunale *aequitatis mater*[131].

V. Le sentenze: archivi e tecniche di registrazione

In età normanna la natura del supremo tribunale regio (senza sede fissa e composto principalmente da *fideles* variabili per numero e qualifica) come anche la forma precipuamente orale dei procedimenti non favorivano certamente la registrazione e conservazione delle sentenze, e quando ciò avveniva era funzionale essenzialmente all'interesse delle parti.

Per quest'epoca abbiamo notizia solo di carte di giudicato, di *scripta memoriae* e *notitiae iudicati* contenenti sintesi delle specifiche liti ed il dispositivo della sentenza, redatte dal notaio della curia. Prive di qualsiasi argomentazione di diritto, queste 'carte' servono a comprovare situazioni giuridicamente garantite in quanto giuridicamente 'dichiarate'. Firmate dai giudici e munite di sigillo, esse erano consegnate alle 'parti richiedenti' che avevano interesse a conservarle ed è proprio grazie agli archivi, in special modo di enti ecclesiatici, che parecchi di tali documenti ci sono pervenuti.

Si tratta di *memoriae* scritte in lingua greca o latina[132] (a seconda della 'nazionalità' dei contendenti) espressamente fatte redigere in forma scritta,

---

130 Cfr. *De Gregorio,* De iuditiis, 150. Non è semplice dire se l'affermazione per cui «id quod servat M. C. totum Regnum servare debet» debba intendersi riferita ad una realtà consolidata ai tempi dell'illustre giurista messinese (che esprimeva anche gli orientamenti del potere regio) e non, piuttosto e come appare più probabile, solo ad un suo personale convincimento, significativamente suffragato con la citazione di un'*auctoritas* che faceva riferimento ad una realtà politico-istituzionale (quella napoletana) sostanzialmente diversa.

131 Cfr. *Niccolò Intriglioli,* Decisionum aurearum Magnae Regiae Curiae Regni Siciliae liber primus (Panormi 1609) dec. 7, 33b.

132 Le carte di giudicato redatte in lingua greca seguivano, di norma, il formulario greco, per cui iniziavano con la formula d'invocazione e la data (dalla creazione del mondo). Quindi faceva seguito la *narratio* con l'indicazione del nome dei giudici e delle parti, l'esposizione dell'oggetto della controversia e l'indicazione del luogo del giudizio. Il documento veniva chiuso dalle sottoscrizioni dei giudici e dei testimoni, talora seguite dalla firma del notaio scrivente e dal sigillo. Le carte redatte in lingua latina, invece, seguivano il formulario latino, per cui d'ordinario si aprivano con la formula invocatoria e la data (dalla nascita di Cristo). Seguiva il testo, articolato in esposto e disposto, con l'indicazione dei nomi dei giudici e delle parti oltre che dell'oggetto della lite e del luogo. Nella *corroboratio* vi era l'indica-

talora – come annota il giustiziere Goffredo di Moach nel 1172 – «ne de his terminis aliqua in posterum suboriatur dubitacio ... hanc memoriam scribi feci cum subscriptis testibus» o anche «ad cauthelam archiepiscopatus ... factum est presens ad perpetuam memoriam instrumentum et archiepiscopatui traditum» – come si legge nella decisione, ancora del 1172, della causa fra Leo Chelones e l'arcivescovo di Messina. La memoria poteva essere redatta in uno, ma anche in più esemplari: «ad huius sane nostrae constitutionis iudicium duo scripta, unum et idem continentia, unum pactensibus aliud episcopo per manus Vidonis nostri notarii scribi et subscriptorum testium manibus confirmari, nostro sigillo insigniri praecepimus», si legge, ad esempio, nella sentenza regia del 1130 che risolveva la vertenza fra i pattesi ed il vescovo di Lipari. Talvolta poteva essere utilizzato anche lo strumento notarile della *charta partita:* «ad perpetuam autem concordiam utriusque ecclesiae praesens scriptum utique dedimus ecclesiae mediantibus quibusdam apicibus qui partiti fuerunt ut si quando de predictis divisis oriretur discordia per munimentum huius scripti sopiretur», come, ad esempio, si legge in una sentenza, del 1159, del gran giustiziere della Gran Corte Raimondo di Tusa[133].

Sia l'assenza di documentazione che gli stessi testi delle *memoriae* pervenuteci ci confermano non solo la mancanza di un obbligo di redigere in forma scritta le sentenze, ma altresì la carenza di qualsiasi forma di registrazione delle stesse, anche per uso della corte. Dalla *charta iudicati* riguardante la già ricordata controversia del 1172 fra Leo Chelones e l'arcivescovo di Messina per la proprietà di alcune terre nel casale di Larderia risulta, ad esempio, che «magnae vero supremae curiae iudices Iohannes Burdonus et Bartholomeus de Platia et Iodicus Persicus, audita reverendissimi archiepiscopi responsione, eumdem interrogarunt dicentes utrum testibus probare posset quod asserit». Quello che si chiedeva di provare testimonialmente all'arcivescovo messinese era proprio una precedente sentenza a questi favorevole, relativa al possesso di *tenimenta* di terra a Larderia, pronunciata dalla stessa Gran Corte e da quello invocata.

L'obbligo della scrittura per gli atti processuali in genere e per le sentenze in particolare veniva stabilito solo dalle costituzioni fridericiane. Il compito di redigere per iscritto i verbali del processo era affidato al *notarius ad acta curiae* che, secondo quanto attestato dal Gregorio, doveva provvedere alla tenuta dei *libri curiae,* ordinati secondo l'anno indizionale ed acquistati annualmente dal medesimo notaio[134]. Le costituzioni, però, non

---

zione del notaio redattore, mentre il documento si chiudeva con le sottoscrizioni dei giudici e l'eventuale sigillo. Rari sono gli esempi di carte di giudicato redatte nella forma delle 'carte partite'.

[133] Anche per i documenti citati cfr. *Romano,* Tribunali, 226 - 9, 286 - 9.

[134] *Gregorio,* Considerazioni, 231.

dispongono nulla in ordine alla registrazione dei procedimenti e delle sentenze (scritte) e, peraltro, non resta alcuna documentazione di una prassi ordinaria di registrazione dell'attività giurisdizionale, in genere, della Regia Gran Corte o delle sue sentenze, che avrebbero potuto anche essere scritte in unico originale consegnato alle parti. Credibilmente potevano esistere dei *quaterni* della cancelleria del tribunale tenuti dal notaio di curia e, con probabilità, anche dei fascicoli degli atti ordinatamente raccolti. Di essi non abbiamo però traccia, come non rimane traccia degli archivi normanni e svevi, andati dispersi o distrutti. Resta, invece, documentato l'uso delle *notitiae sententiarum* redatte dai notai a richiesta delle parti *ad cautelam et futuram memoriam* e ad esse consegnate.

Se l'obbligo della scrittura, pur tendenzialmente, favorisce l'adozione di un sistema ordinario di registrazione, almeno degli atti giudiziari più importanti, verso questa medesima direzione spingono, oltre che motivi tecnici, a partire dalla fine del Duecento ed a causa dei continui e rilevanti mutamenti socio-politici che interessano l'isola, anche esigenze di documentazione oltre che un clima di sospetti e conflittualità. Abbiamo così che, intorno alla metà del Trecento, appare quasi universalmente seguita in Sicilia da parte di tutti gli uffici e le magistrature centrali e periferiche la prassi di registrare gli atti prodotti[135]. È certo, comunque, che, come si è poco innanzi ricordato, il notaio Rinaldo Picigna ed il giudice Niccolò Palazzo da Castrogiovani transuntano, nel 1326, una cedola della Regia Gran Corte traendola proprio da un «quodam quaterno cedularius appellato in quo huiusmodi cedule registrantur»[136]. E se conosciamo carte di giudicato rilasciate dalla Regia Gran Corte ancora nel 1340[137], è probabile che nei medesimi anni si fosse ormai consolidato l'uso di tenere dei libri *(quaterni)* di sentenze da parte della cancelleria del medesimo tribunale. La mancanza, per quell'epoca, di archivi dei tribunali regi (probabilmente dispersi sia a causa delle travagliate vicende politiche dell'isola che della mancanza di una sede fissa della corte e dei suoi tribunali, peraltro funzionanti ora a Palermo, ora a Messina e, più tardi, anche a Catania) non ci consente però di disporre di una documentazione, se non significativa, almeno probante; e se non abbiamo notizia di libri contenenti registrazioni di sole sentenze, queste appaiono annotate in calce ai fascicoli processuali o scritte in fogli autonomi.

Un'abbondante documentazione d'archivio resta, invece, a partire dagli inizi del Quattrocento, quando tutti gli atti processuali venivano raccolti in appositi *quaterni,* ordinati a cura del mastro notaio, e le sentenze riportate

---

[135] *Burgarella,* Diplomatica, 196.

[136] Cfr. *Romano,* Tribunali, 245 e supra nt. 116.

[137] Palermo, Archivio di Stato, Tabulario di S. Maria di Malfinò, per. 238.

sui margini del libello o in calce ad esso erano annotate in appositi *quaterni sententiarum,* utili per riscontri di natura fiscale e dai quali potevano essere tratte delle copie legali per le necessità delle parti. In una copia autentica di una sentenza pronunciata dal *legum doctor* Martino delle Torri, quale giudice delegato, eseguita da «Philippus Piscis totius regni Siciliae regius puplicus notarius» leggiamo, ad esempio, che al notaio veniva richiesta una copia «in puplicam formam reddactam» di una «sentenciam seu provisionem offici magistri notariatus ipsius magne curie, pro eodem Andrea Carioso, per nobilem et egregium dominum Martinum de Turribus decretorum doctorem ut iudicem delegatum auctoritate sue commissionis latam reddactam in quaterno ac penes me supradictum notarium ut conservatorem ipsius existentem» e che «sentenciam ipsam seu provisionem scriptam et reddactam in predicto quaterno legimus»[138].

La forma di registrazione nei *libri processuum,* almeno a giudicare dai rari esemplari pervenutici, era assai scarna: l'intestazione del giudice, il nome dell'imputato e dell'accusatore, la formula di condanna o la nota di assoluzione (priva di motivazione) e quindi l'indicazione dei giudici e del notaio. Nei *registra sententiarum,* invece, oltre ad un breve transunto delle sentenze, si leggevano i nomi dell'imputato e dell'accusatore, l'indicazione del reato e della pena[139].

Solo dalla prammatica del viceré Monteleone del 1533 sappiamo che era fatto obbligo al mastro notaio della Regia Gran Corte di tenere un 'quinterno separato' nel quale dovevano registrarsi *sententie, banni* e *foriudicationi* facendone «una mentione summaria et nella margine di ogn'una di esse si facci postilla come si cancellano o si commette la stipulatione o si pagano»; registri che andavano consegnati periodicamente al procuratore fiscale[140]. Lo stesso doveva tenere non solo un'aggiornata giuliana delle sentenze, ma provvedere a registrare le stesse entro quindici giorni dalla data della pronuncia.

Seppure disordinati (a causa delle vicende belliche) e non consultabili, nell'Archivio di Stato di Palermo si conservano alcune migliaia di volumi

138 Palermo, Archivio di Stato, Conservatoria del Registro, v. 5, 210v - 212v.

139 L'esempio maggiormente significativo pervenutoci (almeno fra quelli allo stato noti) è un «Liber sententiarum anni presentis...» (Palermo, Archivio di Stato, Tribunale del Real Patrimonio, sentenze, v. b. 1/d, – ex n. p. 1557 –, segnalato da *Antonino Giuffrida,* La giustizia nel medioevo siciliano (Palermo 1975) 29; *Id.,* Giustizia e società, in: Storia di Sicilia, 3 (Napoli 1980) 553) contenente le registrazioni di alcuni procedimenti criminali della Regia Gran Corte per gli anni 1497 - 8. Da questa giuliana risulta evidente l'esistenza di un registro dei processi, almeno a giudicare dalle frequenti annotazioni «fuit comprobata cum libro processuum fol. ...».

140 Pr. III. 9, §. 12, in Regni Siciliae Pragmaticarum Sanctionum, II, 60.

di atti processuali della Regia Gran Corte[141]. Purtroppo la consultazione dell'intero fondo non è consentita e risulta assai difficile ricostruire i vari processi, dato che l'archiviazione degli atti non avveniva per procedimenti bensì per fasi processuali. Abbiamo così fascicoli di 'termini', 'contumacie', 'conclusioni', 'scritture e produzioni', 'esecuzioni', 'interlocutorie e sentenze', 'decreti', 'opposizioni', 'cedole', 'effetti decisi'. Comunemente il fascicolo di maggiore interesse appare quello degli 'effetti decisi' che conserva il libello processuale, i verbali concernenti l'escussione dei testi, le allegazioni e, talvolta, in calce le sentenze, spesso annotate in breve sintesi anche sul risvolto esterno del libello o sulla copertina del fascicolo, con l'aggiunta di una nota relativa all'appello o all'esecuzione.

Le sentenze registrate presentano una forma estremamente concisa e sono assolutamente prive di motivazioni, mentre non risultano né i *vota* pronunciati dai singoli giudici né la *decisio* del tribunale. È proprio tale prassi seguita nelle registrazioni che lascia presupporre che i vari *libri sententiarum* obbedissero ad obiettivi di controllo e documentazione dell'ufficio ed a scopi fiscali. Diritti da pagare all'erario e necessità connesse ai termini di appello ed alle procedure di esecuzione rendevano indispensabile la tenuta di simili registri, assolutamente inutilizzabili, però, sia per fissare un *usus* del tribunale che per potere essere fonte di 'precedente'. Il che sembrerebbe provato dall'assoluto disinteresse per questo materiale: nessun notaio, giudice o avvocato siciliano riteneva utile, infatti, raccogliere tali materiali in sillogi per uso pratico.

Un diverso interesse risultano avere invece suscitato i *vota* e le *decisiones* dei giudici della Regia Gran Corte, anche se la loro rilevanza va valutata alla luce dello speciale contesto normativo siciliano.

VI. Le *decisiones* della Regia Gran Corte e la loro *auctoritas* nel sistema giudiziario del Regno di Sicilia

Le nostre conoscenze sulla dottrina giuridica e sulla giurisprudenza siciliana fino alle soglie del secolo XVI sono alquanto limitate[142]; ciononostante si può affermare che, almeno fino al Seicento, i precedenti giurisprudenziali non sembrano essere tenuti in gran conto e comunque non è data loro un'importanza determinante neanche come *auctoritates,* come sem-

141 Il fondo della Regia Gran Corte (in sede civile e criminale), custodito presso l'Archivio di Stato di Palermo e allo stato non consultabile, nel 1940 risultava costituito di ben 24.000 registri, andati in larga parte dispersi in seguito alle vicende belliche. Cfr. Guida generale degli archivi di stato italiani, 3. N-R (Roma 1986) 313.

142 Per informazioni sul punto, cfr. *Romano,* 'Legum doctores', 259 - 64, 303 - 45.

brano provare anche le rare sillogi di *decisiones* pervenuteci[143]. Dal sistema giudiziario dell'isola, peraltro, non era consentito ad alcun tribunale di 'creare' norme o, comunque, di stabilire 'precedenti' giudizialmente vincolanti.

Già nelle costituzioni fridericiane che regolavano il sistema normativo e giudiziario del *Regnum,* disponendo la graduazione delle varie fonti[144], non vi era spazio per i precedenti giurisprudenziali, di fatto privi di qualsiasi valore normativo. Le *notitiae sententiarum* note sembrano avere l'esclusiva funzione di 'strumenti' di prova rilasciati *ad cautelam* della parte prevalente e, comunque, *ad futuram memoriam* di una situazione di diritto 'giudizialmente dichiarata' con riferimento ad una specifica concreta fattispecie. No si ha, invece, notizia di sentenze allegate con funzione di 'precedente' giurisprudenziale in alcun modo vincolante per il magistrato chiamato a decidere.

La distinzione fra potere normativo e potere di giudicare appariva chiarissima: il sovrano mentre delegava la seconda 'funzione' a giudici regi, riservava la prima a sé stesso, regolamentandola in un sistema di fonti che, essenzialmente, si articolava in *leges regiae, consuetudines et statuta civitatum* e *ius commune*[145].

---

143 Tra le opere edite in Sicilia nel XVI secolo, l'unica raccolta di decisioni della Gran Corte risulta essere quella del giudice catanese Francesco Milanese, che nel 1597, a Palermo, dava alle stampe la seconda parte delle 'Decisiones tribunalis Magnae Regiae Curiae Regni Siciliae' (preceduta da un'edizione veneziana del 1595 delle 'Aureae decisiones Magnae Regiae Curiae Regni Siciliae'). Appare, peraltro, significativo che solo nelle edizioni a dichiarata impronta praticistica posteriori al secondo ventennio del XVII secolo venga messa in risalto, sin dal titolo, l'utilizzazione delle fonti giurisprudenziali dei tribunali maggiori. Cfr., ad esempio, *Antonino Amato,* Variarum forensium et practicabilium resolutionum liber primus in quo quaestiones in dies fere occurentes controversae dilucide continentur, quae iuris proprii siculi interpretatione et decisionibus tribunalium exornantur (Panormi 1616; e 1627); *Id.,* Variarum [...] liber secundus (Panormi 1634) – libro assai diffuso con ulteriori edizioni: due veneziane, del 1635 e del 1655, e due lionesi del 1656 e del 1668; *Pietro Luna,* Selecta diversorum illustrium sapientissimorumque siculorum, præcipue Blasci Lancea, Io. Aloysii de Septimo, Ferdinandi Boniorni, Raimundi Ramundetta, Modesti Gambacurta, Octavii Corsetti ac aliorum [...] consilia decisiva et allegationes cum decisionibus diversorum Supremorum Tribunalium Regni Siciliæ, tam feudalia, quam allodialia (Panormi 1627); *Francesco Magretti,* Observationes illustratae decisionibus ad constitutiones pragmaticales... (Panormi 1668); *Niccolò Riccio,* Iuridica disquisitio de renunciatione paragii decisionibus Tribunalium M.R.C. et Concistorii S.R.C. Siciliae Regni illustrata (Panormi 1680).

144 Cfr. *const. Puritatem,* C. I. 62 (Constitutiones, 63).

145 In generale, sul problema della graduazione delle fonti normative nel regno di Sicilia, cfr. *Andrea Romano,* Vito La Mantia e le fonti della legislazione cittadina siciliana medievale, Prefazione a *V. La Mantia,* Antiche consuetudini delle città di Sicilia (Messina 1993) XLII* - XLIX*.

Dalla seconda metà del Trecento cominciano a comparire regolarmente nei ruoli dei giudici della Regia Gran Corte prestigiosi esperti di diritto, *legum doctores,* e la loro presenza contribuisce certamente ad accrescere il prestigio dei giudicati della corte medesima, probabilmente attraverso un meccanismo per il quale non era solo l'autorevolezza propria della corte a conferire *auctoritas* al contenuto giuridico delle sentenze, bensì l'*auctoritas* del giudice-*iuris doctor.* Probabilmente, infatti, deriva dalla regolare chiamata di *iuris doctores* all'ufficio di giudici della Gran Corte la circostanza che le soluzioni *de iure* adottate da quel tribunale potevano essere citate a sostegno di specifiche soluzioni.

Proprio alla tarda età aragonese risalgono i primi indizi del formarsi in Sicilia di una giurisprudenza della Regia Gran Corte. Dal *Tractatus super cap. Volentes* del noto giurista e giudice della Regia Gran Corte Gualtiero Paternò[146] apprendiamo infatti che «iudices antiqui intellexerunt illud capitulum in feudo novo tantum». Il riferimento, generico, sembra essere ad una sentenza proprio della Gran Corte nella quale si era 'fissata' in via interpretativa la portata dell'importante capitolo regio. Poco innanzi, sempre Gualtiero osservava che «dum esset mihi commissa causa Chiminne intellexi cap. Volentes quod ... et hic intellectus ita placuit omnibus et ita decisimus omnes et sic unanimiter fuit praticatum et observatum». Il ricordo è di una sentenza della Corte, relativa ad una causa sul possesso del feudo di Ciminna decisa intorno al 1409 mentre il giurista era uno dei giudici, che riproduce il suo *votum,* difforme dall'*opinio* degli antichi giudici. Apprendiamo così che la soluzione di diritto adottata in un precedente giudizio non era da ritenersi obbligatoria nei giudizi successivi vertenti sul medesimo punto, anche che poteva esistere una sorta di 'giurisprudenza consolidata', come porterebbe a credere l'espressione «unanimiter fuit praticatum et observatum». L'ulteriore annotazione, fatta citando una causa per la successione del feudo di Vicari databile intorno al 1416, «Magna Curia in sua opinione persistebat in contrarium» e ciò «non obstantibus oppositionibus nostris», evidenzia l'emergere in seno al tribunale di un grave contrasto interpretativo sulla portata della norma, che verrà risolto ricorrendo all'*interpretatio* viceregia. Ed infatti – nota il giurista – «dominus rex per infantem ita interpretatus est, unde sicut magnifici domini declaretis idem erit lex perpetua firma et inviolabilis». Il trattato del Paternò è databile intorno al 1427: vi si citano sentenze della Gran Corte che hanno affrontato importanti questioni di diritto senza però assumere alcun valore cogente di precedente. Solo l'*interpretatio* regia può dirsi *firma et inviolabilis* e, quel che più conta, *lex.*

---

[146] Il *Tractatus* è edito in *Andrea Romano,* Giuristi siciliani dell'età aragonese (Milano 1979) 168 - 71, ove si leggono anche notizie sul giurista addottoratosi a Padova e giudice del sommo tribunale negli anni 1405, -09, -16.

Ciò non toglie che proprio i giudici della Regia Gran Corte, forti del prestigio loro conferito dall'appartenenza all'autorevole curia e dal possesso di un titolo dottorale fondato sulla padronanza della razionalità del diritto comune, non si limitino al solo accertamento dei fatti ed alla loro qualificazione giuridica con riferimento alla normativa vigente, ma svolgano anche un ruolo di interpreti elaborando una qualificata giurisprudenza. Si è detto che, ad esempio, giudicavano sulla portata del *cap. Volentes* di re Federico III ritenendolo applicabile ai soli feudi nuovi. Ma, sempre esemplificando, gli stessi non esitavano ad estendere la portata del capitolo di re Martino sulla confisca dei beni dei ribelli, qualificando come confiscabili tutti quei beni al momento in possesso del ribelle, anche se di proprietà di terzi. Ed ancora, da un *consilium* del giurista trapanese Giovanni da Taranto traiamo la notizia che la Gran Corte per accertare la sussistenza di una vendita con clausole usurarie, andando oltre i requisiti previsti dal diritto comune (esistenza di un patto di retrovendita a prezzo eccessivamente basso), prevedeva che dovesse essere riscontrata l'esistenza di un elemento soggettivo risultante dall'abitualità del creditore ai prestiti di danaro[147].

È certo, comunque, che a partire dagli inizi del Quattrocento i richiami alla giurisprudenza della Regia Gran Corte sono abbastanza frequenti, in special modo negli scritti destinati ad essere esibiti in giudizio, quali *allegationes* e *consilia.* Così, ad esempio, nei *consilia* del giurista siracusano Guglielmo Perno, uno dei più importanti feudisti siciliani, troviamo ampia documentazione della giurisprudenza del tribunale regio, anche se utilizzata in maniera diversa.

Talora, infatti, il giurista cita, a sostegno dei suoi assunti, opinioni consolidate della Gran Corte, dando testimonianza di una nota *opinio curiae* che viene allegata come rilevante *auctoritas.* Leggiamo, ad esempio, nel volume dei suoi consigli feudali editi: «Et ista est hodie omnium firma opinio et secundum eam sepius iudicatum et ita recte in causa Vicari apparet fuisse determinatum»[148] ed ancora «et hoc iure utimur in 'Magna Curia' huius Regni», oppure «iudicat modo Magna Regia Curia in talibus causis»[149].

Altre volte la citazione della giurisprudenza dell'alto tribunale appare riportata ad *argumentum,* come, ad esempio, quando nota: «Et ita tamen iudicavimus in causa salae» e quindi «secundum hoc optinui in quaestione

---

[147] Sul punto, in particolare, cfr. *Andrea Romano,* Attività mercantili ed usure nel Mediterraneo aragonese. Legislazione, dottrina e giurisprudenza siciliane «de censibus», in: Diritto e Società in Sicilia, a cura di *A. Romano* (Soveria Mannelli) 1994, 264 - 7.

[148] *Guglielmo Perno,* XXIIII consilia pheudalia... (Messanae 1537, rist. an. con Introduzione di *A. Romano,* Messina 1995) 46va.

[149] *Perno,* XXIIII consilia, 4rb.

in pheudo Solarino»[150] o, ancora, «Et hec pars extracta extitit a sententia lata contra dominam Antoniam uxorem magistri Nicolai Carta, lata anno domini MCCCLXXXXV quinte inditionis»[151].

In nessuna citazione, comunque, si fa riferimento a raccolte di giurisprudenza, ufficiali o private, ed anzi, spesso, i rinvii sembrano fatti attingendo a ricordi personali e senza nessun concreto riferimento a fonti controllabili; ad esempio: «Et ita audivi ab illis antiquis iudicibus Magnae Curiae, quod ita iudicaverunt et interpretari hoc capitulum»[152].

Difficile dire, con precisione, quale rilevanza potessero avere le citazioni di precedenti *decisiones* della Gran Corte in successivi giudizi vertenti su analoghe questioni di diritto o, più in generale, sul sistema normativo del regno. Una risposta assai interessante potrebbe venirci dagli stessi scritti di Guglielmo Perno. Nei suoi *notabilia,* infatti, a proposito della portata da dare al tormentato *cap. Volentes,* rammentando la *decisio* a proposito del feudo di Vicari e l'*interpretatio* del viceré che abbiamo visto citate da Gualtiero Paternò nel suo *tractatus,* il giurista osservava: «Quod capitulum ita fuit interpetratum et declaratum in questione Vicari ... et per sententiam viceregis infantis Ioannis terminatum. Quae facit ius, l. fi., C. de legibus, ubi si princeps examinat aliquam causam habet vim legis. Et quia inde fuerunt latae consimiles sententiae ... ubi confirmata per plures alias sententias que in hoc regno fecerunt ius»[153]. L'espressione «per plures alias sententias que in hoc regno fecerunt ius», almeno ad una superficiale lettura, potrebbe portare a credere che una giurisprudenza costante della Gran Corte (se non proprio una singola sentenza) potesse avere in Sicilia forza di legge. In realtà non sono le sentenze (che avrebbero potuto sempre essere variate e contraddette) ad avere 'forza di legge', bensì l'*interpretatio* del viceré e tanto ciò è vero che il giurista sente la necessità di provare, ricorrendo al *Codex* di Giustiniano, la differente efficacia delle pronunzie della Gran Corte e del viceré, che si fondava sul principio «si princeps examinat aliquam causam habet vim legis». Per il resto Guglielmo sembra limitarsi a prendere atto dell'avvenuta recezione, nel foro, dell'*interpretatio,* avente carattere di autenticità, del capitolo regio fornita dall'infante Giovanni. E tale interpretazione trovava conferma in un'altra citazione dello stesso giurista ove, sul medesimo argomento, veniva detto: «ita fuit alias iudicatum, post multas disceptationes, in causa Vicari per serenissimum regem nunc Navarrae, tunc viceregem in hoc regno pro rege Ferdinando eius genitore, me presente. Et inde per aliam sententiam inter dominos Bartholomeum de Iuvenio et Manfridum de Alagona. Quae declaratio cap. Volentes per sen-

[150] *Perno,* XXIIII consilia, 44 rb.

[151] *Perno,* XXIIII consilia, 47 rb.

[152] *Perno,* XXIIII consilia, 45 vb.

[153] *Perno,* XXIIII consilia, 41 va-b.

tentiam habet vim legis, C. de legibus, l. fi., et probatur ff. eo., l. de quibus»[154]. In questa citazione il pensiero del Perno risulta espresso con grande precisione terminologica. Riferendosi alla sentenza del viceré egli, infatti, parla di *declaratio* operata *per sententiam.* Al giurista è assolutamente chiaro che spetta al principe fare le leggi; il tribunale, anche il più autorevole, può solo applicarle, trovandosi costretto a ricorrrere alla *potestas regia* in caso di grave e persistente dubbio sulla reale portata di una norma.

Attraverso gli scritti del medesimo Guglielmo Perno ci sono noti casi di sentenze assunte a precedente obbligatorio, ma, a ben guardare, si tratta, in effetti, sempre di provvedimenti regi che vengono ad inserirsi in un procedimento giudiziario.

Così, ad esempio, in materia di prescrizioni il giurista siracusano notava: «circa hanc tamen pragmaticam fuit noviter inter nos iudices Magnae Curiae deliberatum et disceptatum, an haberet locum stante male fide. Et dum ego fortiter tenerem quod non et in adversum essent omnes collegae, firmantes se ex iure communi quod firmare videtur haec constitutio. Et tamen trutinata et examinata disceptatione in Consilio domini viceregis, secundum meam opinionem declaraverunt et pronuntiaverunt hanc pragmaticam non obtinere stante malafide. Et ita fuit nobis mandatum ut id in decissionibus [sic] *causarum servaremus*»[155]. La citazione risulta di notevole interesse perché, oltre ad attestare un possibile contrasto fra i giudici della Gran Corte (peraltro espresso «fortiter»), ci fa conoscere come, sempre in caso di controversia sulla portata di una norma, non fosse, nella realtà, la sentenza dell'autorevolissimo tribunale d'appello (in questo caso il Consiglio viceregio) ad avere efficacia generalizzata bensì un espresso «mandatum» viceregio, cioé ancora una volta un espresso comando dell'autorità politica con poteri normativi. Il viceré, si badi, volendo che l'interpretazione espressa in via giudiziaria dal suo Consiglio avesse efficacia generalizzata, non si limitava a fare notificare la sentenza di riforma (che avrebbe, evidentemente, avuto valore solo limitatamente al caso in discussione), ma emetteva un apposito «mandatum», che potremmo definire una norma interpretativa.

Ancora una volta nessuna traccia di sentenze registrate per uso generale del foro, ma solo il ricorso a ricordi personali di un giurista che di sé può dire: «tot longissimis temporibus in 'Magna Curia' et Consilio Regio, cum diversis officiis et specialiter ut advocatus fiscalis et tandem ut iudex ipsius Magnae Regiae Curiae usque versatus sum»[156].

---

154 *Perno,* XXIIII consilia, cons. 14, 21vb.

155 *Perno,* XXIIII consilia, 48rb.

156 *Perno,* XXIIII consilia, cons. 24, 42rb.

Non diverso è il caso emergente a proposito dell'interpretazione da dare alla prammatica di re Martino sui beni dei ribelli. È sempre Guglielmo Perno – che sul punto notava «dicebam tunc contra hanc interpretationem» – a ricordare che la prammatica in questione «in Consilio viceregum eo tempore quo eram advocatus audivi a iudicibus Magnae Curiae quod indistincte a diu est intellecta ... iudices ipsi dicebant quod intellecta extitit et iudicata generaliter et indistincte»[157], nel senso che tutti i beni in possesso del ribelle fossero confiscabili, anche se di proprietà di terzi. Il sopraggiungere di una lettera di re Alfonso, nel corso di un processo intentato dal fisco contro Coluccio Tropea da Lentini, che precisava l'interpretazione da dare alla norma, aveva per effetto il cambiamento d'opinione del tribunale e «ita pronuntiatum fuit in Consilio viceregio et conclusum a iudicibus Magnae Curiae, me tunc presente. Quod ita semper fuit habita pro lege et est in viridi observantia et semper secundum hanc fuit iudicatum»[158]. Ancora una volta, non è una sentenza ad assumere valore cogente *erga omnes* bensì una *regia lictera* che, come precisava il giurista, era esplicitamente riferita «pro his ceterisque similibus» e, quindi, «habita pro et pragamatica [*sic*] generali, per l. fi., C. de legibus».

Si può affermare con assoluta tranquillità che se, certamente, in Sicilia fino a tutto il Cinquecento mancavano raccolte di sentenze fatte dalle corti o da privati ed aventi valore di precedenti vincolanti, è del pari vero che le *decisiones* del tribunale della Regia Gran Corte erano in qualche modo note e citate, seppure facendo ricorso ad esperienze personali. Le pronunzie del prestigioso tribunale venivano allegate come *auctoritates,* autorevolissime sì, ma certamente discutibili e non vincolanti per le corti giudicanti. Il ripetersi di pronunzie conformi poteva dar vita ad un *usus curiae* che però poteva essere mutato dal medesimo tribunale in qualsiasi momento e non seguito dalle altre corti, anche inferiori. E va altresì ricordato che la composizione della Gran Corte, limitata dal Trecento ai soli *iuris doctores,* mutava con cadenza periodica.

A giudicare dalla documentazione nota, dobbiamo dire che i registri di sentenze tenuti dal mastro notaio sembra assolvessero solo a compiti di natura 'amministrativa', ma non servivano né a documentare i contenuti delle singole *decisiones,* costituenti dei precedenti obbligatori, né a fornire una 'memoria' agli stessi giudici. Per la Sicilia non abbiamo notizie di tribunali creatori di norme o di una 'giurisprudenza vincolante' e nessuna citazione di sentenza pervenutaci appare tratta da registri di sentenze raccolte per esteso o annotate in sintesi nei dispositivi o regestate per 'massime'.

---

157 *Perno,* XXIIII consilia, 46vb - 47ra.

158 *Perno,* XXIIII consilia, 46va.

Solo a partire dalla fine del XVI secolo, conformemente ad un'abitudine già diffusa in tutta Europa, e che nel meridione aveva trovato l'esempio maggiore nell'opera di Matteo d'Afflitto, si afferma in maniera considerevole l'uso da parte dei giureconsulti e degli avvocati di supportare le loro argomentazioni allegando, insieme alle tradizionali *auctoritates,* anche le *decisiones* delle corti maggiori, e fra queste, naturalmente, soprattutto quelle della Regia Gran Corte.

La forte professionalizzazione della magistratura della Regia Gran Corte, che annoverava fra i suoi giudici solo i giuristi più illustri, contribuiva indubbiamente ad accrescere il prestigio delle decisioni del tribunale. Peraltro il carattere collegiale dello stesso ovviamente conferiva autorità a sentenze adottate col parere concorde dei noti giuristi.

È così che nella Sicilia dell'ultimo decennio del Cinquecento e della prima metà del Seicento si sviluppa e fiorisce una produzione tecnico-giuridica legata all'attività delle corti maggiori, per iniziativa dei più importanti giudici e giuristi che alle speculazioni teoriche sul diritto comune preferiscono le trattazioni professionali legate alla prassi forense.

Il proliferare delle raccolte edite di *decisiones,* specialmente del tribunale della Regia Gran Corte, sembra essere, ad un tempo, la conseguenza e l'origine del consolidarsi di una giurisprudenza dello stesso tribunale, che per il giurista è necessario conoscere.

A proposito dell'esecuzione delle sentenze sappiamo, ad esempio, che «hinc praticamus quod in causis similibus cepta executione sententiae infra annum potest exequi et expediri exequi ultra annum, videlicet infra decem vel triginta annos. Ita fuit decisum in causa vertente inter Francisciellam Brigandì et Dainotta et spectabilem d. Vincentium Romanum sincerissimum regium consiliarium»[159]. Ed ancora, in materia di consuetudini matrimoniali, apprendiamo che «nostrantes de regno inquiunt inter nobiles praesumi more graecorum, et ita decisum per Magnam Regiam Curiam in favorem Nicolai Rosolmino contra eius uxorem»[160].

L'autorità della giurisprudenza della Gran Corte sembra prevalesse nettamente anche su quella di giuristi come Pietro de Gregorio «quorum dicta in Regno habentur pro lege ut dixerunt doctores nostri regnicolae»[161]. Ed appare significativo che Garsia Mastrillo sostenga: «Blascus Lancea et Provinza in quibusdam allegationibus quas ad pennam habeo, ubi testantur ita servari in Magna Regia Curia, quidquid in contrarium dixerit Petrus de Gre-

---

159 *Cimino,* Praxis, §. 23, 51.

160 *Francesco Antonio Costa,* Consilia sive responsa iuris (Messanae 1629) c. 5, 73.

161 *Garsia Mastrillo,* Decisiones Consistorii Sacrae Regiae Conscientiae Regni Siciliae, I (Panormi 1619) d. 64, 137b.

gorio, cuius opinio in hoc non servatur et idem saepe sepius vidimus iudicatum in Magna Regia Curia his nostris temporibus et praecipue in causa donnae Margaritae et donnae Annae de Aragonia sororum ipsius ducis, qui stilus ultimus servari debet»[162]. Del pari risultano frequentissime le citazioni del tipo: «hanc esse opinionem communiter receptam secundum quam iudicamus quotidie in Magna Curia»[163] o «ista est practica Magnae Curiae ... et nos millies practicavimus in dicto tribunali»[164].

Ma, per quanto autorevole, nessuna pronunzia della Regia Gran Corte poteva assumere valore cogente. Assai chiaramente, ad esempio, lo stesso Mastrillo precisava che «sententia erat transacta in rem iudicatam et ... faciebat ius inter partes»[165] e Leonardo Cimino notava «et ita fuit decisum in causa baronis Pettinei contra illustrissimum de Gambacurta marchionem terrae Mottae die 11. martii 1608 ... et ita passim practicatur hodie per tribunalia»[166]. Dal che mi pare risulti assai evidente che le sentenze della Gran Corte avevano forza cogente solo fra le parti del giudizio, mentre i vari tribunali potevano adeguarsi alle soluzioni giudizialmente adottate da quella corte «passim». E, significativamente, lo stesso Cimino, ripetendo antiche posizioni della dottrina, affermava: «sententia autem definitiva principis lata super causa de qua plene cognoscit habet vim legis generalis, l. finali, C. de legibus»[167]. Anche se si poteva definire la «Magna Curia aequitatis mater» e si poteva affermare che «uti mater veritatis et aequitatis semper odit praescriptiones»[168], era evidente che anche la giurisprudenza costante di quel tribunale poteva essere messa in discussione fino a provocarne il cambiamento, anche adeguandosi alla giurisprudenza di un tribunale estero. È Garsia Mastrillo che osserva in materia di censi: «et communem opinionem dicit esse Blascus Lancea, super eadem bulla, et ibidem Saccanus, ubi refert ita semper temporibus suis fuisse iudicatum per Magnam Regiam Curiam ... et secundum predicta iudicavit Concistorium pro Ioseph Solito de mense iunii 1604 confirmando sententiam Magnae Regiae Curiae. Et alias fuit iudicatum in Sancto Offitio pro Octaviolo Burgio contra Iacobum Staiti. Est tamen advertendum quod hodie in Regno est recepta illa opinio ... et ita passim iudicatur novissime in supremis his tribunalibus, per decisionem doctissimi Octavii Corsetti»[169].

---

[162] *Mastrillo,* Decisiones, I, d. 1, 4b.

[163] *Garsia Mastrillo,* Decisiones Consistorii Sacrae Regiae Conscientiae Regni Siciliae, II (Panormi 1620) d. 295, 325b.

[164] *Mastrillo,* Decisiones, II, d. 295, 327b.

[165] *Mastrillo,* Decisiones, I, d. 52, 114a.

[166] *Cimino,* Sol ritus, c. 76, 126.

[167] *Cimino,* Praxis, §. 17, 13.

[168] *Intriglioli,* Decisionum aurearum, d. 7, 33b; d. 28, 82b.

[169] *Mastrillo,* Decisiones, I, d. 94, 199b.

Da tutto ciò sembrerebbe potersi ricavare che in Sicilia l'atteggiamento costante verso il precedente giurisprudenziale fosse simile a quello tenuto nei confronti di qualsiasi altra *auctoritas* e che la sua influenza derivasse dall'autorità del tribunale, dal prestigio dei giudici, da una prassi costante. Le sentenze della Regia Gran Corte, sia che fossero citate nella forma elaborata di una *decisio* edita a cura di un giurista che nella forma originale, erano allegate a sostegno di un'interpretazione sostenuta e mai come precedenti vincolanti, con forza pari alla legge.

Non sembra esistessero 'ruoli' delle sentenze della Gran Corte (come degli altri tribunali supremi del Regno di Sicilia) o sillogi ordinate 'ufficiali' e complete, ma solo alcune raccolte di *decisiones* selezionate, approntate da giureconsulti che avevano esercitato il giudicato, tenendo presente la propria esperienza ed il proprio contributo, e sostanzialmente costituenti delle opere letterarie – a destinazione prevalentemente praticistica – costruite sulla base delle sentenze. Nessuna delle sillogi siciliane di decisioni, peraltro, riusciva ad affermarsi e ad avere un'influenza sul sistema giudiziario locale come la raccolta delle *decisiones* di Matteo d'Afflitto per Napoli, che – come afferma il Cortese – riescono ad assurgere a «fonte primaria per il carattere quasi normativo gradualmente assunto»[170].

I giuristi siciliani, senza fare mai riferimento a repertori originali di sentenze o registri dei tribunali, a partire dagli inizi del Cinquecento, e con un notevole crescendo nei secoli immediatamente successivi, allegano sia le sentenze dei maggiori tribunali (riferendo di processi visti di persona o dei quali si aveva notizia) sia le *decisiones* edite raccolte dai giuristi del Regno, ma anche, ed in misura assai notevole, sentenze e decisioni dei grandi tribunali europei, dando prova della circolazione di una sorta di giurisprudenza 'sovranazionale' prodotta dalle corti più prestigiose, alla formazione della quale anche il tribunale della Regia Gran Corte non restò totalmente estraneo, almeno a giudicare dalla diffusione europea delle edizioni di raccolte di sue *decisiones*.

---

[170] *Ennio Cortese,* Sulla scienza giuridica a Napoli tra Quattrocento e Cinquecento, in: Scuola, diritto e società nel Mezzogiorno medievale d'Italia, a cura di *M. Bellomo,* I (Catania 1985) 131. Un dato che sembra confermato dalla circostanza che in un inventario di libri della biblioteca del *doctor iuris* messinese Giovanni Paolo d'Ancona († 1618) non si trovano opere significative di questa natura. Cfr. *Daniela Novarese,* Studi e cultura giuridica fra '500 e '600. La biblioteca di un giudice messinese, in: Studi e Diritto nell'area mediterranea in età moderna, a cura di *A. Romano* (Soveria Mannelli 1993) 165 - 7.

VII. *Vota* e *decisiones Magnae Regiae Curiae.* Le raccolte siciliane edite e loro diffusione

Il processo di stabilizzazione dei tribunali siciliani che era venuto maturando con la pubblicazione, nel 1569, della prammatica *De reformatione tribunalium* di Filippo II, che definisce la moderna struttura delle magistrature dell'isola, con l'affermazione dei tribunali della Regia Gran Corte e del Concistoro della Sacra Regia Coscienza, unitamente alla diffusione in tutte le regioni d'Europa della letteratura di natura giurisprudenziale, porta ben presto ad un fiorire anche in Sicilia di edizioni di *decisiones* dei maggiori tribunali locali, o meglio di un genere letterario che da quelle trae fondamento e pretesto.

La prima opera siciliana di tal genere data alle stampe è quella del giudice e professore universitario catanese Francesco Milanese († 1595), che metteva insieme in due volumi, rielaborandole, quaranta decisioni del tribunale della Regia Gran Corte in una silloge pubblicata a Venezia nel 1595, e quindi riedita ancora a Venezia nel 1596 e 1602, a Francoforte nel 1600 e a Palermo nel 1624.

Peraltro nei cinquant'anni dal 1600 al 1650 contiamo complessivamente circa 30 edizioni di *decisiones,* che diminuiscono a dieci nei successivi cinquant'anni[171]. Di queste edizioni oltre la metà riguardano sentenze della Regia Gran Corte.

Oltre alle *Aureae decisiones Magnae Regiae Curiae Regni Siciliae* del Milanese, abbiamo, infatti, le *Decisiones aureae Magnae Regiae Curiae Regni Siciliae* del giudice e professore catanese Niccolò Intriglioli († 1604) edite a Palermo nel 1609 e nel 1631; il primo volume delle *Decisiones Tribunalis Concistorii Sacrae Regiae Conscientiae Regni Siciliae* del giudice palermitano Giovan Francesco del Castillo († 1632) edite a Palermo nel 1613 e nel 1626, mentre il secondo volume, *cui ... accedunt aliquae notabiles decisiones et presertim Magnae Regiae Curiae,* viene edito, sempre a Palermo, nel 1622 ed un terzo volume di *Decisiones Magnae Regiae Curiae* cui si aggiungono *aliquae causarum delegatarum* è dato alle stampe, ancora a Palermo, nel 1629; le *Decisiones Consistorii Sacrae Regiae Conscientiae Regni Siciliae* del palermitano Garsia Mastrillo († 1620) in quattro volumi pubblicati a Palermo il primo nel 1606 (e ancora nel 1619 e nel 1623), il secondo nel 1610 (e poi nel 1620), il terzo nel 1621 e l'ultimo nel 1624

---

[171] Su questa produzione, analiticamente, *Romano,* Tribunali, 270 - 85 e, per precisi riscontri bibliografici ed essenziali notizie biografiche, Diritto e Cultura nella Sicilia Medievale e Moderna. Le edizioni giuridiche siciliane (1478 - 1699), con Prefazione di *A. Romano* e Introduzione di *M. A. Cocchiara* (Soveria Mannelli 1994) *ad v.*

(con riedizioni a Venezia, negli anni 1606, 1609, 1612, 1622 e 1624, a Spira nel 1615 e nel '19, a Lione nel 1621, a Colonia nel 1660). Vanno ancora ricordate le *Variarum forensium et practicabilium iuris resolutionum* del giudice palermitano Antonino d'Amato († 1653) edite a Palermo negli anni 1616 e 1627 (il I volume) e nel 1634 (il II volume), mentre della stessa opera si ricordano un'edizione veneziana del 1655 e due lionesi del 1656 e del 1668 ove i due libri sono editi in un unico volume; le *Tribunalium Siciliae decisae observationes* del giudice e professore messinese Mario Giurba († 1649) edite a Messina nel 1646 (e ancora ad Amsterdam nel 1652 e a Colonia nel 1688), e, dello stesso, i *Consilia seu Decisiones criminales* in edizione messinese del 1626 (riediti a Venezia nel 1626, a Genova nel 1645 e nel '54, a Vienna nel 1629 e a Napoli nel 1654) ed il primo volume delle *Decisionum novissimarum Consistorii Sacrae Regiae Conscientiae Regni Siciliae,* edite a Messina nel 1616 e a Palermo nel 1621 (ma anche a Venezia nel 1617, ad Amsterdam nel 1651, a Ginevra nel 1653, nel 1671 e nel 1675 e a Colonia 1654). A Palermo negli anni 1619, 1620 e 1635 vengono edite le *Decisiones novissimae Magnae Regiae Curiae supremique magistratus Regni Siciliae* del giudice palermitano Mario Muta († 1636), mentre delle *Decisiones supremorum huius Regni Siciliae tribunalium* del giudice catanese Mario Cutelli († 1654) il I volume viene edito sia a Messina che a Palermo negli anni 1632 e 1636 ed il II è dato alle stampe a Palermo nel 1652. Le *Decisiones criminales Magnae Regiae Curiae Regni Siciliae* dell'avvocato messinese Girolamo Basilicò († 1670) sono edite a Messina nel 1669 e ancora a Firenze nel 1691. A Palermo, nel 1684, è pubblicato il I volume delle *Disceptationes fiscales notis politicis illustratae et in supremis Siciliae Praetoris definitae* di Ignazio Gastone († 1693), mentre il II volume è pubblicato, sempre a Palermo, nel 1696 e, forse, ancora nel '99. Sempre nella capitale Ottavio Caracciolo e Lanza († 1670), nel 1641, pubblica le *Decisiones Regiae Curiae Praetorianae foelicis urbis Panormi* e Francesco Magretti († 1672), nel 1665, le *Iuridicae controversiae in causa taxationis dotium de paragio unica decisione resolutae per regiam Curiam Praetoris felicis urbis Panormi,* dando spazio e diffusione anche alla giurisprudenza di un tribunale cittadino (la Corte Pretoriana di Palermo).

Le varie raccolte risultano espressamente effettuate, almeno a quanto dichiarano gli autori, comunemente «ad utilitatem advocatorum, ad usum studendi et commodum practicorum et curialium» – come scriveva, ad esempio, Leonardo Cimino – e la loro diffusione si giustificava anche con il favore con cui erano accolte dagli operatori del diritto, che vi trovavano una casistica facilmente utilizzabile per cause analoghe nelle quali, peraltro, non era escluso potessero trovare come giudice proprio l'autore dell'opera.

La maggior parte delle decisioni attiene ad argomenti feudali, anche se non mancano raccolte integralmente dedicate alle vertenze penali (come, ad esempio, quelle di Giurba e Basilicò), fiscali (come, ad esempio, le *disceptationes* di Gastone) o in parte contenenti sentenze in materia di compravendite e censi (come, ad esempio, il II volume del Milanese).

La struttura delle opere è largamente simile, seppure non identica, sia per i criteri di selezione che di riproduzione del materiale. Normalmente sono riportate le sentenze delle quali il giurista ha avuto personale conoscenza come giudice, contribuendo alla loro redazione, o come avvocato (è questo il caso, ad esempio, delle *aureae decisiones* dell'Intriglioli). Le singole *decisiones,* rielaborate e ordinate, assomigliano da vicino a *consilia,* ai quali sono aggiunte in calce brevi sintesi delle rispettive sentenze. Talora, come ad esempio per i *Consilia seu decisiones criminales* del Giurba, la somiglianza è totale, presentando delle elaborazioni scientifiche dei casi completate da una sintesi del dispositivo delle sentenze. In alcuni casi si ha l'impressione che le varie *resolutiones* riproducano più propriamente dei *vota* espressi dai vari giudici, seppure rielaborati, con una notizia della sentenza finale[172] o anche delle *allegationes*[173]. In qualche caso la raccolta appare strutturata come un repertorio, per tema, e si concretizza in una silloge di *conclusiones* e di dottrina con chiare finalità processuali, come nelle *decisae observationes tribunalium* di Mario Giurba. Nel complesso i volumi di *decisiones* dei giuristi siciliani sembrano raccogliere gli esempi di un genere letterario nuovo che appariva come lo sviluppo del simile genere delle *allegationes,* assai diffuso nell'Italia meridionale, e non pare casuale che nei medesimi anni assieme alle edizioni delle *decisiones* fioriscano anche quelle delle *allegationes,* spesso limitate all'edizione di un solo processo[174].

Solo che mentre nelle *allegationes* si ha, di norma, la riproduzione integrale della memoria processuale allegata dal giurista nel giudizio (con possibile annotazione dei termini della sentenza), nelle *decisiones* le argomentazioni delle allegazioni sono riportate in sintesi (talvolta intersecando le ragioni espresse dalle parti) e viene lasciato più spazio alla sentenza riportata per esteso o, più spesso, in sintesi. Le *decisiones* pubblicate,

---

172 Assomigliano, ad esempio, a *vota* completati con l'aggiunta dell'esito del giudizio cui si riferiscono i Responsa decisiva (Panormi 1663) ed i Responsa legalia decisiva (Panormi 1665), di *Filippo Cammarata,* mentre ha più la natura di repertorio il Controversiarum forensium iudiciorum, in quibus variæ ac multiplices materiæ, tam ecclesiasticæ, quam prophanæ in utroque foro frequentius occurentes disceptantur ac resolvuntur, tomus primus, di *Giovan Battista De Grossis* (Catanae 1662).

173 Sembrano, ad esempio, assomigliare ad *allegationes* processuali i *consilia* e *responsa* di *Francesco Antonio Costa,* Consiliorum sive responsorum.

174 Cfr. *Romano,* Tribunali, 277 - 8; Diritto e cultura, *passim.*

comunque, non sono mai sentenze integrali (almeno a giudicare dai possibili raffronti con i fascicoli processuali corrispondenti)[175] e non corrispondono alle sentenze effettivamente emanate, se non nel dispositivo e nei dati relativi alle parti. Di fatto le *decisiones* si pongono come vere e proprie opere letterarie specialistiche per la redazione delle quali le sentenze costituiscono solo una base di lavoro, indispensabile per la costruzione di un'elaborata trattazione giurisprudenziale e dottrinaria. Nessun rapporto diretto, peraltro, sembra esistere fra *decisiones* edite, infarcite di citazioni di *leges* e di *auctoritates* ad opera dei curatori, ed i resoconti delle sentenze stilati dai cancellieri. Ancora più labile appare il rapporto fra *decisiones* e giuliane di sentenze e, comunque, in nessuna *allegatio* o *decisio* ho avuto modo di riscontrare indizi che portino a pensare alla consultazione di resoconti processuali scritti dai cancellieri. Tutte le raccolte edite, inoltre, sembrano riferibili all'iniziativa di privati (giudici-giuristi) e sono particolarmente dedicate all'uso forense «ad commodum practicorum et curialium Magnae Regiae Curiae Regni», mentre mancano notizie di repertori di sola giurisprudenza utilizzati da magistrati per finalità di ufficio o di raccolte fatte predisporre dal potere pubblico, anche se c'è da ritenere che le edizioni di *decisiones* dovessero risultare certamente gradite a tribunali e giudici per la loro intrinseca propensione a celebrare l'autorità della magistratura ed a favorire istanze conservatrici.

Relativamente numerose sono le edizioni dei *vota* espressi da giuristi-giudici nell'esercizio del proprio ufficio e dallo stesso magistrato, editi talvolta con un corredo di *iustificationes* aggiunte a fondamento dell'interpretazione di diritto sostenuta[176]. Non sempre tali *vota,* come spesso risulta dalle edi-

---

[175] Eccezionali si possono ritenere singole sentenze edite, in miscellanee o in fascicoletti autonomi, in forza dell'interesse della controversia cui si riferiscono. Ad esempio, si possono vedere: Decisio unica Magnæ Regiæ Curiæ et a Consistorio Sacræ Regiæ Conscientiæ confirmata in causa spolii de recenti vertente inter Nimpham Maia et Turrigrossa [...] contra Iacobum et Antoniam Bessio iugales, in *Maia I.,* Consultationum ... pars I. (Panormi 1631) 160 - 169 (ed anche in: *Maia I.,* Consultationum ... pars I. (Panormi 1656) 101 - 107); [Sentencia del Tribunal de la Gran Corte] Por don Francisco Ruffo Santa Pau, posseedor de el estado y marquesado de Licodia y principe de Scila, con don Ioseph Branciforti Barresi Santa Pau, principe de Butera, s.n.t.; *Giovanni Francesco Del Castillo – Rocco Potenzano – Simone Sitaiolo,* [Decisio in causa pro validitate testamenti Emanuelis Philiberti principis Sabaudiæ] Serenissimus Carolus Emanuel dux Sabaudiæ donavit, in: *Del Castillo G. F.,* Decisionum ... liber tertius (Panormi 1629) 260 - 281; *Sebastiano Giusino,* Decisio Tribunalis Magnæ Regiæ Curiæ Regni Siciliæ in causa successionis principatus Buteræ, cum dignitate magnatis Hispaniarum, Petrapertiæ et aliorum statuum ac feudorum vacantium ob mortem d. Donnæ Margaritæ ab Austria et Branciforte (Panormi 1662).

[176] Si vedano, ad esempio, *Vincenzo Agrigento – Pietro Amico – Pietro Morfino – Rocco Potenzano,* Iustificationes votorum Magnæ Regiæ Curiæ Regni Siciliæ in causa feudali possessoria ducatus Galterii, s.n.t. (ma Palermo 1640); *Marco Anto-*

zioni, sono stati assunti a base della successiva sentenza e c'è il sospetto che i testi siano stati abbondantemente rivisti, con l'aggiunta di vaste citazioni di dottrina e giurisprudenza, in occasione dell'edizione[177]. In tale forma i *vota* si distinguono assai poco dai *consilia* dei giuristi più tardi e, soprattutto, dai *responsa resolutiva* raccolti da alcuni giuristi a propria gloria e per l'utilità dei pratici[178]. Sostanzialmente non dissimili, anche se

---

nio Marchese, Iustificationes sententiæ datæ in causa petitionis vindicatoriæ et reintegratoriæ septem feudorum nuper erectorum in titulum baroniæ Asprimontis (Panormi 1632); *Mario Cariddi – Cataldo Fimia – Marco Antonio Marchese,* [Iustificationes sententiæ datæ] In causa petitionis vindicatoriæ et reintegratoriæ septem feudorum nuper erectorum in titulum baroniæ Asprimonti (Panormi 1637); *Ottavio Corsetto,* Iustificationes ... in quibus plenissime discutitur an Sindicus urbis Panormi possit pro defensione privilegii comparere et pro cive bannito, ut in iustitiam remictatur, pro terminando articulo contra Fiscum, quod non audiatur? et iudices possint causam terminare non obstante banno et pragmatica, quod iudices non auxilientur bannitis sub pœna in dicta pragmatica contenta?, in: *Baronio F.,* Consilia diversorum siculorum... (Panormi 1656) pp. 102 - 191.

177 I *vota* editi riguardano, in larga misura, controversie di rilievo. Alcuni esempi si possono leggere in: *Alfonso de Agraz – Pietro Amico – Rocco Potenzano,* [Vota in causa Castanie] Pendente in Consistorio Sacræ Regiæ Conscientiæ via appellationis... (s. n. t.); *Vincenzo Agrigento – Vincenzo Gianguereio – Rocco Potenzano,* [Vota in causa castelli Bruchule] In præsenti controversia inter d. Catherina Gantes... (s. n. t.); *Placido Carafa,* Votum decisivum sive definita resolutio pro d. Isabella Iurato Gonzales baronissa Castellucii domina Hyspanæ (Messanae 1654); *Mario Cariddi,* Motivum [in causa inter universitatem civitatis Saccæ, et Regio Fisco assidente, et ducem Montis Alti, baronem Carabi Sancti Bartholomei], in: *Cutelli M.,* Decisiones supremorum... (Messanæ 1632) 391 - 392; *Carlo Caruso,* Votum decisivum in materiam electionis prælati regularis (Panormi 1664); *Id.,* Votum in causa propria cum summario copiosissimo (Panormi 1655); *Mario Cutelli,* Votum [...] in causa baroniæ Asperimontis inter comitem Isnelli actorem ex una et ipsius baronem ex altera, una cum iustificationibus (s. n. t.); *Vincenzo Gianguercio – Baldassarre Maccagnone – Rocco Potenzano,* [Vota in causa super reductione ad Regium Demanium terræ Franchevillæ] In presenti controversia iam diu in hoc Tribunali Regii Patrimonii... (s. n. t.); *Gregorio Leonino,* Votum s. t. u. i. d. don Gregorii Leonini: Prior quidam obtenta superioris venia a Monasterio recedit, sperans inimicorum calumnias (Panormi 1682).

178 In Sicilia la letteratura consiliare non conosce una diffusione pari a quella del resto d'Italia. Fra le più note e consultate raccolte di *consilia* prodotte da giuristi locali, oltre ai già citati XXIIII consilia pheudalia di Guglielmo Perno, possiamo ricordare: *Francesco Baronio,* Consilia diversorum siculorum super privilegio felicis urbis Panormi, quod Fiscus non possit principaliter agere contra cives (Panormi 1656); *Ottavio Corsetto,* Consiliorum feudalium [...] volumen I. (Panormi 1616); *Id.,* Consilia feudalia et quæstiones forenses super ritu Magnæ Regiæ Curiæ Regni Siciliæ (Panormi 1646); *Francesco Antonio Costa,* Consiliorum sive responsorum iuris [...] volumen primum (Messanae 1629); *Niccolò Intriglioli,* Consiliorum seu responsorum liber primus (Messanae 1594); *Id.,* Consiliorum seu responsorum (Panormi 1632); *Luna,* Selecta diversorum; *Francesco Salerno,* Consiliorum sive responsorum iuris [...] liber primus (Panormi 1640; e Panormi 1643). Ai *vota* e ai *consilia* si possono altresì accostare, per contenuti e struttura, anche i *responsa deci-*

spesso più estese e, comunque, specificamente strutturate per essere allegate agli atti processuali con il fine di sostenere i diritti del proprio cliente, sono le *allegationes,* ora raccolte in sillogi[179] ora pubblicate singolarmente[180]. *Vota, responsa resolutiva, consilia, allegationes* si distinguono, comunque, dalle *decisiones* e per l'origine e per l'autorità. Essi, infatti, sono il prodotto dell'attività di un privato, avvocato o dottore di diritto che sia, con finalità di parte e con un'autorità strettamente connessa al prestigio dell'autore. Le *decisiones* riproducono, invece, (seppure non fedelmente, almeno per quello che ci è dato sapere) le pronunzie di una corte di giustizia e, costituendo in sé un 'precedente', propongono soluzioni di diritto prodotte *pro veritate* dall'autorità giurisdizionale, tanto più autorevoli quanto più alto è il livello del tribunale che le ha prodotte. Decisioni collegiali, talvolta adottate a maggioranza, che si distinguono dai *vota,* anche fortemente dissenzienti, espressi dai singoli giudici.

---

siva attestati, particolarmente, dalle sillogi di: *Filippo Cammarata,* Responsa decisiva [...] in quibus celebriores ac arduæ iuris conclusiones circa rem iurisdictionalem, beneficiariam, feudalem, iudiciariam, tutelarem, immunitatem ecclesiarum... [tomus primus] (Panormi 1663) e ... tomus secundus (Panormi 1665); *Placido Carafa,* Responsum resolutivum iurisdictionale et iustificatio [...] pro utriusque iuris doctore d. Iosepho Vassallo (Panormi 1667). Peraltro va notato che nelle fonti spesso si fa riferimento, senza distinzioni, ad un *responsum decisivum* e ad un *votum decisivum.*

179 Fra le raccolte di *allegationes* più note si possono menzionare quelle di: *Pietro Corsetto,* Allegationes pro Regio Fisco (Panormi 1628); *Giovan Filippo Costa,* Allegationum libri duo (Panormi 1613; e Panormi 1640); *Pietro De Gregorio,* Allegationes (Panormi 1600); *Giovanni Battista Romano Colonna,* Allegationes criminales contra Fiscum (Panormi 1656; Messanae 1658); *Giuseppe Scoma,* Allegationes ad intellectum statuti de insinuandis subiugationibus (Panormi 1663); *Id.,* Patrocinia Regii patronatus in variis causis, 4 v. (Panormi 1664 - 1686); *Giovan Filippo Testai,* Allegationes [...] in causis propriis coram diversis magistratibus disputatæ et decisæ [...] liber primus (Panormi 1613); *Id.,* Allegationes [...] in causis propriis coram diversis magistratibus disputatæ et decisæ (Panormi 1623); *Id.,* Allegationes [...] in causis propriis coram diversis magistratibus disputatæ et decisæ [...] liber secundus (Panormi 1640). Si può notare che le citazioni delle allegazioni di altri autori non erano molto frequenti in Sicilia, in special modo negli scritti di carattere scientifico-dottrinale.

180 È il caso, ad esempio, di: *Niccolò Cannizzaro,* Allegationes ... in causa vertente in Magna Regia Curia inter don Marium Buglio et Minafria, baronem Bifare, cum magno procuratore Regii Fisci (s.n.t.); *Rocco Potenzano,* Allegationes pro Regio Fisco [contra Augustinum et Petrum Rivalora fratres] (Panormi 1630); *Giuseppe Scoma,* Allegationes ad intellectum text. in l. hac edictali C. de secundis nuptiis et §. finalis Authent. de nuptiis in causa manutentionis possessionis bonorum hæreditariorum quondam illustris d. Vitalis Valguarnera principis Nixemi pro illustri d. Ioseph Valguarnera principe Nixemi [...] contra dominos d. Pontium et d. Franciscum Valguarnera filios primi matrimonii (Panormi 1679). A partire dagli inizi della fine del secolo XVIII anche nei massimi tribunali siciliani invarrà l'uso di produrre in giudizio, almeno nei processi di maggiore rilievo, le proprie allegazioni a stampa.

Nonostante la composizione della Regia Gran Corte e la sua autorità, anche nei momenti di maggiore crisi del potere politico e di decadenza delle istituzioni, questo tribunale non è fonte normativa a nessun livello. Esso ha il compito istituzionale di applicare le leggi, cosa che i giudici fanno cercando di trarre il massimo profitto. Accanto alle principali magistrature fioriva un'intensa attività di elaborazione pratica del diritto che assicurava un'efficace saldatura fra mondo della teoria e mondo della prassi, in assoluto più vivace di quello teorico-esegetico che viveva con alti e bassi intorno alle cattedre universitarie e spesso si disperdeva in sterili esercitazioni prive di reali agganci con la vita quotidiana. In questo quadro il ruolo principale assolto dalle raccolte di *decisiones* della Regia Gran Corte sembrerebbe essere quello di diffondere la conoscenza delle opinioni del tribunale stesso (peraltro selezionate da giudici ed avvocati interessati all'operazione per esigenze pratiche, economiche, cetuali e di prestigio) e di favorire il consolidarsi di una *communis opinio* e di uno *stilus curiae* quanto più uniformi possibile e d'impianto conservatore.

Certamente i giuristi siciliani conoscono la giurisprudenza delle maggiori corti europee, che citano tenendola in conto[181]. Quanto le decisoni della Regia Gran Corte del Regno di Sicilia fossero note *extra Regnum* è un'indagine, non priva d'interesse, che resta da fare non essendo significativo, se preso da solo, il dato editoriale che vede più raccolte di *decisiones* del tribunale siciliano edite all'estero.

181 Un dato che parrebbe confermato non solo dall'abbondanza delle citazioni di sentenze pronunciate dai più importanti tribunali europei ma anche dalla circolazione e dalla presenza di raccolte di decisioni di quelle corti fra i libri posseduti da giudici ed avvocati siciliani. Per un esempio, *Novarese*, Studi e cultura, 153 - 95.

GIANCARLO VALLONE

Corti feudali e poteri di giustizia nel Salento medievale

I. I tribunali feudali del Principe di Taranto e del Conte di Lecce

È noto che curie o *consilia* con competenza giurisdizionale si ebbero nei grandi potentati feudali, in specie francesi. Ed è ovvio che Gennaro Maria Monti, convinto che il Principato di Taranto fosse «un grande dominio» di tipo francese, cioè con autonomia quasi sovrana rispetto al potere monarchico centrale, valutò la *curia* giustiziale del Principato come una prova di tale autonomia o quasi sovranità; soprattutto quando, nel corso del Quattrocento, Gian Antonio Orsini del Balzo unì nella sua persona oltre al Principato di Taranto, di suo padre Raimondello (che l'ebbe nel 1399), anche la Contea di Lecce ereditata da sua madre, Maria d'Enghien (che ne fu investita nel 1384).

Un indagatore documentale come il Monti, ebbe di questa *curia* giustiziale soltanto notizie indirette; egli riuscì ad indicare appena una relazione del giurista leccese Giacomo Antonio Ferrari († 1587) riportata dal Summonte[1], e una sentenza del 1447 che Pietro Giannone, in una sua rara allegazione, attribuiva al *Consistorium Principis* orsiniano, ch'è anche l'unica attestazione d'un tal nome[2].

Dall'antica relazione, e da altre opere del Ferrari, si poteva ricavare sia la data della istituzione del tribunale: il 1402 (data rimasta assolutamente

[1] *G. A. Summonte,* Historia della città e del regno di Napoli III (Napoli 1675) 454 - 455 (lib. V).

[2] *G. M. Monti,* La condizione giuridica del Principato di Taranto, in: Annali nel Seminario giuridico-economico della R. Università di Bari, 2 (1928) 20 - 22; il Monti aveva già indicato questa sentenza in uno studio dell'anno precedente; e ne dette il testo completo, dal Giannone, in: Quattro chiarimenti, in: Japigia 3 (1932) 228 - 229, ch'è una risposta al primo intervento dell'Antonucci sul punto. Forse un riflesso fornisce il giurista secentesco Gian Girolamo Robertino: *G. Vallone,* Feudi e città. Studi di storia giuridica e istituzionale pugliese (Galatina 1993) 165, 180.

dubbia) sia la sua competenza in appello[3]. Questa era ribadita dal Cutolo e dal Vacca[4]. Su questa, ed altre convinzioni del Monti, intervenne con grande pregnanza ed intuito il magistrato Giovanni Antonucci. Egli sostenne che mancava ogni prova che il tribunale fu istituito nel 1402; e che avesse sede a Lecce; e che Raimondello Orsini avesse nel 1402 il mero e misto imperio (diciamo la giurisdizione civile e criminale); e che il tribunale avesse giurisdizione in grado d'appello.

Le conclusioni di questo dubbio metodico erano però positive: il Concistorio fu creazione posteriore al 1420, quando a Gian Antonio Orsini fu riconosciuto il doppio imperio; fu in origine «un organo consultivo», poi un tribunale feudale che giunse ad usurpare il grado d'appello[5]. La questione tacque per un decennio finché fu scovata una sentenza del 1438 emanata in

---

[3] In verità nella relazione edita dal Summonte, il Ferrari dice che il Concistorio fu istituito «per perpetuo giudice di tutte le città e castelle di quelle provincie», e solo dopo la morte dell'Orsini, re Ferrante «dispose dovesse essere in perpetuo giudice d'appellatione di tutti gli altri provinciali»; dunque si trattava di attribuzioni al nuovo organo regio, il Sacro Regio Consiglio Provinciale. Nell'altra opera del Ferrari, la *Apologia paradossica della città di Lecce* (scritta tra il 1576 e il 1586; ed. 1707; e 1710; n. ed. Cavallino 1977), si afferma invece che a questo tribunale istituito, si badi, da Gian Antonio Orsini «venivano le appellazioni di tutti gli stati suoi, né conveniva di appellarsi dopo loro ad altro maggior tribunale, eccetto che a lui» (p. 432). Più sopra il Ferrari però affermava che al Concistorio o «Consiglio» giungevano «tutte le cause di tutti gli stati suoi», ma che in grado d'appello interveniva una specie di consiglio di Maria d'Enghien, composto da Agostino Guarini e Everardo (= Berardo) Paladini (p. 425). Il testo del Ferrari è notoriamente interpolato, e non è escluso che tali interpolazioni risalissero, come dice anche Laporta nell'introduzione della ristampa, alla controversia celebre per le decime di S. Pietro in Lama; forse anche per queste notizie specifiche sul Concistorio, che con quella controversia avevano un nesso (la sentenza del 1447). Giuste osservazioni sul punto in *G. Antonucci,* Il «Concistorium Principis» degli Orsini di Taranto ›(1963), in: Almanacco Salentino 1970 - 1972 (Galatina 1972) 213 e 215.

[4] *A. Cutolo,* Maria d'Enghien (1929, Galatina 1972), 67 - 68; *N. Vacca,* La corte d'Appello di Lecce nella Storia (Lecce 1931); e, di nuovo *G. M. Monti,* Ancora sulla feudalità e i grandi domini feudali del Regno di Sicilia e sul Principato di Taranto, in: Rivista di Storia del diritto italiano 4 (1931) 541. L'unico accenno documentale che dichiara un potere sulle impugnazioni più che un grado d'appello posseduto dall'Orsini, peraltro assai dubbio e tardo, è nella opera cit. del Summonte vol. III 389 dove si afferma, in occasione della pace tra l'Orsini e Ferrante nel 1462, che il Principe «potesse tenere la giurisdizione sopra tutti i baroni, esistentino dentro del suo Principato, senz'altra appellazione al Re».

[5] *G. Antonucci,* Note critiche. Il «Concistorium principis» degli Orsini di Taranto, in: Japigia III (1932) 89 - 93; la risposta del *Monti* non si fece attendere, ed è nei ‹Quattro chiarimenti› cit.; alla quale seguì un rapido appunto di *Antonucci,* Il principato di Taranto, in: Taras 7 (1932, ma 1933) 3. Quindi toccò al *Monti* ribadire la sua idea: Altre ricerche sull'ordinamento giudiziario e finanziario angioino-aragonese, in: Annali cit. 8 (1, 1935) 19 - 22; ed infine, ancora all'*Antonucci,* Sull'ordinamento feudale del Principato di Taranto, in: Archivio storico per la Calabria e la Lucania 11 (1941) 35 - 40.

grado d'appello da «Berardus de Paladinis de Teramo legum doctor Reginalis et Principalis appellacionum Iudex» (un titolo già attestato per il 1425); e questa costrinse Antonucci ad una ulteriore revisione, in verità aderente alle sue anteriori interpretazioni[6]. Se c'è stata così ampia indulgenza alla bibliografia precedente è non solo per la sua qualità, ma anche per la difficoltà di entrare nel merito terminologico e documentale senza dare a ciascun il suo, e senza evidenziare l'intensa compenetrazione tra fatti e teorie.

Nonostante ciò, è addirittura sorprendente che anzitutto al Monti sia sfuggito l'atto del 12 maggio 1294 conservato nell'ormai perduto Reg. ang. 68, ma assicurato agli studiosi dalle indagini di Perrot e di Longnon[7]. In quest'atto, Carlo II d'Angiò concesse al figlio Filippo la «cognicionem et decisionem appellacionum» nel ducato d'Atene (infeudato a Gui II de La Roche).

La concessione è assolutamente unica che io sappia per tutta l'età angioina; e se ne capisce facilmente la logica: costituire a Filippo una supremazia ed influenza determinante nell'Oriente greco, ad un braccio di mare dalle coste pugliesi, perché Filippo era anche principe di Taranto. Tuttavia, dal tenore del documento, non c'è modo di estendere la concessione degli appelli anche ai feudi pugliesi di Filippo; e cioè al Principato. Invece, dalla documentazione che era d'uso, emerge ora notata per la prima volta, una sentenza del 26 gennaio 1363 emanata «in suppenna prope castrum Tarenti ubi curia regi solet» da «Rogerio de Flumine de Dyano Imperiali Appellationum iudice Principatus Tarenti at aliarum terrarum Imperialis Maiestatis»[8], cioè di Roberto principe di Taranto. Nella fattispecie si decideva avverso una sentenza emanata il 23 marzo 1362 dal capitano di Brindisi su alcuni beni immobili di titolo controverso. Il documento, lunghis-

---

[6] Il documento fu indicato da *L. G. De Simone,* cioè *E. Aar,* Gli studi storici in terra d'Otranto (Firenze 1888) 343, e ripreso da *N. Vacca,* La antiche magistrature e le antiche scuole universitarie di giurisprudenza in Lecce, in: Almanacco Forense Salentino (Galatina 1953) 17 - 26; quindi, nel 1953, il citato intervento di *Antonucci,* Il «Concistorium principis» etc. L'originale si legge nel ms. *Codice diplomatico brindisino* (trascritto da A. de Leo e conservato in Biblioteca «de Leo» di Brindisi) vol. III (B. 59) c. 139r - 143r ed è tuttora inedito.

[7] *Ch. Perrat-J. Longnon,* Actes relatifs a la principauté de Morée 1289 - 1300 (Paris 1967) 83 - 85. In un primo tempo il re Carlo II s'era riservato gli appelli dal Principato d'Acaia e dal Ducato d'Atene; poi, con un ripensamento attestato nello stesso documento, concesse al Principe di Taranto la cognizione degli appelli dal Ducato. Potere questo che non è tra quelli resi al Principe di Acaia nella sanatoria dei conflitti istituzionali del 1296: nr. 191 (163 - 165). La complessità del problema si deduce anche dal distacco che il *Monti* usa nell'esegesi del capit.196 delle *Assise di Romania* nelle: Ricerche sul dominio angioino in Grecia (1933), in: Nuovi studi angioini (Trani 1937) 634.

[8] Codice diplomatico brindisino II (di *A. de Leo,* a c. di *M. Doria Pastore;* Trani 1964) 202 - 211 (nr. 80): cfr. *Aar,* Gli studi 330.

simo, propone una «diffinitiva sententia» (nel senso di non interlocutoria), ed è fondamentale per ricostruire la procedura assai articolata, e con diverse citazioni di *leges*, adottata in quest'importante corte feudale[9].

Per molti versi, questo *iudex appellationum* del Principato, sembra esprimere lo stesso potere, competenza e istituzione del «reginalis et principalis appellationum iudex generalis» attestato nel 1425, e operante nel suo officio nel 1438 (qui con sede in Lecce, avverso sentenza del capitano di Brindisi).

L'istituzione però s'era ampliata perché accoglieva gli appelli dai feudi principeschi (di Gian Antonio Orsini principe di Taranto) ma anche dalla contea di Lecce cioè dai feudi della regina Maria d'Enghien.

È noto che madre e figlio ebbero gestione concorde dell'amministrazione; ma la titolarità dei feudi rimase divisa finché Maria visse, cioè fino al 1446; ed anche allora l'unione sembra rimanesse personale in testa all'Orsini. Ed anche la giustizia di gravame, benché esercitata da un magistrato unico, è definita con doppia derivazione «reginale» e «principesca». Senonché, come non conosciamo alcun privilegio di concessione degli appelli al Principe di Taranto, in quanto tale, nemmeno conosciamo un'analoga concessione per i Conti di Lecce.

C'è in verità un altro documento, anche se non tarantino, che ci costringe a riflettere. In una controversia su un ortale oggetto di prelazione, e nella quale era intervenuta una prima sentenza del baglivo di Lecce dell'otto III 1335, intervenne appello (già in corso il 16 marzo) innanzi al vicario generale del Conte di Lecce, ch'era allora Gualtieri VI di Brienne duca d'Atene. Non è chiaro, per l'incompletezza del documento, se questa «causa appellationis» fu o meno definita in sentenza; è probabile di sì. Certo è che una delle parti si rivolse al Brienne (presente a Lecce l'otto settembre 1335), perché intervenisse in via di grazia (ed è problematico il titolo con il quale il Conte di Lecce e i Principi di Taranto, usavano questo potere, che in dottrina si riteneva esclusivo del sovrano).

Gualtieri, con una sua lettera, accettò la richiesta, delegando, ma in via di grazia, alla decisione (che intervenne il 23 IX 1335), Jean de Crécy suo camerario a Lecce[10]. Ora, lo stesso Gualtieri definisce «causa appellatio-

---

[9] In un altro atto del 14 XII 1371, lo stesso «Rogerius de Flumine» è «prothonotarius nostrus et iudex» del Principe: Codice 265 (nr. 105).

[10] Le pergamene di San Giovanni Evangelista in Lecce (a c. di *M. Pastore,* intr. *P. F. Palumbo;* Lecce 1970) 55 - 59. Anche nel Principato di Taranto avveniva qualcosa di simile. Il monastero di Santa Maria Maddalena di Castellaneta subì uno spoglio, e l'abatessa supplicò il principe di intervenire. Filippo I, il 25 VI 1304 delegò il suo giustiziere ad apprestare un «remedium iuris iuxta formam sacri regni capituli» ma «sine strepitu et figura iudicii absque oblacione libelli». A sua volta il Giustiziere «Henricus de Hervilla» commise il 18 X 1304 l'incarico agli *iudices* di Castellaneta, che il 14 I 1305 emisero sentenza: *E. Mastrobuono,* Castellaneta e i suoi documenti dalla fine del secolo XII alla metà del XIV (Bari 1969) nr. 39

nis» quella svolta dal suo vicario avverso la sentenza del baglivo di Lecce; ma abbiamo chiarissimi elementi per intendere l'espressione in modo diverso da quello apparente. L'appello, o meglio impugnazione, dal baglivo al feudale era in via generale una novità introdotta dalle riforme istituzionali della prima età angioina, e dalla concessione generalizzata della giurisdizione civile ai feudatari.

È certo però che il barone, in quanto ormai giudice «ordinario», poteva istituire un baglivo nelle sue terre, e ne accoglieva le impugnazioni, in applicazione tra l'altro del principio di diritto comune «a dato iudice appellabitur ad eum qui dedit» (quasi che l'attributario della giustizia incaricasse altri a giudicare), dunque si tratta d'una scissione interna al primo grado di giurisdizione civile, che consentiva oltretutto di non turbare la logica magistratuale delle impugnazioni ulteriori, così come fissata nel *Liber Augustalis*[11]. Tuttavia, questa interpretazione può valere anche per il Principato di Taranto, dove è attestato uno «iudex appellationum» fin dal 1363? E dove cioè il *nomen* dell'appello è speso, non occasionalmente, per definire la fase di gravame avverso sentenze baiulari, ma proprio per definire un'istituzione giurisdizionale del Principato? Nella fattispecie del 1363 (e in quella del 1438) questo magistrato giudica avverso sentenza del capitano di Brindisi. Già questo è un problema, perché alla figura istituzionale del capitano sono state dedicate solo pagine evanescenti. Sembra però di intuire che tra fine Duecento e inizio Trecento la magistratura baiulare si rafforzò come centro d'affluenza della giurisdizione civile, tanto che la dottrina coeva tentò di limitarne l'espansione. Nel corso del Trecento invece, il baglivo regredì, a quanto pare, ad una competenza di natura genericamente annonaria integrandosi funzionalmente (cioè anche specificandosi in competenza) con gli *iudices* cittadini, mentre il titolare della piena giurisdizione sembra divenisse appunto il capitano[12], che nelle città feudali è di

(445 - 448). Ancora, Filippo II accolse una supplica da Tarentini e Castellanetani, per una questione di confini con Laterza, e commise una «causa summarie inquisitionis» ad alcuni suoi fiduciari, che fecero relazione «Maiestati nostra... et Consilio nostro»; il Principe decise il 28 V 1373: *M. Perrone,* Storia documentata della città di Castellaneta e sua descrizione (Noci 1896) 35 - 40. Sembra quest'ultimo, a differenza di quello del Brienne, intervento in via di grazia che non segue o s'innesta in procedimenti giudiziari (cfr. anche infra nt. 20).

[11] *G. Vallone,* Iurisdictio domini, 166s e in generale 102s.

[12] Le incerte attestazioni normative del capitano, cominciano a convergere nella figura, poi usuale, di magistrato cittadino dalla fine del Duecento in poi. Ed è ovvio che la letteratura giuridica iniziasse a notarlo, già consolidato, solo verso la metà del Trecento: così Luca da Penne († 1390?) lo definisce: «vocantur hodie capitanei, quia per annum capiunt administrationem» in Cod. 10, 72 (70 *de susceptoribus*), 4 *(neminem)* nr. 10 (ed. Lione 1582) 346a. Altre indicazioni in *Vallone,* Feudi, 12; e, con confusioni, in *R. Pescione,* Corti di giustizia nell'Italia meridionale (Napoli 1924) 173 - 187.

nomina baronale. Il capitano, dunque, non sostituì le preesistenti magistrature locali, e creò perciò il problema del coordinamento. È solo una congettura, ma plausibile, che proprio la specificazione delle competenze negli «iudices dati» (mi limito alle località feudali) creasse l'esigenza di un magistrato sovraordinato, il capitano, delegato dal feudale a ricevere tutte le impugnazioni «ad eum qui dedit», ch'era appunto il feudale. In effetti le tracce antiche del rapporto tra baglivo e capitano, sembrano abbastanza compatte nell'esprimere questa struttura d'impugnazione. Tuttavia, è dal feudale che potevano sorgere ulteriori complicazioni, perché se questi subinfeudava, la concessione istituiva anche nel concessionario poteri giustiziali, e per lo più di livello e natura baiulare. In questo caso, che è frequente e non di rado complesso, perché il suffeudo è spesso una unità abitativa, il giudice «dato» dal primo feudale a coordinamento del feudo, sembra divenire a lume di logica (e purtroppo solo con essa) il capitano; e quindi la sua sentenza avverso sentenza del baglivo suffeudale, può essere di nuovo impugnata «ad eum qui dedit» cioè davanti al barone o a un suo delegato. Questa delega a giudicare l'impugnazione (così come esercizio giustiziale diretto del barone) sembra insomma in entrambi i casi (feudo semplice e feudo con suffeudi), il limite ultimo, o alto, del primo grado (o delle prime cause) della giurisdizione feudale. Col tempo, la delega divenne poi invalicabile (nel senso di istituire un limite in più agli abusi) quando fu proibito ai feudali l'esercizio personale della giustizia[13]. Al di sotto d'un tal limite, però, abbiamo visto di quanto la scindibilità del primo grado potesse complicarsi. A parziale conforto, va detto che fino all'età aragonese questo fenomeno poté circoscriversi alla sola giurisdizione civile, perché le concessioni di doppio imperio (che includevano la giurisdizione penale) furono fin'allora abbastanza rare anche se i Principi di Taranto l'ebbero fin da Manfredi[14]. Cosicché, lo *Iudex appellationum* del Principato di Taranto, interpretato sullo sfondo di queste logiche complesse, serviva bene l'esigenza di una riorganizzazione istituzionale di tutte le istanze interne, si ricordi, al primo grado di giurisdizione d'un potentato articolatissimo come quello ionico. Il *nomen* poi, va preso nello stesso senso nel quale è stata intesa la «causa appellationis» dichiarata, a Lecce, dal duca d'Atene. Insomma, sono impugnazioni o, meno precipuamente, appelli interni al primo grado; il secondo grado si svolgeva invece innanzi la magistratura regia (appello esterno o seconde cause), salvo che non fosse esso stesso infeudato; ma per tutta l'età agioina tali infeudazioni non emergono nel Regno meridionale. E se anche apparissero, sarebbe comunque difficile

---

[13] Forse nell'ultimo trentennio del Quattrocento: *Vallone,* Iurisdictio, 155 - 156 e nt. 107. L'abuso frequente (che sopravvisse) era di impugnare dal delegato al feudale.

[14] *G. Vallone,* Evoluzione giuridica e istituzionale della feudalità, in: *AA. VV.,* Storia del Mezzogiorno IX (Napoli 1993) 94.

riconoscerle *ex actis;* cioè distinguere una qualunque delle fasi del primo grado (innanzi al baglivo feudale o suffeudale o al capitano o al delegato baronale etc.) dal secondo grado feudale. Così come sarebbe pericoloso tentare la distinzione a secondo della magistratura procedente. L'unica chiave resterebbe allora la lettera dei privilegi di concessione, che, se mai fossero stati emanati, certo non sarebbero scomparsi nel nulla. Ora, è vero che la concessione del 1294 per l'Oltremare (questa sì relativa al secondo grado) invoglia a considerare possibile, o maggiormente possibile, l'espansione della attribuzione delle «seconde cause» anche alle terre pugliesi del Principe (e poi, in età orsiniana, anche alla contea di Lecce), magari nella forma di un abuso o usurpazione in qualche modo più fondata. Così come si possono continuare a immaginare privilegi a noi ignoti. Eppure, non lo credo.

In un documento importante del 1347 il principe Roberto riconosceva che la giurisdizione civile (e cioè il potere «ponendi baiulos et removendi..., ordinandi iudices, regendi Curiam, ponendi bannum, imponendi multam...») di Casalrotto in distretto di Mottola, cioè *de principatu Tarenti* spettava al monastero benedettino della S. Trinità di Cava; ma la giurisdizione penale doveva esservi personalmente e inderogabilmente esercitata dai giustizieri principeschi[15]. Più che la doppia feudalità giustiziale sullo stesso territorio (fatto non insolito) noterò tre cose: che i poteri dei Benedettini, relativi alle giustizia civile, sono rigidamente incentrati nella figura del baglivo, onde intuiamo la retrostante magistratura principesca del capitano (in Mottola) destinataria dell'impugnazione; che la giurisdizione principesca in penale è subito esercitata dai giustizieri; che Roberto dichiara di avere in Mottola e nel Principato «merum et mixtum imperium ac gladii potestatem»[16]. Non c'è margine sufficiente per dedurre che al giustiziere spettasse la giurisdizione penale e all'asse baglivo-capitano quella civile; ma è chiaro già per la logica istituzionale professata dal documento, che le due magistrature esprimevano lo stesso livello di attribuzione: quello del primo grado o «prime cause». Né il Principe disponeva di altro; se avesse avuto il privilegio delle «seconde cause» (cioè della prima causa d'appello) l'avrebbe detto: egli invece si dichiara posessore solo del doppio imperio.

---

15 *G. Guerrieri,* Possedimenti temporali e spirituali dei Benedettini di Cava nelle Puglie. Terra d'Otranto (Trani 1900) 218 - 221.

16 In teoria, si potrebbe sostenere che il *mixtum imperium* rientrava nella giurisdizione civile e dunque nella competenza baiulare: così *Marino da Caramanico,* gl. *Locorum* in *const.* I 65 *Locorum baiuli* (ed. *Cervone,* Napoli 1773) 126a; e così anche Andrea da Isernia, commentando lo stesso brano; perciò che il Principe si attribuisca, su Mottola e distretto, proprio il misto imperio, quando dovrebbe riconoscerlo ai Benedettini, varrebbe a fondare la retrostante giurisdizione del capitano (che, comunque sussisteva certamente). Tuttavia per la complessità della materia, anche solo dal punto di vista teorico, vedi *Vallone,* Iurisdictio, 21 - 25.

Si dirà che quel privilegio poteva essere intervenuto dopo il 1347 e prima di quel 1363 quando apparve lo *iudex appellationum;* ed invece no. Nel celebre inventario di beni e diritti che il Principe Gian Antonio Orsini aveva in Taranto, gli si riconosce tra l'altro «utile dominium ipsius civitatis et civium et habitantium in ea ac cum mero et misto imperio et gladii potestate, prout latius continetur in reginalibus privilegiis»[17].

Se l'Orsini aveva solo questo in Taranto e nel suo distretto (ove c'era una terra come Martina), non poteva avere di più nel Principato; ed anzi nelle singole località poteva avere meno, come a Casalrotto dove s'è visto che il Principe di Taranto aveva solo la giurisdizione penale, o come a Laterza, dove la «curia Principalis» dell'Orsini disponeva della «gabellam baiulationis ac bancum justitiae et cognitionem causarum civilium»; il 12 VIII 1429, poi, vendendo all'Ospedale cateriniano di Galatina la terra di Bagnolo, Orsini cedette le cause civili («bancum iustitiae ad recognitionem causarum civilium») trattenendo però le cause penali, cioè il doppio imperio *cum gladii potestate,* e nell'assenso di Giovanna II del 21 III 1430 si concede anche questa riserva «sicut Princeps ipse habet in ipsis terris et locis suis»[18]. Non si dice di più. Ed anche l'idea dell'usurpazione non regge; anzitutto perché negli inventari più tardi il possesso delle seconde cause sarebbe stato censito, al fine ad esempio di vantarne l'acquisto prescrittivo; e, inoltre, il possibile conflitto con la magistratura regia avrebbe anch'esso lasciato tracce[19].

---

17 Il documento è edito da *G. Cassandro,* Un inventario dei beni del Principe di Taranto, in: *AA. VV.,* Studi di storia pugliese in onore di G.Chiarelli II (Galatina 1973) 6 - 57. Altra, parziale, in: Regolamenti contenuti nel Libro Russo del 1400 sulla pesca dei mari di Taranto... (Taranto 1877). Cassandro (p. 7) data il documento tra il 1420 e il 1435; tuttavia una glossa antica al rito 17, 1 della R. Camera della Sommaria, accolto nel commento di Goffredo de Gaeta (ed. Napoli 1681, p. 447) cita un capitolo d'un inventario orsiniano del 13 I 1452 (data errata?), e questo capitolo è identico a quello edito dal Cassandro (p. 30); *Aar,* Gli studi storici 290.

18 Biblioteca Provinciale di Lecce (= BPL) ms. 281 fs. 4. È una copia più volte ritrascritta (la più antica nel 1514) di un antico inventario non datato. I documenti del 1429 e del 1430 si leggono, per estratti in *B. F. Perrone,* Neofeudalesimo e civiche Università in Terra d'Otranto, I (Galatina 1978) 179 - 182 e per regesto in *M. Montinari,* Galatina antica. L'Ospedale di Santa Caterina (Galatina 1941) XIX, XX (doc. 35 e 38). Bagnolo era feudo *in capite a Rege* (e non suffeudo quaternato) come si ricava, tra l'altro, dalla prestazione del *servitium* o *adoha* alla Regia Curia (data l'epoca). Parrebbe invece suffeudo del Principato il casale di Lizzano che Orsini vendette il 16 II 1439 a Francesco de Agello con riserva del «feudali servitio seu adoha»: *A. Pagano,* Storia di Lizzano (Lecce 1994) 176 - 177.

19 Un conflitto, cioè, con il Giustiziere provinciale e con la Gran Corte della Vicaria, (cioè anche con le altre figure istituzionali della sua complessa genealogia): *Vallone,* Iurisdictio, 170 - 171; e *G. Vallone,* Evoluzione giuridica, 96 - 99. Si comprende bene che già la articolazione complessa della giurisdizione feudale di primo grado, avrebbe reso comunque spinoso il contenzioso con la magistratura regia, se non fosse che, *ex lege,* le attribuzioni di questa erano abbastanza larghe da

L'età orsiniana, dunque, emerge anche qui, nell'esame dell'epoca anteriore, a dimostrazione d'una certa continuità istituzionale nel Principato di Taranto e poi nella Contea di Lecce[20]. E già è possibile anticipare che la maggiore quantità di documenti relativi a quell'età non risolve tutti i dubbi, ed anzi forse li aumenta, anche per l'ambivalenza di alcuni termini basilari come, s'è visto, quello di *appellatio*.

II. Il tribunale degli Orsini

Anzitutto va detto che il termine *curia* o *consilium* o *consistorium* ha polivalenza di significati, sia che si tratti di organi regi ovvero feudali: essi possono cioè indicare il nucleo amministrativo generale del sovrano, o del feudatario; o anche la loro corte di giustizia. Nel 1451, quando, per certo, esisteva già il tribunale orsiniano, la *curia* generale del principe si componeva almeno di un «cancelliere», Giacchetto Mangalabeto di Gallipoli; di un «erario», Rinaldo de Lago di Otranto; di un «senescalco», Bartolomeo Prato e di altri minori[21]. Una corte feudale di giustizia era naturalmente possibile solo nel caso che il feudatario avesse poteri di giustizia; ma l'ipotesi di un feudale senza quelli di giustizia civile, fu nel Mezzogiorno d'Italia, e dall'età angioina, del tutto teorica[22]. D'altra parte, è vero che la celebre promessa d'investitura, nel marzo 1399, di re Ladislao a Raimondello non parla di giustizia; ma è anche vero che di lì a due mesi, nel maggio, si concesse il Principato a Raimondello «prout ipsum tenuerunt» i principi suoi predecessori, che per certo ebbero il doppio imperio[23]. I dubbi ad ogni

---

consentire una recezione elastica dell'appello avverso sentenze feudali; insomma c'era *in nuce* quanto bastava a fissare il principio, piuttosto cinico, per cui tutte le sentenze feudali intercorse ne valevano una: *Vallone,* Evoluzione, 100 e rinvii.

[20] La Contea di Lecce potrebbe aver avuto un'espansione istituzionale in analogia del Principato tarantino con il matrimonio di Raimondello Orsini e Maria d'Enghien nel 1384 o 1385, pur rimanendo i due feudi nominalmente separati. Nemmeno sappiamo quando con esattezza i Conti di Lecce ebbero il doppio imperio; per certo nel 1275 Carlo Id'Angiò lo rifiutò a Ugo di Brienne: *Vallone,* Evoluzione, 94. Il 24 IV 1323 Gualtieri VI fu istituito «capitaneum ad guerram» nella provincia di Terra d'Otranto con il doppio imperio, ma niente di più: *G. Guerrieri,* Gualtieri VI di Brienne duca d'Atene e Conte di Lecce (Napoli 1896) 53 - 54; qui alle pp. 58 - 65, un atto del 1344 dà notizia di un'interessante controversia sui confini tra Gualtieri conte di Lecce e il Principe di Taranto, risolta mi pare, in via non contenziosa.

[21] *G. Vallone,* Il testamento di Nicolò Pagano Arcivescovo di Otranto (1424 - 1451), in: Ricerche e studi in terra d'Otranto 5 (1991) 72 nt. 28.

[22] *G. Vallone,* Iurisdictio, 102s.

[23] *Cutolo,* Maria d'Enghien, 51 - 53, 57 e 54; anche il documento del marzo, parla di «tenimentis, territoriis, aliisque iuribus, iurisdictionibus et pertinentiis eorum», frase che, se non fosse per l'epoca, e per il suo contenuto (si concedono altri feudi contenuti nel Principato) parrebbe richiamare quanto in *Vallone,* Iurisdictio, 80 - 94.

modo, cadono anche formalmente per il figlio di Raimondello, appunto Gian Antonio Orsini del Balzo.

Noi conosciamo il privilegio del 4 maggio 1420 con il quale Giovanna II confermò, all'Orsini, Taranto, Ostuni, Otranto, Gallipoli, Polignano, Nardò e tutte le altre «civitates, terras, castra et loca» di Terra d'Otranto e di Bari che «occupata detinentur» dal de la Marche, marito di Giovanna II. Il documento è indirizzato ai prelati, magistrati, baglivi e giudici delle località predette, con l'intimazione di obbedire «ad dictum merum et mixtum imperium cum gladii potestate spectantibus praefato Principi seu eius locumtenentibus, officialibus vel ministris»[24]. Tuttavia, nonostante questo fondamento di legittimità, almeno in prima istanza, del potere giustiziale orsiniano, i problemi restano tutti: (attribuzione del grado d'appello; impugnabilità ulteriore alle corti regie; competenza concorrente della magistratura regia etc.). Prima di entrare in questi temi, sarà bene censire il materiale a nostra disposizione, certo più numeroso, e perciò più fruibile che per l'età angioina.

Anzitutto una sentenza del 26 luglio del 1403; «Maurus de Sancto Ippolito» di Gallipoli, maestro razionale e «consiliarius» di Maria e Raimondello, viene da questi delegato a decidere una controversia sui luoghi di fida tra le *universitates* di Oria e Mesagne[25]. Nel 1425 Maria d'Enghien delega alla decisione su lite per la fida degli animali tra le due predette località, Berardo Paladini e Roberto de Noha «reginalis et principalis appellationum iudex generalis». La lite, introdotta con supplica dei mesagnesi a Maria, fu decisa da delegati il 14 luglio 1425 in Mesagne[26]. In quel torno

---

[24] *L. Pepe,* Il Libro Rosso di Ostuni (Valle di Pompei 1888) 113 - 114; chi volesse una descrizione, al 1431, dei possedimenti feudali di Gian Antonio, legga il documento edito in *M. Perrone,* Storia documentata (Noci 1896) 139 - 140. Il documento del 1420 sembra piuttosto una concessione relativa alle terre del Principato ancora occupate dal de la Marche e consegnate, appunto allora, all'Orsini. Una tradizione non ignobile dal Coniger in poi vuole infatti che il Principato gli fosse concesso (con l'inclusione di Brindisi) nel 1407, e poi nel 1417 dopo che Giovanna II l'aveva dato al de la Marche (a quest'episodio sembra adattarsi il frammento edito in *P. Coco,* Francavilla Fontana nella luce della storia (Taranto 1941) 80 nt. 2). Il documento del 1431 sembra comunque incompleto. Nascondo in nota la congettura che la data istitutiva del 1402, data dal Ferrari, possa essere nata sommando refusi ed errori, dalla lettura del documento edito poi dal Pepe.

[25] *A. Profilo,* La Messapografia ovvero memorie istoriche di Mesagne, II (Lecce 1875) 205 - 209; e *Antonucci,* Il «Concistorium», 214. Dunque nell'età di Raimondello Orsini (1399 - 1406) il meccanismo della delega sembra attestato; e una controversia tra *Universitas* tarantina e capitolo della cattedrale fu sollevata innanzi al Principe, e questi delegò alla decisione Guglielmo de Latinis, da Firenze, vicario generale della diocesi; costui, «de commissioni sibi facta» sentenziò; la decisione non fu appellata e passò in giudicato. La controversia poi riesplose, come si evince da una pergamena del 4 V 1409 conservata nell'archivio capitolare di Taranto (= ACT, V D) presso la Biblioteca vescovile della città.

[26] *A. Profilo,* La Messapografia, 209 - 215, e *Antonucci,* Il «Concistorium», 214.

d'anni nacque una controversia di confini tra Laterza e Castellaneta, che fu risolta, forse previa supplica a Gian Antonio Orsini che la stornò in giustizia, con processo e sentenza. Però, con privilegio da Andria del 29 VIII 1425, l'Orsini stravolse la decisione «non obstante processu et sententia», che fu revocata[27]. Poi tocca a Taranto e Oria litigare per i confini; il Principe delega il suo «consiliarius» Ciccarello Montefuscolo di Nardò e i capitani delle due città alla ricognizione; la delega (o la sua conferma) è del primo settembre 1432; la sentenza, letta dal Principe personalmente è, pare, del 1434[28]. Quindi la citata sentenza del 1438, pronunziata a Lecce in appello avverso la sentenza del capitano di Brindisi da Berardo Paladini «reginalis et principalis appellacionum iudex».

Abbiamo ancora la sentenza del 1447 che ci è giunta indirettamente grazie alle pagine di Giannone e alle ricerche del Monti. Segue una vicenda più documentata: nel 1447 Raguccio de Noha, sostenendo che la sua masseria di Torricella era «feudo nobile» (e quindi soggetta al *militare servitium)* e perciò sottratta alle pretese fiscali dell'amministrazione leccese (e cioè la soggezione alle collette) che includeva invece Torricella come masseria nel suo territorio, avanzò supplica al principe Orsini a che gli si riconoscesse la sua richiesta; ma il Principe addì 17 novembre 1447 aggiunse una «decretatio» alla supplica, e delegò alla decisione il capitano della città e contea di Lecce che, nella persona di Giovanni Effrem, sentenziò il 4 gennaio 1449[29]. Infine posso indicare una nuova sentenza, in originale, del 9 maggio 1453.

Il documento, ampiamente rifilato va, a mio avviso, ricostruito così: nel luglio 1451 comparve, dinanzi al Principe, Greco Tomacelli (quest'è

---

27 Archivio di Stato di Lecce (= ASL), *Scritture Univ. Laterza* fsc. 1, fs. 3, 21 c. 20r - 22v. Altro esempio di stravolgimento, in via di grazia, d'una sentenza precedente, è nel privilegio del 25 ottobre 1446 che l'Orsini indirizzò ai Galatinesi: *M. Paone,* Arte e cultura alla corte di G. A. del Balzo Orsini..., in: *AA. VV.,* Studi di storia pugliese in onore di G. Chiarelli, II (Galatina 1973) 97 - 98.

28 L'atto di delega (o la sua conferma) si legge in *L. Galli,* Storia di Laterza (Palo del Colle 1940) 140s., ed è, per quanto mal trascritto, di grande importanza per la storia della cancelleria orsiniana. La sentenza, o meglio la relazione dell'accaduto, e l'intervento principesco si legge in *F. Tanzi,* Il «Chronicon neretinum», Rivista storica salentina I (1903) 252 - 253 nt. 3; in *Antonucci,* Il «Concistorium», 213 - 214; e per intero, e con varianti in *E. Travaglini,* I limiti della foresta oritana in documenti e carte dal 1432 al 1809 (Oria 1977) 51 - 56 (sempre da un trasunto del 1452). Su questi documenti, e le loro edizioni, v. ora *G. Carducci,* I confini del territorio di Taranto tra Basso Medioevo ed età Moderna (Taranto 1993) 16 - 17.

29 Il documento, *Antonucci,* Il «Concistorium», 213, non lo conosce direttamente, ma da *N. Bodini,* Demani della città di Lecce. Documenti (Lecce 1912) 313s. Bisogna invece leggere l'originale conservato in ASL, *Libro Rosso di Lecce,* 271 - 282. Fra Giovanni Effrem di Bari era reginale capitano della città e contea di Lecce già nel 1444 (?): Il codice di Maria d'Enghien a c. di *M. Pastore* (Galatina 1979) 56.

senz'altro il cognome) barone di Casarano, con una supplica in volgare dove richiedeva la «revocatio» (cioè il ritorno forzato) di due suoi vassalli «obligati ad personalia et realia servicia», rifugiati a Felline, terra del barone Salvatore Tolomei. Alla supplica l'Orsini appose un rescritto nel quale, in data 27 luglio 1451, esortava l'arcivescovo d'Otranto, ch'era allora Stefano Agricoli (il celebre martire del 1480) e «ceteris magnificis» consiglieri (?) a decidere la lite sorta (forse) dinanzi al Giustiziere feudale e al capitolo di Nardò.

Il rescritto pare redatto da «Antonius de Agello». Lo stesso giorno, il 27 luglio, i «consiliarii» del Principe, a Lecce, «hora et loco quibus tunc curiam regere» erano soliti, citarono le parti, e infine, dopo varie fasi procedurali oscurate dalla lacerazione del documento, giunsero a sentenza il 9 maggio 1453[30]. C'è a sufficienza di che trarre qualche considerazione. Anzitutto il Principe, a somiglianza di quanto faceva il Re a Napoli, era il diretto destinatario delle suppliche o petizioni che provenivano da tutti i suoi dominii[31]. Sulla petizione, il Principe delegava l'organo decidente, a suo arbitrio. In verità, siccome la supplica eccita la richiesta di grazia e non quella di giustizia, il Principe potrebbe decidere a sua discrezione, immediatamente[32], ma i documenti superstiti, legati quasi tutti a controversie su confini, mostrano bene che egli preferisce dedurre la grazia in giustizia, investendo, appunto a discrezione, un suo organo giudicante o un singolo della decisione. Nel 1402 fu delegato un «consiliarius», così nel 1432 - 1434; nel 1425 fu delegato il giudice delle appellazioni, che dunque decise come delegato e non in quanto giudice d'appello; nel 1447 - 1449 si delegò il capitano di Lecce e la sua *curia*[33]; nel 1451 - 1453 fu delegato proprio il

---

30 Edita da *L. Idra* – *V. Speranza,* Le pergamene aragonesi dell'Archivio di S. Nicola di Bari. Il regno di Alfonso il Magnanimo. 1441 - 1458 (Bari 1991 ma 1992) 104; 126 - 128; 133.

31 Ritengo del tutto nominali le distinzioni tra aree «principesche» e aree «reginali» del potentato orsiniano, fors'anche viva Maria d'Enghien; è vero che i mesagnesi, nella supplica del 1425, si rivolsero a lei, che era, lo prova il documento del 1431 (supra nt. 24), signora di Mesagne; ma la giustizia o la grazia erano sostanzialmente unitarie.

32 Si può ritenere, in generale, che la supplica dovrebbe intervenire su sentenza, ma vi sono eccezioni: una potrebbe essere attestata dall'altra sentenza del 1451 - 1453 che sembra deduzione da un intervento in corso di causa. I giuristi di diritto comune, trattavano l'argomento nell'esegesi di Cod. 1, 21 (24), 2. Comunque senza un contenzioso dedotto in giudizio (a prescindere dal fatto che vi sia definito) l'intervento principesco può sembrare di tipo amministrativo: ad esempio l'intervento orsiniano del 1454 (?) per l'erbatico tra Galatina e Collemeto: *M. Paone,* Arte e cultura, 96 - 97. E ci sarebbero altri esempi (supra nt. 10 e 20).

33 Erra *Antonucci,* Il «Concistorium», 213 a ritenere analoga a questa, la celebre sentenza del 1447 ricordata dal Giannone; di essa non sopravvive quanto basta a sapere se interveniva su delega principesca al Concistorio, o su diretto intervento giudiziale di questo. Al Giannone si può credere, e se parla di Concistorio, non può

consilium o Concistorio principesco. La prassi sembra questa: alla supplica il Principe appone un rescritto o «decretatio» che individua l'organo decidente, e questo pronuncia nel merito a prescindere dalle sue competenze istituzionali. In ogni caso, queste competenze istituzionali ci sono. Una simile prassi è attestata, si è visto, fin dal 1335, nell'età del duca d'Atene, a Lecce; e a Taranto addirittura dal 1305.

È ovvio che non tutte le controversie si esprimevano in via di grazia; la maggioranza delle controversie si iniziavano e definivano in via di giustizia, dopo la qual via poteva aprirsi l'altra (se non era autonoma). E in via di giustizia operavano le istituzioni principesche.

L'importanza del documento del 1451 - 1453 sta nel fatto di attestare, sebbene non chiarissimamente, l'esistenza del Concistorio e dei suoi «consiliarii»; cioè d'un organo collegiale di giustizia. E qui varrà ripetere che negli altri casi in cui è delegato un «consiliarius», non si allude necessariamente al *consilium* o Concistorio principesco; «consiliarius» qui vale quanto «familiaris» o «fidelis», cioè, al più, membro della curia generale del Principe.

La sentenza del 1438 svela invece un'articolazione istituzionale più ampia e non insolita (1363): dalle curie cittadine si appellava al Giudice delle appellazioni, per altro già attestato nel 1363 e nel 1425. In quali rapporti fossero Concistorio e Giudice di appello del Principe, non sappiamo. Cioè non sappiamo se fossero organi analoghi vissuti con nomi diversi in tempi diversi, o se fossero termini sinonimi dello stesso tribunale; ovvero se consistessero di attribuzioni differenziate (per competenza) d'uno stesso organo; o, infine, se fossero organi diversi coesistenti.

La presenza, attestata nel 1451 - 1453, ma, sembra, incidentalmente, d'un Giustiziere feudale, complica ancor di più il quadro generale, anche perché lo stato del documento è pessimo. La supplica, inoltre, girata dal Principe al Concistorio, non permette di intravedere né i suoi stessi motivi di intervento (su sentenza in qualche modo definitiva?) né l'eventuale posizione d'appello del Concistorio rispetto al Giustiziere (a tacere d'altro: ad esempio l'intervento del capitolo di Nardò). La competenza di questi era, nel caso, su un episodio di *revocatio;* cioè una controversia civile, in senso lato[34]. Dunque è impossibile entrare nel merito dei rapporti tra organi giudiziali dell'Orsini[35]; ma, per certo, esisteva un suo Giustiziere, un Concisto-

pensarsi invece alla curia cittadina di Lecce. A dover pensare, invece, ad una impugnazione dalla curia nel Concistorio (in analogia con la sentenza del 1438) questo parrebbe analogo al Giudice degli appelli. Ma è bene evitare le congetture.

[34] Sull'istituto, v. *Vallone,* Iurisdictio, 83 s. Per l'importanza di questo documento, v. infra nt. 38.

[35] Grazie al documento del 1438 sappiamo che dalle curie cittadine si appellava (in civile) al Giudice di appello; cosicché il concistorio, posto che già esistesse nel

rio o *concilium* con i suoi giuristi o «consiliarii» in senso tecnico[36] e un Giudice d'appello.

Bisogna tuttavia chiedersi se la presenza così intensamente articolata di strutture giudiziali feudali, entra o meno in concorrenza con gli organi regi di giustizia. Sappiamo che fino al quarto decennio del Cinquecento, la giustizia concessa in feudo non ammetteva la concorrenza, o il cumulo, con organi giustiziali regi, purché il privilegio contenesse espressa clausola di esclusività[37]; il privilegio orsiniano del 1420 non contiene una tale clausola; ma è pur vero che esso è anteriore al Parlamento di San Lorenzo quando, nel 1443, si generalizzò la concessione del doppio imperio a tutti i feudali. Insomma è plausibile che nel 1420, dato il carattere eccezionale e il sapore implicitamente esclusivo del privilegio, si concedesse (o confermasse) all'Orsini la giustizia privativa sui suoi feudi. E per le terre demaniali? Ol'Orsini ebbe la nomina a officiale regio nelle terre demaniali insistenti nei suoi domini (manca però ogni traccia documentale) o sopravviveva la competenza dei Giustizieri regi in queste terre[38]. Certo, se l'Orsini

---

1438, sembrerebbe una corte con competenza ristretta; e non d'appello (salvo che gli fosse attribuita una competenza d'appello riservata: vedi anche supra nt. 33). Le ambiguità del Ferrari su questo punto sono ben evidenziate, congetture a parte, da *Antonucci,* Il «Concistorium», 213 e 215; e supra nt. 3. La congiunzione di «reginalis et principalis» che accompagna nel 1425 e nel 1438 la qualifica del Giudice d'appello, fa pensare non ad un tribunale reginale d'appello su quello principesco; ma ad un tribunale d'appello unico per terre Orsini e d'Enghien. Il Ferrari va forse interpretato sulla base dei risultati documentali qui esaminati.

36 Nel documento del 1447 in *Paone,* Arte, 98, si parla di «sentenza data e confirmata per più famosissimi dottori» (e v. supra nt. 32).

37 *Vallone,* Iurisdictio, 162 s.

38 *L. G. De Simone,* Lecce e i suoi monumenti (1874, Lecce 1964^{2}) afferma che Raimondello Orsini «abolì il Giustizierato di Lecce» (p. 199); invece *Cutolo,* Maria, 59 parla di «un giustiziere del Principe, ben distinto dal giustiziere regio». Il *Pescione,* Corti di giustizia, 128 - 130 dà ai giustizieri regi compiti anche nelle terre feudali; ma l'argomento è inesplorato. Un documento interessante per i giustizieri feudali nel 1370 è in *Monti,* Ancora sulla feudalità, 541 nt. 136 o, ad esempio, nel 1344 in *Guerrieri,* Gualtieri VI, 580. Una menzione al 1452 di Giustizieri orsiniani è nel *Libro Rosso di Lecce* 300. L'argomento è però assai complesso. In Asn, *Div. Somm. II Num.,* vol. 240 c. 23r, si dice che Anna Colonna, da Lecce, inviò al marito Gian Antonio Orsini, il 9 marzo 1460, il famoso Francesco Sanguigni, «giustiziere della provincia di Terra d'Otranto». Sanguigni sembra Giustiziere feudale, ma il suo distretto, la Terra d'Otranto, ha *nomen* regio (tracce di ciò anche nel Trecento). È opportuno però ricordare che con il cap. *Ut exercitium* del 1330, re Roberto sancì il potere dei giustizieri e capitani regi di giudicare anche nelle terre feudali (ed. *R. Trifone,* La legislazione angioina (Napoli 1921) nr. 162 p. 242). Aggiungo che tra Casarano e Felline, terre della oscura lite tra feudali del 1451 - 1453, almeno Felline sembra fuori del dominio di Orsini, e ne dovremmo dedurre che la competenza orsiniana (cioè quella dei suoi organi di giustizia) copriva l'intero distretto regio nel quale insistevano i suoi dominii, quasi avesse avuto l'investitura territoriale di regio officiale. Il 10 XII 1463 (da un transunto del 13 IX 1490) i

avesse avuto l'officio di Giustiziere regio provinciale, avrebbe avuto anche la competenza d'appello in forza della federiciana *const.* I 43. La lite dedotta in Concistorio nel 1451 - 1453 è tra due feudali uno dei quali fuori, pare, dal dominio orsiniano: ma è imprudente congetturarvi sopra.

Per il resto i privilegi non parlano neanche di concessione feudale degli appelli, o «seconde cause», e gli storici, infatti, pensano, come sappiamo, ad usurpazioni. Eppure un grado d'impugnazione era implicito nel grande dominio orsiniano. Come tale, cioè a prescindere dagli offici regi che Gian Antonio potrebbe (o anche potrebbe non) aver ricoperto.

La differenza tra questa corte orsiniana e le grandi corti feudali anche del primo Cinquecento[39] sta nel fatto che il Concistorio non doveva raccordare giustizie subordinate dotate di gradi ulteriori di giustizia, cioè delle «seconde» o anche «terze cause». Infatti il privilegio del 1420 obbligava, tra altri, i baglivi e i giudici a contratti ad assoggettarsi al doppio imperio principesco. Ora i baglivi (e giudici a contratti) erano titolari d'una giurisdizione minore che, in applicazione del principio «a dato iudice appellabitur ad eum qui dedit», implicava, anche questo sappiamo, una circoscritta cognizione d'appello a pro del feudale; ma si tratta in realtà, d'una scissione interna al prima grado civile[40].

Siccome il privilegio del 1420 concede all'Orsini anche «feudis et feudatariis», sembra che ogni singolo feudale del potentato, con il suo grado scisso di giustizia fosse a sua volta subordinato (per scissione) ad un ulteriore grado di giustizia, quella principesca. Il punto, che tocca da vicino l'antica questione del Monti, si potrebbe acclarare disponendo di alcune investiture interne (dall'Orsini a feudali). Abbiamo qualcosa, in verità, sia per l'età orsiniana che per l'epoche anteriori; e se anche non si riesce a capire bene quando i documenti indichino un suffeudo quaternato e quando un suffeudo piano (non sempre è sopravvissuta l'indicazione dell'assenso regio), la distinzione, per il profilo che ci interessa, è sostanzialmente irrilevante. Ad esempio il 16 giugno 1308, Filippo di Taranto concesse il casale di «Santa Maria de Vetrana» presso Oria a Vallechino de Yserio «cum

---

casali di Borgagne e Pasolo furono accettati (su loro richiesta) nel regio demanio, e gli si concesse inoltre di passare dalla giurisdizione del Giustiziere (regio) come per il passato, a quella del Capitano di Lecce: *Libro Rosso di Lecce* 332. Non sembra che questi casali facessero parte dei dominii orsiniani; anche per questo il Giustiziere sembra quello regio; ma non è facile ipotizzare le ragioni della seconda richiesta, e dell'assenza d'un capitano locale.

39 Ad esempio dalla città reginale di Molfetta si appellava nel terzo lustro del Cinquecento ad un *Reginale Consilium* di Giovanna III, la «triste regina»: v. *R. Maranta,* cons. 37 nr. 7 (ed. Venezia 1587); e v. *T. Grammatico,* cons. civ. 101 (ed. Lione 1584).

40 *Vallone,* Iurisdictio, 166s.

hominibus, vassallis vineis... iuribus et pertinentiis suis»[41]; poi il 2 dicembre 1323 (o forse 1322) il conte di Lecce (non è mai inutile lo sguardo a quest'altro potentato destinato a unirsi all'altro nel Quattrocento) Gualtieri di Brienne dette assenso da Conversano alla donazione del casale di Cavallino *sub Comitatu* a Goffredo de Noha «cum hominibus, vassallis, tenimentis pertinentiis et introitibus suis»[42]; mentre nel 1336 la terra di Francavilla veniva concessa dal Principe in feudo nobile «cum hominibus, vassallis iuribus pertinentiis»[43]. Insomma, quanto fin qui sappiamo dell'età angioina sembrerebbe negare la concessione suffeudale delle giustizie. Invece nel 1353 il principe Roberto concesse, a Pietro de Tocco, Martina «cum hominibus vassallis... gabellis, baiulationibus, iuribus, iurisdictionibus»[44]; e ancora nel 1367 Filippo II di Taranto concesse alla mensa vescovile brindisina il casale di Principato «cum hominibus, vassallis... iuribus, iurisdictionibus et pertinentiis»[45].

Ciò significa che anche nelle concessioni suffeudali l'esercizio della giurisdizione si considerava implicito (se lo era) nel fatto stesso della concessione, e ciò almeno dopo il 1282. E se ancora nel 1399 Ottone di Brunswick principe di Taranto concesse il feudo di Scaglione, in distretto di Ostuni «cum omnibus iuribus rationibus et pertinentiis»[46] è però in quell'epoca che i documenti cominciano a parlare più chiaro. Il 24 aprile 1406 re Ladislao concesse a Carluccio Maramonte la baronia di Campi «cum hominibus, vaxallis, vaxallorumque redditibus, iuribus, iuridictionibus et pertinentiis» che egli già possedeva «sub Comitatu Licii», ma separandola dalla detta Contea e ponendola «immediate et in capite» dal Re, almeno finché la ribelle Maria d'Enghien non «reduceretur ad nostre maie-

---

41 *Monti,* Ancora sul Principato, 14 - 15 e v'è in calce l'assenso regio. Altre indicazioni da atti perduti in *L. G. De Simone,* Degli Angioini principi di Taranto (Taranto 1866) 13 - 15; interessanti le note autografe nell'esemplare posseduto dalla BPL.

42 *G. Guerrieri,* Gualtieri VI di Brienne, 55 - 56. Se si ritenesse il computo bizantino, l'anno diverrebbe il 1322. L'assenso regio del 1323 si legge in *Coco,* Francavilla, 175 - 177.

43 *Coco,* Francavilla, 179 - 180 (è la conferma regia).

44 *I. Chirulli,* Istoria Cronologica della Franca Martina II (Venezia 1752; ed. Martina Franca 1982) 100 - 104. La concessione *immediate et in capite* dalla Curia principesca del 20 III 1353, è amplissima; si concede inoltre «percipiendum iura, redditus et proventus omnes... cum collectis seu toto eo quod nobis seu nostre Curie competit», dietro servizio d'un milite, per altro inferiore al valore; il tutto «sub spe» dell'assenso regio. Analogie con questo importante documento, presenta l'altro, sempre di Roberto, ma relativo ad un feudo in Acaia, per Giannotto Seripando del 1357, edito in *Monti,* Ricerche, in: Nuovi studi angioini 640 - 644.

45 *P. Coco,* Strane vicende del diruto casale di Principato..., Rivista storica salentina 9 (1914) 238 - 245; edito anche nel Codice dipl. brind. II nr. 92 (233 - 239); cf. anche nr. 10 (44).

46 *Il Libro Rosso... di Ostuni* 205 - 206 (conferma di re Ladislao).

statis obedientiam et fidem»[47], come poi avvenne per il loro matrimonio di lì a poco. Diversi anni più tardi, il 3 gennaio 1463, da Bari, Gian Antonio Orsini del Balzo concesse il casale di Andrano a Gian Antonio Saraceno «cum castello seu fortellitio, feudis, vaxallis, banco iustitiae, territoriisque...»[48]. Ancora il 7 ottobre 1463, da Ruffano, un rogito ci attesta che Giacomo dell'Antoglietta, in cambio d'una parte del casale di Salve, posseduto da Ruggero Sambiasi, permutò la sua parte del casale di Morciano «cum banco justitie civilium causarum, iure platee ⟨et⟩ piscarie, cum tarpeto et iure baiulationis... prout... tenebat et possidebat et prout... princeps Tarenti Joannes Antonius... eidem Jacobo... concessit»[49]. Il *bancum iustitie,* che a un certo punto s'interpretò come il potere di istituire il baglivo per esercitare la giurisdizione baiulare, e cioè civile, sembrò a più antichi esegeti la «virga iustitiae», la titolarità di quella giurisdizione[50]. Ne potremmo dedurre agevolmente che i suffeudali dell'Orsini esercitavano *in terris eorum* la giustizia civile di officio baiulare; e che cioè il loro potere giurisdizionale era limitato alla magistratura baiulare, donde procedeva l'impugnazione agli officiali orsiniani, così come è congetturabile che avvenisse dai baglivi di diretta istituzione principesca. Posso fornire ancora un esempio più tardo, e successivo alla morte dell'Orsini e alla dissoluzione del suo potentato ma, per così dire, parlante. Il 5 aprile 1468 l'università di Lecce, a mezzo del suo sindaco, supplicò che re Ferrante «se degna concedere alla dicta Università le cause de appellacione le quale se vertono in la bagliva de Leze... et de quelle se conosca per li Regi Capitanei de dicta cità et lor corte como per lo passato se ha observato». Il re rispose: «Placet»[51]. Poi però sempre Ferrante, il 16 VII 1472, vietò al Regio Consi-

---

47 *De Simone,* Lecce, 195 - 197; un'edizione più corretta in *U. Congedo,* Maria d'Enghien (Lecce 1899) 87 - 90. In *Aar,* Gli studi storici 227 - 228, altre indicazioni di atti perduti.

48 *Aar,* Gli studi storici, 296 - 299. Il feudo era rientrato nella «curia» orsiniana per la morte improle del celebre «miles» Francesco Spinelli da Nardò. Il 15 maggio 1465 re Ferrante confermò la concessione, al Saraceno, ma di modo che gli derivasse «immediate et in capite a nobis et nostra curia... nullumque alium preter nos... in superiorem et dominum recognoscat». Un decreto dell'Orsini in data 5 VI 1429, con il quale si concede l'assenso alla vendita di un suffeudo (evidentemente piano) del distretto neretino si legge in *A. Frascadore,* Le pergamene del monastero di S. Chiara di Nardò 1292 - 1508 (Bari 1981) nr. 23 (97 - 98).

49 BPL, ms. 327. Copie senza numerazione d'ordine.

50 *C. Pecchia,* Storia politica e civile del Regno di Napoli I (Napoli 1869³) 291, 295, 305. *Andrea d'Isernia,* in *const.* I 63 *Magistri Camerari* (ed. *Cervone,* Napoli 1773) 124a; *Matteo d'Afflitto,* in ead. const. (ed. Venezia 1588) c. 174r nr. 2 - 3. Una tarda concessione dell'*officium baiulationis* è conservata nel formulario aragonese del ms. 80 del Fondo San Martino della Biblioteca Nazionale di Napoli, c. 16v - 17r.

51 ASL, *Libro Rosso* 436. Sembra che Ferrante avesse stornato queste impugnazioni al Maestro Portolano con un privilegio forse del 1466. Questo storno era noto,

glio Provinciale la «iurisdicione de la cognizione de le prime cause» civili e criminali spettanti all'università di Lecce, e di rimettere le cause usurpate «alla corte del Capitanio de essa cità de Leze»[52]. È evidente che in quest'ultimo documento il concetto di «prime cause» ingloba tutta la competenza del capitano, e cioè anche gli «appelli» dal baglivo ricordati per il 1468. Anche la dottrina era su questa posizione: «licet Capitaneus Baronis videatur iudex appellationium sententiae latae per Baiulum; tamen reputatur prima causa respectu secundae; si forte Baro habet privilegium primarum et secundarum causarum, ideo a Capitaneo, qui iudicat post Baiulum confirmando vel infirmando, appellandum est ad iudicem secundarum. Ergo una censetur eademque causa baiulationis Curiae et Capitanei, quasi non sit iudicii variatio in istis modicis»[53]. A questo punto, se anche non tutte le congetture sono state provate, soccorrono però le regole, e il principio generale, che, grazie alla convergenza di tante prove, si è potuto costruire.

---

per le province di Bari, Otranto e Abruzzo, anche in teoria: *A. Moles,* Decisiones... R. Camerae Summariae Regni Neapolis (Napoli 1670) § 9, 1 nr. 19 - 22 (p. 132). Anche a Taranto, d'altra parte, la bagliva era già in età orsiniana un corpo della «dogana»: *Cassandro,* Un inventario, 21, 41 - 42. Il primo febbraio 1489 sempre Ferrante stabilì che il capitano di Lecce ricevesse le impugnazioni dalla bagliva cittadina, solo in assenza del Portolano: ASL, *Libro Rosso* 514.

52 ASL, *Libro Rosso* 1116 - 1117. Ancor più chiaramente il 23 agosto 1475: *Libro Rosso* 1244 - 1245. Sono brani importanti per valutare i rapporti tra la corte (regia) del capitano di Lecce, e il Regio Consiglio Provinciale. Ne può anche derivare qualche suggestione per la relazione tra quest'ultimo organo e il Concistorio orsiniano. Un rogito di not. L. Perrone di Lecce del 21 III 1586 (ASL not. 46/2, c. 397r, 399rv) ricorda che un privilegio di re Ferrante ad Antonello de Noha, barone di Noha, stabiliva le prime cause della sua baronia; mentre altra lettera regia inibiva al capitano di Galatina di intromettersi nella giurisdizione di Noha. Pur nell'ignoranza delle date esatte, è chiaro il rispetto assoluto delle giurisdizioni feudali, di feudi peraltro tutti, all'epoca, *in capite a Rege,* benchè, forse, si potesse pretendere un'antica soggezione di Noha alla Contea di Lecce.

53 È il tardo ma solido *P. Rendella,* Tractatus de pascuis... (1618; Napoli 1726); II *de baronum pascuis,* cap. IX (p. 49). A Galatina dalla curia del Capitano (giudice *ad quem* dal baglivo) s'appellava al viceduca (giudice «secundarum causarum») e da qui alla magistratura regia d'Udienza, come s'evince da un atto del 13 IX 1557 di not. Raimondo Scalfo di Galatina (ASL not. 38/1, c. 106r - 108v). Non si confonda la scissione nel primo grado attestata dal Rendella, con la riduzione ad unità di tutte le sentenze feudali (anche di secondo e terzo grado) inventata a fine Cinquecento dalla pratica forense: vedi supra nt. 19. All'idea di modicità della causa come presupposto dell'organizzazione intraistituzionale delle impugnazioni si richiama espressamente anche un documento più antico, ma utile, del 17 X 1395: la regina Margherita, dietro supplica dell'Università di Barletta, concesse che le sentenze penali del Capitano di città inferiori al valore di tarini 15, fossero inappellabili nella regia Curia, con ordine sia a questa sia al capitano di città di uniformarsi: *N. Barone,* Repertorio delle pergamene dell'Università di Barletta. 1234 - 1658 (Napoli 1904) 87.

Il silenzio parziale dei documenti è dunque sanato; e non è lecito parlare di appelli usurpati o abusati. È chiaro che per rispettare la giurisdizione del baglivo; cioè quella (implicita nella concessione) della giustizia civile al suffeudale; e quella ulteriore concessa espressamente al principe, c'è *in re ipsa* una gerarchia di impugnazioni (o appelli). L'officio di «iudex appellationum» degli Orsini presiede e definisce questa competenza fisiologica per scissione, senza dover ricorrere all'idea dell'usurpazione o della concessione delle seconde cause, almeno fino al reperimento di documentazione contraria. Tutto questo nel civile; nel penale il mero imperio orsiniano sembra fosse di prima istanza fissa (cioè non scindibile), ma anche qui difettano i documenti. Oltre non si può andare; ma, per certo, le varie istituzioni di giustizia del potentato orsiniano si racchiudevano, per quanto in rapporti tra loro insondabili, in queste coordinate.

Falsa, invece, l'idea che dalla giustizia principesca del Concistorio, e foss'anche del Giudice d'appello non si potesse appellare ulteriormente alla giustizia regia[54]. Siccome in definitiva il Principe disponeva, nel penale, solo delle «prime cause», mentre nel civile, anche a voler considerare (direi velleitariamente) il sistema di scissione come dirompente le «prime cause», era certa la possibilità di appellare ai Giustizieri provinciali regi, se mai vi fossero stati, e/o alla Vicaria[55] in forza della *const.* I 43[56].

---

[54] Ad esempio *Vacca,* La Corte 29. La *dec.* 136 del d'Afflitto, relativa ad ulteriore controversia tra Vescovo e Università di S. Pietro in Lama darebbe prova provata di quanto s'è detto, se non fosse insondabile la sua storia anteriore alla fine del Quattrocento, quando d'Afflitto scriveva, e la sua eventuale provenienza dall'epoca e dalla corte orsiniana. V. anche *Vallone,* Iurisdictio, 80 nt. 40.

[55] Sul punto, *Vallone,* Iurisdictio, 170s. Un profilo scientifico della Sacra Regia provinciale Udienza Idruntina, cioè anche la sua continuità con il Concistorio orsiniano in specie sul piano delle attribuzioni e del grado di giustizia, non esiste. Rapidi cenni, ancora i migliori, in *Cassandro,* Lineamenti del diritto pubblico del regno di Sicilia Citra Farum sotto gli Aragonesi, in: Annali del Semin. giurid. ec. R. Univ. Bari VI 2 (1934), 123 - 124. Ricordo soltanto una notizia da *Marino Frezza,* De subfeudis baronum etc. (Venezia 1579) 420 nr. 9: la Udienza otrantina conosceva *ex privilegio* delle controversie sui feudi quaternati e sui feudi piani.

[56] In effetti la lettera della *const.* I 43 (da intendere in conformità con l'inciso finale della *const.* I 40,2 *Magnae Curiae)* parla del Maestro Giustiziere come, tra l'altro, destinatario dell'appello dai giudici inferiori; quindi i giuristi posteriori (d'Afflitto, Frezza, Follerio) lo identificarono con le competenze della Vicaria. Tuttavia già una glossa di Andrea da Isernia, sembra voler intendere come destinatari dell'appello i Giustizieri provinciali, il cui officio si burocratizzò nelle Regie Udienze provinciali. E queste, in effetti, divennero dal Quattrocento il luogo deputato agli appelli dalle corti baronali. Come sappiamo, l'obiezione della competenza solo penale dei giustizieri provinciali era già caduta (non senza dubbi esegetici) con il cap. *Quia nulla,* di re Carlo II (della fine del 1308?) relato da un celebre brano di Bartolomeo da Capua.

Vorrei però sottolineare che queste analisi piuttosto complesse, respingono la comoda ipotesi che tutto quanto sembri turbare la teorica dei tre gradi di giurisdizione, o lo turbi secondo una troppo semplice presunzione di conoscenza, esprima senz'altro un'abuso o una usurpazione. Così come va respinta la altrettanto semplicistica convinzione che ogni istanza (o fase) d'impugnazione corrisponda ad un grado del giudizio. Quando l'abuso c'è, per così dire, si vede. In una terra del Basso Salento, Ruffano, ed in una data in verità tarda, nel 1596, quando Principato di Taranto e Contea di Lecce erano ormai un ricordo, l'amministrazione cittadina giunse fino al Sacro Regio Consiglio per denunciare l'abuso (significativo in sé oltre ogni cronologia) che dalla sentenza del baglivo «si sole appellare al Luogotenente, et po' s'appella al Capetanio, et poi s'appella al Barone. Fuit provisum quod non liceat appellare nisi a Bajulo ad Capitaneum»[57]. Cioè dal giudice dato al delegato di «eum qui dedit». Ma prima dell'intervento del Regio Consiglio, le impugnazioni erano ben quattro, invece delle due (di primo grado) riconosciute. Molta della letteratura, recente ed antica, va rivisitata.

Insomma, almeno ad una notizia del Ferrari possiamo credere; quella relativa alla composizione interna del Concistorio; cioè «un consiglio di quattro Consiglieri iurisperiti, eletti di tutta la Japigia per li più dotti; un di Lecce nominato messer Antonio Guidano, un di Bari chiamato Messer Francesco di Effrem, un di Taranto detto messer Andrea di Agello, ed un di Ostuni nominato messer Gasparro Petrarolo, un avvocato fiscale, il cui nome fu messer Daniele de Muro, un segretario che fu messer Colantonio de' Frisi, un procurator fiscale detto notaio Gio. Pietro de Argenteriis, un mastro d'atti detto notaio Donato Sala, e Capo e Presidente di quello, messer Agostino Guarino»[58]. Non c'è, per ora, da aggiungere altro.

---

[57] Decreta S. R. Consilii in favorem universitatis Ruffani (Lecce 1693) 27; e anche *G. M. Novario,* Tractatus de vassallorum gravaminibus (ed. Ginevra 1686) gr. II 89. *E. Personé,* Poche memorie della famiglia Personé (Napoli 1780) 54, ricorda da un documento perduto, che nel 1572 Marsilio Maramonte, barone del feudo rustico di Ogliastro, nel distretto di Nardò, supplicò e ottenne dal duca Acquaviva che gli ufficiali baiulari di Nardò esercitassero anche nel suo feudo: il feudo rustico era, pare, *in capite a Rege,* e l'esempio e tardo; prova però che non sempre l'uso stesso (non già l'abuso) della giurisdizione (e l'istituzione del baglivo) era conveniente.

[58] *Ferrari,* Apologia, 431: testo più articolato di quello edito dal Summonte. Naturalmente i quattro Consiglieri, ma anche gli altri personaggi sono noti. Antonio Guidano (di Galatina) e Antonio (= Andrea?) Ajello sono i «i due Antonii» che la tradizione vuole esecutori in Altamura dell'Orsini. Aggiungo solo che il 22 marzo 1456 si laureò in diritto civile «Daniel De Muro de Rocha de Apulia»: *C. Piana,* Il «liber secretus iuris caesarei» dell'Università di Bologna 1451 - 1500 (Milano 1984) 37 - 38; viveva ancora nel 1481 a Lecce: *E. Perito,* Uno sguardo alla guerra d'Otranto e alle cedole della tesoreria aragonese di quel tempo, in: Archivio storico per le province napoletane 40 (1915) 327. L'esistenza dei giudici induce l'esistenza del Tribunale.

M. ASCHERI

La Rota della Repubblica di Siena nel secolo XVI

Negli ultimi anni, in particolare per merito di Gino Gorla, c'è stato anche in Italia un fervore di studi intorno ai 'grandi tribunali' in età moderna[1]. Tuttavia, per l'approfondimento dei problemi che interessano in questo contesto siamo veramente ai primi passi. *A fortiori* lo siamo poi per quanto riguarda la Rota di Siena, che non è mai stata oggetto finora di alcuno studio specifico, anche se il suo nome ha meritato qualche notorietà, specie per essere state alcune sue tarde raccolte di 'decisiones' associate a quelle della ben più famosa Rota di Firenze[2]. Il tribunale merita quindi qualche attenzione, e non solo per la sua antichità e per essere stato modello per la Rota perugina[3]: come si vedrà, il suo modo di procedere è interessante per attestare non già la crisi del diritto comune, quanto piuttosto il suo trionfo.

La Rota venne istituita a Siena con deliberazione della Balia, l'organo di governo effettivo[4] della Repubblica di Siena, libera ancora fino a metà Cinquecento, l'11 dicembre 1503[5], evidentemente sotto la suggestione eserci-

---

[1] V. anche per rinvii bibliografici ai lavori di Gorla, il mio Tribunali, giuristi e istituzioni dal medioevo all'età moderna (edizione rivista, Bologna 1995), e gli atti del convegno dedicato a Grandi tribunali e Rote nell'Italia di antico regime, a cura di *M. Sbriccoli* e *A. Bettoni* (Milano 1993), ove si trova un profilo dello studioso recentemente scomparso. Per una riconsiderazione storiografica v. ora *R. Savelli,* Tribunali, 'decisiones' e giuristi: una proposta di ritorno alle fonti, in: Origini dello Stato. Processi di formazione statale in Italia fra medioevo ed età moderna, a cura di *G. Chittolili, A. Molho, P. Schiera* (Bologna 1994) pp. 397 - 421. Quadro d'assieme sintetico nel mio: Höchste Gerichte in Italien zur Zeit des Ancien Régime, in: Frieden durch Recht. Das Reichskammergericht von 1495 bis 1806, hrsg. *I. Scheurmann* (Mainz 1994) pp. 428 - 434.

[2] V. *Ascheri,* Tribunali, cit., ad ind.

[3] Si v. *C. Cutini,* Il tribunale della Rota di Perugia, in: Grandi tribunali e Rote, cit., pp. 297 - 339 (311).

[4] Per un profilo della struttura giuspubblicistica senese v. *M. Ascheri,* Siena nel Rinascimento: istituzioni e sistema politico (Siena 1985).

[5] In Archivio di Stato di Siena (da ora ASSi), *Balia 49,* cc. 92r - 96r (edizione integrale del testo nel mio contributo: Alle origini della Rota di Siena (1503), destinato agli: Studi in onore di Filippo Gallo). Riprodotta in ASSi, *Statuti di Siena 40,* del quale c'è ora la descrizione analitica di *E. Brizio,* Leggi e provvedimenti del Rinascimento (1400 - 1542), in: Antica legislazione della Repubblica di Siena, a cura di *M. Ascheri* (Siena 1993) pp. 161 - 200.

tata dalla recente istituzione, nell'aprile dell'anno precedente, dell'omologo tribunale per il Dominio fiorentino[6].

Mentre però il tribunale centrale fiorentino ha già meritato più studi, quello senese è stato preso in considerazione solo saltuariamente. Il collegamento delle due istituzioni giudiziarie non è soltanto nominalistico, naturalmente. Il fatto è che Siena (come Firenze e altre città interessate dal fenomeno 'rotale', del resto)[7] stava allora vivendo un periodo molto complesso e difficile politicamente, che aveva condotto da qualche anno alla prima e unica signoria virtuale della sua storia, sotto il pugno di ferro di Pandolfo Petrucci[8]. Quel 'Magnifico' Pandolfo, discendente da una famiglia 'popolare' che aveva avuto nel Quattrocento salde radici nel governo cittadino, aveva insediato una signoria in città proprio mentre a Firenze la complicazione della vita politica (sono gli anni del Machiavelli) aveva portato alla nomina di un 'gonfaloniere' a vita, contro tutta la tradizione comunale di origine medievale.

La Rota, qua e là, venne istituita per rispondere quindi a pressanti motivi di politica interna, a situazioni delicate che richiedevano di consolidare l'unità tra i gruppi dominanti, di superare i passati contrasti in modo da

---

[6] Sul quale v. *M. Ascheri,* Firenze dalla Repubblica al Principato: la motivazione della sentenza e l'edizione delle Pandette, nella raccolta: Tribunali, cit., pp. 55 - 83. Tra le due Rote s'inserì cronologicamente quella della Romagna, con sede a Cesena, istituita formalmente da papa Alessandro VI a fine di luglio del 1502, ma forse già decisa a dicembre del 1501: sul punto v. *A. K. Isaacs,* Cesena agli inizi del Cinquecento, in: Storia di Cesena, III: La Dominazione pontificia (secoli XVI - XVII - XVIII), a cura di *A. Prosperi* (Rimini 1989) pp. 16 - 61 (in part. 29 - 39, 45). È una Rota con giudici dottori ma provenienti dalle città del territorio interessato, voluta dal duca Valentino per presentare il proprio governo come portatore di pace e di giustizia (grazie al provvedimento papale poté interessarsi addirittura di cause beneficiali, coinvolgendo quindi sia laici che ecclesiastici). La Isaacs mette questo consiglio di giustizia in relazione all'affermarsi di modelli aragonesi-catalani in Italia nel corso del Quattrocento (v. il lavoro cit. a nota 5, p. 360s.): nel Consiglio di giustizia napoletano, come alla Rota romana (e ora in Romagna) i Borgia fecero prevalere il principio tipico del consiglio di Aragona secondo cui gli uditori dovevano provenire da certe aree geografiche.

[7] Oltre a Firenze, si pensi a Lucca, per la quale v. ora *V. Tirelli,* L'istituzione della Rota di Lucca nel sec. XVI, in: Grandi tribunali e Rote, cit., pp. 227 - 257. Sia per Lucca che per Genova v. poi *Isaacs,* L'istituzione, cit.

[8] Le vicende sono narrate già dallo storico settecentesco Giovanni Antonio Pecci, mentre la più recente storiografia è rappresentata soprattutto da *David Hicks,* del quale si vedrà la relazione svolta al convegno su: La Toscana al tempo di Lorenzo il Magnifico (atti in corso di pubblicazione a cura di *Riccado Fubini*); si v., per bibliografia e alcuni caratteri fondamentali del regime Petrucci (privatizzazione di uffici e beni pubblici) *A. K. Isaacs,* Le campagne senesi fra Quattro e Cinquecento: regime fondiario e governo signorile, in: Contadini e proprietari nella Toscana moderna. Atti del convegno di studi in onore di Giorgio Giorgetti, I (Firenze 1979) pp. 377 - 404.

poter far fronte ai gravissimi pericoli esterni, provocati dalla possente presenza militare straniera (dei Francesi e dell'Impero) in Italia. Questo è il contesto, che è stato seguito dalla Isaacs in un denso saggio che collega le vicende interne italiane agli sviluppi internazionali[9].

In particolare, a Siena la Rota fu istituita quando la città si trovò sotto il pericolo di essere invasa dalle milizie del Borgia, contro il quale aveva congiurato anche Pandolfo Petrucci, che lo conosceva bene come sostenitore dei suoi oppositori. Fu un modo per rafforzare il regime, quindi, perché il nuovo tribunale, composto in via esclusiva di giudici dotti e forestieri, doveva evidentemente rassicurare i vari gruppi politici e sociali poco convinti dell'autoritario governo del Petrucci.

Non a caso nel preambolo costitutivo si dichiara che si voleva assicurare che «se administri ragione *indifferentemente* ad ciascheduno, così in le civili come in le criminali (cause)». È comunque dal complesso del provvedimento che emergono altri dati interessanti. È possibile ad esempio che si siano voluti rassicurare in particolare i debitori e gli abitanti delle comunità dello Stato senese – che occupava un ampio territorio: circa il terzo meridionale della Toscana[10].

Quanto alla tutela dei debitori, si denunciò infatti come 'abusione', come grave abuso, che essi potessero essere perseguiti per più di una volta per lo stesso debito, prevedendosi a loro favore la possibilità di ricorrere ai giudici d'appello in modo che il creditore dovesse pagare tutte le spese[11]. Nella seconda direzione, era previsto: (1) che in caso di liti nate nel 'contado' (ossia il territorio sottoposto al governo della città), quando un abitante del luogo si sentisse 'gravato' potesse ricorrere alla Rota, che l'avrebbe restituito 'in pristino stato' procedendo con 'summaria ragione et de facto', in modo evidentemente da eliminare le spese consuete[12]; (2) che

---

[9] *A. K. Isaacs,* Politica e giustizia agli inizi del Cinquecento: l'istituzione delle prime Rote, in: Grandi tribunali e Rote, cit., pp. 341 - 386.

[10] L'ampio Stato è raffigurato nella carta nel mio saggio: Il Rinascimento a Siena (Siena 1993; anche in ed. inglese: Renaissance Siena, Siena 1993). Gli abitanti dello Stato, secondo la tradizionale comunale, erano esclusi dalla cittadinanza senese e si reggevano (in parte) secondo statuti locali.

[11] Il punto è sottolineato dalla *Isaacs,* L'istituzione, cit., p. 364, nota 49, che ricorda come nel 1523 – quindi nel periodo successivo al predominio dei Petrucci – la legge fu modificata osservandosi che il provvediemnto era stato «male usato», applicato «in grave preiudicio di epsi creditori».

[12] Le norme sui processi del contado attribuiscono quindi grande potere discrezionale ai giudici: nelle cause criminali che non fossero condotte in modo formale, il loro appello si poteva chiudere «come a loro parrà et portarà ragione (= diritto comune) et li statuti del Comune di Siena» (e non quindi quelli locali); in quelle civili sotto i 25 fiorini avrebbero proceduto «come ad loro parrà». Le procedure sommarie si svolgevano il lunedì e il sabato, probabilmente per facilitare chi doveva muoversi anche da lontano.

la Rota aveva 'piena autorità etiam di punire li officiali et levarli da lo officio'[13], provvedendo anche a far eseguire ogni sei mesi in città[14] pubblici bandi perché si venisse a conoscenza di questa possibilità offerta dalla magnanima giustizia centrale dello Stato contro eventuali amministratori infedeli e prepotenti[15].

Quanto alla struttura del tribunale, la Rota da un lato eliminava i giudici della tradizione comunale, ma li inglobava al proprio interno, con il grosso vantaggio quindi di non attentare alla tradizione comunale, e dall'altro garantiva la nomina diretta da parte del governo dei membri del collegio giudicante – mentre prima il podestà portava con sé i giudici collaterali che dovevano godere esclusivamente della sua fiducia. Inoltre, con un solo provvedimento si sistemava sia la giustizia di prima istanza[16] che quella d'appello.

Il tribunale di Rota era infatti composto da cinque giudici, dei quali i due più giovani (dottorati da non meno di tre anni) divenivano giudici di prima istanza rispettivamente nel civile e nel penale per sei mesi soltanto. Il primo giudice ordinario si sarebbe occupato anche delle cause dei danni dati[17], mentre il secondo, oltreché del penale[18], delle cause dei pupilli. Gli

---

[13] «...quanto hanno li Regolatori, non diminuendo però in alcuna parte la auctorità de li detti Regolatori». Si tratta di una magistratura cittadina – cioè retta da 'normali' cittadini, non necessariamente tecnici – che era preposta tra l'altro all'amministrazione del territorio.

[14] Naturalmente, se i bandi fossero stati inviati nel territorio la norma avrebbe un significato più pregnante; comunque, anche così ha il suo rilievo, perché almeno gli abitanti delle terre più vicine erano spesso in città per ovvi motivi commerciali e comunque notizie di questo genere, quando favorevoli, si dovevano diffondere con una certa rapidità.

[15] Di nuovo *Isaacs,* L'istituzione, cit., p. 364 nota 49.

[16] Senza tuttavia intaccare la tradizionale competenza del tribunale di Mercanzia (sul quale si v. nel mio: Siena nel Rinascimento, pp. 111 - 137, e: Tribunali, giuristi, cit., pp. 23 - 54), presso il quale solamente si prevedeva l'intervento del giudice dotto – riprendendo un tentativo di metà Quattrocento – ma, precisava la delibera di Rota, che «non possit ullo modo reddere votum suum». Il giudice dotto era quindi chiamato come semplice consigliere dei mercanti, i quali avevano dovuto evidentemente lamentare la crescente 'recezione' del diritto dotto nei negozi mercantili (v. Tribunali, cit., p. 34 ss.); l'intervento era previsto per le sole cause di valore superiore alle cento lire. In caso di appello, essendo questo primo giudice interessato, sarebbe intervenuto il giudice delle riformagioni. Ci si preoccupava anche che i giudici dotti non alterassero la consueta giustizia 'de plano et equo' dei mercanti, per cui avrebbero dovuto applicare i loro statuti e le consuetudini 'de la corte'. Il governo vuole cioè rassicurare i mercanti, confermando la loro tradizionale autonomia: v. anche *Isaacs,* L'istituzione cit., p. 364.

[17] Assistendo, evidentemente per la sua competenza tecnica, l'Ufficiale e il notaio predisposti all'ufficio omonimo, che avrebbero pronunciato le sentenze in suo nome. La materia dei 'danni dati' si riferisce all'ampio settore dei danneggiamenti a carico delle aziende agrarie.

altri tre dovevano essere invece addottorati da almeno sei anni e costituivano il Consiglio di giustizia vero e proprio, ossia la corte d'appello per tutte le sentenze definitive, interlocutorie e miste dei due precedenti giudici. Che si trattasse della vera novità è dimostrato anche dalla inusitata lunga durata del loro ufficio: tre anni.

La loro sentenza sarebbe stata irrevocabile ove concorde o ove confermasse anche solo a maggioranza la sentenza appellata, ma nel caso in cui mancasse o l'unanimità o la conformità s'apriva la possibilità della terza istanza: o dinanzi ai tre più il giudice ordinario che non aveva pronunciato la sentenza, o dinanzi ai tre più i due giudici ordinari succeduti ai due precedenti[19]. «Acciò che con più ragione si conceda dicta seconda appellatione et che non sia così facile ad contradirsi senza ragione», si disponeva che il giudice dissenziente doveva però dichiararsi tale e «ponere le cause o causa perché discorda da tale sententia». A differenza di quanto previsto a Firenze[20], nessuna norma però si riferiva esplicitamente alla conservazione delle decisioni, e tanto meno alla loro conservazione a disposizione del pubblico.

Della conservazione si parla solo con riferimento agli atti della causa. Si partì col rilevare «quanti scandali nascano ne la vostra città et non ne le altre per perdare li processi de le cause quali sonno male custoditi», come premessa per ordinare che i notai che in qualunque corte comunale rogassero degli atti processuali dovessero raccogliergli «in uno libro legato ogni sei mesi finiti», con l'obbligo di consegnarlo al camerlengo dei consoli dei notai. Questi era in particolare incaricato di provvedere alla custodia degli atti. Per evitare la loro dispersione si sanciva l'obbligo di non far uscire dalla sede dell'arte le carte se non a richiesta del giudice. Le parti le avrebbero avute per il suo tramite, assumendosi le spese del messo per la trasmissione. Si prevedevano copie alle parti, a pagamento, mentre al giudice soltanto si potevano consegnare le carte originali.

Di come sia stata applicata la normativa si sa, però, ancora poco. È noto che alcuni giudici in questi primi anni furono di Montepulciano, città vicina a Siena e ribelle a Firenze[21], con la quale evidentemente Siena

---

18 Ma nei 'malefici enormi' sarebbe stato assistito dal giudice «che terrà lo luogo del podestà in lo modo che soleva intervenire el podestà»: era uno dei tre giudici triennali, che teneva il titolo di podestà e quindi di giudice delle esecuzioni, civili e penali. Un secondo giudice si sarebbe occupato della Mercanzia, mentre il terzo sarebbe stato giudice delle 'riformagioni', ossia consigliere legale degli organi dello Stato. I tre giudici ruotavano ogni sei mesi in questi incarichi ulteriori rispetto alla loro funzione primaria di giudici di appello.

19 Il primo caso valeva per le sentenze interlocutorie, il secondo per le definitive.

20 Su questi punti v. il mio Firenze dalla Repubblica al Principato, cit.

21 Anche i giudici provenienti da Pisa rinviano all'ostilità con Firenze; notevoli anche le presenze di giudici portoghesi in questi anni (e per tutto il secolo furono

voleva rafforzare i legami d'alleanza, e altri neo-laureati dell'Università di Siena legati al regime politico senese. La Rota, che avrebbe quindi dovuto dare una vernice di imparzialità al regime, potrebbe aver dato una prova negativa: questa è l'impressione visto che fu coinvolta nella caduta del governo dei Petrucci[22]. Ma già nel 1516 (4 settembre) si trova traccia di 'capitula addita' alla deliberazione istitutiva[23], e nel 1518 (27 maggio) furono approvate riforme chieste dai procuratori 'et curiam pratichantes'[24].

Si giunse così alle riforme del 1523 (30 marzo), che attribuiscono di nuovo la giustizia penale ad un Capitano di giustizia (come nella tradizione quattrocentesca)[25], le cui sentenze sono comunque sottoposte al sindacato in appello della ricostituita Rota; lo stesso provvedimento[26] sancisce che nelle cause di minor valore si dovrà procedere in modo sommario («debbino tenere ragione sommaria»): la Rota sotto le 25 lire, il giudice ordinario sotto le 10.

Con questo ordinamento delle corti centrali si pervenne alla riforma del 1541, in un momento di gravi conflitti politici che motivarono l'intervento diretto dell'inviato di Carlo V per assicurare la pace cittadina[27].

Infine, la Rota ebbe una dettagliata regolamentazione nel grande statuto che la città si diede nel 1545 – l'ultimo statuto di Siena, destinato a rimanere in vigore fino all'età napoleonica, ovviamente con modifiche varie[28]. Esso confermò la giustizia penale al Capitano (*praefectus Urbis* nel latino

---

frequenti, come si può dire grazie allo schedario (incompleto) predisposto da Carla Zarrilli, dell'Archivio di Stato di Siena, per il gruppo di ricerca coordinato da E. Fasano Guarini, che me ne ha consentitto gentilmente la consultazione; si v. la *Isaacs,* L'istituzione, cit., p. 365 nota 51, che segnala anche due giudici ordinari che erano laureati da un anno soltanto quando furono nominati – contro la regola della normativa istitutiva.

22 *Isaacs,* op.cit., p. 365.

23 Si v. ad es. nella bella raccolta normativa in Siena, Archivio arcivescovile 6519, c. 223rv.

24 Ibid., c. 223v.

25 Il fatto ha chiaramente un significato politico: si trattava di eliminare l'arbitrario tribunale degli Otto di guardia che aveva operato, pare, con criteri prettamente politici a difesa del regime. La serie archivistica del *Capitano di giustizia,* interrotta a fine Quattrocento, riprende infatti da questa data.

26 Testo in MS 6519 dell'Archivio arcivescovile, cit., cc. 223v - 225r.

27 Per cenni e rinvii bibliografici v. la mia introduzione allo statuto del 1545 (v. nota successiva); l'intervento del 1541 nel MS 6519, cc. 231r - 232v. A c. 280r, i 'capitoli' del 4 dicembre 1541, che riservavano all'inviato imperiale la prima nomina del Capitano di giustizia (previsto per un anno riconfermabile), mentre le due elezioni successive avrebbero avuto luogo a cura del Senato di Milano o del Collaterale di Napoli.

28 Ed. a cura di *M. Ascheri et alii,* L'ultimo statuto della Repubblica di Siena (1545) (Siena 1993) ad ind.

classicheggiante dello statuto), che doveva essere signore di castello o cavaliere o 'almeno' giurista in modo che non potesse essere disprezzato: proprio perché poteva anche non essere dotto era previsto che operasse coadiuvato da un vicario giurista almeno da 6 anni (I, 264).

La giustizia civile fu riservata invece a cinque giudici forestieri, come nel 1503: 2 per le prime istanze[29] e 3 per gli appelli e le nullità[30], operanti con l'aiuto di un'équipe di notai cittadini. Anche questa volta si previde il terzo grado di giurisdizione, che per le sentenze definitive comportava il riesame da parte di sei giudici[31], mentre per le interlocutorie prevedeva l'invio d'un *consilium* vincolante da parte del collegio dei sei al giudice *a quo*. Si parla di nuovo di decisione del giudice dissenziente: «ille qui non ierit in sententiam aliorum duorum Auditorum, si diversae fuerit opinionis, sub poena aureorum vigintiquinque fisco applicandorum, si sententia diffinitiva fuerit, eius sententia pariter in scriptis proferre (debet) causas exprimendo nec non rationes et iurium allegationes, quibus precipue motus fuerit ad dissentiendum ab opinione duorum Auditorum, eius in officio collegarum» (I, 278, p. 156 ca. me.). Se si trattasse di sentenza non definitiva bastava che l'opinione fosse scritta non dal giudice ma dal notaio.

Quel che conta è che «singulas quoque decisiones quae fieri contingerint ab Auditoribus praedictis in eorum officio in quibuscumque causis ad eorum pertinentibus officium, eorum completo officio, relaxent et relaxare teneantur et debeant in compendium redactas, et cum allegationibus et motivis iurium in Archivo palatii, in manibus custodis Archivi publici, sub poena florenorum centum, aerario fisci applicandorum; et huius rei ratio erit habenda in sindicatu, et non aliter a sindicatu liberentur nisi per eos effectualiter deposito in publico Archivo palatii decisionum compendio predicto» (I, 278). Non a caso il sindacato, disciplinato subito dopo, doveva essere svolto annualmente da un ufficio comunale, ma integrato da un *doctor* del collegio dei giudici, in modo che fosse presente un elemento tecnico per valutare come era stato svolto il lavoro.

Nello statuto è omesso un fatto interessante che compare nella riforma del 1541, laddove si sottolineava come l'ufficio della Rota e Consiglio di giustizia era importante e che erano quindi necessari provvedimenti, perché «le loro sententie danno et tolghano inrevocabilmente, et che da la buona giustitia nasce la pace et da la pacie el ben vivere universale, considerato

---

[29] Uno è giudice ordinario delle cause civili e dei danni dati; l'altro è giudice del placito (soprattutto per le tutele).

[30] Devono essere iscritti in un collegio di giudici da almeno 10 anni e vengono condotti per 3 anni a partire dal 1 ottobre; ognuno dei tre, come nel 1503, esercita le funzioni di podestà, giudice delle riformagioni e della Mercanzia a turni di 6 mesi (I, 275).

[31] Ossia il giudice ordinario, del placito, il vicario del Capitano e i tre di Rota.

anche ora esser nata nuova praticha indotta da poco tempo in qua, che li giudici di Ruota non vogliano ne le cause dare e dubbi, di modo che il più delle volte chi ha la sententia contra non sa la causa». Perciò si obbligavano i giudici a dare alle parti (o loro avvocati e procuratori, naturalmente) i «dubbi in scriptis sempre che alchuno gli domanderà», e inoltre a «servare et porre in charta tutte le ragioni, dottrine, authorità et cause, per le quali si muovano a giudicare così et ogni sei mesi se ne facci un libro et tenghisi nel archivio di cabella o delle riformationi acciò si vedino le decisioni che si faranno».

Fin qui la normativa. In che modo la documentazione riflette l'applicazione di queste previsioni? Chiariamo intanto che la documentazione pervenuta è abbondante ma molto irregolare e differenziata per il Giudice ordinario (civile) e il Capitano di giustizia (penale). Per il primo giudice abbiamo[32]:

(1) una serie di registri (ossia di volumi cartacei già rilegati prima dell'uso) con il diario delle udienze quotidiane (e quindi con rinvii interni perché una stessa causa è trattata in luoghi diversi) e delle lettere spedite ai giudici del territorio[33];

(2) una ricca raccolta di 'faldoni' (ossia grosse cartelle) con decine e decine di fascicoli processuali residuo dell'attività svolta[34], raccogliendo ogni fascicolo notizia dei fatti più importanti della causa (come documentato nel vol. II di quest'opera);

(3) taluni volumi di 'decisioni'[35], anch'esse in forma di registri cartacei.

Per il secondo giudice si posseggono i vari registri con annotazioni quotidiane[36] delle varie attività svolte, ossia rispettivamente: inquisizioni e loro

---

[32] Oltre a serie che attengono alla 'volontaria giurisdizione' svolta: si v. ad esempio: Giudice ordinario 3048, primo registro conservato delle donazioni insinuate negli anni 1611 - 1624.

[33] Ad es. Giudice ordinario 116, per il 1530, o il 205, per la seconda metà del 1540 (sulla copertina pergamenacea 'civilia').

[34] Ad es. in Giudice ordinario 117 sono conservati 53 fascicoli della seconda metà del 1529.

[35] Il primo conservato è Giudice ordinario 3037, con 44 decisioni non datate (ma riferibili agli anni 1582 - 90) di Cassiano del Pozzo, che sappiamo (dallo schedario citato a nota 21) aver giurato per prendere servizio anche nel 1608. La serie prosegue anche con cartelle che comprendono più registri fino alla cartella 3047, che ha al proprio interno i tomi XIX - XXIV secondo una numerazione settecentesca, con decisioni del 1681 al 1735.

[36] L'ordine delle annotazioni è cronologico, per cui i verbali di un singolo processo sono registrati in più luoghi dello stesso registro, con note marginali che aiutano a rintracciare la pagina; in alcuni volumi c'è anche un rubricario alfabetico con i nomi delle persone interessate: v. ad es. Capitano di giustizia 60 e 64 per due grossi registri di 'inquisizioni' del 1542 (in margine si indica se l'inquisito è stato

sviluppo processuale, accuse ricevute, denuncie presentate[37], tregue e paci concordate tra le parti (e inibenti l'attività del giudice) e 'faldoni' con fascicoli raccoglienti gli atti del singolo processo[38].

Per la Rota vera e propria le serie sono sostanzialmente[39] due: quella dei 'faldoni' con i fascicoli processuali rimasti[40], e quella delle 'decisioni', il cui primo volume conservato[41] risale agli anni 1541 - 1543 ed è relativo all'attività (346 decisioni, senza distinzione in civile e in penale) dei giudici Luca Franceschini, Pietro Calefati (giurista che ha lasciato più tracce della sua operosità)[42] e Matteo Marcolini, con in principio un indice di mano di fine secolo XVII – inizio XVIII (circostanza non irrilevante, come risulterà oltre) indicante gli argomenti delle singole pronuncie. Ogni gruppo di giudici ha lasciato un volume risultante dalla legatura successiva (ma già coeva) dei fascicoli riempiti da ognuno di loro. Le decisioni si succedono senza indicazioni di tempo (salvo l'indicazione generica degli anni di attività del gruppo nella copertina pergamenacea[43]), un giudice dopo l'altro, e in una scrittura relativamente calligrafica, certamente ottima rispetto a quella degli atti processuali. Gli scriventi sono quindi consapevoli che questa è la parte 'nobile' del loro lavoro. Tanto che si sottoscrivono in calce ai fogli o in fine ad ogni decisione. Le decisioni sono state numerate progressivamente per ogni giudice e più tardi rinumerate complessivamente all'interno di ogni volume.

L'obbligo di redigere e depositare le decisioni è stato quindi rispettato, ma tra carte processuali e decisioni non è affatto agevole capire come si

---

condannato o assolto; ci può anche essere indicazione del giudizio della Rota, come in Capitano di giustizia 60, c. 203r); numeri 61, 62 e 65 per le 'accuse'; nel numero 63 ci sono gli atti disposti su richiesta di parte (perquisizioni, interrogatori etc.).

[37] In particolare dai 'sindaci' delle comunità del territorio, che avevano l'obbligo di notificare i reati di cui venissero a conoscenza (e che attivavano l'inquisizione del giudice).

[38] Serie denominata 'Processi penali risoluti' (154 - 209).

[39] Serie minore è quella dei 'compromessi', tenuti a sé, con i numeri 87 - 103 (per gli anni 1558 - 1590). Importante per dare un'idea del lavoro complessivo della Rota la serie di registri in cui venivano annotate soltanto le sentenze: il volume più antico corre dall'aprile 1597 al maggio 1598: in circa 200 carte sono registrate circa 400 sentenze (rubricario all'inizio per rintracciare le parti).

[40] V. Tribunale di Ruota (questa è l'intestazione sulla costola, secondo un ordinamento che possiamo ritenere ottocentesco) 104 - 143 (anni 1504 - 1732).

[41] La serie prosegue fino al numero 52, con decisioni del 1808.

[42] V. la voce di *A. Mazzacane* in: Dizionario biografico degli Italiani, XVI (Roma 1973) p. 644 ss.

[43] Esempi nell'appendice. Più tardi (sec. XVII) è stata aggiunta l'indicazione del numero di serie (T. I = tomus primus etc.). Sul dorso l'indicazione (nell'esempio di cui nel testo) 'Decisiones Rotae a 1541 ad 1543 T. I' è stato aggiunto nel secolo XVIII, quando appunto c'era più interesse a rintracciare le decisioni.

potesse costituire un *case law* specifico in ambito senese. I fascicoli delle cause sono costruiti (indifferentemente quelli in primo grado e quelli d'appello) secondo la prassi quattrocentesca. Apre la 'petitio' (o l'atto d'appello, il 'libellus'), seguono i mandati per la rappresentanza processuale, le 'posizioni' dell'attore, la loro notificazione alla controparte, le varie udienze con le varie eccezioni, le (abbastanza normali) testimonianze sugli 'articoli' indicati dalle parti e in fine al fascicolo – di solito con scrittura più curata – il testo della sentenza – redatta nello stile asciutto dell'età precedente, senza motivazione[44], con sottoscrizione autografa del giudice seguita dall'attestato notarile circa il giorno e luogo della pronuncia, con relativi testimoni.

Dai fascicoli consultati – di assai difficile lettura, a parte l'atto introduttivo e la sentenza, perché redatti *currenti calamo* dai notai della corte – non risultano inclusi in queste raccolte processuali lo scambio di questioni di diritto (i 'dubia' di cui sopra)[45], né l'iter formativo della decisione del (o dei) giudice. Una possibilità è che la 'decisio' finale si potesse ritenere riassuntiva dei problemi di diritto sollevati nel corso del processo e che quindi non si ritenesse necessario conservare lo scambio delle memorie sui punti di diritto tra le parti e la corte. In effetti, la 'decisio' rotale senese è del tutto conforme a quelle a stampa del tipico 'mos rotalis' italiano[46], con il suo andamento fortemente dottrinale, tendenzialmente destinata a replicare a tutte le obiezioni alla decisione scelta infine dal giudice.

La 'decisio' è, cioè, una narrazione al passato («Moti fuimus») dell'itinerario dottrinale a suo tempo svolto dal giudice per giungere alla sentenza, ma l'autonomia tra quest'ultima e la motivazione è tale che mentre la sentenza è conservata nel fascicolo processuale, la 'decisio' è a parte e non veniva neppure redatta contestualmente alla sentenza, ma dopo, quasi fosse una riflessione dottrinale sulla stessa – purché prima di lasciare l'ufficio o entro i sei mesi di cui alla normativa sopra richiamata.

---

44 Ne ho riportato esempi in: 'Giustizia ordinaria', cit., in: Tribunali, giuristi, cit.

45 Non solo a Siena i giudici erano restii a concederli. «Questo dar dubii gli Auditori sempre lo aborirono sì perché bisogna a voler dar dubii relevanti et da persone dotte dilligentemente veder li processi e poi porvi studio», ammette una relazione cinquecentesca bolognese citata da *F. Boris* e *T. Di Zio,* La Rota di Bologna, in: Grandi Tribunali e Rote, cit., pp. 131 - 154 (142s.). È singolare che neppure nell'atto di appello (molti ci sono conservati anziché in Rota tra le carte del Capitano di giustizia, giudice a quo) si dichiarassero concreti motivi giuridici: si chiede che venga pronunciata la nullità perché la sentenza è stata ingiusta e contraria al diritto perché il giudice era incompetente o comunque 'come si dirà' in futuro...

46 Studiato ancora in uno dei suoi 'snodi' centrali da *G. Gorla,* Procedimento individuale. Voto dei singoli giudici e collegialità 'rotale': la prassi della Rota di Macerata nel quadro di quella di altre Rote o simili tribunali fra i secoli XVI e XVIII, in: Grandi tribunali e Rote, cit., pp. 3 - 78.

Al suo interno la decisione ingloba le argomentazioni *verosimilmente* addotte dalle parti nel corso del processo in fogli poi (di regola)[47] non conservati nel fascicolo proprio perché la 'decisio' ne deve tener conto («Ad primum dubium... Ad secundum... respondetur») per così dire 'costituzionalmente'. Ma questo modo di procedere non solo non ci permette di valutare il lavoro degli avvocati, ma non ci consente neppure di accertare fino a che punto il giudice dovesse contenersi entro gli ambiti argomentativi proposti dalle parti e entro quali limiti invece potesse spaziare oltre, proponendone di propria iniziativa. Le posizioni 'teoriche' degli avvocati perciò non vengono citate direttamente, ma attraverso le citazioni di dottrina e di giurisprudenza (di altri tribunali: Rota Romana, d'Afflitto etc.)[48] da loro utilizzate e influenti, in positivo o in negativo, sulla decisione del giudice adito.

In questo primo Cinquecento la Rota senese non ha ancora raccolte di decisioni a stampa, e i giudici sembra che non avessero interesse a citare i precedenti del tribunale dalle raccolte manoscritte depositate. Un controllo eseguito sul IV volume di decisioni conservate[49], consente di accertare che la Rota continua a citare i 'dottori', in particolare del '400 (Paolo di Castro, Alessandro Tartagni etc., ma anche i più recenti Felino Sandei e Filippo Decio, che aveva anche insegnato a Siena), o le raccolte dell'Afflitto e della Rota romana, ma non la propria giurisprudenza.

Gli stessi volumi delle decisioni sono in una scrittura accurata, all'opposto degli atti processuali, e quindi verosimilmente predisposti proprio perché ne fosse facilitata la consultazione. Tuttavia, la prassi non sembra tenerne conto, e l'assenza di repertori e di indici antichi che facilitassero la loro consultazione confermano che non era *necessaria* la loro consultazione in questo primo periodo di attività della Rota.

Si vince la causa (e quindi anche si motiva da parte del giudice) utilizzando quella dottrina di diritto comune (giurisprudenza compresa di altri 'grandi tribunali') che fosse consultabile da parte di chiunque, cioè quella a stampa. Il giudice di Rota non pretende che l'avvocato gli ricordi la giuris-

---

47 Solo occasionalmente si possono rintracciare brevi memorie difensive (scritte in modo fortunatamente un po' più chiaro della scrittura notarile di corte) con citazioni di dottori: ad es. in Capitano di Giustizia 157 ci sono *defensiones* non firmate per un inquisito mantovano nel 1541 con citazioni del Tartagni, Bartolomeo Socini e Ippolito Marsili, e per un altro processo *responsiones et allegationes* di un accusatore che cita Bartolo, il Socini (IV vol. dei *consilia*) e Ippolito Marsili.

48 È la situazione descritta in: Tribunali, giuristi, cit., p. 89 ss. (dall'originale in tedesco dell'Handbuch der Quellen und Literatur der neueren europäischen Privatrechtsgeschichte, hrsg. *H. Coing*, II.2 (München 1976) pp. 1113 - 1221).

49 ASSi, Tribunale di Ruota 4; anni 1556 - 1558, giudici Selvatico Guidi (52 decisioni), Gerolamo Papponi (51) e Gaspare Pinario (uno dei tanti portoghesi, 49).

prudenza della corte, né l'avvocato si cura di farlo, perché sa che il giudice non ne è al corrente e non si prende cura di essa (di solito almeno). Il giudice avrebbe dovuto svolgere un lavoro ulteriore rispetto a quello corrente che avrebbe avuto un senso preciso ove il giudice fosse stato a vita in quella sede. Invece, già sapendo che dopo il triennio sarebbe passato ad altro tribunale[50], il giudice non si curava che di aggiornarsi sulla dottrina di diritto comune 'generale', quella che gli sarebbe stata utile anche altrove.

Depone in questo senso anche il MS 6519[51], ricco di annotazioni marginali che attestano un uso certamente dotto del volume – probabilmente nella corte vescovile[52]. Ebbene, la mano circa di metà Cinquecento molto diffusa nei margini confronta nelle sue annotazioni i testi normativi senesi con la dottrina di diritto comune, ma senza mai citare l'uso del foro senese! Lo stesso dicasi per un'altra interessante raccolta manoscritta, che attesta comunque interesse per la giurisprudenza rotale senese. Un manoscritto (eccezionalmente) ci tramanda in copia una selezione del volume delle decisioni ufficiali citate, degli anni 1541 - 1543[53]. Ebbene, le note marginali di cui è corredato, anche se non frequenti, rinviano alle posizioni dei 'dottori', e non a decisioni rotali che pure quelle confermassero o meno.

I 'dottori' – e i giudici della Rota sono tali – per farsi capire da tutti hanno bisogno di rifarsi alle dottrine a tutti accessibili, che sono appunto (ormai) quelle circolanti a stampa. Forse, in questo primo tempo di diffusione delle decisioni dei nuovi tribunali dotti, si pensava che citare decisioni manoscritte sarebbe stato come motivare insufficientemente le proprie opinioni, perché in modo non riscontrabile con facilità. Bisognava fondarsi sulle dottrine accessibili a tutti per avere credibilità. Gli avvocati nelle loro comparse utilizzavano i dottori, e altrettanto facevano i giudici nel rispondere. Siamo quindi in piena efficacia del diritto comune dottrinale: gli

---

50 Sulla mobilità dei giudici, importante perché spiega anche l'omogeneità del mondo 'rotale' italiano, v. ora i primi dati d'una ricerca svolta in più sedi esposti dalla coordinatrice nazionale *E. Fasano Guarini,* Per una prosopografia dei giudici di Rota. Linee di una ricerca collettiva, in: Grandi tribunali e Rote, cit., pp. 389 - 420 (seguono dati particolari di *B. G. Zenobi* su Avignone, *A. Gardi* su Bologna, *C. Penuti* su Ferrara, *C. Bitossi* su Genova, *A. M. Napolioni* su Macerata, *M. Bonvini Mazzanti* su Urbino).

51 La raccolta normativa dell'Archivio arcivescovile citata.

52 Si noti l'elegante legatura in pelle e la cura calligrafica del testo.

53 Siena, Biblioteca Comunale, MS H V 42; di mano del secondo '500, 169 decisioni; la 34, ad es., corrisponde alla 5 del giudice Franceschini in ASSi, Tribunale di Ruota 1. Nella stessa Biblioteca il MS E IV 14, di mano del secondo Cinquecento, reca un'adespota 'Praxis iuxta consuetudinem Senensem' (dai libri di Antonio Sestigiani), che reca la formula sia della sentenza definitiva di prima istanza che d'appello, ma caratteristicamente senza neppure ricordare le 'decisiones', pur ormai 'rituali' da tempo.

stessi statuti di Siena sono ricordati perché danno problemi di interpretazione, ma questi vengono risolti secondo gli schemi tipici del diritto comune.

Le decisioni della Rota senese avrebbero cominciato a far parte del mondo delle opinioni utilizzabili dal momento in cui fossero state trasferite a stampa, ad uso di tutti. Ma per quelle senesi la tradizione sotto questa forma a disposizione degli operatori del diritto comincia solo relativamente tardi. Nel 1564 solo alcune decisioni sono inserite in una raccolta più ampia del giudice Pietro Benintendi[54]; poi, nel 1587[55] dal giudice Gerolamo Magoni, lo stesso che fu coinvolto in ancora oscure vicende che condussero tra l'altro a far vietare in Toscana la circolazione d'una sua raccolta di decisioni. Una prima questione era emersa nel 1577 quando un giudice allora alla Rota fiorentina (Giuseppe Ludovisi) aveva pubblicato una raccolta di decisioni lucchesi: un'edizione successiva (Venezia 1586) aveva dovuto accogliere anche il nome del Magoni – evidentemente leso nel suo 'diritto d'autore'. Ma quando questi si occupò anche di decisioni della Rota di Firenze (dove, guarda caso, era stato operoso il Ludovisi), con un'edizione del 1588[56], provocò un bando granducale che ne vietava la circolazione perché «né vista, né approvata»[57].

Nella Firenze della Controriforma tutto si voleva controllare e non si vedeva favorevolmente la diffusione di atti che erano pur sempre 'statali'. L'orientamento doveva finire per avere presto ripercussioni anche a Siena. Tanto è vero che nel 1590, nell'ex-capoluogo ormai inglobato nel granducato di Toscana, si obbligarono i giudici a non stampare e a non far stampare le proprie decisioni[58]. Vero è che nel secolo successivo tali divieti saranno nella prassi superati, ma, visti questi precedenti, non è un caso che per giungere ad una raccolta specificamente dedicata alla Rota senese si debba attendere quella del Marzi-Medici del 1628[59]. L'opera però ebbe solo due edizioni, a quanto pare, e non è neppur sicuro che avesse una grande circolazione.

---

54 Già giudice a Siena negli anni 1526 - 29 e poi negli anni '40. La sua raccolta è ufficialmente dedicata a quelle bolognesi: v. *Ascheri,* Tribunali, cit., p. 213.

55 È una raccolta ufficialmente lucchese: v. ibid., p. 215, poi accresciuta con decisioni fiorentine: v. ibid.

56 Si v. il mio Tribunali, giuristi, cit., p. 215.

57 Si v. *E. Fasano Guarini,* I giuristi e lo Stato nella Toscana medicea cinque-seicentesca, in: Firenze e la Toscana dei Medici nell'Europa del '500, I (Firenze 1988) pp. 229 - 247 (234), e v. già il mio: Tribunali, giuristi, cit., pp. 121 e 175 nota 313 per lavori di J. Hilgers e A. Panella, ove anche riferimento al più generale controllo della stampa; si v. poi p. 173 nota 289 per disordini a Lucca in sede di sindacato del Magoni nel 1592.

58 Si v. il mio: Tribunali, giuristi, cit., p. 121.

59 Ibid., p. 224.

Per trovare massicce citazioni di giurisprudenza senese bisogna giungere alle raccolte del '700 (De Comitibus e Neri Badia)[60], ossia del secolo che si avvia verso una giurisprudenza 'regionale' toscana. Allora, mentre circolano anche con larghezza 'voti' e decisioni singole, in forma di 'volanti' stampate per il singolo processo, diviene normale ricordare la giurisprudenza locale.

Ma prima essa non gode di alcun privilegio. Anzi, sembra meno credibile della dottrina con più ampia diffusione. Il deposito e la pubblicità delle decisioni non avevano avuto infatti la funzione di creare una giurisprudenza locale *erga omnes,* che valesse a sostituire con il tempo la dottrina di diritto comune, ma soltanto di dare maggior credibilità alle pronuncie giudiziarie in un mondo fortemente turbato dall'invadenza eccessiva della politica e dalle faziosità da essa indotte nell'amministrazione della giustizia[61]. Solo con la crisi definitiva del mondo comunale e l'altrettanto definitivo rafforzarsi degli ordinamenti principeschi le decisioni cominceranno invece ad essere riguardate anche in Toscana come un'alternativa plausibile, nella crisi crescente del diritto comune: una opzione relativamente 'certa' contro il caos delle opinioni dottrinali.

Nel Cinquecento l'esistenza di motivazioni autentiche e pubbliche (anche in penale!) coesistente con uno scarso interesse per la giurisprudenza (mancanza di 'ricordi' di giudici, di 'reports') sembra attestare la perdurante piena vitalità del sistema del diritto comune quanto meno in Toscana: delle 'auctoritates' dei dottori liberamente circolanti al di là delle frontiere politiche, tra ordinamenti statali ben diversi. Con conseguenze ovviamente anche paradossali: in Toscana si dà ampio credito alle decisioni napoletane (in quanto fini elaborazioni dottrinali, naturalmente, e non in quanto espressione di quell'ordinamento...) e si vieta la diffusione delle proprie! L'idea che sembra sottostare a un atteggiamento del genere è che se altri si sono ormai sottoposti al giudizio internazionale mettendo in circolazione le proprie decisioni – come appunto hanno fatto i Romani e i Napoletani – tanto meglio: si utilizzeranno per quello che sanno proporre di buono, come avviene per ogni altra opera dottrinale. Ma le 'proprie' decisioni, anche se di giudici dotti e preparati, è bene tenerle riservate, per evitare che possano essere criticate, travolgendo con ciò anche l'autorità e l'immagine dello Stato.

L'argomento si spiega solo storicamente, com'è ovvio, nel quadro del tutt'altro che lineare, plurisecolare processo di costruzione dell'assolutismo statale[62]. Non può sfuggire un suo profilo che potrebbe apparire – come

---

60 Ibid., ad ind.

61 V. ad es. *J. Hook,* Justice, authority and the creation of the Ancien régime in Italy, Transactions of the Royal Historical Society, 5th series, 34 (1984), pp. 71 - 89.

62 Istruttivo ad es. l'evolversi del rapporto Stato-Chiesa: v. *A. D'Addario,* Aspetti della Controriforma a Firenze (Roma 1972) pp. 144 - 175.

dire? – un po' 'schizoide': da un lato si vieta la diffusione della propria giurisprudenza per non coinvolgere la maestà del proprio Stato, ma dall'altro si riconosce implicitamente l'incapacità dello stesso Stato di dare una piena regolamentazione ai rapporti sociali ammettendo (di nuovo implicitamente) che i giudici possano tranquillamente ricorrere alla giurisprudenza altrui! Era una contraddizione, e fu presto risolta – come s'è detto, 'aprendo' la giurisprudenza locale[63]. Rimaneva comunque fermo – sul punto non ci sono pronunce, perché era del tutto ovvio – che quel ricorso al *case law* straniero era possibile *imperio rationis,* non certo *imperio iurisdictionis*...

[63] Di cui si è largamente servito *Gino Gorla* in più saggi. V. ad es.: Il Museo Guarnacci di Volterra, la Fabbrica di Porcellane Ginori e i palazzi di Firenze, in: Foro italiano 1972, V parte; Breve addizione a il Museo Guarnacci..., ibid., 1977; Appunti sui 'Tribunalia' e 'Magistratus' con funzioni amministrative e giudiziarie operanti fra i secoli XVI e XVIII nello Stato pontificio e nel Granducato di Toscana, in: Foro italiano 1990; A decision of the Rota Fiorentina of 1780 on liability for damages caused by the 'ball game', Tulane Law Review 49 (1975), pp. 346 - 357.

BERNADETTE AUZARY-SCHMALTZ
ET SERGE DAUCHY

Le Parlement de Paris*

Le vaste rayonnement du Parlement et l'abondance des sources qui relatent l'histoire et le fonctionnement de l'institution ont conduit les organisateurs du projet *Case Law in the Making* à prévoir une répartition chronologique.

La présentation des recueils d'arrêts du Moyen Age (tome I) et leur collation avec les registres (tome II) a été assurées par Bernadette *Auzary-Schmaltz* (ingénieur de recherche, Paris), Serge *Dauchy* (chargé de recherche, Lille) s'étant chargé de l'examen des recueils des Temps Modernes (tome I) et de leur comparaison avec les sources (tome II).

L'histoire générale de l'institution et des sources nécessitant une présentation affranchie de barrières chronologiques, la répartition de la tâche s'est faite par thème, une collaboration s'étant néanmoins instaurée entre les auteurs pendant l'élaboration de cette étude.

Dans le premier volume, sont traités successivement:

1. Le Parlement de Paris: Cour souveraine du royaume de France.
2. Les archives du Parlement de Paris.
3. Les recueils d'arrêts privés au Moyen Age.
4. Les recueils privés de 'jurisprudence' aux Temps Modernes.

Dans le second volume est présentée la collation des recueils privés avec les registres de la Cour:

1. Le Parlement de Paris au Moyen Age.
2. Le Parlement de Paris aux Temps Modernes.

---

* Cette étude a pu être réalisée grâce au soutien apporté par le C.E.H.J. (CNRS – Université Paris II – Archives de France). Nous remercions en particulier Mme Chavarot et Mme Lemaire, ainsi que M. le Professeur Hilaire.

I. Le Parlement de Paris: Cour souveraine du royaume de France[1]

Le Parlement de Paris, contrairement à ce que pourrait laisser penser son nom, n'est pas une institution représentative mais une cour de justice. C'est probablement même la plus connue des anciennes cours supérieures de l'Europe occidentale. Cette notoriété, la cour souveraine du royaume de France la doit tant au prestige de sa fonction qu'à son ancienneté, à l'importance de ses compétences et à l'étendue de son ressort. L'histoire du Parlement de Paris est étroitement liée à celle de la royauté elle-même puisque cette cour exerce le droit souverain par excellence des princes que restera, tout au long de l'Ancien Régime, l'exercice de la justice. Le Parlement ne pouvait donc se développer comme cour souveraine du royaume qu'après la consolidation du pouvoir royal. L'institution a d'ailleurs largement contribué à asseoir l'autorité royale, l'appel à la cour supérieure constituant le signe le plus tangible de l'appartenance au royaume. Mais sa puissance et son ambition étaient telles que le Parlement fut aussi une institution politique redoutable, représentant à de nombreux moments de son histoire une menace pour la monarchie. Narrer les vicissitudes de l'institution c'est presque écrire l'histoire de la monarchie. Présenter son organisation et son personnel, c'est étudier la rationalisation, la centralisation et la professionnalisation de la justice. Enfin, l'analyse des contentieux permet de retracer l'évolution du droit et surtout d'entrer dans l'Histoire, comme le relevait déjà le célèbre jurisconsulte français Dupin qui exerçait les fonctions de procureur général au milieu du XIXe siècle: «l'histoire seule du Parlement de Paris serait une grande partie de l'histoire de France et la plus importante sans doute puisque ce serait celle de notre législation, de notre gouvernement, de notre droit public intérieur; mais cette histoire est encore à faire: elle est tout entière dans les registres et dans les archives. Qui jamais aura la patience, le courage et le loisir de l'en tirer?».

Dans cette brève présentation on trouvera d'abord un aperçu succinct des origines du Parlement de Paris, son organisation et ses principales fonctions. Ensuite seront abordés les rapports de la cour souveraine avec le pouvoir politique et avec les parlements de province et sa contribution au développement du droit formel et matériel.

1. Les origines du Parlement de Paris

Les origines du Parlement de Paris remontent aux XIIe et XIIIe siècles, moment où sont réunies les conditions nécessaires pour transformer une délégation occasionnelle de la justice en cour de justice permanente et sou-

---

[1] Par Serge Dauchy.

veraine[2]. La royauté impose alors sa compétence judiciaire au détriment des justices seigneuriales et municipales. Dans un domaine royal agrandi de façon spectaculaire, le roi met en place, au-dessus des prévôts, de nouveaux juges royaux, les baillis et sénéchaux. Parallèlement, on abandonne également les anciens modes irrationnels de preuves pour généraliser une nouvelle procédure empruntée aux officialités[3]. Le pouvoir royal peut ainsi soumettre à l'appel les jugements prononcés par les juges royaux devant sa cour avant d'étendre également cet appel hiérarchique aux décisions rendues par les juridictions des grands vassaux du roi. Il en résulte un afflux important et continu de procédures judiciaires devant la *curia regis,* nécessitant la formation d'une structure spécialisée dans leur traitement. Les premiers signes d'évolution sont perceptibles dès le règne de Philippe Ier. Les actes royaux de cette époque font état d'une distinction entre les féodaux, appelés *optimates* ou pairs du royaume, et les conseillers permanents nommés *curiales.* Cette spécialisation des tâches judiciaires se poursuit et se renforce encore sous le règne de Louis VII (1137 - 1180) puisqu'un corps de juristes professionnels, que les actes désignent sous le nom de *judices nostri,* apparaît dans l'entourage royal. Un noyau permanent, indépendant de l'élément féodal, est créé auquel le roi confie les affaires courantes pour ne garder par-devers lui que les litiges concernant les grands du royaume et les procès à caractère politique[4]. Chacune de ces sessions,

---

2 De très nombreuses études ont été consacrées aux origines et à l'histoire du Parlement de Paris; les principales monographies étant: *F. Aubert,* Le Parlement de Paris de Philippe le Bel à Charles VII (1314 - 1422), t. 1: Son organisation, t. 2: Sa compétence et ses attributions (Paris 1887 - 1890); *Ch.-V. Langlois,* Les origines du Parlement de Paris, dans: Revue historique, t. 42 (Paris 1890), pp. 74 - 114; *F. Aubert,* Histoire du Parlement de Paris de l'origine à François Ier (1250 - 1515), 2 t. (Paris 1894); *G. Ducoudray,* Les origines du Parlement de Paris et la justice aux XIIIe et XIVe siècles, 2 t. (Paris 1902); *E. Maugis,* Histoire du Parlement de Paris de l'avènement des rois Valois à la mort d'Henri IV, 3 t. (Paris 1914 - 1916) et *J. Shennan,* The Parlement of Paris (Londres 1968).

3 L'ouvrage de référence en matière de procédure civile reste *P. Guilhiermoz,* Enquêtes et procès. Etude sur la procédure et le fonctionnement du Parlement au XIVe siècle (Paris 1892). Sur ses origines et son évolution, on consultera *P. Fournier,* Les officialités au Moyen Age. Etude sur le développement, la compétence et la procédure des tribunaux ecclésiastiques ordinaires en France de 1180 à 1328 (Paris 1880); *E. Glasson,* Les sources de la procédure civile française, dans: Nouvelle revue historique de droit français et étranger, t. V, 1881, pp. 401 - 433; *J. Tardif,* La procédure civile et criminelle aux XIIIe et XIVe siècles ou procédure de transition (Paris 1885). La relation entre le développement de la procédure romano-canonique et les efforts de centralisation du royaume a été explicitée par *J. Hilaire,* La procédure et l'influence de l'Etat: autour de l'appel, dans: *J. Krynen* et *A. Rigaudière* éds., Droits savants et pratiques françaises du pouvoir (XIe - XVe siècles) (Bordeaux 1992), pp. 151 - 160.

4 La genèse des institutions royales est retracée, entre autres, par *F. Lot* et *R. Fawtier,* Histoire des institutions françaises au Moyen-âge, 3 vol. (Paris 1957 -

tenues à périodicité régulière et réunissant un personnel qualifié à la composition de plus en plus stable est désignée dans les documents de cette époque sous le nom de *Parlamentum*[5]. En quelques décennies, cette section 'judiciaire' va se détacher de la *curia regis* et former une institution distincte qui se sédentarise dans le palais du roi à Paris et il existe d'ailleurs une étonnante continuité puisque l'Ile de la Cité est encore occupée de nos jours par le Palais de justice. Le Parlement de Paris devient ainsi une cour supérieure permanente dont l'activité s'étend sur presque toute l'année puisque les sessions débutent à la Saint-Martin d'hiver (le 11 novembre) pour ne se terminer qu'en août de l'année suivante. La sédentarisation donna de surcroît lieu à l'organisation d'un greffe permettant la rédaction uniforme et l'expédition des décisions judiciaires. Leur conservation sous forme de registres allait donner naissance à la série des 'arrêts et jugés' – dont les quatre premiers volumes sont appelés *Olim* (1254 - 1318) – et constituent la base indispensable au développement d'une jurisprudence. A partir de la fin du XIVe siècle on dispose également d'autres registres contenant la transcription des délibérations de la cour, des plaidoiries, des amendes prononcées, des accords entérinés par les conseillers et des sentences criminelles.

2. L'organisation du Parlement de Paris

Par une ordonnance de 1345[6], Philippe VI a fourni au Parlement les bases indispensables à son établissement en tant que cour de justice centrale et souveraine: la stabilité du personnel judiciaire qui perçoit des appointements fixes et, dans la mesure du possible, versés régulièrement ainsi que l'organisation interne de la cour. Ainsi, dès le XIVe siècle, le Parlement de Paris est divisé en trois chambres. La Grand'Chambre, dont les autres ne sont que des émanations, est la seule habilitée à rendre des arrêts. C'est également devant cette Grand'Chambre que les avocats plaident les causes qui ne sont pas instruites par écrit. On ne plaidait à l'origine que le matin. Mais, autre signe de l'augmentation constante des contentieux, dès le début du XVe siècle il fallut prévoir des sessions supplémentaires. La Chambre des Enquêtes est chargée de l'instruction des pièces écrites des dossiers et elle juge les appels des sentences rendues sur procès par écrit. Ces procédures sont engagées après que la Chambre des Requêtes (ou

---

1962) et par *J. Ellul,* Histoire des institutions, II, 1: Institutions françaises du moyen âge à 1789 (Paris 1956).

[5] On en retrouve la plus ancienne mention dans un acte de 1239 édité par *Ch.-V. Langlois,* Textes relatifs à l'histoire du Parlement depuis les origines jusqu'en 1314 (Paris 1888), n° 36.

[6] *E. de Laurière,* Ordonnances des roys de France de la troisième race recueillies par ordre chronologique, t. II (1723), pp. 219 - 224.

Requêtes du Palais) s'est prononcée sur la recevabilité des litiges portés devant la cour[7]. Elle perdra cette raison d'être dès lors que la procédure sera bien fixée et jugera aux Temps Modernes les titulaires du privilège de *committimus* par lequel les bénéficiaires étaient autorisés, quel que soit leur lieu de résidence, à plaider directement devant Parlement de Paris. Il faut encore signaler l'existence d'une section criminelle composée de conseillers laïques. Elle décharge la Grand'Chambre des affaires de sang que les conseillers clercs ne pouvaient connaître en raison de leur état. En 1515, François Ier l'érige en Chambre criminelle, appelée aussi *Tournelle* criminelle car des magistrats de la Grand'Chambre et de la Chambre des Enquêtes y servent à tour de rôle. Cette tournante avait pour but de ne pas charger toujours les mêmes conseillers des affaires pénales et d'éviter l'endurcissement d'hommes amenés à prononcer des sentences capitales[8]. Durant les siècles suivants, le nombre sans cesse croissant de litiges obligera le Parlement à multiplier les Chambres: ainsi le Parlement de Paris comptera au XVIIIe siècle cinq Chambres des Enquêtes et deux des Requêtes.

Les magistrats étaient nommés par le roi qui consultait préalablement son chancelier et les membres de son conseil. Après avoir obtenu un droit de présentation des candidats à nommer, l'ordonnance de 1389[9] accorde au Parlement le droit d'élire les nouveaux conseillers, introduisant ainsi dès la fin du XIVe siècle une cooptation de fait. Les présidents de chaque chambre dont le premier est le président de la Grand'chambre, sont également élus par leurs pairs et, après approbation du roi, installés par le chancelier. Les élections sont en principe libres, mais il arrive très fréquemment que le roi, la reine ou les princes exercent des pressions auxquelles il n'est pas toujours possible, ou souhaitable, de se soustraire. Les clientèles princières n'étaient donc pas négligeables, tout comme d'ailleurs les solidarités féodales et bourgeoises. Pour être conseiller, on ne devait – du moins officiellement – pas posséder un diplôme universitaire en droit romain ou en droit canonique, qualification qu'on exigeait, au contraire, des procureurs et avocats. Les ordonnances prévoient tout au plus qu'une commission de conseillers nommée par le roi doit examiner les candidats et éliminer ceux qui n'auraient «ni l'âge ni les connaissances voulus». A partir de la fin du XIVe siècle, on constate pourtant que presque tous les candidats, tant laïques que clercs, possèdent une licence en droit et, si le diplôme juridique n'a jamais été imposé par la législation royale, il semble bien qu'il n'est déjà plus possible au XVe siècle d'accéder à la charge de conseiller sans

[7] *F. Aubert,* Les requêtes du Palais (XIIIe - XVIe siècles), dans: Bibliothèque de l'Ecole des Chartes, t. LXIX (Paris 1908).

[8] *J.-M. Carbasse,* Introduction historique au droit pénal [Collection Droit fondamental] (Paris 1990), pp. 111 - 113.

[9] *E. de Laurière,* op. cit., t. VII, p. 224 sq.

formation universitaire. Cette évolution marque le professionnalisme accru des juges mais apparaît néanmoins comme contradictoire puisque les conseillers sont tenus de juger les appels non selon le droit romain – considéré comme l'instrument abusivement utilisé par l'Empereur pour tenter d'établir sa supériorité universelle – mais en se basant exclusivement sur les coutumes et les ordonnances, matières qui n'étaient pas enseignées dans les universités.

A la fin du XIVe et au début du XVe siècle, à la suite de la minorité puis de la folie de Charles VI, le royaume traverse une crise profonde. Le Parlement de Paris est alors l'enjeu de la lutte fratricide entre Armagnacs et Bourguignons. Le principe de la cooptation est détourné de sa véritable finalité qui était de pourvoir l'institution de conseillers compétents et indépendants et on voit, au contraire, la cour souveraine livrée au clientélisme princier. Après l'entrée des troupes anglaises et bourguignonnes à Paris, le dauphin établira même en 1418 sa propre 'cour souveraine' à Poitiers, le Parlement de Paris rendant alors ses jugements au nom d'Henri, roi de France et d'Angleterre. Si les deux cours affirment leur légitimité exclusive et prétendent à ce titre exercer chacun le droit souverain de juger en dernier ressort, les conseillers font pourtant preuve d'indépendance et ils semblent ainsi les seuls encore capables d'incarner la continuité de l'Etat. Le 'schisme' ne prendra fin qu'en 1436 lorsque Charles VII installera à nouveau sa cour souveraine à Paris. Le roi y réunira les conseillers des deux parlements, exprimant ainsi sa volonté de restaurer et de pacifier le royaume. Cet épisode de l'histoire de France marquera profondément et durablement l'organisation judiciaire puisqu'il aboutira à la reconnaissance de l'inamovibilité des juges[10]. Louis XI accordera ce statut à l'ensemble des officiers royaux[11]. Puis, durant les deux siècles suivants, les conseillers obtiendront l'hérédité de leurs charges, ceci avant que le pouvoir impose la vénalité des offices[12]. A partir du XVIe siècle, les rois vont élever la vénalité au rang de système cohérent de gouvernement, la création et la vente de nouveaux offices devant renflouer les finances royales. En 1521, François Ier crée quelque cinquante offices de conseillers et de présidents qui tous sont 'mis en vente' par le monarque. La résignation en faveur d'un héritier donne également lieu au paiement d'un *droit de relief* fixé à un dixième de la valeur de l'office. Les magistrats ont ainsi été obligés d'ac-

---

[10] *Fr. Autrand,* Naissance d'un grand corps de l'Etat. Les gens du Parlement de Paris (1345 - 1454) (Paris 1981). On consultera également, pour retracer les événement de cette époque, *J. Favier,* La guerre de Cent Ans (Paris 1980) et *B. Schnerb,* Armagnacs et Bourguignons. La maudite guerre (Paris 1988).

[11] *J. Kubler,* L'origine de la perpétuité des officiers royaux (Nancy 1958).

[12] Les principales études en la matière restent *G. Pagès,* La vénalité des offices dans l'ancienne France, dans: Revue historique, t. 169 (1932), pp. 477 - 495 et *R. Mousnier,* La vénalité des offices sous Henri IV et Louis XII (Rouen 1945).

cepter la vénalité pour conserver les offices dans le patrimoine familial. Contrairement à ce qu'on pourrait croire à première vue, la vénalité a renforcé l'inamovibilité des magistrats. Comment pouvait-on encore révoquer un officier qui avait acheté sa charge? L'hérédité et la vénalité des charges ont alors fait l'objet d'une réglementation rigoureuse, surtout en ce qui concerne le montant des droits, sans cesse plus nombreux, à acquitter en cas de vente d'une charge ou lors d'une résignation en faveur d'un héritier désigné. La plus connue de ces taxes est sans aucun doute la *paulette*, introduite par Henri IV en 1604 sur proposition de son secrétaire Charles Paulet. Celle-ci officialisa la transmission héréditaire des offices contre paiement d'une taxe annuelle dont le montant correspondait à un seizième de la valeur de la charge. Toute mobilité vers des fonctions supérieures peu nombreuses et de plus en plus souvent confiées à des commissaires révocables devint dès lors quasiment impossible. La stabilité du corps tourne dès lors à l'enracinement. Une carrière parlementaire devient donc l'objectif que les officiers de justice souhaitent atteindre et on s'attache à garder l'office, d'autant plus qu'un des principaux attraits de la charge de conseiller au Parlement était qu'elle procurait la possibilité d'accéder à la noblesse, qui conférait de nombreux avantages tels l'exemption de taille. Ainsi se répandra, aux Temps Modernes, l'image de ces grandes familles de parlementaires, constituant la *noblesse de robe* et qui ont fourni à la cour souveraine plusieurs générations de conseillers, d'avocats et de procureurs[13].

Tout au long de son histoire, le personnel du Parlement va considérablement augmenter en nombre. L'ordonnance de 1345 prévoyait trois présidents, 44 conseillers clercs et 29 conseillers laïques. Au milieu du XVIe siècle on dénombre quelque 150 officiers, leur nombre passant à 260 dans la première moitié du XVIIIe siècle. La Grand'Chambre comporte alors neuf présidents à mortier chargés d'assister ou au besoin de suppléer le premier président et 33 conseillers (12 clercs et 21 laïques). Les cinq Chambres des Enquêtes comptent chacune trois présidents et 32 conseillers et les deux Chambres des Requêtes, trois présidents et dix à douze conseillers.

3. Les fonctions du Parlement

Investi d'une délégation permanente du roi, le Parlement rend, en son nom, la justice en dernier ressort. Juridiction d'appel avant tout, le Parlement de Paris se prononce sur les sentences des tribunaux de droit

---

[13] *J. F. Bluche,* L'origine des magistrats du Parlement de Paris au XVIIIe siècle (Paris 1956); *Idem,* Les magistrats du Parlement de Paris (1715 - 1771) (Paris 1960) et *J. Félix,* Les magistrats du Parlement de Paris (1771 - 1790): dictionnaire biographique et généalogique (Paris 1990). Voir également *F. Sword,* Robe and Sword. The regrouping of the French aristocracy after Louis XIV (Harvard 1953), p. 53 sq.

commun. Il reçoit aussi en appel les décisions des justices seigneuriales, des pairs et de quelques tribunaux d'exception ainsi que des appels comme d'abus des décisions des juges d'Eglise. Dans certaines circonstances enfin le Parlement est juge de première instance: il est compétent, de manière exclusive, pour les affaires de régale ainsi que celles qui touchent les princes de sang et les apanages.

Le Parlement est parallèlement titulaire d'un pouvoir réglementaire qu'il exerce sous la forme d'arrêts de règlement[14]. A la différence des arrêts ordinaires qui n'avaient autorité de chose jugée qu'entre les parties en cause, les arrêts de règlement étaient obligatoires *erga omnes*. C'étaient de véritables actes législatifs qui étaient publiés dans tout le ressort de la cour et devaient être appliqués par tous. Ils étaient parfois rendus à l'occasion de procès qui soulevaient une nouvelle question de droit et avaient donc pour but de remédier à des problèmes juridiques spécifiques auxquels ni les coutumes ni les dispositions normatives n'apportaient de réponse. La cour pouvait alors donner, pour l'avenir, force obligatoire à la solution qu'elle venait d'adopter. Mais, bien plus fréquemment, les arrêts de règlement interviennent en matière administrative: ordre public, réglementation de la vie économique, de la construction ou de l'urbanisme. Cette réglementation de 'police' était bien évidemment subordonnée à la législation royale et elle pouvait faire l'objet, en cas de conflit, d'une cassation par le Conseil du roi. C'est par le biais de l'arrêt de règlement que le Parlement de Paris a, par exemple, imposé son 'style' aux tribunaux inférieurs dans le courant du XVᵉ siècle.

Le Parlement se trouve également associé à la procédure législative par le biais de l'enregistrement. La cour souveraine était, en effet, chargée d'enregistrer les ordonnances royales, une formalité préalable et indispensable à la mise à exécution de toute disposition législative. Les conseillers ont parfois mis cette compétence à profit pour peser sur les décisions en faisant valoir leur *droit de remontrances*, i.e. la possibilité de refuser l'enregistrement des lois. Ce droit est le plus souvent utilisé pour suggérer des modifications ou des améliorations aux textes soumis, mission qui incombait d'ailleurs à la plupart des cours de justice d'Ancien Régime. Si, en revanche, l'exercice de cette prérogative menait à une épreuve de force avec le monarque, celui-ci adressait au Parlement des lettres de jussion. En cas de second refus, le roi convoquait un lit de justice, procédure suprême par laquelle il ordonnait personnellement aux chambres réunies l'enregistrement de l'ordonnance[15].

---

[14] *G. Deteix,* Les arrêts de règlement du Parlement de Paris (Paris 1930).

[15] *S. Hanley,* The Lit de Justice of the Kings of France. Constitutional Ideology in Legend, Ritual and discourse (Princeton, New Jersey 1983).

4. Le Parlement et le pouvoir politique

Durant tout le Moyen Age et jusqu'au XVIe siècle, le Parlement de Paris apparaît comme un symbole politique personnifiant la souveraineté du monarque français. Très tôt déjà, la royauté avait dû faire face aux aspirations universelles des empereurs germaniques. Dans l'entourage du roi, les juristes chargés de développer une réponse juridique aux prétentions impériales avaient alors proclamé que *rex Franciae est princeps in suo regno*[16], maxime qui sera entérinée et répandue par les conseillers de la cour souveraine. Le rôle du Parlement est tout aussi important en matière de politique intérieure. Lorsque le roi rattache de nouvelles principautés au domaine royal, il soumet d'abord leurs habitants à la compétence de sa cour souveraine. Le territoire sur lequel le souverain règne effectivement se confond ainsi avec le ressort du Parlement qui devient de ce fait le fer de lance de la politique royale. On peut d'ailleurs en mesurer l'importance aux efforts déployés par les ducs de Bourgogne et premiers Habsbourg pour soustraire le comté de Flandre à la compétence du Parlement[17].

La vocation première de l'ancienne *curia regis* avait été de conseiller le suzerain, il semblait donc légitime de reconnaître au Parlement une participation dans la gestion des affaires du royaume. A la fin du Moyen Age les magistrats considéraient déjà que la délégation du droit souverain de rendre la justice ne signifiait pas pour autant que leur rôle soit réduit à celui d'un instrument docile, obéissant aveuglément aux aspirations politiques du monarque[18]. Mais les ambitieux conseillers parisiens, outrepassant leur simple mission de conseil, tendaient rapidement à abuser de leur indépendance et ils prétendaient bien souvent dicter au souverain sa politique[19]. Le Parlement s'érige, entre autres, comme le gardien des lois fondamentales du royaume et s'accorde en conséquence le droit de rejeter les décisions royales contraires à ces lois. A partir du XVIe siècle, le Parlement va de surcroît affirmer certains droits politiques en s'appuyant sur son droit de remontrances. Le Parlement est alors d'autant plus en position de force que le pouvoir

---

[16] *A. Bossuat,* La formule «le roi est empereur en son royaume». Son emploi au XVe siècle devant le Parlement de Paris, dans: Revue historique de droit français et étranger, t. XXXIX, 1961, pp. 371 - 381.

[17] *S. Dauchy,* Le Parlement de Paris et les Pays-Bas bourguignons, dans: Tijdschrift voor Rechtsgeschiedenis, t. LXI, 3, 1993, pp. 367 - 373.

[18] Voir à ce sujet l'aperçu d'*E. Glasson,* Le Parlement de Paris. Son rôle politique depuis le règne de Charles VII jusqu'à la Révolution, 3. t. (Paris 1901).

[19] Les relations entre le Parlement de Paris et le pouvoir au Temps Modernes ont fait l'objet d'une analyse par *J.-L. Harouel,* Parlement de Paris, dans: *F. Bluche,* Dictionnaire du Grand Siècle (Paris 1990), pp. 1151 - 1153. Voir aussi *J.-L. Harouel, J. Barbey, E. Bournazel,* et *J. Thibaut-Payen,* Histoire des institutions de l'époque franque à la Révolution (Paris 1986).

le sollicite et le mêle aux affaires d'Etat. En 1593, il est consulté sur la succession au trône et rend le célèbre arrêt Le Maître qui, tout en affirmant le principe de catholicité, écarte au nom de la loi de masculinité la candidature de l'infante d'Espagne. Puis, à la mort de Henri IV, c'est au Parlement que Marie de Médicis demande la régence. Rien d'étonnant s'il se permet en 1615 puis à nouveau en 1648 d'exercer sa tutelle sur le pouvoir et d'affirmer qu'il est le seul organe apte à conseiller le monarque. Mais Louis XIV, qui n'avait jamais pardonné la Fronde aux conseillers, a rabaissé la superbe des parlements et en particulier celui de Paris. Ils ont été replacés au rang de cours supérieures – la souveraineté étant l'apanage du roi – et par la déclaration du 24 février 1673 il limita considérablement leur droit de remontrances. De surcroît, le premier président de la Grand'Chambre n'est plus un officier coopté par les conseillers mais un commissaire désigné par le roi et révocable *ad nutum*[20]. A la mort de Louis XIV, le régent voulant outrepasser les limites de ses attributions, aura recours aux services du Parlement de Paris, lui restituant en même temps son droit de remontrances, c'est-à-dire les moyens d'une contestation politique.

5. Le Parlement de Paris et le droit

Le Parlement de Paris a tout d'abord joué un rôle actif dans l'unification de la procédure appliquée devant l'ensemble des tribunaux de son ressort[21] et les décisions judiciaires contiennent très souvent des dispositions à ce sujet. La généralisation de la procédure romano-canonique n'a pas seulement été le résultat d'une réception passive, la juridiction d'appel y a elle-même largement contribué. Ainsi le Parlement adresse encore aux XIVe et XVe siècles de nombreuses injonctions aux juridictions inférieures interdisant le recours au duel judiciaire, pourtant limité depuis l'ordonnance de saint Louis de 1258, ou ordonnant de manière plus générale le respect du style de la cour souveraine. Le Parlement a également développé et imposé sa propre organisation des voies de recours[22]. Celles-ci sont d'ailleurs à la base des recours que prévoient encore les codes de procédure civile dans la plupart des pays européens. La jurisprudence du Parlement de Paris fut aussi décisive dans le processus d'uniformisation du droit positif, entre

---

[20] *A. Hamscher,* The Parlement of Paris after the Fronde (1653 - 1673) (University of Pittsburgh 1976).

[21] Voir la synthèse présentée par *R. C. van Caenegem,* History of European Civil procedure, dans: International Encyclopedia of Comparative Law, XVI.2 (Tübingen 1973).

[22] Cf. *S. Dauchy,* Les voies de recours extraordinaires, proposition d'erreur et requête civile (de l'ordonnance de Saint Louis jusqu'à l'ordonnance de 1667) [Travaux et recherches de l'Université de Droit, d'Economie et de Sciences sociales de Paris, Série sciences historiques n° 26] (Paris 1988).

autres par le truchement des arrêts de règlement. Notons que le Parlement fut étroitement associé à la rédaction officielle et à l'homologation des coutumes aux XVe et XVIe siècles. L'ordonnance de Montils-lès-Tours de 1454 prévoyait déjà que les coutumes mises par écrit devaient être vérifiées par le Parlement avant qu'elles puissent être promulguées. Par lettres patentes de 1497 Charles VIII précisera son rôle d'arbitre en cas de désaccord entre les Etats des pays et les commissaires parisiens.

Ce bref survol du rôle déterminant du Parlement de Paris dans le développement du droit français et européen soulève également le problème des sources formelles du droit, c'est-à-dire les modes d'expression des règles du droit positif dans le ressort de la cour souveraine[23]. Durant tout l'Ancien Régime, la principale source du droit français restera la coutume. Les difficultés engendrées par la diversité des coutumes – dont de très nombreuses n'ont jamais été mises par écrit – ont d'ailleurs probablement contribué à leur rédaction et à leur homologation. Avant cette rédaction officielle, les dispositions de la coutume devaient être prouvées par les parties et ce n'est qu'en cas de désaccord qu'une enquête était menée par des commissaires.

La législation en général et les ordonnances royales en particulier ont d'abord pour objectif de compléter la coutume dans le domaine du droit privé et constituent la principale source de droit public. Le maintien de l'ordre et la police mais aussi la monnaie, le commerce et l'industrie seront de plus en plus réglementés par des ordonnances qui prendront, à la fin du XVIIe siècle, l'aspect de véritables codes.

La jurisprudence, la doctrine et le droit savant ne peuvent pas être mis sur le même pied que la coutume et la loi; en effet, ils n'ont pas un rôle directement créateur de droit. Ainsi, les conseillers ne sont pas liés par leurs décisions et celles-ci ne constituent donc pas des précédents judiciaires. La jurisprudence n'a donc pas joué un rôle essentiel avant que des arrêts commentés soient édités. Le droit romain, enfin, n'a jamais fait l'objet d'une réception officielle au Parlement et ceci essentiellement pour des raisons politiques. La décrétale *super speculum* promulguée en 1219 par le pape Honorius III sur les instances du roi de France fait état de la *Francia* «où les laïcs ne vivent pas sous le régime du droit romain» et en 1278 Philippe II avait interdit aux avocats d'alléguer du droit romain ou canonique dans leurs plaidoiries[24]. Dans la pratique, on constate au

---

[23] Les sources du droit alléguées devant le Parlement de Paris dans les appels provenant de la Flandre ont été analysées dans *S. Dauchy,* Un aperçu de la litigiosité dans le royaume de France à la fin du moyen âge. Les appels flamands au Parlement de Paris (1320 - 1520), dans: *H. Mohnhaupt* et *D. Simon* éds., Vorträge zur Justizforschung. Geschichte und Theorie, t. 1 (Francfort 1992), pp. 45 - 77.

[24] *W. Ullmann,* The prohibition of Roman law at Paris, dans: Juridical Review, t. 60, 1948, pp. 177 sq. et *S. Kuttner,* Papst Honorius III und das Studium des Zivilrechts, dans: Festschrift Martin Wolff (Tübingen 1952), pp. 79 sq.

contraire que les avocats étayent fréquemment leur argumentation par des allégations de droit savant. Vu l'absence de motivation formelle des décisions, il n'est pas possible d'en mesurer l'impact, mais il est probable que les conseillers ont été influencés par un droit qu'ils avaient étudié dans les universités, ceci lorsque les autres sources faisaient défaut ou semblaient contradictoires.

6. Le Parlement de Paris et les parlements de province

Jusqu'au XVe siècle, il n'existe dans le royaume qu'un seul parlement qui siège à Paris. Les appels provenant des pays de droit écrit posaient néanmoins problème. Le Parlement avait d'abord envoyé en Languedoc une délégation de conseillers parisiens, spécialistes du droit romain et des coutumes méridionales, qui tenaient sur place des *Grands Jours*. Puis, on avait créé au sein du Parlement de Paris une chambre distincte appelée *Auditoire de droit écrit*. Mais l'augmentation constante des causes d'appel et les difficultés découlant de l'éloignement des plaideurs ont abouti en 1443 à la création du Parlement de Toulouse. L'extension du domaine et le respect des identités des principautés annexées ont ensuite conduit la monarchie à en créer toute une série d'autres. Presque tous prennent la suite, soit immédiatement, soit après un délai parfois séculaire, de l'ancienne juridiction souveraine du territoire concerné. Sont ainsi institués les parlements de Grenoble (1453), Bordeaux (1462), Dijon (1477), Aix (1501) et Rouen (1515). Créé en 1553, le parlement de Bretagne, après une période d'alternance avec Nantes, se fixe à Rennes en 1561. Puis viennent les parlements de Pau (1623) et Metz (1663). Le parlement de Dole, créé en 1674, est transféré deux ans plus tard à Besançon. Institué en 1686, le parlement de Tournai est ramené à Cambrai en 1709 en raison des défaites françaises, et finalement installé à Douai en 1713. Le dernier sera le parlement de Nancy érigé en 1775. L'étendue des ressorts des parlements de province varie considérablement, mais leur structure est à l'image de la cour parisienne: grand'chambre, chambre des requêtes, chambre des enquêtes et tournelle criminelle. Comme le Parlement de Paris, ces cours sont souveraines au civil comme au criminel. Certaines offrent, en outre, la particularité d'être à la fois chambre des comptes, cour des aides et cour des monnaies. Par ailleurs, tous les parlements sont chargés de l'enregistrement et de la publication des lois, ce qui décuple les possibilités d'une opposition politique à la royauté. Malgré l'existence de ces parlements provinciaux, le Parlement de Paris ne connaît pas de rival et on continue d'ailleurs à parler du 'Parlement' tout court, comme au temps où il était le seul dans le royaume.

En 1790 l'Assemblée Constituante décrétait l'abolition du Parlement de Paris, mettant ainsi un terme à plus de cinq siècles ininterrompus d'activité judiciaire et politique[25]. Il nous reste aujourd'hui les milliers de registres et autant de liasses de minutes qui s'alignent dans la galerie du Parlement aux Archives Nationales à Paris. Cette documentation constitue une source incomparable et presque inépuisable pour l'histoire judiciaire, mais aussi sociale, économique, religieuse et politique du Moyen Age et des Temps Modernes. Le Parlement a tranché des conflits entre les plus hauts dignitaires du royaume, mais il était également le dernier recours de nombreux plaideurs anonymes qui soumettaient à la cour d'appel leurs soucis quotidiens. On peut estimer que la cour souveraine a traité à peu près un million de litiges, rendant quelque 400.000 arrêts civils et pas moins de 200.000 sentences criminelles, activité à laquelle il faut encore ajouter les contentieux traités durant les divers Grands Jours et l'homologation de nombreux accords.

Mais, le Parlement de Paris fait aussi partie intégrante de l'histoire européenne. Le Parlement a inspiré à des degrés divers l'organisation judiciaire de plusieurs pays et continue à travers les codes napoléoniens à marquer le droit et la procédure bien au-delà de ce que fut autrefois son ressort.

II. Les archives du Parlement de Paris[26]

1. Présentation et description des sources

Les archives du Parlement de Paris constituent une magnifique collection unique en Europe occidentale, qui s'étend sans interruption de saint Louis à Louis XVI, des Croisades à la Révolution. En effet, le 15 octobre 1790, le Parlement de Paris – la plus ancienne et la plus prestigieuse des juridictions royales de l'Ancien Régime – cessait, en vertu d'un décret de l'Assemblée Constituante, les fonctions qui avaient été siennes pendant plus d'un demi-millénaire. Ses archives mises immédiatement sous scellés, furent confiées à Terrasse, ancien commis au greffe du Parlement et transférées en 1847 du Palais aux Archives nationales. Les registres reçurent la lettre X comme lettre de série[27]. La série X comprend 26800 articles; à l'heure actuelle, elle est divisée en cinq ensembles de documents:

X1 Parlement civil
X2 Parlement criminel
X3 Requêtes du Palais

---

[25] *A. Grün,* Notice sur les archives du Parlement de Paris, dans: *E. Boutaric,* Actes du Parlement de Paris, t. I (1254 - 1299) (Paris 1863), pp. II - XII.

[26] Par Bernadette Auzary-Schmaltz.

[27] Avant la formation des archives du Parlement, les membres de la *Curia regis* déposaient leurs enquêtes dans le Trésor des Chartes, nom donné à l'édifice annexe de la Sainte-Chapelle du Palais où étaient déposées les archives du roi depuis le XIIIe siècle (actuelle série J des Archives nationales).

X4 Chancellerie du Palais

X5 Communauté des procureurs

Chacun de ces ensembles étant lui-même subdivisé en deux sous-ensembles: 'A' pour les registres et 'B' pour les minutes. Il faut noter que X1 comporte un troisième sous-ensemble 'C' constitué par les registres factices des accords. C'est dans les sous-séries X1 et X2 qu'il faut chercher les archives proprement dites du Parlement, émanant de l'activité de ses chambres – Grand'Chambre, Chambre des Enquêtes, Tournelle – et de ses greffes. Nous avons privilégié les archives du Parlement statuant au civil, les praticiens de l'Ancien Régime s'étant eux-mêmes principalement intéressés aux matières civiles.

Contrairement à certaines autres juridictions, les contentieux traités par le Parlement de Paris n'ont pas été conservés sous la forme de dossiers rassemblant l'ensemble des pièces se rapportant à une même affaire. Il faut, dès lors, reconstituer le dossier d'après différents types de sources appartenant à plusieurs sous-séries du Parlement[28] dont il convient préalablement de préciser les caractéristiques les plus importantes. Dans la présentation des différents types de pièces relatifs à un procès civil, nous décrirons systématiquement d'abord les registres, puis les minutes.

Les plus connues et les plus anciennes sont bien sûr les *arrêts et jugés*. Ils constituent le premier témoignage de l'activité judiciaire du Parlement par ses plus anciennes décisions connues sous le nom d'*Olim*[29]. Jusqu'au début du XVIe siècle, ils sont conservés dans des registres en parchemin qui contiennent aussi des lettres. Rédigés en latin dans un style très formaliste, les arrêts et jugés statuent généralement sur le fond, mais on trouve aussi un très grand nombre de décisions préparatoires et interlocutoires. On appelle 'jugés' les décisions rendues par la Chambre des Enquêtes alors que les 'arrêts' sont prononcés par la Grand'Chambre, soit sur plaidoiries, soit en conseil. Cette distinction sera abandonnée en 1514, le Parlement ne prononçant plus que des jugés qui, conformément à l'ordonnance de 1539, seront rédigés en français à partir de cette date.

Les minutes des jugés sont conservées de manière continue à partir de 1547[30]. L'ordonnance de mars 1344 prescrivait que le conseiller qui rappor-

---

28 Pour rassembler les pièces d'un procès, il faut aussi considérer dans un souci d'exhaustivité des documents n'émanant pas du Parlement, tels les lettres de rémission (Trésor des Chartes, série JJ) et les actes conservés dans les archives des institutions ecclésiastiques et des villes.

29 Les Olim ou registres des arrêts rendus par la Cour du roi sous les règnes de Saint Louis, de Philippe le Hardi, de Philippe le Bel, de Louis le Hutin et de Philippe le Long, publiés par le *Comte Beugnot* (1839 - 1848) 4 vol.

30 Un rouleau de décisions prononcées en mai 1505 et rédigées par le rapporteur a été classé parmi les minutes (X1B 1).

tait sur la cause devait, dans les six jours suivants la mise en délibéré de l'affaire au conseil, rédiger lui-même la minute et en donner lecture à la Chambre. Après y avoir éventuellement apporté les corrections nécessaires, la minute est remise au greffier qui la transcrit dans les registres: leur contenu et leur rédaction ne diffèrent en rien de ceux des minutes. Ecrites sur feuilles volantes et réunies en liasses, les minutes se présentent de façon identique jusqu'en 1790: outre la narration des faits, le dispositif et la date, on y trouve la signature du président, les noms des conseillers qui ont pris part à la décision et l'indication du montant des épices, ces deux dernières informations étant volontairement omises dans les registres. *On ne trouve donc pas dans les minutes – pas plus que dans les registres – la motivation des jugements.*

A partir de 1364, apparaît une autre série appelée 'Conseil et plaidoiries réunis'. Cette deuxième série fait l'objet d'une transcription dans des registres distincts à partir de 1395.

Le principal intérêt de ces registres du Conseil est de conserver une brève transcription en français de la délibération des conseillers statuant en dehors de l'audience, transcription qui servira de base au conseiller rapporteur chargé de mettre en forme la rédaction protocolaire de la décision.

Le deuxième intérêt de ces registres est de refléter étape par étape les différentes phases d'un procès, de l'ajournement jusqu'à la décision finale, en passant par les demandes de délai présentées par les parties (jour de conseil, jour de vue, essoine) et les mesures provisoires ordonnées par la Cour. La présence de mentions marginales laisse penser que les registres du Conseil constituent le rouage essentiel du déroulement d'une procédure en Parlement. On y rencontre des mentions de trois types: certaines sont relatives au contenu (par exemple: 'Enqueste', 'Clerc rendu'), d'autres sont des renvois à des relations antérieures du procès figurant dans le même registre (par ex.: '*supra statim idem Johanne*') et enfin d'autres font mention des décisions définitives ou interlocutoires (par ex.: '*Pronunciatum*' ou '*Dictum*' suivi de l'indication du jour et du mois). Les mentions '*Pronunciatum*...' (à partir de la fin du XVe siècle: 'Prononcé le...') servent à l'établissement des listes des arrêts et jugés qui figurent à la fin du chaque session et grâce à celles-ci le chercheur pourra trouver la décision mise en forme dans les registres des arrêts et jugés. Il est à noter que seul ce dernier type de mention perdure aux Temps Modernes.

Cette série nous fournit enfin une troisième catégorie d'informations liées à l'organisation interne du Parlement et à son fonctionnement quotidien. Au début de chaque session est indiquée la liste des conseillers et du personnel auxiliaire (notaires, secrétaires, greffiers) qui vont siéger. Le greffier qui tient ces registres note aussi les faits divers qui animent au fil des jours la vie des parlementaires, par exemple la visite de personnages importants; il mentionne également des événements qui dépassent le cadre restreint du Palais (traités de paix) surtout lorsque ceux-ci ont pu avoir des répercussions sur la vie judiciaire (par exemple, l'écroulement du Petit Pont en 1408 empêche pendant quelques jours certains conseillers de venir siéger). Dans cette optique, le 'Conseil' constitue la chronique du Parlement de Paris. Les prétendus journaux tenus par les greffiers du Parlement, comme ceux de Nicolas de Baye et de Clément de Fauquembergue, sont en réalité l'œuvre d'un historien français du XIXe siècle, A. Tuetey[31], qui les a élaborés en recueillant les informations non contentieuses fournies par les registres du Conseil auxquelles il a ajouté des extraits des plaidoiries. Ces deux journaux ne sont rien d'autre qu'une compilation faite à une époque tardive de deux catégories distinctes de sources. La mention des faits divers ainsi que les graffitis dans les marges (par exemple, la représentation de Jeanne d'Arc dans le registre X1A 1481 qui couvre les années 1428 à 1436) disparaissent progressivement dans la deuxième moitié du XVe siècle.

Les minutes, également sur feuilles volantes, sont conservées depuis 1553. Elles présentent l'original des actes dont les registres contiennent la reproduction et sont divisées pour la période moderne, comme les registres de cette époque, en trois catégories distinctes: délibérations, déroulement de l'instance et défauts. Parmi les délibérations, certaines concernent les jugés et les autres les *dicta*. Ces décisions *dites aux parties* (conformément à la mention marginale qui figure dans les registres du Conseil) sont uniquement prononcées oralement et ne font l'objet d'aucun enregistrement. C'est pour cette raison que l'ordonnance de Moulins de 1566 exige que ces minutes soient écrites par le rapporteur et signées par le président.

Les plus anciennes minutes ne nous sont pas parvenues et nous ne disposons pas non plus pour la fin du Moyen Age des brouillons de plumitifs rédigés par les greffiers et des feuilles de délibération qui mentionnaient l'opinion personnelle de chaque magistrat[32].

Les *plaidoiries* en tant que source autonome (par rapport au Conseil) forment une série distincte à partir de 1395. A l'origine, elles se présentent comme le résumé des arguments de chacune des parties, puis progressivement elles deviennent la transcription exhaustive des plaidoyers prononcés par leurs procureurs et avocats. Ce changement est sensible à partir de la

---

[31] *A. Tuetey* éd., Journal de Nicolas de Baye, greffier du Parlement de Paris 1400 - 1417, 2 vol. (Paris 1885 - 1888) et *Idem*, Journal de Clément de Fauquembergue, greffier du Parlement de Paris 1417 - 1435, 3 vol. (Paris 1903 - 1915).

[32] Nous en possédons néanmoins quelques exemples réunis par Nicolas Dongois, greffier en chef civil du Parlement, dans un registre intitulé 'Feuilles de Me Daniel Voisin, secrétaire de la Cour, premier et principal commis au greffe et greffier en chef criminel, décédé en 1622'; cf. *A. Grün*, op. cit., p. CLXIII, n. 1.

deuxième moitié du XVe siècle: la fréquence et le nombre croissant des allégations de droit savant sont parmi d'autres des éléments qui montrent à l'évidence qu'il ne s'agit plus d'un simple résumé des arguments.

On distingue deux catégories de registres de plaidoiries: les plus anciens appelés 'Matinées'[33] auxquels s'ajouteront au début du XVe siècle les 'Après-dinées', à partir de 1401[34]. Ces derniers, d'un format plus petit, sont en outre en papier à la différence de tous les autres registres du Parlement qui sont en parchemin. 'Matinées' et 'Après-dinées' sont confondus dans une même série après 1571. A partir de cette date, les registres des plaidoiries ne contiennent plus la transcription des plaidoyers des avocats, mais elles présentent l'état de l'activité des différentes chambres des enquêtes. On y retrouve essentiellement les décisions de ces chambres désignées sous le nom de 'Arrêt rendu en plaidant' ainsi que des actes concernant le déroulement des procédures devant ces chambres.

Les minutes sont conservées à partir de 1584. Les liasses renferment divers documents: les actes retranscrits dans les registres, les réceptions de procès à juger et les comparutions et quelques plaidoyers.

Il faut encore signaler l'existence d'autres documents archivés dans la série X1A. Certains sont en rapport avec le contentieux, mais comme ils ne présentent guère d'intérêt pour la recherche présente, nous nous contenterons de les citer brièvement[35]. Les registres des Amendes (1399 - 1477) mentionnent les amendes prononcées par le Parlement au civil en précisant le montant[36]. Les registres du greffe contiennent les différentes phases de la procédure telles que les décrit P. Guilhiermoz. Pour la période 1611 - 1790, nous disposons de registres reprenant les conclusions des procureurs généraux. Signalons encore les registres des saisies réelles (1598 - 1790) et les registres d'oppositions sur les biens acquis par le roi (1693 - 1790). D'autres documents sont sans rapport avec le contentieux: la correspondance du Parlement (1376 - 1529); les ordonnances (1337 - 1785) ayant fait l'objet d'un enregistrement par le Parlement; les registres du Conseil secret qui contiennent à partir de 1636 les indications non contentieuses originellement transcrites dans le Conseil, tels la réception des membres et les débats avec le roi[37].

---

[33] X1A 4784 à X1A 4841 (1395 - 1500).

[34] X1A 8300 (1401) à X1A 8326 (1499).

[35] La liste exhaustive figure dans *M. Langlois,* Parlement de Paris, dans: Guide des recherches dans les fonds judiciaires de l'Ancien Régime (Paris 1958).

[36] Voir les conclusions de *S. Dauchy,* Quelques remarques sur les amendes prononcées par le Parlement de Paris au Moyen Age pour 'fol appel' provenant de Flandre, dans: Tijdschrift voor Rechtsgeschiedenis, t. LV, 1987, pp. 49 - 55.

[37] Les registres du Conseil secret au temps de la Fronde ont été détruits sur ordre de Louis XIV.

Il faut aussi noter dans la sous-série X1A les registres des Grands Jours tenus en province par les conseillers du Parlement de Paris: Grands Jours de Troyes (discontinu de 1367 à 1583), Poitiers (idem de 1531 à 1635), Bordeaux (1456 - 1459)[38], Montferrand (1481), Moulins (1534 - 1550), Angers (1539), Riom (1546), Tours (1533 - 1547), Lyon (1596). Les registres de la Cour souveraine en exil à Poitiers, connue sous le nom de Parlement de Poitiers, cotés X1A 9190 à 9201, couvrent la période 1418 - 1436. On constate une évidente ressemblance avec les registres du Parlement de Paris, ce qui n'est pas pour surprendre puisqu'ils sont l'œuvre matérielle et intellectuelle des 'gens du parlement'. Des greffiers venus de la Cour souveraine consignent par écrit les procès jugés par les magistrats parisiens avec lesquels ils ont une collaboration régulière tout au long de l'année judiciaire. Une relative homogénéité dans la composition et la tenue des registres en découle. Comme leurs homologues parisiens, les registres tenus à l'occasion des Grands Jours contiennent à la fois des lettres et mandements et des arrêts et jugés. Ils renferment en outre parfois des décisions prises en conseil, des plaidoiries et éventuellement les accords ou transactions par lesquelles les parties ont mis fin à leurs différents. La langue employée est, comme à Paris, le latin pour les décisions et le français (ou moyen français) pour les plaidoiries et les délibérations des magistrats en conseil[39]. Paradoxalement, on trouve dans les archives du Parlement de Paris des registres de certains parlements de province: le Parlement de Tours (1590 - 1594) et le Parlement de Châlons (1589 - 1594).

Dernier ensemble de la série X1, les *Accords* (sous-série X1C) conservés de manière continue pour la période 1320 - 1540[40] se distinguent des sources décrites précédemment aussi bien quant à la forme qu'en ce qui concerne le fond. Il s'agit de documents dont la rédaction a été laissée aux soins des parties; une grande disparité dans la forme en découle. Ces actes si divers ont été artificiellement, pour des raisons pratiques, présentés en registres par les archivistes du XIXe siècle. L'accord comprend en général plusieurs actes: l'autorisation de s'accorder délivrée par la chancellerie, la promesse d'accord de chacune des parties et l'accord proprement dit passé devant une juridiction inférieure ou un notaire; celui-ci est ensuite soumis

---

[38] *H. Barckhausen* éd., Les Grands Jours de Bordeaux de 1456 et de 1459, dans: Archives historiques du département de la Gironde, t. 9, 1867.

[39] En outre, des informations utiles pourront être trouvées dans *L'Historique des Grands Jours* rédigé par le greffier Nicolas Dongois. En effet, à son retour à Paris en 1665, ce greffier érudit a jugé bon de faire précéder son propre journal, relatant les sessions de Grands Jours d'Auvergne dans lesquels il a officié en tant que greffier civil, d'une recherche historique portant sur les Grands Jours antérieurs (*De l'origine des Grands Jours,* ms. A.N., série U 749 et 750).

[40] Le dernier registre (X1C 264) contient encore quelques accords postérieurs jusqu'en 1640.

au Parlement qui y appose une formule d'entérinement. Leur contenu n'est pas une décision imposée par une juridiction, mais un accord ménagé entre les parties à l'issue d'une transaction, le rôle du Parlement se limitant à en faire respecter les termes. A l'instar d'une décision judiciaire, l'accord vient rétablir la paix entre les parties, peut-être d'une manière plus incontestable dans la mesure où il a été en principe librement consenti. Il est aussi dans la plupart des cas une façon de sortir de la phase juridictionnelle dans des conditions acceptables, en se dispensant de payer les dépens de l'adversaire.

2. La finalité des registres

L'étymologie du terme 'registre' indique une première voie pour aborder la question de la finalité. Parmi les définitions proposées par Du Cange[41], la plus convaincante paraît être celle de Papias: «*Registrum: liber qui rerum gestarum memoriam continet...*». Toutes les juridictions permanentes au Moyen Age semblent s'être préoccupées très tôt de conserver dans un plumitif le compte-rendu des audiences pour garder le souvenir de ce qui avait été fait et décidé, avec pour objectif le souci de pouvoir en fournir la preuve. La justice royale était en retard à cet égard par rapport aux justices de certains princes, pairs du royaume; on ne peut guère savoir, en effet, ce que pouvait être le mode de conservation des décisions du Parlement avant les *Olim,* mais en revanche il en va différemment des sentences de l'Echiquier de Normandie conservées dans les premières années du XIIIe siècle. La mutation qui s'est opérée seulement au XIVe siècle à la Cour du roi[42] s'explique par la conjonction de plusieurs éléments: d'abord, c'est le moment où on passe d'une civilisation orale à une civilisation de l'écrit; ensuite, on constate un accroissement du nombre des causes jugées au Parlement à cause du développement de l'appel et du fait de l'élaboration de la théorie des cas royaux. En sorte que le record de Cour, par lequel on sollicite la mémoire des juges pour qu'ils se remémorent les termes des décisions rendues, n'est plus un moyen suffisant et adéquat pour assurer le bon fonctionnement de la justice. La collection des *Olim* prouve en elle-même l'enregistrement des décisions du Parlement. Une décision de 1301[43] atteste clairement l'existence des 'registres de la Cour' puisque la comtesse de Vendôme demande pour prouver son *intentio* que la Cour les examine; le Parlement accepte sa proposition, mais il refuse de fournir une copie des

---

41 Glossarium mediae et infimae latinitatis (Paris 1840 - 1857), 7 vol., V° *Registrum.*

42 Sur l'historique des registres du Parlement, on consultera avec profit *A. Grün,* Notice sur les archives du Parlement de Paris, p. XII sq., in: Inventaires et documents ... Actes du Parlement de Paris par *E. Boutaric* (Paris 1863).

43 *Olim,* op. cit., t. II, p. 453, n° 7.

registres à la partie adverse sans indiquer les raisons de ce refus. Cet arrêt est conforme au principe de la non-communication des registres aux parties, ou en tout cas, d'une communication très strictement limitée.

Parmi les ordonnances des XIVe et XVe siècles qui jalonnent la réglementation relative à la tenue des registres, celle du 8 avril 1342[44] pose des exigences quant à la capacité des greffiers, appelés notaires: ils devront être «suffisants pour faire lettres, tant en latin, comme en français, comme dit est, selon ce que l'office le requiert»[45]. Une ordonnance du 28 janvier 1373[46] porte création de trois offices de notaires secrétaires du Parlement de Paris, précisant une spécialisation des fonctions entre greffe civil, greffe criminel et présentations. Enfin, une ordonnance du 28 octobre 1446[47] dispose que les conclusions et plaidoyers devaient être fixés par le registre; c'était d'après les termes qu'il leur donnait que l'état de la cause se trouvait définitivement arrêté pour que la Cour y fasse droit. Aussi, les avocats disposaient-ils de deux jours pour voir le registre du greffe et, au besoin, le faire corriger.

La finalité de l'enregistrement est donc, semble-t-il, purement interne, en ce sens que la tenue des registres a pour seule fin de faciliter le fonctionnement de la juridiction:

- La présentation matérielle des registres du Conseil, dans lesquels l'enregistrement commence toujours par l'indication du noms de parties («Entre ... et...»), montre le souci du greffier de repérer rapidement les différentes étapes d'un procès et les mentions qu'il porte dans la marge ont la même utilité (cf. supra, Description des sources).
- La trace écrite que constitue le registre gardé avec précautions au greffe fixe définitivement et de manière indiscutable les contours du litige et peut de ce fait servir à écarter des plaideurs qui tenteraient de réitérer une action ayant déjà fait l'objet d'un jugement. La 'chose jugée' est par

---

[44] *Isambert,* Recueil général des anciennes lois françaises, t. 4, art. 5.

[45] Nous avons relevé les titres et qualités énoncés par les greffiers dans les *incipit* de deux registres du Conseil. Incipit du registre X1A 1473 commençant le 13 novembre 1385: «*Incipit registrum ... registratum per me Johannem Jouvence, Domini nostri regis clericum, prothonotarium ac grefferium dicti parlamenti pro octavo anno quo registum dicti parlamenti tenui*»; incipit du registre X1A 1479 commençant le 12 novembre 1407: «*Incipit registrum manuale consiliorum per me N. de Baye, Cathalanensis dyocesis clericum et subdiaconum ecclesiarum Cathalanensis et Suessionensis canonicum, artium liberalium magistrum, in jure civili licentiatum et bachalarium in canonico jure in forma licencie, prothonotarium et secretarium Domini nostri Karoli sexto regis et hujus sue parlamenti Curie grapharium indignum*».

[46] X1A 8653, f° 397^v^ - 398.

[47] Ordonnance de Montils-lèz-Tours, art. 27: *Isambert,* op. cit., t. 9, p. 161; *E. de Laurière,* Ordonnances des Roys de France de la troisième race recueillies par ordre chronologique, t. XIII, p. 478.

ce moyen prouvée. On constate que cette finalité étroite ne connaît aucune modification notoire jusqu'à la fin de l'Ancien Régime.

Enfin, sans doute, on peut penser que cette volonté de conserver la mémoire des jugements traduit aussi de la part des conseillers un souci de cohérence. Les citations de précédents, au moins en matière de procédure et de compétence, qui sont nombreux à la fin du XIVe siècle (cf. 'Le Parlement de Paris au Moyen Age: collation de recueils privés et de registres de la Cour', dans le deuxième volume) montre que, si le juge n'est pas lié par le précédent judiciaire, il y est attentif[48]. Les parties sont d'ailleurs bien conscientes que la citation de précédents, qui est faite *pro et contra*[49] conformément à la méthode scolastique en honneur au Moyen Age, peut influencer la décision des magistrats; à cette fin, leur avocat n'hésite pas à motiver les prétentions de leurs clients, tout spécialement lorsqu'il s'agit de trancher des conflits de compétence entre villes ou institutions ecclésiastiques et princes territoriaux en alléguant des jugements rendus par le Parlement, jugements que ces institutions peuvent prouver en montrant des copies authentiques et scellées qu'elles ont obtenues à l'issue de procès antérieurs consacrant leurs prétentions et qu'elles conservent à cette fin dans leurs chartriers[50]. En clair, c'est aux parties qui les invoquent que revient le soin de *trouver* et de *prouver* les précédents, les enregistrements de la Cour ne constituant qu'un archivage à usage interne.

Si l'on n'ose pas encore parler d'une véritable jurisprudence, il est néanmoins incontestable qu'une *manière de juger* se dégage d'une suite de décisions prononcées dans des cas identiques, définissant ainsi de nouvelles règles de procédure ou de compétence (cf. par exemple, la compétence de la justice royale sur les clercs faussaires, dossier n° II dans le deuxième volume).

La présomption que l'on porte à ces registres une attention croissante en tant que source subsidiaire du droit – compilations de décisions judiciaires – est renforcée à la période moderne par la multiplication des recueils d'arrêts. Comme leurs auteurs, tant avocats que magistrats, semblent souvent avoir puisé directement les décisions qu'ils commentent dans les registres mêmes (cf. infra, 'Les recueils privés de 'jurisprudence' français aux Temps Modernes'), on peut penser que les conseillers du Parlement de leur

---

48 Voir infra, dans: 'Les recueils d'arrêts privés au Moyen Age', la réfutation par la Cour d'un précédent cité dans un procès relaté par Le Coq à la Question 34 (Dossier n° II).

49 Après avoir cité des précédents, on prend soin de mentionner qu'il n'existe 'aucun arrêt contraire': cf. *Jean Le Coq*, op. cit., question 221.

50 On trouvera des exemples dans *S. Dauchy*, De processen in beroep uit Vlaanderen bij het Parlement van Parijs (Bruxelles 1995) [Verhandelingen van de Koninklijke Academie van België, Klasse der Letteren n° 154], pp. 125 sq.

côté attachaient de plus en plus de prix aux précédents, ce qui expliquerait le succès de cette littérature arrêtiste.

III. La reconstitution des dossiers

La reconstitution des dossiers à partir de ces différentes sous-séries a donné des résultats très variables selon les cas. Il s'agit d'un exercice aléatoire puisque la reconstitution parfaite d'un dossier suppose la conservation de toutes les pièces qui lui appartiennent. Le dossier-type 'idéal' se compose de textes émanant des registres de plaidoiries, du Conseil et des arrêts-jugés. D'autres profils de dossiers sont fonction du caractère plus ou moins complet de la reconstitution. Celle-ci est tributaire de deux sortes d'éléments. Des raisons externes, tout d'abord, expliquent que certaines pièces relatives à un procès soient manquantes: parmi ces raisons, on pense en premier lieu aux aléas de la conservation des documents et on constate que certaines séries sont déficitaires (Conseil et plaidoiries particulièrement); l'incurie de quelques conseillers qui ont conservé par devers eux une partie de leurs dossiers nous en a définitivement interdit l'accès[51]. Enfin certaines pièces gravement endommagées et demeurant illisibles, notamment parmi les plaidoiries (d'une écriture toujours très cursive) datant du milieu du XVe siècle, nous privent des informations qu'elles contiennent. D'autres motifs propres à la procédure elle-même justifient l'absence de source. C'est tout d'abord l'abandon du procès, soit que les parties n'aient pas eu les moyens suffisants pour le poursuivre (une procédure en Parlement coûte cher[52]), soit qu'elles aient décidé d'y mettre fin à l'issue d'une transaction: le dossier d'un tel procès ne comporte ni décision du Conseil, ni arrêt, ni jugé. En second lieu, on ne trouve de plaidoiries enregistrées que pour les procédures qui se déroulent devant la Grand'Chambre; un litige porté devant la Chambre des Requêtes (procès par écrit), par exemple, ne peut être éclairé par l'argumentation présentée par les avocats des parties. Par ailleurs, nous

---

[51] Ainsi par exemple Maître Gilles de Clamecy, conseiller au Parlement, sommé d'ouvrir son hôtel «pour avoir certains proces qu'il a et qui ont esté longuement poursuiz et demandéz» (X1A 1480, f° 94 - 4 juin 1417).

[52] En se référant seulement à la bibliographie la plus récente, on peut trouver des éléments d'appréciation des frais de justice devant le Parlement dans la thèse d'*A. Rigaudière,* Saint-Flour, ville d'Auvergne au bas Moyen Age. Etude d'histoire administrative et financière (P.U.F., Paris 1982), t. II, p. 741 sq. On consultera également avec profit les tableaux de frais dressés pour deux procès introduits au Parlement par deux villes flamandes au XVe siècle: Damme (1426 - 1428) et Bruges (1432 - 1435). Ces deux procès relativement brefs coûtent aux villes qui les ont engagés respectivement 843 et 1658 livres parisis: *S. Dauchy,* The Cost of Pleading in the Parlement of Paris in the Fifteenth Century, dans: *F. Battenberg* et *F. Ranieri* éds., Geschichte der Zentraljustiz in Mitteleuropa. Festschrift für Bernhard Diestelkamp zum 65. Geburtstag (Weimar-Cologne 1994), pp. 181 - 193.

avons pu constater au cours de ce travail de regroupement des sources concernant une même affaire qu'à maintes reprises des arrêts ou des jugés dont une décision du Conseil prévoyait l'enregistrement ne se retrouvaient pas dans la série des arrêts et jugés; cette remarque est surtout vraie pour la période 1425 - 1432 pendant laquelle la tenue des registres d'arrêts et de jugés (X1A 65, 66 et 67) est extrêmement perturbée. Enfin, une dernière raison peut expliquer qu'un dossier ne comporte pas de décision finale (arrêt ou jugé): un accord intervenu entre les parties et enregistré par le Parlement est venu clore la procédure. Enfin, la longueur des procès rend d'autant plus difficile la collecte des pièces, elle augmente en conséquence la longueur des dépouillements. Il faut, de surcroît, tenir compte des deux facteurs suivants: d'abord, la première pièce d'un dossier n'est pas nécessairement celle par laquelle la demande en justice à été introduite; elle constitue seulement la première trace écrite de cette demande. Ensuite, même lorsque la dernière pièce est une décision finale faisant présumer la fin du litige, on remarque que la décision pourtant définitive rendue par la Cour ne conclut pas réellement le procès, souvent parce que des difficultés surgissent au moment de l'exécution du jugement.

Les lacunes de la documentation rendent parfois insaisissable le raisonnement juridique qui a pu être celui des conseillers; alors qu'à cette défaillance s'ajoute l'absence de motivation en droit des jugements français jusqu'à la Révolution, on peut mesurer la difficulté à percevoir l'élaboration d'une jurisprudence.

IV. Inventaires et instruments de recherche

Le bref aperçu que nous donnons ne prétend nullement être exhaustif. Nous nous contenterons de signaler les principaux inventaires qui donnent accès aux archives du Parlement de Paris et les instruments de recherche existants pour l'étude de la jurisprudence:

a) Inventaires publiés:

[*E. Campardon*], Répertoire numérique des archives du Parlement de Paris, série X (Paris 1889).

M. Langlois, Parlement de Paris, dans: Guide des recherches dans les fonds judiciaires de l'Ancien Régime (Paris 1958).

J. Favier (s.l.d.), Les archives nationales. Etat général des fonds, t. I: L'Ancien Régime (Paris 1978), pp. 649 - 663 (série X).

J. Favier (s.l.d.), Les archives nationales. Etat des inventaires, (Paris 1985), pp. 211 - 242 (série X).

b) *Instruments de recherche:*

1° Editions de textes:

A. Beugnot éd., Les Olim ou registres des arrêts rendus par la Cour du roi sous les règnes de Saint Louis, de Philippe le Hardi, de Philippe le Bel, de Louis le Hutin et de Philippe le Long, 4 vol., (Paris 1839 - 1848).

Ch. V. Langlois, Textes relatifs à l'histoire du Parlement depuis les origines jusqu'en 1314 (Paris 1888).

P. Guilhiermoz, Enquêtes et procès. Etude sur la procédure et le fonctionnement du Parlement au XIVe siècle (Paris 1892).

R. C. van Caenegem éd., Les arrêts et jugés du Parlement de Paris sur appels flamands, conservés dans les registres du Parlement, t. I: textes (1320 - 1453); t. II: textes (1454 - 1521) (Bruxelles 1966 - 1977), [Commission des Anciennes Lois et Ordonnances de Belgique].

C. T. Allmand et *C. A. J. Armstrong* éds., English suits before the Parlement of Paris (Londres 1982), [Royal Historical Society, Camden fourth series, vol. 26][53].

2° Analyses publiées:

E. Boutaric, Actes du Parlement de Paris, t. I (1254 - 1299); t. II (1299 - 1328) (Paris 1863 - 1867).

H. Furgeot, Actes du Parlement de Paris, t. I (1328 - 1342); t. II (1343 - 1350) (Paris 1920 - 1961), avec index par *J.-P. Laurent.*

S. Dauchy, Regestes des appels flamands au Parlement de Paris reconstitués d'après les registres du Parlement et les sources conservées dans les archives de Belgique et du Nord (Bruxelles, sous presse) [C. R. A. L. O. B.].

3° Inventaires analytiques manuscrits sur fiches et index du C. E. H. J.[54]:

Inventaire analytique manuscrit sur fiches, concernant au civil, les registres de Lettres, Arrêts et Jugés cotés X1A 5 à 31 (1319 - 1384) et les registres des Grands Jours de Troyes cotés X1A 9182 à 9188 (1367 - 1409)[55].

---

[53] De nombreux extraits des registres du Parlement sont également édités dans *P.-C. Timbal e. a.,* La guerre de Cent Ans à travers les registres du Parlement (1337 - 1369) (Paris 1961) et *Idem,* Les obligations contractuelles dans le droit français des XIIIe et XIVe siècles d'après la jurisprudence du Parlement, 2 vol. (Paris 1973 - 1977).

[54] Sur les travaux du Centre d'Etude d'Histoire Juridique, créé en 1953 par P.-C. Timbal dans le but d'explorer et rendre accessibles les archives du Parlement, voir entre autres *P.-C. Timbal,* L'exploitation des archives du Parlement de Paris: une méthode et ses résultats, dans: Rechtsgeschichte und quantitative Geschichte. Arbeitsberichte, herausgegeben von *F. Ranieri* (Francfort 1977), pp. 23 - 35.

Index méthodique manuscrit sur fiches des noms de matières, concernant les deux premiers volumes des *Olim* (publiés par *A. Beugnot)* par *J. Hilaire* et *B. Auzary-Schmaltz.*

Index méthodique manuscrit sur fiches des noms de matières[56] et de parties, concernant les registres du Parlement civil cotés X1A 5 à 31 (1319 - 1384), ainsi que des Grands Jours de Troyes et du Parlement de Poitiers.

Un traitement informatique a été appliqué à l'intégralité des registres de Lettres, Arrêts et Jugés cotés X1A 17 à 21 (1361 - 1369) et X1A 28 (1378 - 1379)[57].

Les archives nationales disposent, en outre, d'un index de noms de parties sur fiches manuscrites de la série des Accords (complet) et de la série du Conseil pour la période 1364 - 1483.

---

[55] Notons également l'inventaire analytique manuscrit du Parlement de Poitiers cotés X1A 9190 à 9199 (1418 - 1436) et, au criminel, les registres X2A 6 à 9 (1351 - 1382).

[56] Les matières présentées sous la forme d'un ensemble de mots-clés formalisé et organisé, sont réunies dans un cadre juridique et méthodique publié par *J. Metman* et *P.-C. Timbal,* Thesaurus d'histoire médiévale du Centre d'Etude d'Histoire Juridique (Paris 1983).

[57] *J. Metman* et *B. Auzary,* Les archives judiciaires et leur traitement informatique, dans: Informatique et histoire médiévale, Collection de l'Ecole française de Rome (1975), pp. 361 - 377.

BERNADETTE AUZARY-SCHMALTZ

Les recueils d'arrêts privés au Moyen Age

Dans l'ensemble de la littérature qui fleurit au cours de la seconde moitié du XIVe siècle ainsi que l'a noté Fr. Olivier-Martin[1], le recueil d'arrêts tient une place particulière au milieu des coutumiers et des styles de procédure. Au XIVe siècle, il n'existe pas en tant que tel mais on le rencontre intégré dans des œuvres à caractère mixte tels que coutumiers et styles de procédure. Le plus ancien de ces recueils, que l'on peut considérer comme le prototype, est le *Stylus Curie Parlamenti*[2]; il est assorti de citations d'arrêts que son auteur, l'avocat Guillaume du Breuil, a entendus prononcer au Parlement où il exerçait ses fonctions. Par son contenu composite, il doit être rapproché du *Style de la Chambre des Enquêtes*[3] qui se présente comme un répertoire de règles de procédure illustrées par des décisions de la Cour. Nous avons sélectionné trois recueils contemporains pour conduire cette étude, qui s'inscrivent chacun à sa manière dans cette tradition. Les *Questiones Johannis Galli*[4] possèdent incontestablement ce caractère composite, tellement typique des œuvres de ce temps car, malgré ce qu'annonce l'incipit[5], elles sont davantage qu'un recueil d'arrêts; à ces arrêts choisis en fonction de l'intérêt qu'ils offrent aux yeux de l'avocat qui les a collectés entre 1383 et 1398 s'ajoutent des ordonnances royales, plusieurs notables de droit (compilations de règles de droit reconnues comme usages établis) et des *casus*. Quant aux *Notes d'audiences prises au Parlement de Paris de 1384 à 1386 par un praticien anonyme*[6], l'éditeur signale[7] les difficultés qui se présentent pour déterminer la nature exacte de ce recueil:

---

[1] Histoire de la coutume de la prévôté et vicomté de Paris (réimpression de l'édition de 1925) t. I, p. 93.

[2] L'édition de référence est celle de *F. Aubert* (la plus récente): Guillaume du Breuil. Stilus Curie Parlamenti (Paris 1909).

[3] Publié par *P. Guilhiermoz,* Enquêtes et procès (Paris 1892).

[4] *M. Boulet,* Questiones Johannis Galli (Paris 1944).

[5] «*Sequuntur plura notabilia arresta que vidit et audivit pronunciari in curia Parlamenti et alibi, Magister Johannes Galli, quondam regis advocatus*» (incipit du manuscrit de Paris, cité par *M. Boulet,* op. cit., Introduction, p. CLV).

[6] *Fr. Olivier-Martin,* Notes d'audiences prises au Parlement de Paris de 1384 à 1386 par un praticien anonyme, dans: R.H.D., 1923, pp. 513 - 603.

[7] Op. cit., p. 517.

l'incipit a disparu, les informations concernant aussi bien la nature que l'auteur du recueil sont donc perdues; le bilan du contenu dressé par l'éditeur dans son introduction montre néanmoins que l'ouvrage se compose majoritairement (80 des 119 paragraphes) de la relation d'affaires plaidées au Parlement dans lesquelles un avocat a invoqué une coutume notoire dans telle province ou un style pratiqué devant telle juridiction. Le troisième recueil utilisé appartient à une catégorie différente. Il s'agit du *Grand Coutumier de France*[8] ou *Coutumier de Jacques d'Ableiges*. A la fois coutumier et style de procédure illustré de décisions judiciaires, cette compilation achevée entre 1385 et 1389[9] présente un caractère hétérogène fortement marqué[10], accentué par le fait que les nombreuses copies qui ont été effectuées du vivant de l'auteur et ont servi de base à l'établissement de l'édition n'ont pu être épurées – faute de comparaison avec l'original – des additions et variations apportées par les 'disciples improvisés' de d'Ableiges.

Œuvres composites par nature, ces trois recueils présentent des caractéristiques communes et des traits propres, dont il faut maintenant dresser le tableau. Quant à la forme d'abord, aucune édition n'a pu être faite d'après le manuscrit original, ni même d'après un manuscrit que l'éditeur aurait pu considérer comme prototype; chaque éditeur a donc dû procéder à l'établissement du texte en s'aidant de plusieurs manuscrits. Pour les *Questiones,* M. Boulet a utilisé comme manuscrit de base le manuscrit de Paris[11], corrigé par ceux de Londres et de Turin et subsidiairement par l'édition de du Moulin de 1558; les *Notes d'audiences*... ont été éditées à partir de deux manuscrits de la Bibliothèque nationale[12] que Fr. Olivier-Martin[13] qualifie de «copies assez médiocres... assez éloignées de l'original... [et qui] dérivent d'un modèle commun». L'édition du *Grand Coutumier* posait des problèmes beaucoup plus complexes: l'existence de plusieurs copies contemporaines de l'original, jointe au grand succès qu'a connu ce coutumier dès le XVe siècle expliquent le grand nombre de manuscrits retrouvés en France et à l'étranger; Fr. Olivier-Martin en a relevé dix-huit[14]; les éditions imprimées du XVIe siècle ont eu pour base des manuscrits aujourd'hui disparus et l'édition la plus communément utilisée de nos jours, faute de pouvoir

---

8 Nouvelle édition par *E. Laboulaye* et *Dareste* (réimpression de l'édition de Paris 1868, Scientia Verlag Aalen, 1969).

9 Voir sur la rédaction du *Grand Coutumier* la notice de *P. Petot* et *P.-C. Timbal,* Jacques d'Ableiges, Extrait de l'histoire littéraire de la France, t. XL (Paris 1968), pp. 23 sq.

10 On y trouve aussi des ordonnances (Livre I), des notables de droit (Livre IV).

11 Ms. 4645 de la Bibliothèque Nationale.

12 Ms. français 5259 et ms. 135 du Fonds Dupuy.

13 *Notes d'audiences*..., p. 514.

14 Histoire de la coutume de... Paris, t. I, pp. 93 - 96.

disposer d'une bonne édition critique, est celle de 1598, établie par Charondas le Caron[15].

Ces différentes informations concernant les sources, qui constituent autant de réserves quant à leur aptitude à remplacer l'original, étaient nécessaires avant d'aborder l'examen de leurs caractéristiques intrinsèques, à savoir le but poursuivi par leurs auteurs et leurs méthodes de travail.

En entreprenant cette collecte de données, chacun des auteurs n'avait d'autre dessein que celui de se constituer une documentation personnelle[16], indispensable pour ces trois juristes de métier à une époque où la vie judiciaire se trouve confrontée à une civilisation de l'écriture, selon l'heureuse expression utilisée par J. Hilaire et Cl. Bloch[17]. L'intérêt spéculatif que ces différentes entreprises attestent se double pour Jean Le Coq d'une nécessité professionnelle évidente: recueillir des décisions rendues par la juridiction devant laquelle on plaide permet de se constituer une base documentaire fiable, constamment enrichie donc remise à jour en permanence, et de disposer ainsi d'informations introuvables ailleurs. En effet, la consultation des registres dans lesquels la Cour consignait ses décisions ne semble jamais avoir été libre, pas même pour les avocats. M. Boulet[18] considère que Jean Le Coq, comme ses confrères avocats ou procureurs, n'a certainement pas eu accès au greffe du Parlement. On sait que les collections d'archives que la Cour s'est constituée, à peu près à partir du milieu du XIIIe siècle, semblent bien avoir été destinées à un usage strictement interne. L'obligation «de garder le secrez de la cour» et de ne pas divulguer l'opinion personnelle de chacun des conseillers qui pèse sur les juges[19] interdit toute publicité des registres. La Cour a conservé ses actes «avec des précautions particulières», la communication des registres aux parties, à leurs avocats ou représentants devant être autorisée expressément[20]. Cette tendance restrictive est ancienne (elle apparaît dans une ordonnance de Charles VIII de 1490[21], qui prévoit la communication aux parties, avocats et procureurs au greffe et en présence du greffier) et elle semble avoir été constante: un édit de 1716 ordonnera

---

15 Publiée par *Laboulay* et *Dareste* en 1868.

16 *Fr. Olivier-Martin* (*Notes d'audiences…*, p. 524) attribue cette motivation aux praticiens consciencieux de l'époque.

17 Connaissance des décisions de justice et origine de la jurisprudence, dans: Judicial Records, Law Reports and the Growth of Case Law, éd. *J. H. Baker* (Berlin 1989), pp. 52 sq.

18 Op. cit., Introduction, p. XXVI.

19 *E. de Laurière,* Ordonnances des roys de France de la troisième race, t. II, p. 223: ordonnance du 11 mars 1344, art. 14 - 15.

20 Voir l'Introduction de *A. Grün,* pp. XLVIII sq., dans: *E. Boutaric,* Inventaires et documents. Actes du Parlement de Paris, t. I (Paris 1863).

21 *E. de Laurière,* op. cit., t. XIV, p. 270: ordonnance du 28 décembre 1490, art. 50.

encore aux greffiers en chef de ne communiquer les registres «qu'à personnes convenables et avec la sûreté requise»[22]. Des raisons analogues, dictées par le besoin de se constituer une documentation[23], ont probablement motivé le praticien anonyme dont on peut conjecturer la qualité d'avocat (ou d'avocat-stagiaire) puisque son assiduité à l'audience[24] nous autorise à le faire. Quant au *Grand Coutumier de France,* en dépit de son titre qui pourrait faire croire qu'il s'agit d'une œuvre officielle[25], il est l'œuvre d'un bailli royal qui, pour se 'divertir' de ses fonctions qu'il exerce à Evreux à partir de 1385, s'adonne à l'étude. Le fruit de ses efforts est ce large exposé de droit parisien que l'auteur réservait à l'usage familial[26]. L'utilisation personnelle à laquelle ces travaux étaient destinés est encore confirmée par le fait que leurs auteurs ont négligé de leur donner un titre. Le Coq parle de son 'papier'[27] et d'Ableiges de sa 'petite compilation' ou de son 'livret'[28]. L'œuvre anonyme n'avait pas une autre destination, le petit nombre de manuscrits le prouve à défaut de connaître les intentions que l'auteur avait dû annoncer dans l'incipit aujourd'hui manquant.

Quant à leur façon de travailler, les auteurs eux-mêmes n'ont pas jugé utile de s'en expliquer puisqu'ils poursuivaient des visées qui leur étaient propres, le seul critère étant sans doute la facilité de consultation. Alors que la technique de rédaction utilisée par J. d'Ableiges reste à peu près inconnue, les éditeurs des *Questiones* et des *Notes d'audiences*... ont formulé des hypothèses – très voisines – sur la manière de travailler de Le Coq et sur celle du praticien anonyme, hypothèses qui paraissent tout à fait fondées. Fr. Olivier-Martin[29] remarque que les notes du praticien anonyme prises au jour le jour en assistant à l'audience étaient consignées sur un 'papier', c'est-à-dire un cahier composé de quelques feuilles de papier et muni d'une couverture permettant de l'identifier rapidement. M. Boulet[30]

---

22 *A. Grün,* ibid. Et voir sur cette question infra, la partie consacrée aux Temps Modernes.

23 Sur la formation des juristes, voir les intéressantes remarques présentées par S. Dauchy dans le chapitre traitant des recueils aux Temps Modernes.

24 *Fr. Olivier-Martin,* o.c. *(Notes d'audiences...),* p. 514.

25 Reproche que l'on peut formuler plus fermement encore à l'égard du titre attribué à cet œuvre par certains historiens du XVIIIe siècle: 'Coutumier de Charles VI', ainsi que l'on remarqué *P. Petot* et *P.-C. Timbal,* op. cit., p. 24.

26 *P. Petot* et *P.-C. Timbal,* op. cit., p. 49.

27 *M. Boulet,* op. cit., Introduction, p. XXX.

28 *P. Petot* et *P.-C. Timbal,* op. cit., p. 23. Cette humble appellation n'a pas empêché que le *Grand Coutumier* a bénéficié d'une diffusion imprévue; il a dès l'origine rencontré un grand succès chez les praticiens parisiens, en sorte que ces notes, en passant de main en main, se sont enrichies de toutes sortes de gloses et d'interpolations.

29 *Notes d'audiences...,* p. 519.

30 Op. cit., Introduction, pp. XXIX sq.

reprend cette hypothèse, qui est largement corroborée par la pratique de l'époque, ainsi que le note A. Giffard[31]; Jean Le Coq transcrivait lui-même les notes qu'il avait prises à l'audience, les mettait régulièrement en ordre et les conservait sur des feuillets ou des cahiers de papier qui n'étaient pas reliés entre eux, ce qui permettait d'intercaler des additions postérieures en évitant le procédé de la note marginale, impossible pour des ajouts d'une certaine ampleur. Par cette manière de travailler sur cahiers libres, qui semble leur avoir été commune, les deux avocats se conforment à la technique adoptée par les praticiens de leur temps, qui remplace le procédé sommaire et inadéquat des gloses marginales.

Comme leurs œuvres sont de la même essence, un dernier parallèle peut être fait entre Le Coq et le praticien anonyme en ce qui concerne la présentation de la matière recueillie. Cette observation permet de tirer des conclusions quant au degré d'évolution intellectuelle des auteurs. Jean Le Coq, avocat renommé, est un personnage en vue dans le milieu judiciaire parisien; devenu avocat du roi en 1387, il est à l'apogée de sa carrière lorsqu'il entreprend son recueil. C'est donc en praticien averti, confiant dans sa propre compétence, qu'il dégage avec une rigueur dépourvue d'hésitation les principes de droit posés par la Cour à l'occasion des causes qu'elle a jugées. Ses *Questiones* exposent les faits qui sont la cause du litige, le lieu où il se déroule, le nom des parties en présence, leurs prétentions, leurs arguments; elles rapportent enfin la sentence et la discutent. Dans la plupart des cas, Jean Le Coq pose le problème de droit sous une courte rubrique, par exemple dans la Qu. 44 qui est reprise dans le dossier n° I[32]: «*An dominus possit facere persecutionem ratione delicti facti in personam suorum subditorum*», puis il donne un bref résumé de la sentence «*Fuit dictum per arrestum*», en mentionnant éventuellement les prétentions des parties. Chaque fois qu'il le peut, il indique les motifs qui ont déterminé la décision, en précisant «*Ratio fuit...*» ou, plus prudemment, «*Ratio potuit esse...*», hypothèses fort bienvenues puisque les décisions ne sont pas motivées. Certaines questions sont développées plus longuement, peut-être parce qu'il a plaidé ces causes; l'avocat a alors adopté le plan traditionnel de la discussion scolastique: exposé des faits, arguments *pro et contra,* réponses aux objections et solution; ce schéma est celui de la Qu. 34 relatant une affaire plaidée par Le Coq[33]. Comme le remarque M. Boulet[34], une telle relation «implique un effort de composition accompli, à tête reposée, dans

[31] Etudes sur les sources du droit coutumier, dans: R.H.D., t. XXXVII, 1913, p. 620.

[32] Cf. tome II de cette publication, 'Le Parlement de Paris au Moyen Age: collation de recueils privés et de registres de la Cour'.

[33] Citée ibid., dans le dossier n° II.

[34] Op. cit., Introduction, p. XXXIV.

le silence d'un cabinet de travail». On peut ajouter que les citations de causes postérieures analogues attestent aussi que la rédaction est une œuvre réfléchie, enrichie sans cesse par l'addition de cas semblables nouvellement jugés, recueillis soigneusement par un juriste soucieux de pouvoir fonder d'autant mieux son argumentation devant les juges qu'il pourra *évoquer un ou plusieurs précédents* sur lesquels ils ont eux-mêmes statué. C'est une mention de ce type que J. Le Coq a ajoutée au dernier paragraphe de la Qu. 44: le procès qui y est relaté se déroule de février 1385 à janvier 1386; puis, l'avocat a remis l'ouvrage sur le métier pour consigner à la fin de la Question une nouvelle affaire qui s'y rapporte et qui a été jugée en 1389[35], procès dans lequel Maître J. Le Coq avait requis «pour le procureur du roi» que le défendeur soit puni pour bris de sauvegarde.

Cette documentation abondante, classée de manière mi-chronologique, mi-thématique a été élaborée par un homme d'expérience qui y a travaillé pendant près de vingt ans. Il en va différemment pour les *Notes d'audiences,* travail plus modeste aussi bien dans son ampleur que dans sa conception. L'éditeur indique que le texte qu'il publie a été établi à partir de deux manuscrits relativement brefs (35 folios pour le plus long) alors que les trois principaux manuscrits qui ont servi à l'édition des *Questiones* comportent tous plus de 130 feuillets[36]. Le document du praticien anonyme ne possède pas à l'évidence les mêmes qualités de composition. Il est structuré de façon uniforme en paragraphe qui se succèdent de manière chronologique sans qu'aucun regroupement par thème ne vienne faire la preuve que l'auteur a exercé sa réflexion *a posteriori.* «Ce n'est pas un ouvrage composé méthodiquement, avec des prétentions scientifiques, mais un simple recueil de notes prises au jour le jour par quelque praticien assidu aux audiences du Parlement» ainsi que Fr. Olivier-Martin l'a justement remarqué dans son introduction[37]. A la différence de J. Le Coq, le praticien anonyme ne résume pas, en général, le point de droit qu'il évoque; il énumère seulement les affaires qui ont été présentées à l'audience en les introduisant laconiquement par *item.* Certaines fois, pourtant, il ajoute un commentaire personnel par lequel il marque son adhésion ou sa critique. Très exceptionnellement, il propose une véritable discussion du cas, tout à fait 'à la manière de' Le Coq; ainsi, par exemple, dans le paragraphe 80 où il est question des avocats pensionnaires, question qui l'intéresse particulièrement s'il se destine au barreau. Quelquefois enfin, il résume fermement la doc-

[35] L'édition des *Questiones* donne à penser que le procès cité dans ce dernier paragraphe est en fait un précédent puisqu'il porte la date – erronée – de 1382; on verra dans le tome II (dossier n° II) comment ce procès a pu être retrouvé et daté de manière sûre.

[36] Le ms. de base, celui de Paris, compte 189 feuillets (format 72 × 70 cm).

[37] Op. cit., p. 519.

trine qui résulte d'une décision de la Cour; c'est le cas dans le paragraphe 98[38]: «*Ex quibus nota quod...*». En dépit de ces tentatives – peu nombreuses – qui apportent un élément dynamique dans cette chronique laborieuse, le recueil tronqué de son incipit et de son explicit semble bien être le cahier de notes d'un 'étudiant', soucieux de transcrire tout ce qu'il entend, qui nous est parvenu à l'état brut; sa transmission par deux manuscrits seulement atteste clairement que ces papiers personnels ont eu une circulation des plus limitées. Aucune comparaison n'est possible du point de vue de la diffusion avec l'œuvre de J. Le Coq qui, bien que destinée à un usage privé, a beaucoup circulé dès le XVe siècle, après la mort du célèbre avocat; encore moins avec le *Grand Coutumier* que d'Ableiges avait composé pour l'instruction de ses neveux[39], mais qui en réalité a connu une large diffusion à la fin du XIVe siècle et au XVe siècle.

Pour poursuivre valablement l'examen comparatif des recueils en envisageant maintenant leur contenu, il faut considérer ceux qui présentent le plus de similitudes, les *Questiones* et les *Notes d'audiences*. Reconnaissons à Le Coq, comme le fait M. Boulet[40], sa primauté d'auteur de *recueil d'arrêts* car son ouvrage peut bien être qualifié ainsi, malgré la présence de 'scories' archaïsantes que sont les ordonnances royales et les 'notables de droit'. Le travail du praticien anonyme est de la même nature bien qu'il ne présente pas les caractéristiques d'une œuvre aussi élaborée. Si le résultat n'est pas du même niveau, la démarche est bien identique et, dans le besoin de se documenter qui les animait, ces deux praticiens contemporains ont fait preuve l'un et l'autre d'une certaine subjectivité inhérente à ce type d'entreprise menée à des fins personnelles.

Le constat des similitudes existant entre ces œuvres entreprises à des fins utilitaires invitait à poursuivre la comparaison sur le plan intrinsèque: il a paru alors intéressant de repérer des procès répertoriés par les deux auteurs et d'examiner la manière dont chacun les présente. Cela est possible pour les années 1384 à 1386[41] pendant lesquelles les deux praticiens ont fréquenté l'audience. Parmi les affaires qu'ils relatent l'un et l'autre, nous avons sélectionné deux questions de droit qui, sans être atypiques, ne sont pas non plus représentatives d'une orientation dominante propre à chaque recueil. En effet, la première affaire choisie concerne la responsabilité délictuelle, la seconde touche à la délimitation de la compétence royale face à la justice ecclésiastique. Or, Le Coq dans sa collection de cas investigue des domaines très variés (droit public, procédure, droit privé), mais

[38] Cité dans le tome II de cette publication (dossier n° II).

[39] *Fr. Olivier-Martin*, op. cit., p. 524.

[40] Op. cit., Introduction, p. XIV.

[41] Le praticien anonyme a fréquenté l'audience pendant ces trois années seulement alors que Le Coq a officié à la cour depuis 1383 et jusqu'en 1398.

on remarque cependant qu'il a consacré une plus forte proportion de ses *questiones* au droit public[42]. Quant au praticien anonyme, il est bien difficile de se faire une idée de ses goûts d'après un travail aussi impersonnel, cela autorise parfaitement François Olivier-Martin à dire qu'il est «éclectique dans ses choix»[43].

Le premier point de droit (cf. tome II, dossier n° 1) est relatif à l'action offerte au seigneur pour poursuivre les faits délictueux subis par ses sujets. Par son arrêt du 16 février 1385, rapporté par J. Le Coq à la Question 44, la Cour reçoit la demande de l'évêque de Reims: il présente ses conclusions contre Jean dit le Grand Foynon, qui a maltraité ses sujets, les habitants de Mons, où l'évêque a toute justice. Cette jurisprudence a été confirmée par une autre décision de 1386 rendue au profit de l'évêque de Laon[44], que Le Coq a rapportée à la suite de la précédente[45]. Le praticien anonyme cite aussi l'affaire concernant l'évêque de Reims, mais il néglige la question de fond (l'action doit-elle être ou non ouverte à l'évêque) pour s'attacher au déclinatoire de compétence proposé par l'avocat de Foynon en prétendant qu'il était clerc; son commentaire porte seulement sur cet aspect du litige.

Le second (dossier n° II) touche au délicat problème de la compétence de la justice royale face à la justice ecclésiastique, plus précisément la question posée par Le Coq est celle-ci: un clerc prisonnier de la cour séculière doit-il être rendu à la cour spirituelle? Le procès cité en référence oppose en 1384 un clerc, Mundus, emprisonné au Châtelet sur l'ordre de la Cour qui l'a ensuite élargi, à l'évêque de Paris qui réclame qu'il lui soit rendu. Le Coq a été désigné par la Cour (par 'distribution' de conseils) pour défendre la cause et de ce fait il relate l'affaire avec précision. Il énumère d'abord les arguments de l'évêque présentés en sept points, dont le dernier énonce deux *précédents judiciaires;* il donne ensuite ses propres 'raisons' qui tendent à réfuter celles de l'évêque. Parmi ces arguties d'avocat (voir la première raison donnée par Le Coq), quelques points nous semblent devoir être relevés. Le quatrième point (des deux plaidoiries) porte sur la partition entre le *délit privilégié,* dont la connaissance appartient à la justice royale, et le *délit commun,* qui doit être sanctionné par la juridiction ecclésiastique; on remarque d'abord l'emploi d'une terminologie relative-

---

[42] Op. cit., Introduction, p. LXIV.

[43] Op. cit., p. 527.

[44] L'édition de M. Sautel date par erreur cette décision de 1382, ce qui fait croire qu'il s'agit d'un précédent; or il n'en est rien: les instruments de recherche dans le fonds du Parlement dont on dispose maintenant ont permis d'identifier de façon certaine les parties et de retrouver la décision qui a, en réalité, était présentée au conseil le 16 février 1385, l'arrêt mis en forme ayant été rendu le 13 janvier 1386 (cf. édition de textes dans le tome II).

[45] Cette mention postérieure prouve le soin avec lequel Le Coq a enrichi sa documentation.

ment nouvelle[46]; de plus Le Coq propose la prééminence de la justice royale, comme si «le délit privilégié tenait le délit commun en état». Le cinquième point évoqué par Le Coq montre que l'avocat s'intéresse au sort de celui qu'il défend puisqu'il veut éviter à son client élargi par la Cour (c'est-à-dire placé dans une sorte de liberté conditionnelle) de connaître un sort plus dur s'il était rendu à l'évêque qui le mettrait en prison. Enfin, dans son septième point, l'évêque citait deux précédents: l'un concernant l'évêque de Châlons, qui a obtenu restitution du clerc Guy d'Enaumont pour juger le délit commun, l'autre évoqué de manière plus allusive «au sujet d'Aymery Trousset, clerc non marié». Le Coq réfute brièvement ces allégations de précédents dans son septième point, mais il sera plus explicite dans le paragraphe final où il indique la solution du litige: il note que la décision a été prise «non obstant les arguments de l'évêque» car, en ce qui concerne Enaumont[47], il avait été repris dans les prisons de l'évêque de Châlons et conduit ensuite au Parlement; or, dans le cas présent (celui de Mundus), il n'en était pas ainsi. Le cas de Trousset a, en revanche, beaucoup intéressé le praticien anonyme si on en juge par l'ampleur des développements qu'il consacre à ce procès. Bien que Le Coq ait été l'avocat de Trousset, c'est le praticien anonyme qui relate en détail son procès dans deux longs paragraphes (98 - 99): Le Coq a d'abord proposé (§ 98) un déclinatoire de compétence parce que Trousset est clerc et qu'il s'agit d'un 'crime personnel' (Trousset a commis un faux). Le conseil de la partie adverse, qui n'était autre qu'Oudard de Molins[48], autre grande figure du barreau parisien, avait proposé à titre de précédent[49] un arrêt rendu contre J. Curiat: ce dernier qui jouissait de la qualité de clerc avait néanmoins dû répondre en Parlement d'un faux commis dans des lettres du Châtelet.

La Cour déboute le client de Le Coq et décide de connaître de l'affaire. Le Coq demande alors (§ 99) à la Cour de faire défense au cardinal de Laon, juge ordinaire de Trousset, de molester ce dernier tant que le procès est pendant en Parlement; il obtient satisfaction[50] et, d'après la relation donnée par le praticien anonyme, Arnaud de Corbie qui présidait la Cour en a décidé ainsi «quia, quamdiu Curia cognoscit de fractione salvagardie per clericum, episcopus non potest cognoscere de principali delicto per quod delictum fuit salva gardia fracta *et hoc est notabile*».

---

[46] *Fr. Olivier-Martin* note la première occurrence de l'expression «délit commun ou fait non privilégié» dans un arrêt du 4 mars 1381 (L'assemblée de Vincennes de 1329 et ses conséquences. Etude sur les conflits entre la juridiction laïque et la juridiction ecclésiastique au XIVe siècle (Paris 1909), p. 273, n. 4).

[47] Voir textes publiés dans le dossier n° II, dans le deuxième volume.

[48] Devenu comme Jean Le Coq avocat du roi en 1391 (*E. Maugis,* Histoire du Parlement de Paris de l'avènement des rois Valois à la mort d'Henri IV (Paris 1916), t. III).

[49] Arrêt de janvier 1382.

[50] Arrêt du 17 mai 1385.

Les questions de compétence disputée entre juge royal et juge ecclésiastique intéressaient manifestement beaucoup les praticiens de l'époque: Le Coq a plaidé plusieurs procès qui s'y rapportent[51]; le praticien anonyme leur porte un intérêt particulier, à tel point qu'il néglige parfois le problème de fond pour s'intéresser au privilège du for (cf. supra, à propos du Dossier n° I). Et Jacques d'Ableiges reprend dans le Livre IV du *Grand Coutumier* le procès de Jean Curiat contre l'évêque de Paris en 1382, il cite à ce propos un précédent de 1380 ou 1381 que les deux 'arrêtistes' parisiens semblent ignorer[52]. Il faut dire que la question était d'actualité dans les années 1380, car le Parlement prétend alors connaître des délits commis dans l'exercice de leurs fonctions par les clercs officiers royaux. Ceux-ci ne peuvent donc alléguer valablement leur privilège pour décliner la juridiction royale; une 'jurisprudence' nouvelle est en train de se mettre en place timidement[53].

Que la place 'privilégiée' que ce problème de compétence, révélateur de la progression du pouvoir royal, s'est vue attribuer dans cette étude soit un hommage rendu à ces trois juristes attentifs à l'évolution du droit de leur temps.

S'il est tout à fait clair comme l'ont remarqué J. Hilaire et Cl. Bloch[54] que la méthode de J. Le Coq «permet une utilisation des décisions très précise pour une éventuelle citation devant la juridiction dans une plaidoirie», peut-on pour autant en conclure que le poids de ces précédents pouvait être destiné à emporter la conviction du juge? Il semble bien, au terme de cette étude, que la jurisprudence a de fait dès le Moyen Age une certaine autorité. Plusieurs raisons permettent de le penser.

La première, et on peut dire que c'est un bon indice de *l'utilité* de la jurisprudence, c'est la fréquence des citations de précédents dans les registres du Parlement, qu'il s'agisse de décisions ou de plaidoiries, au civil comme au criminel. Cette fréquence également constatée par M. Boulet[55] incline à penser que cette démarche n'était pas sans objet.

Un deuxième argument ressort de l'apport de la jurisprudence à l'égard des coutumes, spécialement dans l'administration de la preuve de la coutume et même dans l'élaboration de certaines coutumes procédurales. Certains auteurs ont déjà remarqué le rôle important que les décisions judiciai-

---

[51] Voir par exemple Qu., 34, 35, 60, 117.

[52] Ces procès que nous avons pu identifier sont retranscrits dans le Dossier n° II, *in fine.*

[53] Évolution observée par *Fr. Olivier-Martin,* op. cit., p. 271.

[54] Connaissance des décisions de justice et origine de la jurisprudence, dans: Judicial Records, Law Reports and the Growth of Case Law, éd. *J. H. Baker* (Berlin 1989), p. 64.

[55] Op. cit., Introduction, p. LVIII sq.

res ont joué pour préciser, compléter et faire évoluer la coutume en lui permettant de s'adapter aux nécessités du temps[56] et A. Sergène[57] a noté qu'en matière de coutumes, la citation mentionne en général un seul précédent; c'est donc à ce dernier que l'on reconnaît une *force probatoire* suffisante qui dispenserait l'avocat de toute autre preuve. Ce changement dans le mode de preuve, changement qui est en fait une simplification, explique sans doute le soin que prennent les praticiens de consigner les précédents dans leurs recueils. En ce qui concerne notre recherche, les précédents cités dans les deux dossiers ne touchent pas le fond du droit; ils concernent la procédure et la compétence, domaines qui, par la lacune des textes normatifs, s'élaborent à partir des décisions de justice. Aussi peut-on dire, en l'occurrence, que la jurisprudence est créatrice de coutumes procédurales ou de styles.

Il faut en troisième lieu rappeler le rôle essentiel de la jurisprudence en matière criminelle. La 'coutume jurisprudentielle' joue un rôle considérable dans le système de l'arbitraire des peines en usage pendant tout l'Ancien Régime[58]. Le juge pénal, qui a pour chaque infraction la responsabilité d''arbitrer', c'est-à-dire de choisir la peine adéquate en fonction de la gravité de la faute et de la culpabilité imputable au délinquant, décide «à la lumière de la jurisprudence antérieure»[59].

Un ultime argument, et non des moindres, ressort de la pratique des arrêts de règlement. Dès le XIIIe siècle, le Parlement rend des arrêts d'une portée bien différente de celle des décisions judiciaires puisque ces dernières ont seulement autorité de la chose jugée entre les parties au procès, alors que les arrêts de règlement sont des *dispositions obligatoires pour tous* qui, à la différence des ordonnances, émanent de l'initiative du Parlement et non de celle du roi. Ces arrêts de règlement établissaient une sorte de législation provisoire «en attendant une loi et pour en tenir lieu dans l'intervalle»[60]. Rendus à l'occasion d'un procès, ils intervenaient dans les domaines les plus variés ainsi que les quelques exemples qui suivent vont le montrer pour le XIVe siècle. Dans le domaine de la procédure, un arrêt de règlement de

---

[56] *M. Boulet,* ibid. et *J. Hilaire* et *Cl. Bloch,* op. cit., p. 66.

[57] Le précédent judiciaire au moyen âge, dans: R.H.D., t. XXXIX, 1961, p. 254.

[58] Voir l'analyse donnée par *J.-M. Carbasse* des pouvoirs de juge pénal dans son Introduction historique au droit pénal (P.U.F., Paris 1990), p. 167 sq.

[59] Dans le même sens, voir les conclusions de *Cl. Bloch* à propos des: Peines appliquées aux faux monnayeurs en France par la Chambre des Monnaies (fin du XVe siècle): «Si les juges font enregistrer ces renseignements [relatifs à l'activité professionnelle des délinquants], n'est-ce-pas dans le but de pouvoir retrouver au fil du temps ... toutes les données qui les ont conduits à prononcer une peine plutôt qu'une autre?», dans: Tijdschrift voor Rechtsgeschiedenis, t. LVIII, 1990, p. 87.

[60] *A. Esmein,* Cours élémentaire d'histoire du droit français (Paris 1892), p. 509.

1320 précise le style de la cour[61]; un autre de 1340 vient conforter une ordonnance qui limitait le nombre des huissiers au Parlement[62]; un autre fixe les règles pour évoquer devant le Requêtes du Palais des causes pendantes devant le prévôt de Paris[63]. En matière criminelle, deux arrêts de règlement rendus dans la seconde moitié du XIVe siècle viennent limiter l'emploi de la question[64]. Afin de définir les privilèges municipaux de la vicomté de l'Eau à Rouen, le Parlement rend en 1380 une décision très significative à l'égard de la valeur que les conseillers eux-mêmes accordent aux décisions rendues au sein de la Cour puisqu'ils érigent en arrêt de règlement une décision rendue antérieurement: à l'occasion d'un différend entre la ville de Rouen et certains marchands normands qui entendent faire circuler librement leurs marchandises sous le pont de Rouen, la Cour se fonde sur un arrêt de 1315, dont se prévalent les marchands, pour trancher en leur faveur et, le 5 juillet 1380[65], elle ordonne à l'Echiquier de faire publier l'arrêt ancien par les baillis et vicomtes du duché de Normandie dans leurs circonscriptions «*ad finem quod nullus super hoc ignoranciam pretendere valeret*».

Il est assez curieux de remarquer que, dans le débat ouvert depuis une cinquantaine d'années sur la valeur de la jurisprudence moderne entre les auteurs qui voient en elle une source du droit[66] et ceux qui, au contraire, lui reconnaissent une simple autorité[67], un consensus semble se dégager pour accorder à la jurisprudence *une inspiration possible pour le juge,* mais pas une règle obligatoire, situation somme toute assez proche de celle que nous venons de décrire pour la fin du Moyen Age[68].

---

61 X1A 7, f° 130 (19 janvier 1320): consécration des usages de la cour, notamment en matière de complainte.

62 X1A 9, f° 96 v° (6 mai 1340).

63 X1A 21, f° 402 (8 juillet 1368).

64 X2A 9, f° 83 v° (6 juin 1377): il sera désormais interdit de questionner *ad vertibulum;* X2A 9, f° 130 (28 août 1378): interdiction d'utiliser le carcan.

65 X1A 29, f° 166: en faveur d'un marchand de Bayeux; une décision identique a été rendue le 11 mai 1380 au profit de plusieurs marchands de Caen et de Honfleur (X1A 29, f° 151 v°).

66 Voir en particulier les conclusions de *E. Serverin* (De la jurisprudence en droit privé (P.U.F. de Lyon 1985), p. 329 sq.) qui considère comme une réelle source du droit une partie de la jurisprudence de la Cour de cassation.

67 Voir l'état de la question dressé par *J. Carbonnier,* dans: Droit civil. Introduction (P.U.F., Thémis, Paris 1991), §. 148.

68 Après avoir évoqué les arrêts de règlement rendus par le Parlement, il convient de noter que la Cour de Cassation a été amputée de cette fonction normative qu'exerçait le Parlement sous l'Ancien Régime; en effet, l'article 5 du Code civil interdit «aux juges de prononcer par voie de disposition générale et réglementaire sur les causes qui leur sont soumises».

SERGE DAUCHY

Les recueils privés de 'jurisprudence' aux Temps Modernes

Dans les traditions romaniste et canoniste autant que dans la pratique coutumière médiévale, le rôle des décisions judiciaires comme source du droit est généralement considéré comme étant limité. Les jugements sont plutôt un instrument de connaissance de la coutume qui contribue à l'établir et à la prouver[1]. Mais la jurisprudence va évoluer avec la centralisation et la rationalisation de justice. Les 13e et 14e siècles constituent ici une période charnière. A cette époque, le développement de l'appel affirme l'autorité de la Cour souveraine du royaume où siègent toujours davantage de juges professionnels aptes à créer le droit. Les conseillers et avocats du Parlement seront d'ailleurs les premiers à s'intéresser aux contentieux en tant que source subsidiaire du droit, établissant même des recueils d'arrêts à leur propre usage (ceux-ci sont présentés dans la partie consacrée au Moyen Age). Cette littérature arrêtiste se développe surtout à partir de la seconde moitié du 16e siècle. On voit alors apparaître de très nombreux recueils d'arrêts qui, grâce à l'imprimerie, connaissent une large diffusion et sont parfois réédités à plusieurs reprises. Ces recueils sont, pour nombre d'entre d'eux, de véritables ouvrages de doctrine coutumière qui, en contribuant à répandre les décisions des cours souveraines du royaume, ont élevé la jurisprudence au rang de source à part entière du droit français[2].

---

[1] *Ph. Godding,* La jurisprudence (Turnhout 1973), p. 11 sq., [Typologie des sources du moyen âge occidental, fasc. 6]. On consultera également *A. Sergène,* Le précédent judiciaire au moyen âge, dans: Revue historique de Droit français et étranger, t. XXXIX, 1961, pp. 224 - 254 et 359 - 370.

[2] *J. Hilaire* et *Cl. Bloch,* Connaissance des décisions de justice et origine de la jurisprudence, dans: *J. H. Baker* éd., Judicial Records, Law Reports and the Growth of Case Law (Berlin 1989), [Comparative Studies in Continental and Anglo-American Legal History, Bd. 5], pp. 47 - 68 notent que «La création de nouveaux parlements et, au milieu du XVIème siècle, la création des sièges présidiaux ne pouvaient qu'accroître le poids de la jurisprudence: d'autant qu'à partir des coutumes rédigées le rôle des cours était moins désormais de reconnaître la coutume en lui accordant la consécration judiciaire que de procéder à l'inévitable interprétation et de combler les lacunes».

Il n'y a que peu d'auteurs qui se soient intéressés aux recueils d'arrêts. Ils constituent, pour les historiens du droit, davantage une source d'information, parmi d'autres, qu'un objet de recherche en soi. Nous disposons néanmoins de l'étude particulièrement exhaustive et, de surcroît, très récente de Gerhard Walter consacrée à cette littérature juridique[3]. Dès lors, il ne semble pas utile de rédiger une nouvelle présentation générale des recueils «de jurisprudence» français publiés aux Temps Modernes, tout au plus suffira-t-il d'en rappeler quelques caractéristiques essentielles. La principale de ces caractéristiques, commune à l'ensemble des ouvrages – qu'ils soient désignés sous le nom de *Recueils d'arrêts, Décisions, Codes* ou *Questions notables* –, réside incontestablement dans le fait qu'ils résultent tous, sans exception, d'initiatives privées. En France, aucune juridiction d'Ancien Régime n'a entrepris, voire envisagé la possibilité, de publier les décisions qu'elle rendait. Les cours de justice se contentent, conformément aux dispositions contenues depuis le début du 14e siècle dans les ordonnances relatives au fonctionnement du Parlement, de faire enregistrer par le greffier les décisions et plus tard également les délibérations des conseillers et les plaidoiries. La dénomination de recueils «privés» n'implique donc pas qu'ils ont été rédigés à l'usage propre de son auteur, mais bien qu'ils résultent de l'initiative de praticiens particuliers.

I. Le *Recueil d'arrêts notables* de Georges Louet

L'option choisie pour effectuer cette étude comparative a donc été de sélectionner un recueil privé d'arrêts – principalement rendus par le Parlement de Paris – puis d'établir la comparaison entre les causes citées et les registres rédigés par l'institution elle-même. Notre choix s'est porté sur le *Recueil d'arrêts notables* de Georges Louet qui apparaît, à plusieurs égards, comme particulièrement représentatif des très nombreux ouvrages édités entre le 16e et le 18e siècle. De surcroît, cet ouvrage a connu à l'époque une réelle notoriété comme en témoignent les nombreuses éditions ainsi que les renvois répétés faits par d'autres arrêtistes.

Georges Louet était, comme la grande majorité des auteurs de recueils privés, directement rattaché à la Cour dont il a publié les décisions[4]. Il est

---

3 *G. Walter,* Bibliographie der französischen Rechtsprechungssammlungen des Ancien Régime, dans: Ius commune, 1975 (5), pp. 210 - 299 et *Idem,* dans: *H. Coing* éd., Handbuch der Quellen und Literatur der neueren europäischen Privatrechtsgeschichte, t. II/2 (Munich 1976), pp. 1223 - 1263. On trouvera quelques éléments dans *J. Brissaud,* Cours d'histoire du droit français public et privé, 2 t. (Paris 1904); *E. Chenon,* Histoire générale du droit français public et privé des origines à 1815, 2 t. (Paris 1926 - 1929); *A. Esmein,* Cours élémentaire du droit français (Paris 1925^{25}) et *A. Isnard,* Catalogue générale des livres imprimés de la Bibliothèque Nationale, t. I - VIII: Actes Royaux (Paris 1910 - 1960).

né à Angers vers 1540 et mort à La Rochelle en 1608. Archidiacre de Tours et doyen d'Angers, il fut reçu conseiller clerc au Parlement de Paris le 4 janvier 1584 par résignation de Jean de Laubespine fait évêque de Limoges. Après avoir prêté serment à la Ligue le 26 janvier 1589, il fait partie des conseillers transfuges de Paris qui demandent leur intégration au Parlement de Tours; après enquête sur ses lettres patentes datées du 10 juin 1589, il sera reçu le 5 février 1590. A partir de 1594 il siège à nouveau au Parlement de Paris et, pour services rendus à l'occasion de la délicate question de l'annulation du mariage entre Henri IV et Marguerite de Valois, il aurait obtenu du roi la première charge vacante de président des Enquêtes. Il décéda pendant une commission judiciaire alors qu'il venait d'être nommé évêque de Tréguier[5].

Spécialiste du droit canonique et, en particulier, des matières bénéficiales, Georges Louet a joui tout au long de l'Ancien Régime d'une grande renommée grâce à son *Recueil d'arrests* dont la première édition date de 1602. Cet ouvrage a connu de nombreuses éditions, revues et complétées au 17e siècle par Gabriel-Michel de Roche-Maillet (en 1610), par Julien Brodeau, avocat au Parlement, (en 1614, 1616, 1620, 1627, 1633, 1643, 1650, 1655, 1661, 1668 et 1678) et encore au 18e siècle (1742) par Nicolas-Guy du Rousseaud de la Combe, également avocat au Parlement[6].

La confrontation du recueil de G. Louet avec les registres du Parlement a été entreprise à partir des éditions en deux tomes de 1712 et de 1742. La première de ces éditions tardives est une réimpression de la dernière version revue par J. Brodeau (1678) augmentée de quelques nouveaux arrêts signalés dans la préface[7], la deuxième étant celle revue par Rousseaud de la Combe[8].

---

4 *G. Walter,* op. cit., pp. 1241 - 1242, note que les auteurs sont essentiellement des avocats rattachés aux cours souveraines (50% des auteurs dont on connaît la profession) ou des conseillers et présidents (30%).

5 *E. Maugis,* Histoire du Parlement de Paris de l'avènement des rois Valois à la mort d'Henri IV, t. III: Rôle de la Cour par règnes (1345 - 1610) (Paris 1916), pp. 266, 277, 289 et 303, et Nouvelle biographie générale depuis les temps les plus reculés jusqu'à nos jours, sous la direction du *Dr. Hoefer* (Paris 1862), t. 31.

6 *G. Walter,* op. cit., p. 1257.

7 «*Et dans cette nouvelle & derniere Edition de l'année 1712 les addition qu'on y a faites sont tirées des Arrêts du Parlement de Toulouse par M. de CATELLAN, des Arrêts du Parlement de Tournay par M. PINAULT, des Plaidoïers de M. de BORBERON, Avocat General au Parlement de Metz, des œuvres de M. AUZANET, de la Coûtume de Paris par M. de PLESSIS, du Traité des Communautez de M. DENIS LE BRUN, du Tome cinquiéme du Journal des Audiences du Parlement de Paris par M. LA GUESSIERE & M. NICOLAS NUPIED, de la douziéme partie du Journal du Palais* in quarto, *& des Arrêts augmentez dans la nouvelle Edition du Journal de tous les Parlemens de France par MM. GUERET & BLONDEAU en deux volumes* in folio, *& des Arrêts des differens Tribunaux de France par M.*

La structure de l'œuvre repose sur le classement alphabétique des questions de droit très diverses qui sont traitées, chacune de ces questions constituant un chapitre identifié par la première lettre du titre suivi d'un chiffre romain. Ainsi la question analysée dans le cadre de cette étude est intitulée 'Chirurgiens & Apotiquaires préferez à tous autres creanciers, même à la veuve pour ses conventions' et correspond au chapitre C. XXIX. L'ensemble des titres est repris dans la table des matières figurant au début des deux volumes.

Chaque chapitre est précédé d'un sommaire où sont énoncés les intitulés des sous-parties numérotés en chiffres arabes. Le développement juridique proprement dit débute invariablement avec l'arrêt commenté par G. Louet, probablement tel qu'il avait été rédigé et présenté par l'auteur lui-même dans l'édition de 1602. N'ayant pu retrouver un exemplaire de cette version originale, nous ne pouvons l'affirmer avec certitude, mais plusieurs indices semblent néanmoins l'attester. D'un point de vue matériel, ce premier paragraphe, couvrant toute la largeur de la page, se distingue clairement du reste du texte imprimé en colonnes. Dans la marge on peut aussi relever, en face du texte, la mention A[uteur]. La façon de citer les arrêts, sur laquelle nous reviendrons plus loin, correspond d'ailleurs aux règles communément en vigueur au début du 17e siècle. Vient ensuite le commentaire – très fourni – de J. Brodeau qui s'engage généralement par «voiez ce que dit notre auteur» ou «cet arrêt allégué par l'auteur», attestant sans le moindre doute que ce qui précède doit bien être attribué à G. Louet.

La démarche de J. Brodeau vise un double objectif: tout d'abord commenter l'arrêt rapporté par Louet en alléguant des arguments nouveaux puisés dans les coutumes, les ordonnances, le droit savant et même la littérature ou en établissant des parallèles avec d'autres questions; ensuite apporter de nouvelles décisions – empruntées à d'autres recueils d'arrêts ou directement tirées des sources – conformes au précédent cité ou précisant encore davantage la question qui y fut soulevée. On peut relever l'approche différente des deux 'arrestographes' – ainsi que les ouvrages de l'époque appellent les auteurs de ces recueils – dans les passages consacrés aux 'chirurgiens et apothicaires' et reproduits dans le second volume de ces actes. On remarque que Louet ne va pas au-delà d'une simple notification de l'arrêt alors que Brodeau s'étend en longues digressions sur les médecins antiques et les frais funéraires auxquels on assimile les honoraires des

---

AUGEARD; toutes lesquelles nouvelles additions, au nombre de 600 celebres Questions, sont distinguées par une marque de cette maniere».

8 En ce qui concerne les passages sur lesquels repose le travail de collation, ces deux éditions sont rigoureusement identiques, tant du point de vue du contenu que de la présentation.

chirurgiens et apothicaires pour expliquer qu'ils constituent des créances privilégiées, développant son propos par de fréquents recours au droit romain et à de nouvelles décisions judiciaires. Les éditions tardives du *Recueil d'arrests notables* illustrent ainsi l'évolution qui a marqué cette littérature juridique entre le 16e et le 18e siècle. En effet, les plus anciens arrêtistes se contentent de reproduire *in extenso* des décisions judiciaires, souvent de façon chronologique et tout au plus pourvues d'un titre et de quelques lignes résumant la question de droit qui y est abordée. D'autres ne font que résumer les informations essentielles, c'est-à-dire le nom des parties, l'objet du litige, les arguments de fait et de droit allégués par les avocats et, enfin, le dispositif et la date du jugement. Leur titre est souvent révélateur ainsi, par exemple, les *CCXXVII arrests celebres et mémorables du Parlement de Paris* de Barnabé Le Vest ou les *Cent notables et singulieres questions de droit décidées par arrests mémorables des cours souveraines de France* de Jean Chenu. A partir du milieu du 17e siècle, les ouvrages se présentent plutôt comme des traités où l'arrêt a pour fonction d'introduire un développement juridique, parfois il n'est même guère plus qu'un argument parmi d'autres sur lequel repose le raisonnement de l'auteur. Les recueils sont alors davantage structurés, privilégiant souvent certaines matières ou tendant, au contraire, à devenir de véritables dictionnaires.

Pour conclure la présentation de l'œuvre de G. Louet, notons encore que chaque chapitre se termine par une 'Addition nouvelle' où sont réunies quelques décisions supplémentaires – n'ayant souvent qu'un lien très lointain avec la question traitée[9] – prononcées tant par les parlements des pays de coutumes que par ceux des pays de droit écrit. Ces arrêts sont rapportés de manière très succincte: tout au plus signale-t-on la juridiction concernée, le nom des principales parties engagées, la date du prononcé et le dispositif. Enfin, en marge du commentaire de J. Brodeau et de l'addition sont indiqués les titres (annoncés dans le sommaire) ainsi que la date et, en peu de mots, le dispositif de tous lcs arrêts cités.

II. Les sources et la méthode de travail des arrêtistes

Il n'est probablement pas nécessaire de s'étendre sur les sources des arrêtistes que sont – sinon exclusivement, du moins essentiellement – les contentieux tranchés par les parlements, mais aussi ceux portés devant d'au-

[9] Ainsi dans le chapitre consacré à la créance privilégiée des chirurgiens et apothicaires, la *Nouvelle addition* comprend plusieurs arrêts rendus par les parlements et qui traitent de sujets aussi divers que les qualifications des apothicaires et chirurgiens, la défense qui leur est faite de pratiquer la transfusion sanguine et d'autres questions qui touchent à l'exercice de la médecine en général.

tres juridictions[10]. En revanche, on ne sait que peu de choses en ce qui concerne leur méthode de travail: en d'autres termes, comment recueillent-ils leurs informations? Il est, en effet, à remarquer que les membres du Parlement étaient, du moins dès la fin du Moyen Age, tenus à un certain devoir de réserve. Il ne leur était pas permis, pour reprendre les termes de l'ordonnance de 1507, de divulguer «*les secretz de nostredicte cour aux serviteur de nosdictz conseillers et aultres gens*»[11]. Mais cela ne signifie pas pour autant, contrairement à ce que prétendent certains auteurs, qu'ils ne pouvaient pas consulter les registres. La même ordonnance (art. 54) enjoint, au contraire, les conseillers «*qu'ilz soient curieux de voir et visiter les arrestz de nostredicte court, et les stiles et observations d'icelle, affin de sçavoir et cognoistre la forme de dicter les arrestz et d'appliquer les extraitz*». En revanche, leur communication à des tiers devait être strictement contrôlée afin de préserver le principe du secret des délibérations en conseil qui auraient fait l'objet d'une rédaction dans des cahiers distincts, insérés dans les registres[12]. Il semble néanmoins peu probable que les conseillers aient dépouillé les registres, tels des historiens, afin de réunir les sources de leurs travaux. Quant aux avocats, il est invraisemblable qu'ils aient eu accès aux registres de la Cour. On peut penser qu'ils se sont principalement appuyés sur leur propre expérience, commentant dans leurs recueils essentiellement les causes qu'ils avaient eux-mêmes plaidées ou, lorsqu'il s'agit de conseillers, celles dont ils avaient eu connaissance en tant que rapporteur. On peut citer, à titre d'exemple, les *Questions notables de droit décidées par plusieurs arrests de la Cour de Parlement* de Claude Le Prestre: la grande majorité des causes publiées a été jugée par la cinquième Chambre des Enquêtes dont l'auteur fut successivement conseiller et président. Ainsi l'arrêt du 12 mars 1611 qu'il rapporte pour démontrer que la créance privilégiée des apothicaires est assise sur les meubles et aussi sur les immeubles, arrêt qui sera repris par Brodeau, porte dans les registres la signature de Le Prestre en sa qualité de conseiller-rapporteur. Les conseillers et plus encore les avocats pouvaient réunir des informations en prenant des notes durant les audiences. Plusieurs historiens accordent un crédit

---

[10] On dispose, en outre, de quelques recueils consacrés aux arrêts du Conseil d'Etat et aux décisions du Conseil Privé: *S. Roulliard,* Les reliefs forenses, 2 t. (Paris 1610); *T. Mongeot,* Arrêts notables du Conseil d'Estat et privé du Roy... (Paris 1655); *J. Gaultier,* Les Plaidoyez, 2 t. (Paris 1662); *M. Augeard,* Arrests notables des differens tribunaux du Royaume sur plusieurs questions importantes de droit civil, de coutume, de discipline ecclesiastique et de droit public, 3 t. (Paris 1710 - 1718).

[11] *F. A. Isambert e. a.,* Recueil général des anciennes lois françaises depuis 420 jusqu'à la Révolution, t. XI (Paris 1827), p. 480: art. 53 de l'ordonnance du 14 novembre 1507.

[12] *J. Hilaire* et *Cl. Bloch,* op. cit., p. 59.

important à cette méthode de travail, dont il existe des exemples anciens comme les *Notes d'audiences prises au Parlement de Paris de 1384 à 1386 par un praticien anonyme* (cf. supra, B. Auzary-Schmaltz), et que l'organisation du Parlement semble de surcroît dicter. Ils consultaient aussi leurs confrères pour savoir s'ils n'avaient pas connaissance de contentieux qui pouvaient enrichir leur propos; c'est peut-être la raison pour laquelle les arrêtistes mentionnent fréquemment le nom des avocats qui ont plaidé la cause qu'ils commentent. Antoine Mornac signale même dans la préface de son *Recueil d'arrests du Parlement de Paris depuis 1588 jusqu'en 1620* (éd. 1721) qu'il a régulièrement consulté le rapporteur des causes qui l'intéressaient afin d'obtenir plus de précisions sur les parties, l'objet des litiges, les arguments des parties et même les motivations des juges. Enfin, les recueils d'arrêts et de plaidoyers publiés forment pour les arrêtistes une dernière source non négligeable mais elle aussi indirecte. Ils identifient généralement avec minutie leur documentation, mentionnant l'auteur, le chapitre et le numéro de la question, mais sans nécessairement vérifier les informations. Ceci expliquerait que certaines décisions citées par plusieurs auteurs restent introuvables dans les registres et dans les minutes, des erreurs de date qui se seraient glissées dans la première édition ayant par la suite été répétées.

La précision des renseignements contenus dans les recueils, en particulier les sources du droit diverses alléguées par les avocats des parties, peuvent laisser penser que le devoir de réserve et l'interdiction de reproduire les registres – une interdiction que les auteurs ne font d'ailleurs que contourner habilement en résumant ou en paraphrasant les originaux – n'étaient pas rigoureusement imposés. On peut énumérer plusieurs exemples où conseillers et avocats transcrivent mot à mot la décision rapportée sans toujours tenter de le dissimuler. Ainsi, Jean Chenu fait précéder sa transcription *in extenso* de l'arrêt du 19 avril 1580 relatif à la créance privilégiée des apothicaires de la mention «*extraict des registres du Parlement*»[13].

---

[13] Recueil de reglemens notables tant generaux que particuliers, donnez entre Ecclesiastique, pour la celebration du service divin: Iuges, Magistrats, & autres Officiers Royaux, & des Seigneurs Iusticiers inferieurs & subalternes pour l'exercice de leurs Offices, rang, seance, prerogatives, institutions & destitution d'iceux, auquel sont adioustees cent rares & singulieres Questions de Droict decidees par Arrests memorables, partie d'iceux prononcez en Robbes rouges. Le tout extraict des Ordonnances Royaux, Arrests du Conseil privé & autres Cours souveraines de France, par *Iehan Chenu* de la ville de Bourges, advocat en Parlement, 3e éd. (Paris 1606), pp. 370 - 373; voir la transcription dans le second volume. Dans le recueil de G. Louet, la présentation de l'arrêt du 8 février 1596 comporte également des phrases entières qui ont littéralement été copiées des registres ou des minutes; celles-ci étant l'original rédigé par le rapporteur que le greffier reporte, parfois des mois voire des années plus tard, dans les registres, il est impossible de vérifier quel support matériel les auteurs ont utilisé.

Il serait erroné de conclure de ce long développement consacré aux décisions des cours souveraines que la jurisprudence constituait la seule et unique source des recueils d'arrêts. Les arrêtistes, ainsi qu'on peut le vérifier dans l'œuvre de G. Louet, utilisent abondamment les ordonnances royales et les coutumes et ils se réfèrent, en outre, fréquemment au droit romain, au droit canonique voire même aux auteurs antiques et bibliques; cela mériterait également une étude plus détaillée.

III. La finalité des recueils privés d'arrêts

La finalité des recueils privés d'arrêts est une question que les historiens, à l'instar de G. Walter[14], abordent souvent parallèlement à l'interdiction qui était faite aux juges d'Ancien Régime de motiver leurs décisions, une disposition qui frappait tout particulièrement les arrêts des cours souveraines. Cette interdiction est énoncée pour la première fois dans l'ordonnance du 11 mars 1344 qui stipule que «*Depuis que les Arrests sont prononciez & publiez, il ne loist à nul, quel que il soit, dire, ne reciter, de quel opinion li Seigneur ont esté. Car en ce faisant, il enfraindroit son serment que il a fait, de garder & non reveler les secrez de la cour*»; et le législateur ajoute, en outre, que «*Comme peut advenir que aucun Seigneur, par inadvertence, le dit...pour ce, se au conseil ne demourassent que li Seigneur, & li registreur de la Cour, & allassent tous autres besoigner*»[15]. Cette interdiction est probablement fondée sur l'idée que la justice a été déléguée par le roi au Parlement. Comme «*le roi ne tient que de Dieu*», ainsi que le formulent les documents d'époque, il n'était pas concevable que les conseillers, qui rendent les arrêts au nom du roi, soient tenus de motiver leurs décisions et de laisser ainsi aux justiciables la possibilité de discuter les arrêts. La Cour du roi ne connaissant, en outre, aucun supérieur, elle pouvait même s'écarter du droit pour juger, le cas échéant, en équité[16]. La délégation de la justice – que le roi a tout loisir de retenir – a également des répercussions directes sur l'organisation des voies de recours. Ainsi les plaideurs qui introduisent une proposition d'erreur «ne peuvent venir contre un arrest sinon que on allègue *errorum proprium* ou le dol des parties», mais en aucun cas parce que «les juges ont erré en droit»[17]. On peut dès lors penser que le «devoir

---

[14] *G. Walter,* op. cit., pp. 1237 - 1244. Voir également *t. Sauvel,* Histoire du jugement motivé, dans: Revue du droit public, t. LXXI, 1955, pp. 1 - 53.

[15] *E. de Laurière,* op. cit., t. II, p. 223 - 224, ordonnance du 11 mars 1344, art. 14 et 15.

[16] *P. Guilhiermoz,* Enquêtes et procès (Paris 1892), p. XVIII. Voir également *J. Hilaire* et *Cl. Bloch,* op. cit., p. 59. L'auteur du *Style de la chambre des enquêtes* (début du 14e siècle) fait, à ce sujet, un devoir au rédacteur d'arrêts d'utiliser des formules pour cacher les motifs des décisions de la Cour et donne toutes les hautes raisons qui, selon lui, justifient le secret.

de réserve» et le «secret que les membres de la Cour juraient d'observer» impliquaient davantage l'interdiction formelle de motiver les décisions judiciaires, d'ailleurs réitérée par de nombreuses ordonnances tout au long des 15e et 16e siècles[18], que la publication des arrêts; ceux-ci ne mentionnant, pas plus que les registres du Conseil, la motivation en droit des jugements rendus. Quelques auteurs prétendent bien, dans leur préface, qu'ils présenteront «tant les faits sommaires et moyens des parties, que les raisons et motifs des juges»[19]. En réalité, ils ne font que confronter la disposition de la Cour au raisonnement des parties et à l'intervention du procureur du roi, essayant de découvrir de cette façon quels arguments auraient pu inciter les juges à se prononcer en faveur de l'une d'entre elles[20]. Mais, ce rapprochement qu'affectionne également G. Louet, ne peut en aucune manière être considéré comme une divulgation des motifs juridiques qui sous-tendent la décision judiciaire ainsi qu'on l'entend aujourd'hui. Une telle infraction au secret observé par la Cour aurait d'ailleurs inévitablement été sanctionnée par la censure royale qui, en revanche, ne semble jamais avoir pris ombrage à la publication de textes copiés littéralement des registres.

Le véritable objectif des arrêtistes est donc différent et on peut en trouver des indications dans leurs œuvres. Dans la dernière édition du *Recueil* de G. Louet, l'approbation d'éditer délivrée par le censeur royal signale que «cet ouvrage a été regardé dans les impressions précédentes comme un des plus utiles à ceux qui fréquentent le barreau». Cette littérature juridique prétend donc, avant toute autre chose, être un instrument de travail pour les praticiens et leurs auteurs les destinent tout spécialement aux avocats. N'oublions pas que plus de la moitié des auteurs appartient à la profession. Dans ces «manuels», ils pourront puiser les arguments les plus à même de convaincre les juges, c'est-à-dire les dispositions de la coutume et des

---

17 *S. Dauchy,* Les voies de recours extraordinaires: proposition d'erreur et requête civile (Paris 1988) [Travaux et recherches de l'Université de Droit, d'Economie et de Sciences Sociales de Paris, Série sciences historiques n° 26].

18 Ainsi, l'ordonnance du 28 octobre 1446 qui assortit, pour la première fois, cette interdiction de sanctions: «A certaines ordonnances faictes, afin de celer et non revéler les secretz de nostredicte court, adjoustons et ordonnons que s'aucun officier de nostredicte court, soit président, conseiller, greffier, notaire ou autre, révèle doresnavant en aucune manière les secretz d'icelle court, il soit privé pout tout un an entier, de l'émolument de ses gages deuz à cause de son office», *F. A. Isambert,* op. cit., t. IX, p. 151, art. 4; et les ordonnances de 1453, ibid., t. IX, p. 244, art. 109 et 110; de 1535, ibid., t. XII, pp. 432 - 434, art. 36 - 44; et de 1549, ibid., t. XII, p. 157, art. 13 et 14.

19 C'est le cas de *J. Bouvot,* Nouveau recueil des arrests de Bourgogne…, 2 t. (Genève 1623 - 1628).

20 Les arrêtistes font souvent précéder le dispositif de la cour par quelques mots révélateur à ce sujet comme «En suivant cela, la cour…», «Contrairement à ce que dit le défendeur, la cour…», etc.

ordonnances royales, les allégations de droit savant et, bien sûr, les précédents judiciaires. L'éditeur de notre *Recueil d'arrêts notables* met également en avant que «cette compilation fait voir en même tems la Jurisprudence Romaine et la Jurisprudence Françoise» et pour souligner encore davantage son utilité, il précise que *«la plûpart des Auteurs, dont ces Arrêts sont tirez, disent qu'ils ont été donnez suites aux raisons alléguées par Monsieur Louet, & par son Commentateur, comme on le peut vérifier en les cherchant dans leur source»*. Ainsi, les collections de décisions commentées qui ont été publiées sous l'Ancien Régime apparaissent comme un instrument essentiel dans la formation pratique des membres du barreau. L'enseignement juridique dans les Universités ne comprenait, jusqu'à la réforme de celles-ci par l'édit de 1679, que le droit romain et le droit canonique et non le droit coutumier français en vigueur devant les tribunaux royaux[21]. Seuls la doctrine et les conseils prodigués par les aînés pouvaient compléter cette formation théorique. Dans les recueils publiés, ils trouvaient en effet, les instructions nécessaires pour construire un plaidoyer selon les formes requises et pour rassembler les bases juridiques de leur argumentation.

Faut-il en conclure que la jurisprudence constitue, en France, une source du droit à part entière sous l'Ancien Régime et que le royaume aurait même connu une certaine forme de *case law*?

On peut assurément répondre par l'affirmative à la première question. La jurisprudence constitue bien, au même titre que le droit savant, une source de l'ancien droit français. Mais on peut tout au plus qualifier la jurisprudence de source subsidiaire car les magistrats ne motivent pas leurs décisions – dans l'acception actuelle du terme – en recherchant eux-mêmes des précédents dans les registres de la Cour. Ainsi que B. Auzary-Schmaltz l'a noté, la finalité des registres des arrêts et jugés n'était pas d'établir une collection de précédents judiciaires. En revanche, si les conseillers n'étaient pas liés par leurs propres jugements, il est indéniable que les arrêts constituaient un argument essentiel, pouvant déterminer les décisions des parlements et plus encore celles rendues par les juridictions inférieures. Les recueils d'arrêts présentent, à ce titre, un double intérêt. Ils livrent aux praticiens des cas précis, leur permettant de soumettre à la Cour les précédents qui se rapprochent le plus de l'affaire qu'ils plaident. Ensuite, les éditions successives augmentées de nouveaux arrêts rendus par l'ensemble des parlements du royaume, équivalent à de véritables mises à jour des connaissan-

---

[21] *P. Ourliac* et *J.-L. Gazzaniga,* Histoire du droit privé français de l'An mil au Code civil (Paris 1985), p. 159 sq. On consultera également, à propos de l'édit de 1679, *C. Chêne,* L'enseignement du droit français en pays de droit écrit (1679 - 1793) (1981), et *Fr. Olivier-Martin,* Les professeurs de droit français et l'unification du droit civil français, dans: Mélanges Sugiyama (1940), pp. 263 - 281.

ces juridiques. Les avocats confrontés à une question de droit y trouvent les décisions les plus récentes qui ont pu, elles-mêmes, être rendues sur la base de précédents plus anciens[22]. Peut-on formuler des conclusions similaires en ce qui concerne les conseillers? Est-ce qu'ils consultaient des collections privées de jurisprudence avant de se prononcer et rédigeaient-ils des recueils à cette fin? Rien ne permet actuellement de l'affirmer ni de l'infirmer. Il nous semble dès lors prématuré de trancher péremptoirement la question relative à l'existence d'un *case law stricto sensu,* c'est-à-dire un droit essentiellement fondé sur la jurisprudence, en France sous l'Ancien Régime. En revanche, si on accepte une définition plus souple selon laquelle le droit a été influencé par les précédents judiciaires, on peut parler de *case law* et nul doute que les recueils privés d'arrêts y aient largement contribué. La littérature arrêtiste a donc bien agi comme un miroir révélant aux cours leur propre jurisprudence, mais un miroir quelque peu infidèle du fait de l'absence de motivation des arrêts.

[22] Ceci est d'ailleurs la définition donnée par *Cl. de Ferrière,* Dictionnaire de droit et de pratique (Paris 1724), de la jurisprudence: «Jurisprudence des arrêts est l'induction que l'on tire de plusieurs arrêts qui ont jugé une question de la même manière dans une même espèce».

JEAN BART

Les archives judiciaires du Parlement de Dijon

Le titre même de cette contribution en trace les limites. D'une part, seules les pièces issues de l'activité juridictionnelle de la Cour seront analysées ici, à l'exclusion de tous les témoignages ou relations de l'action ou des attitudes politiques des magistrats, individuellement ou en corps, qui, jusqu'à présent, ont surtout retenu l'attention des historiens. D'autre part, seul le parlement *royal* qui s'installe au cours des dernières années du XVe siècle à Dijon après le rattachement de la province au royaume de France a laissé des archives importantes, voire volumineuses. Quelques épaves seulement nous sont en effet parvenues de la Cour ducale qui, avant la chute de Charles le Téméraire (1477), siégeait à Beaune, ou à Saint-Laurent-lès-Chalon pour les terres d'oultre-Saône faisant partie du duché[1], alors que les possessions comtoises des Grands Ducs d'Occident – la Franche-Comté – alimentaient la pratique judiciaire du Parlement de Dole. Il ne sera donc question ici que de la jurisprudence du Parlement *de Dijon* – terme préférable à celui de 'Parlement de Bourgogne', moins courant et non officiel. Pour bien saisir la richesse comme la variété des archives venues jusqu'à nous, il convient d'abord de tracer brièvement les grands traits de la composition de la Cour dijonnaise, d'analyser ensuite sa compétence et la répartition des causes en son sein, de décrire enfin les principales masses documentaires conservées aujourd'hui.

I. Les chambres

Georges Chevrier a décrit naguère les péripéties – dues entre autres à l'opposition du Parlement de Paris – de la création d'une Cour souveraine décidée par Louis XI en 1477, qui ne sera définitivement fixée à Dijon qu'en 1494 sous le règne de son successeur.[2] Ces débuts difficiles ont été

---

[1] Le plus ancien des sept registres arrivés jusqu'à nous a été publié par *Pierre Petot,* Registre des Parlements de Beaune et de Saint-Laurent-Chalon (1357 - 1380)... (Paris 1927). Les six autres sont conservés aux Archives départementales de la Côte-d'Or, sous la forme de petits *in folio,* aux cotes B 11 402 à 406 et B 11 411.

[2] *G. Chevrier,* Les débuts du Parlement de Dijon (1477 - 1487), in: Annales de Bourgogne, t. 15 (1943), p. 93 - 124.

suivis d'un siècle et demi d'une croissance elle-même tumultueuse, car, comme tous les autres parlements du royaume, celui de Dijon s'est élargi et diversifié par la création de plusieurs chambres et, par conséquent, par l'augmentation de son personnel, ce qui fut rarement du goût des officiers déjà en place. A l'origine et pendant quelques décennies, la juridiction est une, réunissant deux présidents, douze conseillers et deux chevaliers d'honneurs, mais dès le premier tiers du XVIe siècle elle est subdivisée: en 1524, la décision est prise de distinguer deux chambres, ce qui ne sera effectivement réalisé qu'en 1537. Alors, l'une, considérée comme la première et la plus prestigieuse, est volontiers désignée sous le nom de *Grand'chambre,* mais nous verrons que dans les arrêts, on l'appelle tout simplement *le parlement* et que cette dénomination lui est réservée. La seconde, à l'exemple du Parlement de Paris, reçoit le nom de *Tournelle,* et pour les mêmes raisons: les magistrats qui la constituent y siègent par roulement. Une nouvelle chambre – la troisième par ordre chronologique de création, mais la dernière selon l'ordre des honneurs ou des préséances et aussi en raison de sa compétence limitée au premier degré – apparaît en 1575: la *Chambre des Requêtes du Palais* qui, à l'instar de son homologue parisienne, devait connaître en première instance, à charge d'appel devant *le parlement* (ou Grand'chambre), des procès civils des privilégiés bénéficiant du *committimus* et des églises de fondation royale. Mais la mise sur le marché de nouveaux offices consécutive à cette création s'est heurtée à l'hostilité des officiers déjà pourvus, à tel point que l'édit d'Henri III portant 'fixation et établissement d'une Chambre des Requêtes en ce Parlement' n'a été enregistré que sur lettres de jussion, et que la nouvelle chambre ainsi que ceux qui la composaient furent, dit-on, toujours mal considérés: les *commissaires aux requêtes* ne purent, pendant longtemps, prendre le titre de *conseillers du roi au parlement* et durent subir bien des vexations. Un peu plus tard cependant, en 1589, le même Henri III édicte l'installation d'une autre chambre dite *des enquêtes,* en même temps que les bailliages royaux d'Auxerre, de Mâcon et de Bar-sur-Seine sont enlevés au ressort du Parlement de Paris pour venir grossir celui de la Cour de Dijon. Mais la situation politique du moment autant que l'hostilité des magistrats locaux empêcha la réalisation de ce projet, si bien que les trois bailliages ci-dessus mentionnés n'ont jamais été rattachés au Parlement bourguignon. Quant à la *Chambre des Enquêtes,* elle ne vit le jour qu'en 1630, après de nouvelles lettres de jussion. Entretemps, les terres relevant du Parlement de Dijon avaient été agrandies par l'effet du traité de Lyon qui rattachait au royaume la Bresse, le Bugey, le pays de Gex et le Valromey, anciennes possessions savoyardes qui devenaient ainsi, judiciairement parlant, bourguignonnes. Surtout, après un grave conflit relatif à la création décidée en 1627 d'une Cour des Aides et Finances dont les offices furent d'abord attribués à la Chambre des comptes, le Parlement de Dijon recueille le contentieux fiscal et joue ainsi, à partir de 1630, le double rôle de Parlement et de Cour des aides. Son ressort – des plus modestes par rapport à celui des autres parlements du royaume – intégrera celui du Parlement de Dombes après la transformation de ce dernier en sénéchaussée (1771). Quant à son personnel, il réunira autour du Premier président neuf présidents à mortier, deux chevaliers d'honneur, six conseillers clercs, soixante-six conseillers laïcs, et le conseiller garde des sceaux de la chancellerie du Parlement, outre les *Gens du Roi* groupant sous la houlette du Procureur général, deux avocats généraux et huit substituts.

Pour être complet, signalons l'existence, au sein ou à côté du Parlement, de la *Table de marbre,* compétente en matière d'eaux et forêts en première instance mais aussi en appel lorsque les gens du Parlement siégeaient avec elle en nombre double. En outre, trois autres chambres circonstancielles doivent être mentionnées: la *Chambre neutre,* sorte de juridiction des conflits entre la Chambre des comptes et le Parlement, de composition paritaire, la *Chambre de l'Edit de pacification* ou *Chambre mi-partie,* composée de catholiques et de réformés qui, dans les années 60 du XVIe siècle, devait résoudre les conflits opposant des adeptes des deux religions mais qui ne fonctionna pas vraiment, et la *Chambre de révision* instituée à la suite du rattachement de la Franche-Comté au royaume de France par le traité de Nimègue, pour jouer le rôle tenu jusque là par le Grand Conseil de Malines à l'égard des arrêts rendus par la Cour de Besançon. Composée de neuf parlementaires dijonnais et de deux bisontins, elle devait connaître de la révision des arrêts civils rendus par le Parlement de Besançon, mais sa durée fut éphémère. Enfin, comme partout, pendant les vacances judiciaires qui allaient de la fête de l'Assomption à la Saint Martin d'hiver (du 15 août au 11 novembre), certaines affaires criminelles mais aussi civiles estimées pressantes étaient expédiées, à partir de 1554, par une *Chambre des vacations*. Constituée de magistrats issus de la Grand'Chambre, de la Tournelle et de la Chambre des Enquêtes, elle devait siéger, d'après un règlement de septembre 1681, du lendemain de la Notre-Dame de septembre à la veille de la fête de Saint Simon et Saint Jude (donc du 9 septembre au 27 octobre). Cette chambre statuait de la même manière que les chambres ordinaires et ses arrêts seront insérés parmi ceux des autres chambres.

En somme, quatre chambres ont fonctionné de manière régulière – sous réserve des aléas dus aux troubles politiques[3] – pendant les derniers siècles de l'Ancien Régime: la Grand'Chambre, la Tournelle, la Chambre des

[3] C'est le cas, en particulier, à la fin du XVIe siècle pendant des guerres de Religion. Au moment de la Ligue, les parlementaires restés fidèles au roi quittent Dijon et réorganisent la Cour à Flavigny puis à Semur-en-Auxois. Au XVIIIe siècle, l'activité juridictionnelle du Parlement subira, bien sûr, le contre-coup des crises politiques de la fin de l'Ancien Régime.

Enquêtes et celle des Requêtes. Leur jurisprudence a laissé des témoignages massifs (plus de 300 mètres linéaires de documents) sous forme de registres ou de liasses qui constituent des ensembles complets ou presque à partir de la fin du XVIe siècle et qui sont conservés aujourd'hui aux Archives départementales de la Côte-d'Or dans la série B et la sous-série B II[4]. Mis à part un certain nombre de registres inventoriés par Joseph Garnier[5], la grande masse des arrêts ou pièces diverses issus du Parlement dijonnais est accessible grâce à un 'registre placier' manuscrit composé au cours du XIXe siècle, instrument fort précieux puisqu'il permet de consulter les documents, mais qui doit être utilisé avec précaution, sans attacher au classement opéré alors une trop grande confiance. Ce présent et modeste article est simplement destiné à faciliter son décryptage. Cet objectif a déjà été poursuivi, il y a plus de vingt ans, dans une note beaucoup trop brève, à l'occasion du colloque tenu lors de la commémoration du cinquième centenaire de la création du Parlement et Grand Conseil de Malines.[6] Il s'agit ici de la compléter et de la préciser.

II. Compétence des chambres et répartition des causes

Toute la difficulté des recherches de jurisprudence dans les fonds du Parlement vient du fait que le classement du 'registre placier' a été opéré par chambres ce qui semble logique eu égard à l'organisation moderne des tribunaux dont les sections ou chambres ont des compétences bien définies, mais qui ne convient absolument pas pour les juridictions anciennes, en tout cas pas pour le Parlement de Dijon. Pour bien saisir la manière dont les arrêts ou décisions diverses que celui-ci rendait étaient conservés ou classés, il faut abandonner tout cartésianisme et considérer que les exceptions sont parfois plus importantes que la règle elle-même. Cependant, d'une manière générale, les arrêts étaient distingués, quelle que soit la

---

[4] Toutes les cotes d'archives issues de ces séries seront désormais citées sans indication de dépôt.

[5] B 12 230 et s.; Inventaire sommaire des archives départementales antérieures à 1790, rédigé par *J. Garnier*..., Côte-d'Or, Série B, t. VI (Dijon 1894), 379 p. impr.

[6] *J. Bart,* Note sur l'utilisation des archives du parlement de Dijon, in: Concilium magnum 1473 - 1973, Commémoration du 500e anniversaire de la création du Parlement et Grand Conseil de Malines. Colloque Bruxelles-Malines (Bruxelles, A.G.R.-A.R. 1977), pp. 173 - 180. N'oublions pas davantage l'étude très fouillée de *Jean-Claude Garreta,* Les archives du Parlement de Dijon. Etude de sources, in: Mémoires de la Société pour l'histoire du droit et des institutions des anciens pays bourguignons, comtois et romands, t. 23 (1962), p. 203 - 244, mais cet article est surtout destiné à recenser les recueils factices ou les pièces dispersées permettant de compléter ou de combler dans une certaine mesure les lacunes des séries d'archives. Celles-ci sont cependant brièvement analysées (pp. 228 - 232).

chambre qui les ait rendus et malgré l'existence de deux greffes différents, criminel et civil, selon le type d'audience qui les avaient produits. La distinction entre les audiences du matin et celles 'de relevée' n'a, en l'occurrence, pas grande importance, pas plus que celle des audiences publiques et des audiences à huis clos; en revanche, la tenue des audiences et leur finalité opéraient des distinctions – banales pour les juristes anciens au point qu'ils ne nous donnent guère d'éclaircissements à ce sujet –, mais qui aujourd'hui demeurent parfois obscures.

La *summa divisio* semble être, à Dijon comme à Paris, celle qui oppose les arrêts rendus par les magistrats assemblés au cours de l'audience, au terme d'une ou de plusieurs séances, et ceux qui sont l'objet de délibérations plus longues et réfléchies, à la suite de l'examen de pièces écrites et du rapport d'un conseiller chargé plus spécialement de l'affaire: les arrêts rendus *en conseil* selon le vocabulaire parisien[7]; à Dijon, on parle plus volontiers des 'procès de commissaire', ou des 'arrêts rendus sur le rapport des procès par écrit'. Les autres décisions étaient prises au terme de deux types d'audiences: les audiences 'par avocats' et les audiences 'd'instruction'. Les unes et les autres étaient réparties dans la semaine selon un ordre établi à l'avance qu'un auteur du XVIIIe siècle, sans doute bien informé puisqu'il s'agit d'Antoine Garreau, procureur au Parlement de son état, rapporte de la manière suivante:

> Les Audiences publiques de la Grand'Chambre se tiennent le lundi, le mardi et le jeudi matin et s'il est férié le jeudi, l'audience est remise au lendemain. Celles de relevée ou du soir sont lundi, le mardi et le vendredi. Les Audiences Publiques de la Tournelle se donnent le mercredi et le samedi matin. L'entrée pour les procès par écrit de commissaire se fait dans toutes les chambres le jeudi et le samedi de relevée et certains autres jours à ce destinés et les après dinées des veilles des mêmes jours et des jours fêtés.
>
> Les procès par écrit de l'ordinaire se jugent tous les matins et le soir dans chaque chambre qui n'est point occupée à l'Audiance par avocats ou aux procès de commissaire. Les Audiences d'instruction se donnent dans les trois chambres le matin dès l'entrée, tous les jours qui ne sont point fériés ou extraordinaires.
>
> Tous les arrêts aux Audiences par avocats ou sur le rapport des procès par écrit peuvent être donnés par dix juges et ceux d'instruction par deux juges seulement...[8]

---

[7] Cf. *M. Langlois,* Guide des recherches dans les fonds judiciaires de l'Ancien Régime aux Archives nationales (Paris 1958), p. 74. Pour les comparaisons Paris/ Dijon, voir aussi, bien sûr, dans le présent ouvrage, les contributions de Bernadette Auzary-Schmaltz et de Serge Dauchy.

[8] Description du gouvernement de Bourgogne, suivant les principales divisions temporelles, ecclésiastiques, militaires et civiles, avec un abrégé de l'Histoire de la Province ... par le sieur *Garreau* (seconde éd. Dijon, A. de Fay, 1734), pp. 249-250.

Le même auteur indique les principes de compétence:

> La Grand'Chambre connaît en matière civile de toutes les appellations verbales; la Tournelle juge par écrit les affaires du grand Criminel et à l'audience tant celles-là que celles du Petit Criminel non apointé; on décide en la Chambre des enquêtes les affaires du Petit Criminel qui sont réglées. Chacune de ces chambres juge en matière civile les procès par écrit distribués aux conseillers qui y servent[9].

En définitive, les trois chambres d'appel ont une compétence générale. La Tournelle, par exemple, rend au moins autant de décisions en matière civile qu'en matière criminelle et il est des procès très importants, soulevant des problèmes de fond fort discutés, qui sont tranchés par la Chambre des Enquêtes, entre beaucoup d'autres: l'affaire de la succession Lavirotte posant la question de la validité du testament du fils de famille, résolue aux Enquêtes par un arrêt du 19 juillet 1726, qui a suscité une abondante littérature.[10] En outre, certaines affaires pénales sont jugées par la Grand'Chambre. Aussi avec précaution et peut-être une pointe d'humour, Garreau, après avoir exprimé les principes de compétence ajoute-t-il: «*Il y a plusieurs exceptions à ces règles générales*». De toute manière, lorsqu'un procès a été confié pour rapport à un conseiller, l'affaire suit ce dernier dans la chambre où il 'tourne'. Et la rotation est assez rapide: chacune des trois chambres d'appel comporte un certain nombre de présidents qui, eux, sont fixes (quatre à la Grand'Chambre dont le premier, quatre à la Tournelle et deux aux Enquêtes), ainsi que deux conseillers clercs et dix-huit conseillers laïcs qui 'tournent' à la Saint-Martin et à Pâques (donc environ tous les six mois), de la Grand'Chambre à la Tournelle, de la Tournelle aux Enquêtes et des Enquêtes à la Grand'Chambre. Toutefois le Doyen du Parlement – le conseiller le plus ancien – demeure en permanence à la Grand'Chambre, et le plus récent reste aux Enquêtes. Ajoutons encore que les *évocations* ou jugements des causes venues du Parlement de Grenoble ou éventuellement d'autres parlements du royaume selon la décision du Conseil privé, dans lesquelles les gens de ces cours étaient impliquées par parenté ou alliance, sont de la compétence de la Grand'Chambre, mais le conseiller rapporteur désigné pour telle ou telle de ces causes peut parfaitement siéger ailleurs; alors, dans ce cas, lorsqu'il viendra rapporter à la Grand'Chambre, un conseiller de celle-ci s'en ira le remplacer et emmenera avec lui ses propres dossiers.

---

[9] Ibid.

[10] Cf. entre autres: Arrest Notable du Parlement de Dijon, du 19 juillet 1726, sur la question si un fils de famille en Bourgogne peut disposer de ses biens par testament ou donation à cause de mort, sans le consentement ou autorité de son père. Et si une pareille disposition, faite par un fils à son père, de son consentement, intervenu en l'acte, est bonne et valable. Avec quelques dissertations pour et contre sur cette matière, servant d'éclaircissement à la coutume de Bourgogne (Dijon, A. de Fay, 1728).

Mais comment les causes ordinaires étaient-elles réparties au début de la procédure? Un règlement royal daté du 10 novembre 1662 a cherché à le préciser et ce texte fut interprété, par le Parlement lui-même en mars 1663[11] aux fins d'application. Ainsi, les dispositions de l'article V sont expliquées de la manière suivante:

> 'Articles accordés et arrestés dans la Compagnie sous le bon plaisir du Roy, pour l'explication et exécution dudit règlement'
>
> La distribution générale se fera sur le Registre d'Arrest en Arrest, et ce faisant toutes les causes concluës des Rolles et autres procès conclus au Greffe dans lesquelles causes et Procès, les parties auront produit de part et d'autre, se distribueront, sçavoir également entre les trois Chambres en ce qui est des procès de Commissaire, et quant à ceux de l'Ordinaire, les Enquestes en auront les deux tiers, et dans l'autre tier la Grand Chambre en aura les deux tiers et la Tournelle l'autre tier, laquelle distribution se fera par lesdits sieurs Premier Président et autres Présidens des Grand Chambre, Tournelle, et Enquestes, chacun à celuy des Conseillers de la Chambre qu'il avisera, sans que les Procureurs puissent remettre les causes qui auront esté dans un Rolle, et conclues par l'Arrest général à un nouveau Rolle, à peine de l'amande, et deffenses seront faites aux Procureurs de mettre d'autres causes aux Rolle, que celles qui sont de qualité à pouvoir estres jugées à l'Audiance, et ordonné à eux de se communiquer respectivement, et restituer les pièces avant que de mettre leurs causes au rolle, à peine de l'amande.

Malheureusement, les rôles ne nous ont point été conservés[12], toutefois, la translation des arrêts eux-mêmes, sous diverses formes, permet de combler cette lacune.

III. Les ensembles documentaires

Si l'on néglige les épaves isolées, quatre types de pièces, registres ou liasses, dont les indications se complètent et parfois se confondent, sont à distinguer.

---

[11] Ces deux documents ont été imprimés cote à cote à destination des juristes bourguignons: Règlement fait par le Roy pour le Parlement de Dijon, concernant la Grand Chambre, et les séances, et fonctions des officiers de la dite Cour. Avec les Articles arrestez audit Parlement, les Chambres assemblées pour l'explication dudit règlement, escrits en marge d'iceluy. Et l'ordre estably pour la direction des menuës nécessités du Palais (Dijon, Pierre Paillot, 1663). Une autre édition a été faite chez Jean Grangier, à Dijon, en 1695. Un exemplaire de chacune d'elles se trouve conservé en B 12 069. En outre, les deux textes ont été reproduits par *Garreau,* op. cit., p. 250 et s.

[12] L'auteur du registre placier a indiqué sous la rubrique 'Grand'Chambre', aux cotes B II 36/1 et 2, deux 'Registres des distributions des causes, 1746 - 1789', mais ces deux documents concernent la Table de Marbre et non la Grand'Chambre.

1. Les 'plumitifs des audiences'

Ainsi sont désignés les registres où se trouvent relatées au jour le jour, plus ou moins sommairement, les décisions prises. Conservés nombreux à partir de la fin du XVIe siècle, ils sont propres à chaque chambre, ce qui se comprend puisqu'il s'agit d'une sorte de relevé d'activité.

D'abord, sous les cotes B II 25/1 - 210, se trouvent 207 registres (car trois sont portés actuellement manquants[13]) rangés sous la rubrique 'Grand'Chambre'. Ils couvrent une période de près de deux siècles: 1598 - 1789. Ecrits comme une sorte de *memento,* ils donnent un certain nombre d'indications sur le travail quotidien du Parlement, mais les renseignements fournis, toujours signés par le magistrat qui a présidé la chambre, diffèrent avec le temps. Ils sont plus riches et détaillés sur le fond des affaires au début de la période alors qu'au XVIIIe siècle, les mentions sont devenues stéréotypées. Ainsi, dans le tout premier registre[14] (de la Saint-Martin 1598 à la mi-août 1599), on peut saisir l'argumentaire des avocats des parties ou des gens du roi, avec parfois référence à des sources générales du droit: lors de l'audience du vendredi 12 mars 1599, 'de relevée à huis clos', les magistrats dijonnais connaissent d'une affaire portant sur les donations entre époux et sur les formalités des testaments; des avocats restés célèbres – au moins aux yeux des historiens du droit bourguignon – plaident:

> Despringles[15] pour l'apelant dict que mariage fut contracté ... (qu') il a esté réservé (aux époux) de se pouvoir donner telle portion de leurs biens que bon leur semblera...
>
> Guillaume[16] pour l'apellé dict que aiant perdu son frère il n'a voulu négliger sa succession...
>
> Despringles a répliqué et dict que ... la coutume ne porte point qu'il faille avoir des notaires royaulz pour les testamentz, un notaire de barronye et de scel autentique est capable pour les recevoir...
>
> M. Le Goux[17] dict que la cause est de conséquence. Il y a heu plusieurs dificultés résolues mais la principale n'a point été tranchée. De plus Germain qui a reçu le testament n'étoit point notaire...
>
> La Cour dict qu'elle en délibèrera en conseil sur les pièces que les parties mettront par devant le greffier...

---

[13] B II 25/17 (1614 en partie); /69 (1647 en partie); /79 (1652 en partie).

[14] B II 25/1.

[15] Jean Depringles ou Despringles (1550 - 1629) qui mourut doyen des avocats au Parlement, composa un commentaire sur la coutume du duché de Bourgogne.

[16] Jean Guillaume, reçu avocat en 1595, préparera au début du XVIIe siècle un recueil d'arrêts rendus en interprétation de la coutume dont une partie sera publiée plus tard par le président Bouhier.

[17] Guillaume Legoux de Vellepele, avocat général.

On peut déjà conclure de cette décision que les 'procès par écrit', tranchés après délibération en conseil, sont mentionnés dans ces premiers plumitifs, mais ils en disparaîtront par la suite. Dans la marge, figure parfois la lettre 'R' signifiant que l'arrêt a été enregistré. En tout cas, la structure des notices qui couvrent couramment plusieurs feuillets est toujours la même: intervention de l'avocat de l'appelant, réponse de celui de l'intimé, réplique du premier, conclusion du ministère public et décision du Parlement. Il en est ainsi le 11 mars, dans une affaire de mainmorte où les plaidants invoquent 'les règles de droit' ou 'la coutume'. Même chose le 26 mars, dans une curieuse cause relative aux 'femmes remariées que l'on apelle folles vieilles' et qui, à Chalon (sur-Saône) sont l'objet de sanctions pécuniaires selon une 'ancienne coutume' de la ville. Un avocat remarque:

> Il semble que la nature abhorre les folles vieilles qui se remarient et telles nopces sont deshonnestes, (aux grands) dommages des enffans du premier lict, cela n'aporte que des procès et divisions entre les enffans...

Mais, un siècle plus tard, de telles mentions ont complètement disparu des plumitifs. Est seulement indiqué plus ou moins brièvement le *dictum* ou dispositif de l'arrêt rendu à l'audience, ou le renvoi à une autre audience. Les parties, en revanche, sont beaucoup mieux identifiées et la composition de la chambre est en général indiquée. Prenons, à titre d'exemple, le plumitif rédigé à partir de la Saint-Martin 1758[18]. A la date du 16 novembre, quelques lignes font part de la rentrée solemnelle de la Cour: «*Première audiance publique tenuë en Parlement à Dijon le jeudy seize novenbre 1758 du matin par...*» Suivent les noms de tous les magistrats qui y ont assisté. Puis, en quatre lignes il est dit que l'un des deux avocats généraux a prononcé un discours destiné aux avocats sur l'élégance du style et que le Premier président en a fait un sur l'émulation. «*Après quoi, la première cause du rolle publique a été apellée et remise à lundy prochain*». Ce jour-là, 20 novembre, est effectivement mentionnée la tenue d'une 'Audiance d'instruction', 'en Parlement' (c'est-à-dire à la Grand'Chambre), le matin à huis clos. Les noms des parties sont indiqués; le procureur du demandeur requiert défaut; les procureurs des défendeurs s'en remettent à la prudence de la Cour qui donne défaut. Le même jour, le matin également, a lieu une 'Audiance publique' tenue par la même chambre qui examine une affaire de succession testamentaire. La matinée ne suffisant pas, l'audience se poursuit le lendemain matin, avec les mêmes magistrats auxquels s'ajoutent deux conseillers supplémentaires. Après avoir indiqué que les avocats des parties ainsi qu'un avocat général ont été entendus, le rédacteur du plumitif donne la teneur de l'arrêt rendu: «*La Cour faisant droit en l'instance dit que..., condamne...*». Une autre cause vient à la même audience, seul l'avocat des appelants est entendu, c'est pourquoi «*La Cour a continué la*

---

[18] B II 25/183.

cause à lundy prochain». Et il lui faudra quatre audiences avant d'en terminer et de rendre son arrêt le 1er décembre. Entre temps se sont poursuivies des 'Audiances d'instruction' et des 'Audiances par avocats'. En marge de chaque arrêt, se trouve l'abréviation 'ft' signifiant que son texte a été reporté en forme sur un autre registre.

Les plumitifs de la Tournelle sont conservés sous la cote B II 43: 1 - 16 pour la période 1702 - 1790. Ils se présentent à peu près sous la même forme que ceux de la Grand'Chambre à la même époque et mêlent, bien entendu puisque la compétence de la Tournelle est double, les affaires civiles et les affaires criminelles. Ainsi, toujours à titre d'exemple, dans le 'plumitif d'audiances depuis la Saint-Martin 1755 jusqu'au 27 octobre 1759'[19] (cette dernière date montre que les affaires traitées par la Chambre des vacations sont intégrées dans le registre), nous trouvons, à la date du 19 janvier 1758, le matin à huis clos, une audience d'instruction en matière civile, une autre le surlendemain. Puis, après un intervalle d'une semaine, le lundi 30 janvier, toujours le matin à huis clos et en matière civile, une 'Audiance par avocats sur placet', le lendemain, une audience d'instruction, le surlendemain, 1er février, une autre, mais le même jour et également le matin, se tient une 'Audiance publique criminelle' avec plusieurs affaires, et ainsi de suite, de semaines en semaines.

Pour la Chambre des Enquêtes, ce que le registre placier des Archives de la Côte-d'Or appelle 'registres des andiences' est également un ensemble de plumitifs qui se trouvent conservés, pour la période 1674 - 1789, sous les cotes B II 58/1 - 9. Mais l'un de ces neuf registres, le troisième (1698 - 1709), est porté manquant depuis 1941. D'autre part, le dernier comporte deux parties: la première contient effectivement le 'plumitif des audiences de la Chambre des Enquêtes du 8 janvier 1781 du matin à huis clos au vendredy quatorze août 1789 du matin à huis clos', alors que la seconde, reliée par erreur à la première, est un ensemble de cahiers relatifs aux 'Audiances des Requêtes du Palais du 19 décembre 1782 au 7 septembre 1789'.

Car la Chambre des Requêtes agissait de la même manière que les autres formations du Parlement, quoique sous une autre forme. L'auteur du classement moderne des archives judiciaires a distingué les 'registres et carnots des audiences ordinaires' et les 'registres et carnots des audiences extraordinaires'. Il semble que les premiers, seuls, placés sous les cotes B II 47 B/1 à 139 (1597 - 1782)[20] soient de véritables plumitifs. Les seconds[21] apparaissent comme des registres de transcription des *sentences* rendues, car

[19] B II 43/14.

[20] En réalité: 1597 - 1789 puisque, comme on l'a vu, les derniers cahiers ont été malencontreusement reliés avec les plumitifs de la Chambre des Enquêtes.

[21] B II 48/1 - 102 (1586 - 1717).

l'infériorité des Requêtes du Palais est marquée aussi par la désignation de ses décisions qui, données en première instance, ne peuvent pas recevoir le nom d'arrêts. Toujours est-il que la série des plumitifs est longue de près de deux siècles. Les feuillets de ces registres sont, contrairement à ceux des autres chambres, divisés en deux colonnes. Dans la colonne de droite, sont rapportés les noms des parties et de leurs procureurs, et dans celle de gauche, la teneur de la sentence est brièvement indiquée. La composition de la chambre est détaillée avec toujours, comme c'est la règle aux Requêtes, deux conseillers qui tiennent la présidence, et un nombre variable de magistrats qui les assistent.

Ainsi, quelle que soit la chambre considérée, les plumitifs, sans fournir, sauf à l'origine, de renseignements précieux sur les débats juridiques de fond soulevés par les procès, demeurent utiles comme points de repère permettant de suivre le déroulement d'une affaire et d'identifier telle ou telle décision citée par la doctrine. Cependant, d'autres registres complètent les renseignements donnés par les plumitifs.

2. Les 'registres des audiences'

Rédigés après coup, ils contiennent les textes *in extenso* des arrêts ou sentences rendus à l'audience, en matière civile, toutes chambres d'appel confondues, d'une part, en matière criminelle, de l'autre. Nous savons que les audiences sont qualifiées soit d''audiences d'instruction', soit d''audiences par avocats'. Les premières sont tenues par deux magistrats seulement, en présence des procureurs des parties, mais les avocats n'y participent pas. La très grande majorité des arrêts ainsi rendus sont préparatoires ou incidents, ou bien concernent l'exécution d'un arrêt préparatoire antérieur, mais, exceptionnellement, on trouve aussi dans ces registres des arrêts définitifs. Est toujours indiquée la chambre qui a pris la décision et la structure des arrêts est à peu près toujours la même. Après les identités des parties et de leurs procureurs, les paragraphes de l'arrêt se présentent de la manière suivante:

La cause appelée,
Ouï X procureur du demandeur lequel a conclu aux fins de sa requête,
Y procureur du défendeur a conclu à ce que...
La Cour ordonne ... (ou condamne, ou donne défaut, ou met l'appellation à néant...)
Fait à l'audience d'instruction tenüe en parlement (ou à la Tournelle, ou aux Enquêtes) le... du matin à huis clos (ou de relevée).

Comme leur nom l'indique, les 'audiences par avocats' sont des audiences ordinaires, publiques ou à huis clos, réunissant au moins dix magistrats, au cours desquelles les défenseurs des parties plaident, et qui se terminent, au bout d'une ou de plusieurs séances, par le prononcé de la décision. Ainsi, les 'registres des audiences par avocats' retiennent les textes, *in extenso* également, des arrêts rendus de cette manière. La chambre est, ici aussi, toujours indiquée et le texte se présente en général comme suit:

> [identité des parties, de leurs procureurs et de leurs avocats]
> La cause appelée, lesdits avocats ouïs...
> Ouï aussi X substitut du Procureur du Roi en ses conclusions...
> La Cour parties ouïes et le Procureur Général du Roi ... ordonne (ou condamne)
> Fait à l'audience par avocats ... le...

Logiquement, nous devons retrouver dans de tels registres, 'd'instruction' ou 'par avocats', toutes les affaires mentionnées dans les plumitifs des différentes chambres et, d'après quelques sondages, il semble bien que cela soit le cas. Mais pour le chercheur, les deux masses documentaires ne font pas double emploi car les hasards de la conservation font que la chronologie des différentes masses documentaires n'est pas identique. En matière civile, pour les 'audiences d'instruction', nous disposons d'une longue série de registres allant de 1554 à 1790, avec cependant des lacunes importantes au XVIe siècle, mais la série est ininterrompue à partir de 1579[22]. Les registres des 'audiences par avocats', eux, sont moins nombreux, ils n'existent que pour la XVIIIe siècle[23]. En matière pénale, la série des 'registres des audiences criminelles' est lacunaire jusqu'en 1647 et ininterrompue de cette date à 1784[24]. Y sont répertoriées ensemble les 'audiences d'instruction' et les 'audiences par avocats', ces dernières étant de loin les plus nombreuses. On s'aperçoit d'ailleurs, à la lecture de certains arrêts, que, tout en demeurant des 'arrêts d'audience', c'est-à-dire prononcés sur le champ, ils ont fait l'objet d'un délibéré pendant une suspension de séance. Par exemple, dans une affaire 'évoquée' du Parlement de Besançon, la Tournelle dijonnaise, le 14 mars 1781 au terme de seize audiences, après avoir entendu les cinq avocats des parties ainsi que l'avocat général Guyton de Morveau – que ses talents de chimiste et la Révolution vont bientôt rendre célèbre – décide:

> La Cour ordonne qu'il en sera présentement délibéré sur le registre,
> L'audience retirée, Messieurs rentrés en la Chambre du Conseil de la Tournelle, et après qu'il en a été délibéré sur le registre, l'arrest formé, Messieurs étant remontés à l'audience publique et ayant repris leurs places l'audience rentrée, il a été prononcé ainsi qu'il suit.
>
> La Cour parties ouïes et le Procureur Général du Roy en ses conclusions ... condamne...[25]

---

[22] B II 24/1 - 311 et 24bis/1 et 2 (Registre des audiences du parlement royaliste de Semur et de Flavigny [1589 - 1595]).

[23] B II 26/1 - 147 (1704 - 1782).

[24] B II 42/1 - 38.

[25] B II 42/38, 14 mars 1781.

Outre la relation des 'audiences d'instruction' et 'par avocats', les mêmes registres contiennent les décisions prises lors des 'audiences de miséricorde' qui avaient lieu quatre fois par an et au cours desquelles étaient dénombrés les prisonniers détenus à la Conciergerie du Palais ou dans d'autres prisons royales de Dijon. Les magistrats pouvaient décider l'élargissement de certains d'entre eux, souvent prisonniers pour dettes, mais pas uniquement. Les prisonniers se présentent 'aux pieds de la Cour, têtes nues et à genoux', ils sont assistés de l''avocat des pauvres' qui est entendu, ainsi que le représentant du Ministère public. Après quoi, «*La Cour séant à l'audiance de miséricorde ... a ordonné et ordonne que la dite partie de X (avocat des pauvres) demeure présentement élargie des dittes prisons et le geôier bien et valablement déchargé...*»

Enfin, pour être complet, rappelons que la Chambre des Requêtes conservait dans ses 'carnots d'audiances' à la fois des plumitifs et des registres de sentences, avec la même distinction entre 'audiences d'instruction' et 'audiences par avocats'[26].

3. Les 'arrêts par écrit de commissaire'

Rendus aprés délibération en Conseil sur le rapport d'un conseiller commis à cet effet: le 'commissaire', dans le langage du Palais, ils se trouvent conservés à part et nous sont connus grâce à deux types de documents: liasses et registres. D'abord, par des liasses de minutes. Ainsi, pour les arrêts civils, nous possédons 286 liasses rangées par l'auteur du registre placier sous la rubrique 'Grand'Chambre' mais qui, en réalité, contiennent des arrêts rendus par les trois chambres d'appel, de 1574 à 1790, avec des lacunes jusqu'en 1602, mais de manière continue ensuite[27]. Très variables en volume, du simple feuillet à des cahiers de plusieurs dizaines, voire d'une centaine de pages, les arrêts se présentent tous de la même manière, avec, dans la marge, la date[28], le nom de la chambre où l'affaire a été tranchée, le nom des procureurs des parties. Le texte lui-même contient l'exposé de la demande ou de la cause tel qu'il résulte des conclusions des procureurs des parties, puis le dispositif précédé toujours de la mention:

> Vu aussi les conclusions du Procureur Général du Roy et ouy le rapport de X conseiller commissaire cette part député,
> La Cour faisant droit sur le tout...

L'arrêt est toujours signé par le président de la chambre et par le conseiller rapporteur. Enfin le montant des 'épices et vacations' ainsi que celui

---

[26] Cf. supra, notes 20 et 21.

[27] B II 27/1 - 286 'Arrêts minutes du parlement'.

[28] Avant l'ordonnance de 1667 qui a supprimé cette formalité, figure aussi la date de la prononciation.

des 'conclusions' sont indiqués, de même que la taxe d'enregistrement de 3 sols par livre.

En matière pénale, tous les arrêts, ont été rangés à tort sous la rubrique 'Tournelle' alors que certains sont rendus, on le sait, par les deux autres chambres. Trois types de pièces s'y rencontrent. Correspondant aux 'arrêts minutes' civils et présentant les mêmes caractéristiques, les 'Arrests définitifs criminels' remplissent 42 liasses, la première correspondant à l'année 1561, les autres couvrant la période 1582 - 1590[29]. Elles concernent les affaires de 'grand criminel', mais on y trouve aussi quelques arrêts civils rendus par la Tournelle et rangés ici par erreur. D'autres liasses intitulées 'Arrêts d'audiences au criminel' semblent réunir les arrêts du 'petit criminel'[30], comme cela est indiqué sur certaines décisions. Enfin, vingt-deux liasses contiennent, pour la période 1699 - 1790, des 'arrêts sur requête'[31] qui interviennent en cours de procédure criminelle, sur requête de particuliers poursuivis ou incarcérés qui réclament par exemple contre un décret de prise de corps, ou bien, plus rarement, du Ministère public[32]. La requête, signée du procureur du requérant, est exposée, assortie de pièces écrites; un conseiller a été désigné pour les examiner. Le Ministère public est entendu. L'arrêt est signé par le président de la chambre ainsi que par le rapporteur, comme un arrêt définitif.

En marge de la quasi-totalité des arrêts, au civil comme au criminel, le greffier a porté la majuscule *R* signifiant que le texte a été transcrit sur un registre. De fait, toujours sous la rubrique 'Grand'Chambre', sont conservés, pour la période 1625 - 1790[33], 363 gros in-folio dits 'registres des arrêts définitifs'. Les quarante plus anciens de cette suite – plus exactement trente neuf car l'un d'eux ne peut être dépouillé en raison de son état[34] – ont fait l'objet d'un inventaire sommaire imprimé[35]. De tels registres étaient certainement destinés à conserver solennellement la mémoire des arrêts rendus. Pour le chercheur d'aujourd'hui, leur avantage vient du fait que leur lecture est, d'ordinaire, plus aisée que celle des minutes. Cependant les deux types de documents ne font pas double emploi. En effet, la

---

29 B II 46/1 - 42.

30 B II 45/1 - 17 (1649 - 1790).

31 B II 44/1 - 22.

32 Contra: *J.-C. Garreta,* op. cit., p. 231 qui laisse entendre que la requête vient toujours 'du procureur du roi'.

33 B II 23/1 - 363.

34 B 12 252, in-folio 450 feuillets (Saint-Martin 1643 - 1er mai 1644). D'après l'inventaire imprimé, «par suite de l'humidité causée par les pluies, les feuillets de ce registre agglutinés les uns aux autres ne peuvent se détacher sans tomber en poussière. Reliure en parchemin en aussi mauvais état. Dépouillement impossible».

35 Cf. supra, note 5.

conservation des minutes est antérieure de plus de cinquante ans à celle des registres; d'autre part, ceux-ci contiennent uniquement le texte des arrêts sans les renseignements externes figurant sur les minutes; enfin, certaines minutes – peu nombreuses – ne sont pas reportées sur le registre. Il est difficile d'en connaître la raison. On pourrait penser que seuls les arrêts *définitifs* et non les *préparatoires* sont l'objet d'un enregistrement, mais quelques sondages montrent que tel n'est pas toujours le critère du choix. Pour avoir une vision complète de la jurisprudence, il est donc préférable de dépouiller les liasses de minutes. Ceci est vrai également des sentences rendues par la Chambre des Requêtes. Leurs minutes sont en effet conservées dans cinquante liasses allant de 1609 à 1779[36].

4. Les procès-verbaux

Si les masses documentaires jusqu'ici décrites réunissent les décisions prises par les différentes chambres du Parlement, il est une autre catégorie de pièces, encore peu sollicitées en raison sans doute de leur caractère disparate, qui constituent une source particulièrement abondante et riche d'informations précieuses, sous la forme de procès-verbaux divers. Sous l'appellation 'procès-verbaux d'exécution des arrêts' de la rubrique 'Grand'Chambre' – série et titre trompeurs –, sont réunies cent quarante trois liasses[37]. La pièce la plus ancienne remonte à 1547; la dernière date de 1790; c'est dire que cette suite est la plus longue qui nous soit conservée. Le contenu des liasses est des plus variés. Outre des grosses d'arrêts, en particulier d'arrêts de règlement, de très nombreux procès-verbaux d'exécution d'arrêts dressés par les conseillers rapporteurs – dont certains sont fort volumineux[38] –, des procès-verbaux d'exécution de sentences arbitrales, des rapports d'experts, des procès-verbaux de 'veues de lieux', des enquêtes diverses, 'enquêtes secrètes', 'réponses cathégoriques', et bien d'autres choses encore. Ce qui permet de pallier partiellement la disparition des 'sacs' de procédures. Au XVIIIe siècle, la richesse des liasses devient encore plus grande car les procès-verbaux ou rapports sont volontiers accompagnés de plans ou dessins. La même variété se retrouve dans les archives de la Chambre des Requêtes où 24 liasses ont été conservées, de

---

[36] B II 49/1 et 1bis-49 du registre placier, aujourd'hui cotés B 12 230 à B 12 592. Dans leur très grande majorité, les arrêts enregistrés sont des arrêts civils.

[37] B II 29/1 - 143. La première liasse contient des pièces datées de 1547, 1566, 1572, 1573, 1580, 1583, 1584, mais ensuite la série ne connaît pas d'interruption.

[38] Entre autres, par exemple, le 'procès verbal d'exécution d'arretz contenant la visitte des chastiaux, maisons, moulins, fourgs, estangs, bois et autres choses dépendans de l'évesché d'Autun'. La visite a duré huit jours, du 26 août au 2 septembre 1659, et le résultat de chaque jour est fidèlement consigné.

1609 à 1790[39]. On y trouve, par exemple, dans une affaire opposant, en 1754, le Chapitre cathédral de Langres à la Chartreuse de Dijon au sujet des limites entre les justices de Gevrey(-Chambertin) et de Brochon, un rapport des deux experts nommés par les parties: Jean Lamarre, commissaire en droits seigneuriaux et notaire royal en la résidence de Saint-Léger-sous-Beuvray, pour les religieux de la Chartreuse, et Edme de La Poix de Fréminville aussi commissaire en droits seigneuriaux et notaire royal de la ville de Marcigny – auteur célèbre de *La Pratique pour la rénovation des terriers et droits seigneuriaux,* (1746 - 48, 1752 - 57) – pour les chanoines de Langres, et les experts ont joint à leur rapport un 'plan géométrique'[40]. De quelque chambre qu'elles proviennent, les pièces rangées sous la rubrique 'procès-verbaux', présentent donc toujours un caractère concret, voire pittoresque, qui contraste avec l'apparence stéréotypée des arrêts ou sentences.

Outre ces quatre masses documentaires qui permettent d'avoir une vue globale de la jurisprudence du Parlement, il faut simplement signaler, faute de pouvoir les analyser ici en raison des dimensions limitées de cette contribution, l'existence d'autres documents qui, par leur volume et leur contenu, présentent également un grand intérêt. Il s'agit d'abord des *Décrets* dont quatre-vingt-dix-sept liasses sont conservées pour les chambres d'appel, de 1600 à 1790[41], et, pour la Chambre des Requêtes de vingt 'carnots de décrets'[42] et de cinquante liasses de 'Décrets, criées, saisies, ordres'[43]. On sait que ce sont, selon la chambre considérée, des sentences ou des arrêts rendus à la suite de la vente d'immeubles saisis. Soulignons aussi le profit que le chercheur peut tirer des actes par lesquels le Parlement était amené à homologuer des décisions prises en dehors de lui et qui sont transcrits dans deux séries de registres[44]. Ajoutons que les archives de la Table de Marbre sont assez complètes à partir du début du XVIIe siècle et qu'elles sont réparties de la même manière que celles du Parlement[45]. Enfin, le fonds du Parlement de Dombes, supprimé en 1771 et remplacé par une sénéchaussée siégeant à Trévoux, a été transféré dans les archives du Parlement bourguignon, et l'on y trouve les mêmes genres de liasses ou registres[46].

---

39 B II 50/1 - 24.

40 B II 50/23, 8 mai 1754.

41 B II 30/1 - 97.

42 B II 54/1 - 20 (1656 - 1760).

43 B II 55/1 - 50 (1610 - 1786).

44 B II 38/1 - 8, 'Homologations de sentences arbitrales' (1765 - 1784). B II 39/1 - 11, 'Homologations d'arrêts, délibérations, jugements etc.' (1683 - 1789).

45 B II 72 et s.

46 B II 89/1 - 25, Audiences (1598 - 1726); B II 90/1 - 18, Arrêts minutes (1649 - 1669); B II 91/1 - 13, Plumitifs (1608 - 1771); B II 92, 93, 94, Arrêts (1587 - 1771) etc.

En définitive, les archives judiciaires de la Cour de Dijon sont riches, variées et... complexes. Puisse cette complexité ne pas rebuter les chercheurs, et cette présente et modeste note les inviter au dépouillement!

MICHEL PETITJEAN

Les recueils d'arrêts bourguignons

Si le monde des juristes, juges, avocats, notaires, retient depuis longtemps l'attention des chercheurs du Centre Georges Chevrier[1], l'histoire des arrêtistes n'a pas encore été écrite. C'est que ces derniers furent particulièrement nombreux – la liste n'en a pas été dressée – et que leurs recueils, pour la plupart, n'ont pas été publiés. Ceux-ci nous sont parvenus souvent en plusieurs manuscrits, dont la filiation serait à établir, car ils sont parfois recopiés les uns sur les autres avec d'insignifiantes variantes ou des ajouts plus subtantiels. Leur étude, en effet n'est pas négligeable pour la connaissance du droit provincial. Elle est même d'autant plus importante, ici, que la coutume, rédigée avec précocité et maladresse, a dû faire l'objet d'une constante interprétation, jusqu'à la fin de l'Ancien Régime. Avec la doctrine, la jurisprudence devait combler les lacunes du texte officiel qui n'avait guère plus que formulé quelques règles résultant de l'usage et laissé de côté des pans entiers du droit. Les décisions de justice, les arrêts rendus par les tribunaux et par le Parlement, installé à Dijon après le rattachement de la Bourgogne à la couronne de France[2], devaient servir à l'élaboration du droit bourguignon.

Importance des recueils d'arrêts

La jurisprudence, en elle-même, constitue une source fondamentale du droit. C'est même – on le sait – une source à caractère *quasi* sacré, puisque l'autorité d'une décision de justice repose sur l'autorité du souverain qui tient, lui-même, de Dieu son pouvoir. Dans cette conception, les Parlements

---

[1] Centre Georges Chevrier, Université de Bourgogne, UMR-CNRS 5605.

[2] A l'époque ducale, Beaune avait tenu le rôle de capitale judiciaire. Dans cette ville – préférée à Dijon où la justice des évêques de Langres avait été trop menaçante aux origines du duché de Bourgogne – avaient été fixés les tribunaux supérieurs: Cour d'appeaux et Parlement – cf. *E. Champeaux,* Les Ordonnances des ducs de Bourgogne sur l'administration de la justice du duché, avec une introduction sur les origines du Parlement de Bourgogne, dans: Revue bourguignonne publiée par l'Université de Dijon, t. 17 (1907), n°s 2 - 3. Sur l'installation du Parlement à Dijon, cf. *G. Chevrier,* Les débuts du Parlement de Dijon (1477 - 1487), dans: Annales de Bourgogne, t. 15 (1943) pp. 93 - 124.

– celui de Dijon, depuis 1477[3] – jugeant en dernier ressort avaient une autorité presque infaillible: *res judicata pro veritate habetur.* Autrement dit, la justice rendue par une cour souveraine s'apparentait à la vérité. Certes, les juges ne sont pas infaillibles et peuvent se tromper comme les autres hommes, mais on doit en conscience s'en tenir à leurs jugements, comme s'ils n'avaient pu faillir. Chacun doit se plier sans broncher à leurs décisions, qui incarnent la justice et la loi, tant qu'elles subsistent. D'où, l'on entrevoit l'intérêt que pouvaient offrir les recueils d'arrêts. S'y trouvaient consignées toutes les maximes réglant la société. Ceux qui les ont composés en étaient d'ailleurs tout à fait conscients. Leurs compilations devaient, à leurs yeux, servir de guide pour la conduite à tenir dans les situations du moment et pour éviter aux plaideurs de faire fausse route dans leurs démarches juridiques: avertir sur la manière de bien établir un contrat, de fixer utilement les conventions d'un mariage, de bien faire un testament, bref de conduire efficacement toutes ses affaires et de ne pas s'exposer aux risques d'une procédure.

Source primordiale du droit bourguignon, la jurisprudence devait être connue de chacun, des plaideurs et surtout de leurs défenseurs. Les recueils d'arrêts ont donc pour but de faire connaître aux intéressés les principales décisions judiciaires. De tels ouvrages s'adressent d'abord aux avocats, qui, à Dijon, par suite de l'absence d'une université jusqu'au XVIIIe siècle[4], devaient se former eux-mêmes au contact de la pratique et par un apprentissage auprès de leurs aînés. C'est pourquoi, à l'instar des auteurs d'ouvrages dogmatiques, les arrêtistes entendaient-ils eux-mêmes faire œuvre didactique, fût-ce simplement en faveur des jeunes membres de leur famille qui voulaient à leur suite embrasser la carrière judiciaire. Ils ont œuvré non pas surtout pour les doctes, mais d'abord pour eux-mêmes et – quelques-uns l'affirment clairement en introduction de leur ouvrage – pour les jeunes et les débutants non encore rompus aux complexités juridiques, dont le niveau des études et des connaissances était souvent à déplorer[5].

---

[3] Auparavant, le duché de Bourgogne ayant été constitué en apanage, les jugements rendus par le Parlement ducal étaient susceptibles d'appels au Parlement de Paris, là où théoriquement – disait-on – se terminaient les procès bourguignons.

[4] La Faculté de droit de Dijon ne fut créée sous forme d'une Université qu'en 1723. Avant cette date, il n'y avait pas d'école de droit officielle, mais le droit était enseigné par des professeurs privés, des avocats surtout, tel Jean Girard, dont l'enseignement paraissait fort apprécié au XVIe siècle. *P. Perrenet,* Un professeur de droit dijonnais au XVIe siècle, Jean Girard, dans: Mémoires de la Société pour l'histoire du droit et des institutions des anciens pays bourguignons, comtois et romands (M.S.H.D.B.), 6e fasc. (1939), pp. 195 - 202 et du *même auteur:* Le Palais de justice de Dijon. Les cours souveraines (Le monde du Palais, Rennes, 1936).

[5] «J'ai moins écrit pour les doctes qui n'ont pas besoin de mes recherches, que pour les commençans et ceux qui sont moins verséz dans la science du droit, je

Auteurs...

Ce sont surtout les avocats qui ont cherché à consigner les usages de la province tels qu'ils résultaient de la coutume ou des constructions doctrinales[6]. Ce sont eux encore qui ont voulu rassembler dans des recueils les décisions des tribunaux susceptibles de faire jurisprudence. Cela n'étonnera pas, puisque dans leurs conseils ils se fondaient sur les arrêts rendus pour des faits et des circonstances comparables aux causes qui les occupaient. Formés par les études au droit romano-canonique, ils devaient s'efforcer d'apprendre par eux-mêmes les principes du droit coutumier[7] et surtout de connaître l'énorme jurisprudence qui, depuis la rédaction de la coutume, en 1459, s'était peu à peu constituée et servait à interpréter les règles brèves et souvent fort complexes du texte officiel. Il était donc normal que les avocats aient cherché à rassembler toute cette jurisprudence, arrêts de réglement, avis de la cour en des recueils qui leur serviraient d'abord à préparer le travail du Palais, dont la mission leur incombait naturellement. Abstraction faite des recueils anonymes, la cohorte des avocats-arrêtistes est restée dominante du XVIe au XVIIIe siècle: Job Bouvot, Bernard Cousin, Bernard Durand, Bernard Martin, Philibert de la Mare, Maletête, Jean des Pringles, Jean Guillaume,[8] François-Claude Jehannin, Jean-Auguste de Chevanes, Nicolas Perrier, Jean Melenet, François Perrier, Guillaume Raviot, tous avocats réputés en leur temps ont compilé la jurisprudence du Parlement de Bourgogne. Seulement quelques officiers de ce Parlement, présidents, conseillers, un greffier, les ont imités.

---

leur ai indiqué les sources». Introduction au Recueil d'arrêts de *François Perrier* par *Guillaume Raviot*, n° XCVI.

[6] Cf. mon article sur: Le rôle des avocats dans la formation du droit coutumier bourguignon, dans: Revue de la Société internationale d'histoire de la profession d'avocat, n° 5 (1993), pp. 35 - 49.

[7] Si les juristes bourguignons allaient faire leurs études juridiques dans les Universités françaises ou italiennes, ils ne pouvaient qu'apprendre sur place les rudiments du droit coutumier, à partir d'un enseignement ayant pour cadre la coutume et conçu à la mode des glossateurs, comme le montre Le Coutumier bourguignon glosé (fin du XIVe siècle), ed. *M. Petitjean, M. L. Marchand* et *J. Metman* (Editions du C.N.R.S., Paris, 1982).

[8] Le petit recueil d'arrêts rendus en interprétation de la coutume que nous a laissé cet avocat, né en 1570 et mort en 1629, n'est qu'un fragment d'un ouvrage plus important dont il nourrissait le projet: la publication en latin des arrêts les plus remarquables rendus de son temps, avec les principales raisons des parties, à la manière de l'ouvrage d'Anne Robert pour les arrêts du Parlement de Paris. Cf. l'Histoire des commentateurs de la coutume du duché de Bourgogne, en tête des: Œuvres de Jurisprudence de M. *Bouhier*, par M. *Joly de Bévy* (Dijon 1787), p. XXXVI.

...et Types

Comme nombre de ces arrêtistes avaient l'intention, a-t-on dit, de faire œuvre didactique, leurs ouvrages offrent habituellement un aspect méthodique, voire systématique. Ils sont conçus par matières juridiques, ordonnées alphabétiquement et sont généralement pourvus de tables finales dressées dans le but – pas toujours atteint – d'en faciliter la consultation. Beaucoup de ces compilations appartiennent ainsi à un double genre: ce sont à la fois des ouvrages doctrinaux et des recueils d'arrêts, répertoires de droit et de jurisprudence où l'auteur traite les questions à la manière d'un docteur rapportant avec ses propres thèses, l'opinion des auteurs, donnant d'abondantes références aux textes des *corpora* et émaillant son exposé des décisions de justice qui lui paraissent déterminantes. C'est sous cette forme que se présentent, par exemple, les *Arrêts notables du Parlement de Dijon recueillis par M. Nicolas Perrier,* l'un des plus importants recueils bourguignons tant par le volume de son contenu que par sa notoriété. Ce recueil dont plusieurs copies nous ont été conservées[9] revêtait une grande valeur aux yeux des juristes de la province, puisque c'est dans cette compilation qu'a puisé abondamment François Perrier dont le recueil fut publié par Guillaume Raviot au XVIIIe siècle[10].

Si bien que les deux arrêtistes parmi les plus connus, Nicolas et François Perrier – qui n'étaient pas parents[11] – ont suivi la même inspiration. Ils ont l'un et l'autre composé un recueil méthodique: les articles ou questions de droit font l'objet d'un exposé très construit, avec références aux droits savants, au droit coutumier des autres provinces, aux auteurs: romanistes du

---

[9] Vide infra.

[10] Introduction, n° XCVIII: «J'ai puisé dans diverses sources. Les recueils de Mr de la Mare, autre fameux avocat..., celui de Mr Maltête, l'une des lumières du barreau de son siècle..., mais principalement celui de Nicolas Perrier, qui a vécu avec moins d'éclat, mais qui n'a pas moins mérité l'estime de tous les connaisseurs, m'ont fourni beaucoup d'hypothèses et d'arrêts dont j'ai profité».

[11] Nicolas Perrier, surnommé l'aîné, était né à Saint-Jean-de-Losne en 1628. Il mourut en 1694. Reçu avocat, il ne put s'illustrer au barreau à cause d'une mauvaise élocution, mais connut la renommée dans les consultations. François Perrier, surnommé le jeune, naquit à Beaune, le 14 janvier 1645 et mourut le 3 octobre 1700. Reçu avocat à Paris, il plaide assidument à Dijon. Il a laissé un recueil de 350 arrêts publiés et annotés par l'avocat Guillaume Raviot. Ce dernier, bien placé pour comparer les deux hommes, pensait que Perrier-l'aîné était 'plus sçavant et plus jurisconsulte' que Perrier-le-jeune, mais que ce dernier était plus 'méthodique' que son prédécesseur, comme cela se voit d'ailleurs à la lecture des deux recueils. Selon le même Raviot, Nicolas Perrier fut sans doute le praticien le plus versé dans la science du droit qu'ait connu la Bourgogne. Le Président Bouhier le tenait en pareille estime. Nicolas Perrier a composé aussi des Observations de droit et de coutume, selon l'usage du Parlement de Dijon (imprimées à Dijon, chez Jean Grangier, en 1688, in-4°-), op. cit., p. XXXIX.

Moyen Âge, commentateurs des coutumes, tractatistes et, enfin, sont rapportés les arrêts du Parlement de Bourgogne et évoquée, à l'occasion, la jurisprudence des autres Parlements.

Fiabilité

Si l'on aperçoit toute l'utilité que peuvent présenter les recueils d'arrêts pour la conservation des maximes du droit, on mesure aussi les dangers auxquels ils exposeraient si leurs auteurs ne s'étaient pas entourés pour les confectionner de toutes les précautions que l'on est en droit d'exiger[12]. Car pour se plier aux décisions de la justice, pour s'y rallier sans réserves, encore faut-il en voir les raisons. Autrement dit, les arrêts compilés dans les recueils de jurisprudence et les ouvrages doctrinaux doivent être motivés, afin que le lecteur soit suffisamment persuadé de leur bien-fondé.

C'est ainsi que les commentateurs de la coutume, qui ont voulu appuyer leur exposé sur les décisions des tribunaux, n'ont pas tous fait preuve d'une assez grande prudence. Les arrêts qu'ils ont rapportés se trouvent mêlés à leur discours et peuvent prêter le flan aux critiques d'absence de motifs et de mauvaise datation. C'est, par exemple, les reproches qu'encourt l'ouvrage de l'avocat Jacques-Auguste de Chevanes, auteur d'annotations sur la coutume[13]. Sous sa plume, les décisions judiciaires destinées à l'éclaircissement de la coutume risquent au contraire de donner une fausse idée des règles du droit bourguignon. Car elles sont rapportées pêle-mêle, sans avoir fait l'objet d'aucun tri préalable et sans que s'en découvrent les motifs, jamais précisés. Le risque est évident: on pourrait en déduire de fausses maximes, d'autant plus trompeuses et dangereuses pour l'avenir qu'elles sembleraient fondées sur de solides décisions des tribunaux. Aussi, de Chevanes a-t-il été accusé d'avoir cité ses arrêts sur de faux mémoires, de n'avoir pris aucune précaution pour les vérifier et d'avoir fait preuve d'une totale négligence tant pour la date des arrêts que pour le nom des parties[14].

Commentateurs et arrêtistes, pour la plupart, n'ignoraient pas les dangers et quelques-uns ont cherché à s'en prémunir par une déclaration de prin-

---

[12] Sur cette question et sur les discussions des contemporains, voir *C. Chêne,* L'arrestographie, science fort douteuse, dans: Recueil des mémoires et travaux publié par la Société d'histoire du droit et des institutions des anciens pays de droit écrit, fasc. XIII (1985), pp. 179 - 187.

[13] Coutumes générales du Pays et Duché de Bourgogne avec les annotations de M. Bégat, Président, et du Sieur de Pringles, avocat audit Parlement, revues, corrigées et augmentées de plusieurs arrêts... (Chalon 1665).

[14] Cf. l'Histoire des commentateurs..., op. cit., p. XXXVIII, où le Président Bouhier relève quelques-uns des pièges de cet ouvrage: deux arrêts qui semblent contraires, alors qu'ils ne le sont nullement; un principe de droit que l'auteur tente de confirmer par un arrêt qui, en fait, avait jugé le contraire...

cipe. L'auteur du premier recueil imprimé, l'avocat Job Bouvot, qui s'intitulait jurisconsulte chalonnais, fort d'une expérience du barreau de quarante-six années, quand il composa son ouvrage, affirmait avoir toujours indiqué le fait et l'argumentation de ses arrêts, afin que chacun puisse y trouver les raisons qui avaient inspiré les juges. En dépit de cette précision initiale, un sévère jugement peut être porté sur son œuvre distribuée sous forme de questions notables où les décisions judiciaires, noyées dans la réponse circonstanciée apportée à chacune d'elles, sont très difficiles à retrouver. Le Président Bouhier[15] lui reproche d'avoir recueilli ses arrêts «avec plus de travail que de choix et de discernement». Les arrêts qu'il cite ne sont pas sûrs, car il ne s'agit pas de jugements qu'il a lui-même vu rendre, mais il n'en a eu connaissance que sur le rapport d'autrui et son style confus rend malaisée la vérification de ses démonstrations. Il fait état de la jurisprudence d'autres tribunaux présentés comme des cours souveraines, qui ne le sont pas toujours, et présente, à l'occasion, ses propres allégations comme des décisions de justice. Enfin, la date de ses arrêts est souvent erronée, si bien qu'il est assez difficile de les retrouver dans les registres du Parlement.

On a cherché parfois à se mettre à l'abri de cette dernière critique, tel Pierre Taisand, illustre commentateur de la coutume de Bourgogne. Dans son commentaire imprimé, l'un des monuments les plus importants de la littérature juridique bourguignonne, en dépit des critiques essuyées[16], sont rapportés plus de six cents arrêts généraux ou particuliers du Parlement de Dijon qui, précise-t-il, lui ont été communiqués directement par plusieurs et principaux officiers de ce tribunal et par les avocats les plus illustres ou leurs héritiers[17]. Tous ces arrêts qu'il a minutieusement vérifiés devraient,

---

15 Ibid., p. XXXIII. Fils d'avocat, Job Bouvot naquit à Chalon en 1558, fut reçu avocat à Dijon le 7 juin 1580 et mourut dans sa ville natale en 1636. Il avait été l'élève de Cujas. Bouvot ou Bonnot? Cf. *A. Bailly,* Job Bouvot, jurisconsulte imaginaire, dans: M.S.H.D.B., fasc. 43, 1986, pp. 213 - 215.

16 Voir, par exemple, les critiques de l'avocat Pierre Lemulier, son contemporain et condisciple, dans mon article: Un homme de loi semurois: l'avocat Pierre Lemulier, dans: Annales de Bourgogne, t. LXII, 1990, pp. 5 - 24.

17 «...Les arrêts que je cite ont été pris dans des sources très pures, je veux dire dans des recueils d'arrêts qui ont été rendus au rapport de ceux qui me les ont communiqués ou en des procès dont ils étaient juges ou sur les plaidoyers des plus célèbres avocats de ce Parlement, morts et vivants, qu'ils ont eux-mêmes retenus et mis dans leurs recueils avec beaucoup d'exactitude et sur la foi desquels ils ont plaidé, écrit, consulté pendant un grand nombre d'années. De sorte que l'on doit compter sur la fidèlité des arrêts insérés dans cet ouvrage, m'étant surtout attaché à n'y oublier aucune circonstance et ayant consulté moi-même les juges qui les ont rendus (qui m'ont dit quelquefois les motifs) ou les registres du Palais, afin qu'il ne me restât aucun doute... Je me suis fait une loi de ne rapporter que des arrêts fidèles». Coutume générale des Pays et Duché de Bourgogne, avec le commentaire de M. *Taisand*... (Dijon 1698), Introduction.

précise-t-il, pouvoir être retrouvés sans difficulté dans les archives du Parlement. Si, malgré toutes les précautions prises, quelques-uns de ces arrêts ne pouvaient pas être retrouvés, cela ne prouverait pas leur fausseté, car Taisand prévient de la possible disparition des registres du Palais, par suite de la liberté prise par les procureurs, les clercs, voire les plaideurs de s'introduire quelquefois dans la chambre du Conseil.[18]

Quelques juristes se montraient encore plus exigeants. Tout en insistant sur l'indéniable utilité des règles jurisprudentielles, ils soulignaient les dangers qu'il y aurait à prendre pour des principes tous les arrêts rendus par le Parlement. L'auteur des *Traités de droit français à l'usage de Bourgogne*[19], l'avocat Gabriel Davot, premier professeur de droit français à l'Université de Dijon, insiste sur l'extrême prudence qu'il faut avoir dans la consultation des arrêts rendus par les tribunaux, dont on connaît rarement les vrais motifs. Car les arguments développés par les avocats dans leurs plaidoiries, si elles inclinent souvent les juges, ne sont pas toujours les seules raisons qui les ont poussés à se prononcer. C'est pourquoi, d'ailleurs, on interdisait au greffier – comme le faisaient les anciens règlements – de consigner les raisons développées par les avocats.

Jean Melenet, l'un des plus savants avocats dijonnais du XVIIe siècle[20], s'est fait l'écho de tous les griefs que l'on pouvait formuler à l'encontre des arrêtistes. Les vrais motifs des arrêts ne pouvaient être connus la plupart du temps par le rapport d'autrui. Melenet estimait qu'il ne fallait point s'attacher aux arrêts et que les auteurs d'ouvrages de jurisprudence ne devraient pas même en faire mention. Pour lui, une seule source de maximes ne saurait tromper: les déclarations du roi, les règlements des cours, les arrêts généraux qui s'y forment et les certificats d'usage délivrés par les Parlements eux-mêmes. Lui, qui voulut aussi faire œuvre d'arrêtiste[21], s'est donc borné à ne compiler que ce genre de décisions, trouvées sur le registre des délibérations secrètes du Palais. Seules, ces décisions lui semblaient sûres: on n'avait pas à craindre que la cour, en pareil cas, se soit déterminée par des faits particuliers, car «on ne retient point dans ce dépost de

[18] Ibid., Arrêt du 13 juillet 1650 ordonnant que «pour avoir révélation de la soustraction de ces registres... monitoire serait expédié à la forme des édits et arrêts, qu'il serait publié et fulminé aux prônes des églises paroissales de la ville de Dijon et dans la chapelle du Palais et que l'arrêt serait lu et publié à l'audience et affiché aux portes du Palais à ce qu'aucun n'en prétendit cause d'ignorance».

[19] Publiés à Dijon entre 1751 et 1767 par son gendre, Jean Bannelier, batonnier des avocats et doyen de la Faculté de droit.

[20] Cf. mon article sur: Le Rôle des avocats, cité supra.

[21] Jean Melenet a laissé plusieurs ouvrages manuscrits sur la coutume de Bourgogne: B. M. de Dijon, ms 2241: Coutumes générales du duché de Bourgogne, conté de Charollois et terres d'outre Saône qui n'usent de droit écrit, par M. *Mellenet*, avocat en ce Parlement.

nostre jurisprudence le résultat d'un arrest intervenu sur des circonstances particulières». D'après lui, tout arrêtiste devrait s'en tenir à ce type de décisions. «Alors, dit-il, la lecture des préjugés serait utile et nulle erreur ne serait à craindre. Mais on doit peu prendre de confiance aux préjugés intervenus sur des hypothèses particulières, car souvent ils n'ont point décidé les questions de droit qui y étaient agitées»[22].

En résumé, l'historien du droit bourguignon qui dispose d'importants ouvrages doctrinaux, commentaires et traités sur la coutume, imprimés la plupart, peut aussi connaître la jurisprudence des tribunaux et du Parlement à travers une abondante série de recueils, la plupart manuscrits. Et les juristes contemporains l'ont eux-mêmes averti des précautions qu'il devra prendre pour leur consultation.

Principaux recueils d'arrêts bourguignons[23]

Recueils imprimés

– *Nouveau recueil des arrests de Bourgogne, où sont contenues diverses notables questions de droit tant coustumier que romain, controversées entre les docteurs, proposées par Me* J. Bouvot, *advocat au Parlement de Bourgongne; décidées par jugements et arrests de la cour souveraine du Parlement de Dijon...*, t. I (Cologny, P. et J. Chouet, 1623); t. II (Genève, J. Stoër, 1628).

L'ouvrage est distribué sous la forme de Questions notables.

– *Arrests notables du Parlement de Dijon recueillis par M.* François Perrier ... *avec des observations sur chaque question par* Guillaume Raviot... (Dijon, 1735), 2 vol. in. f°.

L'ouvrage est distribué en questions au nombre de 350, placées sous autant d'arrêts, point de départ de l'exposé.

---

22 Idée développée par Melenet dans la préface écrite au début du recueil d'arrêts qu'il a lui même composé et reproduite dans toute une série de manuscrits B. M. de Dijon, ms 311 et vide infra. Cf. *A. Laurain,* Les arrêts de règlement du Parlement de Dijon, dans: M.S.H.D.B., fasc. 5, 1938, pp. 205. sq.

23 La liste que nous donnons ici, n'est pas exhaustive. Cf. *J. C. Garreta,* Les archives du Parlement de Dijon. Etude des sources, dans: M.S.H.D.B., fasc. 623 (1962), pp. 203 - 244 (spéc. pp. 232 - 239) où la plupart des recueils que nous énumérons sont déjà indiqués avec de précieuses remarques sur leur utilité – plus ou moins grande – pour l'historien.

Recueils manuscrits

– B. M. de Dijon, mss 1304 à 1310 et 1496 à 1501.

Il ne s'agit pas là de recueils d'arrêts, tels que nous les avons envisagés précédemment, mais d'extraits des registres du Parlement fidèlement transcrits par deux collectionneurs bourguignons. Arrêts rendus entre 1515 et 1753[24].

– Arrêts de la Cour de Parlement de Dijon remarqués par M. VIROT, conseiller en icelle.

B. M. de Dijon, ms 310.

138 arrêts rendus entre l'année 1555 et le mois d'avril de l'année 1578. La date des arrêts n'est pas toujours indiquée. L'auteur mourut en 1579.

– Arrêts notables rendus au Parlement de Dijon depuis le 5 mars 1567 jusques à la fin de 1570, recueillis par Me BERNARD COUSIN, avocat.

B. M. de Troyes, ms 1758.

– Arrêts donnés au Parlement de Dijon.

B. N. fr. 5302.

146 arrêts rendus entre le 14 févr. 1569 et le 28 janv. 1592.

– Recueil d'arrêts du Parlement de Dijon depuis le 26 mars 1613 jusqu'au 30 juin 1617 par MILLIÈRE, conseiller (f° 308 - 382) suivi d'un: Recueil de quelques arrêts du Parlement de Dijon par MALETESTE, ancien célèbre avocat (f° 389 - 434).

B. M. Dijon, ms 2094.

– Recueil d'arrêts.

Arch. dép. de Saône-et-Loire, B 4 et 5.

180 arrêts généraux (tous imprimés, sauf un) rendus entre 1622 et 1744 sur des affaires particulières, mais dont les conclusions, en raison de leur intérêt, sont notifiées à tout le ressort du Parlement.

– Arrests recueillis par feu M. SEGUENOT, depuis 1655 jusqu'à 1666.

B. M. Dijon, ms 312.

– Recueil d'arrêts du Parlement.

B. M. Dijon, ms 314.

Arrêts d'audience surtout rendus entre le 27 janv. 1665 et le 18 mars 1697.

– Mémoires et observations des choses plus mémorables et arrests de la cour de Parlement de Dijon, faictes par le sr (JOSEPH) G(RIGUETTE), greffier, pour servir aux occurances.

B. M. Dijon, mss 308, 1381 et 1403.

---

[24] En tête du ms 1496, on lit: «on ne peut sçavoir la datte du jour et du mois de l'arrêt, parce qu'en ce tems là les arrêts rendus en procès par écrit ne se dattaient point particulierement, ainsi qu'il paroit par le registre, mais une seule datte, qui étoit celle du jour de la prononciation servoit pour tous les arrêts prononcés le même jour».

– Recueil de jurisprudence par ordre alphabétique de matières formé au commencement du XVIIe siècle par un jurisconsulte, auteur d'un recueil d'arrêts.

B. M. Dijon, ms 1432.

Il s'agit d'un répertoire de jurisprudence par matières, présentées sans aucun ordre, avec renvoi par l'auteur à «mon recueil d'arrests».

– Copie du recueil d'arrêts de GENREAU.

B. M. Dijon, ms 320.

– Recueil d'arrêts de JEHANNIN.

B. M. Dijon, ms 349.

Il s'agit d'un répertoire alphabétique de jurisprudence commençant au mot *abolition* et se terminant au mot *uxor* avec une table finale.

– Arrêts notables du Parlement de Dijon recueillis par M. NICOLAS PERRIER, avocat. Avec diverses délibérations secrètes du même Parlement.

B. M. Dijon, mss 944 et 945, 344 et 345, 1188 (daté de 1753), 933 (Tables alphabétiques du recueil); B. M. Beaune, ms 153 (daté de 1781); Bibl. du Centre Georges Chevrier, 2 vol. manuscrits.

– Arrêts du Parlement de Dijon recueillis par JEAN MELENET.

B. M. Dijon, ms 311.

– Recueil des délibérations secrètes.

B. M. Dijon, ms 1502.

– Idem, par M. le Président BOUHIER.

B. M. Dijon, mss 1402, 2292, 2325, 2470; B. N. fr. 14387; Arch. dép. de la Côte d'Or, B 12071.

Ces huit recueils commencent tous par la même préface sur la valeur des arrêts et les précautions à prendre pour en confectionner des recueils. (Cf. supra).

– Répertoire alphabétique de droit et de jurisprudence, de la main de M. DAVOT, premier professeur de droit français à l'Université de Dijon.

B. M. Dijon, ms 348.

– Recueil d'arrêts notables du Parlement de Dijon par M. de B.

Bibl. univ. de Dijon, 178 004, 2 vol. manuscrits datés de 1780.

Il s'agit de FLEUTELOT DE BENEUVRE, doyen du Parlement, mort le 14 mai 1785, âgé de 90 ans.

– Recueil d'arrêts et de plaidoiries à l'usage du Parlement de Bourgogne par ordre alphabétique de matières.

B. M. Tournus, ms 45.

Arrêts rendus entre 1730 et 1791.[25]

---

[25] V. dans la seconde partie: 'Le parlement de Dijon (Bourgogne): collation de recueils privés et de registres de la Cour'.

FILIPPO RANIERI

Entscheidungsfindung und Technik der Urteilsredaktion in der Tradition des deutschen Usus modernus: das Beispiel der Aktenrelationen am Reichskammergericht

Einleitung

Die Entscheidungen des Reichskammergerichts hatten zwar keine formale Präjudizwirkung, genossen jedoch vor allem bei den Praktikern des deutschen usus modernus eine beträchtliche Autorität. Dies gilt sowohl in materiellrechtlicher Hinsicht als auch für die Entwicklung der richterlichen Arbeitsmethode. Die Ausgestaltung des gemeinen Prozeßrechts im Alten Reich des 16. und 17. Jahrhunderts geht – um nur ein Beispiel hier zu erwähnen – vor allem auf die Judikatur der Speyerer Instanz zurück.[1] Das Thema, das hier erörtert werden soll, gilt den Quellen und der Methode dieser judiziellen Rechtstradition, insbesondere ob und anhand von welchen Quellen die Judikatur des Reichskammergerichts sich in ihrem materiellrechtlichen Gehalt analysieren und rekonstruieren läßt. Es gibt kaum Untersuchungen darüber, in welcher Weise, mit welcher Methode und in welchem Umfang die Rechtsprechung des Reichskammergerichts von den Zeitgenossen bei der praktischen juristischen Arbeit herangezogen wurde[2]. Was

---

[1] Dazu vgl. zuletzt *P. L. Nève/R. Sprenger,* Restitution und Supplikation. Über die Geschichte der Rechtsmittel im 16. Jahrhundert, in: *H. de Schepper* (ed.), Höchste Gerichtsbarkeit im Spätmittelalter und in der frühen Neuzeit (Amsterdam 1985), S. 43 - 59 mit der Analyse einer handschriftlich erhaltenen Aktenrelation des Assessors Viglius von Aytta.

[2] Eine Ausnahme stellt einstweilen die vorzügliche Untersuchung von *H. Weller* dar, Die Bedeutung der Präjudizien im Verständnis der deutschen Rechtswissenschaft. Ein rechtshistorischer Beitrag zur Entstehung und Funktion der Präjudizientheorie [Schriften zur Rechtstheorie, Heft 77], (Berlin 1979), zur gemeinrechtlichen Tradition des usus modernus vgl. insb. S. 22 - 23, 28 - 29 sowie S. 61 - 65; darauf aufbauend *M. Kriele,* Normbildung durch Präjudizien, in: *W. Oelmüller* (ed.), Normen und Geschichte. Materialien zur Normendiskussion 3 (Paderborn 1979), S. 24 - 39, wiederabgedruckt als: Das Präjudiz im kontinental-europäischen und anglo-amerikanischen Rechtskreis, in: La sentenza in Europa (Padova 1988), S. 62 - 80. Siehe auch *H.-J. Becker,* Präjudiz, in: HRG, III (Berlin 1974). Zur Präjudizienbildung in der kontinentaleuropäischen Rechtstradition vgl. die bibliographischen Hinweise

die Prozeßakten anbetrifft, so waren sie ausschließlich für den Gerichts- und Kanzleigebrauch bestimmt. Eine Heranziehung derartiger Materialien in praktischer oder wissenschaftlicher Absicht scheint daher bereits wegen der Geheimhaltung, welche die interne Tätigkeit des Gerichts charakterisierte, undenkbar gewesen zu sein. Anders stellt sich die Situation für die gedruckten Sammlungen von Urteilen und Aktenrelationen dar. Sie fanden seit Mitte des 16. Jahrhunderts eine breite Verwendung bei den Praktikern[3]. Die hohe Zahl der Auflagen mancher dieser Sammlungen spricht hier eine deutliche Sprache. Da die Urteile bekanntlich nicht mit Gründen versehen wurden, kommen aber hier vor allem die publizierten Voten und die Aktenrelationen in Betracht. Im einzelnen ist dieser Aspekt der Wirkungsgeschichte der Quellen der kammergerichtlichen Judikatur jedoch – wenn man von der vorzüglichen, aber alten Dissertation von Weller absieht[4] – selten untersucht worden.[5]

Dies hängt mit einem allgemeinen forschungsgeschichtlichen Grund zusammen: das römische gemeine Recht des 16. und 17. Jahrhunderts wird heute noch eher als Professoren- statt als Richterrecht angesehen. Es wirkt hier weiter noch die alte, heute überholte Vorstellung eines historischen Gegensatzes zwischen kontinentaler und englischer Rechtstradition nach. Die judizielle Dimension des europäischen Gemeinrechts ist zwar in den letzten Jahrzehnten immer wieder betont worden: es fehlen jedoch immer noch ausreichend viele Einzeluntersuchungen um erste präzise Aussagen zur Präjudizwirkung der Rechtsprechung auch in der Tradition der Civil Law jener Zeit machen zu können.[6] Dies gilt sowohl für unsere Kenntnisse

---

bei *F. Ranieri* (ed.), Gedruckte Quellen der Rechtsprechung in Europa. 1800 - 1945, I (Frankfurt M. 1992), S. LV - LXXI.

[3] Vgl. hierzu die Hinweise zu den zeitgenössischen Quellen bei *H. Weller,* Die Bedeutung, S. 43.

[4] Vgl. oben, Anm. 2.

[5] Einige Hinweise hierüber bei *H. Weller,* Die Bedeutung, S. 22 - 23 sowie S. 61 - 65.

[6] Vgl. für einen Beispiel einer solchen Untersuchung *A. Wijffels,* References to judicial precedents in the practice of the Great Council of Malines (ca. 1460 - 1580), in: Miscellanea Consilii Magni III. Essays on the History of Forensic Practice/Etudes d'histoire judiciaire (Amsterdam 1988), S. 165 - 181. Zum Thema grundlegend *J. P. Dawson,* The Oracles of the Law (Ann Arbor 1968) und die zahlreichen Arbeiten von *G. Gorla,* nachgedruckt in: Diritto comparato e diritto comune europeo (Milano 1981). Für eine Gesamtwürdigung vgl. *M. Ascheri,* Gino Gorla tra diritto e storia: per il diritto comune europeo, in: Riv. trim. di diritto e procedura civile 44 (1990), S. 947 - 962 m. w. N. Zu der gemeinrechtlichen Praxis bei den italienischen Gerichtshöfen des 16. und 17. Jh. vgl. zuletzt *G. Gorla,* Procedimento individuale. Voto dei singoli giudici e collegialità rotale, in: *M. Sbriccoli/A. Bettoni* (ed.), Grandi Tribunali e Rote nell'Italia di antico regime (Milano 1993), S. 1 - 78, insb. S. 26 - 27 und 41 - 43; *S. Pierangeli,* Diritto romano e Rota provinciae Marchiae (Torino 1992), insb. S. 179 - 188.

hinsichtlich der Arbeit der Praktiker jener Jahrhunderte als auch selbst hinsichtlich der richterlichen Arbeitsmethode zur Zeit des usus modernus. Dieses Defizit der kontinentalen rechtshistorischen Forschung, im Vergleich etwa zum Stand der Geschichte des englischen Common Law, gilt selbstverständlich auch für das Reichskammergericht. Vor allem fehlen hier bis heute spezielle dogmengeschichtliche Studien, in welchen die spezifische Heranziehung und Verwertung von kammergerichtlichen Urteilen systematisch analysiert und nachgewiesen wird; notwendig wäre hier insbesondere eine systematische Analyse der jeweils in der damaligen Traktaten- und Kommentarliteratur zitierten Fundstellen von kammergerichtlichen Urteilen.[7] Eine solche Forschungslücke kann der vorliegende Beitrag selbstverständlich nicht füllen. In einem ersten Abschnitt (I.) sollen hier zunächst die Quellen vorgestellt werden, die uns zur Verfügung stehen, um die Urteile und die Entscheidungen des Reichskammergerichts aus dem 16. - 17. Jahrhundert ermitteln zu können. Im darauf folgenden Abschnitt (II.) soll anschließend gezeigt werden, welche zentrale und unverzichtbare Funktion den Aktenrelationen der Assessoren zukommt, um die damalige kammergerichtliche Judikatur in ihren materiellrechtlichen Dimensionen analysieren und nachzeichnen zu können. In einem letzten Abschnitt schließlich (III.) soll gezeigt werden, welchen hohen Stellenwert und langfristige historische Wirkung die kammergerichtlichen Aktenrelationen und Voten auch in methodischer Sicht in der deutschen Tradition der Juristenausbildung hatten.

I.

1. Die Prozeßakten aus der kammergerichtlichen Archivüberlieferung[8] enthalten in der Regel keine Endurteile, sondern – der Tradition des schriftlichen römischen gemeinen Prozesses gemäß – nur die Parteienschriften, die produzierten Beweisunterlagen sowie die Protokolle der Zeugenverneh-

---

[7] Dogmengeschichtliche und methodengeschichtliche Untersuchungen zur Judikatur des Reichskammergerichts fehlen; vgl. noch die alte Dissertation von *F. Czermak,* Der Besitz in der Rechtsprechung des Reichskammergerichts, dargestellt auf Grund der Observationen von J. Mynsinger und A. Gail (Diss. iur., Frankfurt M. 1953); auch hier werden jedoch nur die Sammlungen herangezogen, ohne einer unmittelbaren Bezugnahme auf die einzelnen Entscheidungen.

[8] Zur Archivüberlieferung der kammergerichtlichen Prozeßakten vgl. *F. Ranieri,* Recht und Gesellschaft im Zeitalter der Rezeption. Eine rechts- und sozialgeschichtliche Analyse der Tätigkeit des Reichskammergerichts im 16. Jahrhundert (Köln-Wien 1985), I, insb. S. 1 - 17 sowie S. 74 - 90; *F. Battenberg,* ‚Reichskammergericht und Archivwesen. Zum Stand der Erschließung der Reichskammergerichtsakten', in: *B. Diestelkamp* (ed.), Das Reichskammergericht in der deutschen Geschichte. Stand der Forschung und Forschungsperspektiven (Köln-Wien 1989), mit umfassenden Angaben zur derzeitigen Erschließungssituation.

mungen. In der Regel ist eine Prozeßakte chronologisch geordnet, wobei die einzelnen Produkte durch Quadrangelnummern durchgezählt sind[9]. Die Endurteile wurden – wie damals üblich, ohne Angaben zu den Entscheidungsgründen – wie auch die Voten und die Aktenrelationen der Assessoren fast nie bei der jeweiligen Prozeßakte aufbewahrt, sondern in speziell angelegten Urteilsbüchern gesammelt. Diese sind für die Speyerer Zeit nicht erhalten geblieben; die Fragmente im Frankfurter Bundesarchiv sind – wie Diestelkamp gezeigt hat – Abschriften privater Provenienz.[10] Archivalisch vollständig erhalten sind nur die Urteilsbücher und die Sammlungen der Aktenrelationen seit der Mitte des 18. Jahrhunderts. Sie befinden sich als sog. ‚Untrennbarer Bestand' in der Zweigstelle des Bundesarchivs in Frankfurt am Main. Für das 16. und 17. Jahrhundert muß man daher auf die gedruckten Quellen zurückgreifen. Damit werden wir mit der umfangreichen Literaturgattung der gedruckten zeitgenössischen Sammlungen von kammergerichtlichen Urteilen konfrontiert. Sie nehmen für jene Zeit eine zentrale Position in der kammergerichtlichen Quellenüberlieferung ein. Diese Werke sind bereits durch eine grundlegende Untersuchung von Gehrke umfassend beschrieben worden. Auch das Coing'sche Handbuch enthält hierüber eine vollständige bibliographische Dokumentation.[11] Hier ist es deshalb nicht erforderlich, ausführlich die Autoren und die Eigentüm-

[9] Die Urteile sind zumeist auch nicht im Quadrangelprotokoll verzeichnet. Zu der inneren Struktur einer kammergerichtlichen Prozeßakte vgl. *E. Weise,* Die Auswertung von Reichskammergerichtsakten, in: Der Archivar. Mitteilungen für deutsches Archivwesen 17 (1964), S. 251 - 260; *W. Deeters,* Erfahrungen aus der Verzeichnung von Reichskammergerichtsakten im Niedersächsischen Staatsarchiv in Wolfenbüttel, in: Archivalische Zeitschrift 71 (1975), S. 12ff. Für eine vollständige Edition einer kammergerichtlichen Prozeßakte vgl. *F. Battenberg,* Ein hessischer Appellationsprozeß des späten 15. Jahrhunderts. Der Streit des Marburger Bürgers Siegfried Goldschmidt mit Heinrich Bender um eine Bürgschaftregreßforderung, in: SZ Germ. Abt. 98 (1981), S. 56ff. Zu weiteren modernen Editionen von Aktenmaterial siehe die Literaturhinweise bei *Ranieri,* Recht und Gesellschaft, I, S. 27ff.

[10] Siehe die Fragmente im Frankfurter Bundesarchiv: Ältestes Urteilsbuch 1573 - 1601, Sign.: RKG. III. 1; Urteilsbuch 1631 - 1683, Sign.: RKG. III.2; zu deren privater Provenienz vgl. *B. Diestelkamp,* Der Stand der Arbeiten zur Erschließung der Quellen des Reichskammergerichts, in: Consilium Magnum. Commémoration du 500e anniversaire de la création du Parlement et du Grand Conseil de Malines. Colloque. (Bruxelles 1977), S. 199ff., insb. S. 200 Anm. 6; *derselbe,* Das Reichskammergericht im Rechtsleben des 16. Jahrhunderts, in: Rechtsgeschichte als Kulturgeschichte. Festschrift für A. Erler zum 70. Geburtstag (Aalen 1976), S. 435ff., insb. S. 443, Anm. 29; siehe auch *W. Deeters,* Erfahrungen, S. 21.

[11] Vgl. *H. Gehrke,* Die Rechtsprechung- und Konsilienliteratur Deutschlands bis zum Ende des Alten Reichs (Diss. jur. Frankfurt Main 1972); *derselbe,* Die privatrechtliche Entscheidungsliteratur Deutschlands (Frankfurt Main 1974); *derselbe,* Deutsches Reich. Rechtsprechungssammlungen, in: *H. Coing* (ed.), Handbuch der Quellen und Literatur der neueren europäischen Privatrechtsgeschichte, Bd. II.2 (München 1976), S. 1343ff., insb. S. 1362ff. zu den Quellen.

lichkeit dieser Literaturgattung vorzustellen. Auf die Untersuchung von Gehrke aufbauend und verweisend, auch für die bibliographische Dokumentation, ist es zweckmäßig, sich hier insbesondere auf die Frage zu konzentrieren, ob und inwieweit solche gedruckten Sammlungen uns die Möglichkeit eröffnen, die Rechtsprechung des Reichskammergerichts in ihren materiellrechtlichen Inhalten zu rekonstruieren und zu analysieren.

a) Die erste Form, auch in chronologischer Hinsicht, von solchen Sammlungen eignet sich für unsere Fragestellung kaum. Gehrke spricht hier von einem ‚Register-Typus'. Es handelt sich nämlich um rein registerartige Sammlungen, angelegt offenbar nach der Vorlage der Urteilsbücher, in welchen Urteile und Beschlüsse des Reichskammergerichts ohne sachlich-systematische Ordnung und ohne zusätzliche Ausführungen des Herausgebers nacheinander abgedruckt werden. Meist geschieht dies chronologisch nach der Reihenfolge ihrer Verkündung. Wiedergegeben wird nur der Wortlaut des vom Gericht verabschiedeten Entscheidungsspruchs; Angaben zu Parteien und Sachverhalt fehlen völlig. In den frühen Sammlungen von Seylern und von Barth[12] mit Entscheidungsmaterial aus dem 16. Jahrhundert, werden die Parteien lediglich mit Anfangsbuchstaben gekennzeichnet. Aus dem 17. Jahrhundert liegen die Urteilssammlungen von Blum und von Deckherr[13]

---

[12] Vgl. *Barth, Christian:* Urtheil und Beschaydt am Hochlöblichen Kayserlichen Cammergericht vom Jahr 1495, als dasselbe angefangen/ eröffnet. Hiervor/ zum theil/ durch weylandt Herrn Raphael Seylern ... in Druck gefertigt/ jetzundt aber alles von newem ersehen/ vermehrt/ ergäntzt/ und ferner continuirt (Speyer 1604 - 1605) (dazu *H. Gehrke,* Die Rechtsprechungs- und Konsilienliteratur, S. 126; *derselbe,* Handbuch, II.2, ad vocem); *Seiler, Raphael:* Camergerichts Bei unnd end urthail. Selectissimarum sententiarum in amplissimo summoque sacrae imperialis camerae iudicio, ab anno domini MCCCCXCV. usque ad annum MDLXX. inclusive, publicatarum: ... Die fürnembsten und herrlichsten an dem hochlöblichsten des heiligen Römischen Reich in Deutscher Nation/ Keyserlichen Chammergericht/ vom Jahr 1495. biß auff das Jar 1570 (alles einschließlich) eröffnete Bey und Endurtheil. 3 Teile (Frankfurt M. 1572 - 1573) (dazu *H. Gehrke,* Die Rechtsprechungs- und Konsilienliteratur, S. 126; *derselbe,* Handbuch, II.2, ad vocem).

[13] Vgl. *Blum, Jacob:* Chilias sententiarum cameralium. Das ist: Tausend der fürnemsten und merckwürdigsten/ auff das Concept der erneuerten Cammer-Gerichts-Ordnung/ Reichs-Abschied de Anno 1654. letztere Gemeine Bescheide/ auch jetzigen Stylum gerichteter/ und von besagtem 1654, biß 1664sten Jahr am Hochlöbl. Kayserl. Cammer-Gericht gerichtlich eröffneter/ durch ernannten Authorem außerlesener Urteiln. Denen hinbeygethan eine Zugabe von Hundert dergleichen Urtheiln Anno 1665. ergangen. (Wetzlar 1720) (dazu *H. Gehrke,* Die Rechtsprechungs- und Konsilienliteratur, S. 127; *derselbe,* Handbuch, II.2, ad vocem); *Deckherr, Johann:* Rerum in supremo camerae imperialis iudicii senatu judicatarum duodecennalis periodus: Das ist: An dem Hochlöblichen Kayserlichen und des Heil. Röm. Reichs Cammer-Gericht von dem 1666sten Jahr/ in welchem sich Weyl. Hn. Jacobi Blumen publicirte und Gerichtlich eröffnete Tausend fürneme und merckwürdige Urtheil (Wetzlar 1725) (dazu *H. Gehrke,* Die Rechtsprechungs- und Konsilienliteratur, S. 127; *derselbe,* Handbuch, II.2, ad vocem).

vor; sie wurden ebenfalls nach der Vorlage der Urteilsbücher angelegt. In der Sammlung von Deckherr – die eine Fortsetzung der ersteren darstellt – werden die Namen der Prozeßparteien erstmals angegeben. Selbst bei dieser Sammlung ist es aber sehr mühsam, die Entscheidungen mit den Angaben aus der archivalischen Überlieferung in Übereinstimmung zu bringen. Das Problem von solchen gedruckten Sammlungen liegt also darin, daß ohne jegliche Angaben zu Parteien, Sachverhalt sowie Prozeßverlauf dieses Material sich für unsere Fragestellung kaum verwerten läßt. Diese registerartigen Urteilssammlungen scheinen eher eine Modellfunktion gehabt zu haben. Der Abdruck des Entscheidungstenors allein hatte nämlich nur einen Sinn, wenn man annimmt, daß solche Einträge offenbar als Modell bei der Ausfertigung von vergleichbaren Gerichtsverfügungen dienten. Diese wichtige und bisher, soweit ich sehe, übersehene Funktion dieser damaligen gedruckten Sammlungen von Urteilsregistern ist noch nicht im einzelnen untersucht worden.[14]

b) Die deutsche gemeinrechtliche Literatur des 16. und 17. Jahrhunderts kennt darüber hinaus zahlreiche Werke, in denen die von der Speyerer Gerichtsinstanz angewandten und entwickelten materiellen und prozessualen Rechtsregeln im systematischen Zusammenhang dargestellt werden. Bei der Heranziehung dieser Werke der Kameralliteratur begegnet der Benutzer allerdings fast immer ähnlichen Schwierigkeiten wie den soeben beschriebenen. Auch die berühmten Sammlungen von Gail und Mynsinger[15] eignen sich nicht zur Rekonstruktion der Entscheidung im einzelnen Prozeß. Auch hier nämlich werden die Einzelheiten zum Sachverhalt sowie die spezifischen Erwägungen bei den Entscheidungsgründen des einzelnen Urteils in der Regel nicht mitgeteilt. Ferner fehlen bei den nachgewiesenen Urteilen die Parteinamen völlig oder diese sind auf ihre Initialen abgekürzt und insoweit unkenntlich; infolgedessen ist eine genauere Identifizierung des Verfahrens meistens ganz unmöglich, obwohl das Publikationsdatum des Urteils in solchen Werken in der Regel erwähnt wird[16]. Es handelt sich hier also viel-

---

[14] Siehe hierzu allerding die Hinweise von *H. Gehrke,* Die privatrechtliche Entscheidungsliteratur, Teil I, II, B 2a.

[15] *Gail, Andreas:* Practicarum observationum, tam ad processum iudiciarium, praesertim imperialis camerae, quam ad causarum decisiones pertinentium, libri duo (Köln 1580) (dazu *H. Gehrke,* Die Rechtsprechungs- und Konsilienliteratur, S. 175; *derselbe,* Handbuch, II.2, ad vocem, insb. S. 1363; *W. Sellert,* ‚Andreas Gail', in: HRG, I (Berlin 1971), Sp. 1371 ff.; grundlegend neuerdings *K. v. Kempis,* Andreas Gaill. 1526 - 1587 (Frankfurt M.-Bern 1988), insb. zum Werk S. 178 ff.); *Mynsinger von Frundeck, Joachim:* Singularium observationum iudicij imperialis camerae (uti vocant) centuriae quator (Basel 1563) (dazu *H. Gehrke,* Die Rechtsprechungs- und Konsilienliteratur, S. 174; *derselbe,* Die privatrechtliche Entscheidungsliteratur, S. 36; *derselbe,* Handbuch, II.2, ad vocem, insb. S. 1362).

[16] Zu den Observationen von Andreas Gail und dessen Technik bei der Wiedergabe des Entscheidungsmaterials vgl. *K. v. Kempis,* Andreas Gaill, S. 213 - 218;

mehr nur um eine systematisch angelegte Kompilation der Rechtsregeln, welche in der kammergerichtlichen Judikatur jener Zeit Anwendung fanden.

2. Neben den gedruckten kennt die gemeinrechtliche Literatur auch zahlreiche nur handschriftlich überlieferte Sammlungen, wo die privaten Aufzeichnungen der Assessoren aus ihren Beratungen und Sitzungen während ihrer Speyerer Tätigkeit am Reichskammergericht uns aufbewahrt werden. Es ist davon auszugehen, daß auch die meisten gedruckten Sammlungen zunächst aus derartigen handschriftlichen Arbeitsaufzeichnungen ihrer Verfasser hervorgegangen sind. Ein wesentlicher Verdienst, auf diese Quellen aufmerksam gemacht zu haben, gebührt Nève und Sprenger. Die letzte hat neuerdings die Protokolle und Auszüge aus den kammergerichtlichen Beratungen und Urteilsbüchern, welche der Assessor Viglius von Aytta während seiner Tätigkeit in Speyer in den ersten Jahrzehnten des 16.Jahrhunderts aufgezeichnet hatte, vollständig verzeichnet.[17] Einige von solchen Beratungsprotokollen sind inzwischen ebenfalls vollständig ediert worden.[18] Vergleichbare handschriftliche Aufzeichnungen sind uns für die Assessoren Matheus Neser[19], Adam Mörder[20] und Mathias Alber[21] bekannt. Eine

---

siehe hier auch, S. 272 - 278, ein alphabetisches Verzeichnis der ermittelten kammergerichtlichen Verfahren.

[17] Vgl. *R. M. Sprenger,* Viglius von Aytta und seine Notizen über Beratungen am Reichskammergericht. 1535 - 1537 (Nijmegen 1988), insb. S. 105 - 283 mit dem Register aller in den Aufzeichnungen erwähnten Verfahren; verdienstvoll ist hier der Nachweis von Parallelaufzeichnungen in den Handschriften anderer Assessoren sowie der erhalten gebliebenen Prozeßakten. Zu den Handschriften in der Bibliothèque Royale de Belgique mit den Aufzeichnungen von Viglius siehe *P. Nève,* Viglius von Aytta Berichterstatter des RKG, in: Akten des Colloquiums Rechtsbehelfe, Beweis und Stellung des Richters im Spätmittelalter und der frühen Neuzeit (Köln-Wien 1985), S. 35 - 55.

[18] Siehe etwa *R. M. Sprenger/A. Wijffels,* De actio quanti minoris in de praktijk van het Rijkskamergerecht ca. 1535. Uit de aantekeningen van Viglius van Aytta, in: Lopend rechtshistorisch onderzoek. Handelingen van het tiende Belgisch-Nederlands rechtshistorisch colloquium, *D. Lambrecht* ed. (Brussel 1990), S. 129ff., insbesondere S. 136 - 159 für die Edition; *R. Sprenger,* L'autorité de la communis opinio dans la pratique de la Chambre Impériale de justice (c. 1535): une application de l'actio quanti minoris, in: Miscellanea Consilii Magni III, bereits zit., S. 161 - 164; *dieselbe,* L'emploi du temps à la Chambre impériale de justice à l'epoque de Viglius, ebendort, S. 141 - 144.

[19] Vgl. Bundesarchiv, Zweigstelle Frankfurt Main, unter RKG.Miscellanea Nr. 530; dazu *P. Richter,* Register und Protokolle des RKG als Geschichtsquellen, in: Korrespondenzblatt des Gesamtvereins der deutschen Geschichts- und Altertumsvereine 70 (1922), S. 41 - 49; *derselbe,* Aus dem Reichskammergerichts-Protokoll des Assessors Matheus Neser (1536 - 1544), in: Historische Zeitschrift 29 (1922), S. 439 - 457.

[20] Dazu *H. Rabe,* Der Augsburger Religionsfriede und das Reichskammergericht. 1555 - 1600, in: Festgabe für E. W. Zeeden (Münster 1976), S. 260 - 280. Vgl. ferner die Materialien des Assessors Conrad Büntig (1569 - 1570), vorh. im Landesar-

umfassende Erschließung solcher Sammlungen in den einzelnen Bibliotheks- und Archivbeständen steht allerdings noch aus; dasselbe gilt auch für eine annähernd vollständige Bibliographie der rechtshistorischen Untersuchungen, die zu solchen handschriftlichen Materialien bereits existieren.[22]

II.

1. Ganz anders charakterisiert sich die Quellenlage, wenn man die Aktenrelationen und die Voten der Assessoren heranzieht. Bei den Aktenrelationen werden wir mit einer der wichtigsten Quelle konfrontiert, welche uns die gemeinrechtliche Literatur für die Analyse der richterlichen Arbeitstechnik am Reichskammergericht bietet. Davon existieren zahlreiche gedruckte Sammlungen. Hier seien etwa die Werke von Meichsner, Klock, Thülemar, Ludolf und einigen anderen[23] zeitgenössischen Autoren genannt.

---

chiv Hannover unter: MS. XIII, 817 = MS. II, 276 sowie die Aufzeichnungen von Christoph Hoos (Advokat am Reichskammergericht 1522 - 1546), vorh. in der UB Basel, unter MS. C. VI b, 6 - 12 (früher C. VI.20).

[21] Vorh. in der UB Innsbruck, unter MS. Sig. 176; dazu *G. Dolezalek,* Die Assessoren des Reichskammergerichts und der Nürnberger Religionsfriede vom 23. Juli 1532, in: *G. Dilcher/B. Diestelkamp* (ed.), Recht, Gericht, Genossenschaft und Policey. Studien zu Grundbegriffen der germanistischen Rechtshistorie. Symposion für A. Erler (Berlin 1986), S. 84 - 96.

[22] Für erste Hinweise vgl. *F. Ranieri,* Die archivalischen und literarischen Quellen aus der Judikatur des Reichskammergerichts (16. - 17. Jahrhundert), in: *J. H. Baker* (ed.), Judicial Records, Law Reports and the Growth of Case Law (Berlin 1989), S. 303 - 317, insb. S. 310 Anm. 22; *B. Diestelkamp,* Der Stand der Arbeiten, S. 203 Anm. 24 und S. 206 - 207 Anm. 40; *P. Nève,* Das Plenum des Reichskammergerichts als Spruchkörper. Zwei Jahre während des ‚rechtlichen Krieges', in: Recht und Staat im sozialen Wandel. Festschrift für H. U. Scupin (Berlin 1983), S. 145 - 160.

[23] *Deckherr, Johann:* Relationum, votorum, et decisionum augustiss. imp. camerae iudicii liber singularis (Speyer 1681) (dazu *H. Gehrke,* Die Rechtsprechungs- und Konsilienliteratur, S. 151; *derselbe,* Handbuch, II.2, ad vocem, insb. S. 1366); *Hofmann, Johann Friedrich:* Relationes camerales novissimae ab augustissimi camerae imperialis judicii Dd. assessoribus et assessoratus candidatis elaboratae, in quibus moderna juris et processus cameralis ratio ... selectissima dispositione continetur (Wetzlar 1691) (dazu *H. Gehrke,* Die Rechtsprechungs- und Konsilienliteratur, S. 151; *derselbe,* Handbuch, II.2, ad vocem); *Klock, Caspar:* Liber singularis relationum pro adsessoratu habitarum, nec non insigniorum votorum, decisionum et rerum in camera imperiali ab anno MDC. et quod excurrit, ad hanc usque eatatem judicatarum (Frankfurt 1653) (dazu *H. Gehrke,* Die Rechtsprechungs- und Konsilienliteratur, S. 149; *derselbe,* Handbuch, II.2, ad vocem); *Ludolf, Georg Melchior von:* Symphorema consultationum et decisionum forensium, I - III (Frankfurt/M. 1731 - 1739) (dazu *H. Gehrke,* Die Rechtsprechungs- und Konsilienliteratur, S. 160; *derselbe,* Handbuch, II.2, ad vocem, insb. S. 1368); *Meichsner, Johann:* Decisionum diversarum causarum in camera imperiali judicatarum, adjunctis votis et relationibus,..., tomus I. Vortitel: Decisionum cameralium tomi quatuor, I - IV (Ed. Nico-

Diese Sammlungen sind in der Regel so aufgebaut, daß zu den einzelnen Entscheidungen der jeweilige Prozeßstoff eines kammergerichtlichen Rechtsstreits teilsweise, manchmal sogar vollständig, wiedergegeben wird. In einigen Fällen wird sogar der gesamte Akteninhalt – Appellationslibell, anwältliche Prozeßschriften, rotuli testium sowie die produzierten urkundlichen Beilagen – vollständig, nicht selten in unübersichtlicher Form, nachgedruckt; ebenso werden anschliessend die Aktenrelationen und die Voten der beteiligten Assessoren sowie der Spruchtenor der kammergerichtlichen Entscheidung mit seinem Verkündungsdatum publiziert. Bereits in der Sammlung von Meichsner – das früheste der Werke dieser Art – werden die Namen der Prozeßparteien sowie der beteiligten Anwälte, Prokuratoren und Assessoren vollständig wiedergegeben. Die Identifizierung eines aus den Aktenrepertorien bekannten Prozesses mit einem Fall in einer solchen Sammlung ist insoweit – zumindest bei einer verhältnismäßig guten Kenntnis der archivalischen Überlieferung – ohne große Schwierigkeiten möglich. Im Dokumentationsteil wird unter anderem eine kammergerichtliche Aktenrelation aus der zweiten Hälfte des 16. Jahrhunderts gerade aus der genannten Sammlung von Meichsner abgedruckt. Die Aktenrelationen und die Voten des Assessoren am Reichskammergericht sind für unsere Fragestellung in doppelter Hinsicht von zentraler Bedeutung.

2. Sie eröffnen uns zunächst den Weg, um die Argumentations- und Arbeitsweise der gemeinrechtlichen Richter jener Zeit genau nachvollziehen zu können.[24] Die Entfaltung von Richterrecht in der Judikatur eines Gerichtshofes wird dann besonders deutlich, wenn das Gericht bei der Entscheidungsfindung argumentativ auf eigene Präjudizien zurückgreift. Aktenrelationen und Voten der Assessoren beleuchten uns gerade diesen Aspekt der damaligen richterlichen Argumentationtechnik. Eine enge Bindungwirkung der ‚consuetudo judicandi', im Sinne, daß Präjudizien strikt in künftigen gleichgelagerten Fällen verbindlich seien, wurde zwar in der damaligen gemeinrechtlichen Lehre von niemandem vertreten.[25] Vereinzelt findet man jedoch diese Ansicht bereits in Voten von Assessoren am Reichskam-

---

laus Thessmer, Frankfurt 1688) (dazu *H. Gehrke,* Die Rechtsprechungs- und Konsilienliteratur, S. 148 - 149; *derselbe,* Handbuch, II.2, ad vocem); *Thülemar, Heinrich Günther:* Relationum, decisionum et votorum, ab augustissimi ac supremi camerae imperialis judicii ... assessoribus, et ... assessoratus candidatis elaboratorum et propositorum opus, in duas partes distributum (Frankfurt und Wetzlar 1696) (dazu *H. Gehrke,* Die Rechtsprechungs- und Konsilienliteratur, S. 151 - 152; *derselbe,* Handbuch, II.2, ad vocem).

[24] Vgl. die zutreffenden Bemerkungen hierüber von *A. Wijffels,* L'influence de la doctrine sur l'argumentation judiciaire au début des Temps Modernes, in: Miscellanea Consilii Magni III, bereits zit., S. 145 ff., insb. S. 146 ff.

[25] Zum Diskussionsstand in der gemeinrechtlichen Literatur der Zeit vgl. *H. Weller,* Die Bedeutung der Präjudizien, S. 60 ff.; *K. v. Kempis,* Andreas Gail, S. 208 ff.; allgemein *J. P. Dawson,* The oracles of the law (Ann Harbor 1968), S. 225.

mergericht im 16. und 17. Jahrhundert. Die Aktenrelationen und die Voten erweisen sich dabei als eine einmalige und unverzichtbare Quelle für die Analyse der zur Entscheidungsfindung herangezogenen Argumente im einzelnen Streitfall. Besonders augenfällig ist ein solcher argumentativer Rückgriff auf die ausführliche Erörterung von bereits entschiedenen Parallelfällen in den Aktenrelationen eines Assessors des 16. Jahrhunderts, Caspar Klock, zu verfolgen. Der Aktenreferent verdeutlicht dabei gelegentlich die anfallende Rechtsfrage mit Hinweisen auf frühere, vor der Speyerer Instanz bereits ausgetragenen Rechtsfälle, die durch genaue Parteibezeichnung nachgewiesen werden. Die Rechtsausführungen des Assessors in seiner Aktenrelation machen deutlich den fallbezogenen Arbeits- und Argumentationsstils der gemeinrechtlichen Juristen jener Zeit.[26] „Firmat meam decisionem praejudicium in causa Baden contra die Graffen zu Stolberg – heißt es etwa in einem Votum[27] – ubi dicti Senatus itidem in terminis venditionis redituum venditores facti, non obstante, quod non adeo fortiter obstricti essent, atque nostri Bürgermeister und Rath; item non obstante, quod similiter exceperint, quod nihil perceperint de pecunia vel precio; attamen non exauditi, sed condemnati in solutionem,... fuerunt;... Et quod haec ita comparata sint, praelegam dominis ex praejudicio aliquo, ad hoc pertinenti,...“. Der Parallelfall soll den für richtig befundenen Urteilsvorschlag durch den Nachweis absichern, daß er in Übereinstimmung zur bisherigen kammergerichtlichen Judikatur steht. Solche Voten machen ferner besonders deutlich, daß die damalige richterliche Argumentationsweise auch eine präzise Analyse der herangezogenen Parallelpräjudizien voraussetzte. Es fehlt nämlich gelegentlich auch nicht der Hinweis, daß sich der herangezogene Parallelfall in tatsächlicher oder rechtlicher Hinsicht von dem erörterten Sachverhalt unterscheidet. „Ad praeiudicium a domino Reo conventi in causa Domini Christophori von Bolstatt contra Dominum Abbatem zu Kempten allegatum... – heißt es in einer anderen Aktenrelation[28] – is casus longe diversus est a nostro... Diversum est in casu nostro ubi actores non tantum feudi regulariter capaces sunt, sed etiam in continenti titulum possessionis produxerunt, per quem possessionem justificarunt, et consolidationem naturalis possessionis cum civili impediverunt: quod eo in casu, quo praeiudicium est allegatum, factum non constat. Ut interim taceam valde periculosum esse, praeiudicia in iudicando absque inspectione actorum

---

[26] Vgl. dazu grundlegend *H. Coing*, Europäisches Privatrecht, I. Älteres Gemeines Recht. 1500 - 1800 (München 1985), S. 125 - 126 m.w.N.

[27] So *C. Klock*, Relatio XLIX, Additio Dom. Awers ad votum ad hanc causam ex causa Baden contra Stolberg, in Liber singularis relationum, S. 471.

[28] So Relatio V. nob. Dom. Werneri a Rust., in *C. Klock*, a.a.O., S. 125 Rdn. 431 ff. Siehe auch *J. Blum*, Processus cameralis (Köln 1703), S. 10: „...Nam si casus ante decisus a jam decidendo etiam in minimo differat, allegatum Praejudicium nihil relevat“.

sequi. Levis enim circumstantia vel defectus juris aut facti judicem ad ita pronunciandum movere potuit, qui si non adfuisset, forte aliter pronunciaret". Die rechtshistorische Forschung hat sich bisher mit solchen Quellen kaum beschäftigt. Sie würden uns den judiziellen Charakter des damaligen römischen Gemeinen Rechts deutlich machen. „Quantacumque etiam sit rerum judicatarum auctoritas, – schreibt bezeichnenderweise einige Jahrzehnte später ein Assessor am Reichskammergericht im Vorwort zu seiner Sammlung von Voten und Aktenrelationen[29] – numquam tamen est tanta exemplorum singularium, quae praejudicia vocantur, ut rationes vincant meliores, faciuntque in aliis, specie externa similibus, tempore statuque rerum publica diversis, judicandi regulam". Diese Ansicht sieht unserer Autor gerade in der Praxis des damaligen Reichskammergerichts bestätigt. Die von ihm publizierten Relationen und Voten seien der Beweis, daß die Assessoren von den in Präjudizien ihrer Vorgänger aufgestellten Rechtssätze immer erst nach reiflicher Überlegung im Einzelfall abgewichen wären. „Sic etiam – so Ludolf[30] – constaret publice, ab Antecessorum industria non recessisse Assessores modernos, defungi eos labore non levi et transitorio, sed cum meditatione matura et maxime ardua...". Das Reichskammergericht würde seine Präjudizien als bindend ansehen, solange keine besseren Gründe vorlägen. Weller zeigt in seiner bereits zitierten Untersuchung, daß bezeichnenderweise niemand in der damaligen gemeinrechtlichen Literatur gegen die ‚auctoritas rerum perpetuo similiter judicatarum' mit dem ‚Hinweis argumentierte, in Anbetracht der Bestimmung zur Geheimhaltung sei die für die Präjudizienbindung unerläßliche Wiedergabe der Entscheidungen im Original nicht gewährleistet'. Dies belege – so Weller – ‚um so mehr, daß die Authentizität der öffiziösen Judikatursammlungen außer Zweifel stand'.[31]

III.

1. Ein zweiter, vielleicht noch wichtiger Gesichtspunkt kommt bei diesen Sammlungen hinzu: die kammergerichtlichen Aktenrelationen und Voten stellen nämlich eine bedeutsame historische Quelle auch in methodischer Hinsicht dar. Es geht hier um die sukzessive historische Entwicklung in der deutschen Rechtstradition einer spezifischen richterlichen Arbeits- und Argumentationstechnik, insbesondere um die Ausformung einer besonderen Arbeitsmethode bei der Erörterung der anfallenden Rechts- und Sachfragen. Das Reichskammergericht steht hier am Anfang einer methodischer Tradi-

---

[29] So *G. M. von Ludolf,* Symphorema consultationum et decisionum forensium, I (Frankfurt Main 1731), praefatio.

[30] So *G. M. von Ludolf,* a.a.O.

[31] So *H. Weller,* Die Bedeutung der Präjudizien, S. 64.

tion, welche bis in die heutige Zeit der deutschen Juristen- und Justizausbildung reicht. Die Schriftlichkeit und der mittelbare Charakter des Verfahrens im römischen gemeinen Prozeß, sowie die kollegiale Struktur der Speyerer Gerichtsinstanz haben hier Technik und Stil der Entscheidungsfindung mitgeprägt. Im Zentrum der richterlichen Aufgabe eines Assessors am Reichskammergericht stand das Verfassen einer Relation aus einer Prozeßakte. Die einzelnen Produkte der Prozeßparteien wurden vom Kanzleipersonal in Speyer erst überhaupt zu einem Prozeßdossier zusammengestellt, wenn der Rechtsstreit als entscheidungsreif für eine Relation vor dem Kollegium anstand.[32] Die Notwendigkeit nämlich, das Kollegialgericht über einen Prozeß zu informieren, machte es erforderlich, daß ein Assessor als Relator ein Referat, eine sogenannte *relatio,* zum Inhalt der schriftlichen Prozeßakte anfertigte und den Kollegen vortrug. Bereits in der KGO von 1500 heißt es, „... daß in allen Sachen die Besichtigung der Acten und Gerichtshandlungen, so zu Schöpfung der Urtheile nothdürftig sind, allezeit zum wenigsten zwey Assessoren oder Urtheiler ... befohlen werden, also daß jeder der zwey diesselben Acten, einer nach dem andern lesen, nothdürftig besichtigen, ermessen, und allsdann die Relation davon thun solle ...".[33] In der KGO von 1555 hieß es noch bestimmter, „... der Cammerrichter solle die Acten ... jederzeit zwey Assessoren zu referiren geben" und ferner, daß „die Relation durch sie sämtlich geschehen (solle), und von den Beysitzern keiner, sonderlich deren, die erst neu ankommen, oder des Referirens sonst nicht gar geübt, alleine ohne einen Correferenten zugelassen werden".[34] In den ersten Ordnungen des Reichskammergerichts, selbst in der sonst ausführlichen KGO von 1555, finden sich sonst keine methodischen Regelungen über die Anfertigung von Aktenrelationen. Erst im Jüngsten Reichsabschied von 1654, stößt man in den §§ 143 - 150 auf umfangreichere Bestimmungen, die sich auf die am Reichskammergericht gehaltenen Relationen beziehen.[35] Auch diese Vorschriften betreffen jedoch den äußerlichen Verlauf der Relation; die materielle Ausgestaltung bei der Anfertigung von Relation und Votum blieb den Regeln aus Praxis und Tradition überlassen. Von einer älteren Dissertation von Berger abgesehen, steht die historische und methodische Analyse dieser ‚Relationstechnik' noch aus.[36] Die

---

[32] Zum sog. ‚Komplieren' der Akten in der Praxis der Speyerer Kanzlei vgl. *H. L. Berger,* Die Entwicklung der zivilrechtlichen Relationen und ihrer denktechnisch-methodischen Argumentationsformen (Diss. jur. Frankfurt Main 1975), insb. S. 90 Anm. 1 m.w.N.

[33] Vgl. KGO von 1500 Tit. 18 (wiederholt in der KGO von 1555, Theil I, Tit. 13 § 9); dazu *H. L. Berger,* Die Entwicklung, S. 22 Anm. 1.

[34] Vgl. KGO von 1555, Theil I, Tit. 10, § 4; hierzu Berger, a.a.O.

[35] Abgedruckt bei *Berger,* a.a.O., Anlage I, S. 154 - 155.

[36] Vgl. *H. L. Berger,* Die Entwicklung der zivilrechtlichen Relationen, bereits oben zit., insb. S. 17 - 58 zur Speyerer Zeit des Reichskammergerichts; siehe ferner

bereits erwähnten Sammlungen von Relationen und Voten dürften daher auch für dieses rechtshistorische Forschungsthema eine unverzichtbare Quelle darstellen.

Bereits im 16. Jahrhundert wurden für eine solche Technik der Anfertigung einer Aktenrelation strenge Aufbauregeln entwickelt. Ein derartiger Regelkomplex steht wohl im Zusammenhang mit der methodischen Tradition der Consiliatoren des mos italicus und mit der gemeinrechtlichen Lehrtradition jener Zeit. Dies fand bald seinen literarischen Niederschlag in den prozessualen und praktischen Werken der Rezeptionszeit, die zahlreiche Anleitungsschriften zur Anfertigung einer Aktenrelation kennen. Das Ausbildungsziel stand hier eindeutig im Vordergrund. Eine ähnliche Ausbildungsfunktion erfüllten offenbar auch die bereits genannten Sammlungen von Relationen: die Aktenrelationen der Assessoren am Reichskammergericht dienten hier als Vorbild, und in der Tat gehen auch die praktischen Anleitungsschriften meistens auf die oben erwähnten Sammlungen zurück. Gerade darin wird eine der wesentlichen Funktionen verständlich, welche solche Sammlungen in der Perspektive der Zeitgenossen erfüllten: Sie lieferten nämlich Modelle und Beispiele für die Ausbildung in einer solchen Arbeitstechnik. Die pädagogische Funktion solcher Werke wird besonders deutlich, wenn man ferner beachtet, daß gelegentlich auch sog. ‚Proberelationen' in diesen Sammlungen abgedruckt wurden: es handelt sich dabei um Aktenrelationen, welche Kandidaten für das Amt des Assessorats am Reichskammergericht, die eine ‚Praesentation' erhalten hatten, als Nachweis ihrer Befähigung für die richterliche Tätigkeit anzufertigen und abzuhalten hatten. Solche Proberelationen finden sich seit 1570; hierfür wurden meistens echte kammergerichtliche Prozeßakten zugrundegelegt.[37] Zeugnisse

---

H. Gehrke, Die Rechtsprechungs- und Konsilienliteratur, S. 78 ff.; *J. Schröder,* Wissenschaftstheorie und Lehre der ‚praktischen Jurisprudenz' auf deutschen Universitäten an der Wende zum 19. Jahrhundert (Frankfurt Main 1979), S. 60 - 64; *W. Hulle/ W. Sellert,* Relation, in: HRG, V (Berlin 1987), insb. S. 862 mit einer ausführlichen Bibliographie; *W. Schild,* Relationen und Referierkunst. Zur Juristenausbildung und zum Strafverfahren um 1790, in: *J. Schönert u. a.* (ed.), Erzählte Kriminalität (Tübingen 1991), S. 159 - 176; *E. Meyer-Krentler,* Geschichtserzählungen. Zur Poetik des Sachverhalts im juristischen Schriftum des 18. Jahrhunderts, ebendort; *L. Hoffmann,* Vom Ereignis zum Fall. Sprachliche Muster zur Darstellung und Überprüfung von Sachverhalten vor Gericht, ebendort, S. 87 - 113; *J. Rückert,* Zur Rolle der Fallgeschichte in Juristenausbildung und juristischer Praxis zwischen 1790 und 1880, ebendort, S. 285 - 311. Für historische und vergleichende Hinweise hierüber siehe *F. Ranieri,* Stilus Curiae. Zum historischen Hintergrund der Relationstechnik, in: Rechtshistorisches Journal 4 (1985), S. 75 - 88 umfassend und m. w. N.; *derselbe,* El estilo judicial espanol y su influencia en la Europa del antiguo regimen, in: Espana y Europa. Un pasado juridico comun, *A. Perez Martin* ed. (Murcia 1986), S. 101 - 118.

37 Hierzu vgl. *R. Smend,* Das Reichskammergericht (Weimar 1911), S. 304. Allgemein zu der Einführung von ‚Proberelationen' bei der zunehmenden Professiona-

einer solchen literarisch-pädagogischen Tradition lassen sich bereits in der deutschen prozeßrechtlichen Literatur der zweiten Hälfte des 16. Jahrhunderts nachweisen. Später wird die Anzahl dieser Anleitungsschriften unübersehbar. Berger erwähnt in seiner – übrigens keineswegs vollständigen – Bibliographie dazu mehr als zwanzig solcher Werke aus dem 17. und 18. Jahrhundert.[38]

Im Dokumentationsteil zu diesem Beitrag wird als ergänzende Erläuterung zu den Ausführungen hier, zunächst ein Abschnitt aus einer Lehrschrift am Ende des 16. Jahrhunderts abgedruckt: man findet dort Anleitungshinweise zur Anfertigung einer Aktenrelation, wie man sie in einem beliebigen Lehr- und Anleitungsbuch über die prozessuale Praxis des Reichskammergerichts Ende des 16., Anfang des 17. Jahrhunderts lesen konnte;[39] der Verfasser, den wir nur unter einem Pseudonym kennen, war vermutlich ein Prokurator oder Notar am Speyerer Reichskammergericht[40]. Es folgt anschließend der Abdruck, fast im vollen Umfang, von zwei Aktenrelationen. Die erste stammt aus der Sammlung des Assessors Johann Meichsner und wohl auch aus dessen Feder;[41] sie betrifft eine kammergerichtliche Appellation in einem Erbrechtsprozeß aus Vorpommern aus der zweiten Hälfte des 16. Jahrhunderts, das auch hinsichtlich der aufgeworfenen Rechtsfragen rechtshistorisch beachtenswert ist.[42] Die zweite, in deut-

---

lisierung des Justizpersonals in den deutschen Territorien vgl. *U. Bake,* Die Entstehung des dualistischen Systems der Juristenausbildung in Preußen (Diss. jur. Kiel 1971), S. 6 - 13 zu der preußischen Justizreform.

[38] Vgl. etwa die Angabe infra in Anm. 39; vgl. ferner *Cramer, Johann Ulrich:* Quaenam relationi in supremis Imperii Tribunalibus praemittenda sint, in: Cramer, Oberservationes juris ... Theil I, Nr. 317, S. 710, Ulm 1758; *Hartling, Johann Friedrich:* Dissertatio de arte referendi (Heidelberg 1733); *Homburg, Andreas:* De modo (artis) referendi (Helmstedt 1710); *Knorren, Karl Gottlieb:* Anleitung zu Referirung der Acten (Halle 1755); *Lauremberg, Jacob Sebastian:* Dissertatio de actorum lectione et relatione, nec non sententiarum ex illis conceptione (Rostock 1667).

[39] Vgl. *H. E. Rosencorb* (Rosacorb), Syntagma observationum practicarum recentiorum in supremis Germaniae tribunalibus (Mühlhausen 1605; Frankfurt Main 1646), cap. II, S. 2 - 4 ‚methodus referendi, seu vota concipiendi'. Siehe ferner den Tractatus methodicus processi Camerae Imperialis, in: Symphorema Consultationibus, I (Frankfurt Main 1601), S. 70 - 72 ‚methodus referendi causas in iudicio'; aus späterer Zeit vgl. *H. Bocer,* Disputationum de universo quo utimur iure methodo eleganti conscriptarum, ed. tertia (Argentorati 1634), Classis VI, Disputatio III, S. 349ff. mit dem Titel ‚modus referendi'; *Ch. Besold,* De iudiciario processu et modo referendi seu votandi Dissertatio (Tübingen 1632 und Nürnberg 1641).

[40] Zu Person und Werk vgl. *H. Gehrke,* Die Rechtsprechungs- und Konsilienliteratur, S. 180 m.w.N.

[41] Zu Person und Werk vgl. *H. Gehrke,* a.a.O., S. 148 - 149.

[42] Im einzelnen hierüber siehe *F. Ranieri,* Diritto comune e diritto locale nei primi decenni della giurisprudenza del Reichskammergericht. Alcune prospettive di ricerca, in: Diritto comune e diritti locali nella storia dell'Europa. Atti del Convegno di Varenna (Milano 1980), S. 71ff., insb. S. 80.

scher Sprache verfaßt, ist aus der Sammlung von Johann Otto Tabor übernommen; sie wurde wohl vom Verfasser selbst als Mitglied des höchsten Straßburger Gerichtshofes Mitte des 17. Jahrhunderts angefertigt und vorgetragen;[43] sie bietet zugleich ein gutes Beispiel dafür, wie die kammergerichtliche Praxis der Aktenrelation auch bei den übrigen zeitgenössischen Gerichtshöfen im Alten Reich Eingang fand.[44]

2. Die Anleitungen zur Anfertigung einer Aktenrelation und eines Votums sind im 16. und 17. Jahrhundert weitgehend einheitlich verfaßt: Im wesentlichen wurden darin strenge Regeln zum logischen und sytaktischen Aufbau und zur Formulierung eines solchen Votums vermittelt. Eine kammergerichtliche Aktenrelation strukturierte sich in jener Zeit etwa folgendermaßen.[45] Dabei sei vorsorglich darauf hingewiesen, daß, insbesondere im 16. Jahrhundert, die Zahl und die Untergliederung der vorgeschlagenen Aufbaustationen von Anleitung zu Anleitung durchaus variieren kann.

a) species facti.

Hierunter wurden die Umstände verstanden, welche der prozessualen Auseinandersetzung zugrundelagen. „Inprimis ordo naturae postulat, – schreibt z. B. in seiner Anleitung Besold[46] – ut casus seu facti species, die Herkommenheit deß Hauptstreits nostris dicta, in primo limine relationis, quantum fieri potest breviter ac plenarie narretur,...“. Anschließend folgte eine Prüfung der formellen Verfahrensvorausssetzungen: „Cognita facti species, – schreibt der bereits zitierte Autor[47] – proxima et secunda inspectio est, num processus Iudicarius rite sit observatus,...“. Zu diesem Aufbaupunkt gehörte die Erörterung der Zuständigkeit des Gerichts, der Legitimation von Parteien und Prokuratoren sowie der Ordnungsmäßigkeit der Ladungen.[48]

b) historia processus.

Hierunter wurde meistens die kurze Aufzählung der verschiedenen Verfahrensstationen in den vorangegangenen Instanzen sowie im kammergerichtlichen Appellationsverfahren verstanden.

---

43 Zu Person und Werk vgl. *H. Gehrke*, a. a. O., S. 150.

44 Zur Übernahme des ‚modus spirensis‘ bei den bayerischen Hofräten, vgl. *R. Heydenreuter*, Der landesherrliche Hofrat unter Herzog und Kurfürst Maximilian I. von Bayern (1598 - 1651) (München 1981), S. 104 - 106.

45 Siehe hierüber *H. L. Berger*, Die Entwicklung, S. 39 ff.; *F. Ranieri*, Stilus Curiae, S. 82.

46 So *Ch. Besold*, De modo referendi, S. 2; ähnlich *H. E. Rosacorb*, Methodus referendi, in Bd. II, Dokumentationsteil, Dokument I.

47 So *Ch. Besold*, a. a. O., S. 2 - 3.

48 Ebenso *H. E. Rosacorb*, a. a. O.

c) extractus actorum.

Gemeint war hier die Wiedergabe der Parteienschriften. Diese erfolgte meistens in größter Ausführlichkeit und zum Teil im Original mit der Wiedergabe des Libells des Klägers, der Klageschrift mit dem Klageantrag, sowie anschließend des Libells des Beklagten mit dessen Gegenantrag. Dem folgten die Beweismittel. Waren Dokumente vorhanden, so mußten diese im Original angefügt werden; dasselbe galt für die rotula testium. Ein beachtenswertes Beispiel für die Umständlichkeit einer solchen Wiedergabe des Akteninhalts bietet die Relation von Johann Meichsner, die im Dokumentationsteil zu diesem Beitrag als Dokument II. abgedruckt wird: im wörtlichen Original werden hier sämtliche in der Vorinstanz und im kammergerichtlichen Verfahren protokollierte Zeugenaussagen wiedergegeben.[49]

d) votum.

Gemeint war hier das rechtliche Gutachten zu den von den Parteien aufgeworfenen Rechtsfragen. Auch hier folgte der Aufbau der juristischen Erörterungen strengen Regeln.

aa) substantia actionis, quae sit actio.

Hier zeigt sich deutlich die aktionenrechtliche Denkweise der Juristen aus der gemeinrechtlichen Zeit. „Necesse est, – heißt es in der Anleitung von Rosacorb[50] – ut genus actionis inquiras, et actis diligenter perscrutatis, quae sit causa controversa, quaeve positae actionis causa... Neque vero cogitandum, quod ex una aliqua facti specie, unica tantum nascatur actio; nam saepe plures actiones ex eodem facto competunt,...". Die prozeßrechtlichen Strukturen, welche – aus ihrem historischen Kontext zwar herausgerissen – in Begrifflichkeit und Kategoriebildung jedoch die justinianischen Rechtsquellen noch weiterhin charakterisieren, prägen eindeutig die Denkweise der gemeinrechtlichen Juristen: gefragt wird bezeichnenderweise zunächst also nicht nach der auf dem Fall anwendbaren Rechtsnorm, sondern nach der Klagegrundlage, welche das Begehren des Klägers stützen kann.[51]

---

49 Siehe Bd. II, Dokumentationsteil, Dokument II.

50 So *Rosacorb,* a. a. O.

51 Vgl. hierzu *R. M. Sprenger/A. Wijffels,* De actio quanti minoris, bereits zit., insb. S. 134, wo die Disziplinierung der juristischen Argumentation herausgestellt wird, die durch die Berücksichtigung der in Frage kommenden actiones erreicht wird. Zu dieser typischen Argumentationsweise der gemeinrechtlichen Juristen mit der Prüfung der Frage ‚quae sit actio', welche zu einer rechtlichen Sachqualifikation und so zu einer stringenten Subsumption zwang, vgl. allgemein *A. Wijffels,* Qui millies allegatur. Les allégations du droit savant dans les dossiers du Grand Conseil de Malines, (Amsterdam-Leiden 1985), I, S. 318 - 321 und S. 440.

bb) an probata.

Hier sollte insbesondere geprüft werden, ob die vom Kläger vorgebrachten Tatsachen bewiesen waren und damit das Vorbringen des Klägers begründet war. „Inventa actione, eiusque causis, – schreibt in seiner Anleitung Rosacorb[52] – diligenter est inquirendum, an ea sufficienter ab actore,... probata sit nec ne. Nam si probata non est... reus absolvendus". Hatte der Kläger sein Vorbringen zur Begründung der Klage nicht bewiesen, so war die Klage ohne weitere Erörterung der Rechtsprobleme des vorliegenden Falles abzuweisen. Ein deutliches Beispiel hierfür finden wir in der Straßburger Aktenrelation von Johann Otto Tabor, die im Dokumentationsteil als Dokument III. abgedruckt wird: hier hatte der Beklagte in der ersten Instanz gegen eine unstreitige Forderung die Aufrechung *(exceptio compensationis)* erklärt, konnte jedoch seine Gegenforderung nicht beweisen und war unterlegen; als Appellationskläger in der zweiten Instanz, behauptet er wieder die Existenz seiner Gegenforderung ohne aber weitere Beweismittel vorzulegen. Die Relation schlägt vor, die Berufung zu verwerfen, weil der Beklagte und Appellationskläger sein Vorbringen nicht beweisen könne. Auf weitere rechtliche Überlegungen geht der Referent dabei nicht mehr ein.[53]

cc) an elisa.

War das Vorbringen des Klägers bewiesen, mußte auf die Verteidigungsargumente des Beklagten und dessen Beweise eingegangen werden. Insbesondere war hier zu prüfen, ob trotz geglückten Beweises seitens des Klägers, Einreden vom Beklagten geltend gemacht worden waren, welche das Vorbringen des Klägers erledigten. „Si actio probata est ab actore – schreibt der bereits zitierte Rosacorb[54] – oportet inquirere omnes exceptiones rei et diligenter perpendere, an eae sint relevantes, ad hoc, ut etiam non obstante probatione actoris, nihilominus absolvi reus".

e) Urteilsvorschlag.

Die Relation und das Votum sollen mit einem Vorschlag des Referenten zur Entscheidung abgeschlossen werden. Hier gehört deshalb der Tenor des vorgeschlagenen Urteils mit allen Formalien jedoch, wie damals üblich war, ohne Begründung.

3. Die Aktenrelationen am Reichskammergericht und die ihnen zugrundeliegende spezifische richterliche Arbeitsmethode erlangen ihre volle historische Bedeutung wenn man bedenkt, daß sie bis in die jüngste

[52] So *Rosacorb,* a. a. O.

[53] Vgl. Bd. II, Dokumentationsteil, Dokument III.

[54] So *Rosacorb,* a. a. O.

Geschichte der deutschen Juristenausbildung hineinwirken. Betrachtet man nämlich den oben skizzierten Aufbau einer kammergerichtlichen Aktenrelation – deren Regeln übrigens in die Preußische Allgemeine Gerichtsordnung von 1781 Eingang fanden – so erkennt man hier wesentliche Regeln wieder, die heute noch dem jungen deutschen Rechtsstudent und Rechtsreferendar vermittelt werden.[55] Im Rahmen dieses Beitrags können nur einige wenige Hinweise hierüber gegeben werden. Wenigstens dies sei hier in Erinnerung gerufen: Die Geschichte des deutschen Zivilprozeßrechts im 19. Jahrhundert wird bekanntlich durch die progressive Verabschiedung der Regeln des mittelbaren, schriftlichen Verfahrens des römischen gemeinen Prozesses geprägt. Unter dem Einfluß des französischen Code de procédure civile traten die Mündlichkeit und die freie Beweiswürdigung in den Vordergrund.[56] Die Aktenrelation blieb jedoch in der, insbesondere preußischen, Justizpraxis erhalten. Sie wurde den neuen Prozeßgrundsätzen adaptiert. Wegweisend, vor allem für die Justizausbildung, war die halbamtliche Relationsanleitung des Appellationsgerichts in Naumburg im Jahre 1852.[57] Seit den Reichsjustizgesetzen 1877 war die Aktenrelation für die Richter der Kollegialgerichte formell zwar nicht mehr obligatorisch. Faktisch blieb sie jedoch, vor allem als Proberelation für die praktische Juristenausbildung zwingend in Übung. Auf den wesentlichen Grundlagen des Naumburger Modells beruht auch das von H. Daubenspeck (1884) begonnene und von P. Sattelmacher, später von Sirp, fortgeführte Anleitungsbuch ‚Bericht, Gutachten und Urteil', das immerhin von einigen Jahren in seiner einunddreißigsten Auflage erschienen ist.[58] Bei näherer Betrachtung erkennt man in

---

[55] Dazu ausführlich *U. Bake,* Die Entstehung des dualistischen Systems, bereits zit., S. 13ff., insb. zu §. 2 des preußischen Prüfungsreglements von 1755, wo von „Relationes..., insonderheit aus solchen (Akten), welche schwere und verwirrte Materien enthalten, verfertigen lassen" die Rede ist. Im Jahre 1836 erschien auf Anweisung des Justizministers ein Bericht der Immediat-Justiz-Examinationskommission (abgedruckt in *Kamptz,* Jahrbücher für die preußische Gesetzgebung Bd. 47 (1836), S. 451ff.) mit einer ausführlichen Einleitung zur Anfertigung von Aktenrelationen und Voten. Hierzu *U. Bake,* a.a.O., insb. S. 135; *H. L. Berger,* Die Entwicklung, S. 121ff. und m.w.N.; *F. Ranieri,* Stilus Curiae, S. 85 - 86.

[56] Dazu zuletzt vgl. *Th. Drosdeck,* Die Ablösung der gemeinrechtlichen Beweisdoktrin im 19. Jahrhundert am Beispiel des Königreichs Hannover, in: *A. Gouron u. a.* (ed.), Subjektivierung des justiziellen Beweisverfahrens. Beiträge zum Zeugenbeweis in Europa und den USA (18. - 20. Jahrhundert) (Frankfurt M. 1994), S. 113 - 143, insb. S. 120ff.

[57] Dazu *H. L. Berger,* Die Entwicklung, S. 146 - 150. Die Anleitung ist abgedruckt in: Justiz-Ministerial-Blatt für die Preußische Gesetzgebung und Rechtspflege 15 (1853), S. 72ff.

[58] Vgl. die 31. Auflage München 1989. Zu diesem Werk vgl. *H. L. Berger,* Die Entwicklung, S. 149 - 150. Zu der ‚Relationstechnik' in der heutigen deutschen Juristen- und Justizausbildung, insb. zu der immer wieder hiergegen formulierten Kritik, vgl. ferner die Hinweise bei *F. Ranieri,* Stilus Curiae, S. 76 - 77 m.w.N.; aus

dieser Anleitung zur sog. ‚Relationstechnik', welche die Denkweise vieler Generationen von deutschen Juristen dieses Jahrhunderts geprägt hat[59], trotz der historisch gewachsenen Veränderungen noch die Grundregeln der kammergerichtlichen Aktenrelationen des 16. und 17. Jahrhunderts wieder.

Ohne daß dies den heutigen deutschen Juristen immer bewußt wird, lebt die gegenwärtige Juristenausbildung in Deutschland also noch heute, vielfach wohl unreflektiert, in der Fortsetzung der gemeinrechtlichen Denk- und Ausbildungstradition. Die Anleitung zur Lösung und gutachtliche Behandlung konkreter Rechtsfälle hat immer[60], bis heute, eine zentrale Rolle an deutschen Rechtsfakultäten gespielt.[61] Ein deutscher Jurastudent

---

soziologischer Sicht *W. Schütte,* Die Einübung des juristischen Denkens. Juristenausbildung als Sozialisationsprozeß (Frankfurt M. 1982), S. 47ff.; *J.-M. Scholz,* L'obstacle épistémologique premier de l'historien du droit, in *P. Grossi* (ed.), Storia sociale e dimensione giuridica. Strumenti d'indagine e ipotesi di lavoro (Milano 1986), S. 275ff., insb. 287ff.; neuerdings grundlegend zum Thema *O. Hartwieg,* Die Kunst des Sachvortrags im Zivilprozeß. Eine rechtsvergleichende Studie zur Arbeitsweise des englischen Pleading-Systems (Heidelberg 1988), insb. S. 21, und 126ff., 231ff. (siehe hierzu die wertvollen Hinweise von *Kegel,* RabelsZ 1990, S. 192 - 195).

59 Dazu aus rechtssoziologischer und rechtstheoretischer Sicht *Th. Drosdeck,* Konstitution des Rechtsfalles. Entwicklungstendenzen der Justizsoziologie, in: *J.-M. Scholz* (ed.), El tercer poder (Frankfurt M. 1992), S. 137 - 160, insb. S. 158 - 159: „...Eine Hilfestellung bei der Verwertung von Sachverhaltsschilderungen für die dogmatische Konstruktion erfahren die Richter durch justizintern tradierte Arbeitstechniken, die nach den Erfahrungen der Pilotstudie eine weit größere Rolle spielen, als dies bislang in der rechtssoziologischen Literatur vermutet wurde".

60 Beteiligt waren dabei auch berühmte Juristen: siehe etwa *F. Sturm,* Rudolf v. Jhering: scienza ed insegnamento del diritto romano, in: Studi senesi 1971, S. 23ff.; *A. Stölzel,* Schulung für die civilistische Praxis (Berlin 1894); *Fr. Leonhard,* Anleitung für die juristischen Übungs- und Examensarbeiten (1908); *Zitelmann,* Rechtsfälle für bürgerl.-rechtliche Übungen (Leipzig 1917). Siehe ferner aus der älteren praktischen Ausbildungsliteratur z.B. *v. Berg,* Einige Worte zur Ankündigung eines über die gerichtliche und außergerichtliche Privatrechts-Praxis sich erstreckenden Uebungscollegii für den jungen Juristen (Rostock 1825); aus diesem Jahrhundert *K. Dickel,* Rechtsfälle. Zum Gebrauche bei juristischen Übungen, 3. Aufl. (Berlin 1913); *A. Weinmann,* Gutachten und Urteilsentwurf. Ein Anleitung für Examen und Praxis, 6. Aufl. (Berlin 1930); *W. Neye,* Bürgerliches Rechts in logischer Anwendung (Klausurenlehre) (Berlin 1949); *P. Atzler,* Wie bereite ich mich richtig auf die Referendarprüfung vor? Materiellrechtliche Grundfälle (1. Aufl. 1924 - 30. Aufl., 1968). Zu diesem für die Tradition der privaten Repetitoren typischen Werk vgl. *O. Palandt,* in: Monatschrift für deutsches Recht 1949, S. 253 ‚bewährtes System der praktischen Rechtswissenschaft'; *W. G. Becker,* ebendort, 1951, S. 190; zuletzt *Kegel,* RabelsZ 1990, S. 192; *B. Großfeld,* JZ 1992, S. 23.

61 Siehe für das 19. Jahrhundert *J. Schröder,* Wissenschaftstheorie und Lehre der ‚praktischen Jurisprudenz' auf deutschen Universitäten an der Wende zum 19. Jahrhundert (Frankfurt M. 1979), insb. S. 198 - 211 und S. 262; weitere bibliographische Hinweise zu diesem Aspekt der deutschen Juristenausbildung bei *F. Ranieri,* Educazione giuridica, in: Digesto, 4 Aufl., VII (Torino 1991). Zuletzt

lernt bereits in den ersten Semestern seines Universitätsbesuchs, wie er seine Rechtskenntnisse am konkreten Fall umsetzen soll. Das Erlernen jener spezifischen Fertigkeit, die schriftliche Bearbeitung eines praktischen Rechtsfalles anzugehen, nimmt eine zentrale Stellung in seiner Ausbildung ein. Während seines Studiums lernt er also nicht nur materiellrechtliche Inhalte, sondern vor allem auch eine spezifische Arbeitstechnik kennen – die deutschen Juristen sprechen hier bekanntlich von der sog. ‚Klausurtechnik'. Im Zentrum derselben steht die Anfertigung eines Rechtsgutachtens, wie also der vielfältige Stoff eines verwickelten Falles in einer geordneter und effizienter Erörterung strukturiert werden soll; dies geht bis zur Vermittlung einer Reihe von sprachlichen Regeln zur Gestaltung der schriftlichen Formulierung der Überlegungen, die dabei angestellt werden, und die zu einem Lösungsvorschlag führen sollen.[62] Bei einer realistischen Betrachtung der Ausbildung eines deutschen Rechtsstudenten spielt die Einübung einer solchen Arbeitsweise eine ebenso wichtige Rolle wie das Erlernen des positiven Rechtsstoffes.[63] Im Zentrum der pädagogischen Bemühungen steht hier seit jeher die Vermittlung der Technik des argumentativen Aufbaus eines Gutachtens nach den in Betracht kommenden ‚Anspruchsgrundlagen': genau wie der gemeinrechtliche Jurist sein Votum nach der Frage ‚quae sit actio' aufbauen lernte[64], so lernt der deutsche Rechtsstudent heute

---

zum Thema *K. Michaelis,* Die heutige Juristenausbildung und ihr Verhältnis zur Rechtswirklichkeit, in: Juristische Schulung 1991, S. 798ff., insb. S. 805; *E. Bund,* The study of law and the First National Law Examination in the Federal Republic of Germany, in: Legal Education Two Thousand. Ed. by *J. P. Grant u. a.* (Aldershot 1988), S. 163 - 181, insb. S. 164 - 167.

62 Vgl. etwa *U. v. Lübtow,* Richtlinien für die Anfertigung von Übungs- und Prüfungsarbeiten im Bürgerlichen Recht sowie drei Lösungen praktischer Fälle, 2. Aufl. (Berlin 1986); *St. Puhle,* Dreizehn Schritte zur Klausur. Ein Programm für Referendare zur Bearbeitung von zivilrechtlichen Klausuren und Alltagsakten, in: Juristische Schulung 1987, S. 41ff.; rechtsvergleichend *E. Klein/R. L. Weaver,* Fallmethode oder systematische Stoffpräsentation? Zu den Lehrmethoden an amerikanischen Hochschulen und deutschen Rechtsfakultäten, in: Juristische Schulung 1993, S. 272ff.

63 Siehe etwa *P. Forster,* Frage der Klausurtechnik, in: Juristische Schulung 1992, S. 234ff., insb. S. 235: „... Wer die Klausurtechnik beherrscht, kann im Regelfall auch juristisch denken,... Klausurtechnik und juristisches Denken gehören zusammen"; S. 238: „...Wer das gutachtliche Denken nicht gelernt hat, kann kein guter Jurist werden". Kritisch zu dieser Ausbildungspraxis *B. Großfeld,* Das Elend des Jurastudiums, in: JZ 1986, S. 357 - 360, insb. S. 359; *derselbe,* Rechtsausbildung und Rechtskontrolle, in: NJW 1989, S. 875 - 880; *derselbe,* Examensvorbereitung und Jurisprudenz, JZ 1992, S. 22ff., insb. S. 25 - 26.

64 Das für das römische gemeine Recht typische ‚aktionenrechtliche' Denken ist erst in der deutschen Panktentenliteratur des 19. Jahrhunderts bekanntlich abgelöst worden; vgl. grundlegend dazu *B. Windscheid,* Die Actio des römischen Zivilrechts vom Standpunkt des heutigen Rechts (1856); der Sache nach beseitigt auch die Windscheid'sche Theorie die actio allerdings nicht: so zutreffend *A. Georgiades,*

noch, daß ein zivilrechtliches Gutachten nach den in Frage kommenden Ansprüchen aufgebaut werden soll. Die pädagogische Tradition die einer solchen Denk- und Argumentationsweise zugrunde liegt, und welche übrigens in anderen kontinentaleuropäischen Ländern weitgehend unbekannt ist[65], offenbart die überraschende Fortwirkung in Deutschland der gemeinrechtlichen Wissenschaft bis heute.[66] Damit werden wir mit einer späten, langfristigen Wirkung der richterlichen Tradition des Reichskammergerichts konfrontiert. Die Frage hat bis heute die rechtshistorische Forschung kaum interessiert.[67] Ihre Vertiefung würde der heutigen deutschen Juristengeneration deutlich machen, wie gegenwärtig, wenn auch unbewußt, längst verschüttet geglaubte gemeinrechtliche Denkstrukturen und Denkformen noch sind.

Die Anspruchskonkurrenz im Zivilrecht und Zivilprozeßrecht (München 1968), S. 32 ff. m. w. N.

65 So konnte z. B. geschrieben werden, daß die praktische Ausbildung in der sog. Relationstechnik „jeden Schweizer Juristen in ein von Bewunderung und Grauen gemischtes Staunen" versetzt; so *R. Gmür,* Das Schweizerische ZGB verglichen mit dem Deutschen BGB (Bern 1965), S. 184 ff., insb. 185. Die stringenten Aufbauregeln eines Rechtsgutachtens nach Anspruchsgrundlagen sind z. B. in der französischen Rechtskultur und in derjenigen der übrigen romanischen Ländern völlig unbekannt; wertvolle vergleichende Hinweise hierzu bei *C. Witz,* Droit privé allemand. I. Actes juridiques, droits subjectifs (Paris 1992), S. 479 ff.; hier, S. 553 - 561, die französische Übersetzung eines ‚cas pratique allemand'.

66 Die historische Dimension dieser Ausbildungstradition verkennen die Kritiker derselben (siehe oben Anm. 63). Es ist bezeichnend, daß sie auch von deren Befürworter ganz ignoriert wird; siehe etwa *D. Medicus,* Anspruch und Einrede als Rückgrat einer zivilistischen Lehrmethode, in: Archiv für die civilistische Praxis 1974, S. 313 - 331, mit nur einem Hinweis auf das römische Recht, S. 314; *derselbe,* Allgemeiner Teil des BGB, 2. Aufl. (Heidelberg 1985), Rdn. 77 - 78, S. 35 - 36.

67 Gerade diesem Befund sind meine Ausführungen in *F. Ranieri,* Stilus Curiae, insb. S. 86 ff. gewidmet. Vgl. auch *F. Ranieri,* Juristische Arbeitsstile in historischem Vergleich: beschleunigende Faktoren oder Hindernisse einer europäischen Rechtseinheit?, in: *L. Moccia* (ed.), Il diritto privato europeo. Problemi e prospettive (Milano 1993), S. 59 - 68.

ALAIN WIJFFELS

Grand Conseil de Malines: La rédaction des sentences étendues et le recueil de jurisprudence de Guillaume de Grysperre

Dans la contribution précédente consacrée au Grand Conseil de Malines, un aperçu général des archives judiciaires et des principaux recueils se référant à des décisions de cette cour a déjà été présenté.[1] Afin de répondre au but spécifique du présent recueil, dont l'objet est de préciser la technique et la méthode des archives judiciaires et des recueils (dits) de jurisprudence, cette nouvelle contribution se limitera, pour l'essentiel, à deux aspects particuliers de la question: d'une part, au mode de rédaction des sentences étendues, et, d'autre part, au plus ancien recueil conservé pour le Grand Conseil: celui de G. de Grysperre, dont le texte intégral est publié dans la seconde partie.[2]

I. La rédaction de sentences étendues

Au 16e siècle, les sentences étendues (prononcées au nom du souverain) comportent principalement les éléments suivants: l'identification des parties au procès (y compris les éventuelles modifications au cours du procès, ainsi par exemple suite au décès de l'une des parties), l'objet du litige, le déroulement du procès (du moins certaines phases de la procédure, et notamment celles où l'initiative des plaideurs était décisive: le commencement de la

---

[1] Legal Records and Reports in the Great Council of Malines (15th to 18th Centuries), dans: *J. H. Baker* (ed.), Judicial Records, Law Reports, and the Growth of Case Law (Berlin 1989), 181 - 206. Depuis la rédaction de cet article (en 1986), plusieurs études consacrées au Grand Conseil de Malines ont été publiées; outre la bibliographie de base publiée par *H. de Schepper* et *R. van Answaarden* dans: Miscellanea Consilii Magni (Amsterdam 1980), IX - XXVI, on consultera le supplément par *M. G. M. Snep,* dans: Miscellanea Forensia Historica (Amsterdam 1988), 389 - 402. Un bref status quaestionis sur le Grand Conseil de Malines est paru dans: De centrale overheidsinstellingen van de Habsburgse Nederlanden, I (Bruxelles 1994), 448 - 461 (version française sous presse).

[2] En outre, M. C. H. van Rhee a également soigné une collation de textes relatifs au Grand Conseil, pour la seconde partie, à partir d'un casus traité dans les *Decisiones* de P. Christinaeus.

procédure, les incidents), les principaux arguments (non-juridiques) avancés par les parties, le dispositif.

1. L'absence d'une motivation juridique

La différence essentielle par rapport à un jugement contemporain est sans doute l'absence d'une motivation en droit. Cette constatation doit toutefois être quelque peu nuancée. D'abord, les sentences étendues ne comportent formellement aucune motivation, ni de fait, ni de droit: hormis une brève formule générale,[3] les raisonnements et arguments repris sont ceux des parties, sans que ceux-ci fassent l'objet d'une approbation ou d'une désapprobation de la part de la Cour.[4] Ensuite, contrairement à la conception communément affirmée selon laquelle les sentences étendues ne reprennent pas de considérations juridiques (que ce soit sous forme de motivation de la Cour ou d'arguments des plaideurs), on constate que certaines formes d'argumentations juridiques sont parfois exprimées dans ces sentences: il s'agit notamment d'arguments où la teneur ou la portée d'une source du droit particulier (une disposition coutumière, un acte législatif ou réglementaire) a fait l'objet d'une controverse durant le procès. En revanche, les références au droit savant sont en principe ignorées et, en tout cas, les argumentations parfois fortement élaborées à partir de sources du droit savant (et notamment lorsque des opinions juridiques savantes ont été introduites, à l'instar de *consilia*), sont omises, même sous forme concise.

Ainsi, pour les principes relevant du droit savant, mais en fait également pour les règles du droit particulier, il n'est pas possible de déterminer à partir du texte de la sentence quelle règle de droit a été appliquée ou éta-

---

[3] Du type: «veu et visité en icelluy nostre grant conseil le proces desdites parties et tout ce que par icelluy appert, et consideré ce que fait a veoir et considerer en ceste partie et que peut et doibt mouvoir, Nous, a grande et meure deliberacion de conseil, par ceste nostre sentence diffinitive...»

[4] Il y a controverse quant à déterminer si la sélection des arguments repris dans la sentence étendue correspond ou non à une motivation implicite; c'était la thèse de *C. L. Verkerk,* Een onderzoek naar de motivering van vonnissen van de Grote Raad van Mechelen, dans: Consilium Magnum (Bruxelles 1977), 288; mais *Ph. Godding,* La motivation des arrêts du Grand Conseil de Malines au 16e siècle, TRG 45 (1977), 155 - 157, a démontré que le cas présenté par Verkerk correspondait à l'une des catégories pour lesquelles, exceptionnellement, le droit savant exigeait en principe une motivation. Sans doute, on verra que l'Instruction dont il sera question plus loin semble renforcer la thèse défendue par Verkerk (indépendamment du cas sur lequel il avait fondé sa démonstration). En fait, comme les sentences étendues ne reprennent pas les arguments juridiques (sauf ce qui sera dit en rapport avec les sources de *ius proprium*), l'analyse des arguments mentionnés dans les sentences ne peut élucider la question de la motivation en droit des jugements, et, partant, la possibilité d'un développement jurisprudentiel.

blie. Même lorsqu'on connaît les arguments juridiques développés (du moins par la partie qui a gagné le procès) dans une cause particulière (par exemple parce que le dossier contenant les plaidoiries ou motifs de droit a été conservé, ou parce qu'il existe un recueil de *consilia,* où il est possible d'établir dans quelle cause un avis particulier a été introduit), il n'est guère possible de déterminer le raisonnement juridique ayant abouti à la décision, partant un principe juridique appliqué ou établi par la Cour. En effet, dans les causes d'une certaine complexité, on s'aperçoit que l'argumentation du plaideur victorieux se base sur plusieurs principes (et il est donc spéculatif de se prononcer sur quel principe, ou sur quelle combinaison de principes les juges se seraient fondés), ou encore sur une argumentation comportant des arguments en ordre subsidiaire (et dans tel cas, on ne dispose pas d'éléments permettant de vérifier si les conseillers ont plutôt suivi l'argument principal, ou un argument subsidiaire). Comme on ne dispose d'aucune information sur les délibérés, il n'est pas non plus possible d'évaluer l'importance décisive qu'ont pu avoir des considérations davantage politiques (au sens le plus large: par exemple des principes de morale ou des conceptions quant à l'ordre social), ou l'appréciation des faits (y compris de l'administration de la preuve). L'étude plus approfondie de dossiers particuliers démontre dans quelle mesure ces différentes hypothèses se vérifient dans la pratique;[5] en outre, des recueils plus personnels sur les délibérés dans d'autres cours supérieures de justice à l'époque, confirment que, certainement pour toute forme d'administration de la justice sous forme collégiale, il est extrêmement hasardeux de vouloir reconstituer une motivation juridique des jugements à partir de l'issue du procès.[6]

Cette conclusion implique que, sauf au sein même du collège, les décisions n'avaient guère de chance d'être perçues comme des précédents, à moins peut-être de constituer, selon les conventions du milieu judiciaire gravitant autour de la Cour, un cas-type ou une forme de *test-case.* En fait, un sondage dans la pratique du Grand Conseil des années 1460 à 1580

---

[5] V. notamment: Een kogge en een huwelijksscheepje, dans: *P. L. Nève* et *E. C. C. Coppens* (eds.), Sine invidia communico, Opstellen aangeboden aan Prof. Dr. A. J. de Groot (Nijmegen 1985), 273 - 301 (version française: Une nef sans l'Eglise?, dans: Miscellanea Consilii Magni III (Amsterdam 1988), 187 - 222); Le bénéfice de discussion dans l'ancien droit hollandais. A propos d'un avis inédit d'E. Leoninus et P. Peckius, dans: *G. Macours* (ed.), Cornua legum (Antwerpen 1987), 241 - 260.

[6] V. par exemple: De *actio quanti minoris* in de praktijk van het Rijkskamergerecht ca. 1537. Uit de aantekeningen van Viglius van Aytta, dans: *D. Lambrecht* (ed.), Lopend rechtshistorisch onderzoek. Handelingen van het tiende Belgisch-Nederlands rechtshistorisch colloquium [Iuris Scripta Historica, III] (Brussel 1990), 127 - 159. Ce cas, ainsi que quelques autres (et notamment du Grand Conseil de Malines et de la Haute Cour d'Amirauté à Londres), est traité à l'appui de la même thèse dans un article intitulé: Le juge et le jugement dans la tradition du ius commune (sous presse).

démontre que même les avocats pratiquant régulièrement à cette Cour, ne se référaient que très rarement à un précédent pour étayer l'application d'une règle juridique, et que ces cas plutôt exceptionnels se rapportaient davantage à des applications de règles de droit particulier.[7] Ces cas prouvent que, même dans l'hypothèse d'une connivence entre conseillers et avocats qui aurait pu engendrer des références implicites, le recours aux précédents de la Cour n'était pas exclu, mais n'a pas pour autant été courant.

2. L'objet des sentences étendues

Si les sentences étendues n'avaient pas pour but d'exprimer les motifs juridiques des conseillers, ni leur appréciation des moyens de fait ou de preuves avancés par les plaideurs, quelle était la fonction de ces actes? Il semblerait que l'élaboration de ces sentences suivant un modèle général et leur enregistrement dans les archives de la Cour visaient avant tout des effets procéduraux. Pour la partie victorieuse (ou ses successeurs), la sentence étendue constituait en premier lieu un titre: dans l'immédiat, un titre exécutoire qui lui permettait d'obtenir satisfaction à l'égard de son adversaire;[8] à terme, un titre assurant la sécurité de l'autorité de la chose jugée.

La pratique de l'époque illustre en effet combien la notion de *res iudicata,* strictement interprétée, prenait une place importante dans les litiges, tant à caractère public (où des titulaires d'une autorité, des institutions ou des corporations étaient impliquées), que privé. Afin qu'une décision judiciaire assure la sécurité juridique escomptée, elle devait préciser exactement l'identité des parties, l'objet du litige, les moyens invoqués. Les exceptions couramment opposées au cours des procès à l'invocation d'une sentence antérieure, supposée avoir déjà tranché la controverse soumise à la Cour, montrent comment les effets de la *res iudicata* étaient cernés. Ainsi, *ratione personae,* l'exception de la *res inter alios acta* est l'une des plus fréquemment usitées; cela signifiait qu'il était impératif qu'une sentence précise non seulement l'identité des parties, mais également en quelle qualité elles procédaient; pour l'avenir, ces éléments devaient notamment permettre de trancher si les successeurs des parties intervenant au procès étaient liés ou non par une sentence rendue parfois longtemps auparavant. Dans le cas de parties institutionnelles (par exemple, une ville), l'effet d'un jugement à l'égard de tiers – et la question de déterminer, pour certains

---

[7] References to Judicial Precedents in the Practice of the Great Council of Malines (c. 1460 - 1580), dans: Miscellanea Consilii Magni III (Amsterdam 1988), 165 - 186.

[8] La procédure d'exécution pour dettes a récemment fait l'objet d'une étude détaillée: *C. H. van Rhee,* Execution for Debt against Immovable Property under the supervision of the Great Council of Malines, TRG 63 (1995), 45 - 82.

litiges, qui devait être considéré comme un tiers – pouvait susciter des problèmes délicats lorsque des intérêts permanents d'une telle institution (par exemple le droit de lever un impôt) étaient en jeu. *Ratione materiae,* l'objet du litige, que ce fût un droit ou un bien corporel, n'était pas toujours facile à définir: la portée même d'un privilège, d'une juridiction, d'une exemption... ou, par ailleurs, la délimitation sur le terrain d'une seigneurie, d'un bien-fonds... pouvait facilement prêter à équivoque, ce dont l'un des plaideurs tirait volontiers profit. Plus les intérêts en jeu étaient importants, plus certains litiges sur le même objet – ou à peu près – avaient des chances d'être soumis à nouveau devant les cours de justice. Enfin, *ratione iudicii,* il était important de déterminer quels moyens avaient été avancés au cours du procès – et par conséquent en principe tranchés par la décision. Il n'est donc pas surprenant que ces trois aspects fondamentaux de l'autorité de la chose jugée – visant à prévenir de nouveaux procès sur les mêmes cas d'espèce – correspondent aux principaux éléments que l'on retrouve dans le narré des sentences étendues.

3. La rédaction par le greffier

Un recueil-formulaire manuscrit de la pratique judiciaire, dont la rédaction date vraisemblablement du second tiers ou du troisième quart du 16e siècle,[9] contient également une 'Instruction' sur la manière de rédiger les sentences étendues au Grand Conseil.[10]

Cette Instruction présente plusieurs problèmes d'interprétation. En outre, la terminologie utilisée est parfois équivoque. Comme dans plusieurs actes de ce genre, la finalité des règles ou directives n'est pas explicitée. Ainsi, on note d'une part des instructions fort élémentaires quant à la sélection des pièces du dossier à utiliser (alinéas 1 - 2), mais, d'autre part, le rédacteur de la sentence est à plusieurs reprises supposé reconnaître les moyens importants et les discerner des arguments secondaires (alinéas 5, 7, 10).

Ce rédacteur est, selon une mention à l'alinéa 4, le greffier 'ou son clercq'. Les termes 'formateur de sentence' (al. 5) et 'dictateur de la sentence' (al. 10) semblent se rapporter au rédacteur. Plusieurs mentions dans le texte de l'Instruction semblent confirmer que la sentence étendue était

---

9 Sur ce recueil, *J. Th. de Smidt,* Quelques remarques sur le ms. BPL 54 de la bibliothèque de l'université de Leyde, le manuscrit «PRAXIS», dans: Satura Roberto Feenstra (Fribourg 1985), 533 - 543.

10 Le texte est repris ci-après, dans l'Annexe. Une première édition a été publiée (avec une introduction, un commentaire et un exemple à partir du fonds du Grand Conseil) par *J. M. I. Koster-van Dijk,* Instruction pour le greffier du Grand Conseil concernant la rédaction des sentences (Introduction et édition du texte), dans: Miscellanea Consilii Magni III (Amsterdam 1988), 17 - 41.

rédigée à partir du dictum (al. 1, 5, 7), sans qu'il soit pour autant certain qu'il s'agisse du texte que l'on retrouve dans les registres aux dicta.[11]

L'Instruction présente avant tout des directives de rédaction selon des catégories procédurales. Trois hypothèses principales sont prises en considération: les sentences rendues en première instance (al. 4 et ss.), les sentences rendues soit sur recours d'appel ou de réformation, ainsi que les procédures en 'réduction' (après une sentence arbitrale) (al. 10), enfin, les procédures en matière de décret (al. 11).[12] En fait, l'incipit du premier alinéa indique que l'Instruction est également applicable pour d'autres procédures. Dans les procédures de première instance, des règles particulières sont prévues en cas de défaut (al. 9). La position procédurale de la partie qui obtient gain de cause est parfois prise en compte pour des modalités de la rédaction (p.ex. al. 4 et 10).

Aucune disposition ne parle des arguments juridiques: apparemment, il était évident que ces éléments étaient systématiquement omis lors de la rédaction. Le 'point sur lequel s'assied le procès' (al. 3), que le rédacteur aura préalablement soin de dégager, ne porte pas sur une éventuelle question de droit.

II. Le recueil de G. de Grysperre

De l'ensemble des recueils manuscrits et imprimés qui ont été conservés, celui de De Grysperre est le plus ancien. Quoique datant de la fin du 16e siècle, il ne fut imprimé en partie que deux siècles plus tard. Cette édition, qui ne se préoccupait manifestement pas de produire un texte répondant aux exigences de la critique historique, est à maint égard défectueuse pour tout travail historique. Surtout, elle est fortement incomplète, car pour un grand nombre d'articles ('arrêts'), l'imprimeur se borne à renvoyer au texte correspondant dans un recueil postérieur, celui de P. Cuvelier; il a déjà été relevé que ce procédé avait été suivi dans la tradition manuscrite du recueil de De Grysperre.[13] Sans doute, la version imprimée

[11] Sur cette ancienne controverse, cf. l'introduction de *J. Th. de Smidt* et *Eg. I. Strubbe* dans: Chronologische Lijsten van de Geëxtendeerde Sententiën en Procesbundels (dossiers) berustende in het archief van de Grote Raad van Mechelen, I, 1465 - 1504, p. xix; et *J. Van Rompaey,* De Grote Raad van de Hertogen van Boergondië en het Parlement van Mechelen (Bruxelles 1973), pp. 431 - 432.

[12] Cette dernière disposition, selon *C. H. van Rhee,* o.c., pp. 68 - 69 (et n. 148), ne se réfère pas aux lettres de décret, rédigées sous forme de sentence étendue, mais bien à un acte de notification intervenant avant que ces lettres ne soient scellées.

[13] Notamment dans le manuscrit Stadsarchief Mechelen: Hs. J. Grand Conseil I,2; les références précises au recueil de Cuvelier (et notamment au numéro de folio où se trouve l'arrêt correspondant chez ce dernier) permettent d'identifier le ma-

de ce recueil n'a pas fait l'objet d'un remaniement et n'a pas été tronquée dans la même mesure que ce fut le cas pour le recueil de N. du Fief, mais, en pratique, il faut se rapporter aux manuscrits pour reconstituer l'œuvre de De Grysperre.

1. Agencement général

Très brève, cette collection ne requiert pas nécessairement un agencement spécial. Dans l'édition, la 'Table des Arrêts', où pour chaque article,[14] la question principale est énoncée, peut être rapidement consultée; ces énoncés sont par ailleurs repris, en italiques, au début de chaque article; en outre, cette version imprimée contient une table des matières. Dans les manuscrits, un sommaire de la question est repris dans la marge, ce qui, à nouveau, facilite largement la consultation visant à rechercher un thème particulier.

En fait, comme la plupart des recueils du Grand Conseil, il semble que la collection de De Grysperre suive, en gros, un ordre chronologique, même si cela n'apparaît pas au premier abord. La séquence dans (environ) la première moitié du recueil[15] ne correspond que partiellement à une suite chronologique. En revanche, l'ordre chronologique est nettement mieux reconnaissable dans la seconde partie de l'ouvrage. Vraisemblablement y a-t-il un lien entre cette constatation et celle que dans la première série d'articles, les principaux arrêts cités sont antérieurs à la nomination de De Grysperre en tant que conseiller,[16] tandis que la seconde série correspond à peu près à la première décennie durant laquelle il exerça cette fonction.[17] En outre, on verra que la présentation des 'arrêts' individuels est sensiblement différente d'une série à l'autre.[18]

---

nuscrit Stadsarchief Mechelen: Hs. J. Grand Conseil I, 3bis comme celui constituant un ensemble avec le précédent.

[14] J'utiliserai le terme 'article' pour désigner ce qui, dans les versions manuscrites et imprimées, est désigné comme 'arrêt'; en fait, un même 'arrêt' dans le recueil peut se référer à plusieurs décisions.

[15] Pour faciliter les vérifications du lecteur, la présente contribution renvoie constamment (sauf indication contraire) à l'édition présentée dans la seconde partie.

[16] On relève toutefois quelques références à des décisions postérieures, du temps où De Grysperre était conseiller: articles 8, 17, 18, 40. La mention «et de mon temps» à l'article 12 a peut-être été reprise d'une collection antérieure.

[17] Dans l'article précité, Legal Records and Reports in the Great Council of Malines (15th to 18th Centuries), l.c., la date de 1590, basée sur la version imprimée, est erronée (la sentence en question doit en effet être datée de 1580); en fait, la dernière sentence dont la date est mentionnée est celle du 31.10.1587 (article 68 i.f.).

[18] D'un manuscrit à un autre, la numérotation des articles ou 'arrêts' est différente, notamment en raison d'amalgames ou de scissions; de telles divergences n'affectent toutefois pas la séquence générale des textes. Une divergence plus impor-

La première série, antérieure à la période durant laquelle De Grysperre fut conseiller, contient des références à des décisions s'échelonnant de 1531 aux années '70 (les années '40 n'étant toutefois pas représentées). Hormis les décisions de 1531 et de 1539 citées dans les deux premiers articles, ce sont des décisions des années '60 et '70 qui fournissent l'essentiel de la matière. A plusieurs reprises, un article contient une référence à une décision, suivie de références à des arrêts rendus ultérieurement et censés établir le même principe, ou une application semblable dans un cas quelque peu différent. Parfois, ces ajouts constituent des articles ('arrêts') séparés (parfois très brefs), ce qui tend à brouiller la suite chronologique. Celle-ci n'est d'ailleurs que très partiellement observée dans cette première série, même si l'on ne tient pas compte des décisions postérieures insérées. Il semblerait que certains regroupements par matière expliquent, du moins en partie, la séquence des articles dans cette première série: ainsi, les articles 4 à 8 portent sur des questions procédurales de recevabilité; les charges foncières font l'objet des brefs articles 28 à 30; les droits que des membres du lignage peuvent exercer à l'occasion d'aliénations se retrouvent dans les articles 32 à 39. En revanche, il n'est guère possible de suggérer un ordre quelconque dans les différents articles, disséminés, consacrés au droit patrimonial de la famille (régimes matrimoniaux et successions). Vraisemblablement, tous ces articles sont empruntés à une ou plusieurs collections antérieures. Le fait même que ces articles mentionnent en général le principe appliqué par la décision citée, et parfois d'autres éléments, comme la 'raison' de la décision, indique que, probablement, De Grysperre a eu à sa disposition des notes ou une relation orale d'un ou de plusieurs collègues ou prédécesseurs. Ce recours à des précédents pouvait d'ailleurs être inspiré par des circonstances professionnelles particulières, ainsi lorsqu'au début de sa carrière de conseiller, De Grysperre fut rapporteur dans une cause de révision, ce qui provoqua peut-être son intérêt pour la première cause, traitée de manière plus détaillée, reprise au no. 40.[19]

La seconde série d'articles, à partir du no. 41, respecte en revanche l'ordre chronologique de plus près. Les quelques divergences s'expliquent facilement: à quelques reprises, il s'agit de citer une décision antérieure sur la même question (nos. 45 et 64); pour l'année 1581, les articles 50 à 53 ne

tante concerne cependant les articles 20 à 23 selon le manuscrit bruxellois (B1) ayant fourni la base de l'édition dans la seconde partie: les articles 20 à 23 de cette version se trouvent en effet à la fin dans le manuscrit de Mons (M2: articles 44 à 47); en outre, le no. 69 dans B1 précède le numéro équivalent au 67 de B1 dans le Ms. M2 (soit B1:69=B2:41), mais les deux textes ne correspondent pas tout à fait (se reporter à la note dans l'édition). L'arrêt 59 dans B1 est incomplet (v. également à ce propos la note dans l'édition).

[19] L'intervention de De Grysperre dans la cause en révision d'Utrecht est brièvement mentionnée vers la fin de l'article 40.

figurent pas à leur place, mais sans doute faut-il imputer cette anomalie aux désordres qu'avaient entraînés la prise de Malines et le déménagement précipité à Namur – certaines causes relatées dans le recueil illustrent d'ailleurs indirectement les effets de ces troubles sur l'organisation de la cour.[20] Enfin, la dernière décision (28.04.1584, alors que l'article précédent se réfère à une décision de 1587) omet de mentionner la date de la décision rendue en révision. Pour le reste, la chronologie est respectée.

2. Conception des articles

Il convient de distinguer ici également entre les articles de la première série, fondés sur des informations indirectes, et ceux de la seconde série, où De Grysperre avait pu assister au procès ou aux délibérés, et où, dans certains cas, sa participation à la formation du jugement (en tant que rapporteur) est attestée.

Pour la seconde catégorie, on peut faire état d'un modèle plus ou moins fidèlement suivi selon les cas, et dont les éléments comportent: un casus comprenant la désignation, nominatim, des plaideurs, un résumé de leurs principaux arguments, la décision; celle-ci, à nouveau, peut mentionner différents éléments: la portée du dispositif, un principe appliqué, un motif du jugement, le nom du rapporteur, le degré de consensus parmi les conseillers, et éventuellement, des circonstances particulières quant au collège appelé à juger (ainsi, par exemple, le fait que la décision ait été prise 'les chambres assemblées'); en cas de procès en appel, l'article mentionne souvent si la décision du Grand Conseil confirme ou non le jugement attaqué.

Un exemple-type d'un tel article est l''arrêt' 57: le casus, les arguments et répliques des parties («Briois refuse, soustenant...»; «Du Flos au contraire...»; «Briois persiste...»; «Du Flos le débat par impertinence...»), l'essentiel du dispositif, ainsi qu'une motivation en droit, et des considérations de fait qui eurent quelque poids, enfin la mention du rapporteur. Même si tous les articles ne suivent pas ce modèle avec rigueur, il s'agit clairement du format auquel tend la rédaction des 'arrêts' individuels. Il est par ailleurs remarquable que malgré cette diversité d'éléments incorporés dans les articles, ceux-ci demeurent en général fort succincts: à titre comparatif, on notera que la sentence étendue dans l'affaire de l''arrêt' 57 compte, dans le registre, une trentaine de pages.[21]

---

[20] Article 52: saisie et rançonnement des archives du Grand Conseil après la prise de Malines, alors que le Conseil s'était établi à Namur. Sur ces événements: *J. Th. de Smidt,* De appèlzaken van Holland bij de Grote Raad, Tydskrif vir Hedendaagse Romeins-Hollandse Reg 12 (1949), 81 - 89.

[21] GCM 881, 627 - 642.

Il est également frappant que la concision des articles ne fait pas obstacle, le cas échéant, à des précisions sur les circonstances de fait qui eussent pu être formulées de façon plus abstraite: c'est le cas, notamment, de l'identification des parties; l'arrêt 59 contient même un arbre généalogique destiné à éclaircir les rapports entre les parties au litige. Par contre, l'énoncé du principe (juridique) appliqué tend à être peu explicite, et dans plusieurs cas, le lecteur est simplement renvoyé à l'argumentation de la partie victorieuse, résumée antérieurement.[22] A cet égard, les sommaires marginaux (dont il n'est pas certain qu'ils furent rédigés par De Grysperre) sont parfois plus clairs.

Les articles constituant la première série du recueil ne suivent pas un tel modèle.[23] Il est difficile d'y reconnaître une technique particulière et homogène; tout au plus peut-on relever que dans plusieurs articles, l'accent est mis davantage sur le principe (abstrait) établi ou illustré par la décision que sur les éléments spécifiques de la cause; les arguments des plaideurs et de la décision sont souvent omis, mais les noms des parties et la date de la décision sont en général mentionnés.

3. Matières traitées

Un critère de sélection n'est pas directement apparent: c'est d'autant plus surprenant que le recueil est tellement bref, ne reprenant qu'une fraction infime des causes jugées durant la période dont proviennent les sentences; même pour les années 1581 - 1583, plus fortement représentées, le recueil ne reflète que très imparfaitement l'activité du Grand Conseil.

Dans la seconde série, quelques causes ont vraisemblablement été retenue par l'auteur en raison de sa contribution à la décision en tant que rapporteur; même dans de tels cas, on ne trouve guère une formulation plus

---

22 Ainsi aux articles 43 («pour les raisons que dessus»), 44 («Messeigneurs tenoient la non observance du droict canon et coustume cy dessus alleguee pour chose notoire...»), 48 («pour les raisons que dessus»), 54 («Lesdits couvent et abbés... se fondant... Et ainsy a esté resolu...»), 59 («...Et ainsy a esté jugé...»; «...lequel obiect fut reiecté pour la raison que dessus»), 60 («...ce qu'a esté suivy par arrest...»). Dans d'autres cas, il y a une concordance évidente entre l'argument de la partie victorieuse et la motivation attribuée à la décision. Bien sûr, il faudrait pouvoir vérifier (notamment dans les écritures, pour autant qu'elles aient été conservées, ou le cas échéant dans les sentences étendues) si les arguments attribués aux parties ont effectivement été avancés comme tels; il faut également envisager que l'argument repris dans l'article a pu être le principal argument repris par le rapporteur dans sa *relatio* au collège.

23 Sauf exception: ainsi, l'article 37 (mais il est d'autre part caractéristique que la motivation de la cour est exprimée avec quelque incertitude: «...ayant la Cour vraysemblablement esté meue...»).

élaborée des arguments ou des motifs: malheureusement, le recueil ne nous informe pas sur la rédaction et la présentation des rapports.

Ratione materiae, la sélection s'est apparemment faite en fonction de l'importance perçue des principes appliqués: soit que la décision puisse faire figure de 'précédent' dans une cause ultérieure (ce qui implique que l'auteur envisageait la possibilité d'un cas analogue), soit que le cas présentait plus simplement une curiosité. La sélection des articles portant essentiellement sur une question de procédure s'expliquent aisément, puisque ce type de règles peut s'appliquer dans des causes très diverses. Quant aux décisions relatives aux régimes matrimoniaux et aux successions, il s'agit d'une matière correspondant à une partie importante du contentieux porté à l'époque devant le Grand Conseil, comme il appert notamment des registres aux sentences étendues.

4. Arguments juridiques et motivations

Le principal apport d'un tel recueil est de fournir des informations sur les motifs juridiques ayant, la cas échéant, emporté la décision. A cet égard, le recueil de De Grysperre demeure également très concis, mais il contient néanmoins quelques renseignements que l'on cherchera en vain dans les archives et registres de la cour.

Dans la première série d'articles, le principe de droit appliqué est parfois énoncé tel quel, sans aucune précision; dans certains cas, l'interprétation de la cour est toutefois explicitée.[24] En revanche, plusieurs articles laissent planer un doute quant aux raisons ayant emporté la décision.[25]

Dans les articles rédigés à partir de l'expérience directe de De Grysperre, on entrevoit à quelques reprises les débats qui eurent lieu au cours des délibérés.[26] Cependant, la motivation de la décision se limite en général à l'énoncé d'un principe ou d'une règle. La teneur et l'argumentation des rapports ne sont pas exprimées. Parfois, il est indiqué que des considérations d'équité ont renforcé les motifs juridiques, ou encore, que des circonstances de fait, ou une appréciation des preuves avancées, ont contribué à la décision.

---

[24] Article 4: «...aussy que le procureur general estoit joinct avecq elle, et que le susdit article allégué [scil. art. 14, titre du style de procéder, de l'ordonnance de 1559] debvoit recevoir intelligence, interpretation et restriction par ladite Cour».

[25] Article 5: «...En quoy semble avoir esté suivie la practicque et stil...»; article 37: «...ayant la Cour vraysemblablement esté meue...»

[26] Articles 42, 49, 57, 68, 69: dans tous ces cas, la rédaction de l'article suggère qu'il n'y avait pas unanimité au sein du collège. En revanche, lorsque De Grysperre fait état de la 'conformité' ou 'concordance' des voix, cela pourrait indiquer que le collège était unanime: ainsi dans les articles 54, 55, 61.

A priori, l'importance relative accordée dans les articles aux arguments des plaideurs peut surprendre: en effet, on ne conçoit guère que ces passages puissent jouir d'une autorité particulière. En fait, on s'aperçoit que dans certaines causes, De Grysperre affirme que la décision fut fondée sur tel argument précité de la partie victorieuse. Surtout, il faut constater que les arguments repris dans les articles ont pour la plupart un caractère juridique. Sans doute, ces arguments juridiques ne sont que rarement basés directement sur le droit savant, mais davantage sur le *ius proprium:* ainsi, dans une certaine mesure, la sélection des arguments dans la cadre extrêmement concis des articles du recueil n'est-elle pas entièrement différente de celle opérée par le greffier lors de la rédaction de la sentence étendue. Il est en tout cas frappant de constater que dans les articles de la seconde série, la portée de dispositions coutumières, et occasionnellement de dispositions législatives, semble constituer la raison d'être même du recueil.

5. Recours à des précédents et développements jurisprudentiels

Les références à des décisions antérieures en tant que précédents judiciaires au sens strict, c.à.d. établissant une règle ou un principe susceptible d'être appliqué dans une cause ultérieure, sont, quant aux règles matérielles de droit, plutôt obliques. Pourtant, le recueil contient plusieurs indications de développements jurisprudentiels. En premier lieu, il faut faire état de quelques séries d'articles énumérant plusieurs décisions allant dans le même sens: l'effet cumulatif d'une telle série de décisions implique clairement la formation d'une jurisprudence sur un principe particulier.[27] Ensuite, on relève quelques articles où il est fait mention de mesures de publicité ou d'enregistrement spécialement destinées à assurer une application conforme dans l'avenir: une expression manifeste de la volonté de créer un précédent.[28] Enfin, il faut noter que l'importance des décisions précisant une application du *ius proprium,* et en particulier du droit coutumier, s'inscrivait dans l'ancienne tradition, fortement ancrée au moyen âge, par laquelle la teneur d'une coutume était prouvée (mais souvent aussi, par ce biais, établie de manière plus ou moins créative) par la voie de décisions judiciaires.

[27] Articles 1 et 2; article 3; articles 6 et 7; articles 9 à 18; article 21; articles 28 à 30; articles 35 et 36; article 39; article 40; articles 44 et 45.

[28] Article 32: «...et que note de ce seroit faicte pour selon ce [se] regler doresnavant en cas semblable»; article 51: «...dont par ladite Cour a esté ordonné faire note pour selon ce se regler a l'advenir en semblable[s] cas».

Conclusion

Le recueil de De Grysperre illustre sans doute une conception largement répandue dans le milieu du Grand Conseil vers la fin du 16e siècle quant au rôle des décisions judiciaires dans la pratique de la Cour. Le recueil n'exprime pas tant la volonté de développer le droit ou de créer un droit neuf, mais davantage d'assurer une jurisprudence cohérente: les énumérations, parfois très concises, de jugements semblables, ne citent pas la première décision de la liste comme le précédent qui aurait fourni la base et la justification des décisions ultérieures, ou auquel une autorité particulière serait accordée; les rares cas où il est fait mention d'une mesure visant à assurer une décision semblable à l'avenir se rapprochent davantage de la conception d'un précédent, mais là encore, on a l'impression que l'autorité de la décision judiciaire est subordonnée à celle de la règle établie.

En revanche, la conception des archives de la Cour, et notamment la rédaction des sentences étendues (qui feront par année judiciaire l'objet d'un rassemblement en un registre), apparaît principalement motivée par le souci d'un contrôle de la régularité des procédures et, pour l'avenir, par la nécessité de déterminer aussi précisément que possible la portée de la chose jugée.

Dans le traitement des argumentations et raisonnements juridiques, une distinction entre *ius commune* et *iura propria* s'impose. On constate que dans les sentences étendues, les arguments se rapportant aux sources de cette seconde catégorie ne sont pas systématiquement omis, comme c'est le cas pour les arguments de droit savant. La portée d'une règle de *ius proprium,* en particulier de droit coutumier, retient davantage l'attention de De Grysperre dans sa sélection de décisions. Ces constatations ne sont pas isolées: la pratique, très limitée, de références à des précédents dans les plaidoiries d'avocats au Grand Conseil, est le plus souvent en rapport avec des questions de *ius proprium;* dans le cadre des recours, on a observé que les procédures en révision, dont la recevabilité supposait en principe l'invocation d'une erreur de fait, entraînaient plus facilement des controverses sur une application d'une règle de *ius proprium;*[29] d'une manière générale, la charge de la preuve était plus lourde à l'égard de règles de *ius proprium* (en particulier devant une cour supérieure, où la notion de *ius proprium in loco* tendait à s'effacer) que pour des règles de *ius commune.*[30] Enfin, faut-il rappeler que tant la pratique que la doctrine médiévales avaient établi un

---

29 Les procédures en révision au Grand Conseil de Malines (1473 - 1580), dans: Publication du Centre Européen d'Etudes bourguignonnes (XIVe - XVIe s.) XXX (1990), 67 - 97.

30 *W. Wiegand,* Studien zur Rechtsanwendungslehre der Rezeptionszeit (Ebelsbach 1977).

lien entre la preuve (voire l'introduction) du droit coutumier et sa reconnaissance par des décisions judiciaires? Par contre, la méthode encore prédominante au 16e siècle que suivait le droit savant mettait moins l'accent sur l'application de règles positives de droit matériel, du moins en comparaison avec la méthode qui s'imposera au siècle suivant.

Le recueil de De Grysperre rappelle aussi qu'auparavant, d'autres formes d'annotations ou de collections basées sur des décisions du Grand Conseil circulaient. Durant les décennies suivantes, plusieurs autres recueils de conseillers virent le jour, sans toutefois être imprimés; les manuscrits conservés attestent toutefois que ces ouvrages connurent un certain succès. Cependant, après les recueils de De Grysperre, Cuvelier, De Humayn, Du Fief, la tradition semble s'être perdue pendant près d'un siècle – les manuscrits inventoriés n'indiquent en tout cas pas une poursuite de ces efforts. Les raisons de cette désaffection demeurent incertaines. La publication des *Decisiones* de Christinaeus aurait pu encourager le développement de recueils plus élaborés. Peut-être la confirmation du déclin du Grand Conseil au cours du 16e siècle – comme en témoigne la forte réduction de son ressort, tant en raison de l'évolution internationale que pour des motifs de politique intérieure – a-t-elle en revanche favorisé un repli progressif des conseillers dans le courant du 17e siècle. Il est en tout cas frappant que ce fut le Conseil de Brabant, sans doute la cour supérieure de justice des Pays-Bas méridionaux faisant preuve de la plus grande assurance au cours des derniers siècles de l'Ancien Régime, qui inspira quelques recueils de jurisprudence imprimés plus importants. Malgré sa vocation, le Grand Conseil de Malines n'a guère développé une jurisprudence ayant constitué un apport direct important au développement de l'ancien droit belge.

Annexe

Leiden, Universiteitsbibliotheek, Hs. BPL 54[31]

[133r] Instruction pour minuter, fecter et extendre les sentences quy se rendent et prononchent au grand conseil de l'empereur n*ot*re sire selon la diversité des matieres et proces quy se traictent et demainent.

1. Premiers prendront en leur mains les sacqz et production zur quoy la sentence aura esté rendue, recoeuilleront toutes les pieces suyvant les inventoires, commenchant a celluy de l'impetrant, demandeur, appellant, reformant ou impetrant de proposition d'erreur, et generallem*ent* de celluy provoquant ad iudicium et intentant proces, cum ex p*ar*te actoris ius metiamur, ex p*ar*te ad ius provocantis sit inchoandum. Separera les pieches de celluy commenchant le proces l'une[32] de l'aultre, mectra au costé droict les pieches dont il aura besoing a la confection de la sen-

[31] La ponctuation, l'accentuation et la numérotation des alinéas ont été ajoutées.

[32] Rayé: «de», répété immédiatement après.

ten*ce*, si comme l'impetration ou venue en court, quant venue en court y a eu, la demande et aenspraecke servie pardevant les loyx ausd*its* juges inferieurs que vaillent pour venue en court, mesmes quant au marge ou en fin d'icelle [133v] le jour de l'exhibition de telle demande est couchié, l'acte de ramené a faict avecq la demande ou *con*clusions p*ar* escript s'aulcunes en y a; la replicque et aultres escriptz ulterieurs, escriptures, memoires, additions et supersolutions, requestes civiles et aussy les requestes p*ar* escript dont mention est faicte p*ar* le dictum s'aulcunes en y a,[33] l'acte dispositif, l'acte interlocutoire en faictz ou information d'office quant parties sont appoinctees contraires ou en verification sur poinctz d'office, l'acte sur faictz principaux, et celluy d'avoir servy de reproches et salvations, si comme les enquestes et tiltres, reproches et salvations, requestes par escript dont mention n'est faicte p*ar* le dictum et tous aultres pieches dont l'on n'aura besoing pour extendre la sentence mectra au costé senestre, les lyera ensamble et remectra au sacq.

2. Apres prendra le sacq de l'ad*journé*, deffendeur ou inthimé, receuillera aussy les pieches selon l'inventoire, mectra au costé dextre les pieches que s'ensuyvent, asscavoir l'acte de deffence et response en [134r] quelque matiere que ce soit, pour les responces et conclusions et duplicque p*ar* escript, additions, solutions et aultres escriptz ulterieurs, l'acte dispositif du costé de l'inthimé quant le proces est receu co*mm*e proces p*ar* escript, ne soit que l'appellant ayt levé et l'inthimé non, et pareillement en matiere de reformation et proposition d'erreur, les contredictz sur req*ue*te par escript, actes sur faictz principaulx et conclusions en droict, quant la p*ar*tie ne les aura levé. Et du costé senestre remectra les enquestes, tiltres et munimens, reproches et salvations, les relyera ensamble et remectra au sacq.

3. Ce faict lira et entendra les inventoires, apres procedera p*ar* ordre et a la lecture et intelligen*ce* de aultres pieches servantes a la confection de sa sentence, advisera de comprendre le poinct ou poinctz sur quoy se assiet le proces, et la lecture achevee commenchera p*ar* tel ordre que sens*ui*t:

4. En matiere crue et d'imposition quant l'impetrant aura obtenu, co*mm*enchera le greffier ou son clercq la sentence [134v] p*ar* l'impetration et venue en court, couchera le jour ou saltem le mois que l'impetrant presenta sa requeste sur laquelle son impetration a esté depesché, narrera au plus brief les premises dicelle impetration, et venant au dispositif couchera que sur le contenu esd*ites* p*re*mises l'impetrant a obtenu ses l*ett*res patentes et en vertu d'icelles faict faire commandement ou adjourner selon que les lettres sont. Et sy les l*ett*res de commandement sont au loing libellés, reprendra lesd*its* commandemens, puys pour l'oppo*sitio*n y créé dira que l'huyssier executeur l'aura adjourné a ung tel jour qu'il trouvera p*ar* la relation. Et sy l'impetrant a succumbé et l'adjourné triumphé et que ambedeux les p*ar*ties ont servy de memoires ou escriptures, co*mm*enchera sa sentence p*ar* telz et semblables mot: Comme de ung tel mois (qu'il trouvera p*ar* la relation servante a la venue en

---

[33] Le défaut de ponctuation dans le manuscrit (tandis que l'usage de majuscules n'offre pas une alternative) soulève un problème d'interprétation: où s'arrête l'énumération des pièces à classer «à dextre», et où commence celle des pièces à classer «à senestre»? Une comparaison avec l'alinéa suivant suggère que la série des documents que le greffier remettra au sac sans les utiliser pour la rédaction de la sentence étendue pourrait commencer avec la mention «si comme les enquestes et tiltres...».

court), proces et question se soyent meuz, ayant esté pendans d'entre A., l'imp*etrant* d'une p*art*, et B., adjourné deffend*eur* d'aultre. Pour a raison, prendra regard a ce dont est question. Et puis dira: led*it* imp*etrant* pour obtenir en ses demande, fins et conclusions [135r] cy ap*rez* couchees, disant etc. Reprendra le faict, raisons et moyens y s*er*vans. Et ce faict et les conclusions de l'impetrant couchees, viendra aux faictz, raisons et moyens de l'ad*journ*é en disant: Sur quoy de la p*art* dud*it* adiiourné, ou: A quoy de la part etc.

5. Les conclusions de l'adjourné couchees, sy au regard de celluy quy obtient p*ar* le dictum, soit le demandeur ou deffendeur, samble que les escriptures ne soyent pregnantes pour avoir obtenu, ou que sy l'impetrant obtient, samble que l'adjourné ayt couchié p*ar* ses memoires, raisons et moyens plus pregnante, et que polroient sambler bailler bonne cause a l'ad*journ*é, advisera lors le formateur de sentence de regarder les additions de l'imp*etran*t sy servy en a et reprendra en brief les poinctz et articles quy sambleront donner sollution aux raisons et moyens de l'adjourné.

6. D'aultre p*art*, en matiere crue quant il n'y a venue en court ou que icelle venue en court est fort obscure et les[34] escriptures hinc inde fort obscures et prolixes, et il y a demandes, deffences et conclusions amples p*ar* [135v] escript contenans aulcunes raisons et moyens, ne sera besoing se entruiller en telles escriptures, ains prendant le jour ou que le proces a esté entamé lors passer oultre et descendre aux demandes, r*espo*nces et conclusions, ainsy aulcunement raisonnees, co*mm*e dict est.

7. Ce faict et p*ar*ties oyes, fauldra couchier l'acte dispositif et p*ar* ap*rez* l'acte interlocutoire en enqueste ordinaire et d'office quant tel acte se trouvera au proces, coucher aussy les requestes civiles en leur ordre et observant icelluy es dites et aussy les requestes par escript dont mention est faicte p*ar* le dictum en non aultres, reprendra en brief le dispositif desd*i*tes req*ue*tes civiles et p*ar* escript, ensamble les plus pregnantes raisons et moyens au contraire couchiéz es contredictz, quant l'on a servy de contredictz, et quant non, seullement l'acte de contredict, qui porte tousiours que le contredisant de requeste civile content affin qu'elle soit declairee incivile et desraisonnable, et au surplus de reiection et co*mm*e elle sera trouvee couchee.

[136r] **8.** Sera aussy couché en son ordre que p*ar*ties auront faict leurs enquestes ou l'une la sienne et que p*ar*tie adverse en sera[35] demouree forclose comme ambedeux les p*ar*ties ou l'une tant seullement auront ou aura servy ou employee reproches et salvations, selon qu'il se trouvera porté p*ar* les actes et que finablem*ent* auront concludt en droict. Et ce faict, venu au dispositif de la sentence par telz mots: Et led*it* proces desd*ites* parties furny et mis en estat de juger, elles nous ont instam*m*ent supplié etc. et aultres sam*bla*bles.

9. En matiere crue et d'impetration ou l'adjourné sera trouvé deffaillant, convient reprendre les procedures et deffaulx, reprenant le narré des premiers exploictz, les actes y servants, et ap*rez* l'interlocutoire p*ar* lequel l'impetrant est admiz a veriffier son intendit portant le prouffict de deffault qu'il entend avoir acquitz, les raisons et moyens couchiez en tel intendit que trouvera luy servir a la sentence et p*ar* espec*i*al

---

[34] Rayé: sentences.

[35] Les trois dernières lettres du mot «sera» constituent une correction, écrites au-dessus d'autres caractères, non déchiffrés.

ceulx couchéz ap*rez* l'article portant q*ue* furnissant a l'appoinctem*ent* l'imp*etran*t sert de son intendit, ap*rez* lequel art*ic*le se couchie com*mu*nem*ent* quelq*ue*s art*ic*les des ordon*nances* du grand conseil [136v] qu'est bien requiz d'estre reprins pour tant mieulx iustifier la sentence.

10. En matiere d'appel, reformation ou reduction, le dictateur de la sentence, apres avoir recueillé les pieche*s* des p*ar*ties hinc inde et bien entendu le dictum quant c'est proces par escript, lira et advisera de bien entendre la sentence dont aura este appellé, et le laudum traict en reduction. Ce faict, s'il trouve quelq*ue* p*re*miere venue en court ou proces par escript, commenchera sa sentence p*ar* la date du jour assigné sur icelle venue en court, et ap*rez* formera sa senten*ce* hors de lad*i*te sentence dont a esté appellé ou reformé, et laude dont est reduict, siavant q*ue* telle senten*ce* et laude soient deuement extenduz. Synon aura recours aux escriptures, memoires et aultres escriptz qu'il trouvera au proces p*ar* escript et advisera de prendre les faictz, raisons et moyens que luy sambleront servir a lad*i*te senten*ce*. Reprendra enoultre en brief tout le demené du proces par escript et s'y couchera le dictum [137r] de la sentence dont est appellé avecq la date. Ce faict viendra a l'instance appellatoire et s'il y a anticipation obtenue p*ar* celluy ayant obtenu lad*i*te sentence en touchera sommerement et puis viendra aux griefs de l'appellant, lesquelz il reprendra en brief sy avant que l'inthimé ayant obtenu en ladicte matiere d'appel ayt servy de memoires baillant solutions p*er*tinentes ausd*its* griefz. Aultrement et s'il n'y trouve lesd*its* griefz bien debatuz, ne les couchera, ains touchera en termes generaulx que l'appellant au faict aura proposé les tors et griefz de l'appellation telz que bon luy a samblé, ne fust que l'appellant ayant proposé griefz en p*ar*ticulier et p*ar* specification obtenist et qu'il fust dict bien avoir appellé que lors en tout event, soit qu'il ayt apparentes solutions baillees p*ar* l'inthimé ou non, se coucheront tousiours tels griefz en extendant la sentence et s'il y a requeste civile en fera co*mme* dessus. Et procedera ausurplus en brief les procedures qu'il trouvera en la matiere d'appel, id*em* de la[36] matiere de reformation et réduction.

[137v] **11.** En matiere de decret apres que l'on aura bien entendu le dictum et mis ordre entre les pieches de production, l'on prendra la relation de l'huyssier pour en premier lieu drescher le billet quy se doibt affiger aux huys du palais et ailleurs. Et pour icelluy deuement faire lad*i*te relation au loing veue et incorporee. Et sy besoing est pour la prolixité et multitude des conditions annotee[37] et appostillee pour la memoire l'on couchera en icelluy billet les biens mis en criees et soubhastations et dont la vente se doibt passer p*ar* decret p*ar* bonne specification designation des aboutz, ensamble les charges quy en vuydent et pour quel pris iceulx biens sont demouréz au dernier rencherisseur, affin que tous telz quy poulroient desirer avoir telz biens se puissent reigler selon telles conditions.

[139r][38] Tiltre en franchois

Philippe par la grace de Dieu Roy de Castille, Leon, Arragon, Navarre, Napels, Cicille, Maillorcque, Sardaine, des ysles Indes et terre ferme de la mer Oceans, Archiduc d'Austrice, Duc de Bourgongne, Lothir, Brabant, Lemborch, Luxemborch, Gelre et de Milan, Conte de Hasborch, Flandres, d'Arthois et de Bourgongne Pala-

[36] Les mots «de la» sont répétés par erreur dans le manuscrit.

[37] A la fin du mot: lettre «s» rayée.

[38] Ce qui suit ne fait pas partie de l'Instruction qui précède.

tin et de Haynault, Hollande, Zelande, N*amur* et de Zutphen, Prince de Zwave, Marquis de S*ain*t Empire, S*eigneu*r de Phrise, Salins, Malines, des cité, villes et pays d'Utrecht, d'Overysel et de Groeningen, et dominateur en Asie et Africque.

Tiltre en thois

Philippus byder gratie Godts, Coninck van Castilien, Leon, Arragon, Navarre, Napels, Cicilien, Maillorcke, Sard[i]nie, vanden eylanden Indien en*de* vaster eerde der zee Oceane, Eertshartoghe van Oostenrijck, Hartoghe van Bourgongne, Lothier, Brabant, Lemborch, Luxemborch, Gelre en*de* van Milaenen, Grave van Hasborch, Vlaenderen, Arthois en*de* van Bourgongne Palsgrave van Henegouwe, Hollandt, Zeelant, [39]Namen en*de* van Sutphen, Prince van Zwave, Marckgrave des Heylichs Rijck, Heere van Vrieslant, Salins ende van Mechelen, vander stadt, steeden en*de* landen van Utrecht, Overysel, en*de* van Groeninghen, ende dominateur in Asien en*de* Africke.

---

[39] Rayé: en*de*.

J. TH. DE SMIDT ET C. VERHAS*

Le *Hoge Raad* (La Haye), Cour Suprême de Hollande, Zélande et Frise Occidentale

Introduction

Vers 1445, le recours en appel de la *curia comitis,* la Cour de Hollande (1428), au Grand Conseil du Duc de Bourgogne se développe. Au cours des 15e et 16e siècles, plusieurs milliers de décisions de la Cour feront l'objet d'un appel au Grand Conseil (de 1473 à 1477: Parlement de Malines). Ainsi, dans les Pays-Bas sous les régimes bourguignon et habsbourgeois, le Grand Conseil était devenu le sommet de la hiérarchie judiciaire.

En 1568, la révolte contre Philippe II, menée par Guillaume d'Orange, prit feu. Dans le courant des années '70, une frontière se forma entre, au nord, les territoires combattant pour leur indépendance, et les Pays-Bas méridionaux, sous domination espagnole, où était située la ville de Malines, siège du Grand Conseil. Ainsi, la guerre fit obstacle aux appels des provinces septentrionales à Malines et le prince d'Orange évoqua l'opportunité de créer en remplacement un conseil siégeant en Hollande. Son idée était que cette cour fonctionnerait comme cour suprême pour l'ensemble des Provinces-Unies. En fait, la juridiction de ce nouveau tribunal, appelé *Hoge Raad,* resta limitée aux seules provinces de Hollande et de Zélande.[1]

Le président et neuf conseillers (au début uniquement des Hollandais) entrèrent en fonction le 13 février 1582.[2] Le siège de la cour fut établi à La

* J. Th. de Smidt a rédigé l'introduction et la partie sur les recueils, tandis que Mlle C. Verhas a rédigé la partie sur les archives judiciaires. A. Wijffels a traduit le texte en français.

[1] *A. S. de Blécourt* [et *W. Tonckens J. Lzn*], De geboorte van den Hoogen Raad van Holland en Zeeland, dans: Tijdschrift voor Rechtsgeschiedenis 2 (1921), 428 - 459; *J. Th. de Smidt,* Ons hoogste rechtscollege in het verleden, dans: De Hoge Raad der Nederlanden 1938 - 1988. Een portret (Zwolle 1988), 17 - 31.

[2] Ils avaient déjà été nommés en 1581, et exercèrent leurs fonctions en tant que commissaires en révision, avant même que la cour ne fût établie.

Haye. Le premier jugement fut prononcé le 8 mai 1582, réformant en appel une décision de la Cour de Hollande du 12 mars 1580.[3]

L'instruction du 31 mai 1582, comptant 289 articles, fut édictée par Guillaume d'Orange. Selon son agencement et sa teneur, cette instruction suit largement l'ordonnance de Philippe II pour le Grand Conseil, du 8 août 1559. Le conseil et son instruction survécurent jusqu'à la dernière séance de l'institution, le 10 octobre 1795. Dans le nouveau contexte politique, où la République batave succéda à l'ancienne République, il fut décidé (par arrêté du 30 septembre 1795) de 'mortifier' *(mortificeren)* le *Hoge Raad.* En 1797, on fit encore état de deux anciens concepts de l'instruction de 1582, mais ces textes avaient déjà disparu en 1854.[4]

I. Les archives judiciaires

Les compétences du conseil n'étaient pas exclusivement judiciaires, et, par conséquent, les archives de la cour reflètent également ses activités supplémentaires. Dans la cadre de la présente contribution, les observations suivantes ne concernent que les documents relevant de l'activité juridictionnelle du conseil.

1. Juridiction contentieuse, civile[5]

En principe, les sacs de procédure étaient retirés par les procureurs après le procès. De ce fait, les archives préservées contiennent essentiellement les documents et registres que le greffier était tenu de conserver.[6] Les procès peuvent être reconstitués grâce aux *requêtes* (1.1), *rôles* (1.2), *actes de procédure ('dingtalen')* (1.3), *résolutions* (1.4), *dicta* (1.5) et *sentences étendues* (1.6).

1.1. La *requête*[7] contient la demande par laquelle un suppliant fait valoir qu'il veut intenter une action. C'est la première étape du procès, qui indique immédiatement la nature du litige. Les requêtes étaient rédigées

---

[3] *Th. A. Ariëns,* 400 jaar Hoge Raad, dans: Advocatenblad 1982, 354 - 369.

[4] *R. C. Bakhuizen van den Brink,* Overzigt van het Nederlandsche Rijks-archief (La Haye 1854). Overzigt van het archief der voormalige regtscollegien in Holland. II: De Hooge Raad, p. 196 - 207.

[5] Les procès criminels se retrouvent jusqu'en 1735 dans les mêmes séries que les causes civiles.

[6] Toutes les pièces sont rédigées en néerlandais. Elles sont généralement classées par année, de janvier à décembre. Les vacances judiciaires tombaient au mois d'août: la cour interrompait ses travaux durant ce mois, pour lequel on ne rencontre par conséquent pas de documents.

[7] Le *Hoge Raad:* Collation de recueils..., 1.1.

selon un modèle plus ou moins établi, dont le contenu offre au chercheur les éléments de base quant au litige.[8]

Le suppliant (après une introduction-type) se présente en mentionnant son nom, son domicile, et éventuellement sa profession, et indique en quelle qualité il procède. Ensuite, il esquisse les faits ayant donné lieu au litige: cette narration reprend les principaux éléments de la cause et une motivation de la requête. Le demandeur fait valoir, par exemple, que la prestation qui lui est due n'a pas été accomplie, et qu'il a interpellé (en vain) la partie adverse. Ces éléments justifient la nécessité pour le suppliant de recourir à la justice.

Dans les causes d'appel, la requête décrit brièvement la procédure en première instance, en précisant la date et la portée des jugements intervenus, et confirmant le recours en appel. Dans cette partie, le plaideur explique surtout en quoi il s'estime lésé. Sa narration mentionne évidemment également l'identité de la partie adverse, souvent (mais pas nécessairement) en précisant le domicile, l'occupation et la qualité de l'adversaire. Au 18e siècle, dans les causes où les inventaires ou pièces de procédure devaient être échangés, les requêtes sont rédigées et agencées par articles.

La requête se termine par un dispositif, qui comprend deux éléments: premièrement, une clause de simple mandement *(clausule van simpel bevel),* par laquelle le suppliant requiert un mandement judiciaire spécifique, selon l'objet de ses griefs; cette clause précise ce que le demandeur entend obtenir de la partie adverse. Le second élément du dispositif est une clause justificative *(clausule justificatoir),* comprenant un ajournement en cas d'opposition.

Certains mandements étaient obtenus par dispositif, pour lequel une formule établie était prévue.[9] Dans ce cas, on n'avait pas recours à un dispositif comprenant les deux éléments. Le mandement en appel en est un exemple.

En plus du mandement, le requérant mentionnait les clauses qu'il estimait devoir invoquer au cours du procès. La clause la plus courante (dans les procédures en appel) était celle de relèvement *(relief),* par laquelle le demandeur se protégeait contre d'éventuelles exceptions en raison (notam-

---

[8] Dans la plupart des cas, la partie avait recours à un avocat pour rédiger la requête. De nombreux manuels suggéraient des modèles et expliquaient comment formuler une requête (*J. van der Linden,* Verhandeling over de judicieele practijcq of form van procedeeren, 2e livre, pp. 106 - 111; *R. Hogerbeets,* Van het aen-legghen ende volvoeren der processen voor de respective Hoven van Iustitie in Holland, II praeparatoria et IX Quintus actus; *W. van Alphen,* Papegaij ofte formulierboek).

[9] *J. van der Linden,* Verhandeling over de judicieele practijcq of form van procedeeren, I, 1794; II, 1798; I - II, 1829.

ment) de fautes de procédure de sa part. D'autres clauses fréquemment utilisées étaient celles d'inhibition *(inhibitie),* c.à.d. l'interdiction d'exécuter le jugement attaqué, celles de surséance *(surceantie),* c.à.d. visant à obtenir la suspension de payement, et celles d'autorisation et insinuation *(authorisatie en insinuatie),* c.à.d. afin de citer une partie résidant en dehors du territoire propre à la juridiction. Parfois, le suppliant demandait à obtenir un *committimus,* c.à.d. l'attribution de la compétence sur l'affaire à une juridiction particulière. Si le suppliant voulait modifier ou amplier sa requête à un stade ultérieur, il lui fallait introduire à cet effet une *requête civile.*

La décision de donner suite à la requête, partant d'autoriser, le cas échéant, la poursuite du procès, revenait aux commissaires chargés des audiences au rôle. Les commissaires devaient notamment vérifier s'il n'y avait pas d'obstacles à la compétence et saisie de la cour à laquelle le requérant s'était adressé. Parfois, leur décision n'accueillait qu'en partie la requête du suppliant. La décision se retrouve, suivant une formulation succincte, dans la marge de gauche de la requête, sous forme d'*apostille.* Si la requête était acceptée, on y lit: *fiat ut petitur,* et en outre toute spécification quant aux clauses supplémentaires ou au committimus. Si les commissaires estimaient que la requête n'était pas fondée, ils y répondaient par: *nihil;* si la requête n'était pas recevable telle qu'elle était présentée, la réponse était: *nihil ut petitur;* enfin, si les commissaires estimaient que la cour était incompétente: *nihil hic.*

Les archives du *Hoge Raad* ont conservé les requêtes pratiquement dans leur intégralité pour l'ensemble de la période, de 1582 à 1795. Les pièces sont classées plus ou moins par ordre chronologique, selon la date de l'apostille. A l'origine, il s'agissait de lettres individuelles, qui furent ensuite en principe reliées; cependant, les requêtes manquent pour certains procès.

Les mandements n'étaient pas conservés à la cour, mais remis aux parties.[10] Le mandement permettait de citer la partie adverse et de commencer la procédure contradictoire. Dans certains cas, le mandement était remplacé par un appointement, et notamment dans les causes de moindre importance en première instance, lorsque le défendeur résidait à La Haye ou sous la juridiction hacquenoise *(Haag-Ambacht),* ainsi que pour les citations portant sur des salaires. Le greffier mentionnait l'appointement au-dessous de la requête, mais l'appointement pouvait également être attaché à celle-ci. Ce sont les seuls exemples de mandements adressés aux huissiers conservés dans les archives du *Hoge Raad.*

---

[10] Les intimations (*'intimatiën',* c.à.d. la dernière citation à comparaître) font exception à cette règle; elles ont été conservées pour la période de 1711 à 1795.

1.2 La suite du procès peut être reconstituée dans les *registres au rôle.*[11] Ces registres contiennent, pour chaque séance à l'audience du rôle, un aperçu des causes traitées à cette date. Théoriquement, une seule séance du rôle était prévue par semaine, mais si l'abondance des matières l'exigeait, on poursuivait les audiences le lendemain.

Les registres au rôle étaient tenus selon un système uniforme. A la date de la séance, on mentionne toujours les noms des (deux) conseillers qui présidaient à la séance. Les procureurs étaient tenus d'introduire au greffe pour chaque procès une présentation *(presentatie),* mentionnant les noms, domiciles et position procédurale des parties, ainsi que l'objet de la présentation (p.ex. afin de présenter la demande). Les billets contenant cette présentation étaient transcrits par un greffier dans le registre au rôle, par procureur et dans l'ordre selon lequel ils lui étaient remis. Les procès où intervenait le procureur général (représentant les droits du souverain) étaient traités (et sont mentionnés) prioritairement.

Le substitut du greffier ou un secrétaire faisait lecture du rôle aux conseillers commis à l'audience du rôle, selon l'ordre dans lequel les présentations avaient été enregistrées. Les procureurs des plaideurs s'approchaient alors des conseillers et présentaient l'action prévue. Les registres au rôle contiennent toutefois plus que l'agenda des présentations, car les notules renseignent également ce que les procureurs avaient effectivement présenté. Après la séance, ces notules étaient dictées par les procureurs au substitut du greffier, et inscrites (à gauche) à côté de la présentation afférente dans le registre. Concrètement, il y est mentionné quels actes de procédure ont été effectués par les procureurs, comment la cour en disposa, et dans quels délais la suite du procès aura lieu.

Afin de suivre un procès déterminé dans ces registres, il est pratiquement indispensable de connaître les noms des procureurs intervenant dans l'affaire. Un même procès peut être traité plusieurs fois au cours d'une même séance, et il est donc nécessaire de parcourir toutes les affaires où interviennent ces procureurs. En outre, la pratique démontre qu'on ne peut s'en tenir à consulter les inscriptions faites aux dates correspondant aux renvois dans la marge, car, avant le délai prévu, d'autres actes de procédure pouvaient intervenir (p.ex. une requête civile, une demande reconventionnelle, une complainte, etc.).

Au cours d'une séance, on traitait en premier lieu les affaires déjà présentées antérieurement, ensuite – à nouveau par procureur – les nouvelles causes.

En comparaison avec le style en usage à la Cour provinciale de Hollande, l'enregistrement du rôle au Conseil demeura fort élémentaire: on

[11] Le *Hoge Raad:* Collation de recueils..., 1.2.

n'utilisait en effet qu'un seul registre. De 1582 à 1735, le Conseil a tenu un rôle unique pour les causes civiles et criminelles. Ensuite, ces causes furent enregistrées séparément, sans que la forme des registres au rôle ne fût modifiée.

Au 18e siècle (de 1707 à 1797), il y eut également un rôle aux plaidoiries *(pleitrol),* dont le registre, dans sa partie de droite, comportait également un agenda des présentations, tandis qu'à gauche, on inscrivait la date à laquelle l'affaire était plaidée, et les noms des deux conseillers désignés en tant que commissaires.

Tous ces registres suivent un ordre chronologique. Les registres conservés ne se présentent pas toujours en bon état. La série est parfois interrompue, quelques années manquent entièrement.

1.3 Les renseignements sur la procédure fournis par les registres au rôle peuvent être complétés par les *actes de procédure ('acten van dingtalen').*[12] Quant à leur contenu, ces documents correspondent aux registres au rôle, mais les actes de procédure y sont mentionnés plus explicitement. Souvent, les registres au rôle renvoient dans la marge à ces actes, pour les inscriptions à l'affaire correspondante; les folios de ces actes sont, en effet, numérotés.

Il peut cependant être malaisé de retracer une cause dans cette documentation, car ces actes sont classés de manière très arbitraire. Le but de ces inscriptions demeure incertain, et on ne sait à quel moment précis elles furent rédigées. Vraisemblablement, ces actes étaient inscrits au registre au moment où un procureur sollicitait une copie d'une conclusion particulière. Il semble bien que ces inscriptions ne furent pas enregistrées au moment des actes de procédure auxquels ils se rapportent: ainsi, on rencontre parfois plusieurs actes concernant une même procédure regroupés dans le registre, toutefois sans ordre logique ou chronologique. Partant, il est nécessaire de consulter l'ensemble du registre et de reclasser par ordre chronologique les différentes inscriptions. Les actes mentionnent au début le nom du procureur; parfois, cette mention figure dans la marge.

Tous les actes de procédure ne furent pas transcrits dans ces registres, et cette source ne fournit donc pas un aperçu complet du procès. L'utilité de ces registres consiste à compléter les informations des registres au rôle et des conclusions des procureurs.

1.4 La *conclusion du procureur* est l'adresse finale dans laquelle la partie (par son représentant) résume sa demande. Il s'agit d'une pièce très importante, rédigée par un avocat et présentée par un procureur. Pour la rédaction de ces conclusions, les avocats suivaient certains 'formulaires', en usage à

[12] Le *Hoge Raad:* Collation de recueils..., 1.3.

la cour.[13] Ces formulaires offrent des exemples adaptés selon la nature du litige, et se prêtaient à des adaptations, selon les besoins et les circonstances de la cause. Les auteurs insistent sur la nécessité d'être bref et clair dans les discours. Ces documents ressemblent davantage aux requêtes. Il s'agit de lettres, rédigées par les avocats et datées par le greffier.

Au cours du procès, les procureurs pouvaient être amenés à conclure à plusieurs reprises, selon la complexité de la cause et le nombre d'actes de procédure entrepris. Si les procureurs maintenaient leur conclusions initiales (c. à. d. qu'ils 'persistaient'), il n'était pas nécessaire d'introduire une nouvelle conclusion au greffe.

Les conclusions sont justifiées en se référant à leurs fondements juridiques: elles mentionnent ainsi les autorités et sources de droit invoquées.

Le procureur remettait au greffe la grosse de sa conclusion, et la partie adverse en obtenait une copie. Les conclusions grossées ont été conservées pour la période de 1586 à 1792, les minutes des conclusions pour la période de 1582 à 1795.

L'issue du procès – lorsqu'elle est déterminée devant la Cour – est documentée par les archives suivantes:

1.5 Les *résolutions aux sentences ('resoluties tot de sententies')*[14] permettent d'établir comment les conseillers délibéraient sur les affaires. Il s'agit en effet de procès-verbaux concis des délibérations, établis par le greffier qui y avait assisté.

Le rapporteur, un conseiller désigné par le président pour étudier le dossier de la cause et d'en faire rapport, suggère une solution. Les autres conseillers, informés sur l'affaire par son rapport, soit rejoignaient son opinion, soit exprimaient une opinion différente. La décision était prise à la majorité des voix.

Nous n'apprenons pas quels furent les motifs juridiques sur lesquels se fondèrent les juges. Néanmoins, les résolutions constituent une source de première importance pour l'étude de la jurisprudence de la cour. Dans les causes où les opinions étaient partagées et entrainaient une discussion, les considérations individuelles des conseillers sont parfois exprimées en détail.

Les délibérations exigeaient souvent plusieurs votes. Lorsqu'aucune opinion divergente n'était exprimée, la cause était tranchée selon la solution proposée par le rapporteur. En cas de discussion, la décision de la cour est souvent mentionnée au bas de la résolution. Lorsque le collège n'arrivait

---

[13] *J. van der Linden*, o.c., I, pp. 144 - 150. Plusieurs formulaires de ce genre firent l'objet de recueils, par exemple le Papegaij édité par *Van Alphen*.

[14] Le *Hoge Raad:* Collation de recueils..., 1.4.

pas à une majorité, le greffier notait à cet endroit que l'affaire 'n'était pas en état d'être terminée'. Dans un tel cas, les parties devaient le plus souvent 'comparaître' devant un ou deux conseillers, qui tâchaient de les inciter à un accord. Si cela s'avérait impossible, la cause était réduite aux principales difficultés, que l'on tâchait de trancher point par point, jusqu'à ce qu'une résolution puisse être obtenue. On a déjà relevé que les motivations ayant emporté la décision de la cour n'étaient pas explicitées. Les délibérations demeuraient secrètes.

Les résolutions constituent une série chronologique de 1582 à 1779. Quelques années seulement ont été perdues. Au cours des premières années du fonctionnement du *Hoge Raad,* les résolutions restent très concises. Progressivement, les procès-verbaux devinrent plus élaborés et plus systématiques. Malheureusement, tous les procès ne se retrouvent pas dans les résolutions.

Pour la période 1684 - 1745, on a également conservé les minutes des résolutions.

1.6 Lorsque la décision de la cour était prise, le rapporteur rédigeait le *dictum 'conforme à la résolution' ('dictum zoals geresolveerd'),* reprenant l'essentiel du jugement. En cas de difficulté, une sentence interlocutoire était rendue. L'avantage des dicta 'conformes à la résolution' est que, souvent, le rapporteur établissait une liste des questions à examiner avant de pouvoir les résoudre. Aucune forme particulière n'étant prescrite pour la rédaction des dicta, leur contenu dépend du conseiller qui en était l'auteur. Du moins y a-t-il toujours un rapport de la résolution. Afin de s'assurer que la teneur du dictum soit conforme à la résolution, l'ensemble était relu et signé par une second conseiller, le lecteur. Dans le cas d'une sentence définitive, le texte était repris pratiquement verbatim dans le *registre des dicta 'conformes au prononcé' ('dicta zoals gepronuncieerd').* On peut distinguer l'un dictum de l'autre en collationant les dates: les dicta du premier type mentionnent la date de la résolution, tandis que les registres reprennent la date à laquelle le jugement fut prononcé. Ce dernier dictum constituait la forme finale de la sentence, prononcée en audience publique. Ainsi, le texte était rédigé selon un modèle déterminé, contenant les noms des parties, la nature du litige, et la décision. Les deux séries de dicta ont été minutieusement conservées durant toute la période d'activité du *Hoge Raad;* les dicta y sont repris en ordre chronologique. Quant à la forme, la rédaction dépend en partie de la complexité de la cause.

1.7 Les *sentences étendues ('geëxtendeerde sententies')* constituent l'aboutissement de certains procès. Les jugements du Conseil que l'on rencontre dans les registres aux dicta n'ont pas tous été transcrits et amplifiés sous forme de sentence étendue. Il est probable que la partie victorieuse demandait une telle extension au greffe du Conseil afin de pouvoir faire valoir ses droits. Les sentences étendues n'étaient donc rédigées que sur demande d'une partie, et après que celle-ci eût payé les droits dûs à cet effet. Ainsi, cette collection n'est pas représentative de l'activité générale du *Hoge Raad.*

Quant aux informations qu'elles contiennent, ces sentences représentent néanmoins la source la plus intéressante. La sentence commence par une formule de salutation et une introduction au nom du souverain. Ensuite vient une brève évocation de la manière dont la cause fut portée devant la cour. En degré d'appel, cette partie reprend l'instance dont le jugement fit l'objet du recours, en mentionnant les parties en cause, la qualité en laquelle elles procédèrent, l'objet du litige; le déroulement du procès en première instance est narré, présentant d'abord la version de l'appelant, puis celle de l'intimé. Souvent, il s'agit de la seule source informant sur les motifs réels du litige. La teneur des conclusions antérieures y est reprise. La date et la portée du jugement *a quo* sont mentionnées, et l'objet de l'appel est précisé. Cette partie est suivie d'un exposé du déroulement du procès devant le *Hoge Raad,* reprenant à nouveau les conclusions des parties.

La formule 'savoir faisons' *('doen te weten')* annonce le dispositif. Ce dispositif était sans doute transcrit à partir du dictum 'conforme au prononcé'.

Dans l'ensemble, les sentences étendues sont bien conservées, et classées par ordre chronologique. Jusqu'en 1727, les sentences étendues des causes civiles et criminelles ont été reprises dans les mêmes registres; par la suite, cette série ne reprend que les causes civiles (jusqu'en 1790), tandis que les sentences dans les causes criminelles sont reprises dans des registres séparés (allant jusqu'en 1795).

De nombreux procès n'aboutissaient pas à un jugement définitif. Afin de vérifier si une cause fut terminée par jugement, et à quelle date, on dispose de quelques registres utiles: le 'registre chronologique des sentences et dicta' est une série ininterrompue de 1582 à 1778; les causes terminées y sont reprises par trimestre.[15] De 1700 à 1707, on s'est également efforcé de composer un 'index alphabétique'. Quant aux 'registres des procès servis', établis par procureur de 1582 à 1797, on y trouve quand les pièces de procédures furent introduites (ou 'servies').[16] Enfin, il faut faire mention de 'registres des procès, terminés par la Cour', tenus de 1582 à 1797, comprenant des annotations sur la destination des pièces de procédure.

---

[15] Un index alphabétique de ce registre, sous forme de copie, est conservé aux Archives Générales à La Haye.

[16] Le *Hoge Raad:* Collation de recueils..., 1.6.

2. Juridiction gracieuse

Les sentences de la cour n'étaient pas toujours prononcées à l'occasion d'un litige. Les condamnations volontaires se présentent sous la forme de jugement par lequel une ou plusieurs parties se laissaient 'condamner' à un objet déterminé.[17] Elles s'engagent à des obligations mutuelles, et la cour vérifie qu'elles ont réellement consenti et que leur obligation est rédigée conformément au droit. Les condamnations volontaires n'étaient pas prononcées en audience publique, mais enregistrées.

Le registre des condamnations volontaires pouvait être consulté afin de fournir la preuve des obligations. La rédaction de ces condamnations commence de la même manière que les sentences étendues, mais la suite ne contient pas les arguments des parties, mais bien une copie intégrale de leurs obligations. Les registres comprennent également les actes qui se rapportent à l'accord: procurations, sûretés etc.

Les condamnations volontaires ont été bien conservées pour la période 1583 à 1795, mais les années 1613 et 1752 manquent. Il semblerait que la juridiction gracieuse du *Hoge Raad* gagna en importance à partir de la seconde moitié du 17e siècle. Les procurations pour ces accords furent enregistrés separément de 1582 à 1794.

3. Contentieux où intervient le procureur général

Les litiges où les intérêts publics sont représentés constituent une catégorie spéciale. On peut y distinguer deux types de procès.

Lorsque les intérêts du souverain étaient lésés, le procureur général intervenait d'office. S'il s'avérait au cours d'un procès civil qu'un délit grave avait été commis, le procureur général était averti et pouvait intervenir; à partir de ce moment, l'affaire sera traitée comme intéressant l'ordre public. Lorsque la responsabilité de l'autorité supérieure était engagée, ainsi en raison d'un manquement, le procureur général interviendra comme défendeur.

Les causes affectant le trésor public entraînaient l'intervention de l'avocat fiscal.

Dans les causes civiles, ces fonctionnaires intervinrent parfois en tant que parties jointes, aux côtés du demandeur ou du défendeur. La distinction entre causes purement civiles et celles affectant l'intérêt public n'est toute-

---

[17] *B. J. G. M. Ides Peeters,* Korte inleiding op het verschijnsel willige condemnatie bij de Hoge Raad van Holland en Zeeland in de achttiende eeuw, Inleiding 2 (mémoire inédit).

fois pas toujours très nette. Pourtant, on constate clairement la tendance à traiter ces dernières séparément.

Ainsi, dès 1582, un registre au rôle séparé fut réservé au procureur général. Au début, ce registre fut tenu de la manière décrite pour la série générale des registres au rôle. Le 8 février 1585, une 'nouvelle manière de tenir le registre' fut introduite.[18] A partir de cette date, on prévoyait pour chaque nouvelle cause une page sur laquelle on apportait les inscriptions relatives à chaque acte de procédure. Le registre séparé du procureur général fut terminé l'année suivante. On a vu que dans les séances ordinaires mises au rôle, les affaires où intervenait le procureur général étaient traitées par priorité.

De 1595 à 1607, un autre registre fut tenu concernant les causes du procureur général 'pendantes devant la cour'. Durant les années 1755 - 1760, on tint un registre des 'mémoires du procureur général' introduits en cours de procès. En 1735, on composa des 'extraits des rôles du *Hoge Raad* concernant les causes de l'avocat fiscal et du procureur général' pour toute la période antérieure (1582 - 1734); depuis 1986, ces documents sont conservés dans une autre collection.[19]

II. Les recueils de jurisprudence

L'attention des magistrats, avocats, praticiens et non-juristes qui s'intéressent à la pratique judiciaire s'attache aux décisions des *deux* juridictions supérieures en Hollande et en Zélande. Tous les recueils imprimés reprennent à la fois des décisions de la cour la plus ancienne, la Cour de Hollande, et de la cour suprême, le *Hoge Raad.*

Une seule édition ne comprend que le texte des sentences (ci-après: 1.1). Toutes les autres éditions offrent un sommaire ou un extrait des sentences, accompagné d'un commentaire qui peut être succinct ou au contraire plus développé.[20]

Dans la pratique, on citait tant les recueils imprimés que les compilations inédites.

La première édition annotée de l'*Inleidinge tot de Hollandsche rechtsgeleerdheid* de H. de Groot parut en 1664. Simon Groenewegen van der

---

[18] Archives du Royaume à La Haye (ci-après: ARA), Hoge Raad, inv. 1038, fo. 15.

[19] ARA, Archief Bisdom, inv. 155.

[20] *E. M. Meijers,* Uitgegeven en onuitgegeven rechtspraak van den Hoogen Raad en van het Hof van Holland, Zeeland en Westfriesland, in: Tijdschrift voor Rechtsgeschiedenis 1 (1919), 400 - 421; *L. E. van Holk,* L'origine et l'autorité des recueils de jurisprudence aux Pays-Bas, in: Netherlands Reports to the VIIIth International Congress of Comparative Law, 1970, 1 - 14; *J. Th. de Smidt,* Na Vijfenzestig Jaar, in: Huldigingsbundel Paul van Warmelo (Pretoria 1984), 20 - 29.

Made, l'auteur des annotations, s'y réfère à dix décisions non-publiées de la Cour de Hollande et à dix décisions du *Hoge Raad* à l'occasion de questions sur lesquelles l'ouvrage de De Groot et les sentences des cours proposent des solutions divergentes.[21] Au paragraphe 3.35.8, Groenewegen observe dans sa note 22:

> «...il en a été jugé ainsi à plusieurs reprises par la Cour de Hollande, et dernièrement en juillet 1643, dans une cause où je suis moi-même intervenu comme avocat».[22]

De nombreux exemplaires de l'*Inleidinge* étaient reliées avec des pages vierges alternant aux pages imprimées, ce qui permettait aux étudiants et praticiens d'y insérer leurs propres notes. Plusieurs dizaines de ces exemplaires sont conservées dans des bibliothèques publiques et privées, sans qu'ils aient fait l'objet d'un inventaire ou d'une étude systématique. Par exemple, la collection Meijers (IX. 115) compte une édition de 1667 qui contient des références à plus de 250 décisions inédites datant des années 1679 - 1683.

L'ouvrage sur le droit romano-hollandais *(Rooms-Hollands recht)* de S. van Leeuwen était également un manuel pour praticiens. Dans ce livre, on rencontre également des dizaines de références à la jurisprudence inédite.

D'une manière générale, les préfaces des recueils imprimés et inédits mentionnent qu'une décision de la cour suprême (et notamment du Grand Conseil) faisait autorité en tant que décision émanant du souverain. Mais quelle était l'autorité d'une décision judiciaire? Un jugement pouvait-il constituer un principe s'imposant dans un cas analogue entre d'autres plaideurs? Ou encore: les cours considéraient-elles certaines décisions comme des précédents? La règle du Code de Justinien C. 7.45.13 selon laquelle «non exemplis, sed legibus iudicandum est» tend à restreindre la portée d'une décision, mais un jugement rendu par un président et six ou sept conseillers peut sans doute s'imposer à d'autres en tant que *communis opinio doctorum.*

Par contre, les sentences elles-mêmes ne contiennent ni de références explicites à des précédents, ni des considérations sur la force des préjugés. Cependant, la pratique éprouvait bel et bien le besoin de prendre connaissance de la jurisprudence des cours supérieures, car, comme l'exprimait le conseiller J. van den Sande dans la préface de ses *Decisiones Frisicae* à l'égard d'un avocat:

---

[21] «...waer inne dese Inleidinge van enige sententien van de Hoven van Justitie verschillende is» (dans l'avertissement au lecteur).

[22] «...sulx by den Hove van Hollant verscheydemael, ende nu onlangs op den laetsten juij 1643, geoordeelt is in een sake in de welke ik selfs als advocaet gedient hadde».

«...& hoc magis tua opinio in vulgus probabitur, quod judicati auctoritate munita sit. Similiter... multum momenti erit ad obtinendam victoriam, allegare authoritatem rei in simili causa judicatae».

1. Recueils imprimés

1.1 *Sententien en gewezen zaken van den Hoogen en Provincialen Raad in Holland, Zeeland en West-Vriesland, mitsgaders eenige andere zaken den rechten aangaande. Het eerste deel.* (Rotterdam, Joannes Naeranus, 1662).

(Une seconde partie fut annoncée en 1688 par Isaak Naeranus, l'éditeur des *Hollandsche Consultatien,* T. III. Cette seconde partie n'est toutefois jamais parue).

L'éditeur Joannes Naeranus affirme dans sa Préface que les sentences judiciaires n'ont pas force de loi, mais qu'elles jouissent d'une grande autorité en tant qu'opinions de personnes estimées («...opinien van geachte luiden een groote kracht hebben»), voire même une autorité supérieure à celle des avis et consultations des juristes, car les juges doivent effectuer un choix, tandis que les avocats peuvent souvent se borner à défendre un point de vue unilatéral.

Le livre contient onze textes de privilèges, résolutions etc., ainsi que 151 sentences étendues de la Cour de Hollande, 21 du *Hoge Raad,* et deux du Grand Conseil, c.à.d. 184 notices en tout. 125 sentences de la Cour de Hollande datent du 16e siècle, avant 1580; 15 de la période 1580 - 1600; les 11 autres de la période 1600 - 1649. Pour le *Hoge Raad,* on dénombre 17 décisions des années 1590 - 1600, et quatre de la décennie suivante. Aussi, il est remarquable que dans cette édition de 1662, la grande majorité des sentences dataient déjà de plus d'un demi-siècle. L'éditeur ne nous renseigne pas sur l'élaboration de ce recueil; sans doute s'agissait-il d'une collection d'un particulier, dont les héritiers ont présenté le manuscrit à Naeranus. La qualité des transcriptions est de haute qualité, ce qui suggère que leur auteur aurait pu être un secrétaire ou greffier à la Cour de Hollande, du moins un fonctionnaire occupant une position lui offrant tout loisir pour consulter et copier les registres de la Cour.

1.2 Cornelius NEOSTADIUS, *De pactis antenuptialibus rerum judicatarum observationes.* Lugduni Batavorum: Ex Officina I. Patii, sumptibus A. Meuris, 1614 {407}[23]; Lugduni Batavorum: Ex officina Elzeviriana, 1620 {408}. Avec page de titre distincte: Arnhemii, Typis Jacobi

[23] Les chiffres entre { } se rapportent au catalogue des ouvrages de Neostadius dans *M. Ahsmann* et *R. Feenstra,* Bibliografie van hoogleraren in de rechten aan de Leidse universiteit tot 1811. (Amsterdam 1984).

Biesii, 1657, repris dans: F. a Sande, *Opera quae extant.* Arnhemiæ: Typis & sumptibus J. Biesii, 1658 {409}. Egalement repris dans les éditions de *Decisiones* de 1644 {415} et 1667 {418}.

Traductions néerlandaises: avec une page de titre distincte *Observatien, van gewijsden en sententien, over huwelijcksche voorwaerden, ofte voorhuwelijcks contracten gearresteert.* Rotterdam, B. Wagens, 1654, dans: K. van Aller, *Generale regulen en definitien van beschreve rechten.* Rotterdam, B. Wagens, 1655 {410}. *Vonnissen van huwelijkse voorwaarden met aanmerkingen van K. van Nieustad;* traduction néerlandaise par A. van Nispen dans: *Vonnissen,* 1655 {416}. En 1986 est parue une traduction anglaise du *De Pactis,* d'après la dernière édition de 1667, complétée à l'aide des jugements (sentences, dicta et résolutions) conservés dans les archives de la cour, et comprenant un index des auteurs et des textes des *corpora iuris* auxquels se réfère Neostadius.[24]

Curiae Hollandiae, Zelandiae et West-Frisiae decisiones, necnon aliquot decisiones Supremi Senatus, quibus sententiis Curiae rei judicatae auctoritas tribuitur. [La seule édition qui ne porte pas le nom de Neostadius]. Lugduni Batavorum, Ex officina Elzeviriana, 1617 {411}; Lugduni Batavorum, Typis B. et A. Elzevier, 1627 {412}.

Utriusque Hollandiae, Zelandiae et Westfrisiae curiae decisiones a C. Neostadio collectae. Lugduni Batavorum, Ex officina Elzeviriana, 1644 {415}; Hagae-Comitis, Apud J. et D. Steuckerios, 1667 {418}.

Traduction néerlandaise: *Decisien van den Hoogen ende Provincialen Raade van Hollandt, Seelandt ende West-Vrieslandt.* Leyden, By B. ende A. Elzevier, 1627 {413}. [Une traduction de l'édition en Latin de 1627 {412}].

Traduction néerlandaise: *Vonnissen, van den Hoogen, en Provincialen Raad van Holland, Zeeland en West-Vriesland... in Nederduyts over gezet door Adriaan van Nispen.* Rotterdam, Gedrukt by J. Naeranus, 1655 {416}; *Hollandse praktijk in rechten, bestaande in vonnissen, observantien van oordeelen en consultatien, door K. van Nieustad en J. Kooren. Uyt het Latijn vertaald door A. van Nispen.* Rotterdam, By J. Naeranus, 1655 {417} et *[Decisien van den Hove, ende eenige van den Hoogen Rade in Hollandt van C. Neostadius],* reprises dans: K. van Aller, *Generale regulen en definitien van beschreve Rechten.* Rotterdam, B. Wagens, 1655 {410}.

Cornelis Matthiasz. van Nieustadt (1549 - 1606) fit ses études à Douai. Il devint le premier professeur à la faculté de droit de l'université de Leiden,

[24] Observations on decided cases concerning antenuptial contracts written by D. *Cornelius Neostadius.* Translated by *F. J. Bosman* and *P. van Warmelo;* Archivalia prepared by *J. Th. de Smidt* and *H. W. van Soest.* South African Law Commission, Research Series 5 (Pretoria 1986).

fondée en 1575. De 1580 à 1584, il fut avocat-fiscal à la Cour de Hollande, et de 1584 jusqu'à son décès le 25 juin 1606, conseiller au *Hoge Raad.*

(a) De Pactis

Les sept éditions contiennent les mêmes 23 causes, lesquelles sont toutes en rapport avec des questions de régimes matrimoniaux. Vingt-deux causes furent jugées par le *Hoge Raad* entre 1588 et 1603, une seule (No. XIV) fit l'objet d'une décision de la Cour de Hollande le 18 décembre 1580, et, comme l'indique Neostadius, celle-ci est empruntée à un recueil manuscrit de décisions rédigé par Pelgrim van Loo, conseiller à la Cour de Hollande *(cf. infra).* On peut supposer que les autres 22 causes rapportées par Neostadius lui étaient directement connues, soit en tant que membre de la cour, soit en tant que conseiller-rapporteur (v. not. Dec. X). Les *Observationes* et les *Notae* (y compris celles concernant la décision de 1580) peuvent être attribuées à Neostadius. Parfois, on y rencontre des observations trahissant sa familiarité avec la 'cuisine interne' de la cour, comme lorsqu'il note (Dec. I) que le jugement a été rendu à l'unanimité. Dans la Dec. II, il précise que «M. le Président A. Nicolai nous a confié cette cause pour en rapporter au Conseil». Dans ses notes à cette même *decisio,* il donne un exposé à caractère magistral sur les droits des successions applicables en Hollande, lequel à certainement influencé Grotius.[25] Dans le cas de la Dec. XIII, Neostadius était absent, mais il s'est informé auprès de ses collègues sur les sentiments des conseillers. D'autres exemples pourraient être cités.

Pour la dernière édition du *De Pactis* de 1667, l'éditeur a suivi le même modèle typographique que celui des *Decisien.*

L'œuvre jouit d'une grande popularité et fut souvent citée par les auteurs du droit romano-hollandais. L'édition sud-africaine de 1986 mentionne les références au *De Pactis* figurant dans Rodenburg, *Tractatus de jure conjugum* (1653); Voet, *Commentarius ad Pandectas* (> 1698) et dans les *Praelectiones iuris hodierni ad Hugonis Grotii Introductionem ad iurisprudentiam Hollandicam* (> 1793) de Van der Keessel. Cette édition, comme il a déjà été mentionné, offre également un relevé de tous les *loci* cités par Neostadius provenant des Institutes, du Digeste, du Code et des Novelles, du Décret de Gratien, des collections de Décrétales, ainsi qu'une liste des auteurs cités.[26]

---

[25] *H. de Groot,* Inleidinge tot de Hollandsche rechtsgeleerdheid II.28.

[26] Le *Hoge Raad:* Collation de recueils..., 2.2: Observatio XXIII.

(b) Decisiones

A l'exception de la première édition de 1617, cet ouvrage a été publié sous le nom de Neostadius. Les sommaires des décisions de la Cour de Hollande n'ont toutefois pas été rédigées par Neostadius, mais bien (comme l'a démontré L. J. van Apeldoorn)[27] par Pelgrim van Loo, conseiller à la Cour de 1576 jusqu'à sa mort en 1587. Neostadius avait connaissance de ce recueil, comme en témoigne une remarque dans Obs. XIV du *De Pactis:* «...in latinum translata ex observationibus D. Peregrini Lonii celeberrimi quondam Curiae Hollandiae consiliarii, quas processuum in jure consistentium inscripsit».[28] On ne peut exclure que les promoteurs de la publication – les Elzevier de Leiden – aient utilisé le nom de Neostadius pour assurer au recueil une plus grande autorité, du moins un plus grand succès.

La première édition contient 60 décisions de la Cour, 17 du *Hoge Raad,* et deux du Grand Conseil. Dans l'édition de 1627, le nombre de décisions du *Hoge Raad* s'élève à 102, dans les éditions de 1644 et de 1667 à 127.[29] Les additions sont dues (selon l'avertissement dans le titre de l'édition de 1627) à l'avocat A. de H., dont l'identité n'a pas été établie. Il demeure incertain quelles furent les décisions recueillies par, respectivement, Neostadius et cet avocat; 28 des 127 décisions du *Hoge Raad* sont datées (1586 - 1599), et furent prononcées au temps où Neostadius était conseiller. Les références à 'l'auteur' aux nos. XXV - XXXI portent peut-être sur Neostadius, mais il s'agit à nouveau d'une question inélucidée.[30] Dans l'édition de 1644, on a ajouté les décisions CIV - CVII. La succession n'est ni chronologique, ni systématique. La décision n'est jamais reprise in extenso. Les faits, les considérations de droit et la sentence sont en général résumés en une seule page. Ce texte est précédé d'un mot-clé, parfois accompagné

---

27 *L. J. van Apeldoorn,* Uit de practijk van het Hof van Holland in de tweede helft van de zestiende eeuw. Een handschrift. (Utrecht 1938), pp. 1 - 10.

28 Le manuscrit a été signalé par *E. M. Meijers* dans son article: Uitgegeven en onuitgegeven rechtspraak van de Hooge Raad en het Hof van Holland, Zeeland en West-Friesland, dans: Tijdschrift voor Rechtsgeschiedenis 1 (1918), p. 400. Ce manuscrit, qui porte le titre 'Observationes processuum in jure consistentium in curia Hollandiae controversarum', avait été découvert et fut édité par L. J. van Apeldoorn (v. note précédente). Le recueil contient 46 décisions, dont trois seulement n'ont pas été reprises dans les Decisiones.

29 La traduction de Van Nispen (édition de 1655 {416 et 417}) contient 127 décisions du *Hoge Raad;* la traduction de K. van Aller (édition 1655 {410}) ne contient que les deux décisions du Grand Conseil (Dec. 1 et 2) et sept décisions du *Hoge Raad* (Dec. 4 - 10).

30 A la Dec. XXV, on lit: «Ad hoc Senatu arrestum, an vero auctoris consilium, dubitari potest»; dans les cinq numéros suivants, on retrouve un doute quant à «auctoris hoc consilium videtur».

d'une explication lapidaire. La 'formule' suivie dans le *De pactis* a été adoptée pour cet ouvrage.[31]

Le droit savant n'est cité qu'à une seule occasion. On ne peut reconnaître si l'auteur de ce résumé a emprunté les allégations au dossier, ou s'il les a ajoutées de son propre cru. Dans la dernière édition, celle de 1667, on trouve des 'Notae' et 'Notae ad Notas' en complément; celles-ci contiennent des références à la jurisprudence et à quelques auteurs (p.ex. N. Everaerts), les rubriques ont été amplifiées, la ponctuation a été renforcée.[32]

1.3 Jacob COREN, *Observationes rerum in Senatu judicatarum. Item Consilia quaedam.* Hagae Comitis, Apud A. Meuris, 1633. On connaît deux éditions ultérieures: Hagae Comitis 1642, et Amsterdam 1661; une traduction néerlandaise a été publiée sous le titre: *Hollandse praktijk in rechten, bestaande in vonnissen, observantien van oordeelen en consultatien door K. van Nieustad en J. Kooren. Uyt het Latijn vertaald door A. van Nispen.* Rotterdam, Bij J. Naeranus, 1655 {417}.

Jacob Gerritsz. Coren serait né à Alkmaar. En 1596, il obtint le doctorat en droit (JUD) à Leiden. De 1621 à 1631 (l'année de son décès), il fut conseiller au *Hoge Raad.* Sa vie et sa carrière demeurent encore largement inconnues. L'ouvrage, une publication posthume, contient 41 *Observantien van oordeelen van den Hoogen Raedt,* datant de la période 1621 - 1630. Le recueil suit un ordre plus ou moins chronologique, sans effort de présenter la matière de manière systématique. Coren se réfère régulièrement au droit romain. Parfois, il n'hésite pas à exprimer sa propre opinion, même si celle-ci est différente de la position du Conseil.[33]

1.4 Cornelis van BIJNKERSHOEK, *Quaestiones juris privati.* Lugduni Batavorum, Apud J. van Kerckhem, 1744; également dans: *Opera omnia,* 1767. Une traduction néerlandaise fut publiée sous le titre: *Verhandelingen over burgerlyke rechts-zaaken.* Amsterdam, By I. Tirion, 1747.

Cornelis van Bijnkershoek est né le 29 mai 1673 à Middelburg en Zélande.[34] En 1689, il commença des études en théologie à Franeker, mais il se réorienta vers des études de droit en 1691, consacrées par un doctorat

[31] Le *Hoge Raad:* Collation de recueils..., 2.2: Decisio XLIII.

[32] Le *Hoge Raad:* Collation de recueils..., 2.1.

[33] Cf. quelques extraits de l'Obs. IX, Le *Hoge Raad:* Collation de recueils..., 2.1.

[34] *O. W. Star Numan,* Cornelis van Bynkershoek. Zijn leven en zijne geschriften (Leiden 1869); *L. van Poelgeest,* De raadsheren van de Hoge Raad van Holland, Zeeland en West-Friesland in de achttiende eeuw, dans: Bijdragen en Mededelingen betreffende de geschiedenis der Nederlanden 1988, pp. 21, 25, 29 - 34, 40 - 42, 47, 49.

utr. jur. en 1694. Ensuite, il s'établit en tant qu'avocat à La Haye. En 1704, à l'âge de 31 ans, il fut nommé conseiller au *Hoge Raad,* à l'occasion d'un siège vacant réservé (en principe) à la Zélande, dont Van Bijnkershoek était natif. En effet, lorsque, par un traité de 1587 entre la Zélande et la Hollande, la Zélande avait reconnu le *Hoge Raad* comme cour d'appel suprême, il avait également été convenu que trois conseillers seraient nommés par les Etats de Zélande. En revanche, rien n'avait été conclu quant aux affinités hollandaises ou zélandaises du président de la cour. Aussi, la promotion de Van Bijnkershoek à la présidence, en 1724, la première fois qu'un zélandais occupait cette fonction, fut marquée par de nombreuses intrigues politiques. Cela ne l'a pas empêché de s'acquitter de cette fonction avec beaucoup d'autorité, imposant un respect général.

Les *Observationes Tumultuariae* n'ont été publiées qu'au 20e siècle (infra: 2.1.1). Dans les *Quaestiones iuris privati,* Van Bijnkershoek a traité de la jurisprudence du *Hoge Raad,* tant pour son usage personnel que pour servir à la pratique judiciaire. Dans la Préface 'Ad Lectorem', ce but est exprimé en ces termes:[35]

> «...Pertinent hae Quaestiones magis ad Forum, quam ad Academiam, & pleraeque ad Forum Batavicum. Eas autem praecipue excussit Auctor, de quibus alia ipsius, alia aliorum est sententia: plerisque etiam adscripsit res, ipso Senatore, vel Praeside, a Supremo Senatu judicatas. Sicubi vero non ejusdem sententiae fuerit, cujus Senatu, modeste addidit rationes, quae eum in contrarium moverunt. ... Ubi autem memorat Auctor res, a Senatu, ipso praesente, judicatas, semper iis adscripsit diem, quo lata, non quo pronunciata est sententia... Cum passim in his libris provocetur ad *Observationes Tumultuariae* T.. N.., monendum est, hoc nomine significari commentarios, in quos retulit Vir. Ampl. non tantum res, ipso Senatore vel Praeside, id est, per spatium quadraginta fere annorum, a Supremo Senatu judicatas... Sed cum ipse Auctor ubique eas adhibuerit, religio fuit, ut in omnibus, quae his apparent, sic & hac in parte, aliquid mutare».

Les *Quaestiones* sont divisées en 74 articles, formant quatre livres. La plupart des articles sont rédigés à partir d'une décision du *Hoge Raad,* mais

---

[35] 'Aan den lezer' (p. V): «deze verhandelingen behooren meer tot de Rechtbank, dan tot de Hooge School, en de meeste tot de Rechtbank van Holland. De Schrijver is voornamentlyk getreeden in een onderzoek van de zaaken, omtrent welke hy met anderen in gevoelen verschilde. By de meesten heeft hy ook de Gewysdens van den Hoogen Raad gevoegt, gedurende den tyt, waarin hy Raadsheer of President is geweest... [p. VI]. Wanneer de Heer van Bynkershoek de zaken verhaalt, die in zyne tegenwoordigheit door den Hoogen Raad zyn uitgewezen, heeft hy 'er altoos den dag bygevoegt, waarop de Sententie is vastgestelt... [p. VIII] Dewyl op sommige plaatsen van dit werk aangehaalt wort *Observationes Tumultuariae* T.. N.., moeten wy hier te kennen geven, dat hier door Aanteekeningen verstaan worden, waar in ... zaken, die gedurende hy Raadsheer of President was, dat is gedurende ontrent veertig jaren, zyn uitgewezen... [p. IX] dewyl de Heer Van Bynkershoek zelve die overal heeft aangehaalt, heb ik zwaarigheit gemaakt, om hier in ... iets te veranderen».

rien ne suggère que les considérations de Van Bijnkershoek aient été empruntées aux écritures des plaideurs. Au contraire, tout semble indiquer que Van Bijnkershoek a effectué ses propres recherches, sans se borner à reproduire les arguments des avocats ou les opinions des conseillers. Parfois, pourtant, il mentionne, soit en approuvant, soit en critiquant vivement, les considérations de la majorité ou de la minorité des conseillers; ainsi, par exemple, au No. XVI, où il conclut son exposé en observant:

> «Memini me Senatore vel Praeside bis terve id alias quaesitum esse: sed cum tentata transactione, ut tentari solet in causis dubiis, ea successerit, nihil quicquam decisum est».

1.5 Joannes van der LINDEN, *Verzameling van merkwaardige gewijsden der gerechts-hoven in Holland. Eerste Deel.* Leyden, By A. en J. Honkoop, 1803.

Joannes van der Linden (1756 - 1835) fut pendant un demi-siècle avocat et auteur de nombreux ouvrages sur différents aspects de la pratique judiciaire. Après avoir obtenu le doctorat à Leiden en 1774, il s'installa à La Haye comme avocat. En 1795, il déménagea à Amsterdam. En 1827, après un longue carrière d'avocat, il fut nommé juge au tribunal d'Amsterdam.

Dans la préface de sa *Verzameling,* il explique sa méthode (p. XIV):

> «Mijn doelwit in het samenstellen van dit werk was, om uit de Dingtalen en Proces-stukken zelven, in zaaken over *Juridique Questiën,* (want aan het geen louter *facti* is, heeft het publiek niets)... op te maken het *Casus* van het proces, met woordelijke opgave van de *clausulae concernentes,* en vermelding van alle omstandigheden, welken men kan nagaan, dat eenige *ratio decidendi* gehad hebben; op te geven den summieren inhoud der Dingtaalen, in de zaak gehouden; daar agter te voegen den woordelijken inhoud der Sententie; en eindelijk aan het hoofd van elke *Casus* de gedecideerde *Thesis* in korte woorden...»[36]

Dans la perspective de la publication d'un second volume, il fit appel à ses collègues du barreau, leur demandant de lui communiquer des plaidoyers et écritures, un appel qu'il réitéra en 1806.[37] Ce second tome n'a toutefois jamais vu le jour, l'introduction d'un code civil en 1809 ayant vraisemblablement entravé ce projet.

---

[36] «Mon but, en composant cet ouvrage, a été d'établir à partir des plaidoyers et des pièces relatives aux procès, en ce qui concerne les *questions juridiques* (car le public ne profite en rien de ce qui est simplement question de faits)... le *casus* du procès, en mentionnant littéralement les *clausulae concernentes,* et en faisant état de toutes les circonstances, telles qu'on peut les retracer, ayant contribué à quelque *ratio decidendi;* en outre, de présenter un sommaire des plaidoyers qui furent introduits dans l'affaire, et d'y ajouter les termes mêmes de la sentence; enfin, je fais précéder chaque *casus* par une brève énonciaton de la *thèse*...»

[37] *J. van der Linden,* Regtsgeleerd, practicaal, en koopmans handboek (Amsteldam 1806), p. LXXII.

Le recueil contient une décision du Conseil de Brabant (1787), 18 de la Cour de Hollande (1719 - 1795), 15 du *Hoge Raad* (1727 - 1796), toutes en ordre chronologique. Vingt des 34 causes datent de la période 1774 - 1796. Comme Van der Linden ne débuta sa carrière d'avocat qu'en 1774, il n'a pu avoir une connaissance directe des causes antérieures.

2. Les recueils manuscrits

2.1.1 Cornelis van BIJNKERSHOEK, *Observationes Tumultuariae circa formam procedendi maxime coram suprema Hollandiae Zelandiaeque curia, 1704 - 1743.* En 14 tomes. Texte latin. [Leiden, Bibliothèque de l'Université: P. C. Boeren, *Catalogue des manuscrits des collections d'Ablaing et Meijers,* Collection Meijers 42].

Ci-dessus, sous 1.4 (*Quaestiones,* Ad Lectorem), cet ouvrage a déjà été mentionné. L'auteur s'explique sur le titre en ces termes:

> «Tumultuarias has Observationes vocat, quod ex Senatu domum redux, quotidie, prout quaeque res incidebat, tumultuariae eas conscripserit».

Dans ses *Quaestiones juris privati,* Van Bijnkershoek se réfère à plusieurs reprises au manuscrit de ces *Observationes.* E. M. Meijers, professeur à Leiden, retrouva le manuscrit et en fit l'acquisition en 1918; en 1926, il entama l'édition intégrale.[38]

2.1.2 Willem PAUW, *Observationes Tumultuariae Novae circa formam procedendi maxime coram suprema Hollandiae Zelandiaeque Curia, 1743 - 1787.* En 10 tomes. Texte latin [Leiden, Bibliothèque de l'Université: Boeren, *o. c.,* Collection Meijers 43].

Né à La Haye le 10 janvier 1712, Willem Pauw étudia le droit à Leiden, mais obtint son diplôme à Utrecht en 1734. La même année, il commença à pratiquer en tant qu'avocat à La Haye. En 1741, à trente ans, il fut nommé conseiller par les Etats de Zélande: quoique natif de Hollande, Pauw avait acquis l'office de pensionnaire de la ville de Flessingue, et il était de cet fait éligible à un siège zélandais. En 1743, il épousa une fille de C. van Bijnkershoek. En vertu de son ancienneté, il devint président en 1784. Il occupa cette charge jusqu'à sa mort, le 24 juin 1787. C. van Bijnkershoek avait légué ses *Observationes* à son gendre, avec qui il avait collaboré au *Hoge Raad* de 1741 à 1743. Pauw rédigea un supplément de 1806 *Observationes novae* aux 3317 *Observationes* de Van Bijnkershoek.[39]

---

[38] A titre d'exemple, le texte dans Le *Hoge Raad:* Collation de recueils..., 2.4, reproduit l'Observatio 2452, le cas même auquel se rapporte l'auteur dans ses *Quaestiones,* Livre Ier, no. 16 (cité supra).

[39] *L. E. van Holk,* Mr Willem Pauw (1712 - 1787), raadsheer en president van de Hooge Raad van Holland en Zeeland. Enkele biografische aantekeningen, dans:

Ainsi, on a conservé un recueil de 5123 *observationes* couvrant la période 1704 - 1787. Cette collection, tout à fait unique en son genre, a été éditée à l'initiative de Meijers.[40]

2.2 Johan van Bleiswijk, *Observationes Tumultuariae rerum a Supremo in Hollandia Senatu judicatarum quibus ut senator interfui et quas ac quatenus notandas putavi, 1723 - 1741.* texte latin [Archives Générales du Royaume, Collection Bisdom 139].

Johan van Bleiswijk est né en 1684 à Woudrichem. Il fut avocat avant d'être nommé conseiller au *Hoge Raad* en 1723, une fonction qu'il occupa jusqu'à sa mort en 1748. Dans ses *Observationes,* qui comptent 155 décisions, il suivit l'exemple de Van Bijnkershoek.[41]

2.3 Manuscrit Ockers [Leiden, Bibliothèque de l'Université: Boeren, *o. c.*, Collection Meijers 41].

Ce manuscrit a été attribué par E. M. Meijers à Pieter Ockers(se), notamment en raison de la concordance entre les dates des jugements de la Cour et du *Hoge Raad* auxquels l'auteur se réfère et les années durant lesquelles P. Ockers exerça des fonctions à ces institutions. Né à Zierikzee, Pieter Ockers étudia à Leiden, où il obtint le doctorat le 4 février 1650. Il fut conseiller à la Cour de Hollande de 1654 à 1669 et au *Hoge Raad* de 1669 à son décès le 23 septembre 1678.

Le manuscrit se divise en trois parties: [1] Résumés en latin de 104 décisions de la Cour de Hollande, selon un agencement plus ou moins systématique en sept titres (1656 - 1669); [2] résumés en néerlandais de 57 sentences du *Hoge Raad,* 1669 - 1678 (1701/03); [3] commentaires en latin de 21 sentences (sur les 57 mentionnées sub 2, 1670 - 1678). Ces 21 cas sont tous en rapport avec le droit des successions. L'édition de ce manuscrit est en préparation.

Tijdschrift voor Rechtsgeschiedenis XXX (1962), 358 - 362; *H. W. van Soest,* Hoe vervaardigde raadsheer Willem Pauw zijn Observationes Tumultuariae Novae?, in: Satura Roberto Feenstra... ab alumnis collegis amicis oblata (1985), 585 - 607; *L. van Poelgeest,* De raadsheren..., o.c., pp. 21, 24, 31, 34v, 40 - 45.

[40] Cornelii van Bijnkershoek Observationes Tumultuariae. Ediderunt *E. M. Meijers, A. S. de Blécourt, H. D. J. Bodenstein* [*et alii*] (Harlemi 1926 - 1962), 4 tomes; Wilhelmi Pauwi Observationes Tumultuariae Novae. Ediderunt *H. F. W. D. Fischer, W. L. de Koning-Bey, L. E. van Holk* [*et alii*] (Harlemi 1964 - 1969), 3 tomes; *M. S. van Oosten,* Systematisch compendium (Haarlem 1962); *P. van Warmelo,* Registers op die Observationes Tumultuariae van Cornelis van Bijnkershoek en van Willem Pauw (Pretoria 1982).

[41] *B. van Poelgeest,* Mr Johan van Bleiswijk en zijn *Observationes Tumultuariae,* dans: Tijdschrift voor Rechtsgeschiedenis 55 (1987), 177 - 122; *idem,* De raadsheren van de Hoge Raad van Holland, Zeeland en West-Friesland in de achttiende eeuw, dans: Bijdragen en Mededelingen betreffende de Geschiedenis der Nederlanden 103 (1988), 20 - 51.

Dans les marges et à la fin des décisions, on a parfois inséré des références au *Corpus iuris civilis,* à des auteurs (du moyen âge au 17e siècle), et à la jurisprudence plus récente (notamment du début du 18e siècle). De plus, on a ajouté à la fin les noms des plaideurs.

GERO DOLEZALEK

Litigation at the Rota Romana, particularly around 1700

Few scholars have studied archival material from Rota proceedings after 1500[1]. While the origins of the Rota and its competence and impact in the middle ages have been the subject of many publications[2], the later centuries of the Rota, in contrast, have attracted much less attention[3], although the

---

[1] Best recent study, with a very useful bibliography and introduction in Italian: *Christina Bukowska-Gorgoni,* Causae Poloniae coram Sacra Romana Rota, XV - XVII saec., explanatio singulorum processuum et regesta documentorum (Roma 1995) [Pontificium Institutum Studiorum Ecclesiasticorum, Piazza B. Cairoli 117]. Parallel investigations for Scottish cases before the Rota have been made by *James J. Robertson,* now at the University of Dundee. Also parallel is the research on Danish cases by *Per Ingesman:* see his report Danske processer for den romerske Rota, in: Arkiv. Tidsskrift for arkivforskning 12.3 (1989) 170 - 182. Throughout this essay, the following conventions have been used to mark Latin legal technical terms: *(a)* If they are immediately preceded by the respective English words they are included, in italics, in round brackets: (=...); *(b)* In contrast, if they are used without connection to correspondent English words they are included in single brackets: '...' (and also printed in italics).

[2] A bibliography on the medieval Rota is given in *Coing*'s Handbuch, vol. I, p. 847 - 856. Updates to it are listed in my contribution to vol. 5 of this series, edited in 1989 by *John H. Baker,* p. 69 - 99. A most interesting study on a Rota dossier 1496 - 1498 has been published by *Domenico Maffei,* Il giovane Machiavelli banchiere con Berto Berti a Roma (Firenze 1973), in particular p. 34 - 43 with notes, and p. 142 - 148. The young banker Machiavelli is not identical to the famous homonym politician.

[3] Bibliographical data on the the more recent history of the Rota can be retrieved from *Mario Ascheri*'s article in *Coing*'s Handbuch, vol. II.2, p. 1113 - 1194 (esp. p. 1193 s.) [reprinted in Italian: Tribunali, giuristi e istituzioni dal medioevo all' età moderna (Bologna 1989), p. 85 ss.]. I shall thus only list the farmost important works: *Johann Heinrich Bangen,* Die römische Curie, ihre gegenwärtige Zusammensetzung und ihr Geschäftsgang (Münster 1854) (2nd part, ch. 2: Die Justiz-Behörden der Curie); *Domenico Bernino,* Il tribunale della Sacra Rota Romana, Roma 1717 [prints the text of respective papal constitutions!]; *Emmanuele Cerchiari,* Cappellani Papae et Apostolicae Sedis auditores causarum Sacri Palatii Apostolici seu Sacra Romana Rota ab origine ad diem usque 20 septembris 1870. Relatio historico-iuridica, vol. I - IV, Romae 1919 - 1921 [*Cerchiari*'s long list of judges' dates of office is in part merely based on one unreliable late 18th century manuscript in the Rota archive]; *Iohannes Baptista cardinalis De Luca,* Theatrum veritatis et

old Rota continued its activities until September 1870 when the Italian Church State was annexed to the Kingdom of Italy[4]. My article aims at introducing the reader to Rota records and *'decisiones'* particularly around 1700, and to the special technical vocabulary which the reader may encounter in them.

I. The Type of Judicial Matters Handled by Rota Judges

Until 1834[5] the Rota was never competent *per se* for any matter. The individual *auditores* were mere judicial commissioners (= *judices delegati*)[6], acting in the Pope's stead, on individual appointment *ad hoc,* case

iustitiae (Romae 1669 - 1673 and at least 15 reprints) [see there Liber XV *'De iudiciis'*, pars 2 *'Relatio Romanae Curiae forensis'*; in particular discursus 32 *'De tribunali seu auditorio Rotae'*; *Giuseppe Ermini,* Guida bibliografica per lo studio del diritto comune pontificio (Bologna 1934); *idem,* La giurisprudenza della Rota Romana come fattore evolutivo dello 'ius commune', in: Studi in onore di *Francesco Scaduto,* vol. I (Firenze 1936), p. 284 - 298 [reprinted in: Atti del IV Congresso nazionale di studi romani, vol. IV (Roma 1938), p. 57 - 67]; *Michael Lega,* De veterum decisionum natura et origine earumque collectionibus = Praefatio in: Sacra Romanae Rotae decisiones seu sententiae quae ... prodierunt anno 1909, cura eiusdem S. Tribunalis editae, vol. I (Romae 1912), p. V - LIV; *Raffaele Marchetti,* Notizia delle giurisdizioni che sono in vigore nello Stato Pontificio, Roma 1850, Parte I, Capitolo 2 *'Giurisdizione Ordinaria'*; *Knut Wolfgang Nörr,* Ein Kapitel aus der Geschichte der Rechtsprechung: die Rota Romana, in: Ius Commune 5 (1975) 192 - 209; *Hunoldus Plettenbergius,* Notitia congregationum et tribunalium curiae Romanae (Hildesii 1693), p. 577 ss.; *Richard Puza,* Res iudicata. Rechtskraft und fehlerhaftes Urteil in den Decisionen der Römischen Rota (Graz 1973) [Grazer Rechts- und Staatswissenschaftliche Studien, vol. 29]; *Theodosius Rubeus,* Singularia ex Sacrae Rotae Romanae decisionibus selecta, vol. I - II (Romae 1637); *Renato Saviano,* Il *'Corpus iuris canonici'* e la giurisprudenza della S. Romana Rota come fonte dello *'ius commune'* (Napoli 1954); *Egon Schneider,* Der deutsche Rotaauditor Jakob Emerix (1668 - 1696) und die Jurisdiktion der römischen Rota, in: Festschrift Eduard Eichmann zum 70. Geburtstag (Paderborn 1940), p. 150 - 177; *Iohannes Tanaglius,* Monumenta urbis et orbis supremi tribunalis sive de Sacrae Rotae Romanae auditorio eiusque decisionibus (Liburnii 1654).

4 A survey of the history of the Rota is also given in *Hermann Hoberg*'s recent guide to the materials in the Rota Archive: Inventario dell'Archivio della Sacra Romana Rota (sec. XIV - XIX), a cura di Josef Metzler (Città del Vaticano 1994) [Collectanea Archivi Vaticani, 34], p. 15 - 50.

5 In 1834 the Rota was granted ordinary jurisdiction as an appeal court of the Church State: *Gregorius XVI papa,* Regolamento Legislativo e Giudiziario, §§ 321 - 327, 377 - 382 (§ 327), reprinted in: L'ordinamento giudiziario. I: Documentazione storica (Rimini 1985) [Università degli studi di Roma II. Ricerche sul processo, a cura di *Nicola Picardi* e *Alessandro Giuliani*], p. 729 ss.

6 *Rota,* decisiones recentiores, 391 n. 1 part. 18 vol. 1. This notwithstanding, the Rota judges were by papal statute given the procedural prerogatives of a *'iudex ordinarius'*. That means: the procedural rules for judges with ordinary jurisdiction applied.

by case, in matters where the Pope could or would neither sit himself as a judge nor entrust anyone other than a Rota judge.

In practice this meant the following: Cases in which the Holy See took utmost interest were either decided by the Pope in person or commissioned to cardinals. Day-to-day cases, in contrast, which came to the Pope as a supreme judge were commissioned out *ad partes,* that is: they were commissioned to prelates at or near the place where the litigating parties lived. Only those cases which on the one hand were not vitally important for the Holy See but on the other hand still important enough to keep them under control were commissioned at the papal curia, and mostly *ad Rotam,* as the judges there were especially qualified for this task.

Rota judges were normally given commission to deal with a case in its entirety. They thus had to hear the litigating parties, take evidence, pronounce the judgment and enforce it. In principle, however, it was also possible to delimit the commissioning to a part of the proceedings. For instance, the Pope could appoint someone as *'iudex delegatus'* only for the instruction of the case, or only for the taking of evidence: to examine witnesses, inspect a locality, or scrutinize documents which could or should not be removed from the archive where they were kept.

Partial commissioning occurred especially in matters where Rota judges were entrusted *extra Rotam,* thus in their quality as prelates, and not in their quality as a member of the Rota[7]. For instance, investigations in view of declaring a person to be in bliss, or saint, were often commissioned to Rota judges, however *extra Rotam.*

Many cases which reached the Holy See were expressly commissioned "without further appeal" (= *appellatione remota*)[8]. If the *'commissio'* lacked this clause appeal and further appeals were possible until two successive judgments in the case had come to the same conclusion (= *duae conformes sententiae*)[9]. Appeals against judgments of Rota judges were usually commissioned to a different Rota judge, to be advised by colleagues who had not previously been advisors in the matter[10]. Only in rare cases were such appeals commissioned to a cardinal.

---

[7] Custom at the Rota required that these cases be nevertheless submitted to the Rota for deliberation: *Rota,* Decisiones recentiores, 317 n. 1 part. 11; 556 n. 1 part. 19 vol. 2.

[8] This meant: without further frivolous appeal. It did not hinder appeals against obvious gross mistakes in procedure: *Rota,* Decisiones recentiores, 117 n. 1 part. 3.

[9] Special leave for appeal or *'restitutio in integrum'* could nevertheless be granted by act of grace, to be applied for at the *'Signatura Gratiae'*: *De Luca* (n. 3), n. 58 and discursus 30 *'De Signatura Gratiae'.*

[10] *De Luca* (n. 3), n. 57.

Since the Pope had a double function, namely as the head of the Roman Catholic Church, and also as the sovereign of vast territories in Italy and some territorial remnants in France, the Rota shared this double function: The judges handled secular cases from the Church State as well as ecclesiastical cases from all dioceses under papal guidance[11].

The 16th - 19th century *'decisiones'* of the Rota show that at that time the vast majority of cases was secular: the Rota was mainly an appeal court for the Church State, in civil procedure. Also the bulk of ecclesiastical appeals came from that state[12]. One reason for this was that litigants from territories not far from Rome found it easy and not particularly costly to lodge an appeal at the papal curia, whereas this was difficult and expensive for people living further away.

The amount of catholic church litigation outside Italy had declined anyway because so many territories had broken away from the papacy on grounds of the church reforms in the 16th century. Even in the territories which remained catholic, the church courts lost much of their business to the secular courts. Church courts defended their monopoly of competence in what they regarded as spiritual matters, for instance marriage litigation, but if those matters were appealed to Rome they were usually entrusted to the newly-installed *'Sacrae Congregationes'*[13] and were thus no longer commissioned to the Rota. Only that part of church court litigation which dealt with secular matters was regularly entrusted to Rota judges – but the medieval Rota's main argument, namely prebendary litigation, had almost totally vanished.

Furthermore, governments now tried to impede recourse to any court outside their sphere of influence. This applied as well to appeals to Rome, no matter whether the government in question was catholic or not. The German Reichstag and emperor, for instance, intervened and protested vehemently at the Holy See whenever one of their subjects complained about being summoned to Rome[14].

---

11 *Hermann Hoberg,* Die Tätigkeit der Rota am Vorabend der Glaubensspaltung, in: Miscellanea in onore di Monsignor Martino Giusti Prefetto dell'Archivio Segreto Vaticano, vol. I - II (Città del Vaticano 1978) [Collectanea Archivi Vaticani 5 - 6], vol. II p. 1 - 32.

12 An index to the printed *'decisiones'* according to their diocese of origin is given by *Iohannes Baptista Cantalmaius,* Selectanea rerum notabilium ad usum decisionum Sacrae Rotae Romanae in libris impressis per dioceses extensarum (Romae 1639); continued by *Franciscus Blancus,* Elenchus sive index decisionum Sacrae Rotae Romanae in libris impressis per dioceses extensarum et post indicem Iohannis Baptistae Cantalmaii aeditarum (Romae 1687).

13 Litigation about nullity of a marriage or monk's vow went to the Sacra Congregatio Concilii, but could also be commissioned to the Rota instead: *Marchetti* (n. 3) II (a); *Charles Lefebvre,* La S. Congrégation du Concile et le tribunal de la S. Rote Romaine à la fin du XVIe siècle, in: Apollinaris 37 (1964) 8 - 22.

II. Main Personnel Creating the Records of Cases

Since 1472 the Rota was regularly staffed with twelve judges[15], appointed and sworn in[16] after due examination by their future colleagues[17]. They had to be law graduates and many had served as law professors at some university.

The Rota was supranationally staffed. There was at all times one nominee of the emperor[18], one nominee of the kings of France, Aragon, Castile, respectively, and one nominee from Milan, Venice, Ferrara, Bologna, and

---

[14] Sample case from Aachen, end of 17th century: In the long dispute between the Synodal Court and the Scabinal Court at Aachen, the Synodal Court had used a conflict of jurisdiction arising from the litigation Isabella Chattelein v Johannes Chorus to summon the Scabins to Rome. When the Scabins ignored the summons the Synodal Court obtained a default judgment at the Rota. On 18 May 1683 the Scabins obtained a decree from the emperor's Reichshofrat at Vienna, ordering the City Council of Aachen not to levy execution of the Rota judgment. By 1687 the judgment had still not been executed as the emperor had successfully intervened at the Holy See: *Stadtarchiv Aachen, Hs. 9,* p. 357 - 616. In 1688 the Synodal Court went nevertheless ahead with the procedure. Rota judge Alexander Ursinus issued a second default judgment against the Scabins. So they petitioned the German Reichstag and the emperor to intervene again: ibidem, *Hs. G 17,* p. 6 ss. and p. 46 - 93; *Hs. 9,* p. 554.

[15] Constitution *'Romani Pontificis'* by Pope Sixtus IV, 1472; confirmed in 1770: *'Cum primum supremo'* by Clement XIV.

[16] Many details about the procedure, in general and in individual cases, are given by *Hermann Hoberg,* Die Antrittsdaten der Rotarichter von 1566 bis 1675, in: Römische Quartalschrift für christliche Altertumskunde und Kirchengeschichte 48 (1953) 211 - 224; *idem,* Die Amtsdaten der Rotarichter in den Protokollbüchern der Rotanotare von 1464 bis 1566, ibidem, p. 43 - 78; *idem,* Die 'Admissiones' des Archivs der Rota, in: Archivalische Zeitschrift 50/51 (1955) 391 - 408 [describes a manuscript list of Rota judges, written between 1765 and 1789, which was the main source for *Cerchiari* (see n. 2)].

[17] Examples have been presented by *Hermann Hoberg,* Der Informativprozeß des Rotarichters Dominikus Jacobazzi (1492), Römische Quartalschrift für christliche Altertumskunde und Kirchengeschichte 51 (1956) 228 - 235; *idem,* Der Informativprozeß über die Qualifikation des Rotarichters Antonio Corsetti (1500), in: Mélanges *Eugène Tisserant* IV (Città del Vaticano 1964) [Studi e testi 234], p. 389 - 406; *idem,* Die ältesten Informativprozesse über die Qualifikation neuernannter Rotarichter (1492 - 1547), in: Reformata reformanda. Festgabe für *Hubert Jedin* zum 17. Juni 1965, ed. by *Erwin Iserloh* and *Konrad Repgen,* vol. I - II (Münster 1965) [Reformationsgeschichtliche Studien und Texte, Supplementband 1], vol. I, p. 129 - 141; *idem,* Der Amtsantritt des Rotarichters Antonio Albergati (1649), in: Römische Quartalschrift etc. 49 (1954) 112 - 122; *idem,* Der Amtsantritt des Rotarichters Bernardino Giraud (1762 - 63), in: Studi e ricerche nella biblioteca e negli archivi vaticani in memoria del cardinale *Giovanni Mercati* (1866 - 1957), raccolti a cura di *Lamberto Donati* (Firenze 1959), p. 141 - 165.

[18] *Richard Blaas,* Das kaiserliche Auditoriat bei der Sacra Romana Rota, in: Mitteilungen des Österreichischen Staatsarchivs 11 (1958) 37 - 152.

from Perugia or Northern Tuscany (which alternated in nominating). The remaining three were appointed at the Pope's free discretion, but custom had it that they were from Rome[19].

The judges worked from their private homes and the parties and representatives addressed them there. The *'Rota'* as such had no office rooms for them. It only had deliberation chambers and an archive for old dossiers[20].

Judges were assisted by an *'adjutor'*[21] (in the 19th century called *'auditor secretus'*): a clerk who did secretarial work but often also attended to judicial tasks, in particular if the *'adjutor'* was a highly qualified jurist whereas the judge happened to be first and foremost a theologian. The medieval judges had all been well-versed lawyers, but in later centuries legal qualification was not always the prime concern in nominations.

Judges could also have additional employees to help the *'adjutor'*: these were called *'alumni secreti'* or also *'secretarii'*. Furthermore, the work in a judge's *'studium'* was at times assisted at random by lawyers who were just visitors[22].

It was fashionable to complain about bribery, blackmailing and friends' networking at the papal court – especially between 1400 and 1650. While it is always difficult to substantiate such complaints, it appears unlikely that the papal court should have done much worse than other contemporary courts. It made a bad impression, however, that fees (= *'sportulae'*, also called *'propinae'*) were cashed in by the judge[23] and by other directly

---

19 *De Luca* (n. 3), n. 22.

20 Namely from 1628 onward one stable winter locality at the Vatican, plus (from 1692 onward) for the warmer months a room in the clock tower at the north rim of the Quirinal hill: *Bernino* (n. 3), p. 190; *De Luca* (n. 3), n. 32.

21 Inexperienced new judges might even have two: *De Luca* (n. 3), n. 32.

22 [*Conrad Franz*] *Roßhirt,* Die Verhandlungs- und Entscheidungsweise der Rota Romana als Beweis der Sorge für Gründlichkeit und Schnelligkeit des Verfahrens, in: Archiv für die civilistische Praxis 48 (1865) 195 - 219 (p. 203 § 7 n. 2).

23 The judge, after he had rendered the final judgment (= *sententia diffinitiva*), was given a *'propina'* by the advantaged litigant. Pius IV, *'In throno iustitiae'*, 1561, laid the amount of this fee into the discretion of the litigant, with maximum limits. This was a mere euphemism, since the fee which the winner had paid was calculated among the costs for which he could claim reimbursement from the loser. In effect, the judge's *'propinae'* were thus forced upon the loser. The limit for litigations of low value was ten goldpieces, and for highest values hundred goldpieces. On can in fact come to know how much was paid for which case: it is written on the margin of the original dossiers at the Vatican Archive. Furthermore, litigants were allowed to stock the judge's household with food and drinks, for up to three days' needs. See below, n. 63. The maximum tariffs for treats were repeated in 1611. De Luca (n. 3), n. 30, insists that Rota judges had nevertheless a meagre life, with hardly more that 1000 scudi income per year, so that those without income from other church prebends had to finance their costly staff and household partly

involved court officials[24] instead of going to an impersonal court treasury, and that the judges' households accepted treats[25] and gifts[26]. This feature must however not obscure the fact that many Rota judges, at all times, were impeccably unbiased lawyers who administered speedy and accurate justice.

One salient characteristic which had come down from the middle ages remained conspicuous all the time: the Rota, although regarded as one court, never became a collegiate court in the sense that parties litigated before a bench of judges. It rather remained a conglomeration of individual judges, namely the "Litigation Auditors of the Sacred Apostolic Palace" *(sacri palatii apostolici causarum auditores).* They were under a duty to consult and advise each other regularly – and in that sense one may say that all decisions were carried by a 'bench' –, but each case was entrusted to only one particular judge. This judge heard the case and prepared it for decision. In the end it was the same judge who pronounced the judgment, and it went out in his own name (thus not in the name of the Rota!) and was enforced by him.

The official records of Rota cases were kept by court registrars (= *notarii actuarii*)[27]. In earlier times notaries had been permanently assigned to particular judges: up to four notaries to one judge. Cases had been distributed among these notaries, so that the same case would always be handled by the same notary – if he was available. This changed in 1671 when Pope Clement X drastically reduced the total number of notaries to four (plus aides) and gave them a more independent status, so that they were no longer assigned to certain judges.

Parties could not litigate themselves. They had to appoint a representative, called a *'procurator'* – duly examined, admitted and sworn in at the papal curia[28]. This proctor would set up and sign any requests and submis-

---

from their own family patrimony. The official salary around 1700 was 100 scudi per judge: *Archivio della S. R. Rota, Diaria, n. 186* = diaries of Rota deans, p. 56 (1703), p. 69 (1704).

24 The *'adiutor'* of the judge was paid by the advantaged litigant for the extension of any *'decisio'*, see below, n. 64. The notaries got *'emolumenta'* which were tariffed in detail.

25 See below, n. 63.

26 At Christmas and at the first day of August. *De Luca* (n. 3), n. 30 and 108, explains that these were only small gifts, like candles, cakes, poultry.

27 They formed a *'collegium'*: *Nikolaus Hilling,* Die Errichtung des Notarekollegiums an der römischen Rota durch Sixtus IV. im Jahre 1477, in: Festgabe, enthaltend vornehmlich vorreformationsgeschichtliche Forschungen, Heinrich Finke zum 7. August 1904 gewidmet (Münster 1904), p. 169 - 194.

28 About them see *De Luca* (n. 3), discursus 46 *'De curialibus causidicis'*, n. 97 - 117.

sions which his party needed to make in writing, an he also acted verbally – which was then minuted by the notary in charge.

Furthermore, parties could use the services of one or more of the sworn-in advocates[29]: They pleaded, verbally and in writing, when a decision in the case had to be taken. Oral pleadings took the form of an informal conversation between the advocate and one judge at a time (and/or his personnel) at that judge's private home. The conversations were to an extent public in that those who happened to be present at the time were not excluded, but there was no requirement that the other party be called in to listen.

As a rule, procurators and advocates divided their tasks as follows:

The procurator was the main acting person in the case. He was the *'causae patronus'* making sure that from his client's side all the formalities of litigation were duly fulfilled and procedural pitfals avoided. His main concern were the facts of the case. He collected evidence, submitted it together with summaries and extracts which he had written, and picked out specific points.

This could also require some legal pleading as it had to be pointed out why this or that fact was legally relevant, and why there was a legal presumption for his client's version of the facts, and why the opponent's undertakings to prove certain facts were legally inadmissible or insufficient. The weight, however, was always on the facts of the case.

The advocate, in contrast, was less concerned with the gathering of facts. He focused on their legal evaluation. This included discussions about facts which were in dispute: namely the advocate argued what was proved and who had the burden of proof for those alleged facts which, according to his opinion, had not sufficiently been cleared up. In this regard the advocate's pleadings could at times overlap with those of the procurator – but the emphasis was on legal reasoning.

There existed yet a third type of representative of litigants: the *'sollicitatores'*, also called *'agentes'*[30]. They were an informal profession, not controlled by examination requirements or admission prodeedings. Their work could be a side-line job. The solicitors ran errands: They delivered or picked up papers, deposited fees, queued at the printing office, etc. Another task was to expedite the matter by pushing the judge to set it high on the agenda. This was achieved by persistent molestation: A good solicitor would continually harass the judge, even waylay him in the

---

[29] *De Luca* (n. 3), n. 15 - 68.

[30] *De Luca* (n. 3), n. 127 - 135.

street, until the judge expedited the matter for the sake of ridding himself of the inconvenience.

III. Steps of Proceedings and Respective Records

Litigation at the Rota mainly followed the normal procedural rules of *ius commune,* but papal statutory law[31] and unwritten custom of the court (= *stylus curiae*) also played an important role[32].

Since I have described the normal course of proceedings and record-keeping at the Rota in a previous volume in this series I will now be brief in this regard. My emphasis shall be on details which differ from the medieval course of proceedings, and I shall as well try to introduce the reader to 17th - 18th century Rota jargon.

1. The *'commissio'*

Those wanting to litigate under the Pope as a supreme judge had to file a request (= *supplicatio*) at the Holy See that their case be heard and that an *'auditor'* or other *'iudex delegatus'* be commissioned for that purpose[33]. The request had to contain a brief statement of the facts of the case and of any procedural steps taken so far. It thus served in the function of a document of complaint (= *libellus*)[34] – e.g.:

> *Beatissime pater. Exponitur humillime Sanctitati Vestrae pro parte et ad instantiam Aulii Agerii, quod Numerius Negidius*... (= here follows a summary of the case) ... *Supplicat memoratus Aulus Agerius quatenus Sanctitas Vestra dignemini causam ... alicui ex Vestris sacri palatii apostolici causarum auditoribus ... committere*...

---

[31] In particular *'In throno iustitiae'* of 1561 by Pius IV, printed by *Bernino* (n. 3), p. 228 ss.

[32] On late Rota procedure see *Petrus Ridolphini,* De ordine procedendi in iudiciis in Romana Curia praxis recentior (Venetiis 1696); *Charles Lefebvre,* Antonii Augustini Praxis Rotae; Iacobi Emerix Tractatus seu notitia S. Rotae Romanae. Deux traités inédits sur la procédure de la S. Rote Romaine, publiés avec traduction, notes et compléments divers. (Tournai etc. 1960) [Monumenta Christiana Selecta 8]; this rendered an earlier article by *Lefebvre* obsolete: La procédure du tribunal de la Rote Romaine au XVIIe siècle d'après un manuscrit inédit, in: L'année canonique 5 (1957) 143 - 155; *Roßhirt* (n. 20); *Bangen* (n. 3); *Marchetti* (n. 3).

[33] No longer from 1834 onward in matters of appeal from courts of the Church State. The appellant simply requested the Dean of the Rota to refer the matter to one of his judges. The appellant could suggest one: *Marchetti* (n. 3) I.5.

[34] *De Luca* (n. 3), n. 10.

Certain standard clauses which recurred in a great number of requests were usually abridged, especially towards the end of a document – e.g.: *Statum, etc.; Pro plene, etc.*[35].

Requests were addressed to the Pope and were worded as if he were to read them, but they went to a special papal bureau instead: the *'Signatura Justitiae'*[36]. The *'Signatura'* decided whether the case should be commissioned, and to whom. If the case was sent to the Rota, the *'Signatura'* even decided which judge should have it (= *'auditor ponens'*, also called *'referens'*). The applicant saw to it that the draft for the *'commissio'* be served on the adversary, with a summons 'to explain why the commission should not be signed' (= *ad proponendum quare commissio signari non debeat*)[37].

The commission was dispatched by the *'regens'* of the *'Cancellaria Apostolica'* – which at that time held office near the Basilica Sancti Laurentii et Damasi. The respective decisions were noted on the petitioner's request – e.g.: *De appellatione ad Rotam,* and below: *De mandato sanctissimi domini nostri Papae: Audiat magister Nicolaus, citet, inhibeat, procedat ut petitur et iustitiam faciat.*

Even after a commission had been signed and dispatched, the discontented adversary could still apply for a new hearing in the *'Signatura'*.

The *'commissio'* could on special request contain procedural directives. It could for instance direct that a promulgated excommunication or other *'censura'* against the applicant be lifted or suspended, or that the adversary be summoned by public decree because it was dangerous to summon him in person at his residence or because he had no known abode, or that the proceedings be abridged and simplified (= *sine strepitu et figura judicii*)[38], or that the matter be commissioned together with any other pertaining mat-

[35] These two clauses request that the commissioner shall be declared competent to deal with the matter in all possible stages of proceedings, and that all shortly indicated features shall be regarded as if they had been expressed at length and in great detail. A list of such abridgments of clauses, with explanation, is given in the appendix of the index to the *'Recentiores'*: Sacrae Rotae Romanae decisiones recentiores in compendium redactae ... a nonnullis Mediolanensis athenaei sociis, vol 6 (Mediolani 1730).

[36] Its procedure is described by *De Luca* (n. 3), discursus 31 *'De Signatura Justitiae'*.

[37] *De Luca* (n. 3), n. 9. One such summons, dated 16 December 1684, is recorded in *Stadtarchiv Aachen, Hs. 9,* p. 365 ss.: Johannes Chorus at Aachen is summoned to appear at Rome on 19 January 1685.

[38] Summary procedure was at first regulated by *Clem.* 2.1.2 (*'Dispendiosam'*), but underwent considerable reforms: *'Romani pontificis'* of 1422 by Pope Martin V; *'In throno iustitiae'* of 1561 by Pius IV; *'Litium dispendiis'* of 1592 by Clement VIII. By the 19th century summary procedure had become the normal one.

ters (= *cum omnibus incidentibus, dependentibus, emergentibus, annexis et connexis*).

If the requested directive was neither covered by the general authorization which the Pope had bestowed on the *'Signatura Justitiae'*, nor by the one bestowed on the *'Signatura Gratiae'*, the matter had indeed to be submitted to the Pope in person. The *'Signatura'* prepared and scrutinized such matters thoroughly before referring them to the papal Consistory, in order to cause the Pope as little loss of time as possible. The Pope's decision was minuted on the supplication document by a cardinal who had been present in the Consistory, e.g.: *Placet domini Papae de procedura summaria.* (signed:) *N. cardinalis Casanattus.*

2. Further proceedings before deliberation *in Rota*

A papal messenger (= *cursor*) delivered the petition, now positively endorsed with a 'commissio', to the commissioned judge. The applicant would then approach that judge and request that the adversary be summoned. In an appeal the applicant would also request that the lower court's *'acta'* be transported to Rome and any *'attentata'* be revoked so that everything be restored to the state of affairs as at the moment when the appeal was lodged. The word *'attentata'* meant any attempt to unilaterally change the state of affairs, with or without help by the lower court, at a time when the appeal had already been lodged.

The case remained with the same judge until the instance was ended. The judge could renounce the *'commissio'* – for instance if he felt parties had a reason to suspect that he was biased. The *'Signatura'* then commissioned another judge – on request. If a judge resigned his functions or died, the Dean of the Rota could subrogate another Rota judge[39].

One basic principle of civil procedure under the *ius commune* was that judges hardly ever acted *ex officio* on their own initiative. Almost any judicial activity could only be set in motion by the litigating party who desired it – by filing an appropriate petition to which the judge would then react.

Litigation went through many stages (= *termini*), although it was possible to pack several stages into one appearance before the judge. For each stage the applicant had to obtain a judicial decree to summon (= *citare*) the adversary. If the adversary had not been present when the summons was decreed the applicant had furtermore to attend to the serving (= *'intimatio'*, also called *'insinuatio'*) of the summons. This was easy and caused no

---

[39] *De Luca* (n. 3), n. 6; *Rota,* dec. recentiores 8 n. 4, part. 6; 21 sub n. 2, part. 12; 556 n. 8 and 566 n. 5, part. 19 vol. 2.

delay as long as the adversary had a proctor at Rome, but it was complicated and time-consuming if the summons had to be served at some distant place (= *ad partes*).

The summoned party was offered a choice of three dates to make an appearance in court. He was admonished (= only *monitorie*) to appear at the first or the second date, and firmly ordered (= *peremptorie*) to appear latest at the last date. After the last date had lapsed the applicant could request to procede by default. This required proof that the summons had validly been served. The applicant had thus to "bring back" the summons document (= *reproductio litterarum Rotalium*) together with evidence for due serving: e. g. a sworn statement by a competent court messenger[40], witnessed by some public notary.

In the default procedure the absent adversary party had still to be summoned to each stage of litigation, but this needed no longer be done *'ad partes'*. Simple public announcements in the General Audience at the papal curia would suffice. The summons was read *in Audientia Publica Litterarum Contradictarum* = in Rota jargon: *'per Contradictas'*. If the defaulting adversary changed his mind and came before the judge, he had to accept litigation in the stage in which it now was – and that might be a very disadvantageous one.

At the Rota the parties submitted *'informationes'* to the judge, and the judge then gave the other party a chance to respond. This was different from the procedure at higher courts in the Netherlands where the proctors exchanged pleadings among them without bothering the court. There the judge got the papers only when the exchange had come to an end and a judicial decision had to be made, namely he got two piles of papers: one from each party[41]. At the Rota, in contrast, this could at times happen[42], but normally the judge got the papers continually as they were produced[43].

Exchange of written argument was rapid because the lawyers generally knew in advance what the other side would write and could thus prepare in time. Official interchange of pleading only started three days before the set

---

40 *Rota,* dec. recentiores 634 n. 10, part. 4 vol. 3; 134 n. 2 part. 9 vol. 1; 432 n. 6, part. 13.

41 Cf. my article 'Zivilprozeßrecht' in: *Robert Feenstra, Reinhard Zimmermann* (ed.), Das römisch-holländische Recht. Fortschritte des Zivilrechts im 17. und 18. Jahrhundert (Berlin 1992) [Schriften zur Europäischen Rechts- und Verfassungsgeschichte, 7], p. 76 and 86 - 87.

42 *Rota,* dec. recentiores, 495 n. 40, part. 4, vol. 2.

43 In the *causa Salisburgensis* 1701 - 1705 which I use as an exemple, however, the Rota's archive series *'Positiones'* contains one chronological pile only with papers submitted by the archbishop of Salzburg and another one only with those submitted by the bishop of Chiemsee.

date for the deliberation *in Rota*. Cardinal *De Luca*[44], always extolling the efficiency and dedication of the personnel at the Rota, tells us that judges and proctors and advocates ruined their weekends with hard work to prepare Rota sessions on Mondays. Even if the applicant's *'informatio'* was only delivered on Saturday morning, the answer, and the *'replicatio'*, and the answer to the *'replicatio'* could all be in before Sunday evening. In addition, all the judges were verbally informed[45].

A Rota judge could not decide any legal point on his own – not even in proceedings by default. He always had to seek advice from his colleagues. Their advice was binding. The litigation thus stood under the presage that it had to be set on the court roll for a deliberation *in Rota* and that both parties had to be notified about that date at least one month[46] in advance.

The above mentioned feature could be abused by litigants who wanted to delay proceedings. For instance, if the judge announced that he intended to hear certain witnesses or see certain documents, they could use this as a pretense to raise a legal point and insist that it be discussed *in Rota*. This effected at least one month respite for the maverick party. The only counterbalance to this were the costs which the mischievous litigant would incur, and the proctor's and advocate's fear for their good reputation. It appears that the counterbalance worked reasonably well: On average proceedings at the Rota went quicker than proceedings at the highest courts in our time. Some proceedings, however, pended at Rome for many years.

While the principle, as such, that judges must always seek advice was as old as canon law, and while its implementation in the form that Rota-judges sought advice from each other had been carried through from the medieval origins of the Rota, the practical application by 1700 was no longer the same: the *'dubium'* was formulated differently, and strict rules applied as to which judges were to give advice.

3. The *'dubium'*

In order to file an issue on the court roll for deliberation, the issue had to be shortly characterized in a 'doubt' (= *dubium*). The *'dubium'* announced the question which the judge in charge would pose to his colleagues in the deliberation session[47]. Since the *'dubium'* characterized the issue at hand, it

---

44 *De Luca* (n. 3), n. 39.

45 *Marchetti* (n. 3), I.5, attests that both customs still applied by the middle of the 19th century.

46 *Rota,* dec. recentiores, 446 n. 6, part. 18, vol. 2.

47 Details given by *De Luca* (n. 3), n. 36 ss.

determined, together with the *'litis contestatio'*, the direction in which the proceedings had to go.

Around 1700 the *'dubium principale'* was usually fairly broadly worded. It mentioned the specific disagreement which gave rise to the litigation, and it tried to delineate the case as a whole – e.g.: "Does Baron X, who is an illegitimate son of the late count of Toulouse, hold the count's right of patronage in the parish church at Belvèze?" Or: "Is it true that at Cologne the canons of the church Great St. Martin have higher rank than the canons of the church St. Gereon?"

It could, however, happen that the *'dubium principale'* had to be postponed because an incident isssue, for instance a procedural issue (= *ordinatoria*), had to be deliberated beforehand. The *'dubium incidens'* (also called *'dubium particulare'*) could then, for example, be: "Shall a commission for a witness hearing far from Rome (= *remissoria ad partes*) be granted?"

Up to the beginning of the 17th century, in contrast, if a case presented more than one legal problem, it had been customary to pose each legal problem as a separate *'dubium'* and to word it as an abstract point of law. Legal problems were debated and resolved one by one – e.g.: "(1) Can inheritable rights of patronage over a parish church be bequeathed to an illegitimate son; (2) Is a right of patronage subject to 30 years' prescription time; (3) Does prescription run against a minor if that minor's guardian is insane; (4) Can insanity be proved indirectly – by proving that close family members were heard saying that the person was totally insane?"

A special *'terminus'* was set 'to agree on the dubium' (= *ad concordandum de dubio*). If the litigants did not come to an agreement, or if the judge refused to subscribe to it, this point was submitted for deliberation *in Rota*. It could cause considerable delay as matters of this kind were only debated four times a year in special deliberation sessions – which the Rota jargon styled *'Rotae memorialium'*[48].

4. The deliberation stage of proceedings

Deliberation sessions were regularly held on Mondays and Fridays, but if they happened to be a holiday the sessions could take place on Wednesday or even Saturday[49]. There was a three months vacation during the summer, mainly to give the prelates a chance to escape from the heat in Rome and

[48] Last session before the Christmas vacation, first session after Easter, last session before the summer vacation, first session after it: *De Luca* (n. 3), n. 47.

[49] *Bernino* (n. 3), p. 191; *De Luca* (n. 3), n. 32.

thus from malaria mosquitoes, and there were short vacations around Christmas and Easter.

The sessions *in Rota* were not public. Only the judges were admitted. In former times parties had occasionally been admitted to plead verbally *in Rota,* but this had been abolished under Pope Paul III (1534 - 1549)[50].

In the deliberation chamber the judges' seats were ranked according to seniority in appointment. The most senior judge, rank number one, served as Dean. Rank number two sat on the Dean's right side, rank number three on the Dean's left side, number four and five again at the right and the left side, and so forth. The youngest in appointment date, judge number twelve, came thus to sit opposite the Dean.

Each judge was allowed to submit a maximum of two *'dubia'* per deliberation day[51], and there could thus be up to 24 cases on the roll. It was impossible for the judges to deal with so great a work load in plenary debates. It thus became a habit that judges would only put their *'dubia'* to the four colleagues sitting next to them on the left side[52]. This custom was affirmed by a papal constitution of 1611[53].

The technical word for a deliberation group in Rota was *'turnus'*. Each of the twelve judges was a member of five different *'turni'* which overlapped in part. Judge number 11, for instance, submitted his dubia to numbers 12, 10, 8, 6, but the same judge 11 also sat in a *'turnus'* in which judge number 3 asked advice from 5, 7, 9, 11.

The judge in charge of the case (*'auditor ponens'*, also called *'referens'*) posed the *'dubium'*, answered questions about the case and entered into a debate with his colleagues (the *'corresponsales'*). Other judges could also enter the debate and state their oponion[54], but when the debate came to its end only the votes of the four *'corresponsales'* counted. In the old Rota the *'auditor ponens'* could not vote. This was partly changed in 1746[55] and fully abolished in 1834[56]. If however a matter had been commissioned *extra Rotam,* although to a Rota judge, that judge could always

[50] *Ludovicus Gomes,* Commentarius ad Regulas Cancellariae, in prooemio, cited by *Bernino* (n. 3), p. 192; *Lega* (n. 3), p. XIX.

[51] *Archivio della S. R. Rota, Diaria, n. 186* = diaries of Rota deans, p. 34 = 31 March 1702: Nota quod per errorem fuerunt proposita tria dubia ab R. P. D. Ansaldo, cum alias de stilo non sint solitae proponi nisi duae causae in una quaque Rota.

[52] *De Luca* (n. 3), n. 34.

[53] *'Universi agri dominici'* by Paul V.

[54] *Rota,* dec. recentiores 209 n. 5, part. 18, vol. 1. This was at times regarded as unwelcome meddling: ibidem, 142 n. 8, part. 18, vol. 1.

[55] *'Iustitiae et pacis'* by Benedict XIV.

[56] *Regolamento* (n. 3) § 325.

vote – in exception to the above mentioned principle that an *'auditor ponens'* cannot vote[57].

If the four *'corresponsales'* voted two against two, the matter was postponed to another deliberation session. If the vote then was again two against two, the matter was postponed once more and the fifth and sixth judge to the left of the *'ponens'* voted with the *'turnus'*. If this produced a vote three against three the matter was postponed to a session where all the judges voted[58].

The judges were very reluctant to overthrow an established custom of the court (= *stylus curiae*), or a precedent which had been printed in one of the published collections of *'decisiones Rotae'*. A papal constitution of 1561[59] had ordered that such overruling should only be done for grave reasons, and only with a two thirds majority in a plenary session. The principle had again been inculcated in a constitution of 1611[60]. Thus, if one *'turnus'* deemed it desirable to overthrow an applicable precedent, the matter had to be postponed in order to submit it to a plenary deliberation.

The drafters of the constitution of 1551 had perhaps only referred to the collections of *'decisiones'* from the 14th century – which had enormeous renown and were very widely known –, but by the 17th century the said constitution was at times referred to as if it had meant any printed decision in general[61].

At the discretion of the Dean any matter could be submitted to the full round of judges. It could furthermore happen that the Pope expressly ordered all the judges to look into a particular matter (= *'Videant omnes'*). It also happened that the Pope or a Sacred Congregation or the *'Auditor Camerae'* or any other judicial instance wanted to hear the Rota's opinion

---

57 Example: *Archivio della S. R. Rota, Vota, n. 2* = votes by judge Lancetta (1696 - 1706). On one of his votes, 17 May 1703, he notes *"coram me"* = he was thus the *'auditor ponens'* and could nevertheless vote.

58 With simple majority: *Rota,* dec. recentiores, 113 n. 1, part. 18, vol. 1; *Marchetti* (n. 3) I.5; *Bangen* (n. 3), p. 337; *Lega,* p. XXXVII.

59 Pius IV, *'In throno iustitiae'*: Item decanus et alii auditores, praesertim antiquiores, attendant ne aliquid non solum contra ius, sed nec etiam contra stylum et decisiones antiquas factas in Rota, quae impressae habentur, quoquo modo decidatur, etiam praetextu aequitatis in iure non scriptae, nisi maxima cum ratione et discussione, omnibus votis, seu saltem illorum duabus tertiis partibus, aliter faciendum esse iudicaverit.

60 *'Universi agri dominici'* by Paul V.

61 *Rota,* dec. recentiores, 413 n. 4, part. 16 (*coram Taja,* 5.12.1670, for decisions by Peña, Ludovisius, , Royas, Ninott and Mantica); 337 n. 16, part. 17 recent. (again *coram Taja,* 3.6.1672, for decisions by Dunozetus iunior and Othobonus). Mere *obiter dicta* in decisions, however, could simply be overruled: 196 n. 38 part. 11 recent. (*coram Bichio,* 24.11.1651), referring to older decisions.

on a point of law in a case which pended elsewhere. In such occasions the Rota always staged plenary deliberations.

In contrast to medieval procedure where the *'auditor ponens'* had to wait twelve days for colleagues to come forward and make suggestions, the deliberation procedure around 1700 was much speedier: The *'correspon-sales'* came to the Rota session well-prepared because they had been informed in advance by proctors and advocates, and because they had read the written pleadings which had been delivered to them.

In proceedings by default there were only pleadings from one of the parties. The other party was undefended and could thus not protest against any wrong argumentation or wrong references. This is why the judges scrutinized the argumentations and citations in such cases particularly carefully[62].

After the deliberation session the litigating parties were immediately informed of the outcome. The household members (= *familiares*) of all judges who had voted on the matter were then entitled to a treat by the advantaged party, while the household of the *'auditor ponens'* could expect a double treat[63].

The *'auditor ponens'* and/or his *'adjutor'* then 'extended' the *'decisio'* – that is: they wrote an account of the majority's reasoning and refuted any dissenting argumentation. This was done with the help of minutes taken during the deliberation session, plus any written notes which the other judges had handed over in the session. Often the advantaged party's representatives also helped. The readily drafted *'decisio'* was surrendered to the advantaged party – who had to pay for it[64]. If the draft did not meet its approval, the party could try to demand a revision[65]. Finally the *'decisio'* was printed at the advantaged party's care and expense[66], and printed copies were then delivered to the disadvantaged party.

A *'decisio Rotae'* is an account by the *'ponens'* about the advice which his colleagues gave him[67]. It is by no means a judgment. It merely makes clear what the Rota thinks about the case at present, and what judgment the

---

62 *De Luca* (n. 3), n. 37 extols their zeal in this regard.

63 *Marchetti* (n. 3), I.5. See above, n. 25.

64 *De Luca* (n. 3), n. 108 in fine: at his time the maximum fee was two scudi. It was later changed to three scudi: *Archivio della S. R. Rota, Diaria, n. 186* = diaries of Rota deans, p. 48 = September 1702: "Sanctitas Sua approbavit antiquum honorarium scutorum trium pro extensione cuiuslibet sententiae".

65 *Roßhirt* (n. 3), p. 209.

66 *Marchetti* (n. 3), I.5.

67 *Ascheri* (n. 3) treats this subject on p. 1134 - 1140 and 1162 - 1164. See also *De Luca* (n. 3), n. 51 - 53.

'ponens' will deliver if no new arguments or new evidence material are brought forward in the mean time.

The style and arrangement of *'decisiones'* have been sufficiently described by *Mario Ascheri*[68]. They all end with a stereotypical formula which is usually abridged: *'Et ita, etc.'*. In its extended form it reads: "And so, leaving out other reasons of lighter weight, after pleadings of both parties, it was decided"[69].

The custom of redacting the accumulated legal reasoning into a *'decisio'* had deep roots. There is evidence that already the Rota judges of the 14th century had a habit of keeping note-books for this purpose. Ample evidence of such private note-books has come down to us. After 1500, however, the extension of minutes and notes into a *'decisio'* became an official duty. A papal constitution of 1561 mentions it as a laudable old custom[70], and it further attests that it was also an old custom to hand the *'decisio'* out to the parties. They were thus informally notified about the Rota's view on the case.

The advice which Rota judges gave to a colleague was regarded as a *'consilium sapientis'*. It thus fulfilled the function which in other courts at that time was fulfilled by the judge requesting a legal opinion from a law faculty or a particular lawyer of renown.

The outcome of the deliberation and its reasoning were not secret by law. The judges and other court personnel had only sworn that they would not reveal which judge had said what[71]. In medieval courts, however, the opinion had prevailed that it was wise to keep the reasoning secret.

Some medieval judges had feared that the losing party might be incited to fabricate false new evidence[72]. Another fear was that the painstaking legal research which the judges had done could help the losing party in founding the Heads of Argument for an appeal. Neither argument was very convincing: Someone prone to forge documents or to bribe witnesses could do so even after judgment, namely on appeal; or else if the judgment was not appellable: on a request for *'restitutio in integrum'*. And why should one hinder the losing party from reading the legal sources and literature which the judges had researched? If the judges had done their homework orderly they had nothing to fear.

---

[68] *Ascheri* (n. 3), p. 1162 - 1164.

[69] Et ita, praetermissis aliis levioris ponderis, utraque parte informante, resolutum fuit, etc.

[70] Pius IV, *'In throno iustitiae'*; repeated in 1611 by Paul V: *'Universi agri dominici'*.

[71] Urban VIII, *'Exponi nobis nuper fecerunt'*, 1643, rendered this expressly clear.

[72] Cf. my article as above in n. 2, footnote 16.

After 1500 the opposite opinion eventually prevailed. It was now argued that putting the parties in the picture of what the Rota judges had thought might give the parties more impulse to settle the case amicably, and might give them a chance to come forward and point out any errors, misunderstandings, misreadings and erroneous citations of law texts or legal literature. It was in the interest of good administration of justice that judgments should rest on the best possible evaluation of facts and law and that the parties collaborated to that aim.

The debate must be seen in the context of a general debate 1400 - 1800 about advantages and disadvantages of official disclosure of judges' reasonings to the parties. The Rota opted very early for an enlightened stance while many other courts still drew a tight veil – some of them even up to the late 18th century.

It should be remembered that the official *judgment,* in contrast to the *'decisio'* which preceded it, gave only an account of the facts of the case and no legal reasoning. It would have been unwise to give as well legal reasonings, as C. 7.64.2 said that any expressly stated erroneous legal reasonings rendered a judgment void *ab initio,* even if the losing party had acquiesced and had not lodged an appeal[73]. If a judge was unwise enough to write legal reasonings into the formal judgment document, a mischievous loosing party might use this as a pretext to contend that the reasoning was erroneous and that the judgment was thus void. Only the highest judges (Pope, emperor, kings) could afford to neglect this warning since their judgments could not be attacked anyway.

The principle in C. 7.64.2 was eventually abolished in all *ius-commune*-territories. At those courts, however, where it still applied (e.g. at the Rota), the formal judgments had to be rendered without legal reasoning.

5. Further procedure: new hearing or judgment

After the deliberation *in Rota* litigants could request to summon the adversary "to close the matter" (= *ad concludendum in causa*). A discontented litigant might apply for a new hearing (= *nova audientia*) instead. The Rota decided on such requests four times a year, namely in the above mentioned *'Rotae memorialium'*. The judges were generous in granting the

[73] The emperor Alexander to A. Capito: If, in the inheritance-litigation between you and the grandmother of the deceased, the judge whom the provincial governor had delegated has pronounced that the deceased was able to make a testament even below the age of fourteen years, then it is obvious that his judgment, which goes against such a manifest rule of the law, has no force, and therefore there was not even a remedy of appeal needed, in this situation.

request if the case was to be judged in the last instance. Otherwise, if the case could still be appealed, they often deemed it sufficient that the case could be heard another time on appeal[74].

If a new hearing was granted the *'dubium'* read: *An standum vel recedendum sit a decisis,* and the new submissions by the proctors were styled *'nova facti'* – or, if it was the third hearing: *'tertia facti'*.

Unsuccessful litigants often gave in. They instructed the proctor to acquiesce in the *'decisio'* and renounce any further steps. In the Rota jargon this was called 'Motion of the baby lion' (*'motivum leonelli'* = whose little lion's roar was not as frightening as he had thought).

As long as no new hearing was scheduled, the advantaged party could request the judge to ask his colleagues whether the judgment (= *sententia*) should now be expedited (= *an demandandum pro expeditione*)[75].

Judgment was prepared in writing. The parties were summoned to hear how the judgment was read (= *ad audiendam sententiam*).

Ius commune gave the judge discretion with regard to the costs of litigation. Usually the judgment ordered the loser to reimburse the winner's costs and pay the court fees, as stated in C. 7.51.3, but if the loser had had sound reasons to trust that he would win the case no such order was made.

Thereafter, if the loser had not appealed, the winner could request enforcement of the judgment. The common means to secure enforcement far from Rome was to obtain a piece of writing called *'Litterae executoriales extra Romanam curiam et ad partes'*: This was a circular letter by the Rota judge, addressed to all the secular and ecclesiastical authorities in the respective region, asking them to assist the successful litigant – under threat of ecclesiastical *'censurae'* which would automatically strike the disobedient, and which could not be relaxed by anyone but the Pope or the Rota judge in question.

Threats (= Romana eventualia fulmina):

The loser and any persons whose assistance the winner would implore against the loser's disobedience were given six days to do their best to give the judgment full bearing. The six days counted from the day when the person in question was first shown the *'litterae executoriales'*. If the loser or a person whose assistance had been implored did not comply in time, the disobedient fell into excommunication. If it was an ecclesiastical corporation, all its divine services were suspended (= *suspensio a divinis*) and

---

[74] *De Luca* (n. 3), n. 55.

[75] *De Luca* (n. 3), n. 54.

all its churches, chapels and other localities were burdened with this interdict. If it was the Apostolic Nuntius or an archbishop or bishop, they were forbidden to enter any church.

All clergy members were given power of attorney to enforce these *'censurae'* in the Rota judge's stead, as well as a strict order to do so. They were furthermore ordered to make the excommunication publicly known, by announcing it from the church pulpit on Sundays and holidays, but not before the winner would request them to do so.

Second threat:

Should censured persons withstand excommunication beyond the tenth day after the first public announcement from the church pulpit, then the announcements had to be done in a more impressive form, namely with church bells ringing, with symbolic extinguishing of candle flames and throwing the candle to the ground, with exorcism rites to put the demons to flight who hindered the recalcitrant from coming to their senses, with prayers that God may lead them to better insight, and with the hymn "The Heavens will reveal the iniquity of Juda", and Psalm 35 with the Antiphon "In the middle of life we are embraced by death", in full length, and thereafter clergy should leave the church and lead a procession of all the parishioners to the house of the recalcitrant where three stones should symbolically be thrown at the house, as a remembrance of God's wrath against Korah and Dathan and Abiram who were swallowed by the earth because earth could not bear them any longer[76].

Third threat:

Should the censured persons nevertheless withstand excommunication beyond twenty days after public announcement, then all christians should within six days from notice withdraw from them entirely. All those who did not withdraw would be contaminated by the excommunication.

Fourth threat:

Should this still bear no fruit and should the censured persons persist beyond thirty days, then the matter devolved to the 'secular arm' *(brachium saeculare)* – that means: the secular authorities were requested to arrest and imprison the recalcitrant and sequestrate their assets – until they abided.

---

[76] *The Bible,* Numeri 16, 32 s.

Should the requested secular authorities not step in within six days from notice, then they would themselves become subject to successively aggravated ecclesiastical *'censurae'* – except the Emperor as Rota judges lacked authority to excommunicate him.

Despite the fulminant threats, *'litterae executoriales'* often met strong resistance: Aggrieved persons applied to their secular government or court for an order to stay the execution of the ecclesiastical judgment. Such request had good chances if the aggrieved party had not consented to litigate at the Holy See. Governments, even catholic ones, disliked papal meddling in their territory[77].

IV. The Court Records

Any material belonging to the official papers of litigation was referred to under the global word *'acta'*. This word meant in particular the case folders (= one folder for each case) in which the judge's *'adiutor'* (or before the reform in 1671: the judge's personal notary) accumulated all pertaining documents, in particular the *'supplicatio'* with its *'commissio'*, the Heads of Arguments and other *'informationes'* which the representatives of the parties had handed in, any evidential material, etc.

Each notary furthermore kept one continuous daily record (= *manuale*) in which he minuted whatever was acted before him. Entries in a notary's *'manuale'* were written in mere chronological order. In order to find the information for one specific case, one had to peruse the whole *'manuale'* of the notary to whom the case had been assigned and, if he had been ill or absent during some time, also the *'manualia'* of notaries who had acted in his stead. This was not as time-consuming as one might think as the notaries wrote the case label for each entry very visibly.

In addition, judges kept their personal diaries[78]. It appears that this had initially been an unofficial habit, but it developed into an official duty by the end of the 17th century, due to the above mentioned fact that the number of notaries was reduced and judges could thus no longer rely on having the services of a personal notary at all hours. The judge's diary was often kept by his *'adjutor'*.

Cases at the papal curia were neither referred to under a roll number, nor under litigants' names. In order to refer to a particular case, one simply mentioned the diocese from where it came together with a keyword about the issue and the judge's name.

---

[77] Example from Aachen quoted at n. 14.

[78] For a famous surviving diary see *M. Tocci,* Il diario di Jacob Emerix de Matthiis decano della Sacra Romana Rota (Napoli 1982) [Ius nostrum, serie II.2].

I shall give one example: A monastery near Toledo sold snow (= *nivis*). The local Spanish snow-sellers regarded this as a breach of their trade monopoly and sued the monastery at the Rota – with success! The case was litigated before (= *coram*) judge Hieronymus Priolus. The case label thus read: *Toletana nivis, coram Priolo*[79].

The technical word for the procurator's main piece of work was *'Summarium'*: namely he submitted a parcel of authenticated transcripts of documents, accompanied by a 'summary', i.e. an account of the facts of the case as he saw them, with continuous reference to the enclosed documents, citing text passages from them and summing them up. Strangely enough the evidence documents were called *'jura'* (= 'rights'), although they were considered a part of the fact-finding. The terminology can perhaps be explained by bearing in mind that documents were often submitted in order to prove some contested privilege or other vested right (= *jus*).

The technical word for an advocate's written submission was *'Restrictus iuris'* (medieval usage: *'Allegatio'*). Both the advocates' and the proctors' submissions were globally referred to under the word *'informationes'*, *'positiones'*, or *'memorialia'*, or simply *'scripturae'*.

All papers handed in while a set deliberation date was pending indicate only that date. Since the date when the paper was made and submitted is not indicated it can be difficult to arrange the papers in the Archive chronologically. The notary's *Manualia*, if preserved, can at times offer help as they note which papers were submitted on a certain day.

17th - 19th century Rota dossiers are easy to read because so many *'informationes'* were submitted in print. The parties did this because they wanted to make a good impression. The printing was done at an official papal printing office (= *Typographia reverendae Camerae Apostolicae*) so that one could reasonably assume that all submitted copies were identical and that no fraud by means of deliberate omissions took place. Often the parties needed so many copies that printing was less expensive than hand-copying, anyway. Stacks of printed copies were delivered to the representatives of the other party and thereafter to the *'auditor ponens'* and to each judge who could vote on the matter: one copy for the judge himself, one for his *'adjutor'* or any other lawyer in his *'studium'*, and one surplus copy for control purposes – which was handed over to the adversary's solicitor at his next call[80].

At the deliberation on the case the *'auditor ponens'* got also advice in writing (= *vota*) from his colleagues. The preserved *Vota* in the Rota

---

79 Deliberation on Wednesday, 27 June 1696; published among the decisiones nuperrimae, liber XIV dec. 4.

80 *De Luca* (n. 3), n. 40.

archives are usually short, much shorter than a *'decisio'*. They indicate only the main reasons. Quotations (if there are any) refer mostly to previous *'decisiones Rotae'*. All vota end with the formula "Better insight shall override my present opinion" (= *Salva meliori sententia*). *Vota* were of course kept secret. They are a very interesting source, firstly because of the secrecy and secondly because of the selectiveness of argumentation. The *Vota* show which of the many points submitted by the parties were really regarded as the essential ones.

The *'decisio Rotae'* as extended by the *'auditor ponens'* after the deliberation did not officially form part of the court records. It was merely an 'extra-iudicial' document, drafted for the court's own internal use[81]. It deployed no effect of *'res iudicata'* whatsoever. The judges were free to change their minds, with or without a new hearing. The *'decisio'* was only made known to the parties under canon law's general maxim that judges shall be benign and shall try their best to enhance christian love and understanding between the litigants.

Ius commune required that judgments be prepared in writing and then read. Rota judges thus wrote their judgments on a sheet of paper *(cedula)* which was then archived by the notaries.

The official court records end with the judgment. *'Litterae executoriales'* were issued to the winning parties on request, but they were not archived at the court. They were issued under the name of the *'auditor ponens'*, signed by the Rota notary in charge, witnessed by other Rota notaries and sealed with the Rota Dean's seal[82]. Case winners often multiplied their *'litterae executoriales'* in print. The printed copies sometimes bear an authentication: usually by some local notary[83], and not a Rota notary.

---

[81] *Plettenbergius* (n. 3), p. 591; *De Luca* (n. 3), n. 57.

[82] *Bernino* (n. 3), p. 195, attests that in the 18th century judicial decrees were at times issued under the seal of the *'auditor ponens'*.

[83] Example: *Stadtarchiv Aachen, Hs. G 17,* p. 41 - 45, litterae executoriales 17 May 1688 in the litigation Synodal court at Aachen (backed by the City Council of Aachen) v. Scabinal court at Aachen, vidimated by Johannes Geulen notarius apostolicus (at Aachen?); *Hs. 9,* p. 606 ss. contain another copy of it, without any authentication. I privately own a third copy of this document, bequeated to me by my friend Carl Blell. It has a dry stamp "LIB(erae) IMP(erii) URB(is) AQU(isgranensis) S(i)GI(llum)" with a double-headed eagle – thus the seal of the City Council of Aachen.

V. Pertinent Archival Holdings

1. Archivio della Sacra Romana Rota (now in the Archivio Segreto Vaticano)

The archive contains thirteen series of materials, all with heavy losses over the centuries. All series have been inventorized by the late Hermann Hoberg (1907 - 1992)[84]. His inventories have been printed in 1994[85] – except a few very detailed ones which must still be seen in typescript at the Archivio[86].

Commissiones: This series contains *supplicationes* with notes of commissioning by the *Signatura Justitiae,* 1480 - 1792. They all have a hole in the middle which shows that they were originally archived on a thread.

Manualia actorum et citationum: Daily note-books of Rota-notaries, 1463 - 1800[87]. There exists a detailed inventory in typescript[88] and a shortened version of it in *Hoberg*'s book. Good sample photographs with transcriptions are given in *Maffei*'s book[89]. Up to 1671 each notary was assigned to one particular judge. This is why their note-books were archived under the judge's name. From 1671 onward, however, they are archived under the notary's own name because notaries might then write for several judges. Each volume in the archives contains at least one alphabetical index of the cases concerned. One must however keep in mind that many of the present very bulky volumes have been bound together from several previously independent volumes, each of which has its own index. Often the events in the notary's office (= *in officio*) and those before a judge on grounds of a summons (= *de citatione*) are recorded in two different *'manualia'*.

Diaria: Judges' diaries from 1566 onward[90].

Positiones: Papers submitted by the proctors and advocates, 3837 volumes 1627 - 1870. A very detailed inventory for the first 268 volumes

[84] In the index book-cases in the reading room upstairs, under shelfnumbers 701, 1057, 1072, 1073, 1092, 1094, 1095, 1097, 1106, 1108, 1109.

[85] See above, n. 4.

[86] N. 1057 = *Manualia,* and n. 1072 = detailed inventory for the first 268 volumes of *Positiones*.

[87] *Hermann Hoberg,* Die Protokollbücher der Rotanotare von 1464 bis 1517, in: Zeitschrift der Savigny-Stiftung für Rechtsgeschichte 70, Kanonistische Abteilung 39 (1953) 177 - 227; *Carlo Sangori,* Relazione sull'ordinamento dell'Archivio notarile della Sacra Rota, Roma 1888.

[88] N. 1057.

[89] *Maffei* (n. 2), on p. 142 - 148.

[90] *Hermann Hoberg,* Die Diarien der Rotarichter, in: Römische Quartalschrift für christliche Altertumskunde und Kirchengeschichte 50 (1955) 44 - 68.

of the series exists only in typescript[91]. The other volumes are very summarily inventorized in *Hoberg*'s book. At least in the volumes of 1703 - 1705 which I have seen each piece bears at the end a handwritten note with the name of some judge who was not the *'auditor ponens'*. Maybe the *'corresponsales'* of the *'turnus'* agreed for each *causa* that one of them should read the cause papers particularly carefully, and this is his name.

The series *Informationes* contains the same type of material as *Positiones,* 1626 - 1669.

Processus actorum: contains dossiers from lower courts which have been called up by the Rota, together with respective decrees of Rota-judges, 1500 - 1798, with two inventories[92].

Iura diversa: Documents and witnesses' sayings, submitted as evidence, 1512 - 1882.

Peritiae: Expert opinions, particularly by physicians, surveyors, experts in property value, from the end of the 17th century onward.

Vota: Secret legal advice by *'auditores corresponsales'*, collected by the *'auditor ponens'* and archived at the end of each year by judges' names and roughly by date, 1626 - 1870. *Vota* which the same *'corresponsalis'* gave in the same case at different deliberation dates are often bundled together.

Decisiones, arranged by names of *'auditor ponens'*, 1511 - 1859. There are also a few early volumes of mere rough notes of judges. Systematic collection of *'decisiones'* started only in 1688[93].

Sententiae: Judgments, 1474 - 1803. They are written on sheets of paper which are folded in the middle. The upper half contains the name of the *'auditor ponens'*, the case label, date of promulgation, witness names, and the signature of the Rota notary in charge. The lower half contains the text of the judgment, written in particularly neat handwriting, with the judge's signature. The judge's fee is either noted in the uppermost right corner or in the lowermost left corner. Fees around 1700 were either 10 or 25 or 50 or 100 *scuta aurei.* All judgments have a hole in the middle. They were thus originally archived on a thread, like the *supplicationes.*

---

[91] N. 1072.

[92] N. 1094 (1500 - 1798); n. 1106 is a detailed inventory for the first 100 volumes, years 1500 - 1644.

[93] Lega (n. 3), p. L.

Processus in admissione auditorum: dossiers about admission of new judges, 1492 - 1908, however very few before 1700.

Miscellanea: Documents about privileges of Rota judges, etc.

2. Materials outside the Rota archives

Scattered *'manualia', 'diaria'* and *'registra'* and fragments of them have made their way into many other archives[94] and libraries.

Specimens of *'informationes'* and *'litterae executoriales'* and parties' copies of *'registra'* are also preserved in many local archives, among archivalia of former litigants. Some printed specimens have even wound up in book collections.

Individual *'decisiones'* (= called *'decisiones volantes'*), printed or handwritten, can be found by the thousands in many libraries and archives in- and outside Rome[95]. Published collections of *'decisiones'* are found in all major libraries of countries whose law follows the tradition of *ius commune*.

Separate judgment-documents from the 17th - 18th century are rare because it made little sense to have such documents issued separately. If one wanted to seek enforcement of a judgment one had to request *'litterae executoriales'* anyway, and they included the full text of the judgment, along with the text of the *'supplicatio'* and *'commissio'* and *'decisio'*[96].

'Litterae executoriales' can be found in archival dossiers about litigation which ensued from attempts to enforce the respective Rota judgment. They

---

94 At Rome, the Archivio di Stato has a series of *'manualia'*: *Hoberg,* Protokollbücher (n. 87).

95 They are usually bound together in volumes in rough chronological order. *Ermini* (n. 3), p. 83 - 84 lists a total of 1819 volumes in various libraries at Rome, 110 at Bologna and 110 at Perugia. *Charles Lefebvre,* Rote Romaine, in: Dictionnaire de droit canonique, VII 742 - 771, gives yet another long list. Further indications about 156 items in manuscript collections all over Europe are appended to my article: Die handschriftliche Verbreitung von Rechtsprechungssammlungen der Rota, in: Zeitschrift der Savigny-Stiftung für Rechtsgeschichte 89, Kanonistische Abteilung 58 (1972) 1 - 106. In the Biblioteca Comunale at Trento a whole wall of book cases is densely filled with volumes of *'decisiones volantes'*, in good chronological order from 1700 to 1870. Also the Biblioteca Estense at Modena has 35 volumes: 234 - 236. P.I, 29 vol., years 1700 - 1736; Ms. lat. 253 + 1293 - 1296, years 1668 - 1680.

96 This had been different in the Middle Ages because at that time the Rota judge's task ended with the judgment. *'Litterae executoriales'* could only be obtained from the papal chancery, and to obtain some one had to submit the judgment there. This is why medieval Rota judges issued judgment documents – usually under their own seal, pending on a green silk thread.

are a most valuable source because they combine a full account of the facts and the proceedings with a copy of the *'decisio'* and the judgment.

Furthermore, there exist dossiers of lawsuits before lower courts which gave rise to appeal proceedings at the Rota[97].

VI. 'Reports'? The Published Collections of *'decisiones'*

No 'reports' in the English sense of the word exist for the Rota. There exist, however, many collections of *'decisiones'* that fulfilled the function which English 'reports' fulfilled for the development of English law.

Tens of thousands[98] of *'decisiones'* have been published in collections in book-form. The published collections comprise at least 11.000 pieces from the 16th century, 38.000 pieces from the 17th century, 12.000 pieces from the 18th century and 3000 from the 19th century. Often the *'adjutor'* of a judge published *'decisiones'* after his master's death, but the Rota judges also complained about pirate publications and about the fact that some of the published *'decisiones'* were entirely fictitious[99]. It can only be hoped that the bulk of this vast material was by and large truly copied from original *'decisiones'*.

There exist three types of publications of *'decisiones'*[100]: Collections known under some title comprise *'decisiones'* from several judges. Collections cited under a person's name, in contrast, contain only or mainly *'decisiones'* emanating from that person. Furthermore, there exist collections which are dedicated to one specific topic. They were usually compiled by some academic, to be used as reference material for a treatise on the topic which he had written, and they were thus printed as an appendix to that treatise[101].

---

97 For instance *Archivio Arcivescovile* at Trento, *Atti civili XXV n. 593* = papers of a prebendary litigation 1676 - 1680. The plaintiff lost his case at Trento, but he successfully appealed to the Rota: The respective *'decisio'* is printed as n. 17 *'de iure patronatus'* in the collection appended to cardinal *De Luca's* Theatrum veritatis = *Tridentina jurispatronatus coram R.P.D. Ursino,* Veneris 4. Martii 1689; in the same archive, *Atti Civili XXIII n. 541* contains cause papers 1693 - 1699 in which the same plaintiff tries to reclaim a plot of land which allegedly pertains to the prebend in question. This proves that he had in the mean time successfully enforced his claim. He lost the new lawsuit, though, and he appealed to Rome once more.

98 The content of the various collections overlaps in part. *Paulus Franciscus Perremutus* compiled a listing of duplicates: Conflictus iureconsultorum inter sese discrepantium, vol. I - V, Panormi 1662 - 1671 (vol. IV - V).

99 Discussed by *Ascheri* (n. 3), p. 1138 - 1139. See also p. 1159.

100 Input for the lists which follow has been collected from the articles by *Ermini* and *Ascheri* (n. 3), with few corrections and additions.

101 *Ermini* (n. 3) lists 67 examples, on p. 84 - 87.

There exist furthermore many index works, in part printed together with the respective collection of *'decisiones'*, in part edited separately – and sometimes many years later[102]. Index works from the 19th century also cover contemporary *'decisiones volantes'*.

Collections known under some title

Antiquae (887, 1372 - 1380 with material 1350 onward),
Antiquiores (ca. 1360 - 1365, attributed to 'Bisigneto'[103]),
Novae (495, 1376 - 1381 = by Guilielmus Horborch),
Diversorum [title page: 'Novissimae'] (4247, 1531 - 1604),
Novissimae (616, 1626 - 1630),
Recentiores (12822, 1558 - 1684. The collection comprises only pieces which had not been printed elsewhere in the mean time) [parts I - IV ed. by Prosperus Farinaccius, years 1558 - 1618; parts V - XIV ed. by Paulus Rubeus, years 1618 - 1666; parts XV - XIX.1 ed. by Iohannes Baptista Compagnus, years 1667 - 1678; part XIX.2 ed. by 'adjutores' of auditors, years 1673 - 1684],
Nuperrimae (3569 + appendix 608, 1684 - 1706),
Recentissimae (1707 - 1783, ed. Petrus Iohannes Cocconius),
Decisiones consilii Rotalis ab anno 1800 (115, 1800).

Collections cited under a person's name[104]

Acuña, Petrus Carillo de (303, 1634* - 1644),
Andreae, Martinus (110, 1614 - 1617),

---

102 *Ermini* (n. 3) lists many, on p. 91 - 101. Particularly important are those by *Iacobus Andreas Pizzus* (Romae 1718 - 1719), comprising all *'decisiones'* so far published; the index to the *'Novissimae'* (Viterbii 1612); the index to the *'Recentiores'* (Mediolani 1730 - 1731); the index according to the diocese of origin: see above, n. 12.

103 *Gero Dolezalek,* Bernardus de Bosqueto, seine Quaestiones motae in Rota (1360 - 1365) und ihr Anteil in den Decisiones Antiquae, in: Zeitschrift der Savigny-Stiftung 93, Kanonistische Abteilung 62 (1976) 106 - 172.

104 I mention the judge's name, the number of comprised *'decisiones'* and their range of years, or in some cases (which are marked by an asterisk) the years in which that judge was in office. Chronological order: Thomas Fastolf (1336), Bernardus de Bosqueto (around 1350 - 1360, = *'antiquiores'*), Aegidius Bellamera (756, 1374 - 1378), Ludovicus Gomes (165, 1511 - 1546, printed with Coccinus), Guilielmus Cassador (158 + 57, 1515 - 1523), Marcellus Crescentius (312, 1529 ss., printed with Marcellus Crescentius iunior), Petrus de Benintendis (98, 1540 - 1545), Iacobus Puteus (1409, ca. 1535 - 1551), Paulus Aemilius Verallus (1122, 1551 - 1554), Achilles de Grassis (426, 1546 - 1550), Seraphinus Olivarius Razzalius (1500, 1566 - 1604), Caesar de Grassis (195, 1574 - 1578), Franciscus Mantica (375,

Ansaldis, Ansaldus de (921 + appendix 46, 1696 - 1720),
Arguelles, Gutierrez (118, 1645 - 1650),
Arostegui, Ildephonsus Clemens de (printed 1781),
Barbosa, Augustinus (printed Coloniae 1736),
Bellamera, Aegidius (756, 1374 - 1378),
Benincasa, Alexander (394, 1683 - 1694),
Benintendis, Petrus de (98, 1540 - 1545),
Bichius, Coelius (672, 1631 - 1656),

1587 - 1596), Neapolio Comitolus (168, 1587 - 1591), Franciscus Peña (1689, 1588 - 1612), Iohannes Mohedanus (583, s. XVI.2), Prosperus Farinaccius (278, 1591 - 1604), Iohannes Garzia cardinalis Millinus (449, 1591 - 1605), Alexander Ludovisius (= Gregorius XV papa, 584, 1600 - 1612), Iohannes Baptista Coccinus (2358, 1600 - 1640, printed with Gomes), Iohannes Baptista Pamphilius (= Innocentius X papa, 738, 1605 - 1621), Alphonsus Manzanedo de Quinnones (919, 1605 - 1627), Iacobus Cavalerius (658, 1607* - 1623), Franciscus Ubaldus (897, 1610 - 1625), cardinalis Paleottus (printed with the index to the *'Novissimae'*, see above, at n. 101), Guilielmus Dunozetus (353, 1613 - 1625), Matthaeus Burattus (952, 1613 - 1627), Martinus Andreae (110, 1614 - 1617), Iohannes Baptista Remboldus (648, 1614* - 1626*), Clemens Merlinus (896, 1621 - 1642), Paulus Duran (463, 1625 - 1634), Benedictus cardinalis Monaldus (203, 1626 - 1631, printed behind Ubaldus), Amatus Dunozettus (1889, 1627 - 1652), Petrus Carillo de Acuña (303, 1634* - 1644), Coelius Bichius (672, 1631 - 1656), Franciscus de Roxas (494, 1635 - 1653), Christophorus Peutinger (509, 1639 - 1649), Octavianus Zuccarus (printed Venetiis 1646), Carolus Cerrus (956, 1640 - 1669), Petrus Othobonus (= Alexander VIII papa, 278, 1643 - 1652), Gutierrez Arguelles (118, 1645 - 1650), Franciscus Zarate (122, 1651 - 1658), Iosephus Ninot (89, 1655 - 1665), Angelus Celsus (411, 1646 - 1664), Iohannes Baptista De Luca (see n. 104), Hieronymus Priolus (471, 1653 - 1674), Iohannes Emerix (180, 1656 - 1668), Iacobus Emerix de Matthys (1370, 1668 - 1696), Felix Ubago et Rio (105, 1671 - 1679), Alexander Benincasa (394, 1683 - 1694), Iosephus Molines (1337, 1686 - 1711), Fr. M. Constantinus (printed Romae 1702), Petrus Pacionus (printed Coloniae 1700), Alexander Caprara (762, 1687 - 1706), Ansaldus de Ansaldis (921 + appendix 46, 1696 - 1720), Cyriacus Lancetta (1403, 1696 - 1723), Franciscus Carolus Kaunitz (244, 1702 - 1711), Vincentius Bondinus (printed 1715), Alexander Falconerius (767, 1706 - 1724), Hieronymus Crispus (625, 1708 - 1715), Iohannes de Herrera (237, 1716 - 1721), Thomas Rattus (334, 1722 - 1732), Augustinus Barbosa (printed Coloniae 1736), Carolus Rezzonicus (= Clemens XIII papa, 340, 1730 - 1737), Alexander Tanarius (277, 1734 - 1743), Marcellus Crescentius iunior (506, 1737 - 1738), Ildephonsus Clemens de Arostegui (printed 1781), Bartholomaeus Olivatius (718, 1756 - 1769), Iohannes Maria Riminaldus (800, 1760 - 1785), Iosephus Alphonsus de Very (197, 1763 - 1771), Franciscus Herzan (261, 1771 - 1779), Alexander Malvasius (272, 1784 - 1801), Aurelius Roverella (95, 1786 - 1789), Hercules Consalvus (= Gonsalvus, 73, 1789 - 1798), Antonius Rusconius (163, 1802 - 1808), Ioachim Iohannes Xaverius Isoard (521, 1803 - 1827), Karolus ex ducibus Odescalchis (270, 1816 - 1820), Iohannes Franciscus Marco y Catalan (422, 1817 - 1828), Antonius Dominicus Gamberinus (130, 1820 - 1823), Cosmas de Cursiis (705, 1820 - 1842), Gaspar Bernardus de marchionibus Pianetti (303, 1821 - 1826), Constantinus ex marchionibus Patrizi (110, 1824 - 1828), Petrus cardinalis Marini (640, 1825 - 1845), Theodulphus cardinalis Mertel (74, 1849 - 1853).

Bisigneto = Bernardus de Bosqueto(ca. 1350 - 1360, known as *'Antiquiores'*),
Bondinus, Vincentius (printed 1715),
Burattus, Matthaeus (952, 1613 - 1627),
Caprara, Alexander (762, 1687 - 1706),
Carillo de Acuña, Petrus (303, 1634* - 1644),
Cassador, Guilielmus (158 + 57, 1515 - 1523),
Cavalerius, Iacobus (658, 1607* - 1623),
Celsus, Angelus (411, 1646 - 1664),
Cerrus, Carolus (956, 1640 - 1669),
Coccinus, Iohannes Baptista (2358, 1600 - 1640, printed with Gomes),
Comitolus, Neapolio (168, 1587 - 1591),
Constantinus, Fr. M. (printed Romae 1702),
Crescentius iunior, Marcellus (506, 1737 - 1738),
Crescentius, Marcellus (312, 1529 ss., printed with Marcellus Crescentius iunior),
Crispus, Hieronymus (625, 1708 - 1715),
Cursiis, Cosmas de (705, 1820 - 1842),
Dunozet(t)us, Amatus (1889, 1627 - 1652),
Dunozet(t)us, Guilielmus (353, 1613 - 1625),
Duran, Paulus (463, 1625 - 1634),
Emerix de Matthys, Iacobus (1370, 1668 - 1696),
Emerix, Iohannes (180, 1656 - 1668),
Falconerius, Alexander (767, 1706 - 1724),
Farinaccius, Prosperus (278, 1591 - 1604),
Fastolf, Thomas (1336) (= "Fastolus"),
Gamberinus, Antonius Dominicus (130, 1820 - 1823),
Gomes, Ludovicus (165, 1511 - 1546, printed with Coccinus),
Gonsalvus, Hercules (73, 1789 - 1798),
Grassis, Achilles de (426, 1546 - 1550),
Grassis, Caesar de (195, 1574 - 1578),
Gutierrez Arguelles (118, 1645 - 1650),
Herrera, Iohannes de (237, 1716 - 1721),
Herzan, Franciscus (261, 1771 - 1779),
Isoard, Ioachim Iohannes Xaverius (521, 1803 - 1827),
Kaunitz, Franciscus Carolus (244, 1702 - 1711),
Lancetta, Cyriacus (1403, 1696 - 1723),
De Luca, Iohannes Baptista, cardinalis[105]

[105] On *De Luca* cf. *Ascheri* (n. 3) p. 1188 and *Charles Lefebvre,* J. B. De Luca et le tribunal de la Rote, in: Ephemerides iuris canonici 14 (1959) 300 - 320. *De Luca*'s 'Theatrum veritatis et iustitiae' (Romae 1669 - 1673), a standard encyclopedia reprinted many times, discusses many hundreds of *'decisiones'*. The more recent editions also contain a collection of ca. 1000 *'decisiones Rotae'* which was appended to the work after *De Luca*'s death.

Ludovisius, Alexander (= Gregorius XV papa, 584, 1600 - 1612),
Malvasius, Alexander (272, 1784 - 1801),
Mantica, Franciscus (375, 1587 - 1596),
Manzanedo de Quinnones, Alphonsus (919, 1605 - 1627),
Marco y Catalan, Iohannes Franciscus (422, 1817 - 1828),
Marini, Petrus cardinalis (640, 1825 - 1845),
Merlinus, Clemens (896, 1621 - 1642),
Mertel, Theodulphus cardinalis (74, 1849 - 1853),
Millinus, Iohannes Garzia cardinalis (449, 1591 - 1605),
Mohedanus, Iohannes (583, s. XVI.2),
Molines, Iosephus (1337, 1686 - 1711),
Monaldus, Benedictus cardinalis (203, 1626 - 1631,
printed behind Ubaldus),
Ninot, Iosephus (89, 1655 - 1665),
Odescalchis, Karolus ex ducibus (270, 1816 - 1820),
Olivarius Razzalius, Seraphinus (1500, 1566 - 1604),
Olivatius, Bartholomaeus (718, 1756 - 1769),
Othobonus, Petrus (= Alexander VIII papa, 278, 1643 - 1652),
Pacionus, Petrus (printed Coloniae 1700),
Paleottus, cardinalis (printed with the index to the *'Novissimae'*, see n. 101),
Pamphilius, Iohannes Baptista (= Innocentius X papa, 738, 1605 - 1621),
Patrizi, Constantinus ex marchionibus (110, 1824 - 1828),
Peña, Franciscus (1689, 1588 - 1612),
Peutinger, Christophorus (509, 1639 - 1649),
Pianetti, Gaspar Bernardus de marchionibus (303, 1821 - 1826),
Priolus, Hieronymus (471, 1653 - 1674),
Puteus, Iacobus (1409, ca. 1535 - 1551),
Rattus, Thomas (334, 1722 - 1732),
Remboldus, Iohannes Baptista (648, 1614* - 1626*),
Rezzonicus, Carolus (= Clemens XIII papa, 340, 1730 - 1737),
Riminaldus, Iohannes Maria (800, 1760 - 1785),
Roverella, Aurelius (95, 1786 - 1789),
Roxas, Franciscus de (494, 1635 - 1653),
Rusconius, Antonius (163, 1802 - 1808),
Seraphinus Olivarius Razzalius (1500, 1566 - 1604),
Tanarius, Alexander (277, 1734 - 1743),
Ubago et Rio, Felix (105, 1671 - 1679),
Ubaldus, Franciscus (897, 1610 - 1625),
Verallus, Paulus Aemilius (1122, 1551 - 1554),
Very, Iosephus Alphonsus de (197, 1763 - 1771),
Zarate, Franciscus (122, 1651 - 1658),
Zuccarus, Octavianus (printed Venetiis 1646),

Rota judges were styled *'R. P. D.'* (= *reverendissimus pater dominus*). If a judge referred to a *'decisio'* of a colleague who was still alive he would style him *'R. P. dominus meus'*. A deceased judge, however, was styled *'R. P. D. bonae memoriae'*.

Since the *'decisiones'* in the published collections are numbered, and subdivided into numbered paragraphs, one usually refers to the number and paragraph only. One does not quote the respective date and case label. For example: *dec. 504 n. 7 coram Cavalerio; et Priol. dec. 113 n. 19; et dec. 124 n. 11 coram Celso; ... Rot. divers. dec. 207 num. 2 cum seqq. par. 2* (= from the *"Diversorum"*); ... *Rota, dec. 346 n. 5 par. 10 et dec. 366 n. 5 par. 18 rec.* (= from the *"Recentiores"*, namely decisio 346 in particula 10 and decisio 366 in particula 18).

'Decisiones' which did not form part of a published collection, or which were only printed in an appendix to some treatise, were cited with the label and the deliberation date and name of the *'auditor ponens'*. Any subsections therein were referred to under their beginning words – for instance: *Rota in Isclana beneficii 16. Martii § Et quidem, et 18. Jun. 1696 coram R. P. D. de la Tremoille, et confirmata 5. Decembris eiusdem anni § Numquam autem, coram R. P. D. meo dell'Olmo, et in Compostellana parochialis 17. Junii 1697, in principio, coram me, ... ut plene firmatum fuit in Laudensi canonicatus 16. Martii 1696 coram bonae memoriae Emerix, et per doctores concordatos in Vicentina beneficii 24. Decembris 1688 § Tertia denique, coram reverendissimo domino meo Decano.*

The above mentioned change of habits in formulating the *'dubium'* is reflected in the *'decisiones'*: The older *'decisiones'* raise and solve abstractly worded questions of law. The answers are thus mostly short, and they seldomly indicate enough facts as to allow us to identify the case at hand. One may guess that many of the old *'decisiones'* are connected to other ones which arose from the same case, but it is not visible which ones arose from which case. The younger collections, in contrast, contain long *'decisiones'* which mention the parties' names and many concrete facts of the case and debate all the legal problems of one case together.

Even the more recent collections do not group *'decisiones'* together which arose from the same case on different deliberation days. In many cases a need for deliberation and decision of legal issues arose several times. The respective several *'decisiones'* are thus reported in the published collections as separate items[106].

---

[106] For instance, tomus 3 n. 124 in the *'Nuperrimae'* reports a case *'Coloniensis matrimonii, coram Caccia, 2 aprilii 1688'*. In this case a certain baron Arnoldus de Schenk pleaded that his marriage with Maria Emerentiana d'Ausque was void. The reported *'decisio'* states that Schenk must support his alleged wife during the course

There exist case repertories, arranged according to dioceses and argument keywords and Rota judges' names[107]. They make it somewhat easier to link various *'decisiones'* of a particular case to each other, but this can still not be done mechanically. One must keep in mind that the same kind of issue might provoke several litigations even between the same parties, and that cases could go from one judge to another, for instance if a judge died.

The published collections of *'decisiones'* do not report whether a *'decisio'* gave rise to a judgment and what it ordered. Many cases were in fact amicably settled after the *'decisio'* and thus never brought to judgment. Furthermore, the collections also contain *'decisiones'* which were later superseded by another *'decisio' in Rota* in the same case, namely on appeal or on grounds of a new hearing which had been granted.

It would be very time-consuming and cumbersome to match large numbers of published *'decisiones'* with the official case records in the archives. Although this might prove valuable for socio-legal research and general history, it would not offer additional insights about the judges' reasonings as the archival material does not contain any additional information for such studies.

The *'manualia'* and *'diaria'* make dull reading in this regard because they abound with notifications of power of attorney for proctors, appointments of substitute proctors, notes that XYZ appeared and handed in this and that document, or swore this or that oath, and that judge Soandso decreed this or that deadline, or granted extension for a deadline, and many other technicalities. Almost no clues as to the legal reasoning of the judge are given, and certainly none which would go beyond those which are expressed in the *'decisiones'*, anyway.

The proctors' and advocates' *'informationes'* are more interesting in this regard: They contain much legal argumentation, often backed by long strings of quotations from *ius-commune*-literature.

---

of the litigation, and that he must bear her procedural expenditure, because this is part of due support. Tomus 3 n. 245 in the *'Nuperrimae'* reports another *'Coloniensis matrimonii, coram Caccia, 5 maii 1692'*, which indeed belongs to the same case and decides as follows: While Schenk has a right to prove by witnesses that his alleged wife had before marriage been a mistress of Schenk's uncle Caspar, and that the marriage was thus null, the wife had as well a right to bring counter-witnesses as to her good reputation and chaste life before marriage. The case may have given rise to yet other published *'decisiones'*. Yet another example: Vol 3 dec. 137 in the *'Nuperrimae'* contains a *'decisio'* which concedes the archbishop of Salzburg archiepiscopal rights over the bisdom Passau (Lunae 26. Novembris 1691, coram Priolo). The bishop of Passau requested and obtained a new hearing, yet he lost his cause again: vol. 4 dec. 18 in the *'Nuperrimae'*, Veneris 13. Februarii 1693, coram Priolo.

[107] By *Cantalmaius* and *Blancus* (see n. 12).

When comparing *'informationes'* to the subsequent *'decisio'* one often notices that entire text passages have migrated from the former to the latter – with strings of quotations of literature and all. This is no wonder, particularly not if one keeps in mind that the advantaged party's representatives used to 'help' the *'adjutor'* of the judge in extending the *'decisio'* and paid him for his work, and that they could request that the *'decisio'* be 'revised' if they were not content with it[108].

VII. Authority of Precedents

Rota judges around 1700 continually cited Rota precedents. This was their main reference authority besides the Corpus Iuris Canonici and Corpus Iuris Civilis.

The lower courts in the Church State usually followed the *'decisiones'* of the Rota almost blindly[109]. Academic writers both in Italy and outside treated opinions of the Rota with utmost respect[110].

The continuous reference to precedents was encouraged by the above mentioned rule that established custom of the court (= *stylus curiae*) and *'decisiones'* which had been published in print could only be overruled by a two-thirds majority in a deliberation of the full Rota.

Advocates and proctors searched eagerly for favourable precedents with which to coax the judges of the *'turnus'* into the right direction as the four deciding judges had to abide by any such precedent if they wanted to rid themselves of the case right away. They would not lightly burden themselves with the incommodity of waiting for a plenary session of the Rota – which would cause considerable delay if the court roll was as full as it usually was.

The *'auditor ponens'* could, however, anticipate the difficulty: If he thought the Rota should rather overrule a precedent which had been quoted to him, he could in advance go to his Dean and persuade him to put the matter immediately on the roll for the full round of judges, instead of the regular *'turnus'* of five judges only. This may explain how the Rota could overturn its precedents as frequently as *De Luca* tells us it did[111].

---

108 See above, at n. 65.

109 References to contemporary literature about the practically binding force of Rota decisions are given by *Ascheri* (n. 3), p. 1126 s.; *Bernino* (n. 3), p. 199 - 200.

110 *Th. Rubeus* (n. 3) and *P. F. Perremutus* (n. 97) report in detail which Rota-doctrines were taken over by writers and which were rejected, and vice versa.

111 *De Luca* (n. 3), n. 102.

Contributors

Professore *Mario Ascheri,* Professor of Legal History at the University of Siena, Via Duprè 99, I-53100 Siena (Italia)

Dr. *Bernadette Auzary-Schmaltz,* ingénieur de recherche au CNRS, Centre d'Etude d'Histoire Juridique, Archives Nationales, 60, rue des Francs-Bourgeois, F-75141 Paris Cédex 03 (France)

Professor *J. H. Baker,* St Catharine's College, GB-Cambridge CB2 1RL (England)

Prof. *Jean Bart,* professeur d'histoire du droit, Université de Bourgogne, 4, Boulevard Gabriel, F-21000 Dijon (France)

Professor *W. H. Bryson,* Professor of Law, University of Richmond, Richmond, Virginia 23173 (U.S.A.)

Dr. *Serge Dauchy,* chargé de recherches au CNRS, Centre d'Histoire Judiciaire, Université de Lille II, Place Déliot 1, BP 629, F-59024 Lille Cédex (France)

Professor *Gero R. Dolezalek,* Department of Law, University of Aberdeen, High Street, GB-AB9 2BB Aberdeen (Scotland, Great-Britain)

Professor *R. H. Helmholz,* Ruth Wyatt Rosenson Professor of Law, University of Chicago, 1111 East 60th Street, Chicago, IL 60637-2786 (U.S.A.)

Dr. *D. J. Ibbetson,* Magdalen College, GB-Oxford OX1 4AU (England)

Dr. *Michel Petitjean,* directeur de recherche au CNRS, Centre Georges Chevrier UMR 5605, 4, Boulevard Gabriel, F-21000 Dijon (France)

Prof. Dr. *Filippo Ranieri,* Professor für Europäisches Zivilrecht an der Universität Saarbrücken, Fachbereich Rechtswissenschaft, Postfach 15 11 50, D-66041 Saarbrücken (Deutschland)

Professore *Andrea Romano,* Università degli Studi di Messina, Facoltà di Scienze Politiche, Via T. Cannizzaro 9, I-98122 Messina (Italia)

Professor *J. Th. de Smidt,* Emeritus Professor of the Universities of Leiden and Amsterdam, Spaarnelaan 8, NL-2012 RK Haarlem (The Netherlands)

Professore *Giancarlo Vallone,* Professore di Storia delle Istituzioni parlamentari, Facoltà di Scienze Politiche, Università degli Studi di Pisa, Via Serafini 3, I-56126 Pisa (Italia)

Dr. *C. H. van Rhee,* Molengraaff Instituut Privaatrecht, Nobelstraat 2A, NL-3512 EN Utrecht (The Netherlands)

Drs. *C. Verhas,* Research Fellow NWO, Gravensteen, Pieterskerkhof 6, NL-2311 SR Leiden (The Netherlands)

Professor *Alain Wijffels,* Professor of Legal History, Research Fellow, Gravensteen, Pieterskerkhof 6, NL-2311 SR Leiden (The Netherlands)

MIX
Papier aus verantwortungsvollen Quellen
Paper from responsible sources
FSC® C105338

Printed by Libri Plureos GmbH
in Hamburg, Germany